THE GRANT THAT MAXWELL BOUGHT

THE GRANT THAT MAXWELL BOUGHT
Facsimile of Number 225 of the Original 1952 Edition

by
F. Stanley

Foreword
by
Marc Simmons

SANTA FE

New Material © 2008 by Sunstone Press. All Rights Reserved.

No part of this book may be reproduced in any form or by any electronic or mechanical means including information storage and retrieval systems without permission in writing from the publisher, except by a reviewer who may quote brief passages in a review.

Sunstone books may be purchased for educational, business, or sales promotional use. For information please write: Special Markets Department, Sunstone Press, P.O. Box 2321, Santa Fe, New Mexico 87504-2321.

Library of Congress Cataloging-in-Publication Data

Stanley, F. (Francis), 1908-1996
  The grant that Maxwell bought / by F. Stanley ; new foreword by Marc Simmons.
    p. cm. -- (Southwest heritage series)
  Originally published: Denver : World Press, 1952.
  "Facsimile of number 225 of the original 1952 edition."
  Includes bibliographical references.
  ISBN 978-0-86534-652-9 (pbk. : alk. paper)
  1. Maxwell Land Grant (N.M. and Colo.)--History. 2. Land tenure--New Mexico--History. 3. Land tenure--Colorado--History. 4. New Mexico--History, Local. 5. Colorado--History, Local. I. Title.
  F802.M38S73 2008
  978.9'2--dc22
                           2008003308

WWW.SUNSTONEPRESS.COM
SUNSTONE PRESS / POST OFFICE BOX 2321 / SANTA FE, NM 87504-2321 /USA
(505) 988-4418 / ORDERS ONLY (800) 243-5644 / FAX (505) 988-1025

The Southwest Heritage Series is dedicated to Jody Ellis and Marcia Muth Miller, the founders of Sunstone Press, whose original purpose and vision continues to inspire and motivate our publications.

CONTENTS

THE SOUTHWEST HERITAGE SERIES / I

FOREWORD TO THIS EDITION / II
The Controversial F. Stanley
by
Marc Simmons

A MAN'S REACH / III
from
The F. Stanley Story
by
Mary Jo Walker

TRIBUTE TO F. STANLEY / IV
by
Jack D. Rittenhouse

FACSIMILE OF NUMBER 225 OF THE ORIGINAL 1952 EDITION / V

I

THE SOUTHWEST HERITAGE SERIES

The history of the United States is written in hundreds of regional histories and literary works. Those letters, essays, memoirs, biographies and even collections of fiction are often first-hand accounts by people who wanted to memorialize an event, a person or simply record for posterity the concerns and issues of the times. Many of these accounts have been lost, destroyed or overlooked. Some are in private or public collections but deemed to be in too fragile condition to permit handling by contemporary readers and researchers.

However, now with the application of twenty-first century technology, nineteenth and twentieth century material can be reprinted and made accessible to the general public. These early writings are the DNA of our history and culture and are essential to understanding the present in terms of the past.

The Southwest Heritage Series is a form of literary preservation. Heritage by definition implies legacy and these early works are our legacy from those who have gone before us. To properly present and preserve that legacy, no changes in style or contents have been made. The material reprinted stands on its own as it first appeared. The point of view is that of the author and the era in which he or she lived. We would not expect photographs of people from the past to be re-imaged with modern clothes, hair styles and backgrounds. We should not, therefore, expect their ideas and personal philosophies to reflect our modern concepts.

Remember, reading their words and sharing their thoughts is a passport back into understanding how the past was shaped and how it influenced today's world.

Our hope is that new access to these older books will provide readers with a challenging and exciting experience.

II

FOREWORD TO THIS EDITION

The Controversial F. Stanley
by
Marc Simmons

As a professional historian, I've often been asked my opinion of the author who wrote under the pen name, F. Stanley. According to his 1996 obituary, he published 190 books and booklets on New Mexico history, quite a record by any standard. The problem is, F. Stanley has been almost universally condemned for the innumerable flaws that litter his writings. However, behind the man and the work lurks a curious story.

He was born Louis Crocchiola in New York's Greenwich Village on October 31, 1908 to Italian immigrant parents. After receiving a Bachelor's degree in English at Catholic University in Washington, DC, Louis entered the priesthood in 1938. On that occasion, as was allowed, he formally added the new names Stanley and Francis to his birth name, Louis Crocchiola. Thereafter, he was called simply Father Stanley.

Shortly after his ordination, the young priest was diagnosed with the beginnings of tuberculosis. Following medical advice of the day, the Church sent Father Stanley to Hereford, Texas in the Panhandle, hoping the arid climate might cure him. It did! Something else occurred at the same time. Father Stanley fell under the spell of the Southwest, leading him to become one of the most prolific historical writers of his day.

In 1940 he applied for pastoral work in New Mexico, since he was fluent in Spanish and thought he could be most useful there. The Archbishop of Santa Fe accepted him, assigning Father Stanley first to the Guadalupe church in Taos and then to the San Miguel church at Socorro.

During the 1940s, he served six or so different parishes in northern or eastern New Mexico, thereby becoming familiar with rural and small town life. It was while stationed at Taos, though, that Father Stanley caught the writing bug through mingling with local authors. But later as he was transferred by the Archbishop from one parish to another, he would begin looking into the history of his temporary residence and compiling a file of notes.

His first book, *Raton Chronicle*, appeared in 1948. Then in rapid succession F. Stanley published full-length histories on Cimarron, Socorro, Las Vegas, and the Maxwell land grant. Soon to his line of books, F. Stanley added an ongoing series dedicated to a single small town or fort that other writers had ignored. These little booklets remain easily recognizable with their canary yellow covers and crimson red lettering, plus the New Mexico state emblem, the Zia sun symbol. Eventually, these small works alone numbered 123 titles.

Remarkably, F. Stanley personally financed all of his publications, often going deeply into debt. The several printers he used were generally tolerant of the delay in paying his bills.

Even more stressful for Father Stanley was the harsh criticism his writings received from historians and book reviewers. They unmercifully picked apart his unedited and untidy prose, pointed out frequent mistakes, and condemned the neglect of standards in the composition or format of his books.

For one example, a serious slip occurred in the naming of F. Stanley's longest work, a history of the New Mexico state capital in three volumes, titled *Ciudad Santa Fe*. Under the old Spanish system, Santa Fe in reality never achieved the rank of a *ciudad* (chartered city), but retained the status of a town (*villa*). The author had missed that pivotal fact and thus launched his three volume set with a conspicuous error on the covers.

In 1985 Mary Jo Walker, a librarian at Eastern New Mexico University, Portales, published a sympathetic biography, *The F. Stanley Story*. The book contains quotes from interviews given by Father Stanley in which he defends himself and his methods.

His main plea was: "Pardon the mistakes, but say a kind word for my effort." Painfully aware of his failings, he claimed that his intent was merely to assemble fugitive information from obscure courthouse records, old newspaper files, and archives so that others more able could pick up the thread where he left off and carry on.

After publication of Walker's biography, some historians, myself included, began to look more charitably toward Father Stanley Crocchiola. The fact is, despite his deficiencies, he managed to make in his own quirky way a not insignificant contribution to our regional history.

Today, F. Stanley books and booklets are worth collecting. I'm always happy when I can add another one of his to my personal library. I just wish he was still around so that I could tell him that.

One of the earliest treatments of the historic and controversial Maxwell Land Grant was published by F. Stanley in 1952, titled *The Grant That Maxwell Bought*. Although other books on the subject have appeared since, serious readers still need to go back and examine what Father Stanley had to say. Otherwise, small nuggets buried in his pages, and nowhere else, may be missed.

Sunstone Press in choosing to include *The Grant That Maxwell Bought* in its honored Southwest Heritage Series is wisely making this book available again to the reading public.

III

A MAN'S REACH
"Take him for what he is worth"
from
The F. Stanley Story
by
Mary Jo Walker

It is difficult to say to what extent negative criticism and neglect may have personally affected Father Stanley. Some of his works in the 1970s showed considerable care in preparation, but no more so than his major efforts in earlier decades. He knew his own limitations as well as any of his critics did, but he believed quite sincerely that the flaws in his work were largely literary in nature and therefore of little overall significance; or alternatively that they represented realities over which he had little control, such as his limited time or the cost of typesetting footnotes. His first reactions may be surmised from comments in the foreword to *Dave Rudabaugh*.

> I used to apologize for my mistakes. Come to think of it, why should I? I tried; that's more than my critics did. I investigated to the best of my ability, often going sleepless and hungry in order to attain the facts. No patron has come along the way. I had to rough it alone.... The book may not be literary, but it is factual. In the long run, truth survives.

Two years later, in *The Duke City*, he confessed from a somewhat different perspective:

> I am grateful for all criticism—constructive or otherwise.

And in *Satanta and the Kiowas*, 1968, he pled:

> Let my mistakes be my Calvary, and let my readers be my confessors from whom we hope to obtain pardon and forgiveness.

Simply and with a kind of humble determination, he persevered for many years, his principal resources being his formidable drive and his eagerness to help preserve the history of the region he loved so well. No doubt he attempted too much; probably, as with so many of us, his reach exceeded his grasp. His hope, which he stated over and over again, was that his books would provide guidance for others and "prove a...contribution to Western Americana." That purpose and his dedication to it do not serve to be lightly dismissed.

Taken as a whole, with all its human flaws, F. Stanley's work stands as a unique contribution, as much a part of the written record "as Coronado's visit." Even Ramon Adams acknowledged that "he deserves a full measure of credit for supplying hitherto unpublished information," for putting something into print about obscure places and people, for adding to the body of recorded knowledge about the Southwest. Whatever the final evaluation may be, however, it is certain that F. Stanley has earned a place in southwestern history in his own right.

F. Stanley (circa 1953). *Photograph courtesy of Golden Library, Eastern New Mexico University.*

IV

TRIBUTE TO F. STANLEY
by
Jack D. Rittenhouse
from
The F. Stanley Story
by
Mary Jo Walker
Albuquerque, New Mexico / March, 1984

Some historians write because they hope their writing will bring them money or promotion or tenure. Some write to espouse a cause. A few write because they must, because it is the only way they can quench an inner thirst or scratch an itch of curiosity. The last class is the happiest, and F. Stanley is in this group.

The term historian has many shadings. Among academic people, a historian is a certified scholar whose commission of rank is a degree of Doctor of Philosophy in history, and whose income results from full-time teaching or writing history. Some of these go on to glory and excellence in their work; some gain renown as researchers or as teachers, become a historian's historian, but find writing a difficult task. Many bank their inner fire when they don their doctoral robes and are content to plod along as routine teachers, living as comfortably as a toad in a puddle of buttermilk, looking upon their diploma as a union card.

The grass roots historian is another type, curious about people and places around them. Their writings are their only certification. Some become antiquarians, with a dilettante interest in ancient things and more curious about precision in minutiae than in the social significance of their subject. The term antiquarian has a different meaning among historians than among bookmen.

Still another type of historian is the buff, an individual who is an enthusiast or devotee of a specific subject. When it comes to sheer bulk of knowledge about a subject, or even to accuracy on a point of information, I have seen many buffs who outclassed PhDs. I personally know only three individuals who have their own microfilm readers at home, and all three are buffs. They travel great distances to look at a gravestone or a courthouse record, which is not to say that professional historians and grassroots historians also do not do this, of course.

We owe much to the grassroots historian and the buff. They are the prospectors who discover new lodes. They are curious about people and places and customs, combining the interests of the folklorist and the historian, and if they are good at what they do, they find their work accepted and even honored.

F. Stanley is one whose curiosity and inner fire has drawn him to the study of people and places and events that had gone unnoticed until he saw them. He advanced knowledge in many directions, lit many candles to dispel darkness.

His works are only beginnings, and he knows this. In a sense, history writes itself merely by occurring, and thus there is the axiom that history is not written but rewritten. Another New Mexico local historian, Fray Angélico Chávez, once spoke to El Corral de Santa Fe Westerners and said that history is not a static, pure thing that can be discovered once, written down, and preserved intact forever. Instead, he said, history is a living, growing body that must be nurtured... and which occasionally requires surgery.

F. Stanley has wandered across the Southwest like a Johnny Appleseed of history, planting seedlings in the form of booklets and leaving their later nurturing to others. Later historians will convert these seedlings into trees, by pruning, fertilizing and grafting. The work will require more research, more verification, correction and amplification. But F. Stanley planted the first seed.

The historian who uses only *one* source for his work is a fool, but the historian who refuses to review any source is an idiot. Any source may have errors caused by lack of information, or poor proofreading, or hasty writing. But some questionable bit of old-timer's lore may raise the possibility of truth; it is then up to the later historian to prove or disprove the fact. Once, when I was gathering information about the New Mexico ghost town of Cabezón, I read an old-timer's memoir that mentioned a stage line running through the town. Nowhere else did I find any mention of this, and I sought to verify the story. A usually reliable professional historian scoffed at the notion that the town had ever been on a commercial stage line. Then a museum curator found a printed timetable of the Star Stage Line, listing the route and showing Cabezón as a stop. Although many dissertations do not list F. Stanley works as sources, the padre's booklets have nonetheless been studied for similar possible clues. Given the time and resources, F. Stanley himself would have gone farther; he leaves that to others.

His severest critics often have been people who never wrote a recognized book, or whose books themselves are not without the flaws of typesetters and human errors, or whose dyspeptic nature made them discard a sculpture because of a chip.

The body of work produced by F. Stanley will become part of the vast lore about the Southwest. It will remain as long as libraries stand and will be consulted and used by generations as part of the grassroots literature. Future writers will correct its errors, just as their mistakes will be corrected by still later scholars. But someone had to start it, and F. Stanley was the man.

V

FACSIMILE OF NUMBER 225
OF THE ORIGINAL 1952 EDITION

THE GRANT THAT MAXWELL BOUGHT

THE GRANT THAT MAXWELL BOUGHT

by

F. STANLEY

Copyright — 1952
F. STANLEY

*No part of this book may be reprinted
without express permission of the author.*

PRINTED BY THE WORLD PRESS
Denver, Colorado, U.S.A.

LIMITED EDITION

of

THE GRANT THAT MAXWELL BOUGHT

THIS BOOK NUMBER

| 225 |

of an edition limited to two hundred and fifty volumes

Sincerely,
F. Storey

FOREWORD

This is the story of the Maxwell Land Grant, a vast tract of land in northeastern New Mexico and southeastern Colorado. It is told mostly from the point of view of documents and court trials, rather than from hearsay, old wives tales and "hand-me-down" accounts. Here we examine the lives (briefly, or our tale would never end, especially since new material is being found every day on Beaubien, Maxwell and others) of those who petitioned for it, received it, dreamed great hopes for it, sold it. Also of the companies that struggled to keep it and of the Anti-Grant War that was fought to keep the squatter on land he thought was his. McMains, Pels, Springer, Allison, Tolby — all pass in review for they all helped to focus the attention of the nation on this little corner of New Mexico. We simply put down the facts. We draw no conclusions nor do we form an opinion one way or another. The Grant was, is and always will be a controversy. Perhaps both sides perpetrated wrongs because both sides thought they were right. We merely tell the story. Let the reader make his own decisions

Keleher, Walker, Porter, McPherson, McCullough and a host of others have gone over the ground taking one stand or another; as I happened to live on former Grant property for several years I decided to add a volume to the growing library on the subject. Thousands of volumes have been written about Shakespeare and the subject seems never to be exhausted. The same is to be said for the Maxwell Land Grant whether it be a novel by Ferguson or a scholarly treatise by Keleher. Look in vain for another section of land in the nation that produced so much comment from the press or absorbed the attention of the entire world. Because of this bit of land a Supreme Court Justice almost lost his life; a president of the United States wanted to horse-whip a man; a minister was looked upon as a killer; a cattle man became a killer; vigilantes rode into the night burning and killing; the Anti-Grant War was waged in two states taking more lives than the Lincoln County War that brought Billy the Kid his fame.

A history of this sort is necessarily dry but it will not be if you look upon the Maxwell Land Grant not as a piece of land but as a person—a rather seductive person—beautiful, strong, stretching forth inviting arms to invite you into a web, a blood-draining web, and once within it all happiness left you. Miranda, Beaubien, Maxwell, Collingson, Sherwin, Whigham, Pels, McMains—all died unhappy even though many died rich. Only the uneducated Carson had the foresight to scat pronto before it strangled him, too.

Someone once remarked that the true story of New Mexico would only be written when the story of the Maxwell Land Grant was written. In a sense that is true if you wished to eliminate the Conquistadores and the followers of St. Francis. Let us rather qualify that statement by saying that the history of Americans in New Mexico is more to the point. Sometimes it seems that the author is wandering from the subject when he brings in the Texas-Santa Fe Expedition, Clay Allison, McMains and others but a close study will reveal that they are spokes in a wheel that lead all to the hub. To write the complete history of the Grant would mean to hunt up a man like Folger to build a library to house the many tomes. And one life-time of writing would not fill one corner of it. Hollywood has found Kit Carson. Someday it may discover Maxwell, Allison and Beaubien. To my mind Allison has always been a more interesting character than Billy the Kid.

At this point thanks are in order. The author wishes to thank Mary Lail and Mrs. Alpers of Cimarron. These two know more Cimarron history than a hundred authors who have written it; Vita Abreu, Mrs. Davis, Mrs. Henry Abreu, Mrs. Clothier Webster, Mrs. G. Abdulla and Margaret Webster — all of Springer — relatives of Beaubien and Maxwell — who gave generously of portraits, documents and time. To James Barber, editor of the Raton Range; Frank Pieffer, publisher of the paper; the Raton Historical Society; Mr. Crampton; Librarian Evelyn Shuler, Emily Long — all of Raton for the use of their files. To Mr. Gaylord and the staff of the American School of Research for their hours of patience. To the Colfax County Courthouse staff for their help with the courthouse records. To the library staff of Highlands University, always ready to render assistance. To the Rocky Mountain Coal Company, the Maxwell Land Grant Company, the Santa Fe Railroad, and all other officials who made this work possible from the day we wrote the first note in 1943 to the last note in 1952.

We wish to thank Mrs. Dulle and Theresa Vijil, granddaughter of the former Governor Donaciano Vijil, who were so good about typing and helping with the notes. To all old timers who helped with tales of Anti-Grant days, thanks. To Msgr. Schoeppner and Rev. V. Burke for the use of the church archives, my appreciation. To Rt. Rev. L. FitzSimon, Bishop of Amarillo, for the use of his most complete collection of Southwestern Americana, my sincere gratitude. All others who in any way helped please accept my thanks.

PECOS, NEW MEXICO *February 22, 1952*

CONTENTS

Chapter One --Beaubien and Miranda

Chapter Two --Lucien B. Maxwell

Chapter Three --Buying Up the Grant

Chapter Four ---------------The Maxwell Land Grant & Railway Company

Chapter Five -- Cimarron

Chapter Six --Indians on the Grant

Chapter Seven ---------------------------------------Land Grants in General

Chapter Eight ------------------------------The Beales and Reyeula Claim

Chapter Nine ------------------------The Maxwell Land Grant Company

Chapter Ten -------------------------------------General O. P. McMains

Chapter Eleven -- Clay Allison

Chapter Twelve ----------------------------------Ghost Towns on the Grant

Chapter Thirteen --------------------------------Living Towns on the Grant

Chapter Fourteen --The Picture Story

Chapter One

CARLOS BEAUBIEN AND GUADALUPE MIRANDA

Sometimes one writes about an era, or a man, only to find that while it isn't noisy, its noisome to a degree, even in print, because the central character or his time, breathes vapors of historical gas that works like a sulphur on the reader's imagination. Men like Maxwell bring the soilure of sweat of human being; the seemingly unbearable stench of horses hoofs burning in a smithy; yet, he must be made a stranger in an obviously inhuman world created by humans who walk faster and faster through gun smoke and taverns instinctively trying to get something over with, only to end up as pale, sallow people, most of them, with warped bodies and sullen or patient mouths and tired eyes. In spite of themselves they make history.

Spend a spring or summer at Cimarron and you will see how quickly the air, the sky, the river force you to change your moods varying from contempt for the life you lived before you came to know Cimarron; and melancholy and tenderness and the thirst for the power of Joshua to command the sun, the ever brilliant and glorious New Mexico sun, to stand still. A gentle wind, warmed by the sun, suffused with the sounds of an idle world, pours into you. There is the view into the past where men had fought, drunk, hated one another, and loved the women of Cimarron. Each one came to Maxwell's ranch with a thousand gleaming desires or a thousand dark desires. The sun bakes this into you. Each found his way to Cimarron with dreams and fantasies, for here was a way of life, not for men with white, spermatick necks, but for the brave, because the strong are not really dangerous, but the weak who inspire strong men to attempt what they have not the strength nor the courage to accomplish.

Maxwell was so strong, so extravagant, so certain and so lost. Living his life as a cattle-baron at Rayado, and again at Cimarron, he hurls that great massive shoulder of his as strength against spectral barriers like a wave whose power explodes in hidden mid-oceans under timeless skies because he wants all; feels the thrust and power for everything but gets nothing. Finally, he is destroyed by his own expansion, devoured by his own hunger, tied down by his wealth that enslaves him, for he dies so poorly rich that his unhappiness is mistaken for material poverty.

Sit down on the banks of the ever flowing Cimarron. Let the wind speak. It has a hundred voices that bewitch as the sun bakes and the river enchants. Soon you see the faces—Beaubien, Miranda, Pancho Griego, Clay Allison, Maxwell and Captain Keyes. You settle back and your story is born.

Our story runneth thus—

South of Quebec, on the St. Lawrence River the equinoctial rain was over. The weather was quite warm for that time of year, as it often happens in that section of Canada after the first frosts, so that all the drab, foot worn streets of Trois Rivieres, forming as they did a crazy quilt pattern of houses endlessly similar, stuck like rows of boxes along the ridges of the surrounding hills. Two half grown boys are assisting the parish curate to look for herbs and mushrooms. One of the boys is emaciated looking and at first appearance one is inclined to pity him and invite him in for a meal to help put some flesh over those bones. But in reality he is wiry and healthy. His name is Charles Hipolyte Trotier. All his life he is to keep that hungry look.

Charles was an altar boy and faithful about serving Mass. This was an outing promised by the good priest in recompense for services rendered. The baker's wife had fixed up a special box for the occasion, and her best effort was a splendid apple pie. Charles was a wonderful altar boy but he was not above sampling apple pie especially when the curate was off in the woods in quest of such uninteresting things as mushrooms. So come lunch time the curate had no pie. The outing was over. Charles was marched home in disgrace and the thrashing he got weighed him down more than the pie. Paul Trotier, Sieur de Beaubien and Louise Adelaide Durocher Beaubien were indignant and horrified that their boy should steal anything from a priest. And to eat the curate's apple pie! His soul was lost. Yes, absolutely in Hades. What would the neighbors say? The Trotiers were not capable parents. The disgrace would be the talk of the village. Charles hung his head in shame. His future was certain. He was to be the town criminal. He went to his room and cried.

The next day it rained. For a long time after breakfast he sat by the kitchen window wondering about his fate. Suddenly he knew that he wanted to be a priest. The incident of yesterday was forgotten as parents and curate rejoiced in the newly found vocation. Charles began his studies with his pastor and for a time seemed perfectly happy.

Canada was but a petty undertaking until Colbert assumed control of the colonial policy in 1667. Guided by his dictates, France was willing and able to capture direct control of overseas effort, as England never tried to do with but few exceptions. Since 1663, France's power on the St. Lawrence was secure. The population reached twenty-five hundred, mostly centering around Quebec. Content to stay at home, they were not attracted by any company system to undertake to win fortune in the wilderness. It was better to stay at home and keep your scalp. They knew of the world beyond them through a few adventurous fur traders. A few overcame their timidity and ventured down the Great Lakes region, even down the Mississippi, to give France a strategic hold on the continent. La Salle was the hero of every school boy's dreams. The fantastic tales told him by Don Diego de Penalosa, who was out to break Spain for injustices inflicted upon him, made a national hero of La Salle.

But that was the beginning. Like a double-edged sword, the religious impulse of the adventuresome Jesuits and the race-amalgamation ideal typified in the fast rising class of coureurs de bois, men who thrust off the security of the hearth to enter the untrammeled and forbidden places through the fur trade, the St. Lawrence as well as Quebec became places to open the eyes of the English and the Spanish. More French colonists flocked in. The feudalism of New France, under which the seigneurs labored in the fields with their tenants and married their daughters, taking a winter off now and then to enjoy the cosmopolitan city of Quebec. These differed from the other adventurous Latins in Spanish America, as Charles was later to find out, not because they were not just as bold but because the Crown had a tighter hold on the Spaniards than France had on Canada. Another reason for the expansion of the fur trade was the land holding system evolved by the French which excluded any form of freehold save in a few isolated cases which were exceptional. Inadequate, to say the least, for pioneers and dangerous to agricultural expansion and the growth of a prosperous society, more and more French-Canadians took to the woods and streams so that soon they founded another reckless breed of men known as the Mountain Men thus affecting greatly the lives of Beaubien, Pley, Trujillo, Clouthier, Maxwell, Carson and others to fit into the story of the Maxwell Land Grant. The original purpose was solidarity and tenacity of occupation, but it awakened many Canadians to a venturesomeness dormant in them until they breathed the air of the forest and drank from clear streams so that the woods became home and the wilderness their resting place.

Meantime Charles Beaubien became restless. The curate could read the signs. The boy's eyes were on his books but his heart was with the fur trappers. He sent Charles home with a note to his parents. They understood. Into the scene comes Stephan Burroughs, son of one of New England's better known ministers. He was a tall, friendly, handsome man with ideas in advance of his time. He was also an expert counterfeiter. While in New England he fell in and out of love with more women than it was ever the lot of Robert Burns to know. Mothers cautioned their daughters against him. His father gave him a choice between behaving himself or leaving home. He chose the latter. Soon everyone was talking about him. No one had anything good to say about him or for him. He stole his father's sermons and preached from them to suit his purposes. He took to stealing other things and found himself in and out of jail constantly. The charges were always the same: robbery, adultery, counterfeiting. He was as much in the news as the growing pains of the young American Republic. For many years his record stood as the most arrested young man in New England. He entered Dartmouth college in the hopes of reforming himself but he was expelled upon his first mis-adventure. He had an insatiable thirst for amusement that over-balanced his volatile temper so that he was known as a rogue no matter what his own interpretation or mis-interpretation of his deeds.

He forever carried about him an air of injured innocence because he was taught by his reverend father to look upon himself as the salt of the earth, and whatever his exploits he had the innate desire for good despite the fact that his path was evil. At least, so he claimed in his memoirs (re-printed in 1924) that he was always in search of the truth but just couldn't find it. He sailed for France on a privateer remaining in that country just long enough to acquire a polish in the language which was to be of such help to him at Trois Rivieres. Returning to America he opened a school on Long Island. Again in hot water for "subverting religion" because he taught Hume, Voltaire and Rollin, he defended himself by saying that he only taught to supplement the Bible and out of date hymn books.

He next moved to Georgia. Here he opened another school which barely afforded him a living so he opened up a land office. Before long he was back at counterfeiting. Here he was at an advantage for the new coinage system had not as yet been established and French and Spanish coins were in circulation. He was caught; his ears cropped; his body lacerated; pilloried; the dungeon. Next he was taken in irons to the jail at Northampton and chained to the wall. But he was evidently a superman. No sooner left to himself than he managed to set the building on fire. He was taken out of the burning building and placed in a dungeon elsewhere but he escaped.

Burroughs was now looked upon as in league with the devil. How could a man with an iron band around his waist and bolted to the floor escape except with the aid of the powers of darkness? He next made his way to Worchester where he was picked up by the authorities and again jailed. He escaped. Hunted down, he was captured and placed in a bomb-proof cell in Boston Harbor. In 1800, he was asked to leave New England. Tossing a coin as to whether he should go North or South, he decided on Canada. There he continued as a counterfeiter, but was not jailed. The officials reasoned with him and gave him some religious tracts to read. These made an impression on him and soon he was studying the doctrines of the Catholic Church. Following his baptism in that religion, he went to Trois Rivieres. There he opened a school. When Beaubien found that he had no vocation he went with Burroughs and in this school learned some English as well as the exploits of his teacher which only served to charm him. His mind was made up. He would see the world even as Burroughs did but without the evil that made the teacher so notorious.

Burroughs insisted that travel and observation was a better education than all the books in the world. Many of the French Canadian trappers from the area became such because of the encouragement given them by this teacher from New England. He painted worlds for them they never believed existed. He told them of the woods, and the free life of democratic America. Burroughs stayed for a time with the Beaubiens who were not too pleased with his influence on Charles. Last of all did they want a wanderer in the family. Charles was never a very bright student any more than he was ever to become a brilliant businessman. He never lost his French accent. America fought and won the War of 1812. Beaubien waged a long war with himself between duty to his parents and the call of the wild. Finally, he took off one day and joined a party of trappers headed south for St. Louis, which is probably why he took such a fancy to Maxwell when he found out at Taos that the youth likewise took off to become a trapper.

Beaubien, despite his boldness, was of a shy and retiring nature. All his life he never pushed himself forward. If he had, he probably would have been named governor of the territory instead of Donaciano Vijil. General Kearny was impressed by him so he settled for the office of judge. His bashfulness is further seen in the fact that he would not appeal for the Grant alone but on a partnership basis; his shrewdness is seen in the fact that he selected a political figure for a partner. Such a partner as Guadalupe Miranda was needed most especially for colonization, reform and business with the government. As it turned out Miranda was totally unnecessary. He seems merely to have given the power of his name.

St. Louis was not the largest city in Missouri when Beaubien went there. It was just as French as Quebec although one would look for Spanish influence since it was in Spanish hands before France took over. Even the Louisiana Purchase failed to down the French culture of the city and it wasn't until the coming of Catron and others that the two Latin cultures blended into the American. Because it was mainly a French-Canadian town Beaubien found himself at home there. In 1804 it boasted one hundred and eighty houses. A small sloping hill ascended to what was later to be known as Third Street and beyond this an extensive prairie afforded plenty of hay and pasture for the cattle and horses of the residents of the village. The town had two long streets that ran parallel with the river, along which the homes of the settlers were scattered at intervals. At the far end of the village could be seen several incomplete, dilapidated, abandoned stone towers erected in 1797, but serving no particular purpose except as ornaments for travelers to inspect and villagers to spin yarns about. The levee in 1809 was marked by a perpendicular ledge of rocks and the village was bounded on the west by Third Street. There were only a few buildings west of Second Street and in the whole village one would not come upon a brick building which struck Beaubien as rather strange for the tales he heard of the place prepared him for dwellings of gold and pavements of silver. When he got his first glimpse of the village his stomach turned at the squalor. His birthplace in Canada was cleaner, bigger and more attractive. Burroughs must have been dreaming. If this were a change for the better, then somebody was telling fairy tales.

In 1806 St. Louis had eighteen hundred people, two hundred homes, mostly whitewashed, which gave a considerable advantage as an approach but nothing more. The town was full of gardens and fruit trees. Beaubien was to learn to love gardens simply because it was the thing to do in St. Louis at the time. He always cultivated a garden in Taos. As money was scarce he worked for his board and room. The village was incorporated in 1808, the first to do so west of the Mississippi. On July 3rd of that year Auguste Chouteau, Edward Hempstead, Bernard Pratt, Pierre Chouteau and Alexander McNair were elected first trustees and Joseph Garnier was made the town clerk. In December 1808 a meeting was called to convene on Sunday at the home of Auguste Chouteau to consult with reference to municipal affairs. In those days, meeting on Sundays were deemed appropriate, a throw back to Spanish days. Among the subjects engaging the attention of the village authorities were the ferry and rates of the same, slaves and patrols. "Any free person," ruled the city fathers, "associating with slaves at their dances and other amusements" was subject to a fine of ten dollars. If a free white person, a free negro or mulatto was found in the company of an unlawful meeting of slaves, he was subject to a fine of three dollars, and on failure to pay the same such a person received on his back or her back twenty lashes well laid on. The whipping post was then located on the site of the future courthouse.

In 1809, the officials began to campaign for streets and sidewalks despite the heavy traffic from Indian trading expeditions that fitted out there. The following year the first ordinance of the village levied a license tax on tavern keepers, merchants, barges, carriages, slaves, wheels of fortune, billiard tables and every dog over and above one for each family. The dog tax was fixed at two dollars an animal. Despite all this taxation the total revenue from all sources amounted to the meagre sum of $529.68 from which the clerk, Garnier, received $115.86 for his services, and Charless, the printer, $114 for printing the laws.

All this was not lost on Beaubien. When he wrote out the laws governing the villages and cities he would found on the Grant as well as on his son's Grant one can see the influence of the laws of St. Louis in his work. Auguste Chouteau for whom he clerked and gardened, was like a second father to him. For many years Beaubien sought to pattern his life after him and whatever part he took in civic affairs it was only because Chouteau did so. Auguste wrote to his father and told him that his son was in good hands so that all seemed patched up between Charles and his parents. If Beaubien decided against becoming a Mountain Man it was only because he acquired the airs of a gentleman from Auguste.

When Beaubien came to St. Louis he was told that if he wished to remain he would have to join one of the fire companies. The town boasted two. One was commanded by Pierre Dodier; the other by Bernard Pratte. Charles joined the latter. The failure to obtain money to pay for a fire engine by means of a lottery as authorized by the Act of 1817, resulted in the re-organiaztion of these two companies into the North and South Fire Companies. Two years later two small rotary fire engines were purchased in Cincinnati, the money being secured by private subscription. Beaubien contributed constantly to the maintenance of both engines while he was in St. Louis. I believe another reason in petitioning for the Grant was a certain sense of pride. He would put up model villages and write and tell the city fathers in St. Louis where they were wrong. If he saw anything wrong he never mentioned it but stored it away in his memory as a mistake he would not repeat. That he would one day own a vast tract of land he never for a moment doubted. That much Burroughs taught him —confidence in himself.

The new marketplace in St. Louis was built in 1812, and the rent for a stall was fixed by ordinance at ten dollars a year. This was the year that the first brick house was built on the corner of Main and Chestnut. The home belonged to Manuel Lisa. The plat for the town was completed in 1818. In 1819 the first contested village election took place. In this election political and not municipal questions were made paramount. This was important from Beaubien's viewpoint since the rest of his life in New Mexico would be run on this basis. He would satisfy politicians in order to benefit municipalities. Here he was to fail dismally since politicians in New Mexico, even after the American Occupation, had a way of keeping the masses subjugated so that any social project such as Beaubien hoped to focus through his Grant was defeated from the start. That is why he sold the Grant to Maxwell, and why he induced other inheritors of the Grant to sell. Successful in that political election were Julius De Mun, Thomas McNight, William Carr Lane—who was to be a life long friend of Beaubien's especially when their paths crossed in New Mexico—Henry Von Phal, Pascal Cerre and Joseph Charles, the printer. Defeated were Fremon Delaurier, Alexander McNair, J. P. Cabanne, M. P. Leduc, Antoine Daugin and Thomas H. Benton (who later became quite successful and put through the bill for a road to Santa Fe and inspired America with the coast to coast idea of Manifest Destiny). The population of St. Louis in 1821 when Beaubien left St. Louis was 5,600. Carr was the first mayor.

Beaubien realized more and more that he would never live the dreams of Burroughs if he remained in the Chouteau employ. He talked it over with Fremon Delaurier and it was decided that he should attach himself to a caravan going to Bent's fort. Bent could use a young man of his clerking experience. It seemed to be an uneventful trip for he never mentioned it either to any of his children nor to Maxwell or Carson in later life. There are no documents extant to tell us how Beaubien fared in Colorado. I believed he destroyed these because his instincts were too domestic and he always wished to consider himself a gentleman of old France. Not that he put on airs, it was just that he never forgot that he was a Beaubien. He could have gotten along much easier if he remembered to use the name of Trotier once in a while. Later Beaubiens were totally unaware that this was their family name. He had tried a stall on the market place for a time and found he was quite successful. But it did not make him lord of a manor house. There were times when he came in contact with Menard of Kaskaskia but he never associated the name with himself. It was to be years later when the grandson would come into the family through marriage.

The success of the Becknell brothers stirred him to no end. Here was the answer. Burroughs would now become a reality. A short time at Fort Bent and he ventured off again to Santa Fe. There he was able to connect with some Mountain Men who introduced him to Armijo, Salazar, Ulibarri and Miranda. Beaubien had the happy facility of adaptability and before long he was just as much Spanish as they were. When the Spanish flag gave way to the Mexican he applied for and received papers as a Mexican citizen. Because of the number of French-Canadians at Taos he went there to marry, live out his days, die and be buried. It was at Santa Fe that Beaubien first met Guadalupe Miranda, the school teacher, secretary to General Armijo and Secretary of the Department of New Mexico. Miranda was a polished gentleman of the old school. Beaubien loved to be associated with gentlemen. It was go from the start. Miranda was six years older than Beaubien and his friendship went a long ways to start Beaubien off on the right track both in business and with people of influence. American occupation was remote and Texas invasion even less likely since the Republic of Texas was yet to be.

No matter how great a family name Beaubien and Maxwell brought to New Mexico, a distinguishing trait of the inland as well as the coastal settlements seemed to be one of uniform poverty. This did not mean actual lack of food, clothing and shelter. There was game in the forest, and streams could always be relied on for trout and bass. Paul Trotier probably had nothing more to offer Louise Adelaide Durocher than his title of Sieur de Beaubien. Perhaps because the French character acted jointly with the circumstances of the fur trade to create a contrast with the state of wavering diplomacy and the re-appearing warfare between colonists and natives along the St. Lawrence even after the French gave the country up to the English. Very few Canadians accumulated fortunes that could in any way compare with the Dons of New Spain or even with some of the Spanish Dons of New Mexico. Try as Beaubien did in his years at Taos, he was never able to retire to live the life of a Don. True, he spent quite a bit of money trying to colonize southern Colorado in an effort to be called the father founder of something or other; he was never to be a man of wealth, certainly not as Burroughs thought he would or as his son-in-law Lucien B. Maxwell did. Nor was any other French Canadian trapper who sat behind the walls of Taos to lament his swift flying years that separated him from desire and effort because he failed to die in the Land of Enchantment without enchanting riches.

Yet Charles could not fail to see that all of the trappers returned to Trois Rivieres richer than they left. He drifted from Canada to St. Louis to Fort Bent to Santa Fe to Ranchitos de Taos always dreaming of these returning men who seemed to have conquered the world, but the years were passing him by and he still struggled for a living. In 1833 a group of French Canadians at Chicago petitioned the Holy See for a pastor. One of the signers was a Beaubien, younger brother to Charles. That is all that is known about him. So Charles was not such a failure after all. His name is on Senate documents, presidential reports, in every newspaper of the land that was printed from 1880 to 1893. Perhaps Burroughs was right after all. And it was all because of the Maxwell Land Grant.

The Santa Fe Trade that was so encouraging to Becknell, Glenn and Cooper was now out of their hands as too vast an industry as is always the history of a thing that is big. The Santa Fe Trail was shop talk that could not fail to impress Beaubien. If Becknell had not been successful Beaubien would have lived and died in St. Louis and there never would have been a Maxwell Land Grant.

Taos, at the time Beaubien saw it, was the most important place in the province outside of Santa Fe and possibly Albuquerque. In July, or sometimes in August of each year, a bustling activity advertised the grand fair held mostly for the benefit of the Comanches and Plains tribes. Although forbidden by law, tradesmen generally went in various directions to meet prospective customers. The Indians for the most part, brought in deerskins, buffalo hides, and, most important for barter, captives. These latter were exchanged for knives, horses, mules, beads, trinkets, blankets and other implements. For a man of Beaubien's trading experience this was the place to settle down. This place was of further advantage to him when Wolfskill opened up the northern trail to California from Taos in 1831. By this time Beaubien was married, had several children and owned his own business. Taos was not on the main road of the Santa Fe Trail as we know it, but a cutoff. It was considered a port of entry into Mexican territory from the fact that the earliest pack trains entered by that northern mountain route. Later years so systemized the customs that anyone entering the route would be met by troopers of the Taos Company, even though the customs house was moved to Santa Fe. But heavy business continued to be conducted at Taos. By a law of February 17, 1837, this plaza was re-opened as a port of entry and in reverse order the customs business was conducted at Santa Fe.

Taos was hardly more than a village of a little over a thousand souls when Beaubien enters the picture. Built around a plaza it boasted more hard drinking, bailes, fights, dance halls, hotels and business houses than Santa Fe. The parroquia was originally in the hands of Franciscans but shortly before Beaubien's arrival Padre Martinez became the pastor. The padre had been at Tome, then transferred to his birthplace at Abiquiu. He had a brother at Ranchos de Taos whom he frequently visited. It was these visits to his brother that had made him acquainted with Taos. Politically minded, he requested the Mexican Deputation to take measures in having the Taos Church placed in the hands of Saecular priests, giving as his excuse, the limited number of Franciscans and these worked more for the provincial than for the bishop. He named himself as pastor if it were acceptable to the authorities. And it was. Furthermore, the business carried on by the Ayuntamiento of Taos was so tremendous that it ranked with Santa Cruz, Albuquerque and Santa Fe as a "Villas" at least in practice. Padre Martinez was appointed pastor of Taos on July 14, 1824, and was well established and entrenched by the time Beaubien approached him regarding his marriage to the Lovato girl.

The padre and the future owner of the Grant got along well enough until the petition for the Grant went into effect. We know this from several letters that the padre wrote begging the authorities to re-consider giving all that land to a foreigner. Martinez did not trust Beaubien's motives. The government had already been over-exploited; poor people could till the land to advantage without being told by Beaubien that they were on private property. So the Grant was a controversy from the very start. That the educated padre recognized the vastness of the land involved at the very beginning was a strong factor in favor of the Maxwell Land Grant Company when the case went to the Supreme Court several decades later.

Padre Martinez had nothing to gain by fighting Beaubien, Bent, Carson and others as land grabbers. He was only interested in the kingdom of Taos. Neither the Los Animas nor the Sangre de Cristo nor the Miranda-Beaubien tracts touched Taos—yet he fought them all. The padre was sincerely interested in giving the land over to colonists for the expansion of the Mexican government.

"In this parish of San Geronimo de Taos, on the 11th after having obtained the required dispensations for the day of the month of September, of the year 1827, I, the priest, Don Antonio Jose Martinez, pastor of the same, stranger here on July 3, of this year, in favor of Charles Hippolito Beaubien, which dispensation came from the city of Victoria in Durango, and having published the required Canonical banns in the plaza of Taos, on three days that were feasts having solemn Masses, as the Holy Council commanded, which days were September 2,8,9 of this month, the 13th Sunday after Pentacost, the Feast of the Nativity of the Blessed Virgin Mary, the 14th Sunday after Pentacost, and as there seemed to be no impediment to the marriage, and after much investigation and diligent care following the publication of the banns, I united in the bonds of Matrimony 'in facie ecc.' Carlos Beaubien, bachelor, the legitimate son of Pablo Beaubien and Maria Louisa Carlora Durocher, citizen of the placita of the Most Pure Conception of the Virgin Mary del Ranchito de Taos—and—Maria Paula Lovato, single, also a citizen of the same placita. The sponsors being Santiago Martinez and Maria de la Luz Lucero, residents of Fernando de Taos; the witnesses being Jose Tafoya and Gregoria Martin, residents of Fernando de Taos. The marriage took place in the church of Our Lady of Guadalupe." (Parish Records —Book M page 39.)

For the sake of avoiding confusion let us explain that there are four villages known as Taos. At the time of the marriage neither Beaubien nor his bride lived in what we know as Taos. They lived in a little village north and west of Taos (Immaculate Conception or Ranchitos), not to be confused with Ranchos de Taos (San Francisco) which is south of Fernando de Taos (Guadalupe), the pueblo of Taos (San Geronimo) being the northernmost of the four. Marcos and Basil Lajeunesse had a trading post at Ranchitos. Beaubien worked for them as well as Paula's father. She came to the store quite often and a romance sprung up. After the violent death of one of the Lajeunesse brothers the survivor took Beaubien in as partner. After a time he sold out to Beaubien who opened a store at Fernando de Taos, leaving the Ranchitos store in the hands of Lee who became his brother-in-law. Later Joseph Pley took charge, then Maxwell. Another store was opened in Mora and Pley went there. Taos was the metropolis and the place for a successful businessman to live. There Beaubien built his house. The Ranchitos property also grew the crops for the horses and feed for the goats. Just when Beaubien disposed of the Ranchitos property I have not been able to find out.

The first child born to the Beaubiens was Narciso. He was not baptised at Taos. Nor could I find any baptismal records for any of the Beaubiens. This leads me to believe that the children were taken to Santa Fe for Baptism. The first daughter was Maria da la Luz or Luz as she was called. She married Lucian Maxwell and was co-owner with him of the entire Maxwell Land Grant. Other children were Leonore, Juanita, Teodora, Petrita and Pablo. All were short and in later life very rotund except Teodora who was tall and slender. Virginia Maxwell Keyes was to be very much like her. All are part of the history of the Grant because, with the exception of Narciso, all shared in the ownership. Business prospered from the start. It had to because of the ever increasing Santa Fe trade. But it never made a rich man of Beaubien. He was not lacking for company. Bent, Ledoux, Charette, Roubidoux, Carson and so many others made his home their calling place. The natives soon recognized him as a friend and advisor.

One of the frequent visitors was Guadalupe Miranda. He was a student. In Mexico Iturbide had dethroned the Viceroy Apodaca and created a triumvirate consisting of generals Nicolas Bravo, Guadalupe Victoria and Pedro Celestino Negret. On April 14, 1823, the national coat of arms and flag was established by an act of Congress. Santa Anna was made governor of Santa Cruz, but was quite dissatisfied with the appointment. Under the constitution of 1824, New Mexico, together with Upper and Lower California and Colima, were admitted into the Republic of Mexico as territories, the authorities in each place to continue in power until the legislature should be installed. Guadalupe Victoria was made president, followed by Guerrero who was definitely on the outs with Santa Anna. His revolt succeeded and placed Gomez Pedraza in power. Santa Anna finally took over the government and was dictator when Miranda and Beaubien applied for the Grant.

All this time Miranda was in Mexico acquiring knowledge. He studied with the Dominicans for a time; then with the Franciscans. He came to know Santa Anna and was loyal to him to the day of his death. If Beaubien was frail looking, Miranda was just the opposite. Six feet tall, he weighed two hundred and twenty pounds. Squared shouldered he rarely got into a fight because no one cared to pick one with him. Always neatly dressed, he never carried a gun even when traveling through Indian country. He was born in Chihuahua and came to New Mexico on business. He liked it so much he decided to stay. He opened a private school in Santa Fe at the parroquia under the auspices of Friar Juan Rafael Rascon, the Franciscan pastor. He had a grand time teaching the children of the Dons Spanish, Latin, Greek, and a little philosophy since it seemed likely that Santa Fe would soon have a bishop of its own. Miranda was in hopes that Friar Rascon would be named first bishop, and even wrote up the by-laws governing a minor seminary. Miranda was a pius Catholic and was never known to say a harsh or cruel word. He was ever ready to help anyone in distress and would have made a model friar if he felt that it was his vocation.

When Santiago Abreu became jefe politico on April 24, 1832, his brother, Marcelino, who was conducting a public school at Santa Fe, resigned the position as head master to help him. He was not successful as a politician. Aware of Miranda's devotion for the Vicar-General at the parroquia he asked Friar Rascon to exert his influence over Miranda advising him that the vacancy should be filled promptly and the position paid five hundred pesos a year. In addition Abreu was willing to build a new and more modern school. Santiago also spoke to Miranda about accepting the position. The Abreus loved education and knew that Miranda would carry out a program to suit their tastes. It was because Friar Rascon asked him that he accepted. One obligation imposed upon Miranda was that he must report any student failing to attend school to the Deputation through the Ayuntamiento. All went well for a time until Albino Perez came to Santa Fe as the new governor. A revolution broke out at Santa Cruz and gained momentum over the province. As a result the Abreus lost their heads and Armijo was ushered into the governor's chair, after de-capitating Gonzolez, the Taos Indian, who tasted glory for a day, only to perish in just as short a time. Miranda could not join in the revolt because Perez was lawfully constituted authority. When Santa Anna recognized Armijo, Miranda pledged his loyalty.

Under Armijo, Guadalupe Miranda, besides being Secretary of the Province, was also Armijo's private secretary and Collector of Customs for the government on its northern frontier, the Arkansas river. Miranda and Armijo were on the best of terms. If there was any graft to be obtained, the governor sent lesser officials to obtain it, knowing that it was against Miranda's conscience to do any dirty work for him. In his trips from Taos to Santa Fe, the former school teacher visited the governor quite often and told him of Beaubien. Just who it was that first mentioned the idea of a grant is hard to say. I am inclined to think that Armijo brought it up.

Other fast moving events were shaping the course of history in America and Texas. Governor Armijo's spies informed him that the republic to the east of him was fitting out an expeditionary force for the capture of Santa Fe. Texas claimed all the territory west of the boundaries she then had to the Rio Grande, which meant that Santa Fe belonged to Texas. This claim of Texas is important to remember because it was a major argument used by McMains against the Maxwell Land Grant Company. The Texans insisted that part of New Mexico was included in the treaty of peace with Mexico following the Texan War of Independence. Since the Mexican government would not turn the land over, Texans would take by force of arms what they considered as theirs. Armijo called together his captains, Padre Leyba, Padre Martinez, Salazar, Ulibarri, Bueno, Cortez and others to decide what course to pursue. Guadalupe Miranda was commissioned to write up patriotic propaganda in order to stir up the people to defend their country against the invader. Little matter whether they could read or not. Someone could read the circulars to them in the plaza of each community.

Miranda stayed up all night writing a rather bombastic edict that was sent the next morning to the printer C. de Baca who was working for Padre Martinez at Taos. The padre owned the only workable press in New Mexico at the time. Miranda's proclamation had to suit the personality of Armijo and the people were to be told that it was the governor's own writing. The scholar would have preferred a more classic approach. Months with Armijo gave him an insight to the man that has been lost to the world forever since he never put his impressions on paper. Armijo could strut like a peacock in or out of uniform but he could hardly read much less write as a man that befits his station. In this he was like Kit Carson. He had enough reading and writing to get by on but for his day this is saying a lot since many others in high places could do little more in the field of letters.

The threat from Texas came shortly after Miranda and Beaubien received the Grant. This explains why little or no colonization was done on the Grant. It takes time to survey property especially the size of some states in the East. We must remember that Beaubien not only had his finger in what was to be known as the Maxwell Land Grant, which of course is erroneous because it is the Miranda-Beaubien Grant, but also in the Sangre de Cristo and the Las Animas Grants. All in all he owned land that covered an area larger than Delaware, Connecticut and Rhode Island. He was possibly the largest individual land owner in the history of the United States. We speak here of history since the break with England. The Reavis and Beales Grants were not admitted by the Supreme Court. While they were certainly much larger the claims were proven false or forfeited. Beaubien boasted ownership of land from the site of the present city of Pueblo in Colorado to Springer, New Mexico over to Costilla, New Mexico and up to Fort Garland in Colorado. It was an empire. If he had the ability of Maxwell for making money; the cunning of Waddingham; the popularity of Dorsey; the education of Miranda; the personality of Chaffee, the two Beaubien girls living today—the last of the name and line —would be queens of what is known as the Kingdom of Colfax. Beaubien set out to be a baron; he became a king. All he gave to the enterprise was the noble name of Beaubien. He ruled alone because Miranda was too busy with the affairs of state to worry about what he owned or what he could do with his share of the Grant. He moved in political circles. He was above all a patriot. He loved Mexico and had the gumption to die in his own fatherland. A man is physically dead who does not love his country. The difference in the two men is that Miranda never forgot that he was a Mexican; Beaubien was a French-Canadian who became a thorough American. Beaubien lies buried in American soil. That honor no one shall ever take away from him. An the place that contains his grave is a state monument. He deserves the honor because he did his bit for the progress of the nation even though he failed in the progress of Beaubien. He founded towns, cultivated soil, wrote laws, worked for law and order which is more than can be said for Miranda or even Maxwell. Beaubien failed in business because he put himself aside finally to make America his business. In this he showed his gratitude to a country that gave him all in recognizing his claims.

The Texan threat produced trying days for Beaubien. What if they won? Would they recognize his claims. He had been so loyal to Armijo. These Grants were given in recognition for his loyalty. He would have to sit tight and await the outcome. Miranda was doing his part to arouse the people. He went from village to village stirring the people to heights of patriotism such as they had never known before. His black, beady eyes sparkled as he painted scenes of victory in his nasal, polished tones. Everywhere he went the enthusiasm of the people was aroused to such a pitch that victory seemed assured long before the battle was fought. Indeed, there was to be no battle. The Mexican took over without bloodshed as the Americans were to take over without bloodshed with this difference; that Salazar committed some atrocities that today would rank him with the Nazis.

Some years ago an editor of a Southwestern magazine attempted, in several installments, the story of Maxwell and his land grant. It is pitiable the way he spoke of Beaubien and Miranda. He was under the impression that Miranda was the wife of Carlos Beaubien. In the second article he lamented the fact that Miranda turned out to be a very virile man. All his life he attempted to uplift the masses. What he could never figure out was why Armijo was so victorious with the Texan expedition and such a failure against General Kearny. Miranda became a one man crusade in Dona Ana, El Paso and Mesilla in the hopes of arousing the people to push back the invader. It was only towards the end of his life several decades after the approach of Kearney that he finally conceded that America was here to stay. Whatever his lights we must admire his courage. He is the forerunner of McMains —a fighter of lost causes; thus lost himself.

In the '30's the Texans formed a republic independent of Mexico. In doing so, they set as their boundary the Rio Grande to its source and thence by a line due north to the 42nd parallel. This boundary, if established, would include a large part of the land in the Department of New Mexico. Under the circumstances the claim set up by Texas might be regarded merely as a magnificent assertion to be traded upon for such advantages as it might be able to bring. That the Texans themselves regarded it in this light is evident from the course adopted by the authorities in connection with the expedition that set out in 1841. McMains constantly harped on this claim in the struggle for the Anti-Granters.

From 1838 to 1841, the president of the Republic of Texas was General Mirabeau B. Lamar. A crusader, journalist and a native of Georgia, he found his way to Texas in 1835 because he wanted to take an active part in the revolution. He was ambitious and many called him a visionary. He had at heart the assertion of Texan authority on the upper Rio Grande which of course meant New Mexico. His aims were two-fold: To divert the Santa Fe trade to Texas; to bring about a change of government in New Mexico where he had heard that the people were ripe for revolution. The troops of the expedition, headed by General McLeod, marched thirteen hundred miles from Austin to Antonchico, near Las Vegas. These were two two hundred and seventy volunteers in six companies under Captains Caldwell, Sutton, Houghton, Hudson, Strain and Lewis. Lewis was captain of the artillery. He knew a little Spanish and later proved himself the Benedict Arnold of the army. Fifty more were attached to the column in some capacity or other. Indians, drought, hunger, physical exhaustion made the little army a sorry sight by the time it reached Antonchico so that it had to throw itself on the mercy of Armijo. Damasio Salazar accepted their arms in the name of the Mexican government and imprisoned them at San Miguel del Bado. Here they first met General Armijo and his troops. Miranda, who was with Armijo, took pity on them but did not intervene since they were enemies of the state.

President Lamar was not as visionary as he is painted. To him the annexation of New Mexico was as real as it was necessary. Texas was financially broke. The trade that went to Santa Fe could be diverted to Austin. In 1837, George S. Park, a Texan who had escaped from the Comanche Indians and joined a caravan for Santa Fe, wrote from that town to Austin: "If Texas would open communications with Santa Fe it would be possible to secure peaceably that important position in the interior of North America; that key which will unlock to the enterprise of North Americans the valuable country of California on the shores of the Pacific. New Mexico would offer no resistance."

This was the beginning. As it turned out, America and not the Republic of Texas was to see the Pacific. On May 1, 1841, Manuel Alvarez, the United States Consul at Santa Fe called in General Armijo and Guadalupe Miranda for a special conference. All the Americans, to say nothing of the Texans, in Santa Fe wanted the republic to the east to take over. All of Taos county except Padre Martinez, Carlos Beaubien, Lee, and several others were in favor of the invaders. If the Texans won, what would be the position of the American consul? The Texans made a treaty with the Navajos, hoping for an uprising from the western part of New Mexico as they entered the eastern. All this caused the consul some concern and he pleaded with Miranda to find some means to assure the Americans in Santa Fe safe conduct, as well as the protection of American property.

William G. Dryden, who lived in Santa Fe, wrote a series of letters to the president of Texas explaining why he should capture Santa Fe. McMains was later to write a series of letters to the governor of Texas—such convincing letters that the governor was to send a committee to Santa Fe to investigate why that section of the country was not in Texan hands. McMains felt that if Texas took over the Maxwell Land Grant would be dissolved and he could safely petition for the Crow Creek property he had squatted on.

Two others, Rowland and Workman, in ca-hoots with Dryden, were captured at San Miguel del Bado and on Rowland's person was found a letter from the president to Dryden. This Rowland was later released and built a trading post at San Miguel del Bado. He was a great help to General Kearny. Canseco, the Minister of Finance, sent $10,000 to General Armijo for the purpose of defense. General Marian Aristo was placed in command of the troops along the Rio Grande. Canseco sent another $15,000 and a promise of more troops. This accounts for how Miranda's edicts were paid for. Just how much Armijo pocketed is hard to say. He was in the habit of looking out for himself so he probably took at least one sixth as was his custom. Antonio Sandoval of Albuquerque was sent among the Pueblo Indians to buy their friendship probably with a few gallons of Taos Fire-water. Santiago Ulibarri of the new placita of Las Vegas was placed in charge of scouts. The campaign for the Texan invasion was vastly different than the one for the American invasion. Damasio Salazar and Ulibarri offered one hundred dollars to the first one who would send word of the whereabouts of the Texans. It was Armijo's own nephew who led the group of fanatics in the attack on the U. S. Consul's home in Santa Fe when victory favored Armijo. Thirteen U. S. citizens went to Miranda demanding protection. After the capture of the first group of Texans, because of the betrayal by Lewis, Armijo went to Las Vegas where he set up headquarters and awaited word from Salazar. (See the full amount in the October 1923 issue—Southwestern Quarterly Review—the article New Mexico and the Texan-Santa Fe Expedition by Wm. Campbell Brinkley) Wrote the American Consul to Daniel Webster on Feb. 2, 1842, from his hotel room in Washington, D. C.:

" . . . I had received an insulting letter from General Armijo forbidding me to leave the city of Santa Fe until he returned. But this is not all: on the same day, the 16th, a part of the threats that we had heard before from the rabble were to be put into execution. This day in the morning, the Governor with all the regular soldiers and military of Santa Fe for the frontier; a few minutes after they left the public square, the Governor's nephew, Ensign Don Tomas Martin, his most intimate friend and confident, returned to the square in which are all the public offices and stores, galloped to the jail for one of the Texan prisoners and from thence to my office and commenced abusing me in the grossest and most insulting manner. When he arrived at my house he was accompanied by only the Texan prisoner, but as soon as he had entered and I was about to master him, there came to his assistance Sergeant (now Ensign) Pablo Dominguez, employed in one of the military offices, one private soldier and a crowd of the populace. With this help trying to assassinate me, I suppose, I was badly hurt, and at last received from Ensign Martin a severe wound in the face. At this time Don Guadalupe Miranda, Secretary of this Department, came in, appeesed the leaders and sent the multitude out of my house." So, in spite of himself Miranda did do a service for the U. S. government even though he said he would never become a citizen of the country that robbed him of his country.

The successful outcome of the Mexican arms made Miranda jubilant. He plunged deeper into affairs of the state, taking time out to visit Beaubien in Taos and to talk over plans for surveying the Grant. The two discussed the idea of colonizing and planting. One day James Magoffin visited Beaubien and the gravity of manner of the partner told Miranda that all was not as it should be. He asked Beaubien what the trouble was and was told that the U. S. Senate was talking of a coast to coast America. Miranda left for Santa Fe.

And so did Magoffin.

Again Miranda wrote edicts, proclamations and patriotic propaganda. Again Armijo told New Mexicans to gird on the sword against the invader. But Magoffin gave

Armijo facts and figures. This was not a few adventurers from Texas. He now had to deal with Americans under a capable leader. How much Magoffin gave Armijo to prevent bloodshed the general never told. If he gave anything at all. We only have the trader's word for it. It was his stock argument when he applied to Congress for a re-fund. Armijo would never say because it would be admitting that he sold out his country.

Word came that Kearny's troops were already in Las Vegas. It was a blow to Miranda's pride that his own people fired not a shot in defense of their village. But Miranda had not seen the difference in the equipment of the American soldiers and the out of date affairs the alcalde of Las Vegas passed out with which they were supposed to defend their village. Armijo decided to make a stand at Apache Canyon about twenty miles east of Santa Fe. It was a natural fortress. Archuleta, Miranda, Bueno, Cortez and Ulibarri talked over the plans. Padre Martinez was there also. They rode to the canyon. Suddenly Armijo decided to return to Santa Fe, pack his belongings and head south. As Armijo was the head of the government, Miranda had no choice but to follow. Armijo opened all the warehouses in Santa Fe taking all the soap, sugar and furs to sell in El Paso (present Juarez) and Chihuahua. Kearny marched into Santa Fe without opposition. Beaubien visited the general and was appointed judge of the northern district of New Mexico.

Miranda lived in the hopes that the Americans were only passing through New Mexico on their way to California. Daily he awaited word from friends that the path was clear for his return. Said the Santa Fe Republican for September 10, 1847: "We understand that Armijo, Miranda, Archuleta and Ortiz are at El Paso waiting until they deem it safe to return to this territory." On November 6, 1847, a soldier nearby wrote:

"El Paso was taken by a detachment from Col. Lane's command. We learn that the detachment was twenty strong with Captain Stillman, one sergeant and one corporal . . . in all twenty-three men. They entered the town under the direction and guidance of Captain Stillman just as all were going to church and when the plaza was filled with men. Armijo dropped his cloak and fled, and when they encamped Stillman sent him a message to come in, which he did, and took a parole of honor not to leave. He also, we are informed, offered $10,000 to the people if they would drive the soldiers out of town, but could not persuade them to undertake it. Captain Stillman then went up to the Jornada del Muerte where he met the main body of troops. Armijo fled to Chihuahua, thus violating parole. The army captured all of Armijo's sugar and soap of great quantity which he had there and which he was trading in. If he had used more of the latter on himself he and we would not be in our present state of difficulties. Miranda, Ponce, Valverde did not violate parole. Neither did Ortiz."

The American-El Paso Expeditionary Force took possession of El Paso on November 8, 1848. The troops were commanded by Lt. Col. R. H. Lane. As the soldier quoted above wrote, it was first thought that Stillman captured the city and dealt with Armijo. But later investigation showed that it was Sergeant Smith of Company A who went in advance of Lane with twenty men, taking along Captain Stillman, a scout with a knowledge of Spanish. Armijo as well as Miranda made voluntary surrender of himself to Smith. Instead of taking them into custody, Smith gave them parole on the request of several of their friends who were known to be favorable to the American cause. Armijo skipped but Miranda felt that his word was his honor and remained. Smith was promptly clamped in jail pending court-martial. After a plausable explanation to Lane he was released. Whether he was the same Smith who raised a full company in Scotts County, Kentucky and was voted by his men the rank of captain and who walked eighteen miles before breakfast to get into the battle of Monterrey, I have not been able to verify.

Miranda realized that so long as Armijo had money he would seek to buy his way into the governorship again no matter under what flag he served. While never admitting the conquest of his country, he felt that he could at least be friendly with the conquerors. Such a friendship would have its advantages following a treaty of peace. Besides he wished to see Beaubien and continue their plans for the vast tract of land they owned. He was told that the American government permitted land owners to keep their land if they could prove title. Soon he was trusted enough to be given important services to perform. He told his people that it was useless to fight against the superiority of American arms. The howitzers and other large guns would wipe them out. He knew for certain now that America would never relinquish the conquered territory.

Meantime Armijo was offering large sums of money to men in El Paso, San Lorenzo, Chihuahua and other towns if they would form guerilla parties to wipe out an American soldier here and there; to capture advance scouting parties; to bring in information concerning the plans of the main body of troops. No one accepted his money. There are some things money cannot buy. Miranda's star was in the ascent:

"Mr. Miranda, former Secretary of this Territory under Governor Armijo, arrived in Santa Fe from El Paso yesterday. (Dec. 10, 1847.) El Paso is his place of residence. He is an accomplished gentleman and one whose deportment secured the good will of Col. Doniphan's army, and one whose gentlemanly bearing entitles him to a great deal of consideration." (Santa Fe Republican.)

Miranda took advantage of the opportunity to visit Beaubien, and was glad that his partner spoke to General Kearny about the Grant. True the general told him that such matters were out of his jurisdiction but the fact that the general made him judge spoke volumes. Beaubien often made trips to Santa Fe and struck up an acquaintance with all the new officials. He even had himself appointed agent for subscribers for the Santa Fe Republican newspaper. (January 18, 1848.) Armijo continued to agitate in Chihuahua. When he realized at last that the Americans were not interested in him he made overtures to them in the hope that they would give him some position of responsibility if only to save face with his people. In Chihuahua he was just another man; in New Mexico he would be Don Manuel. General Price was informed of Armijo's desire to return to New Mexico. He was granted permission to return. He settled in Albuquerque for a time and then in Lemitar.

When Armijo received news that he was permitted to return to New Mexico he invited all his friends to a banquet, opened a barrel of wine and toasted himself as "Once again Governor of New Mexico." Miranda who was also at the banquet smiled and suggested that Armijo had better wait until he was in Santa Fe before making such a boast. To which Armijo replied that he would not be asked to return to New Mexico unless it was for the purpose of being named Governor. The Americans needed him for they did not understand his people. Miranda did not tell him that if he had understood them better and treated them like human beings, he would not be here making boastful toasts. Besides, the Americans proved that they could get along without him by putting Don Donciano Vijil in office and then Bent who spoke Spanish like a native.

The Taos rebellion lead by Pablo Montoya and Tomacito, a Taos Indian, was the only major strike against American Occupation raised in New Mexico. There were other minor uprisings at Tome, Las Vegas and Mora but none as serious as the Taos affair. Cortez, Bueno and others made attempts elsewhere but no one paid serious attention to them. January 17, 1847—a never to be forgotten day in the memory of Beaubien. Governor Bent was scalped; Luis Lee, the acting sheriff; Cornelio Vijil, prefect and probate judge of Taos county; J. W. Leal, a lawyer; Pablo Jaramillo, brother of Mrs. Bent; Narciso Beaubien—all lost their lives that fatal day. After the killings at Taos the revolutionists marched nine miles north to Arroyo Hondo and killed a few Americans there. Lee's brother walked all the way to Santa Fe to inform General Price of the rebellion. The general began his attack on the pueblo on February 3, for if Kearny captured New Mexico without bloodshed, Price spilt the blood of two hundred to keep it. Of his own men he lost but few. Captain Burgwin lost his life in this battle.

Beaubien was in a daze for a long time following the death of his oldest son. He refused to live in Taos and moved to Santa Fe. He talked to no one, ate nothing for days; just sat in a chair staring into space. After a time he got over it and went back to Taos. But he again saw signs of rebellion and again went back to Santa Fe which explains why Maxwell did not have any supplies for Fremont when sent down from the site of Pueblo to obtain them in the fall of that year. Wrote James Calhoun, Indian agent, on Feb. 2, 1850:

"I took occasion to consult Judge Beaubien of the Supreme Court . . . and the curate (Padre Martinez) not only of Fernando de Taos but also of the Indian pueblo three miles away. The two gentlemen have a controling influence over the Indians and the curate was one of the delegates elected last September by the votes of those Indians (they were not permitted to vote after the Military Government gave way to the Territorial Government of 1851), and Judge Beaubien acted in concert with the successful clique." The Indians were told by some die-hards that the Federal government would destroy them so they took to plundering and the scorched-earth policy as well as plotting some killings. Said the Indian agent: "I am satisfied that Judge Beaubien is incapable of approving such conduct. Judge Beaubien and the priest met with the Indians and gave them a satisfactory explanation of the American policy." Calhoun, through the influence of Beaubien and the padre, was able to meet the Indians and deliver an address in which he frequently used the words " . . . your wise and good priest . . . and the just and upright Judge Beaubien."

All seemed quiet for a time and Beaubien put his house in order. He lost contact with Miranda because the latter chose to live not only in a country apart but in a world apart. He turned the affairs of the Grant over to Maxwell because he now controlled the Sangre de Cristo Grant which was closer to home and here he would put into effect all that he learned at St. Louis. Again revolt flared up. Wrote the Judge on June 11, 1851 to the Indian Agent at Santa Fe:

"I have been an inhabitant of the territory (of New Mexico) and the valley of Taos in particular for many years and I believe that I understand the native Mexican well. There have been indications within the past few weeks sufficient to convince me that a rebellion against the constituted United States authorities is in contemplation among the lower classes of the inhabitantes of the valley of Taos. Every effort has been made to incite the masses by which I mean the vagabond and unoccupied part of the population against the Americans. From information I have had from reliable sources, secret meetings have been held under various pretenses for the purpose of organizing an insurrection, the object of which was the extermination of Americans and the robbery of their property." As a result of this letter a force of artillery was sent to Taos on June 24, 1851.

Constantly in all his letters as well as in his petitions for grants, Beaubien makes reference to the unemployed who are in his eyes vagabonds, schemers, plotters, thieves, killers and of no particular use on earth. It was an obsession with him. There was no such thing as unemployment. He got things the hard way. Anyone else could. America was the land of opportunity. Burroughs had taught him that. He visioned a Utopia somewhat on the plan of St. Thomas More and the Transcendentalists of New England; a sort of admixture of both although he neither read nor heard of either. Possibly Burroughs gave him the idea a long time ago. By his own admission Beaubien was a little read man. He once remarked that he had never read more than five books in his whole life. Miranda the educated; Beaubien the traveler. Was Burroughs right after all?

Through the years Miranda kept up his contact with Beaubien and Magoffin. It was Miranda who took care of the people who wanted to remain Mexican subjects under the Gadsden Purchase and Treaty. It was Miranda who urged the people of Dona Ana, Mesilla, Franklin not to become American citizens. He was sort of clerk for the government at Chihuahua. His oldest son came frequently to visit Beaubien and settled for some time at Santa Fe. His father did not force him to reject American citizenship. While Beaubien forgave the Indians the killing of his son, he never lived down the memory of the boy. When the story of Taos is told more will be learned of Narciso Beaubien.

Some time after the Civil War Miranda moved to Chihuahua where he was living until shortly after 1884.

He died about that time having lived to a ripe old age. He was visited by reporters from the New York Herald in 1882, but had very little to add to what was already known about the Maxwell Land Grant. Several Maxwell Land Grant officials visited him for an estimate of the acreage of the Grant but he could not definitely say except that it was vast, which they already knew. He is buried in Chihuahua, the only possessor of the Grant on foreign soil and this is as it should be because the Grant was made when New Mexico was a foreign country.

Application for the Grant was made on January 8, 1841. There seems to be no question that the petition was drawn up by Miranda in his scholarly Spanish. Miranda's position with the government was probably responsible for Armijo's prompt answer. Within three days the governor saw fit to "grant and donate to the individuals subscribed the land therein expressed, in order that they may make the proper use of it which the law allows." It seems that a petition was put in writing as well as a concession that was already asked for and given by word of mouth. Miranda standing in as he did with Armijo probably had no difficulty in getting what he wanted. It possibly would have taken Beaubien longer. Armijo did make other grants to other French-Canadians and Americans. He was free with the land because it also meant money in his pocket. He demanded one-sixth of all the profits. That was the way he operated. And money was money whether it came from a Mexican or a French-Canadian. Despite Armijo's love for wine, women and song he was able to save enough to end his days in luxury. Whether his nephew Martin got the bulk of his fortune after his death I cannot say. The Martins did move from Santa Fe to Socorro and it is possible that they went through their inheritance in no time since they are rather poor today.

Upon receiving the Grant, Miranda and Beaubien wrote to the Justice of the Peace, Don Cornelio Vijil, of Taos, asking that he place them in possession according to the law, which he did. The padre at Taos was well aware of what was going on. He was intimate with General Armijo, who usually consulted him for advice. Perhaps he was chagrined that two members of his parish did not confide in him, especially two such influential parishioners. He boasted frequently to many that Taos would be a dull place without him, which was probably true. He overboasted his education which was what sickened Kit Carson against him. He wrote Armijo that Miranda and Beaubien were fairly well off and had no need for additional property. If he must give land away, why not give it to the poor? Furthermore a portion of the land in question conflicted with a claim made by Charles Bent. Could Armijo really trust Beaubien and Bent?

Armijo, who always sat up and took notice when a letter came from Padre Martinez, called for a suspension of the Miranda and Beaubien rights until an appeal by the padre could reach the central government in Mexico City. The suspended petition was signed by Don Mariano Chaves who acted as governor pro-tem until Armijo was re-appointed on April 13, 1844. The Assembly feeling that the two men had been unjustly treated, quickly re-instated Beaubien and Miranda. A letter of complaint against Martinez was written by Beaubien and the reasons he put forth for demanding back his property more than justified the action of the Assembly. The fact that Beaubien alone put forth the complaint and made the demand should have left him sole heir to the Grant since Miranda was making no effort to get back what was rightfully his. For some unknown reason Miranda had nothing to say about neither the suspension nor the re-instatement.

Antonio Jose Martinez was born at Abiquiu, New Mexico, on January 17, 1793, of Antonio Severiano Martinez and arMia del Carmen Santistevan. At ten, he attended the Aphebetical School of Abiquiu, until he was twelve. His father bought a ranch at Taos and the young student gave up school for farm work. He spent his spare time in furthering his education privately. In 1812 he married Maria de la Luz Martinez, also of Abiquiu, the daughter of Manuel Martinez and Maria de la Luz Quintana. They were not related. His wife died in 1814, leaving a baby girl named Luz. She died at her uncle's house in 1825. His wife's death aided his decision to uplift his people as a priest. In this he was encouraged by the Bishop of Durango. He left for Mexico on March 10, 1817, to enter the seminary at Durango. He was ordained on February 16, 1822, returning to New Mexico where he was appointed to the Tome parish. After a short time there he was transferred to Abiquiu. In July 1824 he went to Taos where he established a co-educational school, a rather advanced idea for the time. He also maintained a seminary at Taos and had eleven seminarians under his guidance. Padre Lucero of Arroyo Hondo was one of his pupils. He served as a member of the Departamental Assembly in 1830, 1831 and 1836. He published New Mexico's first newspaper. He served in the legislature of the Territory of New Mexico in 1852 and 1853. He became involved in difficulties with his superiors as well as with Bent, Carson and Beaubien. Like Cromwell he lived in advance of his time. He died on July 27, 1867. He lies buried near Beaubien.

Under the treaty between the United States and Mexico, following the Mexican war, citizens of New Mexico might leave the territory or remain either as citizens of the United States or revert to Mexico. They had one year to decide. As a result of this ruling many of the wealthy haciendados withdrew with their peones and movable possessions to the State of Chihuahua. The boundary between the two countries was not at El Paso as it is today, but further north above the village of Mesilla. Miranda, as we have seen, chose to remain a citizen of Mexico despite his wealth and his vast holdings in New Mexico. He was in public office from 1839 until the coming of the Americans and felt he owed his country a certain amount of loyalty. It was a sense of justice rather that moulded his decision. Whatever he had came from the government, he could not now reject the hand that fed him.

In 1853 Miranda was appointed Commissioner-General of Mexico to induce Mexicans in New Mexico to locate and colonize lands south of the Rio Grande. It was he who placed in possession the people that migrated from Mesilla. This portion of Mexico, north of El Paso, came into the hands of the American government with the Gadsden Purchase. Miranda makes his appearance now and then in the history of that area and save for the negotiations covering the sale of his share of the Grant appears no more in our story. He seems to have met with financial reverses which was the real reason for selling such valuable land. His son Pablo, at Santa Fe, received delegation from him to act as his agent in the disposal of his property. He had intended to sell it in 1846 after the arrival of the Americans for he states that Bent had offered to buy it. Since Bent was killed in the Taos rebellion he must have approached Miranda after the latter's return from Chihuahua. He also said that several other persons told of their interest in obtaining his half of the Grant. The advance of Americans made a poor man of him, so he claimed, so he was forced into the humiliation of selling. He had much rather sell to his good friend Beaubien, who placed it in the hands of his son-in-law Maxwell. Pablo Miranda and Maxwell met in Santa Fe to talk over the deal. Young Miranda received one thousand dollars in U. S. currency, a note for an additional thousand to be paid on July 1, 1858, with five hundred more to be paid when the United States Congress would pass favorably on the claim. Added to this Beaubien himself was to receive two hundred and forty-five dollars for expenses paid by him for investigating the legality of the Grant. The rest of our story is now written because of this sale. Had Miranda refused to sell the story would have ended here. But in selling he saved himself the headaches that were to be the heritage of Maxwell, the Maxwell Land Grant and Railway Company, the Maxwell Land Grant Company, the squatters and the host of people in any way connected with them. Viewing it now after the lapse of so many years, Miranda acted wisely in selling. Only the courts remember his name. It was erased from the Grant as was Beaubien's.

Sometimes things come easy to a man as they did for Beaubien at Taos. More often as not they prove to be the calm before the storm. When the rebellion broke loose, Narciso Beaubien, with a trusted Indian slave, was not at the Beaubien residence. Hearing the tumult, the pair suspected what was afoot and hid in an out-house under a straw-covered trough. The insurgents looked for them in vain. A woman in favor of the revolt who saw them go into hiding yelled to the retreating searchers to come back and kill the sucklings lest they grow up to be men of revenge. The two were killed and scalped.

Narcisco had been a student at Cape Giradeau College south of St. Louis. His father selected the school because of his knowledge of it from his own St. Louis days. He had been absent from Taos for five years. On his return trip to Taos all he did was to glorify the place never suspecting that he was going to his death. His father probably had a certain amount of satisfaction as presiding judge at the court that condemned six men to death; five for murder; one for treason. Perhaps not one of them was involved in the death of his son, but they were part of the insurrection that brought it about and therefore equally as guilty. Narcisso was sixteen at the time of his death.

On December 27, 1843 Narciso Beaubien and Louis Lee petitioned for a grant of land which Armijo referred to the prefect three days after he received the request. No doubt Miranda drew up the petition. Armijo, who was acquainted with the entire Beaubien family, was well aware of the age of Narciso at the time. He also knew that the boy was away at Giradeau College. Joseph Pley acted for Narciso. On January 7, 1844, the justice of peace at Taos placed the petitioners in possession of the Sangre de Cristo Grant. Lee's wife was Mrs. Beaubien's sister.

In 1840 Bent and St. Vrain, trappers and traders, and well known to Beaubien who worked for them for a time, established a trading post near Adobe Creek, Fremont county, in Colorado. They told Beaubien that he had complete charge of the post if he were willing to take over. Besides it would be an asset in his Taos trade for there was a slump that year. Beaubien accepted. This gave him plenty of time to examine the country and to put into effect the Utopia he dreamed about in St. Louis. He consulted Manuel Le Fevre, LeDoux, Lajeunesse and Pley. It was the opinion of several of them that the time was not yet ripe for the project. Several insisted that he would be more successful in the Rayado country on his own Grant. Furthermore the country was in bad shape financially no matter how tremendous the Santa Fe trade seemed to be. Burdened by taxes, harassed by Indians, enslaved by dons, the people, for the moment, seemed at their wits end. To ask them to start a new colony would be ill advised at the moment. Carson and Maxwell were of the same opinion.

While Beaubien acted on this advice he did not completely cast it out of his mind. This land must be his someday. Nothing ventured, nothing gained. It would not be difficult to dispose of the property should his project fail. Miranda, when told of it one Sunday after dinner, stated that the Rayado area seemed safer from Indian attack and closer to home. He would speak to Armijo about it. Lee was from St. Louis and well known to Beaubien, an added reason why he was named to be partner with Narciso in the Sangre de Cristo Grant. Whether Beaubien would have succeeded with his plan in Colorado had not both owners been killed in the Taos revolt is a matter of conjecture. The possibility is that he would have gone ahead with the venture in Rayado.

There appears to be no record of settlement on the Sangre de Cristo Grant during the three years succeeding the formal acquisition of the land petitioned for on December 26, 1843. Jose Miguel Sanchez, justice of the peace at Taos, fixed the boundaries for this Grant which was enormous, the Colorado side taking in over 1,000,000 acres. This was also referred to as the Beaubien Grant. Joseph Pley was the administrator of the property following the death of Lee. He found insufficient personal property belonging to the deceased to satisfy the claims against the estate to meet the debts. Accordingly, on May 4, 1948, he sold Lee's half to Beaubien for one hundred dollars. The other half fell to Beaubien as heir of Narciso. This sale is not as rough as it appears to be on the surface. Beaubien took Lee in when he first came to Taos. He fed him, clothed him, loaned him money, fitted him out for his wedding, set him up in his own home following his marriage, gave him a partnership in the store at Taos and bought some ranch property for him near Ranchos de Taos. The hundred dollars was the wiping off of Lee's debts.

Once the property was in his hands he began preaching colonization to the people of Taos so that by the summer of 1851 a band of Taosenos started a settlement on the Rio Culebra near the present town of San Luis in Colorado. Through Beaubien's efforts the colony proved stable and was soon followed by the plazitas of San Pedro (1852), San Acasio (1853) and Chama (1853-54).

Beaubien's first town of San Luis became quite a village and the social problems of the settlers became complex. Judge Beaubien promulgated certain rules for the government of the plaza and now at long last he would prove to the city fathers of St. Louis that he knew how to govern a town as well as establish one. Here are some of his rules:

"Insomuch as no civilized society can endure in good order, peace and union, which constitutes the happiness of civilized peoples and establishes the superiority and advantages which Christians enjoy over the manners of barbarians, we hereby propose and establish these rules:

a. To maintain the cleanliness of the town and not consent that there be placed therein any nuisance.

b. That drunken revels will not be permitted in the presence of the families of the town, nor fights nor similar disorders.

c. That no person from outside be permitted to live in the town without having previously presented himself before the judge or the justice of the peace and received the permission of either whether or not he may have acquired property in the town.

d. It will not be permitted that any obstruction be placed in the entrances or outlets of the town.

e. Everyone who wishes to take a dwelling of lots in the town will have to request it of the judge, paying its value which will have to remain for the benefit of the chapel.

f. All residents will help in some form or another with the construction of the chapel.

       (signed) Charles Beaubien
Witnesses: J. L. Gasper
      Nasario Gallegos

The Sangre de Cristo Grant was sold in 1864 to Governor Gilpin of Colorado who in turn re-sold it to an English company. In 1840 when Beaubien first managed the Bent-St. Vrain post, he had originally intended to settle what was later to be Florence, Colorado. Maxwell was with him at the time. Beaubien died a not too wealthy man because of financial reverses in these ventures. Miranda soon realized that the idea of colonization became a mania with Beaubien whether from honesty since it was a condition of the grants or because he was trying to prove something to somebody in St. Louis who neither cared nor was interested, only Beaubien could tell. Miranda was for settling Rayado; Beaubien, the San Luis Valley especially since the Sangre de Cristo Grant began north of Taos. Beaubien liked Maxwell because he was a good worker. He knew how to till the land and was able to grow better crops than the natives. For a time Beaubien settled in Cimarroncito in the hopes of doing here what he did in Colorado, but he went back to Taos without accomplishing any more than building a little home for himself. Maxwell, Carson, Owens and Holly built at Rayado but Cimarron was to prove more durable. Cimarroncito later became famous for its apple orchards and is now the popular resort of girl-scouts as Rayado is nationally known for its boy-scout movement. The years began to tell on Charles Beaubien and he kept to his bed more and more.

"We are much pained in hearing that this old and highly esteemed resident of Taos is in a low and declining state of health. He came to this country when a young man, and has remained here ever since. He married a Mexican lady at Taos and has a large family of children, chiefly daughters. They are nearly all married. One of them is the wife of Lucien Maxwell, who has become so rich and powerful at his rancho on the route to the states beyond Fort Union (Cimarron). After the acquisition of this country in 1946 Judge Beaubien was appointed one of the judges by the military authority and continued as such until the Territorial Organization of 1851. He has been in merchandise and has not visited the States since his first arrival in New Mexico. He remembers when St. Louis was only a village. He is an amiable, kind, obliging and intelligent gentleman." (Santa Fe New Mexican, Feb. 6, 1864.)

Guadalupe Miranda lived to a ripe old age. According to the New York Herald he was still living in Chihuahua in 1882. After that year he seems to disapear from the records. He is said to have been visited by Maxwell Land Grant officials when McMains brought forth his charges of "fraud." I would place his death about 1884. He is buried at Chihuahua. Beaubien's death received this notice in the Santa Fe papers: "Judge Beaubien died in the midst of his friends, at his residence in Taos on February 10, 1864. When the United States took New Mexico in 1846, Beaubien had been in Taos over twenty years. He came from St. Louis a very young man. General Kearny divided New Mexico into three judicial districts. Beaubien was in charge of the Northern district. He held this position until the military government was suspended in 1851. Since then he has lived the life of a private citizen engaged in merchandize. He was not thoroughly read nor did he pretend to be. As judge he tried to be fair according to the merits of the case and his own lights."

February 10. That was the day that General Ewell's Confederates were resting from action at Morton's Ford on the Rapidan river in Virginia and the Federals thought that the war was about over. It was a cold wintry day in Taos. Amethyst skies and heavy clouds threatened a downpour of heavy snow on the mourners as they marched to the grave with the remains. Padre Alarid, who sang the High Mass, attended the services at the grave. For all the land he once owned, Beaubien could only claim six feet and that not his own. He was buried in the old military graveyard that was to house the remains of Carson, Martinez, Bent and others. Maxwell the new owner was to be buried far away in a place made popular not because he was buried there, but because Billy the Kid found repose in the old military cemetery at Fort Sumner. And because this is the story of the Maxwell Land Grant, here is the petition for the land, as drawn up in Spanish by Guadalupe Miranda. In it we see Beaubien's horror of having anyone unemployed about him. The diction is Miranda's; the thoughts contained, Beaubien's:

The Petition for the Grant

For the years one thousand eight hundred and forty, and one thousand eight hundred and forty-one.

Most Excellent Sir: The undersigned, Mexican citizens and residents of this place, in the most approved manner required by law, state: That of all the departments in the republic, with the exception of the Californias, New Mexico is one of the most backward in intelligence, industry, manufactures, etc., and surely few others present the natural advantages to be found therein, not only on account of its abundance of water, forests, wood and useful timber, but also on account of the fertility of the soil, containing within its bosom rich and precious metals, which, up to this time, are useless for the want of enterprising men who will convert them to the advantage of other men, all of which productions of nature are susceptible of being used for the benefit of society in the department as well as in the entire republic, if they were in the hands of individuals who would work and improve them. An old and true adage says, that "what is the business of all is the business of none"; therefore, while the fertile lands in New Mexico, where, without contradiction, nature has proven herself more generous, are not reduced to private property, where it will be improved, it will be of no benefit to the department, which abounds in idle people, who, for the want of occupation are a burden to the industrious portion of society, while with their labor they could contribute to its welfare, and honestly comply with their obligations. Idleness, the mother of vice, is the cause of the increase of crimes which are daily being committed, notwithstanding the severity of the laws and their rigid execution; the towns are overrun with thieves and murderers, who by this means alone, desire to procure their subsistence. We think it a difficult task to reform the present generation, accustomed to idleness and hardened in vice. But the rising one, receiving new impressions, will easily be guided by the principles of purer morality. The welfare of a nation consists in the possession of lands which produce all the necessaries of life without requiring those of other nations, and it can not be denied that New Mexico possesses this great advantage, and only requires industrious hands to make it a happy residence. This is the age of progress and the march of intellect, and they are so rapid that we may expect, at a day not far distant, that they will reach even us. Under the above convictions we both request your Excellency to be pleased to grant us a tract of land for the purpose of improving it, without injury to any third party, and raising sugar beets, which we believe will grow well and produce an abundant crop, and in time to establish manufactories of cotton and wool, and raising stock of every description. The tract of land we petition for to be divided equally between us, commences below the junction of the Rayado River with the Colorado, and in a direct line towards the east to the first hills, and from there running parallel with said River Colorado in a northerly direction to opposite the point of the Una de Gato, following the same river along the same hills to continue to the east of said Una de Gato River to the summit of the table land, (mesa); from when turning northwest, to follow along said summit until it reaches the top of the mountain which divides the waters of the rivers running towards the east from those running towards the west, and from thence following the line of said mountains in a southwardly direction until it intersects the first hills south of the Rayado River, and following the summit of said hills towards the east to the place of beginning. For the reasons above expressed, and being the heads of large families, we humbly pray your Excellency to take our joint petition under consideration, and be pleased to grant us the land we petition for, by doing which we will receive grace and justice. We swear it is not done in malice: we protest good faith, and whatever may be necessary, etc.

GUADALUPE MIRANDA.
CARLOS BEAUBIEN.

Santa Fe, January 8, 1841.

Santa Fe, January 11, 1841

In view of the request of the petitioners, and what they state therein being apparent, this government, in conformity with law, has seen proper to grant and donate to the individuals subscribed the land therein expressed, in order that they may make the proper use of it which the law allows.

ARMIJO.

Taos, February 12, 1843

Don Cornelio Vijil, Justice of the Peace:

The undersigned Mexican citizens and residents of this department appear before you in the most proper manner provided by law, and state: That having received from the government of the department a grant to the public land set forth in the accompanying plan?, as will be seen by the superior decree attached to the margin, and having no title of possession which will secure our legal property and prevent any one from disturbing us in it, we request you to consider us as having presented ourselves, and without delay execute the same, to be used according to our rights.

We therefore request you to comply with our request, justice being what we impetrate. We swear not to act with malice, and in whatever may be necessary, etc.

GUADALUPE MIRANDA.
CARLOS BEAUBIEN.

In the town of Taos, on the twenty-second day of February, one thousand eight hundred and forty-three, I, citizen Cornelio Vijil, justice of the peace of this precinct, by virtue of what has been ordered in the foregoing decree, proceeded to the land referred to by Don Guadalupe Miranda, and Don Carlos Beaubien, in the foregoing petition, and being there with those in my attendance and instrumental witnesses, which for that purpose were appointed, we proceeded to erect the mounds according as the land is described in the accompanying petition, and which corresponds with the plan to which I attach my rubric; and commencing on the east of Red River, a mound was erected from whence, following in a direct line in an easterly direction to the first hills, another mound was erected at the point thereof; and continuing from south to north on a line nearly parallel with Red River, a third mound was erected on the north side of the Chicorica, or Chacuaco mesa, (table land) thence turning towards the west, and following along the side of the said table land of the Chacuaco to the summit of the mountain, where the fourth mound was erected; from thence following along the summit of said main ridge from north to south to the Cuesta del Osha, one hundred varas north of the road from Fernandes to the Laguna Negra where the fifth mound was erected, from thence turning again to the east, towards Red River, and following along the southern side of the table lands of the Rayado and those of Gonzalitos, on the eastern point of which the sixth mound was erected, from thence following in a northerly direction, I again reached Red River on its western side, where the seventh and last mound was erected, opposite to the first, which was erected on the eastern side, and being registered I took them by the hand, walked with them, caused them to throw earth, pull up weeds, and show other evidences of possession, with which act was concluded, the boundaries being determined without any claim whatsoever to the injury of any third party, as I, the aforesaid justice, in the name of the Sovereignty of the Nation, (which may God preserve,) I gave to the aforesaid Don G. Miranda, and Don C. Beaubien, the perfect and personal possession asked for by them, in order that it may answer as a sufficient title for them, their children, and successors in which I will protect and defend them, and I direct that they be not derived of said land without having been first heard, and judgment rendered according to law. In testimony whereof, I signed, with those in my attendance and instrumental, (witnesses), who were citiezns Jose Maria Valdez, Pablo Jaramillo and Pedro Valdez, who were present, and residents of this precinct. To which I certify.

CORNELIO VIJIL.

Instrumentals—Jose Maria Valdez, Pablo Jaramillo, Pedro Antonio Valdez, — Attending — Buenava Valdeb, Juan Manuel Lucero.

Years one thousand eight hundred and forty-four and one thousand eight hundred and forty-five.

Most Excellent Sir: Citizen Carlos Beaubien, native of Canada, but naturalized, and resident of this department, in the jurisdiction of San Fernandez de Taos, for himself and in the name of his associate, D Guadalupe Miranda, native of the Mexican Republic, appears before you with due respect, and in the most approved manner provided by law and convenient to him, and states that being about to undertake the cultivation of the lands which by virtue of a petition which we presented to the local government of this department on the 8th day of January, 1841, asking that the public lands at the place of "El rincon del Rio Colorado" be granted to us, including the Rayado and Ponil Rivers, etc., and as there was no injury done to any third party, our petition was acceded to, as may be seen by the decree issued on the 11th day of January in the same year by the most excellent governor and commandant general Don Manuel Armijo which is contained on the margin of our deeds. I have been prevented from carrying those projects into effect on account of the decree of the 27th of February last, issued by your excellency, and which through your secretary, was communicated to the prefecture of the first district, in order that paying attention to the petition addressed to your excellency by the curate Martinez and others in reference to a grant of the lands made to the citizen of the United States, to Mr. Carlos Bent, and that all use made of them be suspended, I have to state to your excellency in defense of those lands which are in our possession, according to the titles thereto which are in our possession, that the petition addressed to your excellency by the curate Martinez and others is founded upon an erroneous principle, as the aforesaid Mr. Bent has not acquired any rights to the said lands. It is therefore very strange that the curate Martinez and others pretend to involve our property, as it has no connection with that of that individual; therefore it is to be presumed, the necessary consequence must be, that the curate Martinez and his associates do not know to whom those lands belong, nor their extent, as he states that a large number of leagues were granted, when the grant does not exceed fifteen or eighteen, which will be seen by the accompanying judicial crtificates. They also state in the petition referred to, as I am informed, that those lands are recognized as commons, where the stock of those towns is pastured. Here is another error when the same curate states that is the place where Buffaloes are hunted, very evidently making a palpable contradiction. He also states in his celebrated petition to the supreme government praying that the natives be not allowed to hunt that most abundant game for fear that the race would be extinguished on account of their unnecessary butchery at improper seasons, and it has removed so far that it takes several months to reach it; and being at so great a distance, can it be supposed that traveling at a moderate gait it can be reached in one or two days? Therefore I believe their claims to the lands granted or assigned to Mr. Charles Bent is a fraudulent one; and as the claim is made against that individual, I do not see that we should be deprived of its productions, our object being to place it under cultivation; and not only does the suspension of labor on those lands injure us, for the reason of having incurred heavy expenses, but also a considerable number of families and industrious men, who are willing and ready to settle upon those lands and to whom we have given lands, a list of which individuals I accompany in order that your excellency seeing their number may determine what may be proper; and even if it were beneficial to the entire department that (torn). In order that your excellency may determine if it is just or not, I accompany the documents which attest our title, requesting that they be returned. Therefore I pray your excellency that we be allowed to remain in the free use of our property by which I will receive grace and justice, which I impetrate. I swear it is not done in malice, etc.

CHARLES BEAUBIEN.

Santa Fe, April 13, 1944

Most Excellent Sir: In session today this most excellent assembly, in consideration of your excellency's decree, has resolved upon the following opinion:

This most excellent assembly being informed of the petition of Mr. Charles Beaubien, in which he states for himself and in name of his associate Miranda, that in consequence of an order issued by the most excellent governor Don Mariano Chavez, the free use and benefit of their possession was forbidden them, and that this was done on account of a petition made by the priest Martinez, and the chiefs of the pueblo of Taos, falsely stating that this land was granted to Mr. Charles Bent and other foreigners, the aforesaid statement of the Priest Martinez and associates being untrue, this assembly believing that the order of suspension having been based upon the false statement and in view of the documents which accredit the legitimate possession of Miranda and Beaubien, and their desires that their colony shall increase in prosperity and industry, for which purpose he has presented a long list of persons to whom they have offered land for cultivation, and who shall enjoy the same rights as the owners of the lands, that the government having dictated the step for the sole object of ascertaining the truth, that the truth having been ascertained and the right of the party established, is of the opinion that the aforesaid superior decree be declared null and void, and that Miranda and Beaubien be protected in their property as having been asked for and obtained according to law. This is our opinion, but your excellency may determine what you may deem most proper.

FELIPE SENA.
AGUSTIN DURAN.
ANTONIO SENA.

DONACIANO VIJIL, Secretary.

Santa Fe, pril 18, 1844

In view of the foregoing opinion of the most excellent Assembly of the justice of the cause of the petitioner for himself and his associate Miranda, concerning the grant made to them by Governor General Manuel Armijo, and the illegal petition of the curate Antonio Jose Martinez and associates, in which they state that the lands of the Rincon del Rio Colorado was granted to foreigners, the order of the 27th of February, issued by this government, forbidding the free use of the land in question is repealed, and Messrs. Beaubien and Miranda are fully authoriezd to establish their colony according to the offers made by them when they petitioned for the land which has been granted to them. Let this be transmitted to the prefect, in order that he may issue his orders in accordance with this decree.

In the absence of the secretary and by direction of his excellency the governor.

SENA.

DONACIANO VIJIL, Acting Secretary.

Rio Ariba, April 18, 1844

Let the foregoing proceedings, in which is to be found the superior decree of his excellency the governor of this department dated the 18th instant, be transmitted to the party or parties interested in the land, who is the proper one, in order that he may give ample authority to the petitioners to occupy the land which has been granted to them. The prefect, in compliance with said decree, informs the justices that they are forbidden from hindering the parties interested in said lands.

ARCHULETA.

The undersigned certify, as far as the law allows, and to the best of our knowledge and belief, that there is no objection made to the settlement of the place called Red River, which embraces the Rayado and Ponil rivers, etc., it being well known and certain that it has never been used as pasture grounds for cattle, and that for a long time it has not been used for hunting buffaloes; on the contrary, the settlement of that place would be a benefit to the interior settlements, affording them protection from the enemy in that direction, occupying a great number of idlers who have no occupation in the cultivation of the soil, and relieving this vicinity from a large number of persons who crowd us. The endless difficulties we experience every year on account of the scarcity of water for irrigation would be avoided. But the greatest advantage of the entire department would be, that in case of a war with the Navajo Indians, the stock could be pastured during the entire year in the vicinity of these new settlements, and be protected by them. It is also certain that from here to the Arkansas River there are not more than six or seven days' journey traveling with packs at a moderate pace, from here to Rayado one and one-half days' journey, from the head of Red River to the Arkansas from three to four days.

In order that this certificate may have due force and effect, we pray the justice of the peace of this first precinct to authorize this certificate, and attach his judicial decree thereto, at Taos, the 14th day of March, 1844.

Pablo Lucero, Buenava Valdez, Blas Trujillo, Gregorio Lucero, Jose Miguel Sanchez, Juan Manuel Lucero, Jose Ma. Valdez, Jose Ignacio de Luna, Tomas Romero, Juan Benito Valdez and Jose Gregorio Martinez.

It passed before me, and at the request of the subscribers thereto by the authority which is conferred upon me by law, I authorize the present certificate, the contents thereof being true; and in order that it may appear, I sign with those in my attendance, to which I certify in Taos, on the 18th of March, 1844.

TOMAS LUCERO.

Attending—Rafael Cordova, Juan Jose Gonzales.

Duplicate of the above certificate on the 16th of March 1844, signed by Miguel Antonio Vijil, Antonio Jose Mondragon, Miguel Mascarenas, Manuel Fernandez, Rumaldo Vagas, Jose Ignacio Gonzales, Jose Manuel Martinez, Pablo Vargas, Juan de Jusus Medina and Buenava Lobato.

At the request of the above signed, personally present, I authorize the present certificate, and I know the contents thereof to be true; and in order that it may so appear, I signed with those in my attendance, to which I certify.

JUAN ANTONIO LOBATO.

Attending—Juan de los Reyes Romero, Jose Matias Casias. S. Fernandez de Taos, March 16, 1844.

TESTIMONY.

BEAUBIEN and MIRANDA.—Rayado Christopher Carson, sworn.—Question. Have you any interest in this claim? Answer. I have not. Ques. How long have you known the Rayado Grant, and do you know the principal points in it? Ans. I have known it since 1845, and know its principal points well. Ques. When was the first settlement made on that grant, and where was it made? Ans. I passed there in 1844, with Lucien B. Maxwell, and saw large fields of corn, beans, pumpkins, etc., and a great deal of land cultivated, and several houses built on the big Cimarron, one of the small streams on the grant. Ques. When did you see the next settlement there? Ans. I went there and settled myself with Richard Owens, and several others in 1845; we built houses, and I alone had fifteen acres under cultivation. I left in August of the same year for California. Ques. Do you know what became of the settlement? Ans. I believe it has been occupied from 1844 up to this time, every year. Ques. What other settlement is there on the grant? Ans. Lucien B. Maxwell settled on the Rayado, a stream within the grant, in 1849, and has been there up to this time, and is there now. Ques. What is the extent of the improvements on the grant? Ans. There are about 200 acres of land under cultivation, about $15,000 in buildings, and about 15,000 head of stock on the grant. Ques. Did you make this first settlement with knowledge and consent of St. Vrain and Vijil? Ans. I did; I knew they had a grant. Ques. What relation is Lucien B. Maxwell to Charles Beaubien? Ans. His son-in-law; he holds the land under the right of Beaubien.

C. CARSON.

Sworn and subscribed before me, this 28th day of July, 1857.

WM. PELHAM, Surveyor General.

Chapter Two

LUCIEN B. MAXWELL

On the state capitol grounds at Springfield, Illinois, a statue representing a man trading with a squatting Indian, is shown to all visitors. The mass of sculpture was a gift to the state by Charles Pierre Chateau, one time business partner of the man he thus perpetuates. This statue of Pierre Menard is less terrifying than the one of his grandson, Lucien Maxwell, in Cimarron, New Mexico. Like Beaubien, Pierre was a French-Canadian. Quebec settled, trappers ever restless and on the move, found their way to the Kaskaskia river. Fort Chartres was built and trading was so prosperous that in time the town of Kaskaskia became known as "The Paris of the West."

After 1720, the parish of Kaskaskia became the religious life center of the area. The first church was a log cabin affair symbolic of the wilderness sacrifices of the pioneers. It wasn't recognized for its beauty. Built mostly through the application of parish fees by several successive priests, it was the Holy Grail sought after by foot-weary traders and trappers after severe, trying excursions. Its long walls were ugly to say the least, but of hewn timbers set in perpendicular manner as were the houses of the time. The interior was lime-plastered and apologies for paintings adorned the walls. The floor was of loose boards. The Jesuits set up a college and convent there, so that Kaskaskia became one of the chain of posts by which France sought to hem in English Colonization. Despite France's efforts, the town was taken by the English in 1763. George Rogers Clark took it from them to give America her claim to the Northwest Territory.

Down in Vincennes, Indiana, Pierre Menard was watching Clark's progress. He had nothing against the Americans. In fact, he preferred them to the British. In 1787 he had established himself as a dealer in pelts and furs. He was twenty at the time. In 1791 he moved to Kaskaskia as an American citizen, but he clung to his mother tongue. When invited to become the first governor of the newly formed state of Illinois, he declined the honor mostly because of his lack of English. He did become first lieutenant-governor.

Unlike Beaubien he was not limited in his selection of friends. Everybody was entertained at Menard's. He built a home within view of his beloved Mississippi, five miles north of Chester in Randolph county which was later to be acquired by the state as a memorial to the grandest citizen she ever had, always excepting Abraham Lincoln.

Pierre married twice. His first wife, Theresa Golden, died on July 30, 1804. She was the mother of Marie Odile Menard and Maxwell's grandmother. Other children born of this union were: Mary Josephine, Pierre, Jr., Amedee Hypolite, Bernice Francoise, Francis Gusseau Chauteau. After the death of his first wife, Pierre married Angelique Saucier. Of this union came Francois Pierre, Jean Baptiste Emond, Sophie Angelique, Emilie Matthew, Aucier, Louis Cyprien and Joseph Amedee. Menard lived a full life. His sound judgment made him rich as a merchant and property owner. He served for a time as United States Indian Agent. He retired from public life in 1820 to devote the remaining twenty-four years of his life to enjoying his splendid home, his family, the fruits of his labors, and his business. He died at Kaskaskia in 1844.

Into the store at Kaskaskia one fine day walked Hugh Maxwell, an immigrant from Dublin, Ireland. His father came from England as a soldier and was stationed in Dublin. He took such a fancy to Ireland that when he mustered out of the army he returned to that country, opened up a tobacco shop, married an Irish girl and favored the Irish cause. Hugh was his oldest son. He heard of the opportunities in America and decided to find the end of the rainbow there. In New York he was attracted by the garb of some frontiersmen and joined the party of trappers working for some fur company. He sang, danced, cooked, played cards and made himself likeable to all. He readily adjusted his temperament to life in the wilderness. The trapping party reached Kaskaskia without mishap and there Hugh decided to settle down. He asked Menard for a position as clerk in his mercantile store. His employer took a liking to him and invited him to his home. That was how he met Marie Odile. There was quite a wedding at the new Kaskaskia church, and for miles around you could not find anybody at their homes because they were all at the wedding dance having a merry time and the merriest by far was the lad from Dublin town. After the wedding in 1817, he settled down to clerking at the Menard Trading Post in Kaskaskia.

The first child, a boy, born on September 14, 1818, was carried in pomp to the parish church and baptised, the name imposed upon him being Lucien Bonaparte Maxwell. All his life he was to be in such horror of Bonaparte that he never used it being content to sign himself as B. Various guesses have been made, even by people prominent in the field of history, as to what the B meant. Twitchell and others guessed any name but Bonaparte. It was in comparatively recent times that it was definitely established that this was his middle name. This first-born child was reared in the luxury of the Menard mansion which probably helps explain the large homes he built at Rayado, Cimarron and Fort Sumner.

Of school age he was sent to the Jesuits at Kaskaskia for his education. After classes each day he went to the store to listen to the yarns of the American Fur Company trappers who stirred his imagination with accounts of their adventures. Repeatedly he sought to evade school and join some expedition westwards. He was given a gun to hunt rabbits with, but he used it to practise marksmanship. His grandfather mostly decided what was good for him and what was not. The Maxwells lived with the Menards. Target practice was such a mania with young Lucien that before long he was recognized as the best shot in Kaskaskia. Old Pierre didn't like this too well for he had other plans for the boy that did not include trapping.

Hugh Maxwell was killed in a hunting accident. He had often remarked that the happiest years of his life were those he spent with the Menard family. Pierre now took complete charge of Lucien and his baby brother. History is silent concerning the latter. He did not live to enjoy the ripeness of his manhood.

Lucien Bonaparte Maxwell had soft blue eyes and chestnut curly hair which he wore long in the fashion of the day. Later years changed this description to bald of head and rotund of body. The opposition of his grandfather whetted his appetite for fur trappers to the extent that one night, rifle in hand, he turned his back on the Menard mansion forever. The home, so famous, that it was reproduced for the Chicago Fair in 1890. Now a prized possession of the State of Illinois, it is visited yearly by about twenty thousand people.

They were excellent teachers, those trappers: Big Bill Williams, Jim Bridger, Roubodoux, LeDeux, Charrette, Carson and men of lesser note whose deeds, yet unwritten, were equally as great. Maxwell learned to keep his mind clear and nimble in times of danger; to read signs of an approaching storm in the turn of a leaf; to smell the difference between a friendly Indian and one on the warpath; to take every precaution in maintaining possession of his crop of hair. So, after the manner of his companions he developed an easy, shiftless, unstudied nonchalance that made dormant his dynamic energy which was good in the light of the years to follow. The wilderness taught him more than all the conversations at the Kaskaskia trading post. He inherited his grandfather's gift of a studied calculation and shrewdness in planning any undertaking that rebounded to his benefit although he was to be overcautious in some deals that finally resulted in tumbling his vast empire about his head. Despite the jests of seasoned veterans, the young novice signed a contract with the American Fur Company and astonished even himself by bringing back a small fortune in furs.

He had been absent two years. The American Fur Company, realizing that he was a one-man gold mine to their industry, ordered him back to his traps immediately. It was on this trip that he struck up an acquaintance with Christopher (Kit) Carson. The two were known to each other as acquaintances but now developed a life long friendship that was to bring the two men together for the rest of their lives. Carson's beginnings were not as fortunate as Maxwell's, but his fame was to be more widespread. He was a legend even in life. Born on Christmas Day of the year 1809, in Kentucky, Boone's wandering spirit settled in him and carried him off to Santa Fe before he knew how to shave. He found nothing to satisfy him in the City of San Francisco de la Santa Fe save the yarns of old trapper Kincade who now and then loaned him a spare saddle horse to ride. Kincade was on his way to Taos to greet some Mountain Men friends of his, and Carson accompanied him. The border city of the north took the youth to its heart from the first. He became a trapper and ultimately won first place as America's most famous scout. He attached himself to an Arapaho girl, and following her death, to a Cheyenne woman. This latter threw him out of her tepee—saddle, bag and baggage. Back in Taos he finally awoke to the charms of beautiful Josefita Jaramillo. They were married and he became the father of many children. Both lie buried in the Kit Carson Cemetery in Taos. Carson did not die in Taos.

The famous Indian Fighter was well known also to Padre Martinez. He was eventually baptised by the padre but soon they had a falling out. The padre was too political minded for his calling. Whatever other faults he had did not disturb Carson but he thought Martinez had no place in politics. Not a bragging man himself, it made him sick to see the strutting padre going about as if all of Taos depended on him. And if the truth were told, it did. It was probably through Fremont, who employed Carson as a guide and scout, that the Taos hunter was first publicized in the American press. To his dying day he never capitalized on his glory, remaining completely in ignorance of his fame. Had he acted as Buffalo Bill, his children would have inherited a fortune. Colorado was to be the scene of his death. Poverty was as much a companion in this as it had been in life. His children were cared for by Tom Boggs who cared for them as though they were his own.

If John Charles Fremont did nothing else in his life than marry the daughter of Senator H. Benton, his life would have been full. His father-in-law's influence started him out on his first expedition for an accurate survey of the vast regions of the unsettled west, known to the Federal government only through the exploits of trappers and a few daring pioneer families. In St. Louis, Fremont recruited a company of twenty-two French-Canadian voyageurs, mostly because of their wilderness experience. Many had traversed the terrain the soldier wished to travel. Partly, too, because he was of French extraction. Through these Mountain Men Fremont was introduced to Kit Carson.

It is not clear whether Carson took Maxwell to the Arapahoes because of his relationship with them, or whether Maxwell just established himself among them on his own. This experience was to profit him later on with the Utes and Jicarillas. At the time that Fremont was gathering his outfit together Maxwell was a trader among the Arapahoes. Rather young for this sort of thing but successful as the American Fur Company knew. When Fremont asked his guide who would be best fitted as hunter for the expedition, he promptly named Lucien B. Maxwell, an opportunity that the youth from Kaskaskia did not turn down. Maxwell also had his difficulties. Remaining with his trap line until late fall of 1841, he joined a mule train headed for the west coast. Just before the caravan reached Taos, he came down with yellow fever in a virulent form. The trainmen pitied him, but they could not delay. They went on, leaving him at Taos with his life pretty much in the balance. Trappers seem to have been gifted with as many lives as a cat. Maxwell recovered to take up his work among the Arapahoes.

In Taos Maxwell frequented the Beaubien home more and more. Not because of Carlos as he was called by the Mexicans, but because of his thirteen year old daughter. Oh, he liked Mr. Beaubien well enough but he was very much in love with Luz. Beaubien was satisfied with Maxwell's background. The marriage took place in Taos.

"On this 27th day of the year 1842, I, the pastor, Don Jose Antonio Martinez, after having made diligent search regarding the freedom to marry of Luciano Maxwell legitimate son of Hucche (Hugh—evidently a name not used in these parts) Maxwell and Maria Odilia Manard —settlers of the villa de Karcaria, which pertains to the United States—in this church of Our Lady of Guadalupe —I united him in marriage with Maria de la Luz Beaubien —single—daughter of Carlos Hipolite Beaubien and Maria Paula Lovato—residents of Taos—from which place he also is. I published the banns on three feast days that had solemn Masses—19-20-27 of the current month, and all seeming to be clear without impediment of any kind, after careful investigation I deemed the ceremony could be performed and after the proper interval they were married. The witnesses were Charles Bent and Maria Ignacia Jaramillo. The sponsors were Santiago Martinez and Eugenia Naranjo. Written by my hand on this 27th day of March, 1842."

Maxwell kissed his bride adios, returned her to her father, picked up his gun and joined Fremont. One thing he did promise her was that someday he would build a home for her as big and luxurious as the one he knew in Kaskaskia. For exploits and deeds of valor, Fremont's First Expedition was uneventful, unless you would want to call the trip itself heroic. A few isolated incidents broke up the monotony. Fremont, who believed in being prepared for every emergency, launched, one fine day, a rubber boat to row along the Kansas river. It was stocked with provisions for the trip. A rubber boat was a novelty to the trappers; so was its management. Provisions and men were seen floating on the river, and the boat, bottom up, danced along its merry way. To Maxwell and Carson the provisions were not important, but the coffee was more valuable than life itself. Their efforts saved the coffee but brought them down with a nice dose of the grippe bordering on pneumonia which bothered them little when the medicine was more coffee. After their recovery the party split up, Maxwell going with Fremont up the South Platte, Carson taking the others on a more northerly route. Seventeen miles east of Long's Peak, on the South Fork of the La Platte, in Colorado, was St. Vrain's fort. Here Fremont called a halt. Evidently Maxwell must have proven capable as a hunter because the general makes no complaint against him in any of his reports nor any other account of the Expedition. Fremont had five men with him as they made their way westward. One day a horde of five hundred Indians hurried their mounts to overtake them. The men made for cover. But they were surrounded before they could get to the river which they had hoped to cross in order to take cover in the timberland. So, they decided to have it out where they were. Fortunately Maxwell recognized the leader as chief of the Arapahoes where he had his trading post. He cussed out the chief in his own language for putting such a scare into him. All ended well with the invitation to Fremont and his men to join the Indians in a pow-wow. Maxwell came out with a bundle of dried buffalo meat as a present.

Maxwell was not with Fremont on the Second Expedition, which took place in the following year. But the name of Louis Menard is on the roster. Maxwell was in St. Louis at the time the general organized his Second Expedition and was asked to join but for reasons of his own decided against it. Besides he was most anxious to see Luz. As there was safety in numbers he traveled with Fremont as far as Fort St. Vrain, where the general hoped to procure a supply of fresh mules and horses. He was disappointed, however, but placed his hopes in Maxwell who was traveling south. Maxwell would not only obtain the animals needed but provisions. Maxwell and the general were too hopeful. Fremont was to wait in vain. Provisions were not obtainable. Patriotic Mexicans hit upon a "scorched earth" policy and burnt all they found in the Beaubien warehouse.

Lucien wanted a home for his bride, a big place such as old Pierre Menard wouldn't be ashamed of and Luz would know by its grandeur the things he was accustomed to as a boy. She was convent bred and used to fine things and good living. His own background made him a favorite with his father-in-law. It was French.

Riding out on a hunt with Kit Carson one day shortly after his return from Fort St. Vrain, he came across a spot on the Rayado Creek that arrested his attention. He remarked, as Young did after him at Salt Lake, "This is the place." Help was hired, land cleared and by the fall of 1844 crops of corn, beans, chili, grain, wheat, alfalfa and pumpkins were being gathered into the barns. Kit Carson settled and built at Rayado to be near his friend. They were joined by Richard Ownes, J. Holly and Joseph Pley. In 1847 Maxwell began the big house at Rayado which was completed in 1849, all the time increasing his fields, flocks and herds. He stocked the Rayado tract with sheep and cattle taking in Carson as a sort of silent partner. Another man very much in the background, but a big help to the Maxwell interests, was Joseph Pley. Some have called him a Spaniard; others have said that he was a he was Spanish we concur with their opinion for they French-Canadian. As Beaubien's granddaughters insist that ought to know. He knew how to keep books which was the reason why Beaubien hired him. He also served as clerk in the store at Taos as well as the store at Mora. He took charge of the accounts in the store at Rayado. He had charge of the sutler's post when a military garrison was erected at Rayado.

Maxwell and Luz become the first buyers of large tracts

on the Grant. The purchase of the Rayado tract begins Maxwell's quest for the entire Grant. True most of this tract came as a heritage from Luz's father but it would not have been as large had not Maxwell bought an equal amount so that the Rayado tract was in their joint names.

Carson lived on practically nothing because he had nothing to live on, and his wants were few. Maxwell's ambition for a lot more than merely his head out of water and a finer living for Luz made him enter whole-heartedly into the venture of raising sheep to be sold in California, the profits to go to his wife for the new things she wanted in her home. Now and then the work was interrupted by a call from the United States Quartermaster Depot at Santa Fe that some Utes or Jicarillas had made away with government horses at Santa Fe and Carson and Maxwell would take time out to retrieve the stock for the soldiers. Just what Carson did with his share of the money that came to him from the sale of the sheep is hard to say for he continued in poverty despite the haul. He did have more of a family to take care of than Maxwell and it may be that it was all spent on his children.

Meantime Benton, Fremont's father-in-law, Bancroft, Buchanan and others were selling the idea of California and a coast-to-coast United States to President Polk. The result was the Third Fremont Expedition and on August 3, 1845, he found himself at Bent's Fort on the Arkansas with sixty well-armed, experienced and capable sharpshooters who could give ten times their number a good fight and come out on the winning side with very few losses as they were to prove in California. From the fort Fremont sent a note for Carson who took upon himself the adding of Owens and Maxwell to the list. They were to prove useful in obtaining fresh water for the little army when it looked as if they would have to turn back on the arid plains near the great Salt Lake. In May, 1946, Maxwell and Carson almost lost their lives.

Fremont had been in his tent until midnight reading dispatches and letters from the Bentons. No sooner had he gone to bed when Carson, a light sleeper, heard the thud of a tomahawk. Jumping up he saw a group of Klamath Indians ready to butcher the recumbent figures. The watch must have fallen asleep or were circumvented in some way by the Indians. The Indians killed Basil Lajeunesse, Fremont's (and Beaubien's) trusted friend, and a Delaware scout. Even the cautious Carson had not been expecting the raid for the evening before he fired off his rifle for the purpose of cleaning it, accidentally breaking the tube. His only defense at the moment was his pistol. The Klamath Chief rushed at him. The close range and the suddenness of the attack caused Carson to fire at randon. His shot merely cut the string that held the Indian's tomahawk. Maxwell took a shot at him, hitting him in the leg. As he turned to fall on Maxwell, a trapper named Step fired a shot that struck him in the back, the ball passing near the heart, and he fell. The other Indians seeing their leader down took to flight. All his life Carson said that he had never come across a braver Indian than the one that attacked him that night. If his warriors had followed his example, none of Fremont's men would have lived to tell the tale nor would they have changed the course of history in California and New Mexico. Maxwell's shot distracted the Indians thus saving Carson's life; Step's shot saved Maxwell's life.

The bubble burst. The war with Mexico became a reality and General Kearny ordered Carson to join him as a guide. Carson had fifteen advance scouts under his command but Maxwell was not one of them. He had joined a trapping party that went into winter quarters near the site of the present city of Pueblo. It was while they were both absent from Taos that the Taos rebellion broke out.

"In April, Mr. Maxwell and I concluded to make a settlement on the Rayado. We had been leading a roving life long enough and now was the time, if ever, to make a home for ourselves and our children. We were getting old, and could not expect to remain able to gain a livelihood as we had been such a number of years. Arrived at Rayado, we commenced building and making improvements, and were in a way of becoming prosperous." (From Carson's account of his life.)

Colonel Price commenced his attack on the Pueblo de Taos on February 3, 1849 as the trappers were making their way south towards Taos. As one man in the group related it:

"We were going along when suddenly sound like distant thunder filled the air. We knew it could not be thunder at this time of the year and we figured that a battle was taking place at Taos which was about thirty or forty miles in a direct line but much farther by mountain route which was the only one we had to follow. We were of the opinion that a force of Mexicans had overpowered the few Americans living on the Purgatoire and was now on its way to Bent's fort. Maxwell LeFevre, Lajeunesse (Basil's brother) and Tom were cast down with the thought of their families who might, at that moment, be subject to the lawlessness of the infuriated populace. This was a gloomy night for them and they passed it in anxious wakefulness all through the dreary, dark hours until morning. All managed to get to bed except Lajeunesse and poor Maxwell, both too uneasy to sleep for thought of their homes."

This statement from an intimate friend of his convinces us that Maxwell did have a sincere, affectionate regard for Luz. Somewhere along the line the talk started that Maxwell was a poor sheepherder who married for money. This was evidently begun by someone who had no knowledge of Maxwell's background. Beaubien thought enough of his children not to let them go through a loveless marriage. The chronicle goes on to say that they camped the next night at Rio de Las Animas but Maxwell didn't sleep that night either. And when they camped at the Raton peak, Maxwell and a fellow by the name of Brawford kept guard. Three sleepless nights for Luz Beaubien! He must have been in love indeed.

"On crossing the stream (which the account calls the Canadian but which I believe was the Vermejo) Maxwell, who had heretofore stayed with the crowd (so as not to think too much of what was happening at Taos) now kept some distance in advance as scout. We were strung carelessly along, when he, jerking his mule around quickly, spurred her into a gallop, and diverged from the route, at the same time motioning us to ride a la comanche—with our bodies so that nothing is seen on the opposite side, but part of the leg with which, and the heel of the same, we held on to the saddle cantle. There was no hill but the gradual rise of ground served to conceal any object approaching from the other side. We were quite excited thundering along at full speed, able to sweep the ground with the free hand, and our rifles ready to jerk up to the face, not knowing whether we were trying to surprise a party ourselves. . . . On making the rise we espied a man unconscious of our proximity going with half speed on one horse and leading another, but so soon as he caught a glimpse of the foremost hat, away he lashed his animals in a full run. With loud yells we straightened up in our saddles and with the report of two or three fusils in the hands of as many half frantic Frenchmen, we charged after him as he endeavored to escape. He saw that this was useless so he fired his gun in the air in token of submissiveness and rode slowly towards us. It was Haw, an Indian belonging to George Bent back on his way to the fort. He told us the joyful news that Colonel Price had marched into Taos at the head of two hundred and fifty men and in the battle had killed two hundred Mexicans and Indians and had bombarded and knocked down the Indian walled town of Pueblo de Taos. On mentioning that St. Vrain commanded a company which did considerable service, cheers of exhultation burst from us again and again."

For Maxwell there was the sad news of the death of Narciso. I suppose it is useless to speculate as to just what might have been our story if this oldest child of Beaubien's had lived. Still a teen-ager, he was intensely in love with New Mexico and had his father's vision of colonization. Cut off at sixteen, he would have been twenty-one when the Military government gave way to the Territorial. At this age of arrival to the status of manhood, it is hard to speculate as to just how much of the Grant he would have permitted Maxwell to obtain. As the oldest son he would have had quite an influence over his dad and helped dictate the policy of inheritance and distribution. While it is a cruel thing to say, the Taos Indians did Maxwell a favor. The death of Narciso made him more than just an Indian scout, a trader, a clerk in his father-in-law's store. Charles wanted somebody's shoulder to cry on, and he selected Maxwell's. Just what might have happened had Narciso survived we leave to fireside historians. The fact is that he didn't which makes the Maxwell Land Grant quite a story. In his *Editor's Run* Chase wrote from hearsay on October 23, 1881:

"Not far from 1838 L. B. Maxwell came into the Territory with a company of trappers from Missouri. He was but fourteen (?) years old, but being a brave energetic lad, he was employed by Beaubien as a clerk in his store at Taos. In the course of a few years Maxwell married a daughter of Beaubien's, and thus secured an interest in the Grant. In a few years more he had managed to buy out, for a promise to pay less than $100,000 to all the heirs of both grantees, and thus became proprietor of about sixty miles square of the territory which now bears his name. He soon became the most prominent man in the Territory of New Mexico as a mountain guide, an Indian trader, land owner, freighter and in other capacities.

"Kit Carson a little younger (?) than Maxwell came to Taos from Missouri not long after Maxwell and the two were always fast friends, and about equally influential with the Indians. It was through these two men that Fremont, soon after the Mexican War, became so famous as a Rocky Mountain explorer. On his first trip both served as his guides, and on his second, Kit went alone, and as you have seen it in the picture books, planted the U. S. flag on the highest pinnacle of the Rocky Mountains. After he got through with Fremont, Kit was made Indian Agent and the ruins of his old store are on the home place of M. M. Chase, within forty rods of where I write. Kit was a little man with full blue eyes, light complexion, nervous, quick motion, feminine voice, always talked rapidly, in a high key, and reminded one of a washerwoman under a full head of excitement. He could neither read nor write (government reports he turned in disproved this —He could sign his own name and could read a little. Because of Chase late comers took up the cry that Carson could not read nor write—let such people investigate government reports. We do not agree with all that Chase has to say. After all a man doesn't spend eight hours in a place and then pass himself off as an authority of the history of the place.) but he was an earnest man, penetrating, a good (?) manager (what happened to all the money he made at the store, in California, in Taos, in Colorado, as a trapper, etc.?) especially of Indians, who feared and loved him at the same time. Kit died about ten years ago in his new home on the Arkansas river, in Bent county, Colorado, where the government had given him a tract of land as a reward for his services. His wife died five days before him (in an attempt to cross the river. The carriage overturned, her head struck a stone—her death was tragic) and both were buried on their Colorado Grant but were soon afterwards taken up, brought to Cimarron and buried in Maxwell's yard (which accounts for several travelers remarking about the solitary grave at Maxwell's place). A few months later (since Maxwell was negotiating the sale of the Grant) the Masonic Fraternity took them up, carried them to Taos sixty miles west, and buried them in the home of their first settlement.

"Maxwell continued in Taos until about 1856 (we know he was in Rayado with Carson in 1844 but we give our reader a chance to find out for himself how many so-called historians had led him astray), when he and Carson made a settlement on the Cimarroncito four miles from the present village of that name, where they started a ranch intending to raise stock and make a trading post. But during the year they had several fights with the Apaches and were forced to vacate. They then went to the Rayado river, ten miles from the present Cimarron village, where they fortified. Maxwell had 20,000 sheep, owned the Grant, and was anxious to secure the advantage of his range. The Indians opposed him because they didn't want the country taken up by the whites. Having fortified himself, Maxwell managed to secure a cannon from St. Louis. The next time the Indians appeared, about three hundred in number, they commenced hostilities by killing one of the two men who were gathering hay near the fort. Then they started to charge the fort, when Maxwell opened the mouth of the cannon with a noise such as the New Mexico red-faces had never heard before. It was loaded with grape and opened a path right through them, tearing sixteen of their number into strings. No bunch of Indians was ever more surprised or more prompt in a scramble for concealment. After this they thought that Maxwell was allied in some sort of way with the Supreme Being, and excepting an occasional brush with some stray scout, he was unmolested. Maxwell's force was less than twenty-five men, consisting of two or three whites, a few Mexicans in his service, and a few peons, or Mexican young men bought and owned according to a custom then prevailing in the territory. In 1858, Maxwell removed from the Rayado, built a store on the Cimarron river, around which the village of that name sprung up. From this time on he did very heavy frontier business, taking government contracts to supply forts, trading with Indians, freighting, etc.

"The only opening to civilization was at Kansas City, 720 miles away, from which point Maxwell got his goods by ox-team, following the old Santa Fe Trail, or stage route from Kansas City to Santa Fe, opened in 1850. (The author makes reference here to the stage route and not the Becknell route of 1821.) The trip took four months, requiring two months each way. He owned one train of twenty-six big teams, frequently stocking his store with $100,000 worth of goods. In 1876 (?) Maxwell sold his Grant for $650,000 to a company of English gentlemen who mortgaged it to a Holland company, and, after considerable litigation, it fell into the hands of another company, of which F. R. Sherwin, of Cimarron, is principal member. Maxwell was 53 when he died in 1877 (?). Maxwell was of medium height, thick set, eccentric, sort of half-Indian, half-white, possessing great powers of endurance and a heart as big as an ox; he was a natural born pioneer."

The government sent a detachment of dragoons commanded by Leigh Holbrook to the Maxwell place at Rayado. Among these dragoons was a man by the name of John Holland. He was a jack-of-all-trades, and to him was entrusted the work of building the barracks and fortifications at Rayado. In his spare time he was employed by Maxwell to direct the building of his Manor House on the Rayado. After the fort was built, Holland was the only man who could handle the two cannon (Maxwell sold his to the government) that surmounted the walls, and for this reason was nick-named "El Artillero" by the natives and Indians. He never married and after mustering out of the army continued in Maxwell's employ as a carpenter. He makes his appearance now and then on the pages of New Mexico's history.

Major William Nicholson Grier succeeded Holbrook as commander of the post. When Fort Union was built, the garrison was removed to that place. Rayado is a Spanish word meaning streak. The place was named for an old Ute chief who built a hut on the spot and isolated himself, for some unknown reason, from the rest of the tribe. He was tatooed about the face and over these lines he streaked multicolored paints. There he died. His grave is unmarked. This was long before the advent of Carson, Maxwell, Pley, Abreu and the other settlers at Rayado.

Even with the dragoons stationed there Rayado was not above Indian raids. One time when Carson and Maxwell were visiting for a few days in Taos, the Indians defied the soldiers and made off with all the stock. Upon their return, Major Grier sent troops out and all the stock were recovered save those killed by the Indians. The following March, Carson took twelve wagons to St. Louis for Maxwell to stock them with goods for the trading post and store which the latter decided to open at Rayado. Going was uneventful, but the return trip was full of adventure. The Cheyennes seemed determined that the goods would not reach Rayado. Troops helped Carson deliver the shipment. When Carson returned, Maxwell gathered together eighteen men and placed them under Carson who took them to the Salado, then down the South Fork to the Plains, ending up on the Arkansas River. All were experienced trappers. The men returned over Raton Pass bringing a good layout of furs. Carson remained at Rayado until Maxwell interested him in sheep. He went to the Rio Abajo, bought sheep, entered into partnership with Maxwell and fattened them on the vegas of Rayado; then in company with Henrie Mercure, Jean Bernadette and several hired hands drove his sheep to California, selling them to a Mr. Norris at $5.50 a head. Maxwell trailed behind with his batch and sold his, also, preceeding Carson to Los Angeles where his partner met him and both returned to New Mexico together. Maxwell had also taken advantage of the opportunity of contracting for beef supplies for the soldiers at Rayado, Santa Fe, Taos, Rio Colorado (present Questa) and Fort Union when that fort was completed. Added to this were the Indian contracts for the Utes and the Jicarillas at Cimarron when he settled there.

Ryus states that Maxwell and Carson took the Oregon Trail by way of Salt Lake, making the trip in four months. He stands alone among the authors in saying that the intake on the sale of the sheep amount to nearly one hundred thousand dollars of which they were relieved somewhere along the route. Neither of the two men were the type to permit themselves to be robbed without doing something about it, if they had to trail the bandits to the end of the earth. A few weeks after the hold-up, the author states, they again gathered a flock of sheep, sold them in California and returned to New Mexico by different routes. Upon his return Carson sold his home to James H. Quinn and moved to Taos possibly because Josefita, his wife, was homesick for her kinfolk there.

Maxwell's Manor House at Rayado, by extensions, became a plaza such as one finds in the villages of New Mexico. Squared off, it had an open court in the center. The completed affair had twenty rooms. The warehouse was of adobe and was fifty feet long and twenty feet wide. Maxwell also provided hay and grain for the horses of the troops stationed there. He also operated a hundred pack mule team from Taos to Rayado and Mora where Joseph Pley was clerking for him when Maxwell was home. When he was away Pley usually took care of things for him at Rayado and Taos.

In August 1847, Maxwell induced his father-in-law to

return to Taos. Beaubien was tired of Indian uprisings, Mexican intrigue and the alarmingly rapid changes taking place in Taos, where despite the recent rebellion Americans were coming in and building hotels, mercantile houses and trading posts. Beaubien had decided to settle at Cimarroncito after a short stay in Santa Fe. Maxwell set about putting Beaubien's affairs in order and shouldered the responsibility of his now vacillating father-in-law. It was his courage and zest for hard work that gave back to Beaubien the initiative lost upon the death of Narciso.

Peter Menard Maxwell, named after Pierre Menard, was born in Taos on April 27, 1848. He was baptised by Padre Martinez at the church of Our Lady of Guadalupe in Fernando de Taos. Charles Beaubien and his wife were his godparents. Whether Marie Odilde Maxwell came for the ceremony is uncertain. No doubt she visited New Mexico now and then to visit her son and grandchildren although Maxwell makes no mention of these visits. He did visit his mother whenever he went to St. Louis for supplies. She almost outlived him.

That the reader might have a better portrait of the family, here is the family tree:

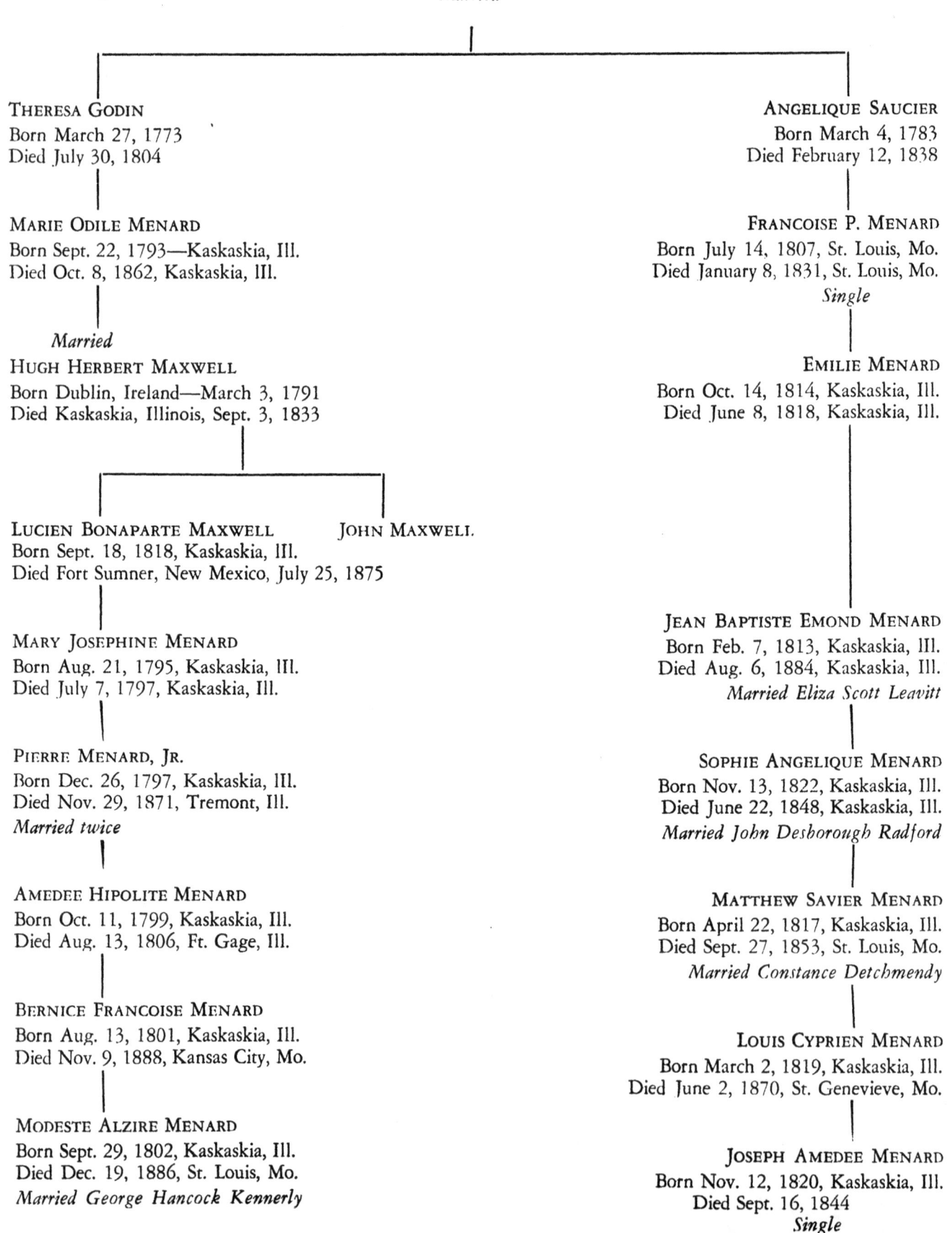

The self styled "General" Cortez of Mora was still stirring up rebellion in Las Vegas, Mora, Taos, Antonchico, Trujillo, Las Colonias, Chaparito, La Questa (present Villanueva) in an effort to overthrow the American government and re-instate General Armijo. Unsuccessful with many of his own people and the Pueblo Indians he sought to arouse the Utes and Apaches along the Cimarron. The Utes would have nothing to do with him, but the Jicarillas listened. He fed them, gave them blankets and fire-water. Word of the possible revolt of these Indians reached Maxwell on July 23, 1850. He called a mass-meeting of citizens at Taos. Before the end of the month he sent a petition to Governor Munroe pleading for a campaign against them. All of Taos county would be interested in raising troops for the affair if he would but give permission. It is interesting to note that among the signers were Kit Carson, Charles Beaubien and Vidal Trujillo (Maxwell's brother-in-law) but very few names of the French-Canadian trappers appeared. The campaign never took place partly because the Indians were not too sure of the promises made them; partly because Cortez was wounded and captured at Las Cruces shortly afterwards. He was later released, and returned to the Pecos country settling at El Macho where he died and was buried. His son and his son's son are also buried there. The family claims kinship to Cortez, the Conquistador.

Seeing that the Indians planned to behave themselves, Maxwell went to Santa Fe where St. Vrain and Boggs had set up a mercantile store and bought a fresh supply of goods for his father-in-law's store at Taos. He left Santa Fe with three wagons of merchandize, pockets bulging with money (he had sold some sheep, goats and steers), accompanied by two native drivers. Near Embudo the train was unexpectedly attacked by Apache warriors much to Maxwell's dismay, for he was confident that they would not go on the warpath. The drivers made for the woods. When certain they were not followed they returned to Santa Fe and reported to the Indian Agent, James Calhoun, that Maxwell had been killed. They returned to Taos with military escort and reported Maxwell's death to Judge Beaubien. Just as he and Luz (she dressed in mourning) set out to see Padre Martinez about a Requiem High Mass, Maxwell made his appearance, none the worse for wear. He had managed to escape his would-be killers and instead of being hunted became the hunter in an effort to salvage his cargo. The Indians, as he hoped, found whiskey in one of the wagons and promptly helped themselves to more than was good for them. When he was certain that they were too drunk to oppose him, he stepped over the prone figures, hitched all the mules to one wagon; tied the wagons one behind the other and returned to Taos in safety, with just the loss of several gallons of whiskey. Twelve days later some one remembered to inform Indian Agent Calhoun to scratch his name off the list of those killed by Indians. He sent a follow-up letter to Washington that he was happy to report that Maxwell was not killed but had reached Taos in safety, with his effects, notwithstanding the number of Indians in the neighborhood.

Lucien was not around when Bishop Lamy came to Santa Fe the first time, but when the dignitary returned from Mexico with the proper papers, both Beaubien and Maxwell were on the welcoming committee. When the Christian Brothers opened St. Michael's College in Santa Fe Maxwell sent his son to them for schooling. As he never put on airs even in the height of his wealth and power he did not expect his children to do so. After a short stay with the Brothers Peter Maxwell was sent to his grandmother in Kaskaskia and attended the Jesuit school there. Neither father nor son ever dressed gaudy nor as people of position and wealth. Lucien was forever going around with his shoes unlaced, soup stains on his shirt, and was not particular if his jacket was on straight or not or if it was dirty. People had to accept him as he was or not at all. He got stouter as the years went by and bald. He was unkempt in dress till the day of his death but this was overlooked because of his extreme kindness and his straightforward dealing with people. There were times when he gave attention to his attire when he was in the banking business and the railroad business but this was mostly to satisfy Virginia who was quite a polished woman at the time. Working the way he did, and living as he did, one could hardly blame him for wishing to retain the frontier spirit even in dress. At times he was cutting alfalfa, at times beef. There were nights he slept in Indian huts or on the plains. Often he was found in his stables taking care of studs he was developing into fine race horses, for racing was a passion with him and he would take his horses far and wide to enter them on the track. Santa Fe, Las Vegas, Trinidad, Denver, Kansas City—anywhere and everywhere wherever there was racing.

It did not take Maxwell long to ascertain that his relatives by marriage had no ambition for developing their inheritance. His father-in-law was so certain of it that he sold the Sangre de Cristo Grant outright. Indeed, it was their lack of interest in his colonizing projects that caused Beaubien to rid himself of the immense strip of land north of Taos and to divide the Rayado tract. Later on when Maxwell was beset with more lawsuits than he could handle he reminded his relatives that they had the same opportunities as he did to develop the Grant but they took the land for granted. Only when he made it something big and powerful did they seek to put their fingers in the pie. But then it was too late.

Maxwell tried his first venture on the Rayado because Col. Sumner was interested in the locality as a centralized spot for a military post. With the soldiers on his land he could rely on them for a certain amount of protection. Also, all stages would stop there and trade would be brought to him. There is no record extant to show how Maxwell arranged this with Col. Sumner but it was not a sale. Rather it was a loan for the land reverted to him when the Rayado post was abandoned. With the garrison settled he opened a sutler's store that eventually became quite a mercantile center. Richard Owens, Holly, Carson, Abreu and several other families working for Maxwell as farmers, teamsters, clerks and gardeners settled about the post that soon had the appearance of a village. There was always the indispensable John Holland. Boggs lived there for a time. He sold his store in Santa Fe and became the chief teamster for Maxwell in making the Kansas City-St. Louis-Rayado route. Whether this Boggs was related to the Boggs of Raton who was to join McMains against the Grant I have not been able to definitely establish. The Boggs of Raton seems to have been his nephew.

Sumner was not satisfied with conditions in Santa Fe. He thought the military there was in line for reform and mostly to get soldiers out of the city he planned a larger post known as Fort Union. He ordered the abandonment of the garrison at Rayado in favor of the new fort. This naturally hurt Maxwell, caused Owens to sell out and helped Carson make up his mind to remain at Taoseno. But Rayado, through the Abreu family, the Charettes and others continued as a village so that eventually a chapel was built there by the Abreus. Phillips of the Phillips 66 family eventually acquired the property and deeded it to the Boy Scouts of America who continue to operate it as Philmont Ranch. The boy scouts, under capable supervision, are re-modeling the old Carson place and expect to maintain it as a shrine for the future scouts to follow. Carson is an ideal of American boyhood and receives the homage he deserves. It would be wonderful if the boy scouts add the Maxwell place and the old military post to the project.

Maxwell was a shrewd business man. If he could establish a mercantile business about a day's journey from the new fort, he would be able to pick up the trade of all caravans coming and going. He could also get all the beef contracts for the military posts of Fort Union, Fort Conrad, Fort Marct, Fort Los Lunas, Fort Craig and Fort Bascom, as well as other cantonments. The site he selected is the present village of Cimarron. He knew this place from the alfalfa and corn fields he had here. Jack Holland built the new Manor House. In this home Maxwell fulfilled his promise to Luz. It was indeed worthy of Pierre Menard. He now becomes one of the first cattle barons of New Mexico.

Cimarron grew. Tom Boggs had a way with him. He was the only one able to induce Mexican families to pack bag and baggage and leave home and friends to settle down to working for Maxwell. So fast did the community grow that it became the county seat of the newly formed Colfax county. Lucien B. Maxwell was elected Probate Judge of Colfax county on Monday, February 26, 1868 by a majority of over three hundred votes over his opponent which is heavy voting for the time and an indication of the popularity of Maxwell. This was shortly after he completed the famous grist mill on the Cimarron which stands to this day. The Civil War did much to make him a wealthy man. Besides the regulars, the Territory quartered many of its militia in far flung posts from Taos to Las Cruces. General Carleton had the duty of keeping New Mexico in Federal hands. All these men had to be fed; their horses taken care of—clothing, blankets and a hundred other necessities that are the by-products of war. Many of the commodities were brought in by freighters over the Santa Fe Trail. Hundreds of covered wagons stoped at Maxwell's in ceaseless procession. No one escaped him. He sold meat, vegetables, grain, flour, merchandise and even induced a few of the drivers to settle in Cimarron. During these war years Maxwell realized a five dollar return to every dollar invested.

Maxwell was in advance of his generation. He was the first in the area to look upon cattle as an industry. He paid high prices to bring in a new breed of sheep, the Cotswold bucks, from Vermont, and five short-horned bulls from Covington, Kentucky. He introduced the mowing machine to New Mexico; rented out pastures to Texans so that they could fatten their beeves for the market; studied how to give New Mexico a sturdier breed of horses, a juicier steak for the table. While he added to his prosperity and wealth, he was not foolish enough to believe that he could operate the vast Grant single handed. His one fault was that he lacked confidence in his son, Peter. He sold large sections of land to Stockton, J. B. Dawson, M. Chase and others. He rented thousands of acres to the government as a reservation for the Utes and Jicarillas. Slouched over a fire of a cold wintery night as a trapper he had dreams of grandeur but this success was beyond his wildest dreams. Often he thought of these lonely nights which was the reason he ordered every stray traveler who came to his door to be fed and taken care of. His hospitality was fabulous because he never permitted himself to forget that he came up the hard way although all he had to do in any crisis was merely to visit his mother but he never availed himself of the opportunity. Only on one occasion was it ever remembered that a guest paid for a meal at his home and that was because a few friends had made him believe that Maxwell was going to kill him so he became insulting and intolerant. When Maxwell got through with him he was a sorry man indeed. As many as fifty at a time sat down to a meal and the silverware used would bring a high price on the market today not only as collectors items but because of their sterling worth.

Maxwell had one large room in his mansion running east and west which was frequented as a gathering place for Indians, trappers, traders, soldiers, merchants and for the favorite game of poker. Next to race horses, Maxwell loved cards and it was a happy day for him when Elkins, Catron, Boggs, Otero, Carson, Pley, Sanderson, Barlow, Stockton and others came in to chat and work hard at a game of poker. This room was kept bare of furniture except a table, a few chairs, some blankets piled high in one corner for Indians and trappers to use since they were accustomed to sleeping on the floor, and a large chest of drawers where Maxwell deposited his receipts from trade, sales, taxes and other income. This drawer was never locked even though at times it contained as much as fifty thousand dollars cash. Maxwell had faith in mankind as well as his trigger finger. There was also enough trusty servants about the place to inform him should anyone be so bold as to help himself from this deposit box. When he thought of it, he emptied the chest sending the money by stage to a bank in St. Louis. Several attempts were made to rob the stage but the drivers, especially Ryus, had such a way of hiding it that no attempted robbery was ever successful. There were times however when a depression hit even Maxwell and he found himself without funds in Cimarron if not in St. Louis. It cost money even in those days to run such a vast enterprise. At times he had as many as five hundred working for him and this constituted quite a pay roll as well as the expense of feeding and housing them. Many times Indians helped themselves to his beeves and sheep and to stop them would put them on the warpath thus risking the lives of many of his charges. Fenton J. Spaulding (not too reliable for facts but interesting reading) in a series of aritcles entitled: Maxwell and His Neighbors remarked:

"About two years ago while throwing down a store building in Cimarron, the workmen unearthed a small box that had evidently been undisturbed for many years. It was opened and found to contain nearly 1,000 flints for the old flint-lock weapons that were in use prior to the time that the ball and cap came into favor. The flints were of two sizes. One kind was about ½ inch by ¾ used for pistols; the other was exactly one inch by 1¼ for rifles. The box was marked: Logansport, Mo. and formed a part of the store stock of Lucien B. Maxwell, one of the greatest characters associated with the Santa Fe Trail. Maxwell was a powerful man weighing nearly two-hundred pounds. His features were strong and his face rugged. He wore his hair long—and his whiskers were bushy and drooping. His chin was clean shaven, square and heavy. An iron frame, and iron nerve, a dead shot with a gun, a born leader among men. . . . Indians swarmed everywhere and Maxwell kicked them about like dogs (?). Nobody registered at Maxwell's. He neither knew nor cared who was in his house. If they displeased him, out they went, otherwise they stayed as long as they wished. There were no locks on any of the doors of his house. Maxwell was quite a business man and taxed people who dealt with him. Sitting astride his horse in the front yard of his subject, for he encouraged colonization on his Grant, he taxed what he thought their living on his land was worth. Sometimes he made a pretense of examining into books and records, but his Indian scouts and outriders kept him informed accurately enough for the purpose. The toll demanded was very small, but always subject to delivery at the Maxwell ranch by the tenant. And it always came in." (Santa Fe Trail Magazine, August 1913.)

Maxwell's purchase of the Grant is covered in a separate chapter. There are a few interesting glimpses of him as Probate Judge. When two men broke into his store and helped themselves to two hundred dollars worth of goods and clothing, then went to his corral for get-away horses, he learned that they were at Rayado peddling the merchandise. He sent a few men to bring them in but they were only able to catch one. This one Maxwell put in chains and kept without food for almost three days. This was not his intention. He had completely forgotten about the man. When he thought of him it was only to have him stripped and lashed. When the man carrying out the punishment would go lightly with the whip, Maxwell would kick him until he put enough power behind his strokes to make the culprit feel it. When some of his Indians misbehaved in Taos the justice of the peace sent some officers to Maxwell asking his help to take them into custody. Maxwell told them that so long as the Indians were on his land the justice himself would have to come for them. He never did.

Maxwell also served for a time as Indian Agent in Cimarron and the government often availed itself of his services for he had the happy facility of keeping the Indians quiet and the settlers happy. People often sought him out for advice and if a settler did not have his rent (tax) Maxwell told him to hold off until such time as he was able to pay. One man who knew him personally and had dealings with him vouched for the fact that one reason why the Indians stayed around his home was because he was the kindest man they had ever encountered. More than once his influence with them prevented an uprising that would have resulted in a massacre. The government appreciated this especially at a time when it was having so much difficulty with the Navajos and Mescaleros.

Meantime Maxwell did not neglect his children. In studying the photographs of the Maxwells it strikes one that Peter and Virginia are the only two who look like their father; the rest favor the mother. Peter was not as tall as his dad and like him was not squeamish about his personal appearance. He was more at home in old clothes and did not like his visits to his grandmother because he always had to be dressed up and formal. Little mention is made of him except that Billy the Kid was killed by Pat Garrett in his home at Fort Sumner. He became quite wealthy as a sheep rancher and owned some property at Las Vegas. His niece told me that late in life he took to drink because something seemed to depress him. Was it the fact that his father sold the Grant for so little considering what others got out of it? Was it financial reverses? His secret was his own and we do not intend to pry into it. She remembers that as a little girl of seven she went from Rayado to visit her uncle in Fort Sumner shortly after Ash Wednesday. The visit was to last a week, but after Easter Sunday Peter finally remembered to get his niece back to Las Vegas. She stayed at the hotel owned by her uncle wondering when she would see Rayado again. Pete found some cronies in town and kept going. The eleven year old girl had to look after herself until Pentacost Sunday(fifty days after Easter) when he finally took her to Rayado. Maxwell was partly to blame. He had no confidence in his son and often called him lazy. On the other hand Peter felt that he didn't have to work because the family was wealthy. Maxwell loved his children but was not demonstrative about it which I think hurt. He gave them all a good education but wanted a hand in their marriages as we see especially in the case of Virginia. In a work like this an author hesitates to go ahead simply because he does not want to pull any family skeletons out of the closet. If he doesn't go into detail he is looked upon as a second-rate historian. Several publishers have turned down this work because they wanted more of the family life and other such material. In the first place it would make the volume too bulky; in the second place after the sale of the Grant the Maxwell children are of no further consequence to the story; in the third place they are entitled to live their lives as they see fit without anyone like me coming along and saying: "I am writing a book about the Grant—How did you get along with your dad?" If people are interested in following up the lives of the Maxwells let them go to Springer, Rayado and Fort Sumner and ask. I am sure they would be graciously received, as hospitable as Maxwell himself would have received them.

Peter was born at Taos. Virginia was born at Rayado. Sofia, Emilia, Odilia, Pablita and Julian were born at Cimarron. All the children were not too tall and in later life had a propensity for plumpness except Sofia who was tall and slender. The girls were sent to St. Mary's Convent at Trinidad for schooling, then to St. Louis. They soon forgot their Spanish which was embarrassing for their mother who knew only Spanish and French but very little English. A few weeks at home had them speaking Spanish once more. Maxwell spoke English, French, Spanish and had a working knowledge of six Indian tongues.

One of the visitors to Maxwell's ranch was a soldier from Fort Union. He was a captain and stationed for a time at Cimarron to look after the stage and mail coaches. General Carleton thought it best that they be quartered at Cimarron rather than the fort as a better protection for travelers, and Maxwell agreed to put them up. It was during this time that the captain and Virginia fell in love.

When Maxwell found out that Virginia had lost her heart to a captain from Fort Union he called her and told her that she wuold have to forget all about her dear captain and concentrate on a wealthy Spanish-American rancher living near Socorro that he had selected for her. An army captain could never give her the things she was used to. Virginia was non-committal. It was one thing to marry money; another to marry for love. Nor had she ever laid eyes on the man of her father's choice. Luz sympathized with her daughter and the captain. Many times when Maxwell was away for days at a time on business she permitted him to visit Virginia and the rest of the children were very good about keeping such visits to themselves. It never occurred to him that his daughter would go on seeing the soldier.

This was the day of the Protestant Missionary Circuit Rider. The rider for this area was Rev. Thomas Harwood, a native of Carolina county, Maryland. Born on October 16, 1829, he was an active member of his church by the time he attained his twelfth birthday. He taught school for five years in Delaware, then turned to surveying in Michigan. In 1858, he was circuit rider in Minnesota, then Wisconsin. He volunteered for New Mexico because more and more people of his denomination were coming here to homestead. He worked at Tiptonville, near Watrous, which became his headquarters. He covered the area included in the Grant. He was well known to Captain Keyes for he often conducted services at Fort Union. The couple consulted him regarding marriage. He advised Virginia to seek out Father Antonio Forchegu, the young padre from France building a church at Cimarron. The priest was sympathetic but firm. Without her father's consent there would be no marriage. If it were a question of two Catholics the priest would take the chance. But the papers had to come through Bishop Lamy who would probably want to know how Maxwell felt about it. The whole affair hinged on Maxwell. Again the couple visited Rev. Harwood. Virginia was convent bred; she knew the difficulties involved. She also knew her father. That he loved her in his own way there was no doubt. He founded Virginia City in her honor. Rev. Harwood saw no way out but to unite the couple in marriage. The ceremony was performed on March 30, 1870, in the grist mill. Isiaah Rinehardt the miller, and his wife acted as witnesses.

Maxwell was in New York at the time talking over a deal with officials of the Atlantic & Pacific Railroad. Nothing was said to him on his return. Suddenly, marching orders came for the captain. His wife had no choice but to go with him. As best she could, Virginia told her father. Parent like he blamed Rev. Harwood and challenged him to a duel. The minister declined as out of keeping with his calling. Besides he had enough of fighting in the Civil War. Maxwell secretly admired his courage which is probably why he never afterwards sought to harm the minister. Later on Rev. Chapelle of St. Matthew's Church in Washington, straightened out the marriage and all the Keyes children were brought up as Catholics. Chapelle became archbishop of Santa Fe. Maxwell sent Virginia a dowry of ten thousand dollars. None of the Maxwell children were destined for ownership of the Maxwell Land Grant.

Captain Alexander Icammel Brooks Keyes was born in Boston when it was at the height of its literary glory. In 1842, Charles T. Brooks, the Unitarian minister of Newport was astounding New England with his translations of Goethe, Schiller, Richer and Ruckert. Emerson, Higginson, Longfellow, Hawthorne, Holmes and a host of less brilliant scholars shamed blacksmiths and servant girls into talking Greek, German and Latin. It was the day of Ichabod, Icammel and Iamblicus. The captain's father cultivated a small farm but a large amount of book learning. He stood in awe of Thoreau, Emerson, Alcott and Margaret Fuller. Transcendentalism transcended his agrarian way of life so abstractly that he could only be concrete in imposing some form of it perpetually in the impossible name he gave his son.

It was a thoroughly New England drenched name as rigid and stiff as the doctrines he professed. Alexander was disciplined from the very beginning which explains why he had no difficulty in adjusting himself to army life. Perhaps with the exception of Peter Longstreet he was the most educated soldier ever to be stationed at Fort Union. The captain also had the New England unbending, stubborn will. Virginia was the girl he wanted to marry. Nothing would stop him. Nothing did. Tall, gaunt, blue-eyed, chestnut hair, he had a love for his country that was worthy of New England. He was at Webster's funeral in October 1852 and saw the multitude like grasshoppers stampede the earth as they took a last look at the statesman who taught them to be Americans. Before him lay the remains of a masterpiece of Yankee blood and sinew whose life had been linked in a chain of interests that progressed into farm, mill and school. He felt so small and lonely against such greatness. He would never forget.

There were tears in his eyes the day Ft. Sumpter was fired upon. He would have entered the army then but to his father the farm at the moment was more important. It was not until October 31, 1863 that he was able to don the uniform of the Mass. Infantry as a buck private. On June 5, 1864 he was transferred to the 1st Mass. Artillery. Three weeks later he was sergeant-major. He was honorably mustered out on October 20, 1865. But post war New England held no appeal for him. He re-enlisted with the rating of 2nd Lt. on February 23, 1866 and assigned to the Twelfth Infantry. On September 21 of that year he was transferred to the 30th Infantry. On February 9, 1867 he was promoted to the rank of First Lieutenant. Shortly after his marriage he was unassigned but spent his time at the various forts in New Mexico. His commission at Bvt. Captain arrived on March 2, 1867. He actually became a captain after his marriage (on December 6, 1873). He was assigned to the cavalry on April 2, 1870. With few exceptions most of his army life for the next fourteen years was spent at various posts in New Mexico.

The differences between the Keyes and Maxwell seem to have been patched up shortly after the marriage which means that the captain was not away from New Mexico very long. The first child born to the couple was a boy born at Fort Stanton and named Maxwell Keyes in honor of Lucien Maxwell. From the day he was born in 1871 to the end of his life he was to know the sound of fife and drum. He enlisted in the 10th Infantry on February 18, 1895 remaining in the army until February 18, 1898. He re-enlisted as a 2nd Lieutenant of the 1st U. S. Cavalry on May 6, 1898 and on August 11 of that year was promoted to the rank of 1st Lieut. A little over a month later he received an honorable discharge but re-enlisted in the Spanish-American War as a 2nd Lieut. He was killed in action at San Ildefonso in the Philippine Islands on November 24, 1899.

General Geoffrey Keyes, so well known for the Sicilian Campaign of World War II, and Maxwell's second grandson, was born at Fort Bayard, New Mexico on October 30, 1888. He attended West Point, graduating in 1913. His father was retired from the army on August 27, 1896 and settled in San Francisco. He died shortly afterwards and was buried at the military presidio in San Francisco. Virginia is also buried there.

Maxwell was not always swimming in riches. On one occasion when Charles Goodnight brought a herd of cattle to Ilriff, a rancher in northeastern Colorado, he told Goodnight to go to Fenton, a freighter, and received in partial payment for the herd, a note for ten thousand dollars held against Maxwell. Goodnight knew Maxwell and was a guest at his home in Cimarron quite often. To Goodnight Maxwell was a better risk than either Fenton or Ilriff. He was counting on this money to meet his contract with Chisum, the cattle baron. Maxwell did not have the money. This was quite a blow to the Texan. He talked it over with Maxwell who told him of J. B. Dawson. Goodnight went to see Dawson and took him into partnership. Dawson was experienced but not too interested in being driven by Goodnight who didn't seem to know the meaning of the word rest. Dawson was interested mostly in stopping at streams along the way of the cattle drive to fish and trap. The partnership was canceled in a hurry and Goodnight decided to chalk it up as a loss. Shortly afterwards, in the summer of 1867, the famous Aztec Mine was discovered on the east side of Mt. Baldy and Maxwell, hating mining as he did, nevertheless did not overlook the opportunity to increase his finances. Word got to Goodnight that Maxwell was in the chips again.

Goodnight made a trip from Palo Duro in Texas in the hopes of receiving full payment on the Fenton note. Maxwell lacked the currency but told the cattleman he could pay him in gold. They set out together for Baldy, the new mining town, where Peter Maxwell was in charge of the Aztec mine. Maxwell was surprised to see so little work done at the mine. He turned to Goodnight, and more to shame his son into working, remarked: "Did you ever see a half-breed worth anything?" Goodnight who loved work answered: "No, I did not." The gold was melted into a round ball. Maxwell asked Goodnight if he had an escort.

"No, I am alone."

"Well, you will never get out of Cimarron canyon alive. Thieves infest the place waiting for people like you. And that gold is mighty tempting to them."

Maxwell called upon Ouray, the Ute chief who stayed about the Home Ranch. He gathered together forty-three of his warriors and escorted Goodnight to safety. Goodnight later remarked that it was the only time in his life that he remembered traveling under escort. When he exchanged the gold for currency he found that he had one hundred dollars over the amount due him. Figuring that he made two trips to Maxwell's he thought it was worth the fare so he kept it.

Indians were the first to find gold on the Grant. Seeing that the white man was willing to pay any price for it they usually brought in nuggets in exchange for fire water and fire arms. The story of the gold rush is told elsewhere in the story of Elizabethtown.

Lucien B. Maxwell was one of those who staked a claim about Discovery Tree at Willow Creek, as we gather from a sign posted on the tree on September 14, 1867:

TO WHOM IT MAY CONCERN

THE UNDERSIGNED CLAIM TWO CLAIMS 200 FT. EACH NUMBER 38839 UP FROM WILLOW CREEK AND 200 FT. ON WILLOW CREEK FORMERLY THE PREEMPTION OF G. NORTON & DAVIS

(Signed) WILLIAM MAXWELL AND
MENARD MAXWELL

These two were not Maxwell's children but the children of his brother, John. As soon as the gold rush started they came from Missouri in the hopes of striking it rich. The Maxwells were interested in gold. It certainly would be foolish to think that the owner of the Grant was not aware that there was gold on his property. Indians must have kept him posted. But he was not interested in what prospectors did to the land. When he brought sheep to California he saw what happened there. Maxwell knew that he would be owner in name only. To keep the thousands out of Elizabethtown, Baldy, Willow Creek, Virginia City and other mining camps would have meant bloodshed. When gold was to be found there was no respect for private ownership. He loved mining—but not on his property. He had mining interests in the Black Range and because of these interests he became one of the founders of Silver City, then the little hamlet of San Vicente, today one of New Mexico's major cities. It was at Silver City and not Cimarron that Mrs. Bonney, and her little son, William, came to know Maxwell. Despite what authors say—William Bonney—otherwise known as Billy the Kid—did not ride the range with Maxwell at Cimarron. They seek to place a justification for the Kid's friendship with Peter Maxwell at Fort Sumner. The little nine year old boy first met Lucien at his mother's boarding house in Silver City. If the Kid ever rode in Cimarron, and it is probable that he did, it was after the sale of the Grant. He was sixteen at the time of Maxwell's death and at that time he started working as a cowboy near Fort Sumner. It was then that he struck up a friendship with Peter Maxwell.

Maxwell now started to plunge into various fields that he knew little about, either in an effort to fight off old age, or to sublimate for the disturbance in his way of life brought on by the influx of miners. He founded the First National Bank in Santa Fe, but sold out the following year to Stephen B. Elkins, Thomas B. Catron and others. He bought the Kitchen Brothers Hotel, the former Buffalo House, in Las Vegas which his son kept for a while following his death and sold. He sunk a fortune into the Atlantic and Pacific Railroad project. He sold his share of the Sangre de Cristo Grant to William Gilpin for a consideration of six thousand dollars. I know of no fitting tribute to the man than that found in the Santa Fe New Mexican on April 23, 1864:

"Lucien B. Maxwell who lives about sixty miles northeast of the county seat (at that time Mora) on the Cimarron river, is one of the most marked men, in the qualities of his character, to be found in the territory. He is a native of Kaskaskia, Ill. He was with Fremont in his exploring tour to Oregon. He came to this country and married the daughter of the late Charles Beaubien. After selling his sheep in California he moved to Rayado about fifty miles from Mora, and began the settlement and cultivation of the place. He began the raising of stock. Under all his disadvantages he increased rapidly in property, and soon built and furnished a house in spacious and elegant style. Soon afterwards he sold his establishment and moved to Cimarron, ten miles further on the frontier, and there began another improvement. It has been continued with wonderful energy and success. The grain raised in his fields by himself, peons and renters is immense in quantity. He has about 20,000 head of sheep, 1500 head of cattle, chiefly cows, ad of improved breeds from the States, and about 200 mares and horses and heavy interests in merchandizing. He has built a magnificent house, a mill (completed in November 1864), a large barn and other out-buildings and other houses for his numerous peons and laborers. His intrinsic character is strong, positive and solid. With these he is so complete in truthfulness, integrity and courage. His spirit is proud and defiant and as independent and self-sustaining as the eagle on a mountain cliff. With all this he is one of the kindest, most generous and charitable men that lives. He yearly gives more to the Indians who swarm to his ranch and dwelling house than does the government. His hospitality is profuse. Nothing about him is mean or diminutive. He is beloved and esteemed by his neighbors and dependents. (The natives affectionately called him Luciano.) He is a man of no personal parade. He is severely plain and unostentacious. His energetic soul would face a regiment of tortures sooner than indulge for a moment the consciousness of a mean action."

Maxwell's relationship with Carson was the best in his life outside his own immediate family. He gave Carson a share in his mercantile store and some real estate. Carson sold these to Pedro Neares. Carson gave him the order for all the wheat, corn, cattle to supply the troops he commanded during the Civil War. Carson also ordered all his supplies for the campaign of Adobe Walls from Maxwell. In Carson's will, after his death was found the following:

"It is my will, that my administrator get security for the promissory note of $3000 drawn in my favor, and signed by Lucien B. Maxwell of Cimarron, New Mexico, and failing in that to collect the note, and loan the money on good security and at the highest rate of interest to be used by him for the support of my children."

Maxwell also owed Carson money for cattle he bought from him and in turn sold to Frank Pape. Maxwell seems to have straightened this out after Carson's death. Here is an interesting note found in the diary of an old timer dated September 26, 1855: "Twelve head of cattle valued at twenty-five dollars a head, were driven off Rio Ocate by Indians—property of Lucien B. Maxwell."

For the campaign of Adobe Walls 200 Utes went in a body to Maxwell and told him they would be willing to serve under Carson and attack the Kiowas if he gave the word. That is how Carson obtained the Indians. Other diaries contain:

"Maxwell is at his father-in-law's doing a very prosperous business as a merchant and a contractor for the troops."

"Spring of 1852 Maxwell and Carson went on a beaver hunt after selling sheep in San Francisco. Maxwell went to Los Angeles by steamer but Carson by land because he became sea sick very easily." (The two met in Los Angeles in October 1853.)

"Kit Carson is out hunting with Lucien B. Maxwell."

"Lucien B. Maxwell came in (to Taos sore, exhausted and beggared. The Utes and Mountain Apaches had jumped him twice on the mountain branch of the Caravan Trail from Bent's Fort to Taos. Maxwell had been surrounded by Apaches at Green Horn river and succeeded in driving them off when he was joined by General Elliot Lee, of St. Louis and Charles Horn (the only white man to escape the Arroyo Hondo massacre). On being joined by these Maxwell started off for Taos, having in all fourteen men. In the Raton mountains he was again attacked by the Apaches, was himself badly hurt by a spent ball and General Lee, Town, Jose Cardenas, Paschal Riviere were killed. Lee escaped the Taos massacre. Town and the Frenchman were killed in the Raton mountains. Indians robbed Maxwell of eighty-two animals, and everything else he possessed, even to the last rifle." (*Sabin in Kit Carson Days.*)

Tired of fighting squatters and beginning to feel the effects of age, Maxwell bought the abandoned fort at Fort Sumner in New Mexico. The sale of the Grant is told elsewhere. Peter liked the change and set about to ranching sheep with a will. He soon became the largest sheep rancher in the Pecos valley.

No sooner settled at Fort Sumner than Indians ran off with one thousand head of cattle and sheep in the spring of 1871. Maxwell rode to Fort Union to enlist the aid of the army. Captain James F. Rondalet went after them and succeeded in bringing back five hundred. His job accomplished, he gave them no further thought. When Maxwell came to Fort Union for his property the animals were nowhere to be found. They had scattered and many a native and Ute Indian had barbeques the like of which was never witnessed since in the area.

In 1875 Maxwell came down with a summer cold he could not shake off. Realiizng he had developed pneumonia he sent Peter to Las Vegas to get a doctor and a priest. Father Pinard was a friend of the family. Almost in sight of Las Vegas a rider overtook Peter and told him that Maxwell had passed on. That was on July 25, 1875. The tombstone that marks Maxwell's grave in old Fort Sumner (several miles from the present town) was not erected by the state of New Mexico but by people from Colorado. Here is his epitaph:

LUCIEN B. MAXWELL

A native of Kaskaskia, Ill., a fur trader and trapper who by industry, good fortune and trading became sole owner in 1864 of the largest single tract of land owned by any one individual in the United States.

Maxwell founded the First National Bank of Santa Fe, New Mexico and invested $250,000 to help build the Texas-Pacific Railroad.

Dynamic — Charitable — Lavish — One of the great builders of the American West. Died in Quiet Retirement July 25—1875 at Fort Sumner, New Mexico. Born September 14, 1818.

Not every fellow that met Maxwell slapped him on the back and called him a wonderful fellow. There were times he had to leave his race horses, and his friends to walk about a block to the long adobe building called the court-house. It reminded one of an Iroquois hut, long and narrow it was, its yeso coat snow-white in the sun. No Iroquois home witnessed the stormy scenes enacted in that court-house. A few court cases are cited in order to impress upon the mind that Maxwell was not so powerful that he was not opposed in some of his dealings and actions:

Lucien Maxwell & Luz Maxwell, and The Maxwell Land Grant & Railway Co.
vs
Guadalupe Thompson, Administratrix c/o George W. Thompson, her husband, Charles Bent & Alberto Silas Bent
Sept. 2, 1871

William M. Ronarth et al
vs
Lucien B. Maxwell   Sept. 5, 1871

John McRea
vs
Lucien B. Maxwell   To Collect a debt

Andrew Stewart
vs
Lucien B. Maxwell   To Collect a debt

The Territory of New Mexico
vs
Lucien B. Maxwell   Contempt of Court

Lucien B. Maxwell
vs
Charles P. Pease   Assumpsit

The Territory of New Mexico
vs
Lucien B. Maxwell
Neglecting to hold Probate Court

Lucien B. Maxwell
vs
John B. Williams, John B. Burns, Federick Huffman, and Joseph Schimel

Besides Joseph Pley, Holland and Abreu, Maxwell formed minor partnerships with many others so that he could be said to be the head of a corporation even before the corporation of the Maxwell Land Grant and Railway Company. This latter appears in the courthouse records for the first time on Monday, April 3, 1871, in Vol. I page 247. Yet, Maxwell is brought before the courts by Patrick Cullen and Peter Kinsinger for failing to pay them the four hundred and seventy-six dollars he owed them as part of his contract in the co-partnership. The debt was made on October 8, 1870 and not paid still on April 6, 1871, which a man of his means could readily afford. "Upon reading and filing the petition of the said Patrick Cullen and Peter Kinsinger, praying the court to appoint three competent auditors to adjust the accounts of the said partners in the co-partnership business set forth in the said petition." (Court House Record Vol. 1 April 6, 1871.) The three men appointed to look into the matter were John Faulkner, Thomas Martin, Thomas Coglow. The case must have been settled out of court for no further mention is made of it.

When Maxwell sold out to the Maxwell Land Grant and Railway Company, he retained the Home Ranch until he could find another place to live. When he was certain of the home at Fort Sumner he also deeded the thousand acres involved to the same company. That he was happy at Fort Sumner is proven by the interest he took in the place in making it as much like the Home Ranch as he possibly could. His son Peter made out well at Fort Sumner and accumulated as vast a holding in the Pecos Valley as his father had at Cimarron. The deed and a letter prove these points.

DEED FOR THE SALE OF THE HOME RANCH— MAXWELL'S MANOR HOUSE AT CIMARRON..

L. B. MAXWELL & THE MAXWELL LAND GRANT & RAILWAY CO. } MEMO OF AGREEMENT.

B. Maxwell agrees to sell and deliver possession to the Maxwell Land Grant and Railway Company the real and personal property described in the annexed schedule.

The above to take effect any time within three weeks from the present date in payment to Lucien B. Maxwell of $50,000 and the balance of the purchase money namely, $75,000 to be secured by a bond and mortgage upon the whole property both real and personal bearing interest at the rate of ten (10) percent per annum, this mortgage to be paid off any time within one year from date at the option of the purchasers. Upon payment of the $50,000 a title bond for a deed to be made on final payment to be executed by L. B. Maxwell in favor of the purchasers for the whole property seal and personal.

If there should be a serious discrepancy between the amount of the merchandise as per inventory and the amount specified in the schedule a proportionate deduction to be made.

Witness our hands the 24th day of August, 1870.
   L. B. Maxwell
   The Maxwell Land Grant & Railway Co.
     By: John Collinson,
       President.

SCHEDULE A. Referred to in the preceeding contract.

All that portion of all the land of the Beaubien and Miranda Grants situated in Colfax County, Territory of New Mexico, Known as the Home Ranch of Cultivated lands,—with the buildings and appurtenances thereon and belonging thereunto; said Home Ranch supposed to contain about one thousand acres more or less, which was reserved in a certain conveyance executed by us to Jerome B. Chaffee, April 30, A.D. 1870, and acknowledged before J. G. Abreau, a Justice of the Peace of same date, also lot _____ Block _____ in Elizabethtown, on which is situated a stone building, also placer mines, a lease dated January 1st A.D. 1868, for ten years for claims numbers six-by-six, sixty-five and one-half of number sixty-four, above discovery tree in Willow Gulch, a lease dated January 1st A.D. 1868, for five years for six hundred feet long and from bank to bank wide on Willow Creek beginning at J. H. Taylor's Co. claims and running up the creek; a lease dated January 1st A.D. 1868, for ten years on Willow Creek numbers sixty-one, sixty-two, sixty-three, and one-half of number sixty-four up from discovery tree and about 700 feet long and from bank to bank wide; a lease dated January 1st A.D. 1868, for ten years for 1,000 feet along, and from bank to bank wide on Willow Creek, beginning at Kinsey & Lees lower stake running down the creek, a lease dated January 1st, 1868, for five years for 1,200 feet long and from bank to bank wide in Willow Creek beginning at the Huz and Cos line, and running up the creek, a lease dated January 1st A.D. 1868, for five years for 900 feet long by 300 wide on Johnson's Flat beginning at the junction of Limerick Gulch and Johnson's Flat: a lease dated January 1st A.D. 1868 for three years for 1200 feet long and 300 feet wide on Grab Flat, commencing at the mouth of Grab Flat on the right hand bank of Willow Creek about two hundred yards above Last Chance and Willow Creek Junction; a lease dated January 1st, A.D. 1868, for three years for 1500 feet long by 300 feet wide, on Michigan Gulch, beginning on what is known as Mitchell's Claim and running up Harden and Company's; a lease dated January 1st., 1868, for one year with privilege for ten years in Willow Creek 600 feet long and from bank to bank wide, beginning at the lower line of the Arizona Company claim and running down the creek; a lease dated January 1st A.D. 1868, for 20 years for 600 feet long and from bank to bank wide in Limerick Gulch, beginning at the dam of the Arizona Company and running up the bank; a lease dated January 1st, A.D. 1868, for five years on Grouse Gulch, 300 feet long by 300 feet wide beginning at Piner Co. upper line and running to Moor's; a lease dated January 1st, 1868, for ten years for 300 feet square on Michigan Meso also an undivided half interest in a certain thirty day stamp quartz mill in Ute Creek known as the Montezuma Mill, together with the ground on which the same may be situated; the divided west half of the Comstock lode being 1500 feet in length in East side of Baldy Mountain; one undivided one-twelfth interest in the Aztec lode situated in the East side of Baldy Mountain and all other real estate owned by me in Colfax County, New Mexico, not including the aforesaid conveyance to Jerome B. Chaffee, also all buildings, tenements, mills, rights, franchises, privileges, improvements, belonging to or appertaining to said tracts of lands of every description, including mines and minerals, and the remainder reversions rents, issues, and profits thereof, and all the rights and titles, interest and estate of them, the said Lucien B. Maxwell and Luz B. Maxwell in and to the same. Also all the merchandise contained in three stores estimated to be of the value of $50,000, also all the stock upon my estate consisting of two thousand sheep, two hundred head of cattle and yearlings:

One hundred head of horses and mules and all farming utensils and other personal property on the Maxwell Ranch, including twenty wagons, excepting only two family carriages, buggy harnesses and two pair of best horses and mules to work them.

   L. B. Maxwell
   The Maxwell Land Grant and
     Railway Company
     By: John Collinson, President
Filed at 6 o'clock P.M. Aug. 27th A.D. 1870—J. Lee, Clerk

           Fort Sumner, New Mexico
           December 9th, 1871
Honorable T. Rush Spencer
Surveyor General of the Territory
of New Mexico.
Sir:

The undersigned Peter B. Maxwell, John Holland and

Vidal Trujillo, settlers and owners of improvements on the public lands lying on the East bank of the Pecos River in the County of San Miguel and comprised in the late Military Reservation of Fort Sumner; — together with forty-one other settlers upon said lands, to-wit: Juan Gonzales, Martin Garcia, Cruz Trujillo, Miguel Salazar, Felipe Orrelas, Ventora Serra, Miguel Trujillo, Eugenio Martin, Pablo Trujillo, Leandro Martin, Jusus Sylva, Meatias Mez, Francisco Rivera, Miguel Armendanis, Manuel Gonzales, Rito Villanreal, Leanders Lovato, Jose Simon Lucero, David Martin, Rito Lusano, Jose Gillan, Vicente Chavez, Jose Rena Damasio, Martin, Juan de Dios Padilla, Juan Luis Cortez, Catasino Garcia, Rafael Dominquez, Antonio D. Medina, Labriano Valdez, Alejo Baca, Ignacio Lovato, Seledon Trujillo, Aepomicens Lopez, Fernando Seguno, Francisco De Herrera, Antonio Jose Chavez and Juan de Jesus Ortega—respectfully make application for the survey and subdivision of the Township in which said lands are situated, under the provisions of the Act of Congress of June 2nd, 1862, as amended by the act of March 3rd, 1871.

The undersigned have appointed and empowered I. Houghton Esq., their attorney to arrange with your office all matters pertaining to this application and request that he be so considered by you.

                     P. M. Maxwell
                     John Holland
                     Vidal Trujillo

The lands for which the 44 settlers make application for survey and upon which they have filed their "Declaratory Statements" in the Office of the Register of the United States Land Office at Santa Fe—as nearly as can be ascertained, fall in Township No. 1, North Range No. 23, East, which is "written the range of the regular progress of the public survey."

The tract of land occupied by these settlers comprises 7040 acres, mostly under cultivation, the buildings and improvements thereon purchased by the applicants from the War Dept. and formerly pertaining to Fort Sumner —together with other buildings and improvements of the present settlers.

The dam and acequia constructed by the Military Authorities, having been destroyed by flood, and abandoned—the present settlers have reconstructed the same at a cost of $7,000.00 and are now expending labor and money for their completion and extension.

The settlement upon the tract comprises over fifty families and within the Township in which it is situated, a population of from 200 to 250.

These applicants—under the provisions of the Acts referred to and instructions of the General Land office of May 6th, 1871, are undoubtedly entitled to a survey of the Township or Townships within which the lands occupied and improved by them are situated. Upon their depositing the amount estimated in accordance with these instructions for payment of the cost of the same as required by said Act.

Applicants are prepared to make the required deposit. As their Attorney respectfully ask to be furnished, at your earliest convenience with a statement of the estimated amounts, in order that the deposit may be made at once— and the survey executed as soon as practicable;—as the settlers are anxious to obtain a legal right to the lands in their possession without delay—by purchase and payment.

                     Respectfully submitted,

                     J. Houghton, Attorney for
                     Applicants for Survey—
                     January 8, 1872

Not acted on as the T. mentioned not known to be and believed not to be the one the settlers really desired surveyed. New application after ascertainment of T., made by M. Brunswick, April 25, 1872, and money for two townships, (2 and 3 of R. 26 E.,) deposited by Peter Maxwell April 26, 1872.

Chapter Three

BUYING UP THE GRANT

Maxwell has often been blamed as unfair to Beaubien's children for the meagre sums he gave them in exchange for their shares in the Grant. If we examine the matter closely we will find that he gave what he thought was a fair price. He was always known as honest and kind; who much more with his relatives? Judge Beaubien changed his will repeatedly. Every time that a child was born in his family or everytime that one married he made a new will. Unlike most fathers he did not wait for his death to leave an inheritance to his children which was especially so in the division of the Grant. Young Narciso, through his father, and as the first-born, received with his partner, Stephan Louis Lee, the Sangre de Cristo Grant. It has been stated by many authors that Beaubien, following his son's death, sold the Sangre de Cristo Grant for a few hundred dollars. This is very wrong. Beaubien did not sell the entire Grant to Gilpin but only the northern part. Strange to relate, Beaubien did not receive the U. S. Patent for the Sangre de Cristo Grant until December 20, 1880 after both he and Maxwell were dead.

Beaubien's last will was made on January 16, 1864. The beneficiaries under his will were his six children, his wife, Lucien B. Maxwell and Federick Muller. The children expressly named are Leonora Trujillo, Paul Beaubien, Petra Abreau and Juana Beaubien. His two other children were the wives of Maxwell and Muller and their maiden names were Luz Beaubien and Teodora Beaubien. His wife was named in the Will as Pablita Lovato. The Will designated and appointed Federick Muller and J. Abreu as "Administers and Executors." This comes as a surprise knowing how well Beaubien got along with Maxwell. Beaubien evidently tried to avoid jealousy among his children by eliminating Maxwell's name as executor. A record in the Taos county courthouse dated January 12, 1869 stated that Muller and Abreu carried out the injunctions of Beaubien's will.

Frederick Muller was appointed Guardian for Pablo Beaubien who was under age. On April 7, 1864, Maria Pablita Lovato, Luz Beaubien and her husband, Lucien B. Maxwell; Teodora Beaubien and her husband, Frederick Muller; Leonora Beaubien and her husband, Vidal Trujillo; Petra Beaubien and her husband, J. G. Abreu, Juana Beaubien and her husband, Joseph Clouthier; Pablo Beaubien by his Guardian, Fred Muller sold most of the Sangre de Cristo Grant to William Gilpin for $15,000. Charles Beaubien on July 7, 1853, gave a Quit-Claim to Lucien B. Maxwell, Joseph Pley and James H. Quinn for a consideration of five hundred dollars. On September 6, 1864, Lucien B. Maxwell and his wife conveyed an undivided one-sixth part of the Sangre de Cristo Grant to William Gilpin for $6,000. On January 27, 1858, Joseph Pley and Benigna Lee, Lee, his wife; Maria de la Luz Tafoya, widow of Stephen Louis Lee, sold their interest in the Sangre de Cristo Grant to Ceran St. Vrain for one thousand dollars who in turn sold his share to Gilpin for $20,000. Thus the Sangre de Cristo Grant passes from the hands of the Beaubiens, Maxwells and other relations mentioned in Beaubien's will.

When Beaubien permitted Maxwell to settle at Rayado he asked nothing in return until almost fifteen years later. There were several reasons for this. Other members of the family were not faring as well as Maxwell; Bent's heirs were questioning their right to the Sangre de Cristo Grant; St. Vrain was also being difficult with Beaubien's heirs through the newly founded Federal Land Office at Santa Fe. Beaubien wished to make certain that Maxwell would have a nice tract of land that would be unquestionably his own. Besides, it guaranteed Maria de la Luz's future. So, the property the judge gave his son-in-law by word of mouth, he now deeded to him for a consideration of five hundred dollars. This was on September 14, 1858.

Joseph Pley—either a French Canadian or a Spaniard—depending on which member of the family you ask—was also administrator of the estate of S. L. Lee. He decided that Beaubien had the right to Lee's share of the Sangre de Cristo Grant because of debts accruing to Beaubien.

The first of Beaubien's daughters to die was Leonore. She died at Rayado on December 8th of the year prior to the sale of the Maxwell Land Grant. Her husband, Vidal Trujillo went to Fort Sumner with Maxwell and entered the sheep-ranching business there with Peter Maxwell. He is buried near Maxwell in the old military cemetery at Fort Sumner. The second daughter to pass away was Juanita. She is buried at Taos. The third was Teodora. She also is buried at Taos. Luz was the fourth. She is buried next to her husband at Fort Sumner. Petra, the last daughter to die is buried at Rayado. Pablo the remaining son died at Fort Sumner. He had a son called Pablo who was killed in World War II. Just two girls, Pablo's daughters Margaret Beaubien and Maria Beaubien carry on the name. When they marry the name will vanish forever. These two are the last of the Beaubiens.

Considering what the Sangre de Cristo Grant was sold for, Maxwell was offering a fair price for the Maxwell Land Grant. All were acting as free agents in selling to him. He imposed himself on no one and he was really hurt when they filed suit for more money or their land back. I would not be a bit surprised if this were not the reason why Joseph Pley pulled stakes and disappeared from this section of the country entirely. Business is business and if you sell a piece of property for a thousand and the fellow you sell it to re-sells it for ten thousand then chalk it up as your own hard luck. This is the way Maxwell felt about it. He was worried, too. Sick at Fort Sumner, he could have probably fought it off as he did so many times before, but lost the will to live with so many law suits on his hands and most of those from people near and dear to him. Perhaps he would have done better as far as his relatives were concerned had he resold the land to them. The value of the land increased only when the gold rush began. Therefore the sale at the time was in proportion to the gold rush at Baldy, Elizabethtown, Virginia City and Willow Creek. Prior to the discovery of gold there was no question about the buying and selling of the Grant. If we use various spellings for the names of the people concerned it is because these various spellings appeared on the documents.

Through Beaubien, Maxwell was given first choice in the purchase of Miranda's property. Teodora Beaubien had married Frederick Mueller (or Muller) who did not seem to have the faculty for turning a penny as Maxwell had. Nor did they later seem to have the confidence in the validity of the grant as her brother-in-law. Court costs may also have influenced their desire to get rid of a piece of property whose ownership seemed even more vague with the American occupation. They sold their share of the grant to Maxwell for the consideration of five hundred dollars. If other members of the Beaubien had stamina, they must have developed a philosophy of defeatism when they saw their relative by marriage add and add to his domain. Maxwell next acquired the inheritance of Joseph Clouthier and Juana Beaubien for the sum of three thousand and five hundred dollars.

Vital and Eleanor Trujillo lived in Mora. As many of her father's interests were in that town, Eleanor must have gone there often and met Vital who became her husband. The peculiar thing about the deed to Maxwell is that she did not sign her name as Beaubien but as Eleanor X. Trujillo. All of Beaubien's family was educated so the secret of the X she carried to her grave. J. G. Abreu married Petra Beaubien. They sold to Maxwell for the same sum as Vital Trujillo. This is the first deed to mention Cimarron. Petra did not sign as Beaubien; she merely used the initial B. Pablo Beaubien deeded over his tract to his brother-in-law, of the County of Colfax, for the same sum as the two others. Teresina Scheurich was not a Beaubien but the daughter of Charles Bent, the governor of the conquered territory appointed by General Kearny. She married Aloys Scheurich, who resided at the time in Taos. Bent had acquired this property from Beaubien and in turn willed it to his daughter. Maxwell bought from the Scheurichs for six thousand dollars. Up in the Greenhorn country in Colorado lived the other Bent girl with her husband, Alexander Hicklin. The Hicklins got rid of their share of the grant for the sum of six thousand dollars also. Maxwell was now the largest individual land-holder west of the Mississippi, if not in the United States. It was not as easy as all that. Some of the family repented their rash sales. A feud commenced that ended in court in favor of Maxwell. It seems that Guadalupe Miranda, Joseph Pley, Luz Beaubien, Maxwell and a few others were hailed to court by Alfred Bent, Alexander Hicklin, Theresa Bent, Aloys Scheurick and Ceran St. Vrain who claimed that Charles Bent was entitled to one-fourth of the grant petitioned for by Carlos Beaubien and Guadalupe Miranda. St. Vrain was a partner of Bent's; the rest were either blood relatives or relatives by marriage. Whatever way their counsel advised, Maxwell had not the power to buy from them. Kirby Benedict, Chief Justice at the time of the suit, decided in favor of Maxwell. The Bents lost heart, not appealing to the higher courts. Another reason for not appealing was that Maxwell sold out soon after this and moved to Fort Sumner. They may have been content to let well enough alone, but one can feel certain that in their hearts they felt they were done an injustice by Lucien B. Maxwell.

Joseph Clouthier was most affectionate towards his wife, and probably would have held on to the land had his wife been satisfied with it, for a Frenchman knows the value of the soil. He was born at Henryville, near Quebec, in 1836. Of a venturesome disposition, he left home when a young man, and in 1849, started for the then almost entirely unkown great West. At Westport, Missouri, he accepted a job driving a freighting team to old Fort Bent where he stopped for a while to do some clerking in the commissary store. He eventually settled in Taos about the close of the Civil War, where he resided up to a few days prior to his death, when he went to Las Vegas where he died.

Soon after locating in Taos he married Juanna Beaubien, daughter of Carlos Beaubien. Their married life was an unusually happy one and the grief over the loss of his wife the December before his own death actually hastened the end for him. He had five children: Mrs. Jaramillo and Mrs. Adair of Taos, Mrs. Sena and Alfonso Clouthier of Santa Fe, and J. P. Clouthier of Fort Sumner. His remains were brought to Taos and placed next to those of his wife whose loss he so sincerely mourned. He was well known throughout the entire Territory, particularly among those of ante-railroad days and beloved by all who knew him. His brother became a well known merchant at Springer. Joseph Clouthier died on October 18, 1893.

J. G. Abreu was born in Santa Fe in 1823, one of the four or five sons of Santiago Abreu who was killed near Santo Domingo in the Jose Gonzolez rebellion of 1837. Coming from an ancient and prominent family, he had crossed the continent at least twice before the advent of railroads. He worked for a time as interpreter for the Perea brothers, merchants of Bernalillo. He carried the U. S. mail fom Santa Fe to Fort Leavenworth in Kansas during the winter of 1848-49, which was the second mail carried across the country between these two points; the first having been carried by Tom Boggs who was associated with Bent, Beaubien and Carson and who took care of Carson's children after his friend's death. He served for a time as a guide to California for a party of Americans. He took to mining but had no luck. Finally he drifted into the Rayado country where he worked for Joseph Pley, a partner of Maxwell's. He lived with Pley and became acquainted with one of Beaubien's daughters, eighteen years his junior. They married and she bore him nine children. He bought part of the Rayado tract in 1859.

Of the others who deeded land to Maxwell very little is known, save of the Sheurick family which was also related to the Bent family. The Sheuricks played a prominent part in Taos affairs. It was they who took care of Governor Bent when he was scalped by the Indians in the uprising which took Narciso Beaubien's life. Their home was neglected for a time until converted into an art gallery. It still exists but as a private residence. Aloy Sheurick's descendants live in Clovis, New Mexico. Hicklin and Muller moved to Colorado as far as can be ascertained; Trujillo made his residence in Mora; Pablo Beaubien did not survive the transfer of deed very long and is said to have died a young man. The Bents did not give up the fight and it dragged on for years. Since Mrs. Scheurick was a Bent she sided in with her relatives in fighting for what they considered their rights.

Docithe A. Clothier was born in St. George, Canada on May 5, 1853. He attended elementary school, following which he remained at his father's farm until he was seventeen years of age. He then went to Sheridan, Kansas, and worked as a clerk for Chick & Co. until he was twenty-seven. He worked for a time with Otero, Manzanarez, finally with Beaubien and Maxwell. He bought land on the Grant and established the famous Clouthier Ranch. In 1878, he formed a partnership with H. M. Porter and eventually bought out the interests of Brown & Manzanares. In 1885, Porter went to Denver and Clouthier in connection with others continued the business as the Spring Mercantile & Banking Company. He managed the affairs of the company until 1888 when he resigned as director but maintained his connection with the firm. When Porter retired the business was valued at $95,000, which was quite a return for the $15,000 invested. Clouthier then went into real estate and divided his time between his second-hand store and real estate. He was elected county treasurer in 1880, serving three terms. He married Josephine Abreu, Beaubien's granddaughter, on Oct. 1, 1882. His daughter married a Webster and the Webster girl married an Abdulla. These descendants of Beaubien's live in Springer, New Mexico.

TRANSFERS OF TITLE

DEED

L. PABLO MIRANDA TO LUCIEN B. MAXWELL

This Indenture, made this seventh day of April, in the year of our Lord one thousand eight hundred and fifty-eight, by and between L. Pablo Miranda, agent for Guadalupe Miranda with full power of attorney to act in the premises, as if his said principal was personally present and would do of his own right; of El Paso, in the State of Chihuahua, and Republic of Mexico, of the first part, and Lucien B. Maxwell, of the County of Taos and Territory of New Mexico, in the United States of America, of the second part, Witnesseth: That the said party of the first part, for and in consideration of the sum of one thousand dollars, lawful money of the United States to him duly paid before the delivery hereof, the receipt of which is hereby acknowledged, and for the further sum of one thousand dollars to be paid on the first day of July, A. D. one thousand eight hundred and fifty eight, the receipt of a promissory note for the payment of said last mentioned sum is also hereby acknowledged, and also for the further sum of five hundred dollars to be paid when the Congress of the United States of America shall have passed favorably on the hereinafter mentioned claim or grant; Also, the sum of two hundred and forty-five dollars to be paid to Charles Beaubien for expenses paid by him the said Beaubien, for the investigation of the legality of the said claim or grant; making the sum total of two thousand seven hundred and forty-five dollars; hath bargained and sold, and by these presents doth bargain and sell, grant and convey to the said party of the second part, his heirs and assigns forever, all the right, title, interest and claim whatsoever that the said party of the first part now has or may hereafter have, in and to a certain tract or parcel of land, lying and being in the County of Taos and Territory of New Mexico, known as the Beaubien and Miranda grant, or Rayado claim, which said claim was confirmed by William Pelham, Surveyor General of the Territory of New Mexico, in the month of September in the year one thousand eight hundred and fifty-seven:

To have and to hold, all and singular the above mentioned right, title, interest and claim whatsoever, unto the said party of the second part and to his heirs and assigns forever.

In witness whereof, the said party of the first part hath hereunto set his hand and seal the day and year above written.

L. PABLO MIRANDA. (SEAL)

Signed, sealed and delivered in the presence of

FRED MULLER.
CHARLES BEAUBIEN.

TERRITORY OF NEW MEXICO,
COUNTY OF TAOS,   } SS.
Second Judicial District,

Be it remembered, that on this seventeenth day of April, A.D. 1858, before me, James Barry, clerk of the District Court for the Second Judicial District of New Mexico, personally appeared L. Pablo Miranda, to me well known to be the person whose name is subscribed to the foregoing instrument of writing, and acknowledged the same to be his act and deed for the purposes therein mentioned.

In testimony whereof, I have hereunto set my hand and affixed the seal of said court at office in Fernando de Taos, the day and year above written.

JAMES BARRY, Clerk

DEED

CHARLES BEAUBIEN AND WIFE TO L. B. MAXWELL.

This Indenture, made this fourteenth day of September, in the year of our Lord eighteen hundred and fifty-eight, by and between Charles Beaubien and Maria Panla, his wife, parties of the first part, Lucien B. Maxwell, the party of the second part, all of the County of Taos and Territory of New Mexico, Witnesseth: That Charles Beaubien and Maria Panla, his wife, parties of the first part, for and in consideration of the sum of five hundred dollars, lawful money of the United States to them in hand paid by the said Lucien B. Maxwell, the party of the second part, at or before the ensealing of and delivering of these presents, the receipt whereof is hereby acknowldged, has remised, released and quit-claimed, and by these presents doth forever remise, release and quit-claim, unto the said Lucien B. Maxwell, the party of the second part, and to his heirs, administrators, executors and assigns, all that certain tract or parcel of land known as the Rayado, being two and one-fourth miles, extending from the Plaza built by the said Lucien B. Maxwell, the party of the second part, and his dwelling house, being the centre forming a square, extending on each side from said house two and a quarter miles, north, south, east and west, lying and being in the County of Taos and Territory of New Mexico, together with all and singular the tenements, hereditaments and appurtenances thereunto belonging, or in anywise appertaining, and the reversion and reversions, remainder and remainders, rents, issues and profits thereof. Also, all the estate, right, title, interest, property, possession, claim and demand whatsoever, as well in law as in equity, of the above described premises, and every part or parcel thereof, with the appurtenances: To have and to hold, all and singular the above mentioned and described premises, together with the appurtenances thereunto belonging, unto the said Lucien B. Maxwell, the party of the second part, and to his heirs, executors, administrators and assigns forever.

In witness whereof, the said parties of the first part have hereunto set their hands and affixed their seals the day and year above written.

    CHARLES BEAUBIEN.   (SEAL)
    MARIA PANLA BEAUBIEN.   (SEAL)

Signed, sealed and delivered in the presence of

    GABRIEL VIGIL.
    FRED MULLER.

DEED

MULLER AND WIFE TO MAXWELL.

This Deed, made and entered into this fourth day of April, in the year of our Lord eighteen hundred and sixty-four, by and between Frederick Muller and Teodora, his wife, of the town of Fernando de Taos, County of Taos, Territory of New Mexico, parties of the first part, and L. B. Maxwell, of the County of Mora, of Territory aforesaid, party of the second part, Witnesseth: That said parties of the first part, for and in consideration of the sum of five hundred dollars to be paid to them by the party of the second part on the delivery of this document into the hands of said L. B. Maxwell.

Have, as we hereby do, grant, bargain, sell, remise, convey and quit-claim and transfer unto said party of the second part, his heirs and assigns, the following described real estate, situate, lying and being in the County of Mora, Territory of New Mexico, and included within the boundaries of a grant known as the Grant of Beaubien and Miranda, under the Republic of Mexico, and afterwards confirmed by the Government of the United States, and a copy of which is on file in the Surveyor General's office, in the city of Santa Fe, in said Territory, to which reference is hereby made; to wit; All the right, title, interest, estate claim and demand of said grantors, heretofore acquired by said Teodorita by inheritance from her father, the late Charles Beaubien, of said County of Taos, (deceased,) being her undivided interest in said grant, as one of the surviving heirs of said Charles Beaubien, decedent.

To have and to hold the above described premises, together with all and singular the rights and privileges, hereditaments, easements, appurtenances and immunities belonging and appertaining thereto unto him said party of the second part and to his heirs or assigns forever.

The said parties of the first part and administrators, themselves, heirs and executors, for and in consideration of the premises, hereby covenant and agree to and with the said party of the second part, his heirs, executors and administrators, that they and each of them will forever defend in law or equity, the title to the above described premises against the lawful claims of any or all persons claiming under said Frederick Muller or Teodorita, grantors herein named, but against the claims of no other person whomsoever. Said Frederick Muller and his wife are not to be held responsible in any manner, now nor hereafter, on account of said sale.

In witness whereof, we have hereunto set our hands and seal this fourth day of April, in the year of our Lord eighteen hundred and sixty-four.

    TEODORA BEAUBIEN.   (SEAL)
    FRED MULLER   (SEAL)

Signed, sealed and delivered and acknowledged in the presence of

    I. B. LEROU.
    WM. G. BLACKWOOD.

DEED

CLOUTHIER AND WIFE TO MAXWELL.

This Deed, made and entered into this fourth day of April, in the year of our Lord eighteen hundred and sixty-four, by and between Joseph Clouthier and Juana his wife, of the town of Don Fernando de Taos, County of Taos and Territory of New Mexico, parties of the first part, and Lucien B. Maxwell, of the County of Mora, of Territory aforesaid, party of the second part, witnesseth: That said parties of the first part for and in consideration of the sum of three thousand five hundred dollars, the receipt of which is hereby acknowledged, by two notes of seventeen hundred and fifty dollars each, to be paid by the said party of the second part, viz.:—The first note of seventeen hundred and fifty dollars, payable the fourth day of the month of August, in the year of our Lord eighteen hundred and sixty-four, and the second and last note of seventeen hundred and fifty dollars payable the fourth day of the month of October, in the year of our Lord eighteen hundred and sixty-four.

Have, as we hereby do, grant, bargain, and sell, remise, convey and quit-claim and transfer unto said party of the second part, his heirs and assigns, the following described real estate, situate, lying and being the County of Mora, Territory of New Mexico, and included within the boundaries of a grant known as the Grant of Beaubien & Miranda, under the Republic of Mexico, and afterwards confirmed by the Government of the United States, and a copy of which is on file in the Surveyor's General office, in the city of Santa Fe, in said Territory, to which reference is hereby made: to-wit:—All the right, title, interest, estate, claim, and demand of said grantors, heretofore acquired by said Juana by inheritance from her father, the late Charles Beaubien, of said County of Taos, deceased, being her undivided interest in said grant, as one of the six surviving heirs of said Charles Beaubien, decedent.

To have and to hold the above described premises, together with all and singular the rights and privileges, hereditaments, easements, appurtenances and immunities thereto unto him said party of the second part and to his heirs and assigns forever.

The said parties of the first part, administrators, themselves, heirs and executors, for and in consideration of the premises, hereby covenant and agree to and with said party of the second part, his heirs, executors and administrators, that they and each of them will forever defend in law or equity the title to the above described premises against the lawful claims of any or all persons claiming under said Joseph Clouthier and Juana, grantors herein named, but against the claims of no other person whomsoever. Said Joseph Clouthier and his wife are not to be held responsible in any manner, now nor hereafter, on account of said sale.

In witness whereof, we have hereunto set our hands and seal this fourth day of April, in the year of our Lord eighteen hundred sixty-four.

        JOS. CLOUTIER   (SEAL)
        JUANA BEAUBIEN. (SEAL)

(Signed, sealed, and delivered and acknowledged in the presence of
        FRED MULLER.
        F. MAXWELL.

DEED
TRUJILLO AND WIFE TO MAXWELL.

This Deed, made and entered into this twentieth day of July, in the year of our Lord one thousand eight hundred and sixty-four, by and between Vital Trujillo and Eleanor his wife, of the town of Mora, County of Mora, Territory of New Mexico, parties of the first part, and L. B. Maxwell, of the same county and territory aforesaid, party of the second part, witnesseth: That said parties of the first part, for and in consideration of the sum of three thousand dollars, to be paid to them by the party of the second part, on delivery of this document to the party of the second part, have, as we hereby do, grant, bargain, sell, remise, convey and quit-claim and transfer, unto said party of the second part, his heirs and assigns forever, the following described real estate, situate, lying and being in the County of Mora and County of Taos and Territory of New Mexico, and included within the boundaries of a grant known as the grant of Beaubien and confirmed by the Government of the United States, and Miranda, under the Republic of Mexico, and afterwards a copy of which is on file in the Surveyor General's Office, in the city of Santa Fe, in said Territory, to which reference is hereby made, to wit: All the right, title, interest, estate, claim and demand of said grantors heretofore acquired by said Eleanor by inheritance from her father, the late Charles Beaubien, of the County of Taos, (deceased), being her undivided interest in said grant as one of the surviving heirs of said Charles Beaubien (deceased). To have and to hold the above described premises, together with all and singular the rights and privileges, hereditaments and appurtenances and immunities belonging and appertaining thereto, unto him the party of the second part, and to his heirs and assigns forever. The said parties of the first part and administrators, themselves, heirs and executors, for and in consideration of the premises, hereby covenant and agree to and with the party of the second part, his heirs, executors and administrators, that they and each of them will forever defend in law or equity the title to the above and within described premises against the lawful claims of any and all persons claiming under said Vital Trujillo or Eleanor his wife, grantors herein named, but against the claims of no other person whomsoever. Said Vital Trujillo and his wife are to be held responsible in any manner, now nor hereafter, on account of said sale.

In witness whereof, we have hereunto set our hands and seals this twentieth day of July, in the year of our Lord eighteen hundred and sixty-four.

        VIDAL TRUJILLO.   (SEAL)
        LENOR X. TRUJILLO. (SEAL)

Signed, sealed, and delivered and acknowledged in the presence of us.
        FERD MAXWELL.

DEED
ABREU AND WIFE TO MAXWELL.

This Deed and Indenture, made and entered into this first day of February in the year of our Lord one thousand eight hundred and sixty-seven, by and between Jesus G.

Abreu and Petra Abreu, his wife, formerly Petra Beaubien, of Rallado, in the County of Mora and Territory of New Mexico, of the first part, and Lucien B. Maxwell, of Cimarron, in the same county, of the second part, witnesseth: That the said parties of the first part for and in consideration of the sum of three thousand five hundred dollars, to them paid by the party of the second part, the receipt whereof is hereby acknowledged, have granted, bargained and sold, and by these do grant, bargain, and sell, alien, enfeoff convey, and confirm unto the said party of the second part, his heirs and assigns, all the right, title, and interest, property, claim, and demand which they have or may have to certain tract of land, situated in said County of Mora and Territory aforesaid, and described as follows: (to wit):

The grant and donation of land known as the Beaubien and Miranda Mexican Grant, ceded by the Mexican government to Charles Beaubien and Guadalupe Miranda, some time in the month of January, in the year of our Lord one thousand eight hundred and forty-one, and confirmed to said Beaubien and Miranda by an act of Congress of the United States, and for a further description thereof reference is hereby made to a copy of said grant on file in the office of the Surveyor General of the United States for New Mexico, at Santa Fe, in said Territory. The said premises hereby conveyed being in effect, all the undivided right, title and interest of said grantors, to said above described tract of land, heretofore acquired by said Petra Abreu under and by virtue of the last will and testament of her father, the said Charles Beaubien, late of the County of Taos, in said Territory, deceased.

To have and to hold said hereby granted and bargained premises, with all the rights, privileges and appurtenances thereunto belonging or in anywise pertaining, to him the said party of the second part, his heirs, executors and administrators, for the consideration aforesaid, do hereby covenant and agree to and with the said party of the second part, his heirs and assigns forever, to warrant, secure and defend the title to the above described premises against the lawful claims and demands of all persons whatsoever, claiming through them or their heirs, but against the claims or demands of no other person or persons whatsoever.

In testimony whereof, the parties of the first part have hereunto set their hands and affixed their seals the day and year first above written.

JESUS G. ABREU. (SEAL)
PETRA B. ABREU. (SEAL)

DEED
PAUL BEAUBIEN TO MAXWELL.

This Deed, made and entered into this the first day of January, in the year of our Lord one thousand eight hundred and seventy, by and between Paul Beaubien of the County of Taòs, Territory of New Mexico, party of the first part, and Lucien B. Maxwell, of the County of Colfax, Territory aforesaid, party of the second part, witnesseth: That the said party of the first part, for and in consideration of the sum of three thousand five hundred dollars ($3,500.00) (the receipt of which is hereby acknowledged), have as we hereby do grant, bargain and sell, remise, convey, quit-claim and transfer unto said party of the second part, his heirs and assigns, the following described real estate, situate, lying and being in the County of Colfax, in said Territory, and partly in Colorado Territory, and included within the boundaries of a grant known as the Beaubien and Miranda Grant, under the Republic of Mexico, and afterwards confirmed by the Government of the United States, and a copy of which is on file in the Surveyor's General's office, in the city of Santa Fe, in said Territory, to which reference is hereby made, to wit: All the right, title interest, estate, claim and demand of said grantor, heretofore acquired by the said Paul Beaubien by inheritance from his father, the late Charles Beaubien of said County of Taos, (deceased), being his undivided interest in said grant, as one of the six surviving heirs of said Charles Beaubien, deceased.

To have and to hold the above described premises, together with all and singular the rights and privileges, hereditaments, easements, appurtenances and immunities belonging and appertaining thereto, unto him the said party of the second part, and to his heirs and assigns forever.

The said party of the first part, for themselves, their administrators, heirs, executors, for and in consideration of the premises, hereby covenant and agree to and with said party of the second part, his heirs, executors and administrators, that they and each of them will warrant and defend in law or equity the title to the above described premises against the lawful claims of any or all persons claiming under the said party of the first part, but against the claims of no other person whomsoever.

In testimony whereof, I have hereunto set my hand and seal the day and year first above written.

PAUL BEAUBIEN. (SEAL)

Signed, sealed, acknowledged, and delivered in presence of
CHAS. F. HOLLY.

DEED
SHEURICK AND WIFE TO MAXWELL.

This Deed, made and entered into this third day of May, A.D. eighteen hundred and sixty-six, by and between Aloys Scheurich and Teresina Scheurich, nee Bent, his wife, of the Town of Don Fernando de Taos, in the County of Taos, and Territory of New Mexico, parties of the first part, and Lucien B. Maxwell of "El Cimeron," in the County of Mora, and Territory aforesaid, party of the second part, witnesseth: That the said parties of the first part, for and in consideration of the sum of six thousand ($6,000.00) dollars, to them in hand paid by the said party of the second part, the receipt of which is hereby acknowledged, have granted, bargained and sold, aliened, enfeoffed, conveyed and confirmed, as by these presents they do grant, bargain and sell, alien, enfeoff, convey and confirm, unto the said party of the second part, his heirs and assigns, the following described real estate, situate, lying and being in the aforesaid County of Mora, and Territory of New Mexico, and known and described as the Rayado Grant, heretofore granted to Carlos Beaubien and Guadalupe Miranda, by Governor Armijo, on the eleventh day of January, A.D. 1841, and which is bounded and described as follows to wit: Beginning on the east bank of the Rio Colorado, at a mound of rocks; thence running, in a straight line eastward, to the first hills, to another mound of rocks; thence, continuing from south to north, on a parallel line with the river Colorado, to the third mound of rocks, on the northern edge of the table lands of Chicorica o Chacuaco; thence turning westward, and following the edge of the said table lands of Chacuaco, to the top or comb of the Sierra Madre, to the fourth mound of rocks; thence, from north to south, following the top of the said Sierra Madre, to the Cuesta del Osha, one hundred varas (100v.) to the north of the road to Fernandez, and to the Laguna Negra, to the fifth mound of rocks; thence, turning anew to the east, towards the Rio Colorado, and following the southern edge of the table lands of Rayado and Gonzalitos, to the eastern point of these table lands, to the sixth mound of rocks; and thence, following in a northerly direction, until the said line strikes the Rio Colorado, on the western bank of said river, where the seventh mound of rocks was placed.

To have and to hold the one undivided one-twelfth (one 12th) interest of, in and to the above described real estate, together with all and singular the rights, immunities, hereditaments, privileges and appurtenances thereunto belonging, or in anywise appertaining, unto the said party of the second part, and his heirs and assigns, forever; the said one-twelfth undivided interest being the entire interest, estate, claim and demand of the said Teresina Scheurich, nee Bent, of, in and to the real estate above described, as a child of, and one of the heirs of Charles Bent, late of the Territory of New Mexico, deceased; and the said grantors hereby covenant, to and with the said grantee, his heirs and assigns, that the above described interest, hereby conveyed, of, in and to the said real estate, is free and clear of all encumbrances, and that they, the said grantors, their heirs, executors and administrators, shall and will warrant and defend the title to the same, unto the said grantee, his heirs and assigns, for ever, against the lawful claim or demands of all persons whomsoever.

In witness whereof, the said parties of the first part have hereunto set their hands and seals, the day and year first above written.

ALOYS SCHEURICH (SEAL)
TERESINA SCHEURICH, nee Bent.

Signed, sealed and delivered in presence of
ADOLPH LETCHER.
WM. G. BLACKWOOD.

DEED
HICKLIN AND WIFE TO MAXWELL.

This Deed, made and entered into this thirty-first day of May, A.D. eighteen hundred and sixty-six, by and between Alexander Hicklin and Estefana Hicklin, nee Bent, his wife, of "Greenhorn," in the County of Huerfano, and Territory of Colorado, parties of the first part, and Lucien B. Maxwell, of "El Cimeron," in the County of Mora, and Territory of New Mexico, party of the second part, witnesseth: That the said parties of the first part, for and in consideration of the sum of six thousand ($6,000.00) dollars, to them in hand paid by the said party of the second part, the receipt of which is hereby acknowledged, have granted, bargained and sold, aliened, enfeoffed, conveyed and confirmed, as by these presents they do grant, bargain and sell, alien, enfeoff, convey and confirm unto the said party of the second part, his heirs and assigns, the following described real estate, situate, lying and being in the aforesaid County of Mora, and Territory of New Mexico, and known and described as the Rayado Grant, heretofore granted to Carlos Beaubien and Guadalupe Miranda, by Governor Armijo, on the eleventh day of January, A.D. 1841, and which is bounded and described as follows, to wit: Beginning on the east bank of the Rio Colorado, at a mound of rocks; thence continuing, from south to north, on a parallel line with the River Colorado, to the third mound of rocks, on the northern edge of the table lands of Chicorica o Chacuaco; thence turning westward, and following the edge of the said table land of Chacuaco, to the top or comb of the Sierra Madre, to the fourth mound of rocks; thence, from north to south, following the top of the said Sierra Madre, to the Cuesta del Osha, one hundred (100 v.) varas to the north of the road to Fernandez, and to the Laguna Negra, to the fifth mound of rocks; thence, turning anew to the east, toward the Rio Colorado, and following the southern edge of the table lands of Rayado and Gonzalitos, to the eastern point of these table lands, to the sixth mound of rocks; and thence, following in a northerly direction, until the said line strikes the Rio Colorado, on the western bank of said river, where the seventh mound of rocks was placed.

To have and to hold the one undivided one-twelfth (one 12th) interest of, in and to the above described real estate, together with all and singular the rights, immunities, hereditaments, privileges and appurtenances thereunto belonging, or in any wise appertaining, unto the said party of the second part, and his heirs and assigns, forever; the said one-twelfth undivided interest being the entire interest, estate, claim and demand of the said Estefana Hicklin, Nee Bent, of, in and to the real estate above described, as a child of, and one of the heirs of Charles Bent, late of the Territory of New Mexico, deceased. And the said grantors hereby covenant to and with said grantee, his heirs and assigns, that the above described interest hereby conveyed, of, in and to the real estate, is free and clear of all encumbrances, and that they, the said grantors, their heirs, executors and administrators, shall and will warrant and defend the title to the same unto the said grantee, his heirs and assigns, forever, against the lawful claim or demands of all persons whomsoever.

In witness whereof, the said parties of the first part have hereunto set their hands and seals, the day and year first above written.

A. HICKLIN. (SEAL)
ESTEFANA HICKLIN. (SEAL)

Signed, sealed and delivered in presence of
MAT. RIDDLEBARGER.
L. RICKABAUGH.

IN THE
SUPREME COURT
OF THE
TERRITORY OF NEW MEXICO

WILLIAM BENT,
Plaintiff in Error
vs.
GUADALUPE THOMPSON, ET AL.,
Defendants in Error

BRIEF ON THE PART OF PLAINTIFF IN ERROR.

In the year of Grace 1865, Albert Bent departed this life, leaving three children of tender years as his sole heirs-at-law.

In the year 1867 a certain paper writing was admitted to probate and recorded in the Probate court of Taos county, as his last will and testament.

This record, as was proven at the hearing in the present case (fols. 92, 95), was made without the examination of the attesting witnesses, or any other witnesses.

The heirs, having arrived at their majority, and having been informed of the record of probate, now seek to impeach the validity of the paper upon petition alleging that if ever signed or acknowledged by their ancestor, the same was so signed and acknowledged while he was no longer of sound mind. The Probate court of Taos county, after hearing all persons in interest affecting the probate, adjudged the paper no will, and rejected it. The District court upon appeal held this to be beyond the jurisdiction of the Probate court.

The questions, therefore, present are, whether a record so made without notice to the hearing of the heirs, and without the examination of witnesses is absolute and conclusive, or may be relieved against, and if so, by what process.

1.

THE PROBATE COURT HAD JURISDICTION
TO ENTERTAIN AND ALLOW PETITION.

By the laws of New Mexico in force at the time of the death of Alfred Bent, the petitioner and his infant brothers were the direct heirs of the ancestor, and succeeded to all his property rights.

Comp. L. 1865, ch. 4 SS 1,2, p. 44.

And although the statute permitted the ancestor to disinherit the heir and give his succession another direction, yet before any writing with this purpose could have its effect, it was required (as indeed, the law everywhere requires), that the testator should be of sound mind and memory, that his wishes should be set down in writing and attested with certain formalities, and that the writing so subscribed and attested should receive the approval of the court of probate appointed for the purpose, and be there recorded.

And in order to the effectual probate and establishment of such a paper, it was essential that the heir should have his day in court with opportunity to confront and interrogate those asserting or seeking to establish the document, and this not only upon the broad principle, which it is safe to assert is recognized in every jurisprudence, that no person shall be condemned and deprived of any right unheard, but by the express provisions of the constitution (5th amendment), that "no person shall be deprived of life, liberty or property without due process of Law."

At the common law two forms for the probate of the last will of a decedent were recognized. The first, known as the probate in common form, when the executor presents the will before the judge or ordinary, and in the absence of parties interested, and without citing them, produces witnesses to establish the same.

1Wms. Ex. (325) 6 Am. Ed.

And, second, in solemn form, or per testes, where the widow and next of kin are cited to be present at the probate of the will and to examine the witnesses and those propounding the same.

Id. (333).

Where probate was made in common form, the heirs of any person having an interest were entitled at any time within thirty years to cite the executor to make proof of the will in solemn form.

Id. (334).

And this right of the next of kin was so highly regarded that acocrding to the authorities it was a matter of common right, 'and the mere acquiescence of the next of kin to the probate in common form is no bar to the exercise of this right, even though he has received a legacy as due him under the will, for he is still at liberty to call in the probate and put the executor on proof of that identical will per testes."

Id. (336).

In the American states the probate of the will of a decedent is generally regulated by statute.

In most jurisdictions some form of notice to the heir is required in the first instance, so that where this is the case every probate may be said to be in some sort a probate in solemn form. Generally, however, even in the states last referred to, the heir is allowed to impeach the will at any time afterwards by proceedings either in the Probate court or by bill in equity.

In other states, either by express statutory regulation or by reason of the absence of regulation, the probate in common form without citing the heir is admitted. But, as we believe, in every one of the states where probate in common form is permitted, the provision of the common law requiring a subsequent probate in solemn form on petition of the heir, is recognized as in force.

Thus in Noyes vs. Barber (4 N.H. 412), it was held that probate in solemn form must be understood to be a probate made after all persons whose interests may be affected by the will have been duly notified and have had an opportunity to be heard on the subject. That notice to the guardian was not to be deemed notice to the wards, and that no probate could have the effect of probate in solemn form unless guardians of the children were appointed having no interest adverse to the interest of the ward, and such guardians were duly notified of the time when the will was to be offered for probate and had opportunity to be heard. In this case the probate in common form made in 1818 was set aside in 1828.

George vs. George (47 N. H. 44), recognises the same distinction.

So, in Brown vs. Gibson (1 Nott. & McC. 326), decided in 1818. The case shows that the will of Brown was proven in comon form in 1814, that in 1818 the citation had issued at the instance of heirs requiring the executor to appear before the ordinary to prove the will in solemn form, and that upon hearing of all parties the probate in common form was revoked and the will disallowed on account of the insanity of the decedent. The first resolution of the court is in these words: "The probate of a will in common form may be revoked either on a suit by citation or on appeal."

Randolph vs. Hughes (89 N. C. 429), is to the same effect. And the court say: "The authorities unequivocally assert the right of persons interested in a decedent's estate, when the will has been proved without citation or notice to any of them, to require a recall of the probate and an order for repropounding the script, unless lost by the laches or unreasonable delay in its enforcement." And the court cite with approval the words of Sir John Nichols in Bell vs. Armstrong (2 Eccl. Rep. 139): "The next of kin, as such merely, are entitled to call for proof per testes of any decedent's will of common right." The court say that the same principle was announced in Ralson vs. Telfair (1 Dev. & Bat. 482), and in Ethridge vs. Corprew (3 Jones 14), in which last case Pearson, J., declares that "no one should be deprived of his rights without an opportunity of being heard. The next of kin are entitled of common right to have such probate set aside so as to give them an opportunity of contesting its validity and having a probate per testes."

In Hamberlin vs. Terry (7 How. (Miss.) 143), the court say, arguendo, that the first probate of a will is a mere incipient step, and is not conclusive upon the heirs and distributees, and may be opened, and, if necessary, set aside.

In Cowden vs. Dobyns (5 Sm. & M. 82), and Garner vs. Lansford (12 Sm. & M. 558), the same doctrine is reiterated.

Wall vs. Wall (30 Miss. 96) re-asserts the same doctrine.

So, in Hubbard vs. Hubbard (7 Oreg. 44), the court, adverting to the distinction between probate in common form and probate in solemn form observed in English courts, declare that "both these forms have been substantially adopted in most of the states by statute, and that in Oregon, while the only one adopted by the positive enactments of the legislature is that in common form, yet that the heir may afterwards assail the will by direct proceeding, and that it then becomes incumbent upon the person seeking to maintain its validity to reprobate the same de novo by original proof in the same manner as if no probate thereof had been had."

In Sowell vs. Sowell (40 Ala. 243), the same doctrine was asserted, and the court cite Roy vs. Seigrist (19 Ala. 810), Stapleton vs. Stapleton (21 Ala. 587), Bradley vs. Andress (27 Ala. 596), and Lovett vs. Chisholm (30 Ala. 88).

Roby vs. Hanon (6 Gill. 463), and Clagget vs. Hawkins (11 Md. 386), are to the same effect.

In Walker vs. Perryman (23 Geo. 317) the two forms of probate are distinguished, and it is held that knowledge of the pendency of the first proceeding will not bar the heir of his right to solemn proof.

In Lively vs. Harwell (29 Geo. 508), it is held, in order to make solemn probate not only must notice be given to the next of kin, but this notice must be a reasonable notice, and a five-days notice was held insufficient.

In the case of Rogers vs. Winton (2 Humph. 178), it appears that this same distinction between the two forms of probate has long been observed in the courts of Tennessee. There it appears that in 1835 the heirs of a decedent applied for leave to contest the validity of a will probated by the widow in the year 1816, and the probate was annulled.

In Gibson vs. Lane (9 Yerg. 475), it appears that upon proceedings substantially identical with those taken in this case, the heirs-at-law of Gibson were allowed in 1834 to vacate the probate of their ancestor's will made in 1816. The court say the proceedings were regular, and cite with their approval the case of Satterwhite vs. Satterwhite (1 Eng. Con. Ecc. 151, 425), where it was held that a will could be called in and a probate contested after twenty years from the probate in common form.

In Burrow vs. Ragland (6 Humph. 481), a bill was filed in the chancery court to annul a will before that time admitted to probate. The bill was dismissed in the court below for want of jurisdiction, and this decree was affirmed in the Supreme court, the opinion citing with approval what is said in Williams on Executors touching the probate in solemn form and common form. The court say: "The design and object of this bill is to enforce the executor to prove it in solemn in form the chancery court. This cannot be done for want of jurisdiction, but to have this done the complainants must cite the executor to appear before the County court for that purpose, which being done, the parties are entitled to their issue on the will and to a trial in the Circuit court. * * * * The executor, having chosen to prove the will in common form, the complainants if they wish it proved in the solemn form must proceed against him by citation in the County court, from which the case will be removed for trial under statutory provision, to the Circuit court."

The same doctrine is either asserted or countenanced in every single one of the American text writers.

Lomax Wills.
3 Redf. Wills, Ch. L, S 3.
Schouler Exr. SS 67-70.

The absolute right of the heir, therefore, to reinvestigate the probate of a paper alleged to be the will of his ancestor, when such probate has been allowed without citation or notice to him, and without his attendance, is established not only by reference to the common law of the English courts (which is expressly declared by the statute to be the rule of decision in New Mexico, Comp. L., 1884 S 1823), but by concurring opinions of the courts in all the state where probate in common form is permitted, and the American text writers.

THE LAPSE OF TIME INTERVENING BETWEEN THE PROBATE AND THE INITIATION OF THIS PETITION IS NO BAR.

The court will not fail to observe that by the petition in this case it appears that the petitioner had come to his majority less than three months before the initiation of his petition.

But, as appears by the authorities, if he had been of full age, if he had been at the time of the probate, if he had accepted a legacy thereunder, this still would have been no bar.

1 Wms. Exr. 336.

The American cases assert the same doctrine: "It is laid down by Godolphin that the probate of a will in common form may be re-examined at any time within thirty years after such probate."

Noyes vs. Barber, 4 N. H. 412.

"The probate of a will in common form may be revoked either by citation or on appeal at any time within thirty years."

Brown vs. Gibson, 1 Nott. & Mc. C. 326.

"The proposition that no lapse of time will exclude the inquiry whether certain papers constitute the will of a party, is supported by almost any number of authorities."

Claggett vs. Hawkins, 11 Md. 387.

III.

THE PROCEEDING BY PETITION AND CITATION TO THE EXECUTOR AND TERRETENANTS WAS THE PROPER PROCEEDING.

No other proceeding would, indeed, appear to be admissible, or, indeed, practicable. How shall the court enter upon the inquiry, and how shall the heir assert his heirship and deny the will, unless by petition? How shall the executor be brought in, unless by citation? Some formality of allegation must be required. Certainly none of the forms of action at common law apply. Neither debt, trespass, trespass on the case, covenant, detinue or replevin will suffice. Equity has no jurisdiction either to allow or revoke the probate of a will.

In re Broderick's Will, 21 Wall. 503.

The only process open to the heirs, therefore, was by petition in the probate court. This was the form of proceeding adopted in every one of the American cases cited. It was the form prevailing in the English courts, and as the Supreme court of Mississippi well declare, the forms of procedure in the English courts are, in the absence of statutory regulations, "necessarily in force in our probate courts.'

Cowden vs. Dobyns, 5 Sm. & M. 90.

The form of proceeding here adopted is also countenanced in the Supreme court of the United States.

McArthur vs. Scott, 5 S. C. Rep. 670, 671, S. C. 113 W. S. 340.

It is respectfully submitted, therefore, that the judgment of the District court is erroneous, and must be reversed.

CALDWELL YEAMAN,
WELLS, MCNEAL & TAYLOR,
FOR PLAINTIFFS IN ERROR.

Chapter Four

THE MAXWELL LAND GRANT AND RAILWAY COMPANY

In 1843, Maxwell was to be introduced to a graduate from West Point, who was to be of immense assistance to him years later in the disposal of the grant. Of course Maxwell did not know this at the time since the man who introduced them, Fremont, was too interested in his own exploits to be concerned about happenings in New Mexico. Besides, Maxwell was a comparative new-comer to the Beaubien family at the time. William Gilpin became quite friendly with Beaubien when stationed with the Army of the West in New Mexico and was known for his exploits against the Navajos, Utes and Apaches. He was quite popular at Abiquiu. Gilpin explored Western Colorado and crossed Cochetopa Pass in 1844. He was dispatched to Washington with the report of the Fremont Expedition of 1843. He served in the Mexican War with the rank of Major. In 1864, he headed a campaign against Indians hiding in the San Juan Mountains. He was also in charge of the campaigns against the Indians molesting traffic on the Santa Fe Trail during the summers of 1847 and 1848.

Gilpin was from Missouri. Following the war he resigned from the army and settled down to the practice of law. He married Julia Pratt Dickerson. Always attracted by the thought of gold and mines in the West he made frequent visits to Taos where he enlisted the aid of Carson and Maxwell as scouts in his expeditions for minerals. In 1860 he published a book entitled, *The Central Gold Region* which may or may not have been responsible for the gold rush to Colorado. It helped in any event to interest soldiers and prospectors in the Colorado and New Mexico areas. Back in the army as Colonel Gilpin, he organized the First Regiment Colorado Volunteers. He was always considered a man of calm judgment, a thinker and scholar as well as a good business man. He made a sound investment when he bought the Sangre de Cristo Grant from Beaubien, re-selling it at an immense profit to an English combine. Naturally Maxwell approached him about the purchase of his immense tract. While Gilpin himself was not interested in the purchase, he would talk to some who might be. Wealthy people who respected his judgment and who would not hesitate to invest in the property. President Buchanan, in one of his last official acts, created the Territory of Colorado on February 28, 1861. President Lincoln appointed Gilpin as first territorial governor on March 22nd. On May 27, 1861, Gilpin entered Denver in that official capacity. His high station acquainted him with many men of political and material importance whom he introduced to Maxwell.

A concatenation of circumstances combined to bring about the disposal of the Grant by Maxwell: the suggestion of friends that the old days were passing and he was being crowded out by squatters, prospectors and traders; gold-crazy hordes; settlers who refused to turn East when no gold was to be found, but who decided to remain to plant the fields about them into another type of gold; ranchmen who decided that here was the place to raise sheep and steers; the possibility that the Indian Agent would convince the government that the Grant would be ideal as an Indian reservation for the Utes and Jicarillas; the old wanderlust of moving to new places and opening new tracts; the breaking up of the family through the marriages of the children; his own refusal to slow-up and admit that he was ageing. His zest for work was proven in the energy he threw into new railroad deals, the founding of Silver City, the opening of the bank in Santa Fe, the store in Mora and food contracts with the government. Another more remote possibility was the alarmingly accumulating number of lawsuits in which he was becoming involved. He was also tired of telling a new batch of prospectors every day that they were on personal property.

Maxwell was inherently a lonely man, wrapted in his own thoughts, plans, schemes and desires. He possessed the hearty laugh of one who tolerates you but at the same time wishes you would leave him alone. His hospitality was princely. He pleased his guests and gave them all he had from the bottom of his heart, retaining the core for a few cronies who alone understood the man as a whole, who received complete hospitality without externals. Maxwell could put on a smile or wipe it off like an actor on stage. He wanted guests; yet seemed bored with them. He had a hearty handshake but it could have been you or the King of Siam or a scrub-woman. Men like Maxwell had two hands—one for the family; one for intimates like Carson, Dold, Boggs, Beaubien. Any other handshake was like a senator making much over constituents but forgetting immediately the door closed on their backs. Big talk for everyone but the few met in silence and smoked cigars and pipes, every exhalation a message of confidence and friendship. Just how many intimates were in the passing parade can be gauged from the number of years that were permitted to elapse before anyone thought of placing an adequate marker on Maxwell's tomb in Fort Sumner. And the ones to place it there were not from New Mexico.

Over and above all Maxwell was shrewd enough to read the handwriting on the wall and keep abreast of the

[47]

signs of the times. The heavy production of cheap foodstuffs, the advance of the industrial revolution spurred on by progressive invention, the application of factory methods in the East of manufacture, forced an increase of ease and well-being to the general American public trying to live down the Panic and the late Civil War. Now the average home had better food, better furniture, better clothing, more books and magazines out of which was to emerge a higher standard of living and men of wealth were to be satisfied with nothing less than a palace no matter how ugly the architecture. By 1869 America had become bath-room conscious and every home that could afford it put in a zinc-lined bathtub of black walnut or pine. Marcotte and his cabinets seemed to be in such demand that he sighed with relief when he learned that he had imitators all over the nation. The parlor with its ingrain carpet, its mahogany center table, its polished air-tight stove with pipe passing through the painted board which closed a discarded fireplace, its piano with a be-ribboned guitar tilted against it, and its pyramidal whatever you might call it in the corner. There was time for reading Beadle's Dime Novels of the exploits of Carson, Fremont, Crockett, Big Foot Wallace, Custer, the Wide Open Spaces that beckoned them West in spirit, if not in action. The aftermath of the Civil War forced Maxwell to take the course he did in spite of himself. Several authors have reiterated the statement that Maxwell died in poverty. There are several reasons for denying this. First of all, his son, Peter, was the richest sheep-man in the Pecos valley; secondly, none of the Maxwell children ever claimed to be impoverished by their father's death; Maxwell was not the type to let everything slip through one hand for he was always taking in with the other; the Maxwell legend of poverty is now being questioned by modern authors.

Among the legion of the army of opportunity seekers who came to New Mexico were Catron and Elkins, lawyers. They had attended the University of Missouri together prior to the Civil War. Thomas Benton Catron enlisted with the Confederates while Stephan Benton Elkins enlisted with the Union forces. Their friendship continued throughout the war, although Elkins came to New Mexico before the war was ended. Here he was elected to the legislature in 1866, when but twenty-five years of age. He was twenty-nine when he replaced Maxwell as head of the bank in Santa Fe. He and Catron were said to have sworn to each other that they would both be senators somewhere in the United States before they died. Whether this was true or mere legend I have not been able to clear up. Both did become senators in any event. Later on Elkins settled in West Virginia where he took an active part in the political life of the state there as well as the educational. Elkins College is named for him. Catron was attorney-general of the Territory of New Mexico and Elkins United States attorney. Through their political friends they learned that Gilpin was talking to a number of persons concerning the sale of the Grant. One such person was Jerome B. Chaffee whose daughter later married President Grant's son.

Governor Gilpin was born on October 4, 1822 on the old Brandywine battlefield. His father had taken a tract for a homestead. At the age of ten he was sent to England for an education. At fourteen he entered the junior class of University of Pennsylvania. After graduating from college he entered West Point, finishing at the academy in 1836. He was commissioned 2nd Lieutenant in the 2nd Dragoons under General Harney at St. Louis. He marched to Florida to engage in the Seminole War. He resigned from the army in 1841 to settle at Independence, Missouri, where he practised law. He had studied law at West Point. He served two years as secretary of the legislature. From 1848 to 1861 he maintained law offices at Independence. He always claimed to be the founder of Portland, Oregon. While at Independence he struck up a friendship with Jerome B. Chaffee. Together they talked of the gold regions of Colorado and the underground wealth to be found there. While it may have been Gilpin who influenced Chaffee to join in the purchase of the Maxwell Land Grant, it was Eben Smith who induced Chaffee to leave Missouri for Colorado.

Eben Smith was the leading spirit behind the early operations of the Mine & Smelter Supply Company of Colorado. Born in 1831, he came to know ores as no other man in the country. He met Chaffee in St. Louis in 1860 where the two learned from Gilpin about the Colorado Fifty-Niners. Loading a stamp mill on a covered wagon at St. Joseph the pair started for the new bonanza and arrived in Denver on May 26, 1860. Their idea was to start a mill to treat ores in Colorado. The Gilpin Company was their goal but by the end of 1860 the two men started the Smith & Chaffee Stamp Mill at Lake Gulch. They settled in Central City. There they met David Moffat of railroading fame and founded the First National Bank of Denver in 1878. Chaffee & Smith bought one-half interest in the H. A. W. Tabor's Little Pittsburg Mine at Leadville. Chaffee was elected to the Colorado Senate and was one of the leaders of the "Denver Crowd" in the fight for Colorado's statehood. Chaffee was one of the orginal thirteen members of the House of Representatives that met on September 9, 1861. Chaffee county in Colorado was named after him in 1879. He died in 1886.

Chaffee was a native of Niagara, New York, where he was born in 1825. He spent his boyhood in Michigan, where he became a bank clerk, then a banker. He then settled in Missouri and finally Colorado.

Chaffee eventually became owner of the Bob-tail Lode and Tunnel Company, from which there was an annual income of close to five hundred thousand dollars. The name was said to have come from a bob-tailed ox used to haul a drag made by stretching a rawhide across a forked stick for conveying pay-dirt to the gulch for sluicing. Making money became a fever with Chaffee. He invested in every industry he thought would bring him profit. His election as senator under the Constitution of 1866, which was vetoed by President Johnson, and the long controversy over it, brought him conspicuously before the public eye as a man fit to lead.

Chaffee had been a delegate in every presidential nominating convention since that of the Free Soil Party in 1856, and was a leader of the Republican Party in Colorado, a capitalist, and liberal in dispensing his money for the use of the political party of his choice. When he took his seat in congress he began agitating for Colorado's admission into the Union as a state, and persisted in it through both terms. He obtained the authorization of a treaty with the Utes for the cession of that portion of their lands in the San Juan country whose mineral wealth had made it coveted by prospectors. One of his most important measures was advocating a change in the rules of the House of Representatives so as to give the territories a representation in the committee on territories, establishing a custom which greatly influenced and increased the power of delegates. Under this rule he could be considered the first delegate to report a bill directly from a committee to the House. He was the author, and secured the passage, of a bill enlarging the powers of the territorial legislatures. He also influenced the establishing of a mining code, besides greatly extending the mail service, and busied himself with projected railroads. He felt pleased that Colorado thought enough of him to name a county after him. Important discoveries at Leadville and Salida made it for a time one of the more important counties of the state.

A man of such fame, importance and wealth was bound to be known outside of his own territory. Over in San Francisco, the owner of one of the largest taverns in the city, was Wilson Waddingham. He invested every penny of his income in lodes, real estate and other enterprises that paid off. He was bartender in his own saloon in order to meet people and make contacts. Customers usually gave him tips on new investments which he would promptly investigate. After making certain that the risk was in his favor, he would make a deal that helped increase his assets. One day several customers from Colorado came in and the talk reverted to Chaffee. Waddingham waited on his customers with one ear cocked. Chaffee would be a man worth knowing. He had enough accumulated wealth to feel on a par with another wealthy man. Suddenly he sold out his business in San Francisco and was seen in and about Leadville and Salida. Like Midas everything he touched turned to gold. He and Chaffee were seen together often. When Gilpin told them of the large tract of land that Maxwell wanted to sell they seemed pleased.

At this point Tom Catron came up from Santa Fe. Maxwell thought that Gilpin was not pushing the deal because he was not interested in buying the Grant outright as he bought the Sangre de Cristo Grant from his father-in-law. Besides Gilpin did not want to pay the price Maxwell asked. It was different dealing with Beaubien. One day as Elkins, Otero, Maxwell, Thompson and Watts were playing cards at the Maxwell Home Ranch, Maxwell said to Catron. "Why don't you go up to Colorado and push Chaffee, Waddingham and a few of the boys about taking this place off my hands Gilpin doesn't seem to be interested."

Assured by Catron that Maxwell was sincere in selling, for they were a bit doubtful that a man wanted to get rid of land on which gold was found, Chaffee and Waddingham went to an abstract and printing shop and had maps made showing steam ships steaming up the Cimarron river, loading and unloading immense cargoes of cattle, sheep, minerals, and other products of the great Maxwell Land Grant estate. They secured a number of the twelve dollar three-hundred foot square mining leases from Elizabethtown and environs, leases from which Maxwell has never realized a penny of rent, figured them up, put a fabulous return on the Aztec Mine, also making Maxwell out a billion dollar a year income, and scattered their results here and there for certain persons in Colorado, New York, London and Kansas City to read.

Taken into confidence also was George B. Chilcott of Colorado. He was born in Pennsylvania in 1928, moving to Iowa sixteen years later. He served as sheriff for three years from the time he was twenty-five years old. Hearing that Nebraska had greener pastures, he settled there and was elected to the legislature. In 1859 he was caught in the wave of migration to Colorado where he immediately became a member of the Constitutional Convention at Denver, returning to Omaha to spend the winter. Of a splendid physique, he settled in present Pueblo county, hired himself as a farm hand, then after two years took out a claim for himself twelve miles east of Pueblo and brought out his family. He was elected to represent his region at the first two cessions of the Territorial Legislature, and was appointed by President Lincoln register of the United States Land Office for the district of Colorado in 1863, which position he held until he was elected congressman. He was Republican in politics having secured the bill repealing the act which discriminated against the whole region west of Kansas and east of California by charging letter postage on printed matter within these boundaries. He was also fortunate in securing rather important action concerning certain land grants, and appropriations for the public surveys. Later on in life he was appointed to the senate to fill a vacancy left there by the resignation of Henry M. Teller. He had much in common with Chaffee whom he became acquainted with through politics. It was only a matter of time when he would be approached about buying some shares in the Maxwell Land Grant. Many of the public buildings in Pueblo are named for him. He interested himself in the finer arts for the city and to this day Pueblo shows a marked preference for music, education and art as an inheritance from this lover of the public weal. Too often do we see cities forgetting the founding fathers and even if ten citizens in a city the size of New York know its history, the average would be rated as excellent.

Charles F. Holly was not interested in politics enough to run for office, but was induced by friends to make a try. Having won his election he became Speaker of the House for the First Colorado Legislature. Said the Colorado News for September 1, 1861: Holly is a prompt and dignified and firm officer, and will discharge his duties faithfully and well. His residence is at the Boulder Mines where he is engaged in mining and quartz milling." It was Holly who introduced the bill for the establishment of the University of Colorado. He had set out for Colorado in company with William Beck, James Frank Gardiner and George M. Chilcott, by ox-wagon from Omaha, Nebraska, to Denver on March 15, 1859. He spent the next few years in the mining industry and later entered partnership with James F. Gardiner in a shingle mill in Douglas county to haul shingles to Denver.

Holly studied law and became a lawyer of note. He accumulated a small fortune by speculating in gold and silver. Almost any speculation paid off in those days if you had the finance to see it through and the gumption to stay with it. These were the three the Catron saw: Chaffee, Chilcott and Holly. Waddingham preferred to remain in the background, for the time being, at least. On May 16, 1869, an agreement was entered into for the consideration of twelve thousand dollars whereby they had an option to purchase the Maxwell Land Grant for six hundred and fifty thousand dolars, with the understanding that the property involved covered about two million acres. Almost a month later Maxwell received word that the trio had decided to exercise the option to purchase, and advised him that they were making arrangements to sell the Grant for $1,350,000, which covered more than double the amount specified in the option. Whether they had informed Maxwell that they were interesting British capital in the deal was not made clear. No doubt Maxwell made it a point to watch their every move. He was too anxious to rid himself of the Grant to bother reserving the Manor House and a few acres for himself for the time being.

The fact that Maxwell did not sell his home and several sections of land is proof that he had no intentions at the time he sold the Grant of leaving for Fort Sumner. This came afterwards. He was not going to give up his home until he was certain the Chaffee, Chilcott and Holly would seal the bid. On April 20, 1870 Lucien and Luz Maxwell turned over the Grant for the amount specified above. The sum seems staggering for the times, since most of the land there sold for fifty-five cents an acre at best, and high above the eight cents an acre that Maxwell paid for a good deal of it. Of course Maxwell received over a dollar an acre for it to say nothing of what he received from the Stocktons, Chases, Smiths, Dawsons and others who bought slices here and there prior to the purchase. Then there were the rentals and town plats at Baldy, Elizabethtown, Virginia City, the Moreno Valley, Willow Creek, Cimarron, Ute Park, Vermejo and Rayado. However in the world any one can say that Maxwell died a poor man is beyond me. True he lost much in false starts at railroading but he made up for this by good investments at Silver City and Georgetown. To say nothing of investments at Leadville, Central City and Golden.

On the other hand knowing of the gold at Baldy, Moreno, Elizabethtown, Virginia City and Cimarron Canyon, as well as the coal at later Blossburg, Gardiner, Van Houten, Dawson, Koehler, and other minerals, water rights, grazing, wheat fields, rye, oats, barley, corn, chili, beans and alfalfa, Maxwell sold very cheaply indeed. Several years ago a concern in Texas was interested in the palisades section of the Cimarron Canyon for a consideration of eight million dollars. And this area was but a small fraction of the whole grant. While the deal never went through, it shows at least that they recognized the true value of the land.

Chaffee, Chilcott, Holly and Waddingham now filed for incorporation. They had in mind a railroad from the Raton Pass to the mines of the Grant which would help them to get the ores more quickly to the smelters in Colorado, hence the name: Maxwell Land Grant and Railway Company. To justify the existence of the newly formed corporation, the New Mexico Legislature, through the influence of Elkins and Catron, by an act of that august body, gave it breath and life. Giving up their option in favor of a corporation did not necessarily mean that the parties concerned washed their hands of the Grant. They bought a pie, stuck in their thumbs and were richly rewarded with juicy plums. Acting for the newly formed company which had stockholders in St. Louis, New York, Denver, London and Amsterdam, William A. Pile, Thomas Rush Spencer and John S. Watts of Santa Fe drew up the articles of incorporation:

1. To purchase the whole or part of the Beaubien and Miranda grant, now known as the Maxwell estate, situated in the territories of New Mexico and Colorado.

2. To develop the natural resources of the same.

3. To lay out towns and villages, and to erect houses, manufactories, plant machinery and other buildings upon any property of the company.

4. To make, operate and use railways, tramways, telegraph lines, canals, roads and streets on the property of the said company, and contribute the expense of promoting, making, providing, acquiring and using any railroads, tramways, telegraph lines, canals, roads or streets, to connect with or which may be beneficial to the property of the said company.

5. To mine for precious or base materials, or any other minerals, ores, coals, salts or earths, and to sink wells and in any other way to accumulate and supply water for all purposes.

6. To cultivate stock a part or the whole of the property of said company, and to sell and dispose of the produce and products thereof.

7. To mortgage the property of the company in whole or in part for raising money, and to sell and convey any portion of the real or personal property of the said company, and to purchase real and personal estate.

8. The amount of the capital stock of the company shall be five million dollars.

9. The number of shares of which stock shall consist of fifty-thousand, of one hundred dollars each.

10. The term of the existence of the said company shall be forty-nine years.

11. The number of directors who shall manage the affairs of the company for the first three months of the corporate existence shall be five, and their names are: William J. Palmer, William A. Pile, John S. Watts, John Pratt, and Miguel A. Otero, sr.

12. The stockholders and not the directors shall have the power to make the by-laws of the company.

13. The principal place of business of the company

is to be located at Cimarron, Colfax county, Territory of New Mexico.

The names of the directors are interesting for they are persons who have contributed much to the history of New Mexico as well as Colorado. The most fascinating one of the group was William J. Palmer; the most exciting, Miguel A. Otero, sr. William J. Palmer was born in Philadelphia, Pennsylvania, in 1836. Time was good to him as well as fortune for he eventually became the president of the Pennsylvania railroad. At the outbreak of the Civil War he raised the Anderson cavalry, of which he was, until the close of the conflict, the commander. Following the war he was named the managing director of the Kansas Pacific Railroad, as well as the superintendent of construction. While thus engaged, he made the famous survey of the transcontinental routes along the 32nd and 35th parallels. No amount of argument could induce him, as director of the Kansas Pacific, to adopt one of these, so, impressed with the resources of the Rocky Mts. and the regions about them, he associated with William A. Bell and others to form the Denver & Rio Grande railroad, destined to have as fabulous a history as the Santa Fe. That was in 1870. Colorado Springs owes its fame, prosperity and growth to him and recognizes the fact by way of an immense equestrian statue to him in the center of town. Always an adventurer and a fighter he seldom undertook a task he did not see to completion. He had great dreams for a system of railroads in southern Colorado and New Mexico, to link the West with the North and East. It was mainly for this reason that he took an interest in the Maxwell Land Grant and became part of the Maxwell Land Grant Company. He made several trips to the Grant to decide exactly where the tracks were to be spread. The Get-Rich-Quick schemes that marked every transaction of the company were not of his making. He was an empire builder and as such Colorado holds his memory sacred.

Palmer was president of the Colorado Springs Company as well as the Denver and Rio Grande Railroad. While working with the Kansas Pacific he noted the evil of intoxicating liquors at the "end of the track" and other frontier towns. This caused him to exclude the sale of intoxicating liquors as far as possible from the new town of Colorado Springs. As the best means of doing this he inserted in all the deeds given by the company to purchasers a clause forever prohibiting the manufacture, sale or other disposition of intoxicating or malt liquors upon any portion of the property deeded. This clause was soon violated by several persons, and a suit for a forfeiture of the lands involved was instituted by the company. A judgment by the state district court in favor of the validity of the clause was obtained without much difficulty. The case was then carried to the Supreme Court of the State of Colorado, which affirmed the judgment of the lower court. Under this decision a number of lots were forfeited for violation of the liquor clause. The people of Colorado Springs in keeping with this action always sought to elect temperance officials to govern the city, at least during the lifetime of Palmer.

Of all the governors of the Territory of New Mexico, the one least mentioned is William A. Pile. He is accused of selling many of the Spanish archives as waste paper. He is said to have done this under the impression that there would be no further need for them since New Mexico was now flying the American flag. Whether he did this himself or caused subordinates to do it history does not tell us. More than likely lower officials were worried by the stacks of letters and other documents in the early process of decay, for the day of steel filing cabinets had not as yet arrived, and since the bundles were stacked in corners anyway perhaps they were not considered important.

Pile created Lincoln and Colfax counties, the two with the stormiest histories in the state. He took very little interest in the Grant as he did about all other things pertaining to New Mexico which he looked upon as but a stepping stone to higher honors. He was a polished gentleman and New Mexico was backwoods for him. He repeatedly wrote to the president, a personal friend of his, about other openings. He eventually succeeded in landing the appointment of United States Minister to Venezuela. Just how much further Venezuela was advanced than New Mexico at the time I do not know. Perhaps he was disappointed.

John S. Watts was one of the original justices of the territorial supreme court following the American conquest. He is said to have cast some remarks on the Otero family in a speech at Mesilla which Otero heard about and resented very much. A sort of bloodless duel took place as a result, and in order to patch up their differences friends suggested that both names be placed on the board of directors of the company. It worked.

Watts was a Union man during the conflict between the States. He watched in amazement the Texan Baylor, as well as the Confederate, iSbley, make plans to take over New Mexico for the South. At that time Ariozna was part of New Mexico. tA that time also, Watts was New Mexico Delegate in Congress. It also amazed the Delegate to see so many Southern Sympathizers in the Territory he loved so well. As the invasion of New Mexico became a reality, he wrote to Major General H. W. Halleck, of the War Department, begging help for the oppressed people of New Mexico. He knew New Mexico well, having crossed the plains twenty-six times. Here he had friends and his attitude was friendly. He would resign his position and without recompense of any sort, roll up his sleeves in defense of the territory. He would even serve as a private if it would further the cause. But his love for New Mexico must have worn thin since he did not choose it as the place to die.

The northernmost county in Kentucky is Boone county named after the famous founder of the state. Near the center of the county is the town of Burlington the birthplace of John Sebrie Watts, born on January 19, 1816. He received his primary education at Lexington, then went to Indiana University to study law. He took a liking to Indiana and opened a law office there. He served in the Indiana legislature during the time of the Mexican War. He was appointed associate-justice of the Supreme Court of New Mexico from 1851 to 1854, following which he opened a law office in Santa Fe until elected

Delegate in Congress. He served for two years. President Johnson appointed him Chief Justice of the Supreme Court of New Mexico on July 11, 1868. He resigned the following year but continued to practise law in Santa Fe which was what he was doing when approached concerning the Maxwell Land Grant and Railway Company. Several months prior to his death he decided to return to Bloomington, Indiana, where he died on June 11, 1876.

Of all named on the board, the more widely known to New Mexicans was Miguel Otero. He was a successful merchant and the founder of the famous firm of Otero, Seller & Co. which did successful business at various points in Colorado and later on in New Mexico. It was he more than any one individual who was responsible for the coming of the railroad over the Raton Pass. The railroad was grateful to him and named its first town in the territory after him. There are no houses left in Otero today, nor any indications that a town ever stood on the spot, but it was quite a frontier show-place while it lasted. Otero was also capable as a lawyer, rancher, politician and governor.

Lucien Maxwell and Miguel Otero were intimate friends. Often Maxwell went to Las Vegas to play cards with his friend and Otero was just as home at Cimarron as he was in Las Vegas. Theodore Roosevelt and Otero were quite friendly and the Rough Riders from New Mexico owed a lot to this relationship. He served as Governor of the Territory of New Mexico for two terms. Otero knew every inch of Maxwell's Grant. No mater for what reason he was appointed on the board, he was better able to direct the policies of the Maxwell Land Grant and Railway Company because he, more than any other, was acquainted with the property involved. Of the whole group he alone left memoirs. He was a man of means and influence which is what the company wanted. While he does not openly appear to have had much to say concerning the company, in secret he influenced it more than Palmer and others were willing to admit. And why not? Of the whole group he was the only New Mexican. It was his native land. The others were interested in it only as a matter of dollars and cents. He wanted new towns, railroads, stores, mines, industries because he felt it would advance New Mexico considerably. Of all the members on the board, he alone hoped that the development of the Grant would mean Statehood for New Mexico. He lived to see the property developed as he had dreamed.

Thomas A. Scott and Samuel M. Felton, both of Philadelphia, were made trustees and a first mortgage deeded over on 1,800,000 acres of land including all the mines, mills and farms it contained. These two were wealthy and quite popular in Pennsylvania. They were known to Maxwell through his railroad investments. Samuel Morse Felton, nephew of Cornelius Conway Felton, the American classical scholar, was born in Philadelphia and decided on a railroad career early in life. He was connected for a time with the Chester Creek railroad and the Lancaster railroad. He became president of several railroads during his lifetime.

"Under and pursuant to a resolution passed at a Board of Directors meeting of the said company, at their office in Cimarron, on the 20th day of May, 1870, the company has determined to borrow for its purposes the sum of seven hundred thousand pounds sterling, and also in Dutch currency, and for that purpose to make, execute, issue, negotiate and deliver, under the corporate seal, its mortgage bonds to the amount of seven hundred thousand pounds sterling, or eight million four thousand Dutch guilders, upon the terms and securities hereinafter mentioned, secured by a mortgage and conveyance in trust, of and upon all the right, title, and interest of the company to and in the said estate so purchased by them as aforesaid." (See the Colfax county records.)

On November 1, 1872, a second mortgage was placed against the property in favor of a loan of two-hundred and seventy-five thousand pounds sterling, with the Farmer's Loan and Trust Company of New York named as trustee. G. B. Elkins represented the Maxwell Land Grant and Railway Company while R. G. Rolston represented the Farmer's Loan and Trust Company in the transaction. It soon became apparent that the only ones to gain in the purchase of the Maxwell Grant were the promoters. They were actually looking to plant towns, build railroads, produce crops and introduce industries as stated on paper; they were trying to turn a dollar into two. The stockholders receiving no dividends for all the money they kept pouring into the venture, demanded an investigation. As a result, on March 11, 1878, both mortgages were foreclosed for the benefit of the stockholders and the company was reorganized on May 30, 1880. In those days the stockholders seemed to have had more of a voice in the business in which they invested than today. Perhaps because only the fairly well off could afford to be stockholders. Today even in major industries the average working man seems to be able to purchase a share or two but he doesn't seem able to tell the directors of the company just what he wants done in order to increase the value of his shares, at least not if he holds a share or two when another holds a lot more. Telephone companies have thousands upon thousands of shareholders but these are not called in to hear how their invested money is doing. Every now and then a dividend check is mailed out to them which seems to satisfy them. Here are the bonds and deeds in the transaction from Maxwell to the Maxwell Land Grant and Railway Company and to the Farmer's Loan and Trust Company:

BOND

Maxwell and Wife to Chaffee et al.

Know All Men By These Presents, that we, Lucien B. Maxwell, and Luz B. Maxwell, nee Beaubien, both of Cimarron, in the County of Colfax, Territory of New Mexico, are jointly and severally held and firmly bound unto J. B. Chaffee, George M. Chilcott and Charles F. Holly, in the penal sum of twelve hundred thousand dollars, the payment of which well and truly to be made to them or their heirs or legal representatives, we bind ourselves, our heirs, executors and administrators firmly by these presents. Given under our hands and seals at the above named place, this twenty-sixth day of May, A. D. 1869.

The condition of the above obligation is such, that whereas, we are the owners of a certain estate of land, situate, principally in the county and Territory above mentioned, and known as the Beaubien and Miranda Grant or Rayado Grant, containing about two million acres of land, be the same more or less, excepting such parcels as have been heretofore conveyed by us; and whereas, the said Chaffee, Chilcott and Holly are desirous of purchasing or inducing other persons to purchase the above described estate or grant, and have paid us the sum of one dollar towards said purchase—the receipt of which is hereby acknowledged—now, therefore, we, the said Lucien B. Maxwell and Luz B. Maxwell, do bind ourselves, our heirs and legal representatives, upon the further payment or tender to us, by the said Chaffee, Chilcott and Holly, or such persons as they may direct, by a good and sufficient deed or deeds of conveyance, and free from all incumbrances, the whole of said estate of land or grant above described, reserving, however, to ourselves the home ranch of cultivated land, with the buildings and appurtenances thereon and belonging thereto—said ranch supposed to contain about one thousand acres, more or less—subject, however, to such conveyances as we have hitherto made of any part or parcel of said Grant or Estate—together with all our right, title, interest and income arising from such conveyances, and together with the following mill and water power and the right to use the same—said mill being situated on said home ranch above reserved; and also, all other buildings, tenements, mills, franchises, rights, privileges and improvements, belonging to or appertaining to said Grant or Estate of every description, including mines and minerals, except only such mines as we may purchase until the consummation of this contract, from persons having at this date interests in mines or minerals upon said Estate.

It is understood that if we desire to include in this sale the home ranch above described, then the amount to be paid us shall be six hundred and fifty thousand dollars.

All the rents, profits and incomes from the said estate, shall belong to us, until the completion of this contract.

Upon the faithful compliance, as above stated by us, then this obligation to be null and void, otherwise to remain in full force and by virtue in law, against us, our estate and legal representatives.

Witness our hand and seals the day and year above written.

                L. B. MAXWELL.   (SEAL)
                LUZ B. MAXWELL. (SEAL)

Signed in presence of HENRY M. PORTER.

BOND

MAXWELL AND WIFE TO CHAFFEE et al.

Know all Men By These Presents, that we, Lucien B. Maxwell, and Luz. B. Maxwell, nee Beaubien, his wife, both of Cimarron, in the County of Colfax, Territory of New Mexico, are jointly and severally held and firmly bound unto Jerome B. Chaffee, of Central City, County of Gilpin, Territory of Colorado, George M. Chilcott, of Excelsior, Pueblo County, Territory of Colorado, and Charles F. Holly, of Cimarron City, County of Colfax, Territory of New Mexico, in the penal sum of two million dollars, the payment of which, well and truly to be made to them or their heirs or legal representatives or assigns, we bind ourselves, our heirs, executors and administrators firmly by these presents.

Given under our hands and seals this twenty-eighth day of January, A. D. 1870.

The condition of the above obligation is such, that, whereas, we are the sole, entire and exclusive owners of a certain grant, tract, or estate of land, and mines, situated principally in the County of Colfax and Territory of New Mexico, and known as the Beaubien and Miranda Grant, containing about two millions of acres of land, be the same more or less, excepting such parts, portions, or parcels, as may have been hitherto conveyed by us, and whereas, the said Jerome B. Chaffee, George M. Chilcott and Charles F. Holly, by them or either of them, their legal representatives or assigns, the sum of thirteen hundred and fifty thousand (1,350,000) dollars, good and lawful money of the United States, any time within six months from the date hereof (said payment to be made at our residence in said county and Territory) to bargain, sell and convey, and we do hereby bind ourselves, our heirs and legal representatives, to convey to said Jerome B. Chaffee, George M. Chilcott and Charles F. Holly, or to such person or persons as they may direct, by a good and sufficient deed or deeds of conveyance, and free from all incumbrances whatsoever, the whole of said estate of land or grant above described, reserving, however, to ourselves the home ranch of cultivated land, with the buildings and appurtenances thereon and belonging thereto (said home ranch supposed to contain about one thousand acres, more or less) subject, however, to such conveyances as we have hitherto made of any portion, part or parcel of said grant or estate, bargained and sold prior to the 26th day of May, A.D. 1869, together with all our right, title, interest and income arising from such conveyances, and together with the flouring mill and water power, and the right to use the same; said mill being situated on said home ranch above reserved; and also all other buildings, tenements, mills, rights, franchises, privileges and improvements, belonging to or appertaining to said grant or estate of every description, including mines and minerals, excepting such mines as we may have purchased or shall purchase until the final completion and full consummation of this contract, from any person or persons, having, prior to the date of May 26th, A.D. 1869, interest in mines or minerals upon or in said estate or grant.

We also covenant, agree and bind ourselves to include within the covenants and agreements of this contract, conveyance and sale the home ranch above described, if we shall at any time conclude to sell the same, at such further sum, price or amount as we may mutually agree upon, and we hereby agree and promise not to sell said home ranch to any other party or parties, until we shall have given the purchaser or purchasers of the said grant or estate, the refusal of the same. All rents, profits and incomes from the said estate or grant shall belong to us until the full and final completion of this contract, bargain and sale.

Upon the faithful compliance as above stated by us, then this obligation to be null and void, otherwise to remain in full force and virtue in law against us, our estate and legal representatives.

Witness our hands and seals the day and year first above written.

       LUZ B. MAXWELL. (SEAL)
       L. B. MAXWELL.   (SEAL)

Signed in the presence of
       SYLVESTER A. GREEN.
       E. B. DENNISON.

ASSIGNMENT OF BOND.

Whereas, heretofore, to wit, on the twenty-eighth day of January, one thousand eight hundred and seventy, Lucien B. Maxwell and Luz B. Maxwell, his wife, executed and delivered to the undersigned, Jerome B. Chaffee, George M. Chilcott and Charles F. Holly, their certain penal bond conditioned to convey to the said Chaffee, Chilcott and Holly, or to such person or persons as they might direct the estate situated partly in the Territory of New Mexico and Partly in the Territory of Colorado, formerly known as the Beaubien and Miranda Grant, but latterly known as the "Maxwell Estate".

And whereas, we the said Chaffee, Chilcott and Holly have, for a valuable consideration, sold and assigned and transferred all our right, title and interest in and under the said bond, to the Maxwell Land Grant and Railway Company, a corporation organized under the laws of the Territory of New Mexico, and have nominated and appointed the said corporation as the party to whom the said Maxwell and wife shall make the conveyance of the said estate, in pursuance of the terms of the said bond.

Now, therefore, these presents witness, that for and in consideration of the sum of one dollar, received to our full satisfaction, and other valuable considerations, received of the said Maxwell Land Grant and Railway Company, the receipt whereof is hereby acknowledged, we the said Chaffee, Chilcott and Holly have, and we hereby do nominate and appoint and designate the said Maxwell Land Grant and Railway Company as the parties to whom the said Maxwell and wife shall convey the said estate; and do hereby request and require them so to do, and we for ourselves, our heirs, executors, administrators and assigns, do hereby release, assign and convey all right, title and interest in the premises, under the said bond or otherwise, to the said Maxwell Land Grant and Railway Company.

Witness our hands and seals the twelfth day of June, One thousand eight hundred and seventy.

      JEROME B. CHAFFEE. (SEAL)
      GEORGE M. CHILCOTT. (SEAL)
      CHARLES F. HOLLY.   (SEAL)

Signed, sealed and delivered in the presence of
       NATHANIEL GILL.

DEED

This Indenture, made the thirtieth day of April, in the year of our Lord one thousand eight hundred and seventy, between Lucien B. Maxwell, of Cimarron, in the county of Colfax, Territory of New Mexico, and Luz B. Maxwell, nee Beaubien, his wife, parties of the first part, and the Maxwell Land Grant and Railway Company, a corporation duly created and organized under the laws of the Territory of New Mexico, party of the second part, witnesseth:

That the said parties of the first part, for and in consideration of the sum of one million three hundred and fifty thousand dollars, lawful money of the United States of America, to them in hand paid by the said party of the second part, at or before the ensealing and delivery of these presents, the receipt whereof is hereby acknowledged and the said party of the second part, forever released and discharged from the same by these presents, and other good and valuable considerations, have granted, bargained, sold, aliened, remised, released, conveyed and confirmed, and by these presents do grant, bargain, sell, alien, remise, release, convey and confirm, unto the said party of the second part, its successors and assigns, forever, all that certain tract or estate of land, with the mines or minerals of every sort thereon and therein, and the buildings thereon erected, situate partly in the said county of Colfax, Territory of New Mexico, and partly in the county of Las Animas, in the Territory of Colorado, and heretofore known as the Beaubien and Miranda Grant, but latterly known as the Maxwell Estate, containing about two millions of acres of land, be the same more or less; for a more particular description whereof, reference is had to the original grant from the government of Mexico to the said Beaubien and Miranda, to the act of Congress of the United States, passed in the year one thousand eight hundred and sixty, confirming the said grant as Grant Number 15, (Statutes at Large, Volume 12, page 71), and the official documents referred to in the said act, and to the official survey, now in course of execution under the direction of United States Government deputy surveyor, W. W. Griffin. Reserving, however, from the said tract the Home Ranch of cultivated land, with the buildings thereon, (except the mill hereinafter referred to), supposed to contain about one thousand acres, more or less; and also reserving an undivided one-half interest in the Montezuma Mill, so called, being a quartz mill of thirty stamps, with its appurtenances, excepting from this reservation of the said Home Ranch, and hereby conveying to the said party of the second part the water power thereon and the flouring mill thereon erected, and the land upon which the said mill is built, together with so much of the land around and adjoining the said mill and water power as may be necessary for the convenient and full and free use and enjoyment of the same; together also, with free and full right of way in any direction and at all times forever to and from said water power and mill, over and across the said Home Ranch, to the said party of the second part, its successors and assigns, and its and their officers, agents and servants. Also excepting from the operation of this conveyance such tracts of land, part of the said estate, hereby warranted not to exceed in the aggregate of fifteen thousand acres, to the parties of the first part, have heretofore sold and conveyed by deeds duly recorded on or prior to the twenty-fifth day of January, one thousand eight hundred and seventy. And also two certain lots of land, one heretofore sold by the parties of the first part to one Peter Joseph, and one heretofore sold to one Valdes, conveyances for which two parcels it is supposed have not as yet been recorded, but which the parties of the first part hereby covenant to have forthwith duly recorded. Also excepting the following mining interests, namely: one-half of the Montezuma Quartz Lode, so called, the said half being fifteen hundred feet by one hundred feet; one undivided sixth part of the Aztec Lode, so called, eight discoveries of quartz lodes, each being fifteen hundred by one hundred feet; and the premises are also subject to six leases of placer claims, each being three hundred feet by three hundred feet. Also, excepting twelve lots in Elizabethtown, the purchase money for which the same have been sold is, however, to be paid to the party of the second part. Excepting also, about six lots of land in Cimarron City, deeds for which have been recorded since January, one thousand eight hundred and seventy. Together with all and singular the tenements, hereditaments and appurtenances thereunto belonging or in anywise appertaining, and the reversion and reversions, remainder and remainders, rents, issues and profits thereof. And also all the estate, right, title, interest, dower, right of dower, property, possession, claim and demand of, whatsoever, as well in law as in equity, of the said parties of the first part, of, in and to the same, and every part and parcel thereof, with the appurtenances: To have and to hold the above granted, bargained and described premises, with the appurtenances, unto the said party of the second part, its successors and assigns, to its and their own proper use, benefit and behoof forever. And the said parties of the first part, for themselves, their heirs, executors and administrators, do covenant, grant and agree to and with the said party of the second part, its successors and assigns, that the said parties of the first part, at the time of the sealing and delivery of these presents, are lawfully seized in their own right of a good, absolute and indefeasible estate of inheritance in fee simple, of and in all and singular the above granted, bargained and described premises, with the appurtenances; and have good right, full power and lawful authority to grant, bargain, sell and convey the same, in manner and form aforesaid. And that the said party of the second part, its successors and assigns, shall and may, at all times hereafter, peaceably and quietly have, hold, use, occupy, possess and enjoy the above granted premises, and every part and parcel thereof, with the appurtenances, without any let, suit, trouble, molestation, eviction or disturbance of the said parties of the first part, their heirs or assigns, or any other person or persons lawfully claiming or to claim the same. And that the same are now free, clear, discharged and unincumbered of and from all former and other grants, titles, charges, estates, judgments, taxes, assessments and encumbrances, of what nature or kind soever. And also that the said parties of the first part, and their heirs, and all and every other person or persons whomsoever lawfully or equitably deriving any estate, right, title or interest of, in or to the hereinbefore granted premises, by, from, under or in trust for them, shall and will, at any time or times hereafter, upon the reasonable request and at the proper costs and charges in the law of the said party of the second part, its successors and assigns, make, do and execute, or cause or procure to be made, done and executed, all and every such further and other lawful and reasonable acts, conveyances and assurances in the law for the better and more effectually vesting and confirming the premises hereby intended to be granted in and to the said party of the second part, its successors or assigns, or its or their counsel learned in the law, shall be reasonably devised, advised or required. And the said parties of the first part and their heirs, the above described and hereby granted and released premises, and every part and parcel thereof, with the appurtenances, unto the said party of the second part, its successors and assigns, against the said parties of the first part, and their heirs, and against all and every person and persons whomsoever lawfully claiming or to claim the same, shall and will warrant, and by these presents forever defend.

In witness whereof, the said parties of the first part have hereunto set their hands and seals, the day and year first above written.

L. B. MAXWELL. (L.S.)

Sealed and delivered in the presence of—(the words "million three hundred and fifty thousand," on first page hereof, being interlined before execution. As to Lucien B. Maxwell)—NATHANIEL GILL.

LUZ B. MAXWELL. (L.S.)

THE MAXWELL LAND GRANT AND RAILWAY COMPANY,
TO
THOMAS A. SCOTT AND SAMUEL M. FELTON.

MORTGAGE DEED.

The Indenture, made the thirteenth day of June, in the year of our Lord one thousand eight hundred and seventy, between "The Maxwell Land Grant and Railway Company," a corporation duly created and organized under the laws of the Territory of New Mexico, hereinafter called "the Company," pursuant to the act of Congress in that behalf, party of the first part, and Thomas A. Scott and Samuel M. Felton, both of Philadelphia, in the State of Pennsylvania, hereinafter called "the Trustees," party of the second part:

1. Whereas, the Company is a corporation with full power to purchase, hold, sell, mortgage and convey real and personal estate, and to execute this indenture;

2. And whereas, the Company has recently purchased in fee simple, subject to certain exceptions and reservations hereinafter particularly mentioned, eleven-twelfths of an undivided grant or estate, situate partly in the Territory of New Mexico and partly in the Territory of Colorado, formerly known as the Beaubien and Miranda Grant, and now known as the Maxwell Estate;

3. And whereas, under and pursuant to a resolution passed at a general meeting of the stockholders, held at Cimarron, New Mexico, on the nineteenth day of May, eighteen hundred and seventy, and pursuant to resolutions passed at a Board of Directors of the said Company, at their office in Cimarron, New Mexico, on the twentieth day of May, one thousand eight hundred and seventy, the Company has determined to borrow for its purposes the sum of seven hundred thousand pounds in sterling money

and Dutch currency, and for that purpose to make, execute, issue, negotiate and deliver, under the corporate seal, its mortgage bonds to the amount of seven hundred thousand pounds sterling, or eight millions four hundred thousand Dutch guilders, upon the terms and securities hereinafter mentioned, secured by a mortgage and conveyance in trust, of and upon all the right, title and interest of the Company to and in the said estate so purchased by them as aforesaid, that is to say: seven thousand of the said bonds for one hundred pounds sterling or twelve hundred Dutch guilders each, numbered from one to seven thousand, inclusive; each of the said bonds to bear equal date herewith, the principal thereof being payable in London or Amsterdam, at the option of the holder, in sterling or Dutch money, on the first day of July, one thousand eight hundred and ninety-five; or if such bonds shall, on any earlier day, be drawn at any of the annual drawings appointed to be held as hereinafter provided, then, on the first day of July next succeeding such drawing, and the interest thereon, at the rate of seven per cent, per annum, in sterling or Dutch money, semi-annually, in London or Amsterdam aforesaid, on the first day of July and the first day of January in each year, until such payment as attached to each bond, at the office of the duly authorized agent of the Company in London or Amsterdam; the said bonds to stand equally secured hereby, without any preference whatever arising from time of issue or otherwise, except as regards bonds drawn at any such annual drawing, and to be issued as required for the purposes aforesaid; and each of such bonds to be duly executed by and under the seal of the Company, signed and attested by its President and Secretary, and the coupons to be signed by or with the name of the Secretary; and upon each of such bonds being so signed and sealed, and the coupons so signed, the said bonds are to be countersigned by the trustees, which countersigning shall be conclusive, and the only sufficient proof that any bond is one of those named in this indenture, and each of which bonds shall be substantially in the following form:

First Mortgage Seven Per Cent, Land Grant and Railway Bond. Principal and interest payable in Sterling or Dutch Currency, free of all United States taxes.

Redeemable at par within twenty-five years, or earlier, if drawn at one of the annual drawings hereinafter mentioned.

£100

This bond is receivable at the par of principal and accrued interest in payment for any of the 1,800,000 acres of land sold under the provisions of the Trust Deed No.

Dutch Guilders, 1,200. Secured by a first Mortgage on 1,800,000 acres of land, including all Mines, Farms, Mills, etc., belonging to the Company.

UNITED STATES OF AMERICA,
TERRITORY OF NEW MEXICO.

THE MAXWELL LAND GRANT AND RAILWAY COMPANY.

Principal payable July first, one thousand eight hundred and ninety-five, or earlier, if drawn at any one of the annual drawings hereinafter mentioned.

Coupons payable in London or Amsterdam, on July 1st and January First, in each year.

KNOW ALL MEN BY THESE PRESENTS, that the Maxwell Land Grant and Railway Company is indebted to Jerome B. Chaffee, or bearer, in the sum of one hundred pounds sterling, or twelve hundred Dutch guilders, at his option, which the said Company promises to pay to the said Jerome B. Chaffee, or to the bearer hereof, in London or Amsterdam, at his option, on the first day of July, one thousand eight hundred and ninety-five; or if this bond shall be drawn on any earlier day, at any one of the annual drawings provided by the trust deed, then on the first day of July next succeeding such drawing. And the Company also promises to pay interest thereon in the meantime at the rate of seven per centum per annum, (free of all United States taxes), payable semi-annually on the first days of January and July in each year, in London or Amsterdam aforesaid, upon presentation and surrender, of the annexed coupons, as they severally become due; and in case of default in the payment of any half-yearly installment of interest which shall have become payable and shall have been demanded by presentation in London or Amsterdam of the coupon therefor, and the continuance of such default for the period of six months after the maturity of such instalment, the principal of this bond shall become due in the manner and with the effect provided in the deed of trust or mortgage securing payment of the same, hereinafter mentioned. This bond is one of a series of bonds, amounting in the aggregate to seven hundred thousand pounds sterling, or eight millions four hundred thousand guilders, and the payment of each and all of which is equally secured by deed of trust or mortgage, duly executed and delivered by the said Maxwell Land Grant and Railway Company to the said Thomas A. Scott and Samuel M. Felton, (trustees), conveying the estate of the said Company, and the appurtenances, property, revenues, franchises and things in the said deed of trust or mortgage mentioned and described. This bond is entitled to the benefit of the sinking fund, and to all other benefits by the said deed of trust or mortgage provided, including the benefit of a provision, whereby, on the first day of July, one thousand eight hundred and seventy-two, and each succeeding first day of July, the yearly sum of sixty-three thousand pounds, or seven hundred and fifty-six thousand guilders, less the amount of one year's interest, after the rate aforesaid, on the bonds remaining due, is to be applied in redeeming such bonds as may be drawn at such yearly drawings in London, as by the said trust deed are provided to be held. This bond shall pass by delivery or by transfer on the books of the Company; and after a registration of ownership, certified hereon by the transfer agent of the Company, no transfer except upon the books of the Company shall be valid, unless the last transfer shall have been to bearer, and transferability by delivery thereby restored. This bond shall continue subject to successive registration and transfers to bearer as aforesaid, at the option of each holder. This bond shall not become obligatory until it shall have been authenticated by a certificate endorsed hereon, and duly signed by the trustees, to the effect that the same is one of those entitled to the security of the mortgage above mentioned.

In witness whereof, the said Company has caused its corporate seal to be hereto affixed. and the same to be attested by the signatures of its President and Secretary, and has also caused the coupons hereto annexed to be signed by the Secretary, this thirteenth day of June, in the year of our Lord one thousand eight hundred and seventy.

WILLIAM J. PALMER, *President*
JOSIAH C. REIFF, *Secretary*

THE MAXWELL LAND GRANT AND RAILWAY COMPANY
TO
THE FARMERS' LOAN AND TRUST COMPANY.

MORTGAGE DEED.

This Indenture, made the first day of November, in the year of our Lord one thousand eight hundred and seventy-two, between the Maxwell Land Grant and Railway Company (hereinafter called the Company), a corporation duly created and organized under the laws of the Territory of New Mexico, pursuant to the Act of Congress in that behalf, party of the first part, and the Farmers' Loan and Trust Company, a corporation duly created and organized under the laws of the State of New York, hereinafter called the Trustee, party of the second part. Whereas, the company is a corporation with full powers to purchase, sell, hold, mortgage and convey real and personal estate, and to execute this indenture. And whereas, the company is seized of or otherwise well entitled to the estate, property and hereditaments firstly hereinafter described and expressed, to be hereby granted for an estate of inheritance in fee simple in possession, free from incumbrances. And whereas, the company is seized of or otherwise well, entitled, in fee simple, to a grant or estate, situated partly in the Territory of New Mexico, and partly in the Territory of Colorado, formerly known as the Beaubien and Miranda Grant, and now known as the Maxwell Estate, being the property secondly hereinafter granted and assigned, subject as to eleven undivided twelfths of the same grant or estate to a certain indenture of mortgage, dated the 13th day of June, 1870, and made between the company of the first part, and Thomas A. Scott and Samuel M. Felton, both of Philadelphia, in the State of Pennsylvania, of the second part, for securing the due payment of mortgage bonds to the amount of £700,000, with interest thereon, at the time and in the manner therein mentioned, and subject also to certain exceptions and reservations in the said indenture particularly mentioned. And whereas, under and pursuant to a resolution passed at the general meeting of the stockholders of the company, held at Cimarron, New Mexico, on the _____ day of _____ 1872, and pursuant to resolutions passed at the Board of Directors of the company at their office at Cimarron, New Mexico, on the ____ day of _____ 1872, the company has now determined to borrow for its purposes such sum in sterling money and Dutch currency as is hereinafter mentioned, and for that purpose to make, execute, issue, negotiate and deliver, under its corporate seal, its mortgage bonds to such amount, in such form and secured in such manner as hereinafter mentioned, and each of such bonds to be duly executed by and under the seal of the company, signed and attested by its President and Secretary, and the coupons to be signed by or with the name of the Secretary; and upon each of such bonds being so signed and sealed, and the coupons so signed, the said bonds are to be countersigned by the Trustees, which countersigning shall be conclusive, and the only sufficient proof that any bond is one of those named in this indenture. And whereas, such bonds are intended to be 2,750 in number, for £100 sterling, or 1,200 Dutch guilders, and numbered consecutively 1 to 2,750, each of said bonds to bear equal date, the principal thereof being payable in London or Amsterdam the first day of November, 1902, or if such bonds shall on any earlier day be drawn at any of the annual drawings hereinafter appointed to be held, then on the first day of January next succeeding such drawing, and the interest thereon at the rate of seven per cent. per annum, in Dutch money, at Amsterdam, as is by such bonds provided, and the said bonds are intended to be substantially in the following form:

First Mortgage seven per cent. Land Grant and Railway Bond. Principal payable at par in sterling or Dutch Currency free of all United States taxes. Redeemable at par within 30 years, or earlier, if drawn at one of the annual drawings hereinafter mentioned. £100.

This bond is receivable at the par of principal and accrued interest in payment for any of the land sold under the provisions of the Trust Deed, dated November 1st, 1872.

Principal payable November 1st, 1902, or earlier, if drawn at any of the annual drawings hereinafter mentioned. Coupons payable in Amsterdam on May 1st and November 1st in each year.

Dutch Guilders, 1,200.

Secured by a first mortgage on certain property fully described in the Trust deed of November 1st, 1872, and by a second mortgage on all the property comprised in a certain mortgage deed, dated the 13th day of June, 1870.

UNITED STATES OF AMERICA,
TERRITORY OF NEW MEXICO.

KNOW ALL MEN BY THESE PRESENTS, that the Maxwell Land Grant and Railway Company is indebted to the Farmers' Loan and Trust Company, or bearer, in the sum of one hundred pounds sterling, or twelve hundred Dutch guilders, at their or his option, which the said company promises to pay to the said Farmers' Loan and Trust Company, or to the bearer hereof, in London or Amsterdam, at their or his option, on the first day of November, 1902, or if this bond shall be drawn on any earlier day, at any one of the annual drawings provided by the trust deed, then, on the first day of January next succeeding such drawing. And the company also promises to pay interest thereon in the meantime at the rate of seven percentum per annum, free of all United States taxes, payable semi-annually on the first days of May and November in each year at Amsterdam aforesaid, upon presentation and surrender of the Annexed coupons as they severally become due; and in case of default in the payment of any half-yearly installment of interest which shall become payable and shall have been demanded by presentation at Amsterdam of the coupons therefor, and the continuance of such default for the period of six months after the maturity of such installment, the principal of this bond shall become due in the manner and with the effect provided in the deed of trust or mortageg securing payment of the same hereinafter mentioned. This bond is one of a series of 2,750 bonds, numbered consecutively from 1 to 2,750, inclusive, and amounting in the aggregate to £275,000 sterling, or 3,300,000 Dutch guilders, and payment of each and all of which is equally secured by a deed of trust or mortgage, duly executed and delivered by the said Maxwell Land Grant and Railway Company to the said the Farmer's Loan and Trust Company (Trustee), conveying the estate of the said company, and the appurtenances, property, revenue, franchises and things in the said deed of trust or mortgage mentioned and described, which mortgage or trust deed is a first lien upon all the property of the Maxwell Land Grant and Railway Company not comprised within the mortgage of the 13th day of June, 1870, and is a second lien upon the property comprised in such mortgage deed. This bond shall pass by delivery or by transfer on the books of the company, and after a registration of ownership certified hereon by the transfer agent of the company, no transfer except upon the books of the company shall be valid, unless the last transfer shall have been to bearer, and transferability by delivery thereby restored. But this bond shall continue subject to successive registration and transfers to bearers as aforesaid, at the option of each holder. This bond shall not become obligatory until it shall have been authenticated by a certificate endorsed hereon, and duly signed by the trustee, to the effect that the same is one of those entitled to the security of the mortgage of the 1st day of November, 1872, above mentioned. In witness whereof, the said Company has caused its corporate seal to be hereto affixed, and the same to be attested by the signatures of its President and Secretary, and has also caused the coupons hereto annexed to be signed by the Secretary, this 1st day of November, in the year of our Lord, 1872.

Dutch Guilders, 42.   Dutch Guilders, 42.

The Maxwell Land Grant and Railway Company will pay to the bearer, in the city of Amsterdam, forty-two Dutch guilders (free of United States taxes, on the _____ day of _____ being six months' interest on bond No. _____.

    No. _____   *Secretary.*

And each of which bonds is to have endorsed thereon a cerificate to effect following, viz.: "We certify that this bond is one of 2,750 bonds of £100 sterling, or 1,200 Dutch guilders, each numbered consecutively from 1 to 2,750, inclusive, secured by the mortgage or deed of trust within referred to."

NOW THIS INDENTURE WITNESSETH, that the company, in consideration of the premises, and of the sum of one dollar to it in hand paid at or before the ensealing and delivery of these presents, the receipt of which is hereby acknowledged, and in order to secure the due and punctual payment of the bonds and interest of the bonds aforesaid to the amount of £275,000 sterling, or 3,300,000 Dutch guilders, issued or to be issued as hereinbefore mentioned, has granted, bargained, sold, assigned, set over, released, conveyed and confirmed, and by these presents does grant, bargain, sell, assign, set over, release, convey and confirm unto the trustees, and to their successors in the trust hereby created, Firstly, All that piece or parcel of land known as the "Home Ranch", containing 1,000 acres, more or less, and being a portion of the land formerly known as the Beaubien and Miranda Grant, but now as the Maxwell Estate, situate in Colfax county, in the Territory of New Mexico aforesaid. And also, all that the southern or south half of lot four (4), block eighteen (18), in Elizabethtown, and the store buildings erected thereon. And also, all that the undivided half of the piece of land on the Creek, known as the Montezuma Quartz Lode, such half being about 1,500 feet by 100 feet. And also of the Thirty Stamp Quartz Mill, situate thereon, and known as the Montezuma Mill. And the divided west half of the Comstock Lode, being about 1,500 feet in length, on the east side of Baldy Mountain. And one undivided twelfth part or interest in the Aztec Lode, situate on the east side of Baldy Mountain, and about six lots of land in Cimarron City, of which the deeds have been recorded since January, 1870. And also, all other, if any, the real estate and hereditaments, situate in Colfax County aforesaid, now belonging to the company, which, previously to the 7th day of September, 1870, belonged to or was owned by Lucien B. Maxwell and Luz B. Maxwell, nee Beaubien, his wife, or either of them, and was included in an indenture of conveyance, dated the 7th day of September, 1870, and made between the said Lucien B. Maxwell and Luz B. Maxwell, of the first part, and the company of the second part, being a conveyance of (among other things) the hereinbefore mentioned premises together with all buildings, mills, mines minerals, rights, franchises, privileges, profits, improvements and appurtenances whatsover to the said hereditaments and premises belonging or in any wise appertaining, or usually held or occupied therewith, or reputed to belong or be appurtenant thereto. And secondly, all the right, title and interest which the company now has, or may at any time hereafter acquire, in or to the aforesaid grant or estate mentioned and described in and as to eleven-twelfths thereof mortgaged by the said indenture of mortgage of the 13th day of June, 1870. And all the estate, right, title, interest, claim and demand whatsoever, both at law and in equity of the company.

To have and to hold the said hereditaments and premises hereinbefore granted, or expressed so to be, unto and to the use of the trustes, their heirs and assigns, subject as to all the premises to the proviso for redemption hereinafter contained, and as to eleven undivided twelfth parts of the property secondly hereinbefore described and intended to be hereby granted to the said indenture of mortgage of the 13th day of June, 1870. In further pursuance of the said agreement, and in consideration of the premises, the company do hereby assign unto the trustees, their executors, administrators and assigns, all that the personal property of whatsoever kind now belonging to the company, or which may or shall, during the continuance of this security, be added to or substituted for the stock and personal property existing at the date of these presents, whether such additional future stock consist of the natural produce of the existing stock, or of stock hereafter acquired by the company; but nothing herein contained shall be construed as to effect the right of the company, so long as it shall remain in possession of the mortgage property, to administer and conduct the business thereof, including the right of continuing to sell the personal property aforesaid, in the usual course of business, substituting for it other stock or chattels, but always in such manner and to such extent as not to reduce, by any sales, changes or substitutions, the value of the security of the trustees below the value thereof at the date of these presents: To have and to hold the chattels and premises hereinbefore expressed, to be hereby assigned unto the trustees, their executors, administrators and assigns, subject to the proviso for redemption hereinafter contained, and excepting out of the hereditaments and premises firstly hereinbefore described and intended to be hereby granted, such parts thereof as have, previously to the date of these presents, been sold or agreed to be sold.

And it is hereby granted, declared and agreed, that the hereditaments, premises, property, rights, franchises and interests, hereby mortgaged or conveyed, are to be had and holden by the said trustees and their successors, upon and for the trusts, uses and purposes following, that is to say:

ARTICLE FIRST.—Until default shall be made in payment of the principal or interest of the said bonds, or some of them, the said company shall (subject to the provisions hereinafter contained, in relation to the sale of the said lands, and approbation and management of the proceeds thereof, and subject to any existing tenancies and arrangements under which any portions of the property are now held), possess, manage and enjoy the said property, and take and use the rents, income, profits, royalties and tolls thereof, as if this indenture had not been made.

ARTICLE SECOND.—All moneys arising from the sale of the said lands and properties, in whatsoever manner such sale shall be made, after paying thereout, as regards any of the property secondly hereinbefore described, all sums which are payable thereout, by virtue of the said indenture of mortgage of the 13th day of June, 1870, and after deducting, as regards the whole of the said lands and property firstly and secondly hereinbefore described, the expenses of executing this trust in respect thereof, shall be received, held and applied by the Trustees, as herein provided, and the same are hereby pledged to and for the payment of the said bonds for £275,000 sterling, or 3,300,000 Dutch guilders, and all such moneys shall be applied by the Trustees, from time to time, as they receive the same. First, in paying to the holders of any coupon or coupons which may be due upon the said bonds hereby secured, the amount of such coupon or coupons, upon due presentation thereof. Secondly, in purchasing and canceling such of said bonds outstanding, secured hereby, as can be obtained at their market value, not exceeding, however, the par value of the same, and accrued interest thereon. Thirdly, in appropriating the yearly sum of £10,000 sterling, or 120,000 Dutch guilders, to redeeming, at par, on the 1st day of January next, after each drawing, such bonds as may be drawn by lot for redemption, one fortnight before the 1st day of November in each year, beginning in the year 1875, each drawing to take place in the city of Amsterdam, under the direction of the company, in the presence of a notary. And fourthly, to the payment of such of the said bonds themselves as shall not have been purchased in accordance with the foregoing provisions, when the same shall become due and payable:

Provided, however, that the Trustees shall from time to time invest all moneys coming to their hands by virtue of this indenture, which shall not for the time be required for any of the purposes aforesaid, in government securities of the United States, or any country in Europe whose public securities are in good credit in the London market, at their current market value, and shall also invest in a similar manner the interest accruing from time to time on such investments, and the accumulations thereof, with the right from time to time to call in or convert any of such investments, and to re-invest in manner above mentioned, or apply the proceeds to paying interest upon, or to purchasing bonds as above, always holding or applying all such investments and accumulations thereof by way of sinking fund to provide for the ultimate redemption of all the said bonds. Provided, further, that if and when the amount of said sinking fund, derived from the sale of said lands, and remaining in the hands of the Trustees, and by them invested in such government securities as aforesaid, reckoning such securities at their market value, shall be equal to the principal of the said £275,000 sterling or 3,300,000 Dutch guilders of the bonds hereby secured, and to the unpaid coupons up to the date of the maturity of the said bonds, the Trustees or their successors may and shall allow all subsequent receipts from sales of any such lands to be received and appropriated by the said company at its pleasure, as if this mortgage or deed of trust had not been executed; and if there should be any of the aforesaid securities or moneys remaining in the hands of the Trustees, by virtue of this mortgage or deed of trust, then the same, after the fulfillment by them of all obligations secured by or incurred under this mortgage or deed of trust, shall be transferred and handed over to the Company.

ARTICLE THIRD.—The Company shall be at liberty to contract for the sale of any parcel or parcels of the said lands, (subject, as regards the lands secondly hereinbefore described, to the said indenture of mortgage of the 13th of June, A.D. 1870), for such consideration as to the Company shall appear to be fair and reasonable therefor; such sale or sales may be made for cash, or on credit, or partly for cash and partly on credit, and whenever full payment shall have been made to the Trustees of the full price of any parcel of the said lands contracted to be sold as aforesaid, including interest on all deferred payments, but in no case before the payment of such full, price, and any accrued interest thereon, the Trustees shall release and discharge the parcel or parcels so contracted to be sold of and from these presents, and of and from the lien of the same, and thereupon the Company may grant and convey the said parcel or parcels of the said lands so as aforesaid contracted to be sold to the purchaser or purchasers thereof, free and discharged of these presents, and of the said bonds had never been made. But it is understood, to all intents and purposes as if these presents and the said bonds had never beei made. But it is understood, declared and agreed that the provisions hereinbefore contained, authorizing the Company to contract for the sale of such lands as aforesaid, are intended to, and shall authorize executory contracts only, and that the right of the Trustees for the benefit of the bondholders secured hereby to the said lands, or the proceeds thereof, is not to be divested or affected to any greater extent or effect than the amount of the payment for such lands actually received by the Trustees; nor shall the title to any such lands pass from the Trustees until actual execution and delivery of the releases and discharge hereinbefore provided to be executed by the Trustees, upon receiving payment for lands contracted to be sold as aforesaid.

ARTICLE FOURTH.—If there shall at any time be default in the payment of any interest or principal upon any of the bonds secured by this instrument, as the same shall become payable, and such default shall continue for six months, the Trustees shall, on requisition of bondholders representing one-fifth of the then outstanding bonds secured by this deed, and on the said bondholders depositing with the Trustees such reasonable sums as the said Trustees shall require to meet necessary expenses, either sell or take possession of, at the option of the said Trustees, the said lands and estates, or any part or parts thereof, and shall exercise either or both of such powers with reference to such parts of said lands and estates as the said Trustees shall elect, and to the extent necessary to raise and pay the amount for the time being due; it being always understood in case of any conflict among the said bondholders, that a written request to sell the whole or any part of the said lands or estates shall be performed and complied with by the said Trustees in preference to a request to enter upon and hold possession of the same; provided, however, that it shall not be deemed or considered a default on the part of the Company that there is any deficiency in the amount of the said drawing appointed for any one or more years for redemption of the capital of the said bonds, so long as the interest on the same is regularly paid.

And it is expressly understood and hereby declared, that in case of any sale or sales of the said lands, or of any part thereof, made by the Trustees under and by virtue of any of the provisions of this indenture, the deeds of conveyance of the Trustees, shall be valid and effectual for the purpose of investing in the grantee therein named a full, perfect and complete title to the premises therein described, free and clear of all lien or incumbrance under or by virtue of this indenture or the bonds hereby secured, and shall include as well the title of the Company as the title of the Trustees.

Any sale or sales shall be effected by public auction either in New York or such other place, and upon such terms as to credit, or partial credit, as the Trustees may think proper or expedient, having first given public notice of the time and place of such sale by advertisement, published not less than once a week for three months in one or more of the principal newspapers in the city of New York, or in case possession shall be taken, the Trustees shall enter into and upon all or any part of the lands, property and premises, rights and interests hereby conveyed or mortgaged, or intended so to be, and each and every part thereof, and exclude the Company as its agent wholly therefrom, and have, hold, use and manage the same, and conduct the business thereof; provided always, that, as regards the property secondly hereinbefore described, all the powers aforesaid shall be exercised subject and without prejudice to the said indenture of the 13th day of June, 1870.

ARTICLE FIFTH.—In case default shall be made in the payment of any half-year's interest on any of the said bonds at the time and in manner in the coupons issued therewith provided, and if such default continue for the period of six calendar months after due demand for such payment, then and in such case the principal of all the bonds secured hereby shall, in case a majority in interest of the holders of the outstanding bonds secured hereby shall, in writing, under seal, so elect, become and be immediately due and payable, anything contained in the said bonds or herein to the contrary notwithstanding; and a majority in interest of the holders of the said outstanding bonds may, by writing, under their hands and seals, declare or instruct the Trustees to declare, the said principal to be due, or waive, or instruct the Trustees to waive, the rights to so declare, on such terms and conditions as such majority shall deem proper, and may annul or reverse the previous election made by the Trustees in their behalf. Provided always, and it is hereby declared, that no such action of the Trustees or bondholders shall extend or be taken to affect and subsequent default, or to impair the rights resulting therefrom.

ARTICLE SIXTH.—The Company hereby covenants and agrees to and with the Trustees, on behalf and for the benefit of the bondholders intended to be secured hereby, that it will, from time to time, and at all times hereafter, upon reasonable request, make, do and execute, acknowledge and deliver all such further acts, deeds, conveyances and assurances in the law for the better assuring unto the Trustees and their successors in the trusts hereby created, upon the trusts, and for the purposes herein expressed or intended, all and singular the lands, premises, property, railways and appurtances, rights, interests and effects hereby mortgaged or conveyed in trust, or agreed or purporting, or intended so to be, whether now owned or possessed by or vested in the Company, or subsequently acquired by or vested in it, and all other property and things whatsoever which may be hereafter acquired in aid of or by way of substitute for, or for use for the purposes of the same; or any part thereof, and all franchises now held or hereafter acquired relating thereto, including the franchise to be a corporation, as by the Trustees or bondholders, or by counsel learned in the law, shall be reasonably devised, advised or required.

ARTICLE SEVENTH.—If the Company shall well and truly pay the sum of money herein, and by the said bonds and coupons attached thereto, required to be paid by it, and all interest thereon, at the times and in manner herein specified, and shall well and truly keep and perform all the things herein required to be kept and performed by the said Company, according to the true intent and meaning of these presents, then and in that case the estate, right, title and interest of the Trustees shall cease, determine and become void, and the rights to the premises and property hereby conveyed, shall revert to and vest in the Company, without any acknowledgment of satisfaction, reconveyance, re-entry or other act, otherwise the same shall continue and remain in full force and virtue.

ARTICLE EIGHTH.—It is mutually agreed, that the term or words "Trustees," and "said Trustees," as used in this indenture, shall be held and construed to mean the Trustees for the time being, whether all or any be original or new, and whenever a vacancy shall exist, to mean the surviving or continuing Trustees, and such Trustees shall, during such vacancy, be possessed of and be competent to exercise all the power granted by these presents to the party of the second part.

Further, that at all times until said bonds, with interest, shall be fully paid, the Company will permit the Trustees or their agents, clerks or attorneys, for that purpose to be duly authorized, fully to inspect all the books of account of the Company, together with its books, reports, memoranda or other papers, and to take such extracts therefrom as may be deemed expedient; and this trust is accepted upon the express condition, and it is further provided and declared, that the said Trustees, or either of them, or any succeeding Trustee or Trustees, may, at any time hereafter, by an instrument in writing, duly signed and forwarded to the said party of the first part, resign its, his or their office, and withdraw from the further execution of this trust; and thereupon, or in case at any time hereafter, either of the said Trustees, or any Trustee hereafter appointed, shall die or be removed by a Court of competent jurisdiction, or become mentally incapacitated to execute the trusts, the President of the Company, with the written approval and assent of the holders of bonds secured hereby, to the aggregate extent of not less than one-seventh of the said bonds outstanding and unpaid, may appoint a Trustee or Trustees to fill such vacancy for the time being, and in such case the new Trustee or Trustees appointed shall, while he or they shall continue to be such, have and possess, and be subject to the rights, powers, estates and duties, as if he or they had been original Trustees hereunder; and during any vacancy in the Trusteeship; the remaining or surviving Trustees shall have power to execute the trusts until the vacancy is filled.

And it is provided and declared, that the due appointment of Trustee or Trustees shall be effectual to vest in him or them the appropriate estate, rights, powers, and duties as herein provided in that behalf, without any new deed or conveyances; but, nevertheless, the Company hereby covenants in any and every such case to make and execute upon request any such deeds, conveyances, or assurances as may be appropriate, for more fully and certainly vesting in and confirming to such new Trustee such estate, rights, powers and duties; and in every case of resignation of a Trustee, the resigning Trustee shall, if requested, made and execute such conveyances or assurances to this successor.

And the Company, for itself, its successors, and assigns, doth hereby absolutely agree to waive, and doth hereby irrevocably waive the benefit or advantage of any and all valuation, stay, appraisement, or extension laws now existing, or which may be hereafter passed by the States or Territories wherein the property to be sold hereunder, or any part thereof, may at the time of sale be situated, or where the said sale may take place, which but for this provision, agreement and waiver might be operative in respect of such sale and transfer, or might be availed of to prevent or postpone the absolute and immediate sale of said premises, property, rights, interests, and franchises, to the highest bidder, upon compliance merely with the provisions herein provided; and the Company doth hereby covenant that it will not in any manner set up or seek, or take the benefit of any valuation, stay, appraisement, or extension law, or other law, to prevent or hinder or delay any of the rights or remedies of the said Trustees or of the bondholders in respect of the bonds hereby secured.

And it is hereby further understood and agreed, that the said or any Future Trustees or Trustee shall be authorized to employ such clerks, attorneys, or agents of any kind as they or he shall require, to act on their or his behalf in carrying out any of the purposes or objects of this trust, and that all expenses of this trust, including a proper and reasonable compensation to the said Trustees or Trustee, the fees of counsel, and the salaries or wages of their agents, with a proper indemnity against liability, shall be retained by the said Trustees or Trustee out of moneys coming into their or his hands; and in case the funds in the hands of the said Trustees or Trustee shall at any time be insufficient for the purposes aforesaid, the said Trustees or Trustee shall, at their option, suspend the further execution of the duties of this trust until the said Trustee or Trustees shall be provided with adequate means therefor, either by the party of the first part hereto or by the holders of the bonds hereby secured.

And it is further agreed and declared, that this trust is accepted upon the express condition that the said Trustees or any future Trustees or Trustee shall not be or become responsible or liable for any destruction, deterioration, determination, loss, injury or damage which may be done or occur to the estates hereby conveyed, or agreed or intended so to be, either by the said party of the first part or its agents or servants, or by any other person or persons whomsoever; nor shall any Trustee, present or future, be in any way responsible for the consequences of any breach on the parts of the party of the first part, its agents or servants, nor for any act, default, or omission of another Trustee, or of any agent or person employed in good faith by the said Trustees, or either of them; nor shall any Trustee, present or future, be or become liable or responsible for any cause, matter, or thing, except his own willful and intentional breaches of the trusts herein expressed and contained: Provided always, and it is expressly declared and agreed, that the Trustee shall be bound, at the request of the Company, to do and concur in all such acts and proceedings as shall be necessary for effectuating a partition of the said estate, or any part or parts thereof, and for that purpose to execute all such deeds and instruments as the counsel of the said Company may judge necessary or proper; and all lands and property acquired by the Company in severalty under and by virtue of such partition, shall be held by the Trustees upon the trusts declared by these presents concerning the property and estates hereby granted and conveyed.

It is further expressly provided, understood and agreed, that if at any time hereafter the parties entitled to the said undivided eleven-twelfth of the said estate and property shall desire to make partition, to the end that said remaining one-twelfth part intended to be included in this mortgage may be ascertained and set apart in severalty, then and in that case it shall be the duty of the said Trustees, upon request, to agree with the said parties upon a fair and equal partition, and the action of the Trustees in the premises shall be conclusive.

In witness whereof, the said Maxwell Land Grant and Railway Company have caused their corporate seal to be hereunto affixed, and this indenture to be signed by their President and attested by their Secretary, and the said the Farmers' Loan and Trust Company have caused their corporate seal to be hereunto affixed, and this indenture to be signed by their President and attested by their Secretary, the day and year first above written.

"That the defendant, the Maxwell Land Grant and Railway Company, and all and every person and party on its behalf having wholly failed, neglected and omitted to pay or cause to be paid to the said Thomas A. Scott and Samuel M. Felton, within the time of thirty days from the second of September A. D. 1879, the said sum of $4,290,868.83 or any part thereof; and it appearing as aforesaid that the said company is wholly unable to pay the same, and that no further allowance of time for the payment thereof would be of any avail to the said company, and that no such further allowance is desired by the same, the said defendant, the Maxwell Land Grant and Railway Company, and all persons claiming under it after the commencement of this action, on September 2, 1879, be, and they are, hereby absolutely and forever barred, foreclosed and precluded of and from all and all manner of the said mortgaged premises, in the said mortgage and this decree mentioned, described, referred to or intended to be so.

"That all and singular the said mortgaged premises and property in the said bill of complaint, and herein named, described or referred to, or intended to be so, and which are hereby adjudged to be covered by the said mortgage to the said complainants be exposed to sale and sold at public auction to be held at Cimarron, in the County of Colfax, and the Territory of New Mexico. (Records Civil & Criminal—Colfax Co. p. 36.)

Aware of the fact that the Maxwell Land Grant and Railway Company collapsed because of the get-rich-quick schemes of its promoters, Frank R. Sherwin of Cimarron, Lucien Birdseye of Brooklyn, New York, and several others took hold of the project in the hopes that they would succeed where others had failed. " . . . . . His certain report, bearing the date of the 25th day of March, 1880, and which was on that day filed with the Clerk of the First Judicial District Court of the Territory of New Mexico, in action aforesaid therein pending . . . . . on the said 22nd of March 1880, at nine o'clock in the forenoon, attended at the door of the courthouse, in the said town of Cimarron, in the place where the said property was so advertised to be sold—to the highest bidder—and there struck off and sold by him, the said Master, to the said Frank R. Sherwin and Lucien Birdseye—at and for the sum of one hundred thousand dollars being the highest and best sum bidden for the property . . . . . "

With Sherwin and Birdseye taking the initiative, the financial affairs of the company were re-organiezd in Holland.

"Be it remembered, that on the 31st day of May 1880, before me the undersigned, Vice-Consul of the United States of America, within and for the said City of Amsterdam, in the Kingdom of the Netherlands, personally appeared before me Frank R. Sherwin and Lucien Birdseye and Catherine Mary Birdseye, his wife—at the same time personally appeared before me Frederick Hendrick Ziegeluar, the vice-president, Peter G. Gerlings, one of the directors, and Alexander W. Grant. . . . "

So, the Maxwell Land Grant Company as we know it today was launched. The eight directors of the new company were: Federick Hendrick Ziegeluar, Peter G. Gerlings, A. A. Salengre, F. A. VanHall, L. Van Stirum, all of Holland; N. K. Fairbank, George M. Pullman, George P. Carpenter both latter from Chicago, and Frank R. Sherwin of Cimarron. The Holland directors controlled more than one-fifth of all the bonds and had secured by mortgage, in default of the payment of interest on other bonds, more than one-half of all the bonds then outstanding. A. W. Anderson, the English Consul in Amsterdam, was appointed secretary for the new company, and Harry Whigham of Cimarron, assistant secretary. As the Maxwell Land Grant and Railway Company mortgaged land to the Farmers' Loan and Trust Company of New York in 1872, to cover payment of 2,750 bonds of the company, payable November 1, 1902, the company had the right in default of payment of interest over six months, to "sell the said lands and estates in the said mortgage or deed of trust;" the property was acquired by the newly organized Maxwell Land Grant Company.

Over in Eliazbethtown and Baldy the gold fever was wearing off. Many of the prospectors thought there was a better living in cattle, crops, so they homsteaded. The beauty and contours of the land blended well with the richness of the soil. The woods abounded in game; streams full of trout. Who were they able to face their relatives and friends back home empty handed? It was best to stay. Here and there they built homes along the Cimarron unaware of Sherwin, Birdseye, or the Grant. Dutch interest in American lands after the Revolutionary War did not commence with the Maxwell Land Grant transaction. As early as 1791, T. Cazanove came over from Holland as American agent representing a number of Dutch firms interested in speculating. The following year six of these firms united as the Holland Land Company with a view of extensive purchases in turn to be sold to the Dutch public at a profit. Cazanove purchased 1,500,000 acres in western New York, and another extensive area in Pennsylvania. In 1796 the company incorporated solely as a stock-selling proposition. It was easy to sell since not a soul in Holland believed their investment would not pay over a thousand percent profit. They were always on the lookout for such deals.

Sherwin's first major problem was the ejectment of squatters. They were to be made to understand that they were living on land not rightfully theirs, and they must vacate all that land along the Cimarron Valley between the fence of what was then the Johnson Ranch in the possession of Henry Lambert and the junction of the Cimarron and Rayado Rivers. To eject so-called squatters in this section, the Maxwell Land Grant Company hired Frank Springer and Thomas Catron, lawyers, to represent them. Their lawsuit involved Pablo Zamora, Manuel Arellano, Manuel Fernandez, Pedro Sanchez, Librado Zamora, and many other Spanish American families who spread out from the Taos district to settle in the valley. It amazed them to know that some one else claimed the land where their sheep and cattle were graizng and had grazed from their father's father's time. No one had bothered to tell them that they were on private property, least of all Maxwell. The court case was to drag on until 1892 when it was finally decided in favor of the Maxwell Land Grant Company. Until the decision was reached, there was to be the spilling of blood, and deeds on both sides of equal regret. Into the picture came one Rev. O. P. McMains who was to stir up more bloodshed, more lawsuits, more national feeling than the Maxwell Land Grant Company bargained for. With the mysterious murder of Parson Tolby and the coming of McMains the Maxwell Land Grant separates from all other land grants in the Southwest as the most written about, the most notorious, the most questioned piece of property west of the Mississippi, and the only one that almost brought about the assassination of a Supreme Court justice of the United States.

Nor was the Maxwell Land Grant and Railway Company without its lawsuits. It was all well and fine for London and Amsterdam to ask what in the world was going on, but it was the squatters and the representatives of the company in Cimarron who had to face the law courts. The following are the more notorious suits brought into court. The list helps shed some light on the workings of the Maxwell Land Grant and Railway Co.:

Lucien B. Maxwell & Luz B. Maxwell; and The Maxwell Land Grant and Railway Co.
vs
Guadalupe Thompson, Administratrix in care of George W. Thompson, her husband, Charles Bent, Julia Bent & Alberto Silas Bent
September 2, 1871

Maxwell Land Grant and Railway Company
vs
Joseph Holbrook   *Ejectment*

Maxwell Land Grant and Railway Company
vs
Jacob Beard & George Thompson   *Ejectment*
For settling on the Beaubien and Miranda Tract.

Maxwell Land Grant and Railway Company
vs
The Atzec Mining Company

Maxwell Land Grant and Railway Company
vs
Edward H. Bergman   *In Chancery*

Maxwell Land Grant and Railway Company
vs
George Thompson & Jacob Baird

Maxwell Land Grant and Railway Company
vs
John Cassaiant
First mention of the Maxwell Land Grant and Railway Company is made in Volume I of the Colfax County Docket and Criminal Record on Monday, April 3, 1871.

Maxwell Land Grant and Railway Company
vs
John Hughes & Israel C. Smith

Maxwell Land Grant and Railway Company
vs
Thomas B. Catron—*It is therefore considered that the said Maxwell Land Grant and Railway Company receive of the said Thomas B. Catron $2,086.76 and the sum of $9.55 as the cost of these proceedings.*

Maxwell Land Grant and Railway Company
vs
Jose Maria Padilla   *Ejectment*

Maxwell Land Grant and Railway Company
vs
Moreno Valley Gold Mining Company   *Assumpsit*

Maxwell Land Grant and Railway Company
vs
William A. Crocker   *Assumpsit*

Maxwell Land Grant and Railway Company
vs
Edward Whiteford et al. *Ejectment*

Maxwell Land Grant and Railway Company
vs
Damacio Lopez *Ejectment*

Maxwell Land Grant and Railway Company
vs
Henry McAlister *Ejectment*

Maxwell Land Grant and Railway Company
vs
Thomas Wiseman *Assumpsit*

Maxwell Land Grant and Railway Company
vs
Juan Aragon *Ejectment*

Maxwell Land Grant and Railway Company
vs
Pedro Sena *Ejectment*

Maxwell Land Grant and Railway Company
vs
Rudolph Irninger *Ejectment*

All the suits were not brought by the company. There were a number in which corporations or individuals hailed the company to court. The more noted were:

John Fumer
vs
Maxwell Land Grant and Railway Company *Assumpsit*

Charles B. Wagner
vs
Maxwell Land Grant and Railway Company *Assumpsit*

Luther Chapman
vs
Maxwell Land Grant and Railway Company *Assumpsit*

Charles F. Holly
vs
Maxwell Land Grant and Railway Company *Trespassing*

Charles F. Holly
vs
Maxwell Land Grant and Railway Company *Ejectment*
(*This was one of the few cases in which an individual sought to oust the company from property which he claimed was his. As the Grant went to the new owners intact, there is no doubt as to what was the outcome.*)

Orson B. Chittenden
vs
Maxwell Land Grant and Railway Company *Ejectment*

Morris Bloomfield
vs
Maxwell Land Grant and Railway Company *Assumpsit*

Edward H. Bergman
vs
Maxwell Land Grant and Railway Company *Assumpsit*

David W. Stevens
vs
Maxwell Land Grant and Railway Company *Assumpsit*

John Hughes & Israel C. Smith
vs
Maxwell Land Grant and Railway Company *Ejectment*

Morris Bloomfield
vs
Maxwell Land Grant and Railway Company *Ejectment*

Federick Miller
vs
Maxwell Land Grant and Railway Company *Assumpsit*

Samuel M. Dodd & James G. Brown
vs
Maxwell Land Grant and Railway Company *Assumpsit*

George L. Appleton et Al
vs
Maxwell Land Grant and Railway Company *Assumpsit*

Bradley Barlow et Al.
vs
Maxwell Land Grant and Railway Company *Assumpsit*
(*This Barlow was part owner of the famous stage line named after himself and his partner.*)

Charles F. Haley
vs
Maxwell Land Grant and Railway Company *Ejectment*

William L. Ewing et Al.
vs
Maxwell Land Grant and Railway Company *Assumpsit*

The Coan & Penbroke Carriage Manufacturing Company
vs
Maxwell Land Grant and Railway Company *Assumpsit*

William M. Rotharthe
vs
Maxwell Land Grant and Railway Company *Assumpsit*

Charles B. Magruder
vs
Maxwell Land Grant and Railway Company *Assumpsit*

Mary Hooper
vs
Maxwell Land Grant and Railway Company *Trespassing*

Bradley Barlow & Jubel Sanderson
vs
Maxwell Land Grant and Railway Company—*The latter failing to appear in court the stagecoach company won the case and were paid $909.22 for damages to their line.*

G. Temple Weightman
vs
Maxwell Land Grant and Railway Company
(Weightman is known in New Mexico for his attempt, as a congressman, to bring the Territory into the Union in 1851.)

Stephen B. Elkins
vs
Maxwell Land Grant and Railway Company *Assumpsit*

Isaiah Rinehart
vs
Maxwell Land Grant and Railway Company *Assumpsit*

Chester H. Lillie
vs
Maxwell Land Grant and Railway Company

Margie E. Stockton
vs
Maxwell Land Grant and Railway Company
(The Stocktons were pioneers in Colfax County, having purchased their land outright from Lucien B. Maxwell prior to the sale of the Grant. They built the famous Clifton House.)

New Mexico and Southern Railroad Company
vs
Maxwell Land Grant and Railway Company

John Collinson
vs
Maxwell Land Grant and Railway Company
(It was Collinson of London who formed a syndicate there to take up the Chaffee option thus forming the company. After the shakeup and re-formation of the company as the Maxwell Land Grant Company, he controlled most of the shares from England to the extent that many called the new corporation the John Collinson Land Grant Corporation.)

The Farmer's Loan & Trust Company
vs
John Collinson; the Maxwell Land Grant and Railway Company; Thomas A. Scott & Samuel M. Felton.

Thomas A. Scott & Samuel M. Felton, Trustees
vs
Maxwell Land Grant and Railway Company

Assumpsit is taken to mean that the party is brought to court for breaking a contract or failing to live up to a contract. All the cases by the company or against the company appear fully in the Colfax County Criminal and Docket records in Raton, New Mexico.

Chase, who wrote his *Editor's Run* in 1882, had this to say about Sherwin:

"But the biggest man in this section of the country (Cimarron) is F. R. Sherwin. If he is not with five or ten millions today, he must be in the near future. Let me explain. (Here he recounts the story of Miranda and Beaubien.) The title was confirmed by Congress in 1860. Maxwell converged his right to a company which organized the Maxwell Land Grant and Railway Company, and incorporated with a capital of five million divided into fifty thousand shares, with a par value of one hundred dollars each. The company borrowed 700,000 pounds sterling of a Dutch company and mortgaged the Grant for security. Payments of interest were defaulted, and in a long string of litigations which followed the stock ran down to a nominal sum, and Sherwin, a sharp, shrewd, penetrating manager, secured a controlling interest in the stock. In 1879, there was a re-organization and a patent issued to the company. The company has a capital of $5,000,000, of which Sherwin owns sixty percent of the whole. In the Grant undisposed of there is still 1,700,000 acres of land. Of this amount 600,000 acres is coal land, and 200,000 of iron, silver, gold and lead, all very rich. One of the gold mines has yielded $60,000 per month with a ten stamp mill. This mine is located twenty-five miles northwest of Cimarron. A coal mine has been recently organized by the Manville Land Company and the A.T.&S.F. railroad, and has been leased by the Maxwell company for fifty years. This involves ten thousand acres. The railroad has opened a mine at Dillon, near Raton. As there is no coal below here, and as the mine is very rich, having a stratum of coal six feet thick; the coal company has prospect of immense profits as they get the mine working. The Maxwell Land Company has also organized a cattle company, with a capital stock of one million dollars, and this cattle company has the grazing of the entire territory of 1,700,000 acres. There is no better grazing land to be found, none better watered or sheltered than that embraced in the Maxwell Grant. Mr. Sherwin has the lion's share in all these companies, and, unless Providence takes a special dislike to this part of creation and punishes it in some unexpected manner, Mr. Sherwin will soon require an extra force of secretaries to count and record his income.

"Mr. Sherwin is a man about forty-five years of age. He was born in Western Massachusetts, emigrated to the West, was wholesale merchant in Milwaukee, afterwards a member of the Louisiana Returning Board (I cannot brag about him concerning that matter) then operator on Wall Street in New York. He then became a broker in London, England, where he got a flea in his ear in relation to the New Mexico land grant. He came over here, and the result is, after a variety of legal struggles and shrewd management: the pivot of the Maxwell Land Grant is in his trousers pocket, and he is rich. Is his title sound, you ask? Every attempt to break it in Washington has failed. Every trial in the Territorial courts, of which there were many, has resulted in sustaining the original Grant and the titles derived from it. . . . .

"In a former letter I spoke of the Maxwell Cattle Company, just formed for the purpose of stocking all the land in the Maxwell Grant not yet disposed of, the number of acres being about 1,700,000. Mr. Sherwin who holds about sixty-six percent of the stock in this company controls them both, and will allow no more land to be sold or leased out of the Grant, and he designs to have all the land controlled by the Maxwell Land Grant Company pass into the hands of the Maxwell Stock Company. This intention virtually puts an end to the increase of settlements in the grazing sections of the Maxwell Land Grant, and holds it as a cattle grazing locality purely. Any future increase must come from the development of gold, silver, iron, copper and coal mines, which are abundant in the hills. Mr. Chase has been engaged to manage the affairs of the Maxwell Cattle Company for five years, receiving therefor a liberal compensation annually with a promise of a better situation at the end of that time. The salaries he receives for the management of the different companies will, if he is president, keep the family from starvation."

Chapter Five

CIMARRON

Cimarron is one of the few places left in New Mexico that is New Mexico. The war did much to make New Mexico like any other place in the nation but Cimarron held out as it held out against summer invaders, sportsmen, millionaires and gamblers. Cimarron defies change. Once the home of Lucien Maxwell, it became the county seat of Colfax county and here Maxwell practised as probate judge the only part he ever played in political life. Here soldiers were garrisoned to protect the caravans moving in and out of the Fort Lyon-Fort Union highway. At first Maxwell used the area for farming and ranching. After moving in from Rayado it became the center of life in northern New Mexico until the gold rush to Baldy and Elizabethtown. Following this it settled down again to being itself. A grist mill, an Indian Agency, a weaver's shop, blacksmith shop, printing press, hardware store, mercantile store, court house, hotel, stage stop, eating place and forage station. That was all there was to early day Cimarron. But this little village was to make quite a name for itself. Here was the stopping off place of Elkins, Catron, Chaffee, Gilpin, Carleton, Carson, McMains, Allison, Buffalo Bill and a thousand other famous and infamous people who marched across the pages of Western history. Sit back a spell while I unravel what took place here at the Capital of the Empire of the Maxwell Land Grant. That is why Cimarron is important to our history. Here were the offices of the Maxwell Land Grant Company; here the general manager lived; here the "big-shots" of the company came to figure out the policies of the corporation; here the Anti-Grant War was planned and fought by McMains, Allison, Hunt and others; here Buffalo Bill signed his contract that was to flare his name across the nation—This Cimarron, this Wild Goat of a place that invited in wild men to drink from its wilder river to flood the pages of history for Cimarron seems to be ever going but like its river never gone.

Cimarron is one of those timeless towns in New Mexico like Cordova, Pecos, Mora and countless others for which the State is so well known. Its heartbeat is in its history rather than in its industry. Here characters appear and suddenly vanish; here they speak for a moment then suddenly hold their peace, depending on how much of the scene they steal. But they are all part of the story of the Maxwell Land Grant. Men whose boots impressed the floors of the bars whether at Maxwell's or Lambert's: these can be vitalized without being cartooned. The Great American Frontier stamped them as parcels of history; connecting links of a chain of events that began with the opening of the fabulous Santa Fe Trail—for we acknowledge that had this Trail not opened and had not Col. Sumner decided on Fort Union—Cimarron would never have been.

Man, even a very prominent man, cannot be said to be entirely one piece or even one color; thus we can look to see in Cimarron, side by side with great achievements the falterings of weakness. Leviathans are great simply because in the midst of their seemingly unhurried lives and in spite of the haltings of the flesh, and at times their own inherent baseness, that succeeded in expressing and creating something over and above themselves and their time. So the heroes of Cimarron remain such whether with a six-shooter or just in a night shirt.

Cimarron as a river sings a song; Cimarron as a town basks in the sun of its past achievements, greatness and glory; Cimarron as a Frontier pushed the outposts just a little farther that Americans might fulfill their quest of Manifest Destiny in moving from Sea to Shining Sea; Cimarron as the home of Lucien B. Maxwell was all that was great and rugged in the heart of a fur-trapper; Cimarron was the capital of the stock industry in those early days, proved to the rest of the nation that New Mexico was more than just a place where stage lines had stops. It was a haven for lawyer, soldier, trader, stockman, dance-hall girl, bar tender and the rest of the frontier breed that while full of faults were not devoid of virtue even though full at times with whiskey and sometimes of lead.

Frontier towns of the 70's and 80's more or less have the same story of six-shooters and bad men. Visitors coming to Cimarron are generally shown the graves of four Negro soldiers from Fort Union supposedly killed by Clay Allison. Actually, these soldiers were buried at the Fort Union cemetery. The four graves are identified as containing the mortal remains of Charles Morris, a Mr. Henderson, who set up type in the early days of the Cimarron News and Press, not to be confused with the Henderson who is said to have killed or wounded fifteen men, the third marker is for a Mr. Carpenter and the fourth for an unidentified person.

Morris was originally from Colorado. He had come to Cimarron with the wife of Chunk Colbert, a bad hombre in his own right. Charles very freely told everyone that his woman was Chunk's former mate and word soon got to Trinidad. Morris needed killing, no doubt about it, thought Chunk, and he was just the man to do it. He went to Cimarron and made an appointment with Morris for a gun battle. That was how Morris was buried at

Cimarron. Of course Clay Allison later took care of Chunk at Clifton House. Charles was killed in 1871. Let us hear from Old Timer George Crocker:

"Two men rode into Cimarron one day. They were riding two gray horses. A matched team. They sold the horses to Henry Lambert, but it turned out that one of the men was a notorious horse-thief. The horses were stolen in Colorado. The day after they sold the horses, three officers from Colorado arrived at Cimarron, having trailed the thieves to Lambert's. There two of the officers got off their horses with their guns in hand and entered the bar. As soon as the thief saw the men, the mutual recognition made him panicky. He jumped from where he was sitting and ran out through the dining room and out the side door and across the street. Just as he reached the steps that went up the porch in front of the Maxwell house, one of the officers that had followed him through the dining room and out the side door shot and killed him before he could mount the steps. It was in the old Lambert's hotel that this incident took place. The bar-room, dining room, and side door were incorporated into the new building. This fellow is buried as you go to the graveyard, across the arroyo and come to the foot of the hill. There, turn to the right and follow between the hill and the arroyo. You should come across the grave at this point. The posse continued its search for the other thief, but he was nowhere to be found.

"The four Negro soldiers were killed by Dave Crockett (nephew of another man by that name of Alamo, Texas fame) in Lambert's barroom. Cimarron was full of Negro soldiers at this time. They were stationed at Fort Union, but were camped here at this time, passing through on an overnight stop on the way to Fort Union. Bushnell's barn was the camp.

"About nine o'clock in the evening, Dave Crockett, Gus Heifner and Henry Goodman were preparing to leave town, but first they decided to stop in at Lambert's for a drink, also for a bottle to take along on the trip. Leaving the bar Dave Crockett was in the lead. When he got to the door, he grasped the knob. The action was simultaneous with someone's turning it on the other side. Crockett managed to pull the door open and seeing a Negro soldier on the other side, drew his gun and killed him. There were two soldiers playing cards just north of the door in the northwest corner of the barroom and another looking over their shoulders kibitzing. Crockett turned on the three and fired twice. Two slumped in the corner. The third started to run out but got as far as the double door leading into the dining room where another bullet dropped him. Why did he kill? The only explanation given at the time was that they were Negroes and he was a Texan. (Note—the soldiers were not permitted to bring in arms consequently they had no defense against civilians many of whom went about the streets of Cimarron armed to the teeth.)

"At our house the family was already abed. After we heard the shots we heard a noise in our back yard. Mother got up, opened the door and looked out. She saw no one. Henry Goodman told us afterwards that he had run from Lambert's after the multiple killing and hid behind a pile of lumber stacked up in our yard. He saw mother when she opened the door.

"Strange as it seems the three men had their horses at the barn which served as a camp for the soldiers. This was a tremendous barn surrounded by a high adobe wall and could very easily be used as a fort. It was here that Sherwin (general manager of the Maxwell Land Grant) kept his horses. It was inadvisable to get their mounts, so they left town on foot. Crockett managed to get to the Dick Steel ranch which is known today as the Springer Ranch. The next day you could see the soldiers all over the hills and up and down the creek and through the brush in search of the killer. He was not found. Gus Heifner, a pal of Crockett's, considered himself a bad man, but I doubt if he ever convinced anyone else that he was.

"Crockett had nerve enough for both. He was a cattleman but sold his stock to locate in Cimarron. Both he and Gus came together. At times they would ride up and down the street shooting off their guns. Upon occasion they would ride into a store on horseback, buy a suit of clothes or whatever they wanted, ride out telling the clerk to charge it to the sheriff. Occasionally, their humor took another twist. If they chanced upon some one they didn't particularly like, they would draw a gun on him and force him into a saloon, then call all the people in from the streets and invite them for drinks, the bill to be paid by their victim. One of these victims was John McCollough. He was postmaster at Cimarron, and brother-in-law to Frank Springer. They married sisters.

"Sheriff Rhinehart with Joe Holbrook and John McCollough as deputies hid behind a well-curb that was in front of the old stage barn. At that time the road running to Cimarroncita or Urraca passed by this well. Crockett had a girl friend out at Mat Crosby's. She was Mrs. Crosby's sister. Gus and Dave often spent the night there as guests. Harry Chandler later lived on this place on the Urraca or Porter place.

"As Crockett and Heifner were leaving Cimarron at midnight (the night following the killing of the soldiers) Crockett was killed. Heifner got away without a scratch. I read, not so long ago, that Heifner was wounded at the time. This was not so. He managed to get to his horse and took off in a dead run never stopping until he reached the Vermejo. Crockett had been warned that the sheriff was waylaying him along the road, but I don't think he was looking for the trap at the well. The pair were at our house just before Crockett's death. They banged at the door until mother got up to ask what they wanted. They were looking for my father. When informed that he was away they inquired for a young fellow, Wheeler by name, who was staying with us at the time. (Wheeler later married and settled in the vicinity of Johnson Mesa. His descendants live in Raton.) Heifner said that both men were in but had sent a woman to cover up for them. At this point Crockett turned to Gus and told him to shut up. They then left for Chittenden's close by. They woke him up and made inquiries because they suspected there was a trap somewhere along the road. They were going from house to house to make sure.

"I talked to Holbrook several years afterwards. He said

that Rhinehart was after him for some time to help in arresting Crockett but he was not interested. Crockett was aware of this and once drew a gun on Holbrook accusing him of aiding the sheriff. This angered Holbrook so he signed up with the sheriff. This happened the same day the soldiers were killed. Holbrook, realiizng his opportunity, borrowed a double-barreled shotgun, loading both barrels. When Crockett and Heifner came along, he got up from behind the well-curb with both barrels cocked, taking a bead on his man. He shouted for him to throw up his hands. Instead of complying Crockett dared him to shoot. He emptied both barrels.

"I believe it was the following Sunday that Heifner rode back to Cimarron with his gun across his saddle riding up and down the main street as if on the lookout for some one. Nothing happened."

Crockett was buried in the Cimarron cemetery near where Parson Tolby's remains rest. He had a marker made at the Cary hardware store over his grave, but someone claiming to be a relative carried it off. Weeds grow there now. The three graves that supposedly contain the remains of the three soldiers killed by Crockett face the Tolby and Crockett graves. Actually the grave of the first is that of John Black. The legend reads: In Memory of John Black, died in Cimarron, May 21, 1872. Age 18. May His Soul Rest in Peace. The second marker reads: In Memory of Pomeroy Laughlin. Native of Ohio. Died in Cimarron May 11, 1872. Age 38 years. The third marker reads: Charles Morris. Native of Tennessee. Died in Cimarron July 23, 1872. Age 32 years.

About the year 1877, a Mr. Maxwell (no relation to Lucien Maxwell) and his boy, not over sixteen years of age, came to this section of the country from "somewhere back East." His wife had not as yet arrived until he could provide a suitable home for her. A ranch was bought with the intention of stocking it with cattle. A Negro worked with the two. Nothing much was noted of these men until one day passing cowboys noticed a team of horses hitched to a wagon loaded with poles standing near the half-constructed house. The next day they came by again and the team and wagon were still there. No one was at the house. Following the wagon tracks back a bit to the trail they came upon young Maxwell's body. Thinking that the boy had been thrown from the load of poles and killed, they went on to the camp they knew Maxwell had out in the hills where he had been cutting logs and poles for his house and corral. They didn't know how to tell him of his boy's death, but they were spared the effort for he was dead with a bullet through the heart. The Negro helper was nowhere to be found. They rode to Cimarron to inform Sheriff Burleson. Knowing that the hired hand often went to Trinidad he wired the authorities there to be on the lookout for him. He was found in a cantina and brought back to Cimarron. He was tried, convicted and sentenced for the hangman's rope. Crocker gives a graphic picture of his end:

"The gallows erected, a grave was dug close by just south of where the Catholic Church now stands over the hill, out of sight of the town. The day that he was to be hanged, word got around that the murderer had a message to be delivered from the gallows. About two o'clock that afternoon, a wagon drove up to A. H. Carey's carpenter shop. There a plain board coffin was loaded on and the wagon driven to jail. The guard brought the prisoner out. He got on the wagon, sat down on the coffin and the procession started for the gallows. At this time you could see men, women and children leaving their houses headed for the place of execution.

"Arriving at the gallows, the prisoner walked up the steps, stood on the platform and addressed the crowd. He made a few preliminary remarks, pointed to his grave, saying that it would be just a few minutes before he would fill the hole. He then told about the double murder.

"He said that the three were out in the camp working with the timber on the morning of the murders. A load of poles had been cut and loaded on the wagon. After lunch the boy started for the ranch with the load. His father walked out to where they had a saddle horse staked close by, to change the stake pin so that the horse might have fresher grass. He then started back to the tent. It was at this moment that he picked up a gun and shot at his employer, but missed him. Maxwell walked up to him and demanded why he shot. He said that he spotted a rabbit and he liked rabbit meat. Maxwell told him to leave the gun alone especially since his marksmanship was so poor as he had come close to hitting him. Maxwell took the gun away from him, setting it inside the tent. The next opportunity was death for Maxwell. He saddled the horse and started for the boy. His excuse to the boy was shortage of provisions at camp. At an unguarded moment he shot the boy. The horses bolted at the sound of the shot, throwing the boy. He rode on to Trinidad.

"It chanced that on that very morning the trains that were doing the freighting from Trinidad had left Maxwell's place for Colorado expecting to return with lumber and other freight. The teamster had a letter from Maxwell to a blacksmith ordering tools and some irons needed by the rancher. When the Negro overtook the freighters he told them that Maxwell had sent him to stop the order on the lumber and freight until further notice. He also asked for and obtained the letter to the blacksmith. In Trinidad he took the letter to the place directed stating that he would call for the irons and tools as soon as the blacksmith would have them ready. He had intentions of returning to Maxwell's to discover the bodies and report foul play. The teamsters and blacksmith would alibi for him. But he went on a drunk and was delayed in Trinidad about a week. He went to the blacksmith's and picked up the order. He was picked up out of Trinidad on his way back. His last words were a warning to young men and boys to beware of wine and women. These were the cause of his downfall. He saw his coffin as well as his grave, but did not stay long in either. That night Dr. Tipton of Tiptonville had the body dug up and loaded on a spring wagon for dissecting. Most of the crowd left before the trap was sprung."

On July 9, 1873, two miners decided to fight a duel in a mining camp near Cimarron. One miner, known as Mosby, was shot in the forehead. A doctor was summoned from Cimarron; examined the wound and pronounced it fatal. The miner who shot Mosby was known as Brown. Taken to Cimarron, he was bonded to the tune of three hundred dollars and told to keep the peace for six months. Released, he skipped the country. He turned up later as Voodoo Brown in Las Vegas where his subsequent adventures after the coming of the railroad lead him into other difficulties and he had to flee that city too. Two days later Mosby was back in the saloon where the fight started and proceeded to drink up courage for another fight. Mosby has a remarkable head on his shoulders. No doubt he had it shot off.

At the time that "Coal Oil Jimmie" and his band of outlaws operated, Cimarron had only three houses besides the Maxwell home. The Jose Gonzolez home on the hill south of the present Catholic church; the Lail home which was then a forage station and stage stop and a home built by John Holland. "Coal Oil Jimmie" took to stealing Maxwell's cattle and a price was placed on his head. Maxwell and the stage line offered a thousand dollars for Jimmie. A fellow by the name of Henry Marks was able to contact two of the outlaws possibly at the Gonzalez home. They agreed to assassinate Jimmie and a companion while asleep, for the reward and their own liberty. The pair had been sleeping in the mountains on their way to hold up a ranch near the flume of the Merino mine. They were killed as agreed and the bodies brought to the stage warehouse (present Lail home) in Cimarron strapped to the backs of burros. They got their reward and a free passage on the route of the company, going east.

Sam Ketchum, the brother of "Black Jack" Ketchum was wounded and captured near Cimarron and brought to the state prison at Santa Fe to await action of the grand jury on charges of train robbery and murder. This gang operated near Folsom. Bob McManus also of the notorious "Black Jack" gang was caught horse stealing near Cimarron. He had been tried by the Federal Court at Las Vegas for stealing mail from the postoffice at Smithville, New Mexico, at which time a son of the postmaster was killed but he was acquitted. This time he was not so fortunate.

With the coming of the railroad over the Raton mountains, the county seat was changed to Springer. The wild-west days subsided. People followed the railroad and forgot the streets once hallowed by Maxwell, Moore, Crocker, Lambert, Springer, Dold, Abreu, Longwell, Allison, Wheaton, Kroenig, Wooton, Carson, Buffalo Bill and a host of other names, whose names crop up now and then in a wild west novel or short story fictionized in the imagination of some writer, but whose true deeds in veracity outshine the fiction that seeks to immortalize them.

For the first time Henry Lambert felt the full force of the breath-taking beauty of the place as he looked down the knoll off the old Gonzales House. It was a halcyon day. The village lay soaked in that luscious leafy fragrance of a too precipitate New Mexico warmth. There was the smell of horses hoofs burning in the blacksmith's shop. The soft wind swept through the high grass so that the blades seemed to be industriously pummeling each other. Here on the hill, the air seemed quite different from the air down by the river. A bluebird sped overhead causing a twilight by his wings as he flew by. Peace and stillness iridescent in the haze of shadow and sun shot chimney smoke, merging with his vision that eternal odor of flowers, or roses and sweet-williams like a musk. Here was the place to live; here the place to welcome the stage; the place to invite the fullness of life. Here was a bit of France cradled between the mountains and the stream.

Henry Lambert was born for freedom. France was his birthplace and October 28, 1838, given as his birthdate. At twelve he left his parental home to learn cooking at Havre. Somewhat later he found employment on a French sailing boat which he deserted when it docked in New York. That was in 1861. The following year he was working on a submarine boat in Pennsylvania. Next he was on a pocket ship off to Liverpool, but America had such a hold on him, that he was back within three months. As a member of the Northern Navy in the Civil War, he was captain's steward. Not to his liking he forsook the Navy for Montevideo, South America. Back again in America within a short time, after serving as cook for a circus, he landed at Portland, Maine. He worked his way down to New York, southward to Washington, D. C., this time as cook for the Fifth Army Corps. For one month he was General Grant's private chef. The urge to move again brought him to North Carolina, but he again enlisted with the Fifth Army Corps as cook for General Warren. Following the war, he located at Petersburg, Virginia, where he opened a restaurant. The discovery of gold at Mt. Baldy closed the restaurant and introduced Lambert to New Mexico.

Lambert was married to a widow, Mary Steep. She died on October 28, 1821, and is buried in the family plot at Cimarron. She was only thirty-five at the time of her death. She was too ill to meet her guests at the grand-opening of the St. James Hotel in Cimarron, but many went to her bedroom to visit her. John Steep, her son, aged sixteen, had died on September 1st, almost two months before.

Henry Lambert spent six months in Elizabethtown in placer mining, following which, he opened the town's second hotel. It is possible that he was in partnership with a Joseph Coleman for in the Mora County deed book on page 269 we find:

Joseph Coleman to Henry Lambert:

Know all men by these presents that I, Joseph Coleman, in consideration of the sum of sixty-five dollars to one in hand paid by Henry Lambert, both of us of the town of Elizabethtown, County of Mora, and Territory of New Mexico, the receipt whereof is hereby acknowledged, have bargained and sold, and by these presents do grant and convey unto the said Henry Lambert, all my right, title and interest in the following described property to wit: a certain of the first part and Henry Lambert of the County of Colfax aforesaid, of the second part:

"Whereas by virtue of a certain writ of execution issued out of the District Court in and for the County of Santa Fe and the Territory of New Mexico in favor of Joseph Holbrook plaintiff and the Maxwell Land Grant and Railway Company, defendant to the said sheriff directed and delivered commanding him that out of the goods and chattels, lands and tenements, moneys, effects, and credits of the said Maxwell Land Grant and Railway Company judgment debtor within this county, he should satisfy payment, he, the said plaintiff did in obedience to the said commands levy on, take and seize all the estate, right, title and interest of the said judgment debtor of, in, and to, the real property hereinafter particularly set forth and described, with the appurtenances:

"And did on the 10th day of May in A. D. 1875, sell the said premises, by public auction in front of the courthouse in Cimarron in said County he having first given notice of the time and place of such sale by advertising the same according to law, at which sale the said premises were struck off and sold to Henry Lambert, for the sum of sixty-seven dollars, he the said Henry Lambert being the highest bidder and that being the highest sum of money so bidden as aforesaid made, executed and delivered to said purchases his deed of conveyance of the said purchase, his deed of conveyance of the property hereinafter named.

"Now this indenture witnesseth that the said party of the first part, sheriff as aforesaid by virtue of the said execution and in pursuance of the statute in such case made and provided for in consideration of the sum of money above mentioned to him in hand paid as aforesaid, the receipt whereof is hereby acknowledged."

There also follows another auction for Block A.S.W. town lot in Eliazbethtown, Mora County, New Mexico situated in lot No. Y in Block No. 3 fronting Second Street 50 feet and running back 40 feet—together with the improvements thereon, to have and to hold the above granted and bargained premises with appurtenances thereof unto the said Henry Lambert, his heirs, executors and administrators to his and their own proper use and behalf forever, on this day of December 28, 1868. Witnesses: Isaac Hattenback and B. B. Walters.

Whether Mat and Andy Calhoun put up the little hotel and bar opposite the Swink Hotel is a matter of dispute. Henry Lambert, recognizing the possibilities in Cimarron, sold his holdings at Elizabethtown and came to Cimarron in 1871. Joe Holbrook, slayer of Dave Crockett, seems to have acquired the hotel. There is no deed showing that Lambert purchased the place in 1871. At this time trouble began brewing between the Maxwell Land Grant people and the squatters. Lucien Maxwell may have sold the property to the people concerned. In those days many deeds passed hands by a mere handshake or an old scrap of paper easily lost. With Maxwell selling to the Grant people and moving to Fort Sumner, the settlers had a thoroughly organized syndicate to deal with. Holbrook may not have retained proof of his proprietorship, consequently his holdings were turned over to the sheriff for public auction.

The sheriff of Colfax County to Henry Lambert—Deed. Block A W Lots 2,3,4,5 Cimarron.

This indenture made May 10, 1875, between John C. Turner, Sheriff of Colfax County, Territory of New Mexico, Lot 1, Cimarron, on May 10, 1875, sold to Henry Lambert for which he paid $102.00. Thus the hotel man was launched on his enterprise with full sanction of the law. The days that his little hotel saw; McMains, Tolby, McCollough, Whigham, Sherwin, Crockett, Dold, Moore, Wheaton, Maxwell, Abreu, Wooton, Kit Carson, Dave Crockett, Clay Allison, Mills, Hixenbaugh, Tom Boggs, Daniel Boone's grandson, Rogers, Buffalo Bill and a host of others whose names are synonymous with American Frontier history; to say nothing of the soldiers stationed at Fort Union, Rayado and Cimarron, who were numbered among his friends. Often the billiard room and bar (present dining room) was the scene of six shooter justice and injustice. It became so common that whenever a man was killed in the billiard room-bar, residents passed it off with the remark, "Seems like Lambert had a man for breakfast." Fred Lambert, a poet and etcher of note, son of Henry, has recorded twenty-six killings at his father's place.

But the hotel as Henry bought it, was not adequate enough for the ever increasing needs of Cimarron. An agreement entered into with Frank R. Sherwin on November 17, 1879, was to produce the Don Diego as it stands today:

"Lots designated therein—Lots 1, 2, 3, 4 in Block A. S. W. in the street known as Barlow Avenue—corner lot No. 1 bordering on the street known as Chavez Street, together with all the buildings thereon, the same being occupied by the second party, and all appurtenances thereinto in anywise belonging, in consideration of the sum of $2,250.00 to be paid within ten years from the date of sale at 7% interest per annum. The mortgage to be paid off in ten years. In the further event, that the said second party shall build a more commodious hotel as is to be hereinafter. If it occur and result that should the first party (Sherwin) fail to keep the agreement he shall pay $5,000.00. The second party (Lambert) will surrender and deliver possession of the Maxwell House now occupied by him for hotel purposes on the north side of the street (this reference may be to the mill—a three story stone building still standing). Party of the second part will build a large and commodious hotel upon the said above premises, contracted to be sold, the cost of same to be not less than $4,000.00 in construction, and pay all taxes due on premises to receiver Thornton and receiver Stratton of said town-site signed in the presence of M. W. Mills.

The new hotel called the St. James, was completed in January 1882 at the cost of seventeen thousand dollars. Lambert put it in use prior to completion, hence authors are confused concerning actual date. The Raton Guard, a newspaper interested in the progress, ran this item in its December, 1881, issue: "The Lambert Hotel in Cimarron is about completed. It costs $17,000.00 and is one of the finest hotels in the Territory of New Mexico." In building his new hotel, Lambert incorporated the bar and billiard parlor into the edifice, thus preserving for future generations the room that saw the frontier blossom. At present it is the dining room, and the bar converted into a lunch counter. Here and there along the ceiling, one may spot a bullet hole, a silent reminder of the good old days when fire-water caused men to steam off their six shooters in wild shooting.

Lambert kept books. That was more than Maxwell did. A glance at the Dec., 1871,—April, 1875, credit book gives an idea of how he checked up on his customers.

M. W. Mills—

July	4	4 beers	$ .60
"	6	Puppe	.75
"	7	Beer—drinks	1.50
"	19	3 drinks	.75
"	25	6 cigars	1.50
"	26	Cigars and pool	3.50
"	28	Pool & billiards	3.25
August	26	drinks	1.00
"	27	drinks	4.00
"	28	drinks	1.25
September	1	drinks	1.25
"	4	drinks	.25
"	18	Pool & cigars	1.50
October	31	Cigars	.75
November	4	4 drinks	1.00

Many names of interest to old-timers appear in the Don Diego registers: Tom Catron, Dr. Longwell (old pioneer doctor at Cimarron, once hunted up for questioning by Clay Allison. He was traced to the Abreu house in Rayado. There Mrs. Longwell answered the door. Asked their business, the men said they wanted the doctor for hanging. Mrs. Longwell told them they were welcome to visit the doctor who was sick in bed with the smallpox and couldn't greet them at the door. They could see him in bed. (They declined the invitation.) John Hixenbaugh, Lewis Kingman, Thomas Vaughn, Charles Springer, Al Allison, James Savage—. All of early Raton: J. W. Wiliamson, J. M. Pearson, George Hoxie, M. O'Brien, Jack Raught—. All of Ute Park: C. M. Bayne, F. A. Lanstrom, B. W. Forster, R. C. Hamilton, E. J. Scott, I. McAuliffe, George Reed, Ed Lear. All of Raton: R. L. Wooten, Sr., of Mountain House, Wooten Canon, Colorado; C. F. Ramsley of Raton; Charles F. Abreu of Rayado; Jas. P. Abreu of Rayado. On June 14, 1899, Gene Lambert, who gave as his residence—any old place—signed the register; Bruce Dawson of Dawson, New Mexico, July 3, 1905. (This is probably one of the earliest dates of Dawson as a place on record); W. B. Stockton of Otero, New Mexico (This is of interest because Clifton House was the earlier residence of the Stocktons) Aug. 8, 1883. A quaint sidelight is the way of registering at the old St. James (now Don Diego—Diego is a contraction of Santiago which means James, Patron Saint of Spain:

Name	Residence	Time	Room	Remarks
J. M. Weight, Esq.	Tinker, by God	July 27, 1883, 7:30	9354	Bum
Albert Venvey	Amsterdam	August 7, 1883, 7:00		Laughs all the time
Pat Chuck	Hot Springs	December 14, 1883, 1:50		Man of 10,000 wants no good grumbles

On the last page of the register dated December 26, 1883, is an interesting item written for want of other paper:

This is to certify that T. E. McCaffey and Jack Cady will run a race in Cimarron with E. McCaffey's sorrel and J. Cady's black for the sum of $1,200.00

E. McCaffey
J. Cady

Henry remarried after the death of his first wife, this time to Mary E. Davis. She was born in 1859 in Liberty, Missouri. It must have been a gala affair in 1883 at the new hotel the day they were united in holy wedlock. She died in 1929, and was buried by her husband Henry who died January 24, 1933. The Old West is at rest.

The story of Cimarron's first press is as interesting as the story of the town itself for it had its beginning in Old Mexico. It goes back to Santiago Abreu, relative of the Abreus who later settled Rayado. Elected to the Mexico Congress in 1825, his duties took him to Mexico City. The possibility of a newspaper in Santa Fe was always on his mind. In his travels as delegate he found just the press he wanted in Chihuahua, but it was years before he was able to ship it to his home city. A press without a printer would just be a press, so a printer named J. Maria Baca was prevailed upon to leave his home in Durango and print the newspaper for Ramon Abreu, the delegate's brother.

The Abreus had use for the press in airing their political views as well as in advertising lands and goods they had for sale. Padre Jose Antonio Martinez differed. He could use the press for educational purposes. From his early days at Abiquiu he was a crusader against illiteracy and ignorance. Indeed, not too many native New Mexicans in 1834 knew the alphabet. His arguments were forceful and Ramon agreed that the pastor at Taos should buy the press to war against illiteracy. Opinions vary as to whether Padre Martinez published the first book ever printed in New Mexico in Taos or in Santa Fe. It was a speller entitled *Cuanderno De Ortogrofia*, dedicated to his brother's children, who came in from Ranchos de Taos to be instructed by him.

It is safe to surmise that the book was actually printed by the padre in Santa Fe, but that he used the name Taos because negotiations were already under way for the sale of the press. The printer was Baca who seems to have been stable equipment. Everytime the press changed hands, he worked for the new owner. From a letter to the legislature, Ramon Abreu seems to indicate that the press was still in Santa Fe in January 1835. This would indicate that Padre Martinez printed his newspaper *El Crepusculo De la Libertad* at Santa Fe. Nor is this far fetched or illogical since most of the people in New Mexico who could read or write congregated at the Capital. Apparently even these did not seem interested for the paper was discontinued after the fourth issue. Various opinions have been forwarded as to its discontinuance. A very plausible one was overlooked. The press may have been moved to Taos.

Padre Martinez in addition to the first co-educational school in New Mexico also ran a seminary for native vocations to the priesthood. Whatever his personal faults, he was sincere in educating and uplifting his people. The bishop at Durango seemd convinced that the boys he trained were prepared for ordination. Book printing went on in earnest. The padre may have foreseen the gathering storm that took the lives of Santiago, Ramon, and Marcelino Abreu. No doubt, if the press were in Santa Fe in 1837, its fate would have been decided then. Padre Martinez became involved in the political situation acting as a quasi-chaplain for Governor Manuel Armijo's forces. His constant trips to Santa Fe, his petty quarrels with Kit Carson, Charles Beaubien, Miranda petition caused him to abandon the publishing business seemingly after 1840, when Beaubien and Miranda were negotiating with Armijo for the property that was to become the Maxwell Land Grant. Besides, the Americans were coming into New Mexico in ever increasing numbers. The omen was not favorable.

So, the press took another trip to Santa Fe: J. M. Baca, the printer again mothering it. Donacious Vigil, who was to play an important part in the American occupation in 1846, bought it, publishing a newspaper, La Verdad, every Thursday. He kept it for almost three years when he sold it to Jose Chavez who used for to propagandize proceedings in the government, printing charged to the government, in the hopes that the people would take a keener interest in governmental affairs and stir their patriotism. Since the masses were uneducated, the *Rayo de Nuevo Mexico* would appeal to just a few. The political interest of the province of New Mexico held little interest for the people of Old Mexico and less for those of New Mexico. Then came Kearny, with the Stars and Stripes. J. M. Baca had to separate from his beloved press. English became the official language and Baca knew about as much English as Kearny knew Spanish.

Hovey and Davis decided to cater to the ever increasing influx of Americans. Besides, the soldiers under Sterling Price and the staff at the new Fort Marcy could use a newspaper of interest to them. They made it a point to have G. R. Gibson, their editor, print news of military importance to boost the Fort Marcy sales. That was in 1847. In view of the fact that New Mexico was turned over to General Kearney without the loss of one life, or the firing of a bullet, the motto of the paper was strange: "We Die, But Never Surrender." The paper died. The press was buried away as were the ambitions of Hovey and Davis.

Meantime up in the north country the Maxwell Land Grant and Railway Company was organizing to add its page to the unique history that is New Mexico's. Whatever might be said for the other forty-seven states, New Mexico stands apart in its history. Conquistadores, Franciscan Martyrs, Colonists, Indian raids, Pueblos, politics, French Canadian trappers, scouts, invaders, flags of several nations, land grants, rustlers, Mormon battalions, outlaws, oil, copper, killers, province, territory, state, she could be said to have more history under one finger-nail than many states have in a body. J. M. Baca was thought enough of to merit a death notice. Born in 1802, he died at the age of 65 content in the knowledge that Spanish was just as official as English in Civic affairs. It still is.

While the press may be said to be dormant, it was not defunct. John Collinson, president of the Maxwell Land Grant and Railway Company decided that a newspaper would be mightier than the sword in dictating the policy of the grant Company. It was also a way of advertising the company to people interested in townsites, mining, stock-raising, farming, but not squatting.

There was a man in Santa Fe who was in English print everything that J. M. Baca was in Spanish. This would be the ideal man to edit the paper. Collinson brought the press and drew up an agreement with this printer named Alexander Patrick Sullivan. Collinson contacted O'Sullivan on September 22nd, 1870, and an agreement was drawn up between them:

"Alexander P. Sullivan, in consideration of the covenants on the part of the party of the second part hereinafter contained doth covenant and agree to and with the said Maxwell Land Grant and Railway Company that he will, as soon as the said company shall prepare a suitable building established at Cimarron In the County of Colfax, in the said Territory of New Mexico, a substantial job-printing office and to publish at said place a twenty-four column weekly newspaper to be known as the *Cimarron News* for one year from the date of this agreement to be printed on clear white paper of good quality and with good clear and legible type. The first issue of said paper to be on the first day of October, next (October, 1871) and every week thereafter said paper to be devoted particularly to advancing the interest of said Maxwell Land Grant and Railway Company and the said Alexander P. Sullivan hereby binds himself during the terms of this contract to use his best endeavors, by all honorable means and ways, to promote the interest of the said company and aid in the development of the resources of its property and the resources of Northern New Mexico and the said Alexander P. Sullivan agrees and further binds himself that provided he should desire at the expiration of the term of this contract to sell or dispose of said printing office and paper he will sell same to the Maxwell Land Grant and Railway Company in preference to any other person or persons, said company paying to him the same price offered by any other purchaser.

"And the said Alexander P. Sullivan further agrees and binds himself to furnish the said company one column for such advertisement as said company may deem proper during the term of this contract for the sum of five hundred dollars payable ten months from the date of the first issue of said newspaper. And the said Alexander P. Sullivan further agrees and binds himself to pay over to the said Company all moneys received by him for subscriptions to the said newspaper until the circulation of the same shall reach five hundred and all subscriptions above that number shall be paid to Sullivan exclusively for his own use and benefit.

"And the said Maxwell Land Grant and Railway Company in consideration of the covenants on the part of the party of the first part doth covenant and agree for one year from the date of this agreement to and with the said Alexander Patrick Sullivan to guarantee a subscription of five hundred copies of said newspaper at the rate of five dollars for each copy to be paid as follows: Twelve hundred dollars of said amount to be paid at once, five hundred dollars at the end of three months and the remaining eight hundred dollars at the end of six months from date of the agreement; and to furnish the said Sullivan a suitable building for said printing office at a yearly rent not to exceed ten percent of the cost of the same and further to pay the said Sullivan five hundred dollars within ten months of the date of this agreement for the use of said column of advertisements etc."

This agreement was signed by both Sullivan and Collinson. There is no indication in any of the deed books that Sullivan ever purchased property at Cimarron. Either he just rented or never fulfilled the contract for his name is scarcely remembered at Cimarron. The paper was taken over by Frank Springer, Whigham and Henderson. The editors pledged themselves to give the readers unbiased reports on all the news items of the city, county, and Territory. They called it the liveliest and spiciest paper in all New Mexico. At first the paper was printed in the old forage and government station (present Lail house) then in the A. H. Carey Hardware Store on the northeast corner of what was then the public square of old Cimarron. A Spanish edition was also added but old Baca was resting in his grave, so another Spanish editor must have been found in either Taos or Santa Fe for this column.

If Clay Allison destroyed the old Abreu press, most of it must have been recovered and repaired, for there is no indication that a new press was bought. Besides, the Cimarron wasn't so deep, but that a few men couldn't wade in and recover the press. An interesting item in a newspaper in Cimarron in 1878 states that another edition would not be forthcoming until the editors could give the readers a report on the county and territorial elections. Special arrangements had been made to get the territorial reports by telegraph. Allison had moved from Otero and the Cimarron country by 1878, therefore, if the Cimarron News and Press were re-published in 1878, the complete press did not remain at the bottom of the Cimarron as many people believe. The only other explanation is that another individual not connected with the Maxwell Land Grant Company (which seems uncertain since the company would not tolerate it) may have brought in a press as a private enterprize. After this 1878 date no further mention is made of the paper which was discontinued. Cimarron quieted down, people came and went until it became almost a ghost town. Suddenly, in 1907, the town revived, and so did the Cimarron News and Press. On January 10, 1907, the first issue appeared with this notice: The type used in this heading is from the old plant of the Cimarron News and Press and was used for a heading for the paper in the seventies." The editorial paid tribute to the earlier paper:

"The history of Colfax County when fully published will contain many a chapter devoted to the thrilling vicissitudes of the old News and Press. The papers were established in 1870, and told of the joys and sorrows, the fortunes and failures of those stalwart pioneers of the early days, who realizing the massive fortunes latent in the hills and wealth of the valleys and mesas of Colfax County, struggled against all odds of fate, in the days when the land was young. The equipment of the old plant was not as complete as the present business needs would demand, and often the editor was office-boy, compositor, stenographer, bookkeeper, pressman, local hustler and job man. At other times the paper flourished and boasted of a mechanical force, and an able corps of editors. The names of well known Colfax County men at the head of the editorial columns of a period of the issues of the old paper, and some of the most able editorials we have ever read appeared in these issues. Some of the old papers tell of stilling events, now forgotten almost, by even the principal actors, some of whom are still living in Cimarron and vicinity. On one occasion the *Cimarron News and Press* was put entirely out of active service by the unkindness of certain citizens of the locality. Many of the older inhabitants of the town remember the incident when Clay Allison was a well known character who was connected with a number of exciting events during the seventies, the times which tried men's souls, and brought out all the good or all the bad in the character of the individual. In some manner the *Cimarron News and Press* incurred the displeasure of this gentleman, and one night, accompanied by some half doezn of his friends, Allison paid the town a visit. They stopped a few moments at Lambert's Hotel where they put a few marks on the black board, and then across the plaza to the newspaper office. The editor and those connected with the paper at the time were absent, but the door yielded to a few well-directed jars from a pole and the party entered. When they got back to Lambert's again, they were covered thoroughly with printer's ink. Whether they believed in the efficacy of this medium or not, they were daubed with a goodly quantity of it. Lambert's facetious query as to their having been to the printing office was cut short by the threat that something would happen to him if he mentioned the occurrence, and the party left. The press of the Cimarron newspaper was found battered to pieces, and every movable thing in the office, including cases, stands and types, were dumped in the Cimarron river. Years after when the youth of Cimarron wanted ammunition for their bean shooters, they went down to the river and gathered up silent messengers of thought, ruthlessly scattered among the sands. Even this crude criticism of the paper did not deter the publishers of the paper, and we find the paper continued for some time after with new material and part of the old. Some of the material of the '70's now forms a part of the *Raton Range* plant, where we understand it is carefully preserved, for the good it has done in years past. The heading of this paper, though rather unique and old-fashioned, was set from the original type in which the heading of the paper of the '70's was set. Some of the letters are somewhat battered, but the head appears very much as it did more than thirty years ago. Old residents of the country will, we hope, recognize the old head."

One of the men connected with the *Cimarron News and Press* in the early days was William Raymond Moley. He was employed by the Maxwell Land Grant people and took over, for a time the editorship of the paper. He was the editor at the time that Clay Allison destroyed the press. This is the same Morley who gave the Santa Fe Railroad the advantage over the Rio Grande in the fight for the Raton Pass. The new *Cimarron News and Press* was short-lived as the old. Only three volumes are buried in the vaults of the Colfax County Courthouse archives at

Raton. The new paper was published by the Cimarron Publishing Company which was owned by Alb. E. Schooeder. Shortly after he revived the old *Cimarron News and Press,* George E. Ramley started another newspaper called the *Cimarron Citizen.* On March 4, 1908, he printed the first issue with this announcement:

"With this, the first edition of the *Cimarron Citizen* the Citizen wishes to announce to Cimarron and to the world at large that its first, last and continuous effort will be for the betterment, advancement and promoting of each and every legitimate and deserving enterprise which tends to upbuild Cimarron, especially, and also increase the commercial welfare of the Cimarron Valley, Colfax County and the territory of New Mexico. The Citizen believes that by working for the interest of the territory surrounding us, it is also working for the interest of Cimarron and incidently, for its own interests. And while it would like to pose as a paper whose only aim is the good of the community and the inhabitants thereof, it frankly expects to get something out of the future itself. But it believes that the only way this future affluence will come, is by helping along everyone and everything, in every possible manner, and all the time, for without a propsperous and pushing community to back it, the chances are ten to one that the Citizen will be early affected by a heavy frost. To one who stops to think this doctrine, if such may it be called, would hold good to any person or organization. We are all here to make our living and to make it as good as possible.

"We all hope to make a fortune and to make it as good as possible. Therefore, as long as it is fair and above board, that will bring about this result. It has been the history of new communities throughout the country, that only those which recognize the value of pushing and boosting have succeeded in being heard from quickly and in reaching a growth that their resources merit, without waiting for the millenium. So, let us all get together and "bost." Let us help each other and incidently, ourselves. We have the resources. Let us work together and develop them. We have the men with brains and honesty. Shove them along. We have business houses that any city in the Territory might be proud of. Patronize them and spend your money at home.

"Being ONE-HALF MILE FROM HEAVEN, we have some of its climate. We have unlimited water, vast forests, untold mineral wealth, fertile grazing and farming lands. In fact, everything but exorbitant tax assessment and the small-pox is to be found at Cimarron. We have in addition, strong churches and schools conducted with as much efficiency as can be found in the country. Everything that helps to make a good, clean, moral community, we possess. We have the component parts of a prosperous city of 10,000. Why not put them together and watch the wheels go round. The Citizen expects to do more than its share in this work, and will gladly take up any good cause, boost any enterprise, push out any work, granting special favors to none, but giving justice to all. If you have anything to push, bring it in and let us help push. If you do have any news of interest, let us publish it. Our moto is not live and let live, but rather "live and help live" and do both well.

Like the *Cimarron News Press,* the *Citizen* was short-lived. Save for a few scattered copies in libraries here and there, the general public is unaware that the paper ever existed.

Then came the hiatus. Many Cimarronians followed Carey and his hardware store to the new town of Raton. Others looked over the hills to the north for employment at Blossburg, Catskill, Peles, and the coal fields. Lumber coal and railroads all around Cimarron. The town was being emptied. Added to this the County seat found its way to Springer; the Maxwell Land Grant people were establishing headquarters elsewhere; McMains' agitating voice was silenced; squatters loaded their belongings into wagons and left as silently as they came. When Allison dumped the press into the river, he drowned the heart of Cimarron. So, the few loyal ones carried on through four decades in silence. Then Cimarron shook off her sleep. The Cimarron Townsite Company started the new town and it looked as if the days of '73; 74; 75 were back again.

The Rocky Mountain Coal Company was interested. With the opening of mines at Koehler, Dawson, Gardiner, Swastica, Brilliant, and the plating of towns at DesMoines, Grenville, Colfax a railroad would be just the thing. By 1907, it had its terminus at Cimarron.

"The St. Louis, Rocky Mountain and Pacific Railroads are considerable in advance of the western lines inasmuch as they have installed their system of telephone-telegraph, and will begin to use it in actual service in the coming week. Trains will be operated by both telephone and telegraph communication, any train or caboose at any part of the line will be able to communicate with the chief dispatcher or with any station at any time". (Cimarron News and Press May 23, 1907). The following week the same newspaper carried this item:

"About the busiest place in Colfax County just now, is up in Ponil Canyon along the right of way of the new Cimarron and Northwestern railroad. Within a stone's throw of the ancient dwelling place of Kit Carson, is being stored the bridge material for half a hundred bridges which the railroad will require to eliminate as much as possible curves and grades, in the ascent up Ponil Canyon. Along through the famous French and Chase ranches are camps of railroad graders, and futher up the canyon are corps of engineers and camps of lumbermen; the former completing the surveys and placing the grade stakes and the latter getting out the ties and building material for the road out of the virgin forests of the upper canyon.

"The Cimarron and Northwestern railway leaves the St. Louis, Rocky Mountain and Pacific railroads at the eastern edge of the Cimarron townsite, where they have more than twenty-five acres of station grounds. Here is already built a large warehouse, fifty by one hundred feet, for the storage of grain, provisions etc., for the various camps, and here are being graded more than a mile and a half of side tracks. These tracks are placed just the proper distance apart so that a double pile of lumber may be placed between, and there will be located the storage yards of the Continental Tie and Lumber Co. The station grounds and lumber yards are on a slight elevation, and constitute a most handsome site for the purpose. The grading for the yard is well along and will be virtually completed ere the end of this week, ready for tracking. Leaving the station grounds the new road will enter the famous French ranch by a slight grade, crossing the French irrigating ditch system by a two-span bridge. In mile two, occurs the heaviest fill on the entire line, a fill of four thousand yards. From this point the railroad enters the chase ranch, cutting off a corner of the famous Chase orchard, where it is necessary to cut down about thirty elegant bearing apple trees, about seventeen years old. After passing the Chase orchard the road hugs the side of the canyon, avoiding the rich agricultural lands and crossing and re-crossing the Ponil river many times. In fact, in the twenty-two miles of the road it will require fifty-one bridges, in addition to a number of channel changes, where the waters of the Ponil will be divided from the old course and the railroad built in their place. The engineering work in the building of the Cimarron and Northwestern is what is termed light mountain work, and when the road is completed will stand as one of the neatest achievements in railroad building in the Southwest. In the twenty-two miles of road there is a climb of 1,400 feet and the maximum grade is two percent. The heavy traffic of course will be down hill, and the capacity of the road will be only limited by the ability of the engine to hold the load back on the down run. One engine can safely handle forty loaded cars. The bridges are all designed for one hundred ton engines, and the rolling stock and road bed will be the best ever used in this character of work.

"On the management of the railroad are among the most agressive men of the Southwest, and their methods of building railroads is somewhat of an innovation. For instance, T. A. Schomberg, who is in charge of the road, has ordered the construction of a telephone line, not only to construction camps along the line, but also to the camps of the locating engineers many miles in advance of the graders. Ordinarily, these camps have no communication with each other or with the grading camps and headquarters and as a consequence much valable time is lost and much expense is incurred in maintaining messenger service. The Cimarron and Northwestern engineers and surveyors may communicate with each other and with all general officers of the road, in Trinidad, (Colorado) by phone, at any time and graders and bridgemen, construction men, all may be directed either from the general offices or from the offices of the engineer in charge.

"Another feature which will facilitate the building of the road is the ease with which material is procured. The securing of material, and especially timber, has usually been one of the greatest drawbacks in modern railroad building. The material for the Cimarron and Northwestern was all purchased before even the grading contracts were let, and as a consequence, immense quantities of it are arriving daily now, and by the time the grade is ready it will be on the ground, ready for use.

"One great advantage which the new road has is the fact that the right of way goes through the immense timber reserves of the Continental Tie and Lumber Company."

"The shops of the St. Louis, Rocky Mountain and Pacific Railroad at Cimarron have been completed for some time, and only a few minor details are lacking now for the most complete shop equipment in the Southwest. The shops have been turning out all classes of railroad and repair work for some time, and are at present making a considerable amount of new work for the storehouse, as well as building a large wrecking outfit for use on the Rocky Mountain lines. The shops are in charge of Master-Mechanic J. W. Records who has planned the arrangement of the equipment, and who is assisted by able machinists in each department.

"The machinery and erecting shop is a building 80 by 100 feet, and is fully equipped with the latest and most perfect machinery used in the building and repairing of locomotives and all classes of railroad equipment. Among the massive and intricate machinery in use in this department are 48 by 48—12 ft. planer with four heads, which is used for heavy locomotive work. This machine planes and smooths cast iron and steel for frames and driving boxes.

"For rod brasses and rod keys and for all light work there is a twenty-four inch shaper. The drill equipment consists of a four foot radial drill for heavy work, and a twenty-eight inch drill for light drilling. A two inch bolt cutter cuts and threads bolts and rods of all lengths and diameters up to two inches. A fifty-five inch boring mill is used to bore out the face of trucks and car and engine wheels. One of the most interesting pieces of machinery in the entire shop is the immense hydrostatic wheel press. The capacity of this press is three hundred tons pressure, and it is used for pressing wheels on and off axles.

"A fifty-eight inch Johnson lathe is in use for all heavier work, and a ten-inch engine lathe fitted with turret head is used for screw cutting and all fine work. A thirty-six inch combination shear and punch is also a most powerful and useful piece of machinery. The shears easily cut three to four inch boiler plate and punch will cut a round hole one inch in diameter through a piece of the best boiler plate an inch in thickness.

"In the wood-working machinery is to be found the bit which bores a square hole through wood. This is a hollow chisel mortiser and cuts a square hole up to twenty-four and a half inches in diameter as rapidly as any auger would bore a round hole. There is a thirty-six inch band saw, and a sixteen inch adjustable circular saw. The blacksmith shop is equipped with four fires, supplied with a number four blower. In this department is a 1100 pound steam hammer. The blacksmith department does all the blacksmith work for the entire line.

"The tool room is equipped with all the latest and best appliances. The boiler room is twenty-two by thirty feet and contains a 270 horsepower, high pressure boiler, which conveys power to a 60 horsepower Atlas engine, high speed.

"A 300 Franklin air compresser furnishes air for the various pneumatic tools and drills and hammer, and supplies the drop pit jacks in the machine shops and round house.

"A 'dummy' engine in use in the Koehler camp for hauling coal trains is being changed from forty inch gauge to standard, and the shops are turning out a fifteen ton derrick, which is of Mr. Record's own designing. This derrick is for general use on the Rocky Mountain route.

"The Cimarron shops are well equipped for fire protection. The water supply is derived from the Cimarron river, from hence it is pumped to large tanks upon the hill near the roundhouse. The elevation of these tanks gives a pressure of fifty-five pounds, and the water capacity is 200,000 gallons every twenty-four hours. Every part of the shops, roundhouse, stone house and the other buildings are equipped with hydrants and hose reels, of which there are a large number, each containing one hundred feet of hose, and conveniently located for use in case of emergency. There is a well trained fire department under the direction of L. A. Guley, who has trained the shopmen in the use of the fire-fighting apparatus.

"J. J. Buick, general storekeeper for the Rocky Mountain route, is in charge of the storehouse, which is a building thirty by sixty feet, and contains supplies for the operation and maintenance of the road. The people of the Master-Mechanic's department are proud of the fact that all of the road equipment of the Rocky Mountain route is in excellent condition, and can be put into service at a moment's notice. The five 90 ton Baldwin locomotives for use in freight service are proving very satisfactory."

But two railroads were not enough for the booming town. More and more attention was focused on its stragetic position:

"H. M. W. Mills, one of the leading lawyers of southern Colfax County, and for forty years a resident in that section has just returned from a trip to Guthrie (Okla.) and Oklahoma City on business. He went there in the interest of the Mountain, Valley and Plains Railroad Company which its promotors are intending to build from the town of Cimarron in Colfax County through olfax, Quay, and Union counties to the town of Higgins in the state of Kansas, on the Kansas Southern Railroad—a distance of three hundred miles,"

"Last Monday afternoon a special train over the Rocky Mountain road pulled into Cimarron with the private car of Superintendant E. J. Dedman. The special was ordered out for the accomodation of a party of officials of the Mountain, Valley and Plain Railroad Company who are now is New Mexico going over some important details incident to the work of building the proposed road—one of the men to examine the route was Frank Harrington who bears the distinction of being the man who shot the famous Black Jack Ketchum, that noted out-law, who was rounded up in Turkey Canyon just west of Cimarron some years ago."

"A corps of seven engineers and assistants in the employ of the Mountain, Valley and Plains Railroad Company, arrived in Cimarron last Friday and pitched their tents on the north side of the mesa just east of the roundhouse. Chief engineer of the road, J. H. Conlen, is preparing to make a thorough survey of the route of the new road between here and Ute Creek, about seventy miles to the east of us. He stated that the new road would come into Cimarron from Springer up the Cimarron river as nearly as possible. Before the road reaches Cimarron, however, it will run off to the northwest, leaving the river and come into the town on the northside of the mesa on which is situated the water tank of the Rocky Mountain road. Arrangements are said to be made with the Rocky Mountain road for the use of their tracks and right of way for coming into Cimarron. It is also stated that the present yards of the Rocky Mountain road will be shared with the new road, and it is probable that some arrangement for the use of the shops of the same road will be made with the new one. It is also the arrangement between the two companies that the present depot at Cimarron will be used as a union depot for the two companies until such time as the growth of Cimarron and the subsequent demands for greater and better accomodations demand the building of a new depot. With the depot of the new company identical with that of the Rocky Mountain, Cimarron will have the best depot and yard accomodations that could be wished, since the depot is located in a most convenient place already. The coming of the corps of engineers to Cimarron, following as it does the statement of President Harrington that the enterprise is already financed, makes the prospects of new railroad facilities for Cimarron in the near future very bright."

Here is an interesting timetable of the St. Louis, Rocky Mountain and Pacific Railroad:

PASSENGER SCHEDULE
In Effect June 15, 1908

No. 1 Daily		Stations		No. 2 Daily
10:00 a.m.	Lv.	DesMoines	Arr.	5:30 p.m.
2:45 p.m.	Arr.	Raton	Lv.	2:30 "
8:30 "	Lv.	Raton	Arr.	12:25 "
4:15		Preston		11:40 a.m.
4:45		Koehler		11:05
5:30		Colfax		10:15
6:35	Arr.	Cimarron		9:25
7:00	Lv.	Cimarron		7:50
7:45	Lv.	Ute Park		7:00

The coal company must have sold to the Santa Fe for later notices mention the railroad as a branch of the Santa Fe. During the recent war there was quite a controversy over the road. Evidently, the other roads were also out of existence for this was the only road mentioned. It wasn't long before the town of so many rails ended by being the town without any.

"With opposition 'reluctantly' dropped, requisitioning of rails on the Santa Fe railroad's branch line through Cimarron was under way Friday without fanfare or ceremony. Even as the work of tearing up the tracks progressed, the Office of Defense Transportation announced in Washington that due to comrplaints over the 'summary character' of government rail requisitioning, hearings would be conducted in such actions in the future.

"The thirty-mile Cimarron rail line, linking Ute Park and Koehler Junction, it was estimated, would be torn up at the rate of about a half mile a day. Mayor F. W. Haegler, who opposed the abandonment of the line, but subsequently agreed to the order requisitioning the rails for war use, informed the Assoociated Press that a suggested patroitic ceremony, not celebration, might be held.

"Mayor Haegler ordered an end to a two months battle by the citizens committee of the community opposing abandonment. The branch line is the only outlet for scores of cattleman to live-stock markets.

"The historic little rail line parallels the old Santa Fe trail which carried the first commerce westward nearly (300) (?) years ago. Ruts worn in later days by the wheels of covered wagons and stages may still be seen along the way. The village of Cimarron, only a few hundred in population, is the largest community on the line."

The people of Cimarron proved more patriotic than historic minded.

The history of every town in the West, during those pioneer days was enveloped in religion, despite saloons, mines, six-shooters and desperadoes. No matter how wild the town there was always to be found the chosen few to lead their people eventually out of the land of Canaan to adjustment. Maxwell and many of his hired hands were of the Catholic faith. The priest that attended Elizabethtown and Rayado also took care of Cimarron. The convent-bred mistress of the Mansion could not let her placita go very long without the religious administration of a padre, nor was it complete without a chapel. The first services were no doubt conducted at her own home. Later on at the Mill, finally in a private building built for the purpose. By 1875, Rev. Anton Fourchegu was installed as the first pastor of Cimarron. He was a big, heavy-set, square-jawed Frenchmen who was liked by all. He was not to remain very long because of the subsequent Maxwell Land Grant deals and the coming of the Railroads over Raton Pass. He later became Vicar-General of the Archdiocese of Santa Fe and was stationed at the cathedral. He lies buried under the main altar of the cathedral at Santa Fe.

The growth of the town furthered the need for a special chapel, consequently the new owners of the Maxwell land communicated with the Archbishop of Santa Fe, deeding over the property on which was to be built an edifice for religious worship:

"The Maxwell Land Grant Company to Archbishop John B. Lamy, as Trustee for the Catholic Church..."

"This indenture made on the 23rd day of September A. D. 1881 by and between the Maxwell Land Grant Company, a corporation duly organized, constituted, and existing under and by virtue of the laws of the Kingdom of the Netherlands and doing business with and in the Teirtory of New Mexico, pursuant to the laws of the said Territory party of the first part, and Archbishop John B. Lamy as trustee for the Catholic Church of the county of Santa Fe, in the Territory of New Mexico, party of the second part:

"Witnesseth that the said party of the first part for and in consideration of the sum of one dollar (and certain improvements to be erected as below mentioned) to it in hand paid by the party of the second part, the receipt of which is hereby acknowledged, has granted, bargained, and sold, aliened, released and conveyed, and by these presents does grant, bargain, and sell alien, remise, release, convey and confirm unto the said party of the second part, and unto his successors in trust forever, the following described lot, tract and parcel of land situated, lying and being in the County of Colfax, and Territory of New Mexico to wit:

"The whole of Block B 4 S. W. of the town plat of Cimarron, Colfax County, New Mexico. It being provided however, that a good and substantial church be built thereon within the term of three years from this date. And it is further provided and distinctly understood and agreed that the above mentioned and described premises are given for the use of and benefit of the Catholic Church to build thereon a church, school, residence of priest, or such buildings as the church may desire for its use and for no other purpose whatsoever, nor can such party of the first part be called against such block if it is used for any other than the aforesaid purpose;

"Together with all and singular the hereditaments and appurtenances thereunto belonging or in any wise appertaining, and the revision and reverious, remaining and remainders, rents issues and profits thereof, and all the right, title, interest, estate, claim and demand whatsoever of the said party of the first part, either at law or in equity of, in, and to the above granted premises with appurtenances;

To have and to hold the premises aforesaid and every part and parcel thereof, with all and singular, the rights, privileges and appurtenances, thereunto belonging in any wise appertaining unto the said party of the second part..."

So the church was built but not the priest's house nor the school for Cimarron was never destined to be a parish center. Priests from Taos, then Springer took charge of the flock. To this day Cimarron is a mission served from Springer with the Oblates of Mary Immaculate in charge.

As Padre Fourchegu was working his way from Rayado to Cimarron to serve his people, other sects were spreading from the East. This was the day of the Circuit Rider. Riding upon the wind and a prayer, into Elizabethtown rode Parson Tolby one fine day to make it his headquarters. With the American Occupation came many people of other faiths into the Land of Enchantment. In 1855, Dr. J. P. Durbin, secretary of the Missionary Society of the Methodist Episcopal Church stated in his annual report that the Society was desperately in need of a man in New Mexico. The man to answer his appeal was the Rev. Dr. Thomas Harwood. Actually, he was the first Methodist Circuit Rider in Cimarron. Rev. Tolby's murder in on the books as unsolved to this day.

"There are numerous needy frontier fields under the care of the Methodist Episcopal Church, but there are few where the task is more exacting, or where the opportunity is more alluring than here at Cimarron, in the mountains of northern New Mexico. Cimarron was one of the first places reached by a Methodist missionary when the Methodist Episcopal Church undertook its missionary work in New Mexico. For years, however, the work had been carried on in an old delapidated frame building, which was absolutely inadequate to meet the need. Last winter, (1919) as already stated, it collapsed. A few hundred feet away from the ruins stands a beautiful brick schoolhouse, but in Cimarron, and in the large territory embracing the two thousand square miles described above, there is not a Protestant church building of any sort."

Yet it was but a few years before when the church seemed to be very serviceable:

"Rev. F. J. Tolby, assassinated in Colfax County in 1875 is said to have a memorial commemorating his death. A monument in his honor will be unveiled, and the day known as Tolby Memorial Day. Toby was a missionary of the Methodist Episcopal Church and a Master Mason. On Sunday, June 29 (1913) the M. E. Church and the Masonic Lodge co-operating, will hold services in his honor. H. E. Frankenburger past master of the Masonic lodge at Cimarron will preside.

"The assassination of the Rev. Mr. Tolby on September 14, 1875 was one of the most atrocious crimes in the early history of New Mexico. The victim was shot to death on the road to Elizabethtown, the assissins having lain in wait for him. It was charged at the time that the murder was a political one as the Rev. Toby had been very outspoken in his criticism of some of the men and political leaders in the affairs of the Territory at the time. The killing created a great deal of excitement at the time in Cimarron where the dead clergyman was popular, and it was thought that the prompt leaving of the county by one or two prominent men who fled to Santa Fe, would have solved the the mystery, and it is wondered why summary vengence was not taken upon them. The church authorities and leading politicians of New Mexico did everything possible to have an investigation made but nothing was ever discovered determinating who his assssssins were. The grave of the dead missionary has ever been kept green by the Masons, and the Memorial service on June 29th will include the unveiling of a monument erected by Cimarron Lodge No. 37 A F and A M and the M. E. Church in New Mexico. It will be unveiled by M. M. Chase, master of the lodge at the time of the assassination. Rev. Dr. Thomas Harward of Albuquerque, who was then superintendant of the M. E. New Mexico Missions will be present at the exercises. The Rev. H. R. Mills is the present pastor of the Tolby Memorial Church at Cimarron." The new M. E. church that replaced the one that collapsed, retained the name of the M. E. Tolby Memorial Church.

Shrouded in mystery is the Cimarron Hermit:

"This signal light of Augustiniani, the hermit priest of Old Baldy, is seen no more, except when the El Povenir, disciples of the martyred hero, called the Brotherhood of Hermits, place a signal on some high jagged cliff overlooking the city, for the sole purpose of perpetuating the memory of this Italian Catholic priest.

"Having read of the Italian recluse, John Marie Augustiniani, who came out over the Santa Fe Trail in 1863, as a misionary among the Indians and of his signal lights, used to assist his followers in protecting themselves from the Utes, we did manifest as much interest as the tenderfoot who felt his gizzard caving in for lack of ballast as this mysterious light would loom up along the palisades of the great Cimarron canyon.

"While digging around among some old papers at Hotel Lambert we found in some worn manuscripts fragments of legendary history of this priest, and the story of his life spent in a cavern near the summit of Baldy. There is a well worn path on the very summit about which the native Indians gathered a legend of this ascetic being. The tale has been handed down until this is the path of the pious priest made as he walked to and fro in devout meditition. Midst the snows and forests of this gigantic peak, Augustianiani tramped in poius solitude, until the last tragic hour of his life in 1867, when the Utes perforated his carcass with arrows; since which time it is hoped he had prayed the rosary and built signal fires in a better land."

Very little is known about this hermit. He must have been known to Carson and Maxwell although neither one ever makes mention of him by word of mouth or by letter. He was also possibly known to the soldiers stationed at Rayado, since Cimarron was not established until after his death. Why the Utes of Cimarron killed him they have not disclosed to this day.

Many demoninations are served in Cimarron today from the surrounding cities. Springer, Raton and Taos being the towns closest to the brave mountain town.

"There has been no little revival of interest in churches and religious matters here in Cimarron during the past month. The Methodists are planning to build a church here, the Presbyterians are thinking of starting a church and holding meetings every two weeks, and now comes Rev. John A. Cutler of Raton, with a plan to start a Baptist church and congregation here in Cimarron. While nothing definate has as yet been decided upon, those of Cimarron who belong to the Baptist church, and they are not few in number, are earnestly talking of obtaining a pastorate here. It is not thought that a church will be built at once, because there are not a sufficient number to undertake so great a task. But if the plan works out properly, weekly services will begin shortly. It is not the plan of the Baptists to hold service but once every two weeks, and to have a pastor come in from the neighboring towns, but it is hoped that sufficient funds can be obtained to rent a hall for the time being and to have a resident pastor in Cimarron. The people are greatly attached to Rev. Cutler and will do everything in their power to induce him to come here and take charge of the church as soon as it becomes organized." (Cimarron Citizen June 30, 1909)

"Last Sunday evening the first services of the Baptist church recently established in Cimarron were held in the Woodmen hall of the Matkin building.

"Rev. J. A. Cutler, who recently resigned from the First Baptist church at Raton, to accept the pastorate here in Cimarron, conducted the services with his usually excellent manner. A large number of people were in attendance and there is every prospect that the new church will become a great factor for good and exert a large influence in Cimarron.

"The Raton Reporter has the following to say about Rev. Cutler:

'The Rev. J. A. Cutler preached his last sermon here on Sunday last and will devote his time hereafter to the Cimarron Baptist pastorate — the family remaining in Raton however, until October next. The reverend wishes to express his appreciation to all the people of Raton for their kindness; the Reporter wishes to express his appreciation to Rev. Cutler alike as a minister and a man. He is eloquent in the pulpit, active in his religion. He preaches and practises the cardinal command of Christ—Charity to all with malice towards none. What is Cimarron's gain is Raton's loss." (Cimarron Citizen Aug. 4, 1909)

The October papers carried no notices of the Cutler family moving to Cimarron. Nor do the Baptists receive any more write-ups which may mean that the church was not as self-supporting as first suspected. This does not reflect on the religious spirit of the people of Cimarron since many cities larger than Cimarron have been in like predicament.

No mater where you turn the pages of American history; no matter how dark the outlook, there is always the ray of sunshine that comes by way of diversion—Plymouth Rock, Valley Forge, Salt Lake City—the outlet saved minds as well as bodies. Maxwell provided most of the entertainment in those early days with his fine race horses. He was the first man to introduce throughbreds into Cimarron and New Mexico. To take care of his fine horses he built immense stables near the Manor house at Cimarron. The fame of the races spread far and wide so that soon he was matching races all over the West and as far abroad as Salt Lake City. It is related that upon one occasion Maxwell matched one of his thoroughbreds against a Texas quarter horse. Prior to the race, Cimarronians emptied their pockets on their favorite. With such large stakes, the owner of the quarter horse, who was somewhat of a gambler, approached Maxwell's jockey in an effort at bribery. When this failed he left the alternative should his quarter horse lose the race. He was quite handy with a gun. Word got around to Maxwell the evening before the race. A sport is a sport and must be accepted. Thus reasoned the Baron of Cimarron. Just before the race, noting that the gambler stood half way up the track with his forty-five cocked for action, Maxwell told his driver, who had a double wrap, to lay on the out side of the other horse. As soon as the danger zone was passed, the jockey turned his mount's head lose and rode for his life. He made the finish line several lengths ahead of the quarter horse. At the finish line Maxwell also on horseback, carbine over saddle bow waiting for an argument. Later on the jockey found out that Maxwell was out to get him if he threw the race. It seemed that both sides had a motive for murder. The jockey lived. The Don Diego preserves a painting of this episode.

The sale of the property to the Land Grant Company did not lessen the Cimarronian love for horses and horse-racing. Frank R. Sherwin carried on Maxwell's stables. He shipped in the noted sire, Uhlan by Voltigeur plus over twenty blooded mares, the horse-society or bluebloods of British racing stock. Added to this all of them were in foal to famous stallions when they reached the Cimarron stud farm. The travel and change of climate played havoc with them and only two colts survived the first year. Sherwin wasn't too lucky with his horses but the CS ranch was more succesful. From this ranch came the steeldusts so popular with the United States army and cattlemen during and after the First World War. A steeldust is a thoroughbred crossed with a mustang. Several of the Cimarron horses such as Socks, Little Joe, Kid, Donay, Chimmney Sweep, and Forever Young were nationally known.

Another favorite sport in the early days was hunting. With the government agency at Cimarron handling meat hunting to bring in the groceries was not necessary as at many frontier towns of the day. National holidays were looked forward to: "Cimarron will have a Thanksgiving festival. A very attractive program of events has been arranged consisting of a turkey shoot, a tug of war, a pony race, a broncho-busting contest, etc. Music will be furnished by the Springer band and at night a grand ball will be given."

Wedding dances, coming out parties, box suppers, church affairs, Masonic outings, all contributed to make life congenial for the community. When the railroad came in you could watch the men lay track and when the station was built you could go down and watch the people coming and going. Old timers have told me that they got quite a thrill out of that especially on Sundays. With the building of new town recreation became more diversified. Many of the town entertainments were held either at the old school or at the Aztec Mill.

"A short time ago, the 'Sporting Editor' of the *Cimarron Citizen* published an interview he had obtained from one Spickelmier, who announced that he had been for twenty two years, off and on, an old ring star, having fought under the illustrious name known to all old timers as the 4 D Kid. In this interview Spickelmier authorized the statement that he had been in training for seven weeks in preparation for a tour of the Pacific coast. He also authorized the editor to publish a challenge to any prize fighter in the Territory of New Mexico or in Colorado to meet him at any weight, at any time, and for any purse and a side bet of five hundred dollars, and our sporting editor being young and unsophisticated, made this announcement believing that the 4 D Kid meant what he said. But alas and alack. Our young affections have been trifled with and our trust in mere man has been cruelly shattered.

"Only a few days after the publication of the article, a sunny faced, breezy, good-natured chap by the name of Flannery, who looked as if he obtained his cheery smile direct from the Emerald Isle, blew off the train and into town just keen for some easy ring money. Hearing of the challenge of the 4 D Kid, he immediately offered himself up as a willing sacrifice to the prowess of the mighty Kid, and asserted that he was willing to be beaten to a pulp and carried out on a stretcher without benefit of clergy or aid of sweet faced Red Cross nurses if he could not side step fast enough and block often enough to avert the calamity. Flannery announced this willingness with a cherub smile, and it was not until the host of ardent admirers of the mighty 4 D Kid had sized up the little lump of sunshine, felt his sturdy arms and thumped his swelling chest, that they were able to worm out of him the fact that he was known as 'Red Mike' and was somewhat of a willing mixer himself. Immediately the fight promoters got busy. They felt that at last a man had been found that could cope with the wiley, shifty footed, hard hitting, machine like science of the old ring veteran, the 4 D Kid and it was anticipated that the fight would be one to long remember in Cimarron. A delegation of self-appointed sportsmen took upon themselves the duty of carrying the wonderful news to the Kid, a duty that was all the more joyful because they believed that they were in effect handing to their old favorite the neat little sum of five hundred dollars as easy money. But again, alas and alack, the man who would far rather fight a buzz saw than eat, wanted six weeks to train and this after a steady training of over eight weeks under the care of some of the best trainers in the country, who had entered Cimarron in disguise.

"With the promise that he would meet Flannery and his backers the next morning and arrange the go, the 4 D Kid took the next train out of town, accompanied by his loving spouse who stated that the Kid had never fought in the ring in his life."

'Cimarron will be again on the face of the map and will be pointed to by all sportsmen as a live and up to the minute town and dwelling place of sportsmen. Last week a subscription list was circulated among the business men of Cimarron and in a few hours over twenty-five pledged themselves to give fifty dollars for the forming of an athletic club here in Cimarron, and in consequence of this subscription list, the Cimarron Athletic Club was formed. The stone building of Fred Nacisso situated on Ninth street southwest of the new school building will be completed at once, and taken over by the club, which now holds a one year lease on the completed building, with option of two years more. The building is fifty by seventy-eight feet inside measurements, and the owner has contracted to put in a maple floor. The first floor will be used as a gymnasium and training quarters for all athletes. If the second floor is built, it will be used for a billiard room, reading rooms and assembly rooms. In the first floor, a shower bath will be installed, and the board of directors has let a contract for the installation of a light plant. It is the intention of the club to let or rent the hall out for lectures, dances and assemblies of all kinds. As the club grows, a physical director will be employed, and he will conduct classes in gymnasium work."

"Last Saturday evening at the Matkin Hall one of the best boxing matches ever held in northeastern New Mexico, was pulled off under the auspices of the Cimarron Athletic Club, the main bout being between Ev. Winters of Raton and Jimmie Burns of Cimarron. After the eleventh round both men showed great distress in wind, and in the fourteenth, both were groggy and weak. Winters however was the least affected and his longer and more thorough training stood him well in stead. Both men rushed the fight in this round and clinches were many. In this in-fighting, Winters got in a blow to the wind and another to the head that did the business, and Burns was counted out. The friends of Winters state that he broke his right hand in the second round. Whether this is true or not the fact remains that his hand was broken and that he put up a game, gritty fight at all times and won the fight fairly and squarely in spite of this great disadvantage. Burns also showed himself to be game and plucky."

The next fight was between Harry Wallace of Cimarron and Will Pettus of Albuquerque. In the fourth round Wallace had a rib broken. He lost the fight on points. Another event looked forward to was the annual St. Louis, Rocky Mountain and Pacific railroad picnic at Ute Park:

"The returns from the station agents and conductors showed that there were over thirteen hundred tickets sold for the round trips from the various towns along the line, and this does not count the railroad employees of Cimarron or Raton. It is estimated that there were fully fifteen hundred people at the event. The main event of the day of course was the big ball game between the employees of the line at Cimarron and the employees at Raton. The Gate City won by a score of eight to seven."

"Last week in Taos in the presence of nearly two thousand gathered spectators, that old veteran of the squared circle, the 4 D Kid, one of the old time favorites and one time sparring partner of more of the best men of their time than one could count on one hand, met his Waterloo. In other words, 4D Kid went up against young Sledge Hammer, better known in Cimarron as Tommy Vest, the barber, and got his, and getting it, got it right. The contest was one of two short exhibitions which were pulled off for the purpose of having a little outside amusement other than the aboriginal sports and dances of the Taos Indians. The old time favorite and veteran of many a hard fought battle, though out-weighing his opponent, by about twenty pounds, was clearly out-classed from the start. He at first waded into his lighter man intending to put him to the hay by mere weight. But Sledge-Hammer Vest side-stepped handily and sent in crushing blow after blow to the stomach and face, and before the third round was ended, the battle was easily the younger man's. The 4 D Kid seemed bewildered and dazed and seemed unable to protect himself or to cover up at all. He was unable to land on his opponent with any degree of certainty, and clearly showed that his balmy days had passed. He has stated that his age being nearly sixty years old, did not affect his ability and strength, but it is evident that he over-estimated himself, and under-estimated the effects of having been so long out of the ring. It is highly probable that this will be the last appearance of the 4 D Kid in the ring. Those who saw the contest state that the Kid must have been an extraordinary man in his prime."

"The following description of the new society game should prove of great interest to the ladies of Cimarron, and it might be well to form a club for the purpose of playing the game to the limit.

"The latest fad in society is the tub cure. In this the patient arises just as the crisp air of the morning is mellowed by the first sunbeam. An ordinary washtub is then filled with hot water, and soap suds, into which various articles of linen are thrown. After they are thoroughly saturated, the patient takes them up one at a time and rubs them briskly up and down on a washboard placed in the tub. This is kept up until the hands, face and arms are a glowing pink. The patient then goes into the open air and hangs all the linen articles on a line stretched for the purpose. The one completing the task first, announces the time to the others over the telephone, and is entitled to a prize. It is an exciting sport and also invigorating exercise.

"This interesting game can be varied and changed in form to suit the most original. Three of four of Cimarron's 'Forty' might form a team and challenge all comers. The game might be made progressive, and the first lady to finish one tub full of clothes might get a punch in her score card. At the end of a certain period, those receiving the greatest number of punches, to be awarded the prize to consist of three dozen patent clothes pins, daintily tied up with blue baby ribbon. Light refreshments can be served after the morning game, and the husbands of those present, should be invited to lend charm and joy to an otherwise pleasant occasion."

"In the near future, in about six weeks from date to be more exact, the band boys of the Cimarron Band will present to the public a 'Nigger Minstrel' show. About thirty voices will be in the chorus and these will be drilled and trained by Mr. Smith, late of Raton, but now of Cimarron, and he will give the benefit of his many years experience along that line.

"In addition to the chorus, the band boys will work up an orchestra from among their numbers, to accompany the singers, and it is planned to have the orchestra composed of not less than eight pieces. There are several old orchestral players among the members of the band. The proceeds from the minstrel show will be used for the purpose of paying off the money still due to the firm from which the band instruments were purchased. The boys are making every effort to meet this debt and at the same time to give Cimarron one of the best bands in the country, and they should be aided in every way possible by every one in Cimarron."

By 1910, the Athletic Hall was leased to stock companies and the people were able to witness such plays as "The Wolf," "The Coward." That same year the Cimarron Opera House was also inviting in stock companies for such performances as "Those Dreadful Twins," "Not a Man in the House" and others. The Matkin Hall in Cimarron was dedicated in 1907. It was built at the cost of six thousand dollars. It was forty-five by seventy-five feet, and was two stories high. It stood on the corner of Ninth Street and Washington Ave. Sam Brewer opened a billiard parlor there in the early days. Some of the first movies were shown at Aztec hall, and at the Cimarron Opera house. Today, the movies are at the Cimarron Theatre. All these are things of the past. Whether stock companies, road shows, boxing matches, polo matches, horse racing will ever return to Cimarron is a matter of conjecture. It is nice to know that this most beautifully located little city once went right along with the best of them. Somewhat the same idea the Bard of Avon once had when he wrote: " 'Tis better to have loved and lost than not to have loved at all."

"E. L. Spickelmeir has been awarded the contract for the erection of a building for the Indian school that will be erected at Taos and has left for that place to start work.

"Spickelmier is better known as the 4 D Kid, and if he can hammer nails as fast and furious as he can hammer his opponents in the squared circle, he is going some. In years past the name 4 D Kid was something that no one in ring circles sneezed at, and when his name was on the bill it was an absolute guarantee of a full house and no four-flushing. He was always making it a point in life to do what he undertook and do it well. We can therefore expect to hear in a short time that the contract has been completed and that he has come back to Cimarron to take either Strong Arm Sullivan, or Sledge Hammer Tom on for anything from a ten round boxing exhibition to a finish go.

"It is stated on good authority that he has promised either one or both these men a go, when he gets back and it is also rumored that both men are in training for the event which both are hoping will come off in the near future. It has not been made public what forfeit, if any, has been posted, but the 4 D Kid has stood ready in the past to post a $50.00 forfeit and a $500.00 side bet, and it is therefore presumed that the stakes are high. It is not thought that the principals will pull the go off in Cimarron because of the antagonism here to prize fights, which the Cimarron people have recently shown, in declaring the fights in Cimarron a thing of the past." (From the Cimarron Citizen, Oct. 27, 1909.)

When O. P. McMains was fighting the Grant people much of his time was spent in Cimarron which was the county seat when he came to New Mexico. After the removal of the seat to Springer, the town started on the downgrade which delighted the heart of the old Agitator. Promptly, he sat down and wrote a poem about it for his paper, the *Raton Comet*. In the July 21, 1882 issue he published this poem:

CIMARRON

Cimarron is nearly dead. Poor town!
She once enjoyed high renown. . . .
Too high, perhaps, for Pride, you know
That lifts one up, oft lays one low.
And Cimarron, alas! was proud.
Queenly her mien; her dress was loud,
Her airs were haughty: For you see,
Nobility's spoiled pet was she;
England's royal sons, whose hair
Was in the middle parted; fair,
Brave, jolly men; gallant knights
In whom fond woman's soul delights
With money—Who can say how much?
And all borrowed from the simple Dutch!
Now these courted Cimarron, the Fair.
They praised her eyes; admired her hair
And made her queen of all the land for
    miles and miles and miles around
An empire vast; and with the sound
Of boisterous mirth, they drank her health.
A bounteous feast would daily spread
Of precious plate, while rudy wine
In silver goblets flamed. 'Twas fine—
Too fine—too utterly too, too.
For all this wealth—I told you true,
With which fair Cimarron they crowned,
Was borrowed; and the very ground
Of her vast empire stolen! So,
When borrowed pelf is spent you know
The jig is up, the Queen is down—
Alas, poor Queen, alas poor Town!
Tis many years since then and now.
Gloom dwells upon her "Doby" brow
Her dress is ancient, shabby, torn;
And there she sits—a poor old crone
Who once in wealth's proud splendor shone.
Forlorn, distressed, used up, played out
While ghostly objects flit about

The fallen fair. Alas, dear me
That such outlandish things can be
And overcome us like a cloud
But, then you know, the queen was proud!

Item—December 4, 1904—Raton Range: "We got to Cimarron in the pouring rain and put up at the local hotel, a reminder of other days, with its spacious rooms, especially the dining room. Then there were the marble washstands and mantle pieces and coal grates in all of the rooms. We also found hot and cold water. The house was built at a tremendous cost in 1880, and has made a fortune for its owner. But today, alas, its glory has passed. Only an occasional passer by stops there as we did." (Quoted by the Will C. Barnes party from Chicago.)

Item—Raton Range June 7, 1907: "Cimarron chosen in 1907 as headquarters for the St. Louis, Rocky Mountain and Pacific Railroad which will there locate its shops. Work of construction is also going on for the shops of the Cimarron and Northwestern Railroad which has its terminal at Cimarron. Cimarron has an unusual number of health-seekers and people of leisure intent upon investment and homebuilding."

Item—Cimarron in northern New Mexico seems to be the place where the first public library was established in the Territory. The date is 1881. Frank R. Sherwin, manager of the Maxwell Land Grant Company, is credited with the founding of the library, and Col. W. H. Reynolds, a director of the Land Grant company was the donor of five thousand dollars and many books from his own private collection for the purpose. Mrs. E. L. Sheldon had charge of the selection of the first books for the library, and she was the first librarian.

Item—Feb. 8, 1886—Harry Whigham acting for the Maxwell Land Grant, leases the Aztec flour mill in the town of Cimarron, together with the ditch rights for the same, and other appurtenances therein belonging for one year, commencing Feb. 8, 1888. This lease is granted upon the express condition that the party of the second part will keep sober and attend his business and that should he become intoxicated, or under the influence of liquor, then his lease shall be void from such time and the same if the rent has not been paid. (signed) George Grubble
Harry Whigham
(receiver)

Item—"Swink's Gambling Hall, now adjoining the Canyon Lunch on the north and used as a garage, was a notorious gambling place, built in 1854 (?) where congregated the sporting elements of those days; the cowboys and the miners and the gun-toting bad men of the region. Piles of money are said to have exchanged hands at the games of Faro, Keno and Roulette, and on one occasion at the insistence of some holdup gang."

Item—July 1922 "Then there came upon the scene Jerome B. Chaffee, who had for years been a congressman from Colorado. He, with associates, secured a bond on the Maxwell Land Grant for $650,000, with reservation of the Maxwell ranch house. He took into his confidence Wilson Waddingham, a bartender from San Francisco. They made maps showing the steam ships running up the Cimarron river, loading and unloading immense cargoes of cattle, sheep and other products of the great estate. They took the twelve dollars, three hundred foot square mining leases that never had paid a cent of rent, figured them up, put a fabulous return on the Aztec, also making out Maxwell out a billion dollars a year income in order to promote their scheme."

Item—Raton Reporter—Feb. 4, 1939—"As a matter of record, the second house in Cimarron was built in 1848-1849. It has been destroyed by fire in 1939. The house now known as the James Lail home in Cimarron caught on fire from a defective flue which did to the old building what time was not able to do. The house was built by Mr. W. R. Whiteman, who came across the plains in 1848 (author's note: His daughter told me he did not come to the Cimarron country until 1857) and built this place as a freighting depot for the Andres Daw stage line. Trips were made twice a year from West Point (Kansas City) to Cimarron. (Note—Possibly for Indian trade—there were no settlers in Cimarron at the time and Maxwell was still at Rayado. The government was stringing out forts near Mora, Wagonmound, Taos, Questa, Rayado at the time—perhaps this is the reason why the stage lines came in.)

"It is believed and told by oldtime residents that the Gonzolez house on the hill, opposite was the first house to be built in Cimarron. The famous old house which recently burnt contained fifteen rooms and had been used as a government forage station, a postoffice, grocery store and many things besides a freighting station. During the early days it also served as an inn where chili, beans, tortillas, goat meat and coffee refreshed weary travellers who stopped there.

"About 1876, the building was used as a newspaper office housing the *Cimarron News and Press*. The construction of the edifice was adobe with hand hewn shingles. It is mentioned in the book: *Fighting Caravan*, a story by Zane Grey and was a famous landmark in the early days of northern New Mexico."

Item—"In the fall of 1875, a newspaper was started in Cimarron called the *News and Press*. It was published by Whigham and Henderson in the county seat of Colfax County (Cimarron) and the editors pledged themselves to give the readers unbiased reports on all the news items of the city, county and territory. They called it the liveliest and spiciest paper in all New Mexico. It was printed in a building on the northeast corner of the public square of Cimarron. It was printed in English and they also published a Spanish edition. An interesting item in a paper printed in 1878 states that another edition would not be forthcoming until the editors could give the readers a report on the county and territorial elections. Special arrangements had been made to get the territorial reports by telegraph."

Item—"In 1936 one found the following hotels in Cimarron: The Swastica, the Antlers, the Don Diego. This last was originally known as the St. James but the name was changed to the Don Diego in the erronious opinion that it was Spanish for St. James. It had forty rooms. Sixteen of these are rented and the rest are used by the Haegler family, the present owners and managers. They have six rooms, with private bath and hot and cold running water. The Swastica hotel in new town has ten rooms, four of which have a private bath. The Antlers hotel, also in new town, has eight rooms.

"The Canyon Lunch managed by Fred Lambert, the son of Henry Lambert, who built the St. James hotel, served as deputy county sheriff for twenty-two years. He spent four years in the Indian service in charge of liquor traffic, seven years with the New Mexico Cattle Sanitary Board as Inspector, three years in charge of Ojo del Espiritu Santo a 300,000 acre land grant. He was nicknamed Cyclone Dick by Buffalo Bill on the night of his birth because at that time a cyclonic wind was blowing, and Buffalo Bill was at Henry Lambert's place at the time. Fred is a writer, poet and author of several books."

Item—"At one time Cimarron had 15 saloons, 4 hotels and a number of business houses within a radius of four blocks. The depression and fires destroyed five business blocks in new town and one block in old town and adversely affected all businesses until 1933 when an attempt was made to establish a polo field and race horse stables within the village limits. Near here Buffalo Bill organized his famous Wild West show. It seems that Cimarron had an entrancing fascination for this famous character that brought him here very often. It was his delight to spend Christmas day here, whenever possible, and give a Christmas party to the children in the dining room of the old St. James hotel, on an occasion giving them as presents, plush-seated tricycles which some of them still cherish as mementos from the old scout."

Item—"The Maverick Club, Inc., was organized in August 1922 by a group of public spirited men led by Rev. G. B. Traveller and Stuart Webster. It is a non-political and non-sectarian organization; in fact the membership includes one Catholic priest, and two Protestant ministers. The objectives are Civic Good Felowship and Education.

"The name 'Maverick' was suggested by a man who now resides in Santa Fe, George E. Remley. The first president was Stuart Webster, who was president from 1922 to 1924. Mr. John J. Nairn was then elected president and has served continuously since. The Club is nationally and internationally known and we have had as guests some prominent people from all over the world. The present officers are John J. Nairn—president—Dr. C. R. Bass and E. G. Haywood—vise-presidents, J. F. Kilbridge—sec'y-treasurer—Herbert E. Coulter—chairman, W. J. Atha and Fred Brooks—Program Committee. The first Rodeo was held July 4, 1924 and it is now an annual affair. The club owns the grounds which were given them by Waite Phillips." *(Letter to the Raton Range dated June 25, 1936.)*

Four miles southwest of Cimarron, one comes upon thirteen hundred acres of the finest farm in the district. Two apple orchards in 1907, produced some of the finest apples this side of the Rockies. That year this farm produced some two hundred and fifty bushels of hay, four hundred bushels of corn, much wheat, barley, and vegetables which were sent to Cimarron daily during the summer months for public consumption. Also familiar to Cimarronians were the milk cans from this farm that kept them supplied with this most necessary nourishment. Added to the value of the farm was the running water, and a large reservoir filled with water near the barns and corrals; two hundred head of cattle; any number of hogs, geese, ducks, chickens, turkeys, hens and other barnyard stock. Connected with the farm were at least four thousand acres of pasture land. Some of the finest horses and mules were raised on this farm. The mansion house was a two-story adobe structure with many and spacious rooms. Nearby were the barns, wagon and tool houses, creamery, out buildings and store rooms. The owner of this little paradise was one Mathias Heck, born in Cologne, Germany, on June 19, 1829. He found his way to the United States in 1844. He lived in several states, arriving in New Mexico in 1862. He served in the Civil War as a member of Co. K—First Cavalry. Was honorably discharged at Santa Fe in July 1866. In 1867 he worked at the mines at Elizabethtown. From there he went to Ocate where he spent nine years in keeping a hotel and mercantile business. He located at his present farm near Cimarron in 1878. In 1867, he married Margaret Blum of Moore, New Mexico. Of this union were born Theodore, John Mathias, jr., Pauline and Katie. He died on June 15, 1909. His grave is to be found in the old cemetery at Cimarron. *(See: Cimarron Citizen, June 16, 1909.)*

"I was just a little girl, only four years old at the time. My grandfather had me on his knee. Suddenly, there was a knock at the door and a tall, well-built man, with the bluest eyes I have ever yet seen came into the room. My grandfather introduced me to him. His name was Clay Allison. My grandfather's name was Thomas O. Boggs." Thus spoke Mrs. M. Heck as she recounted her experiences of early days at Cimarron.

Thomas Boggs was born at Harmony Mission in the Indian Territory in August 1824. He was the son of Governor Boggs of Missouri. At twenty-one, Tom, as he was affectionately called, was with the Mountain Men at Taos. He served as scout and guide with the Fremont expedition, and was an intimate friend of Kit Carson. They were together in many hair-raising and breath-taking escapades. Their friendship lasted till Carson's death when Boggs took upon himself the rearing of his friend's children.

When Boggs settled down in Cimarron he took up with Maxwell where he left off with Carson. Giving up fur trapping he went into the sheep raising business, his wool product bringing him as much as $40,000 in a single year. He married Ronalda Luna of Taos. Boggs was not as fortunate as some in business and later trouble with the Maxwell Land Grant caused him to move on. He settled for a while at Raton, Springer and Clayton. He also lived in Colorado for a number of years.

M. M. Chase, a rancher at Cimarron was born in Wisconsin in 1842. When fifteen years of age he decided to strike out for California. Indians attacked the train he was with, and he was one of the fortunate nine to escape. Chase returned to the middle west until 1860. He then went to Colorado and opened up a meat business. After a half-hearted attempt at mining near what was later to become Central City, he made a contract with the government to supply meat for the troops. This brought him to New Mexico in time, and after the war, he continued his interest in cattle. He purchased a ranch and located on the Vermejo river. Because of Indians, he gave up his ranch to locate at the old Carson place. In Central City he had married Theresa M. Wade. Interested in what the Maxwell Land Grant had to offer he purchased almost a thousand acres of land from them, later adding about another thousand. He started his famous orchard in 1873.

One time when he was in Pecos on a cattle deal, he received word that the Ute and Apache Indians living on the reservation at Cimarron had surrounded the town and were on the warpath because of rations. He was told to return to Cimarron in a covered wagon and to be on the lookout for serious trouble. The matter was settled without his having to lose his scalp.

Albert William Vasev, the cashier of the First National Bank of Cimarron (an institution of the past) did more than any man to make the bank a success. He was born in Illinois in 1876. He married Maude Batterton Kilgore. About the turn of the century he moved to New Mexico, becoming cashier at the bank of Cimarron in 1911.

Albert E. Schroeder, owner and publisher of the Cimarron Citizen was born in Minnesota in 1887. He married Erma Weber in 1912. Coming to New Mexico he was determined to make a success of his newspaper. He would have but Cimarron again struck an hiatus and the paper folded up.

Louis A. Chandler, owner of a large ranch near Cimarron was once postmaster of the town by appointment from President Wilson. He was one of the few famous Cimarronians born in New Mexico. Married to Elizabeth Vance, he started out at an early age to make his own way in life. He was always systematic about his work which accounts for his success as a rancher and postmaster.

Dr. H. B. Masten came to Cimarron as a result of the ill health of his wife. He was known for his pamphlets on consumptives. Well liked and long remembered in Cimarron.

Abe Hixenbaugh like his brother John served for a time as sheriff of Colfax county. He was born in Iowa on Oct. 24, 1867. He married Nona Neff of Raton on August 1, 1890. Hixenbaugh is well known and liked in Cimarron.

William F. Cody (Buffalo Bill) was another outsider who adopted, for a time at least, Cimarron as his home. He was born in Iowa in 1845. When not quite seven his father moved to Kansas where he was killed in the Kansas war. William took on his responsibilities towards the family. He became a pony express rider at the tender age of fourteen. He was known to Carson and to Maxwell. It was Buffalo Bill who named Lambert's son Cyclone, because of the heavy wind that was blowing at the time of his birth. It was at Cimarron that he signed the contract that inaugurated the Wild West show that was to make him internationally famous.

William Ray Morley had everything to live for when he was accidently shot in Las Vegas in 1883. He recogniezd the opportunities at Cimarron enough to be with the Maxwell Land Grant people; to publish the *Cimarron News and Press* and to win the fight for the Santa Fe railroad that brought that line the right of way over the Raton Pass into New Mexico. His life at Cimarron was thrilling enough to make a novel. Too bad his daughter doesn't give him more space in her book, *No Life for a Lady*. But then she hardly knew him. His candle was snuffed out when she was but a little girl.

Of the internationally known figures that filled out the scene at Cimarron, the most widely known and admired was Frank Springer. He was born in Iowa on June 17, 1848. He graduated from the University of Iowa in 1867. He arrived in Cimarron in 1873 where he published the *Cimarron News and Press* as well as being attorney for the Maxwell Land Grant people. At Cimarron he married Josephine M. Bishop in 1876. Not many years later he moved to Las Vegas. His work in Paleontology brought him a degree from George Washington University as well as one from the University of Bonn, Germany. With his equally distinguished brother Charles, he built the Eagle's Nest Dam near Cimarron, which is a fisherman's paradise to this day. These brothers were also responsible for the government of the Maxwell Land Grant as well as for the St. Louis, Rocky Mountain and Pacific Railroad. Together they developed the coal mining and other resources of the region; they helped to enrich Colfax county to the extent that it was known for a time as "The Kingdom of Colfax." Frank Springer was also responsible for the American School of Research at Santa Fe as well as for the Governor's Palace being turned into a museum. When the new state building was built it looked as if the ancient historical Palace would be torn down, but Dr. Springer saved it for New Mexico and the generations to come. Of that Cimarronians may be justly proud. Charles Springer did equally as much for the state and both brothers are enshrined in the hearts of the people of Cimarron.

Last, but by no means least, the Crockers. The Crocker store, like Carey's hardware business, was a landmark in Cimarron. George Crocker was in Cimarron when the Maxwell Land Grant war was on as well as in six-shooter days. He knew Maxwell, Sherwin, Whigham, Morris, Crockett, Whiteman and a host of others, and cherishes the memory of things past at his home in Sandoval, near Albuquerque.

Whiteman came before Cimarron was a place. He knew the Utes and Apaches before they had trouble with the government. Crocker and Whiteman between them could be interesting enough to fill a book larger than all the New York telephone directories put together. As these pioneers go to their rest part of the old West goes with them. This will be the last generation to hear from their lips the tales of Allison, Maxwell, Springer, Carson and old Cimarron.

Chapter Six

INDIANS ON THE GRANT

In the Raton Daily Range for January 4, 1907, appeared an article, little noted, but of interest to the story of the Maxwell Land Grant. Unsigned, it was evidently written by J. R. Foster, the editor:

At the time of the first appearance of Europeans in New Mexico, the territory was but thinly inhabited. The total number of Indians dwelling in or roaming over the region now included in New Mexico were supposed to be less than seventy thousand. Of these about twenty-five thousand were sedentary Indians or Pueblos, leaving about forty-five thousand of what may be called the wild Indians. These were divided into several tribes or bands but our attention is directed to but two—the Utes and the Apaches —because they alone inhabited that part of the territory now known as the Maxwell Land Grant.

The Apaches numbered between seven hundred and fifty to a thousand; the Utes were twice that number. They lived in tents which were pitched on or near the banks of all the streams on the Red River at the north to the Rayado on the south. Most of the time they camped in and around Ute Park and Cimarron on the banks of the river by that name. These tents were covered with buffalo and other wild animal skins at first, but later on the government issued to them regular army tents made of cotton duck.

In the beginning the Indians used the bow and arrow in their hunting expeditions, but later on they came into possession of guns and ammunition, either by purchase, gift or stealth, usually the latter. They never cultivated the soil, so they lived on fish, game and beeves. Maxwell, under contract with the Indian Department, furnished beeves to the Ute nation, the issue of which was made weekly from his own vast herds. The cattle, as wild as those from the Texas prairies, were driven by his herders into an immense enclosed field and there turned loose to be slaughtered by the savages. Colonel Inman, of the United States Army, gives a very graphic and interesting account of one of these slaughters in which he was an eye witness, in the following language: "Once when at his ranch, I told Maxwell that I would like to have a horse to witness the novel sight. He immediately ordered a Mexican groom to procure one; but I did not see the peculiar smile that lighted up his face as he whispered something to the man which I did not catch. Presently the groom returned leading a magnificent gray, which I mounted. Maxwell suggested that I should ride down to the large field and wait there until the herd arrived. I entered the great corral, patting my horse on the neck now and then, to make him familiar with my touch, and attempted to converse with some of the chiefs, who were dressed in their best, painted as if for war; gaily bedecked with feathers and armed with rifles and gaudily appointed bows and arrows, but I did not succeed very well in drawing them from their normal reticense. The squaws, a hundred of them, were sitting on the ground, their knives in hand ready for the labor which is the fate of their sex in all savage tribes, while their lord's portion of the impending business was to end with the more manly efforts of the chase.

"Suddenly a great cloud of dust rose on the trail from the mountain, and on came the maddened animals, fairly shaking the earth with their mighty tread. As soon as the gate was closed behind them, uttering a characteristic yell that was blood-curdling in its ferocity, the Indians charged upon the now doubly frightened herd, and commenced to discharge their rifles, regardless of the presence of anyone but themselves. My horse became paralyzed for an instant and stood poised on his hind legs, like the steed represented in that old lithographic print of Napoleon crossing the Alps, then taking the bit in his teeth, he rushed aimlessly into the midst of the flying herd; while the bullets from the guns of the excited savages rained around my head. I had always boasted of my equestrian accomplishments. I was never thrown but once in my life, and that was years afterwards. But in this instance it taxed all my powers to keep my seat. In less than twenty minutes the last beef had fallen, and the warriors, inflated with the pride of their achievement, rode silently out of the field, leaving the squaws to cut up and carry away the meat to their lodges, more than three miles distant, which they soon accomplished to the last quivering morsel. As I rode leisurely back to the house, I saw Maxwell and Carson standing on the porch, their sides actually shaking with laughter at my discomfiture, they having watched me from the moment the herd entered the corral. It appeared that the horse that Maxwell ordered the groom to bring me was a recent importation from St. Louis, and had never before seen an Indian and was as unused to the prairies and mountains as a street-car mule. Kit said that my mount reminded him of one that his antagonist in a duel rode a great many years ago when he was young. If the animal had not been such a Fourth of July brute, his opponent would in all probability have finished him, as he was a splendid shot, but Kit fortunately escaped, the bullet merely grazing him under the ear, leaving a scar which he then showed me."

The headquarters of the Ute Agency were established at the Maxwell ranch in the early days and the government detailed a company of cavalry to camp there more however, to impress the plains tribes who roamed along the old trail east of the Raton range, than for any effect on the Utes, whom Maxwell could always control and who regarded him as a father. During the later Sixties, efforts were made to remove the Utes from the territory. A treaty was made to that effect in 1868, but the Utes refused to go, and nothing was accomplished except the moving of the agency to Tierra Amarilla. Another treaty was made in 1873, but it was not until 1878 that the authorities succeeded in removing the Utes to their new reservation in Colorado, with which removal they disappear as a tribe in New Mexico history.

The Apaches have likewise had a checkered history. They claimed ownership in the Maxwell Ranch, and when it was sold there was considerable difficulty in satisfying them. The Cimarron Agency was sold in 1872 and an effort made to remove the Indians to Fort Stanton. Not being content with their Fort Stanton home, it was only a few years when the authorities were convinced that a new reservation on the Rio Navajo in Rio Arriba county would be a much better place for them, and they were accordingly moved there, where they have since lived. The baskets made and the blankets wove by the Indians living on the Maxwell Land Grant were very beautiful and of great variety. With few exceptions the baskets and blankets were made by women.

The physical characteristics of the Indians who once inhabited these parts were as follows: A square head with a low but broad forehead, full face and powerful jaw, cheek-bones prominent, lips thick, eyes dark and deeply set; hair long, not absolutely straight but wavy, something like a horse's mane, and like that of a glossy hue; little or no beard; color of skin reddish copper; height of men about the average (5 ft. 8 in.) but looking taller from their erect posture and slender figure; the women rather shorter (5 ft. 2 in.) and many of them with symmetrical figure and pleasing countenance; hands and feet of both men and women small. For the most part the Indians have vanished away and left scarcely a sign of their presence behind them. Along the banks of the streams are found heaps of shells and it is quite common to pick up arrowheads and many rude implements of war. (End of article.)

There is no doubt in anybody's mind that Maxwell got along with the Indians. He was their bread basket. The sale of the Grant was a bombshell for them. It meant work or starve. All the time they thought that they were the ones making the concession in permitting Maxwell to build and live on their land.

General Kearny took upon himself the moral obligation of filling in the necessary positions for governing the newly acquired territory to be held by men whom he found best suited, only after much consultation and deliberation, since he was under orders to continue his march of conquest to California. The office of governor fell to Charles Bent who wrote a letter to the Honorable William Medill, Commissioner of and Affairs at Washington, D. C. (November 10, 1846), informing him that he was the general's choice, and by virtue of his position he felt that he was also the Ex-Officio superintendent of Indian affairs for the Territory of New Mexico, giving in his letter an account of the Indians under his jurisdiction:

"First: I will mention the Apaches or Jicarillas of about one hundred lodges or about five hundred souls. The Jicarillas have no permanent address, but roam through the northern settlements of New Mexico. They are an indolent and cowardly people living principally by theft committed on the New Mexicans, there being but little game in the country through which they range, and their fear of other Indians not permitting them to venture upon the plains for buffalo. Their only attempt at manufacture is a species of potter ware, capable of tolerable resistance to fire, and much used by them and the Mexicans for culinary purposes. This they barter with the Mexicans for the necessaries of life, but in such small quantities as scarcely to deserve the name of traffic. The predatory habits of these Indians render them a great annoyance to the Mexicans.

"Second: The Apaches proper who range through the southern portion of this Territory, through the country of the Rio Del Norte, and its tributaries, and westward about the headwaters of the Gila River. They are a warlike people, and are about nine hundred lodges and from 5,000 to 6,000 souls; they know nothing of agriculture or manufacture of any kind but live most entirely by plundering the Mexican settlements. For many years past they have been in the habit of committing constant depredations upon the lives and property of the inhabitants of this and adjoining territories and states from which they have carried off an incredible amount of stock of all kinds. The only article fo food that grows in their general range is the Maguey and that spontaneously and in very small quantities."

Medill felt that his authority was imposed upon and that Bent had no right over the Indians who were Federal wards. He did some appointing of his own. He hunted up James S. Calhoun, one of Georgia's self-made men. He was owner or part owner of several large vessels shipping out of Savannah and the senior partner in the shipping firm of Calhoun and Bass of Columbus, Georgia. Calhoun was a Whig whose constant talk centered about the exploits of General Zachary Taylor. During the Mexican war Calhoun rendered personal service as captain of a company of Georgia volunteers. Medill, knowing of Calhoun's attachment for the now President Taylor, made, in his estimation, a wise political move in appointing Calhoun as the government's first official Indian Agent from Washington to Santa Fe. The Indian Office was quite evidently at a loss as to just how the Indians of the Southwest were to be taken care of.

Calhoun was quite intelligent and sincerely desirous of helping the Indians. But he found out that "the canyons and valleys of the Red River (Cimarron) afford the usual route through which these Indians pass a very considerable distance in making for the Rio Del Norte (Rio Grande), cross it, and push on to or near the boundary line between the United States and Mexico, ready to rest for a time on the discreet side of it." The Indian Agent was also aware that the Pueblos were a full time job and the Utes and

Apaches of the Cimarron area should have an agent of their own.

Just when the Indians got wind of Beaubien and Miranda's petition is a matter of conjecture. Both were connected with the American Fur Company, enlisting Indian aid in setting traps and bartering for furs. Whatever their claims, the Indians made it plain that the land actually belonged to them. Kicked like a football between Grant owners and the Government, the Jicarillas and Utes (Muache Tribe) insisted that the section they inhabited rightfully belonged to them. They considered Taos their headquarters either because it was the only adobe Indian village in Northern New Mexico of any importance, or because it offered better trading opportunities than Fort Bent, Colorado. Furthermore, a government agency was established at Taos. While the Indians were getting acquainted with the new agencies, Maxwell and Carson took their sheep to California to bring back some of the California gold everybody was going West to obtain. By 1858 Maxwell moved into his home at Cimarron which was to be the headquarters and general hang-out of practically every Indian in the area. Maxwell encouraged the pottery making spoken of by Bent in his letter as well as basket weaving.

Calhoun was soon appointed the first governmental head of the territory, leaving the cares of his former office to another. Superintendent Norton, looking for the cheapest food to give the Indians, consulted Maxwell who was ever ready to turn a dollar. As a consequence, Maxwell became agent for the Indians pocketing the contract that called for feeding the Indians on the Grant at a maximum cost of five hundred dollars a month. A governmental agency warehouse was re-constructed from the stage-coach forage station and warehouse in addition to some other outhouses. The Commissioner of Indian Affairs took exception to Norton's action writing: "Experience has demonstrated that so long as Indians are fed at public expense they will make little or no effort to sustain themselves. Besides, it has not been, and cannot be, the policy of the Department to subsist Indians whose habits are nomadic and whose hunting grounds are unlimited." From the headquarters of the detachment of the First Dragoons stationed at Taos, Lieutenant-Colonel B. L. Beall wrote to his commanding officer at Santa Fe, on March 13, 1850:

"It is well known to you that there is a large party of the Utah tribe, with whom peace has never been made. These Indians have been and still are in the vicinity of Red River, doubtful as yet of the policy of the government toward them. As these Indians are actually, and consider themselves, at war with us, although no hostile demonstrations have been made by them, it is evident that all trading with them must be unlawful and injurious to the interests of the United States. A few days ago I received authentic information that two Frenchmen named Lacombe, of Arroyo Hondo, had gone out to these Utahs taking with them many contraband articles of traffic such as flints, knives, etc. Accordingly acting on the above views, I immediately sent an order to arrest them and bring them before me. They themselves stated that they had a license to trade, and were also invested by the Governor with powers to make peace if they saw fit. This seeming so absurd (as in the case of their ever receiving a license to trade I would have been informed of it) and knowing well that they were men utterly devoid of all character and principle (having been punished for the same offense before) I have acted as above stated, and when they shall be apprehended, will treat them according to their just desserts." Three months later, Calhoun wrote:

"There are, doubtless, quite a number of Utahs who roam with the Apache band, known as Jicarillas, and aid and share in all murders and depredations. In this opinion I am sustained by the military authorities of Abiquiu and Taos, and by the entire Mexican population at and near the former place.

"General Choice also, informs me, the Chiefs seemed to care for no other purchases but powder, and he thinks that the Mexicans supplied them to a limited extent. The Indians said, that without powder they had no way in which to hunt and procure meat and suffering the want of this article they would all starve. The Chiefs expressed great anxiety for the immediate establishment of one or more trading posts.

"I am decidedly of the opinion this is a favorable moment to dispose of the Utahs. They could now be located within certain fixed limits, and by selection of a suitable military post, and establishing there a trading point their well being would be promoted, other tribes could be prevented from making them visits that smack of bloodshed, and their entire submission secured. But to accomplish these results troops, and additional troops are necessary in this territory.

"Since it has ever been the policy of our Government to form treaties with Indian tribes, I give it my opinion, that the two treaties one with the Navajos and the other with the Utahs should be ratified, and the two tribes compelled to comply with the stipulations contained therein.

"In relation to the Navajos, it is proper to mention, they have been committing numerous depredations, and some murders, and carrying off captives during the past week. These Indians ought, and must be, chastised before they will submit to a proper subjection." Troops were maintained at Rayado and later on at Fort Union and Maxwell's ranch.

Norton's position was uncomfortable to say the least. On the one hand Indians demanding food; on the other the influx of ranchers and settlers who set up a constant hue and cry that their cattle and goods were daily being raided, stolen and destroyed. Within one month of Cooley's rebuke, a Ute Indian, deciding that honesty might work, begged, rather than stole a sheep from one of the settlers. Chagrined at the blunt refusal and an order to leave the property at once, he retaliated. Abusive words followed, culminating in gun-play at which the rancher had the better hand, leaving the Indian dead on the spot. War drums and smoke signals. The killer was taken under escort to Fort Union for safety until a proper trial could be had. A kinsman of the deceased Indian demanded the custody of the settler or he would collect every tribesman on the Grant and attack the fort. The commander of the fort insisted that it would be better to take the prisoner to Mora, then the county seat, and have a jury there decide the case. The evidence introduced to the court at Mora seemed insufficient for indictment, so the dispute was carried to Santa Fe where Norton paid the relative four hundred dollars to be distributed among the other relatives of the deceased. It averted a war. Norton's thanks was another rebuke from Cooley for giving money without the sanction of the proper authorities as well as the threat of cutting off Maxwell's five hundred dollars a month.

Into the picture stepped General James H. Carleton, commanding officer in charge of Headquarters of the Department of New Mexico at Santa Fe. He was keenly aware of the necessity of feeding the Indians in order to keep them from depredating and from joining forces with the Southern Apaches and Navajos. Rations were preferable to war. Lieutenant George I. Campbell was stationed at Cimarron with a detachment of troops because the Indians were becoming unruly even for Lucien Maxwell in whom they had unbounded trust and confidence. Carleton sent word through the lieutenant that the slightest hostility would mean an end to the food supply. Each Indian received one-half pound of beef and one-half of wheat meal per day. The cost was $3,000 a month. This was one thousand dollars more than Norton had in mind. Carleton declared that it was not the task of the United States army to manager the Indians but an official Indian agent should be appointed. Erasmus B. Dennison arrived at Cimarron during the month of November and war rumors ceased.

Norton sought to break up the Jicarillas and Utes at Cimarron. Placed on reservations out of his jurisdiction he would not be called upon to answer to Washington if they revolted. He advanced the idea of purchasing the Maxwell property when he was fatalist enough to admit that no amount of persuasion would cause them to leave Maxwell's protection at Cimarron:

"I would respectfully recommend, in behalf of these Indians, the purchase of the Maxwell Grant and in less than one year they would be self-sustaining. There is no avoiding the issue. It is useless to talk of moving them elsewhere for they would resist to the last extremity thus costing the government four times the amount of the cost of the Grant. Two hundred and fifty thousand dollars would be spent in less than one year in fighting to remove them, to say nothing of the loss of life. This is a tract of land forty miles by sixty and containing about 1,500,000 acres. (This seems to indicate that Maxwell was aware of the extent of his property despite McMains and others afterwards who maintained that Maxwell had no idea of the extent of his domain.) There are from 3,000 to 5,000 acres now under cultivation, well watered, with a good system of irrigation, good stone water mill costing $50,000.00, a good saw-mill and barn which cost $10,000.00, a good dwelling, storehouse, and other out buildings suitable for agency purposes, good water and abundant, and wood and timber enough to last many years."

Carson paid a visit to Maxwell sometime before this correspondence and they decided that one answer for activity among the Indians and a safeguard for the Whites, was for the Jicarillas and Utes to smear on their war-paint, gather up their rifles and march against the Kiowas and Comanches. Maxwell would supply the meat and foodstuffs at government expense. Carson would help with guns, shirts, ammunition, and blankets. The result of their action was the battle of Adobe Walls. This was the first concentration of the forces from Cimarron within the memory of the oldest living Indian. On the eve of the battle Carson was kept awake for a time by the war whoops of the two tribes, but after a time it became a lullabye that soothed him to sleep. When the Utahs and Jicarillas found out that they were within hailing distance of the enemy, they discarded their buffalo robes, dived naked into the river in the hopes of cutting away the Comanche horse-herd. They were successful to the extent that there remained hardly a Ute or Jicarilla who was not mounted. They were not above an animated exhibition of horsemanship and bravado in front of the enemy lines. Carson was a little pained that the Utes stooped to killing the Kiowa women found in the village attacked. He proved himself in the retreat before superior numbers after a decisive defeat. It was a victory of which Maxwell was never to hear the end as he distributed supplies at the agency in Cimarron.

Returned to their old stomping ground at Cimarron, the Utes and Jicarillas presented the old problem of rations. A special agent was dispatched with instructions to ship the Apaches to the San Luis Valley, but they could not be moved, offering however, the hope that they would accept a permanent location in New Mexico if offered them, and it suited their tastes. At the end of 1868, the army ceased feeding the Utahs and Apaches, the government separating the former for removal to Colorado even going so far as to discontinue their supplies. In January 1869, when they returned from the winter hunt, they were made aware of the government's attitude but retaliated by killing cattle and molesting the settlers along the Cimarron. Walker, Pope and others agreed that they would have to be removed by military force. The press took up the cry of scalping and raids as a result of the action, but the Agent at Cimarron was of the opinion that the press was unduly exaggerating the outbreak. Nevertheless, General Getty stationed one hundred men at Cimarron. Erasmus B. Dennison was removed as Indian Agent on the charge of habitual drunkenness, being replaced by Charles F. Roedel in December on the recommendation of the Presbyterian board. Not all superintendents looked upon the Indians as a nuisance at Cimarron:

"I do not think the Indians in and surrounding New Mexico are so lazy and indolent as tribes nearer here and bordering upon our own civilization. After they are once reduced to a proper subjugation and made to feel the strength and power of our government and afterwards experience its clemency and kindness, I am of the opinion that they can easily be induced to adopt an agricultural life, that they will prove to be very tractable, and under the guidance of discreet and worthy agents we may yet see some of their rich mountain valleys teeming with the produce of a laborious cultivation. The Spaniards reclaimed from savage life all our Pueblos and made them industrious and honest cultivators of the soil. In a short time we might expect to succeed as well with several of the wild tribes surrounding New Mexico.

"I think there should be appointed at least five agents for the five following tribes: Comanches, Southern Apaches (Mescaleros), Navajos, Utahs, and the Northern Apaches or as the latter are sometimes called, Jicarillas; though the last are omitted by Colonel Calhoun they are entirely separate and distinct from any other tribe and are pre-eminently distinguished for their ferocity and cruelty. They infest our northern New Mexico settlements and have been a greater annoyance to the territory than any other tribe either within or surrounding New Mexico."

With Roedel in, Maxwell complicated matters as far as the government was concerned, by selling out to an English colonizing company. Superintendent Pope was worried since he knew that the English company would not submit to the impositions of the Utes and Apaches, nor be patient with them as Maxwell was. Furthermore the man they revered lost face. The Indians told him point blank that it was not his land to sell since they had tolerated him on their property because he was one of the few Whites they could call a friend. The new owners were having such difficulties with the Indians that they had to be warned time and again to stay out of Cimarron after dark for fear their scalps would dangle from the Utah and Apache tepees. The order was reversed and all Indians were commanded to be out of Cimarron each evening at sundown. Any Indian found in Cimarron after dark would be held and placed in the jail now under construction. On July 26, 1871, Agent Roedel wrote:

"Last fall the Indians were assured by unscrupulous men that their annuity goods were on the way here in order to pacify them about the sale of the Maxwell Grant. When I took charge of the agency in last December without a blanket, or a shirt, or a pound of tobacco, and without a single dollar that could be expended for such, they gradually settled in the belief that I had appointed myself appropriator of their goods to be used for my private use, certainly not a very pleasant state of things for a new agent. . . . If the government cannot appropriate money for clothing and blankets, then it will be well for the government to make the necessary arrangements for a war next spring if not sooner, not merely with the Indians of the Cimarron agency, but with all the Utah tribes; they cannot obtain the means to buy clothing with around here, and there is hardly a deer or an antelope within twenty-five miles of this agency. The country is being rapidly settled and settlers feeling the strength of numbers deem small provocation sufficient cause to shoot an Indian. . . . I beg that relief may be granted speedily, for without such relief we have nothing but inevitable war before us. . . ."

The inefficiency at Washington as well as the inability of officials there to grasp the situation caused Roedel to resign in 1872. Besides the salary of $1,500.00 a year was entirely inadequate. R. H. Longwill, who lived in Cimarron as director of the English company, replaced him pro tem. Negotiations were again started for the removal of the Indians from the Grant property, but they were as stubborn as ever. Now they would consider a reservation in the Cimarron country only. The Jicarillas beat a hasty retreat for a time when they heard that a plague of smallpox was on the way. When they discovered this as propaganda they returned. The new owners of the Grant were nervous. Settlers were giving notice of pulling stakes and moving elsewhere: it was either the Indians or the settlers. The place wasn't big enough for both. To make matters worse, the Indians were not demanding meat but firewater. The orders from Washington were to persuade the Indians to try out the reservation in the San Luis Valley or at Fort Sumner physical violence to be avoided. If still unsuccessful then the agent was to take steps to place them on the location of the Dry Cimarron (over to the east near the present town of Folsom) where they could serve as shock troops against their bitter enemies, the Comanches. But when the question of a military post meant additional expense, the government quietly scratched the suggestion off the records.

J. L. Gould was sent to relieve Longwill as agent, but the latter retained the contract to feed the Indians in the name of the Maxwell Grant Company at the expense of the government. Gould could endure it no longer than five months. Thomas A. Dolan came in August 1873, with the additional commission to negotiate a treaty for the removal of the Jicarilla Apaches, although the agent was not aware that this was part of his job. After a bit of fussing and storming that he was tricked into it, he finally succeeded in persuading Chiefs Jose Layo and San Pablo into signing a treaty. It looked good on paper. They had no intentions of moving, the fact being substantiated by their continued raids on the settlers and the quantities of firewater they gulped. Robert Grisby was employed as special detective to break up the liquor traffic. Apparently he wasn't too successful for a certain woman was hailed before the court seventeen times on charges of selling liquor to the Indians at Cimarron. From the beginning one can say that Washington failed to grasp the situation at Cimarron. "So little is known here (at Washington) of the condition and situation of the Indians in that region that no specific instructions, relative to them can be given at present; and the Department relies on you to furnish it with such statistical and other information as will give a just and full understanding of every particular relating to them, embracing the names of the tribes, their location, the distance between the tribes, the probable extent of territory owned or claimed by each respectively, and the tenure by which they hold or claim it; their manners and habits, their disposition and feelings towards the United States, Mexico and whites generally, towards each other, whether hostile or otherwise; whether the several tribes speak different languages, and when different, the apparent analogies between them, and also what laws and regulations, for their government, are necessary, and how far the law regulating trade and intercourse with the Indian tribes, a copy of which I enclose, will, if extended over that country, properly apply to the Indians there and to the trade and intercourse with them and what modification if any, will be required to produce the greatest degree of efficiency."

"There are wandering tribes, who have never cultivated the soil, and have supported themselves alone by depredations. This is the only labor known to them. The thought of annihilating these Indians cannot be entertained by the American public—Nor can the Indians abandon their predatory incursions, and live and learn to support themselves by the sweat of their own brows unsustained by a liberal philanthropy—This subject—I humbly conceive, should engage the earnest and early consideration of the Congress of the United States."

Major Alexander G. Irvine followed Nolan as Indian agent at Cimarron on the first day of August in 1875. This was the time Parson Tolby made an effort at christianizing the Apaches and Utahs. More and more now they were being relegated to the outskirts of the town as the Grant Company mapped out its plat having enough influence to make it the county seat. Three months after Irvine took office, while distributing the weekly rations to his charges, Juan Barela, half Apache half Ute, and a minor chief, threw the meat back in Irvine's face with the comment that it was not fit for a dog. The agent stooped down, picked it up, threw it back at the Indian at the same time drawing his revolver. So did Barela. They fired simultaneously. The meat-thrower was killed; the major wounded in the hand. The remaining Indians said nothing but walked to their dwellings. The calm before the storm; any settler knew that. Riders were dispatched to Fort Union for troops. General Granger sent thirty cavalrymen who were under the command of Lieutenant George A. Cornish. All winter long they bivouaced, rifles in hand. And the winters at Cimarron are long and cold. Irvine was transferred to the Navajo agency. One of the soldiers, Sergeant James Hickman, was of the opinion that the entire fault did not lie with Barela, declaring so publicly. He event went so far as to substantiate the remark that the meat rationed to the Indians at Cimarron was not fit for a dog; added to this they were being short-rationed. Commissioner Pope had written previous to the Dolan appointment:

"I am now convinced that Cimarron is not a suitable place for these Indians, and that they are surrounded by influences that render their proper control almost an impossibility. They are becoming overbearing and insist that the Maxwell Grant belongs to them, and the Moache Utes refuse to leave it, although it has been sold to the English Company referred to and is being rapidly disposed of to settlers. I have tried several experiments to accomplish the removal but without result."

The Indians were indeed provoked at Maxwell for the sale of the land. In the first place, he had been a steadying force keeping them in check against general uprisings. This was also a protection for the settlers. He was also a great help in obtaining food and if they had nothing to trade he was generous enough to see them through knowing that they considered themselves under special obligations to him. They trusted him as much as he trusted them. He was arbitrator between the Government agency and the family in return for which he lived, by their tolerance, as a baron on the land that was theirs before Miranda knew how to write. For several days after the sale of the Grant Maxwell was not safe in his own house. Why they did not burn his home and scalp him can only be explained away in their deep-rooted affection and the habitual respect they had for him over and above the pain such an action brought to the front.

General Nelson A. Miles, who later attained national fame in his Geronimo campaign, was in Cimarron during December 1875. He had no need to read reports; he saw for himself the lamentable condition to which the Indians had been reduced. He took upon himself to distribute the best beef in town despite the complaints of the settlers. The army agreed with the settlers that military control at Cimarron was not in conformity with its duties. As a result, John E. Pyle, also a recommendation from the Presbyterian board, was appointed Indian agent at Cimarron. His position was short-lived for the agency was formally abolished, San Geronimo Day (September 30th, 1876), on the pretext that the United States Congress failed to appropriate money covering the agent's salary. April 10, 1878, was fixed as the last day for issuing rations. The responsibility for the Indians was placed on the shoulders of Ben H. Tomas, the agent for the Pueblo Indians. He retained Pyle for the time being. Settlers continued to write in echoing the sentiments of Calhoun:

"The Department must not forget that these Apaches are generally the produce of the amalgamations of the Utes and Apaches who roam the country almost to the Pacific. They are called Jicarillas. They are not considered a numerous band, but they are bold, daring, and adventurous spirits; and they say, they have never encountered the face of a white foe who did not quail and attempt to fly from them."

The deadline for distribution of rations was again changed to July 20, 1878. Special Agent James H. Roberts took charge of the Jicarillos and started for Fort Stanton. Four hundred and forty-two commenced the march but only thirty-two under San Pablo reached their destination. The others had turned off their course preferring the reservation at Abiquiu to the fort. San Pablo's men left Fort Stanton to join their brethren at Abiquiu. The agency for Abiquiu actually was not stationed at that place. Since 1872 it was located at Tierra Amarilla to the north and closer to the original stamping ground of the Utahs before the coming of the white man. There was more difficulty in placing the Muache Utahs. Fort Sumner was not very far from the scene of cattle feuds and disturbances at Lincoln. The Utes would fight for whichever side would feed them and give them rifles. On the other hand for them to steal cattle would set the already armed ranchers against them. Three hundred and seven of them were finally settled at Fort Sumner. After a time they took to roving what is now the Ute Park district, finally settling also at Tierra Amarilla. A memorial to the Honorable Secretary of the Interior and Honorable Commissioner of Indian Affairs regarding the Utahs and Jicarillas was made at the 21st session of the Congress of the Territory of New Mexico in 1874:

"Your memorialists, the Council and the House of Representatives of the Legislative Assembly of the Territory of New Mexico, respectfully represent that the Ute and Jicarillas tribes of Indians occupy and range over the northern portion of this territory, having their agency at Tierra Amarilla and a special agent located at Cimarron. These Indians formerly supported themselves by hunting, but as the buffalo are now to be found only at a great distance, and deer and other game have become very scarce, and the country being settled up, the hunting grounds of the Indians are circumscribed and their means of support greatly reduced, and they are now almost entirely, and soon will be entirely dependent upon the bounty of the government for a subsistence. And further, while these Indians have been for a number of years under the care of the government, they have in nowise improved, their intelligence and information have not increased, and they are in no better condition at present than when the goverment first took charge of them. They are today, mere wandering vagabonds, and the only change noticeable in them for some years past is a decrease of energy and a greater love of whiskey and idleness. The appropriations made for their support and the food supplied to their wants, and unfortunately, the special agents employed at Cimarron, for some time past, have failed to acquire the confidence of the Indians or have any authority or control over them. The consequence is that they roam all over the country and for subsistence kill the sheep and cattle of the settlers. These Indians are peaceable and seldom commit acts of violence against the whites, except to castigate persons in charge of herds and those who attempt to prevent their taking such stock as they need.

"Depredations of this character are constantly committed, and the loss and annoyance to the people of Northern New Mexico from this cause is very great; yet in no instance for several years past has there been any retaliation; the people almost universally feeling friendly toward, and sympathizing with, these unfortunate creatures. When remonstrated with, the Indians say they are hungry and must eat; their agent cares nothing for them, nor can they understand his talk; that they are neglected and abandoned and must take care of themselves as best they can. Their situation is truly deplorable, and forces compassion even on the part of those who suffer from their depredations, and whose property is taken to satisfy their wants. While their future, so far as can be anticipated, unless a radical change shall be made in their management, is distressing to consider, we make no compliment of the officers in charge, but we do suggest that the agent to whom the care of these Indians is confided, should be a man not only of intelligence and good character and habits, but he should also be a man of experience, who will interest himself earnestly in the welfare of the Indians; a man who can communicate with them, and a man who will give them his care, friendship and advice; one who has or can acquire their confidence and command their respect, and so be able to guide and control them. In this connection it is well to remember that among the Indians very young men are never entrusted with authority, and are always subordinate to their elders; and in consequence they are not satisfied with very young men as agents. We therefore earnestly recommend that a permanent agency be established at or near Cimarron and that such a man as we have described be placed in charge of the same as agent: That means be adapted to teach these Indians the pursuits of civilized life; that they be taught and induced to cultivate the soil, to give attention to the care and raising of stock, and be by such means rescued from their present deplorable condition and their most unpromising future: That sufficient appropriations be made for their comfortable support, and to carry out the purposes herein suggested.

"We appeal to the government in the name of humanity, for charity's sake, for the credit of our national character, as a duty to these poor people. as also for the interest of New Mexico, to adopt and inaugurate some system, which will, at least, give the Indians an opportunity to advance and improve and become something better than wandering, idle, ignorant distressed vagabonds, which they now are; thus will your memorialists ever pray."

The failure of the Taos rebellion was too much for Juan Antonio Bueno of Taos, who went to Mora and made contact with J. Cortez, a captain in the Mexican army under Armijo. By December 1847, "General" Cortez raised quite an army making his headquarters in the vicinity of Las Vegas. There he committed all kinds of depredations running off, killing and tying up stock and cutting off small parties that chanced to be going that way. James Grolmer, who ran a small trading post in Las Vegas, went to Santa Fe in the hopes of having the military putting a stop to Bueno and Cortez. He admitted that Las Vegas was friendly to Americans but Cortez and his three hundred rebels were a threat to the peace of the community. Among his followers could be seen a number of Utes and Jicarillas from the Cimarron country and well armed, too, as well as mounted. Cortez would order thirty sheep at a time, give the seller a receipt in the name of the Mexican government with the added comment that he would be highly rewarded when Armijo returned to Santa Fe. He would make himself personally responsible for payment. Grolmer brought one such receipt to Santa Fe for the amusement of the soldiers. But they were not amused. There were not fighters walled up in the church of San Geronimo at Pueblo de Taos. These were guerillas striking here and there and hard to track down. More and more of the Indians living on the Grant joined Cortez. Just as soon as news reached Santa Fe that all his men deserted and not a few of the Indians—for it was winter and Christmas was coming on —Captain Armstrong was sent against him with eight men to capture him alive if possible. The trail lead to Antonchico. When Cortez heard that eight men were sent to capture him he enlisted sixty at Antonchico. Armstrong must have been a daring man for he attacked the little army. At the first volley from the soldiers, the rebels scattered, several severely wounded. Cortez escaped. At Chihuahua he was commissioned a captain by General Governor Trias. At the head of new troops he marched towards Mesilla but was wounded before the battle was several minutes old. He escaped to Chihuahua. Sometime later he returned to America and settled at El Macho near Pecos where he is buried.

Armed with new rifles and plenty of ammunition the Jicarillas continued to raid and plunder. Beaubien sought to raise an army to subjugate them, but as everybody else seemed to be having troubles of their own at that time he was not successful. Whenever troops from Taos, Santa Fe or Las Vegas were sent out against them they always managed to elude their pursuers. Usually they found refuge in the bosque at Antonchico a place later used by Billy the Kid for the same purpose. Governor Carr Lane sent Dr. Steck there in the hopes of making a treaty with the Indians:

"In accordance with your instructions I immediately proceeded to Antonchico where, on December 26 (1852) I met twenty-five Jicarillas and seventy-five Mescalero Apache Indians. The principal chiefs were Josecito, Santa Ana and Cuentas Azules of the Mescaleros and Lobo and San Pablo of the Jicarillas. In all my intercourse with them the most perfect good feeling seemed to prevail. They have been living in the vicinity all winter and from reports here have been behaving unusually well. I found them poor and from scarcity of game likely to suffer from want of provisions. After having a talk with them, I distributed among them blankets, shirts, leggings and tobacco, and also made a liberal distribution of corn, as that was what they were most in need of. After receiving their presents they were advised to return to their homes, which they immediately did, and well satisfied with what they had received."

Steck did not say whether or not he took their rifles. No doubt he thought it wise to permit them to retain them as a precaution against Comanche and Kiowa attacks. Steck was to become one of the best Indian Agents in the business, and he was quite influential in settling the Navajos at Bosque Redondo.

General Carleton often visited Maxwell and camped on his Grant. They had known each other since 1851 when Carleton was stationed at Fort Union. These Indians on the Grant are the only ones that I know of that he had personal dealings with. All his other contacts were through his officers and reports. On August 5, 1864, with Maxwell and several other army men, he climbed Mt. Baldy and planted the United States flag on its summit. This was the first time a white man made the ascent. In the following month he sent a company of California Volunteers to Cimarron to help escort the mail from Maxwell's ranch to Fort Lyon in Colorado. From his experiences he set forth these theories concerning the Indian policy as he saw it:

"The Indian Bureau should be placed under the War Department, as it was before the Department of the Interior was created and organized. When under the War Department, which also controls the forces operating in the Indian countries, there would be no conflict of opinion about what should be done in a given case; for, as the fountain whence might emanate instructions, whether to commanders, superintendents or agents, would be one, so the different streams of authority and regulations, descending through these subordinates would be of the same character.... In my opinion the office of Commissioner of Indian Affairs should be abolished, if it be incompatible with the law to have an officer of the army fill it ex-officio. Contemplating the placing of the Indian Bureau under the direction of the War Department; and organizing it systematically, so that its operation should harmonize with those of the troops, and the two run together as parts of the same machine, with no clogs mis-matching, no jarrings, no belts loose. It would be next to impossible to find any citizen who would understand Indian affairs, Indians, Indian countries, Indian wants, and at the same time understand military affairs. But it is easy to find many an officer in the United States Army, who from long service in Indian countries, understands all these matters. I would have not only the head of the Indian Bureau an officer of the army, but each commander of a military department should be an ex-officio superintendent of Indian Affairs for all the Indians in that department; and the commander of one post nearest any one tribe of Indians in that department should be the agent, ex-officio, for that tribe."

Maxwell knew it wouldn't work and told him so. He was going to prove to Maxwell and the world he was right. He tried it at Bosque Redondo and failed miserably.

Chapter Seven

LAND GRANTS IN GENERAL

Land was granted in New Mexico, Texas, and Colorado not because the king of Spain had favorites but because Mexico had to be protected. The choice land and the places known to have gold, silver, copper and other resources for the Crown were actually given to those whom the king could trust and who were capable of enriching the court in Spain. Life in the northern province of Spain centered around Mexico City. There the grandees sought to re-live the splendor they knew in the mother-country. Anything north was exile. Yet, Spain wished to hold on to the frontier country known as Nuevo Mejico. North of New Mexico and extending southward along the eastern frontier into Texas were the ever warlike Comanche Indians. Northwest were the Utes while southeast, south and southwest, ranging from western Texas across the Rio Grande river and along the Gila river to the Colorado river the Apaches roamed where they chose. The Gila group usually united with the Natage and Lipans to invade the settlements at El Paso del Norte (present Juarez), Sonora, and the outposts of Mexico. Governor Anza and several others went on several expeditions against all these tribes to save the settlements and prevent daring raids on Mexico City itself.

Up to 1728, most of the land grants came under the jurisdiction of the Supreme Council of the Indies which controlled the affairs of the Spanish colonies on this side of the Atlantic, in the name of the king. After 1728, authorities in Mexico had more to say, and did. The king was in favor of christianizing the Indians in a hope that it would civilize them and cause them to lay down their bows and arrows. Never having been on this side of the ocean, the rulers of Spain had no idea of what their generals had to cope with save from the reports of the viceroys, missionaries and others, each out of his own mind, thus often conflicting their reports. The viceroys were not too anxious to have missionaries report since more often as not there were complaints against them regarding their treatment of the Indians. Often the queen wrote that they would be directly responsible to her for their conduct in this matter, and repeatedly urged the conversion of the natives under Spanish domination. Mexico ceased to be ruled from Spain when Iturbide took over in September 1821. New Mexico therefore became a province of Mexico. The situation had not changed. The frontiers still had to be protected. The best possible way to do this was to grant land, have it colonized, and let the settlers worry the Indians thus keeping them away from Sonora, Durango, Chihuahua, and El Paso. Also, the officials did not think in terms of acres, they dreamed of revenue. So long as it brought in dividends like stock, and so long as the vast territories were there, they were gracious in giving especially to those who might fatten their pocket-books. On January 3, 1823, the national council of Mexico passed a colonization law, providing for two types of grants of land, one to promoters, who resembled the later American town-site promoters, who were known as Empresarios. These were to sign a contract with the government. The other kind of grant was to individuals. This was given over through common councils, known as Ayuntamientos. It is important to remember this for the decision of the United State Supreme Court touching the 1,714,000 acres of the Maxwell Land Grant was decided on this difference. To the individual was granted eleven square leagues. For colonizing purposes the grant was unlimited and embraced all the land mentioned in the contract. The American government proved that the Beaubien and Miranda tract was for colonizing purposes therefore they were entitled to all the land called for in the petition.

New Mexico was officially designated as a Territory of Mexico on July 6, 1824. It was in 1824 that Mexico became quite definite about grants, or at least it thought it had. It amended, abrogated and repealed at will depending on insurrections and who gained control of the government. In the empresario system, the empresario first presented a memorial to the state government asking for permission to colonize certain waste lands which were designated, as well as the number of families he proposed to introduce. To afford ample choice to the settlers, the tract designated and usually conceded by the government was rather in excess of the appropriation to be finally made. As a rule, after the establishment of the settlement and the completion of the allotments to the colonists, and the assignment of the premium land to the empresario, all the surplus land reverted to the state. This would have probably happened if General Kearny had not taken over New Mexico in 1846, for the empresario was given six years from the date of petition to gather together the colonists if he did not wish to void the contract. New Mexico became American soil before the six years were up. Since in the Hidalgo Treaty, America promised to respect valid Mexican land grants Beaubien and Miranda did not lose their rights to the land. The distribution of the allotments to the settlers was under the control of a commissioner, appointed by the state government, but he had no power to make an assignment without the approval of the contractor. If the contractor failed to introduce the stipulated number of families within the term of six years, he lost his rights and privileges in proportion to the definciency, and the contract was totally annulled if he had not succeeded in settling one hundred families. The premium granted to a contractor was five square leagues of grazing ground and five labores of tillage land for each hundred families, but he could not acquire premium on more than eight hundred families.

Regarding the settlers understood in the contract, each family whose sole occupation was farming, received one hundred and seventy-seven acres but one labor of agricultural land. But if, added to this, he was engaged in stock-raising also, a grazing tract sufficient to complete a square league, less 177 acres. An unmarried man received only one-fourth of this amount. The government of the state alone had the power to increase these quantities in proportion to the size of the families and the activity and industry of the colonists. Eleven square leagues was the limit of land that could be owned by the same hands as prescribed by the National Colonization law. For each square league, or sitio, as it was known, the colonist paid an emptiom sum of thirty dollars to the state, and two-dollars and fifty cents for each labor not irrigable, while irrigable land was a dollar more. These payments were not demanded till after the expiration of six years from the time of settlement, and then only in three installments at long intervals. Contractors and the military were exempt from this quittance. The incoming settler was, moreover, subject to the payment of the commissioner's fees, and to the charges for the sheets of the stamped paper on which the order for the survey was granted and his title deed issued. With other minor items, the total cost of a sitio was about one hundred and eighty dollars.

Governor Armijo had the power to grant the petition made by Beaubien and Miranda as Empresarios. The timing of their request was fortunate because over in Texas President Mirabeau B. Lamar was under the impression that Mexico was holding out on him regarding territory east of the Rio Grande river. He therefore fitted out an expedition to take this land by force if necessary. "With the proofs General Lamar had, that such a feeling existed in New Mexico, he could not act otherwise than he did— could not do other than give the people of Eastern New Mexico an opportunity of throwing off the galling yoke under which they had long groaned. Texas claimed as her western boundary, the Rio Grande; the inhabitants within the boundary claimed protection of Texas." The expedition came to a sorry end, but it did give Armijo a fright. Several years after this, New Mexico was flying the American flag.

The Guadalupe-Hidalgo Treaty of February 2, 1848 gave the inhabitants of the conquered country one year to make up their minds as to whether they wished to continue under American rule or re-move to the old country. Evidently Miranda chose the latter for all his correspondence is from Mexican soil hereafter. At the time of the signing of the treaty and its proclamation by the President of the United States on July 4, 1848, the question arose about the land grants in New Mexico. In order to put together the puzzle, Congress enacted a law creating a Surveyor-General for New Mexico, with the duty to follow the instructions of the Secretary of the Interior. He was obliged to make a full report on all the claims of the land grants, with his decision as to the validity or invalidity of the titles. The report of the Surveyor-General, under the law of 1854, was to be made to the Secretary of the Interior, who in turn was to give the report to the Congress of the United States, with the object of confirming bona fied grants in order to give full support to the promise made by the government to Mexico and to the Treaty of 1848. During the period from 1854 to 1870, Congress confirmed sixty-two Spanish and Mexican land grants, among which was the Maxwell Land Grant. In 1870, Congress changed its policy and declined to act at all on any New Mexico Land Grant Claim! Again, the Maxwell grant was in luck for if Congress would have set it aside, who knows what its history might have been.

When Surveyor-General Julian came into office he worked day and night to try to straighten out the mess, and was of the opinion that men in office before him acted on some fraudulent grants which gave McMains an opportunity to quote him as well as to rant the more. Whatever Julian's opinion or what he had to say in the articles he wrote for the North American Review in 1887, it did not change the fact that Congress, according to its lights, did give a correct opinion concerning the Maxwell Land Grant, and that opinion held. Stephen Dorsey attempted to answer Julian, but as neither one had a direct influence on the Grant save to fire the McMains enthusiasm, the history of the Julian-Dorsey controversy does not fit into the grant.

The salient points to remember about Land Grants are the following:

1. What the Mexican Government and the American government had to say in the Guadalupe Hidalgo Treaty and in the Gasden Purchase.

2. One of the institutions established by Spain in America was a system of land tenure by means of which the royal domain was parcelle dout by the Spanish crown, or by its duly appointed governors, to the loyal subjects of His Majesty, in the form of mercedes or Grants.

3. This practice continued throughout the Spanish regime.

4. No record of any Grant throughout the present confines of the American Southwest are extant prior to 1699. This does not mean that none were given, but simply that we cannot find such records. Some day when all the material of the Archives of the Indies is worked such Grants as prior to 1699 may come to light. If any such documents were here they were probably destroyed during the Pueblo Indian revolt in 1680 or sold as scrap paper by one of the governors of the Territory of New Mexico who felt that English should be the official language since Santa Fe was flying the American flag. This governor has never been forgiven by historians.

5. The Grants of 1699 began when Spain was certain that she once again possessed land she had lost to the Pueblo Indians. It definitely proved that the royal house had no intentions of letting New Mexico go.

6. When Mexico threw over the yoke of Spain royal domain became public domain.

7. The granting of land was continued by the Mexican government in practically the same manner as it had been practiced under the authority of the Spanish crown, except that the validity of any grant that was made rested upon the sanction or confirmation of the Mexican Congress instead of upon the authority of the king of Spain.

8. One must recognize the liberality of the grants the Mexican government made even to those not of Spanish blood. One has to note what took place in Texas although French Canadian trappers took advantage of New Mexico because of its rich beaver streams, Santa Fe Trail trade and commerce.

9. Mexico encouraged colonization and granted large tracts for the purpose of providing homes for the common people who found it difficult to gain possession of private grant of the royal or public domain. Community or pueblo grants were extensively made by both the Spanish and the Mexican governments.

10. Another type of Grant that was neither for the encouragement of colonization, nor for the rewarding of services, was a Grant based upon a purchase price. In nature this Grant was more nearly like the system of land tenure that has been in practise under the government of the United States. The proceeds from the sale of these grants went into the royal treasury and was one of the sources of revenue for the Spanish government. Later the Mexican government made use of the public domain for the same purpose. In this particular respect there is rather close analogy with the practices of the government of the United States, but with this the similarity ends. In other respects, the whole system of Spanish and Mexican land tenures was entirely different from that practised by the United States.

11. The origin and nature of Spanish and Mexican land grants reflect the attitude of the Spanish government towards royal domain in the New World. The ancient laws of Spain declare that the ownership and full dominion of conquered kingdoms belong to the Monarch.

12. Law 11 Title 1 Partida XI—"Wherefore the West Indies having been conquered by the arms of the Catholic King and Queen, Fernando and Isabel, in the 16th century, in consideration of the fact that no person can live without the means of subsistence, and no city can live without the rents necessary for its support, their Majesties thought proper to cede to the towns (poplaciones) of America and to the councils of the same, certain portions of the lands from which to derive their support using the same for pasturage and cultivation certain portions of the lands from which to derive their support, or in the manner that they may be directed by the municipal ordinances."

13. These laws were denominated consejiles or de proprios—and the law quoted above furnishes the legal sanction and basis for that numerous class of grants found in New Mexico known as Pueblo Grants.

14. John Wasson, Commissioner of the General Land Office in Washington, said on July 26, 1882: "Another portion of the conquered lands was distributed by concessions of the king to those who assisted in conquering the country as rewards for their services; and lands were sold also to individuals for the purpose of obtaining means to supply the necessaries of the crown. These lands, donated or sold, were denominated 'de dominio particular' (private property) because the full ownership thereof was transferred to the donees or purchasers, and hence they were truly private property. The usufruit of the remaining lands was ceded by the king to all his vassals, that they might make use of their pastures, woods, waters, and other natural production for the support of their flocks and herds, which lands were called 'common lands' because they were for common use. They are also called 'valdeo' (vacant) because nothing is paid for the use of the pasturage or fire wood that may be cut thereon. They are also 'realengro' (royal lands) because the domain and property thereof are reserved to the king by his right of conquest, although he ceded the usufruit of the same to his vassals."

Chapter Eight

BEALES AND REYUELA

Coahuila, hemmed in by Chihuahua, Tamaulipes and Nueva Leon, had its attraction for men like Doctor John Charles Beales, the London physician. Under Spanish rule it had been known as La Provincia de Nueva Estremadura. While annexed to the government of Texas, after 1824, it was a far richer and more populous country, making it a hotbed of political corruption, injustice, tyranny and oppression. The commandant general ruled it to his tastes. Its most populous towns were Saltillo, Monclova, Parras and Santa Rosa. Some men are too attracted to fertile soil, general climate, and rare atmosphere to be bothered with mutterings about an oppressive government. John Austin and others who had received grants from the Mexican Government were not in favor of joint government with Coahuila. As one master-of-ceremonies toasted: "Coahuila and Texas—they are dissimilar in soil, climate and production; therefore they ought to be dissolved." Pastoral and mining occupations prevailed in Coahuila; Texas was essentially an agricultural country, and cotton, sugar, and cereals were being cultivated to an extent that the central government in Mexico City was jealous of the rapidly increasing number of Americans squatting on Texas soil. The liberal colonization law of March 24, 1825, was repealed; Mexicans alone were permitted to become empresarios in the future; they obtained land at a very cheap price while native Americans were excluded from becoming settlers, while at the same time the rights of colonists were extended.

Austin fought for the rights of the Texans and was arrested at Saltillo in 1834. In July this city also disatisfied pronounced against the State government, formed one of its own, and elected Jose Maria Goribar as Military governor. Immediately, all the acts of the state legislature from January 1, 1833, were declared null and void. This is important to remember in considering the Beales Grant and the Maxwell Land Grant Company's court case invalidating the Saltillo petition.

Beales was an Englishman therefore looked upon with favor by the government. He opened his practice in Saltillo, adding to his prestige in a place where doctors were so sorely needed. He married a relative of Jose Manuel Reyuela who interested him in petitioning the government for a grant of land. Beales was particular. Not just any land would do. Stephen Julian Wilson had a grant but made no settlement nor any attempt to colonize within the six years, prescribed by law. In preparation for the request Beales had himself declared a citizen of Mexico. The petition covered sixty million acres including the tract in the Maxwell Land Grant. Beales and Reyuela placed their petition before the governor of Coahuila in the winter of 1832-1833. In order to fulfill the stipulations of the Grant Doctor Beales went to New York to collect colonists despite Mexican feeling for Americans. The first body of settlers, fifty-seven in number, embarked at New York on November 10, 1833. They entered the Rio Grande Grant on February 28, 1834, settling the town of Dolores, on March 25, 1834, a short distance above Laredo, on the Rio Bravo. Within three months they abandoned the place, possibly because Beales realized that they were about three hundred miles from the nearest point called for in the tract. Again Beales went to New York without success. Reyuela had less confidence than his partner. He sold out to Beales in October, 1833, passing out of the picture. Beales awaited the Texan-Mexican agitation to calm down. He settled in New York, establishing a practice there. He made his will in 1873 naming his son James A. G. Beales as administrator and heir. The doctor died in New York on September 29, 1879. His son was legally appointed his administrator according to the laws of the State of New York. On November 17, 1886, James Beales as such administrator with will annexed, and for himself as one of the devisee's therein named together with Adelaide K. Jaffray, (his sister) and J. Hamilton Jaffray, her husband, Anita Exter, and Eugenia Katherine Beales, his wife by a deed of that date duly executed and acknowledged, conveyed to Newton B. Childs of Kansas City, all the real estate embraced in and described in the grant made by the Governor of Coahuila. Six days later Childs and his wife Nellie, sold to the Interstate Land Company of Colorado, all the right title and interest to all the lands embraced in the grant which included the Maxwell Land Grant property. Part of the grant had been sold for $12,500.00 known as the Arkansas Grant. Childs sold for $250,000.00 and other considerations. The new owners approached the Maxwell Land Grant people asking them to give up their pretentions for a consideration. They refused, saying they would fight their case in the Colorado courts. The Interstate Land people sent squatters along on the Colorado portion of the grant giving them leases for a consideration of One Dollar with the assurance that they would fight their suits for them against the Maxwell Land Grant. The Beales Grant Bubble took the case to Judge Brewer of the Colorado courts, lost, then took it to the United States Supreme Court.

The claim called for all the land along the east bank

of the Rio Grande near the source of the river in Colorado in a straight line west of Trinidad following the stream to about where the town of Anthony, New Mexico, now stands, east to Texas, north to the corner of Oklahoma and Texas. The Interstate Land Company was incorporated under the laws of the State of Colorado, the members being Newton B. Childs of Kansas City, Missouri; James F. Hadley, from the same place; Thomas Carney of Leavenworth, Kansas, Charles Goodnight of Palo Duro, Texas, Willie H. Nelson of Burlingame, Kansas; William H. Lord, from the same town and William V. Childs of Kansas City, Missouri. Of the seven, Charles Goodnight was the best known, and probably better acquainted with the Maxwell Land Grant than the rest. He had dealings with Lucien B. Maxwell, after whom the grant came to be named which was more than the others could say.

Charles Goodnight, about three years older than Kit Carson, was born in Kentucky. In 1845, his family took up the fever of settling in the Republic of Texas. By the time Charles was sixteen, he was hauling freight in Waco. In 1857, he was in partnership with his brother-in-law Wes Sheek, trailing herds up the Brazos River into Palo Pinto Country. After many adventures he settled the Palo Duro country in Texas. As a successful rancher he was approached by Newton B. Childs about the formation of the Interstate Land Company. Since the tract bought from the Beales heirs touched his domain and from a legal viewpoint the company seemed certain of obtaining the property, he became a prominent stock holder. The company had reckoned without the Maxwell Land Grant lawyers.

JUDGE BREWER'S DECISION IN THE BEALES GRANT CASE.

In the circuit court of the United States for the district of Colorado.

The Interstate Land company against the Maxwell Land Grant company; also, the Maxwell Land Grant company against Vicente Preteca et al.

Alexander Graves, Aaron S. Everest, John L. Gerome, counsel for Interstate Land Company.

Frank Springer, Charles E. Gast, counsel for Maxwell company.

Opinion, Brewer, C. J.

The single question in these two cases arises upon what is known as the Beales grant, a grant made in the year 1832 by the governor of the state of Coahuila and Texas. The petition and grant are as follows:

"Petition and grants to Jose Manuel Reyuela and John Charles Beales. For the year 1832 and 1833.

To his excellency the governor of the state of Coahuila and Texas. Sir: The citizen Jose Manuel Reyuela, a native of Saltillo, and there married, and John Charles Beales, a native of England, settled in Mexico, and there married to a Mexican subject, having children, with all due respect to your excellency:

That being very desirous of augmenting the population, wealth and power of the Mexican nation, and at the same time of affording to a certain number of virtuous and industrious families the means of acquiring an honorable subsistence by cultivating a tract of land in the ancient province of Texas, and being moreover acquainted in full with the law of colonization passed by the honorable legislature of this state, on the 24th of March, 1825, by which "empresarios" or colonizing contractors are allowed to undertake to colonize under the conditions and stipulations by said law prescribed, and being anxious to form an establishment that may be useful to a new colony, and at the same time beneficial to the state on account of the advantages to accrue thereout:

We pray your excellency to accept us as such "empresarios" or colonizing contractors, and to permit us to introduce into this state, within the time that may be stipulated, 200 Catholic families of moral and industrous habits, and for the object your excellency will be pleased to grant us the tract of land included within the following limits, viz:

Beginning at a land mark set up on a spot whereat the 32d degree of north latitude is crossed by the meridian of the 102d degree of the longitude west from London, said spot being at the southwest corner of the grant petitioned by Col. Reuben Ross; from thence proceeding west along the parallel of the 32d degree of latitude as far as the eastern boundary of New Mexico; from thence running north on the boundary line between the provinces of Coahuila and Texas and New Mexico, as far as Twenty leagues of the river Arkansas; from thence east to the meridian of the 102d degree of longitude, which is the western boundary of the grant petitioned for by said Col. Reuben Ross, and from thence proceeding south as far as the place of beginning.

Your petitioners as "empresarios" pray for this grant on the same conditions that it was formerly given to the late Stephen Julian Wilson, whose term of six years is about to expire, on May 26 of this year, without the conditions of the grant having been fulfilled in consequence of the grantee.

Besides the conditions which are required by the colonization law of the state, the empresarios and their settlers agree to observe the constitution of the Mexican nation, and the private constitution of this state, as well as the general and local laws that have been or shall be hereafter promulgated. They further bind themselves to comply with the conditions on which this petition is granted and to take up arms in defense of the rights of the nation against the savage Indians, or any other enemies that may attack the country, or in any manner to alter its form of government, or to disturb the public tranquility. And finally to prevent the inhabitants of the United States of North America from trading with the said Indians and providing them with arms and ammunition in exchange for horses and mules.

Wherefore we pray your excellency to be pleased to grant this respectful petition, which we shall consider as a favor conferred on us.

Dated at Saltillo, the 13th day of March, 1832. (Signed) Jose Manuel Royuela, John Charles Beales.

CONDITIONS OF THE GRANT

Terms on which the supreme government of the state accept the proposal of the citizens, Jose Manuel Royuela and John Charles Beales, for colonizing certain land with

200 foreign families such as are not expected by the law of the 6th of April, 1830:

Article 1—The government accepts the proposal made in the foregoing petition, as far as it is conformable with the laws of colonization passed by the honorable congress of the state on the 24th of March, 1825, and consequently assigns to the petitioners the tract of land included within the following limits, that they may establish thereon the proposed colony: It shall begin at a land mark which shall be set upon the spot where the parallel of the 32d degree of north latitude west from London, said spot being at the southwest corner of the grant petitioned for by Col. Reuben Ross; from thence it shall proceed along the parallel of the 32d degree of latitude as far as the eastern limit of New Mexico; from thence it shall ascend north on the boundary line between the province of Coahuila and Texas and New Mexico as far as twenty leagues of the river Arkansas. From thence it shall run east to the meridian of the 102d degree of longitude, which is the western boundary of the grant petitioned for by the said Col. Reuben Ross; and from thence it shall proceed south as far as the place of beginning.

Art. 2—Though the boundaries of the tract set forth in the preceding clause are those assigned to Stephen Julian Wilson, in a grant passed by this government on the 27th of May, 1826, yet this circumstance has not been considered an impediment to the entering into the present contract, insofar as the time allotted to the said Wilson for the completion of said enterprise will expire in the month of May of this present year, without his having to this day performed the same or any part whatsoever. But if, however, in the short time that has to elapse, any number of the families of that empresario should present themselves, then, and in that case, the present grant shall, with due respect to part or parts performed by the first grantee thereof, be null and void to all intents and purposes.

Art. 3—In consideration of the grant herein before specified, the empresarios, or contracting parties, agree to introduce and settle, on their own account, 200 foreign families, conforming themselves as well to the general law of the republic as to the laws of the state in this behalf provided.

Art. 4—All lands whatsoever held under legal titles, that may be included within the limits designated in article 1, shall be respected by the colonists who shall hold under this contract, and it shall be obligatory on the part of the empresarios to see the observance of this clause.

Art. 5—The state retains to itself the right of property over all the surplus lands which shall remain of this grant, after laying off those which belong to the empresarios and their settlers, according to the laws in that behalf provided.

Art. 6—In conformity with article 8 of the law of colonization hereinbefore referred to, the empresarios are bound to introduce the stipulated number of 200 families within the term of six years, which shall be computed from the date hereof, under the penalty of being debarred from all the privileges and advantages afforded by the said law.

Art. 7—It shall be obligatory on the empresarios not to introduce or suffer to remain in the colony, men guilty of atrocious crimes or of bad conduct; as also to endeavor that no person whatsoever shall carry on traffic in arms and ammunition with the barbarous tribes of Indians, in exchange for horses and mules.

Art. 8—Whenever there shall be a sufficient number of men, the national militia shall be duly organized and regulated, according to the laws of the state in that respect provided.

Art. 9—The colony shall be regulated by the person whom this government shall appoint to allot the respective settlements or possessions, and he shall duly observe the laws on colonization in force throughout the state, the general law of the 18th of August, 1824, and likewise the instruction to commissioners, which have been appointed by the honorable congress, taking care to afford protection within the limits of the colony to such persons only as shall be approved of by the empresarios.

Art. 10—All official communications, instruments and other public documents, emenating from the colony, must be written in the Spanish language.

Art. 11—In reference to all matters not provided for or expressed in these articles, the empresarios, or the new settlers holding under them, shall abide and be governed by the federal constitution and the laws of this state.

And his excellency, the governor of the state, as also the citizens Jose Manuel Royuela and John Charles Beales, having agreed in the articles of this contract to grant, and bound respectively to the observance and performance thereof, afterwards signed the same before me, the undersigned secretary of the government.

And having been directed to give the empresarios the certified copy of all the documents relating to the grant, that they may serve them as security, and as formal title (or as a title in form) thereto, the originals will, according to law remain filed and recorded in the secretary's office under my charge.

Dated, City of Leona Vicario, the 14th day of March, 1832.

(Signed) Jose Maria de Letona
          John Charles Beales,
          Jose Manuel Royuela.
Santiago Del Valle, *Secretary*

The foregoing is copied from the original documents filed and recorded in the secretary's office, under my charge whence it was ordered taken by his excellency the governor.

City of Leona Vicario, the 14th of March, 1832.

(Signed)   Santiago Del Valle, *Secretary*.

The same year of the grant, and on October 11, Royuela conveyed by deed to Beales. He remained the owner until his death in 1879. He disposed of his property by will made in 1873, and by sundry conveyances from his devisees the title has passed to the complainant in the one suit and the cross-complainant in the other, the Interstate Land company. The question is presented by demurrers, so that the genuineness and validity of the documents are not open to question.

The contention on the one side is, that this was a grant passing title subject to defeasance, that the grantor never insisted upon any defeasance, and indeed could not, because before the time within which the conditions subsequent were to be performed the state of Texas had revolted from the Mexican government and established an independent nation of its own, and that by this action performance of the conditions was rendered impossible. On the other hand the contention is that the grant was in the nature of a float; that by it certain out boundaries of a large tract were designated within which the grantees, upon performing certain actions, would obtain perfect title to prescribed amounts of land; and that never having performed any of the conditions or thus paid any of the consideration, no title was ever vested in the grantees to any portion of the land. The area of this tract as stated by counsel is over 60,000,000 acres. The fact that arrests attention at the outset is that the claim of title to this tract, an empire in itself, has remained so long unasserted. For over fifty years it has rested quietly, at peace with all the world, and all the world at peace with it. The grantee and single owner lived for forty-seven years after receiving the grant. Litigation at great expense through many years, passing to the supreme court of the United States, has been carried on respecting large bodies of land within this grant, claimed on other and independent titles and now, for the first time, the courts are asked to pass upon this grant. It would seem as though the grantee did not understand the grant to be other than a float as claimed. While of course this does not determine the legal effect of the instrument, it is certainly significant as interpreting the understanding of the parties and it is familiar that oftentimes the conduct of parties to a contract has weight in determining the real meaning of doubtful words or phrases of it.

Again it appears from article 2, that the tract in question was one assigned to Stephen Julian Wilson in a grant of May 27, 1826, and an examination of the terms of that grant shows that it was substantially the same as this. By that as by this, a term of six years was given for the performance of the contract, which term had not expired; and yet as stated in article 2, this fact was not supposed to restrict the power of the government to make this concession. Yet, if, as claimed these grants were deeds with conditions subsequent, title passing subject to defeasance, we should scarcely expect a second grant before actual forfeiture of the first. And in the latter part of article 2, it is provided that if in the short time to elapse before the expiration of the six years, any number of the families of that empresario should present themselves, then this grant with respect to the part or parts performed shall be null and void. In other words, this contemplates that the introduction of a number of families by the first grantee, Wilson, would give him and them title to portions of the grant, a title not acquired until such performance;

a view of the meaning of the contract consistent with that claimed by the demurrant, and opposed to that insisted upon by the complainant.

But these are preliminary matters; we must look to the instrument itself, and to the law under which the concession was made, to determine its real meaning. And noticing the first article of the grant, the article which may be considered as most nearly like the granting clause in an ordinary deed, we find that the language is, that the government assigns to the petitioners the tract of land included within the following limits, that they may establish thereon the proposed colony. Now the word "assign" may mean "convey", although it is not the ordinary word used in respect to land transfers, or it may mean a setting apart of the land as a tract upon which the petitioners can perform their proposed colonization. That the latter is the true meaning is indicated by the purpose for which the land is expressly assigned, to wit: as a place for the proposed colony. The language is not, "granted on condition that they establish a colony", but "assigned" as a place "where they may establish a colony;" and in what may be considered the recital preliminary to the grant, we find the articles are declared to be the terms on which the supreme government accepts the proposal for colonizing certain lands with 200 foreign families. So the colonization was the object of the contract, and it must be assumed that no more rights were intended to be conveyed than those which resulted from colonization.

Again by Art. 4: It is provided that all lands within those limits held by legal titles should be respected by the colonists who held under this contract. True, land previously conveyed would as a matter of law be expected from the grant, but the article also speaks of this as a contract, and implies that colonists under the petitioners would acquire title to some portion of the tract. Of course if this was a grant passing title to the grantees, this article was unnecessary, and it is significant as calling the instrument a contract and settling it over against legal titles.

But article 5 is still more significant, providing that the state retains the right of property over all surplus lands which shall remain of this grant after laying off what belongs to the empresarios and their settlers. In other words, the state retains title to part of the tract, a thing impossible if the instrument was a grant passing title to all. It further implies that only part of the land would belong to the empresarios and their settlers, and that it was to be set apart to them in accordance with the laws of the state. This is exactly the idea contended for by the demurrant, that the instrument taken as a whole was simply a designation of a large tract with given out boundaries, within which the petitioners could by colonization obtain title to certain amounts of land as prescribed by law.

All these provisions of the instrument make strongly against the contention of complainant, and while there are some clauses in the instrument which make in favor of this contention, as for instance, the frequent use of the word grant, the specification in article 3 that in consideration of the grant the empresarios agree to introduce and settle 200 foreign families, and the provision that a certified copy of all of the documents relating to the grant shall be given to the empresarios serving them as security and as formal title; yet if, taking the instrument as a whole there is conflicting provisions, and the real meaning by reason thereof be doubtful, the familiar rule applicable to all concessions from a government, is that the concession or grant is to be construed strictly against the grantee and in favor of the government, grantor (United States vs. Cattle Co., 33 Fed. Rep. 323). So if inquiry was limited to the instrument itself, it would have to be adjudged that it was not a grant passing title, but a designation and setting apart of a tract within which the petitioners might, by performing certain acts, acquire title to some land.

But we are not limited to the instrument itself. It is made in pursuance of the law of the state, and that law must be examined in determining the meaning of the instrument. This would be the general rule, and in addition this grant in terms refers to the law as fixing the rights of the petitioners. The first article declares that the government accepts the proposal, as far as conformable with the laws of colonization passed by the honorable congress of the state on the 24th of March, 1825. Thus the particular statute which we are to examine is expressly referred to and by implication made a part of the contract. Articles 3, 5, 6, 8 and 9 also contain references to the statute, and article 11 directly declares that in reference to all matters not provided for or expressed in this article, the empresarios or the new settlers, shall abide and be governed by the constitution and laws. The act of March 24, 1825, referred to, consists of forty-eight articles. It may be found in Rockwell's Spanish and Mexican law, page 641. It purports to be a colonization law, and the first few articles refer simply to the admission and rights of foreigners. Article 8 is as follows:

"The projects for new settlements, in which one or more persons offer to bring at their expense, one hundred or more families shall be presented to the government, and if found conformable with this law, they will be admitted; and the government will immediately designate to the contractors the land where they are to establish themselves, and the term of six years, within which they must present the number of families they contracted for, under the penalty of losing the rights and privileges offered in their favor, in proportion to the number of families which they fail to introduce, and the contract totally annulled if they do not bring at least one hundred families."

Article 11 defines the unit of measurement. Articles 12, 13 and 14 read thus:

"Article 12—Taking the above unity as a basis, and observing the distinction which must be made between graizng land, or that which is proper for raising stock, and farming land, without the facility for irrigation, this law grants to the contractor or contractors, for the establishment of a new settlement, for each 100 families which he may introduce and establish in the state, five sitios of grazing land, and five labors, at least the one-half of which shall be without the facility of irrigation; but they can only receive this premium for 800 families, although a greater number should be introduced, and no fraction whatever less than 100 shall entitle them to any premium, not even proportionally.

"Art. 13—Should any contractor or contractors in virtue of the number of families which he may have introduced, acquire in conformity with the last article more than eleven square leagues of land, it shall nevertheless be granted, but subject to the condition of alienating the excess, within twelve years, and if it is not done, the respective political authority shall do it by selling it at public sale, delivering the proceeds to the owners after deduction the costs of the sale.

"Art. 14—To each family comprehended in the contract, whose sole occupation is cultivation of land, one labor shall be given; should he also be a stock raiser, grazing land shall be added to complete a sitio; and should his only occupation be raising of stock he shall only receive a superficies of grazing land, equal to twenty-four million square bars."

Articles 15 and 16, like article 14, refer to amounts of land to be given. On September 4, 1827, a series of instructions to commissioners appointed by the legislature for the partition of lands among new colonists was issued by the government. See Rockwell's Spanish and Mexican law, 649. Among them, article 4 reads thus:

Art. 4—"He shall issue in the name of the state, the titles for land, in conformity with the law, and put new colonists in possession of their lands, with all legal formalities, and the previous citation of adjoining proprietors, should there be any."

And article 24. thus:

Art. 24. "He shall take special care that the proportion of land granted to the colonists by articles 14, 15 and 16, shall be measured by the surveyors with accuracy, and not permit any one to include more land than is designated by law, under the penalty of being personally responsible."

References in these articles to article 14, 15 and 16 is to articles in the colonization law. Now article 8 of the law, quoted above, prescribes what the government will do when the petition of an empresario for colonization is presented:

If found conformable with this law, the government will immediately "designate" to the contractors land whereon to establish themselves. This of course does not mean that the government will grant them land, but simply that it will select and designate the place where a colony may be settled. So that when we find in the first article of the grant, that the government assigns a given tract to the petitioners for the establishment of a colony, the assignment is made by virtue of this article eight of the law, and means simply the selection of a place for the colony. Passing on to article 12, we find what the government will give to the empresario specifically declared, to-wit: For each hundred families five sitios of grazing land, and five labors, at least the one-half of which shall be without the facility of irrigation. This article makes plain the meaning of article 3 of the grant, and shows that that means simply that in consideration of the setting apart of this large tract of land the petitioners agree to introduce and settle on that land 200 families. Articles 12 and 13 together provide what shall be given to the empresarios who introduce 800 families and receives more than eleven square leagues of land.

This last article shows a clear intent that no party should obtain title to more than eleven square leagues, no matter what services in colonization he may render to the state. Articles 14, 15 and 16 provide what the individual settlers are to receive, and sections from 12 to 16 inclusive explain fully the meaning of article 5 of the grant, which declares that the state retains title to all the surplus land within the grant, after laying off that which belongs to the empresarios and their settlers. Thus the law makes plain the meaning of the contract, and shows that it was not a conveyance passing title. In other words, the grant must be presumed to have been made in pursuance of the law, and to be limited by the terms of the law. Indeed it is doubtful whether a grant made in excess of the authority given by the law would be valid. This grant in terms refers to the law under which it was made, and shows that it was made in pursuance of the authority conferred by that law, which provides that the government will select a tract of land upon which the empresario may establish a colony, and that if he does he will be paid in land at a fixed rate, and that the colonists that he introduces will also receive definite amounts of land. This grant, made thus in pursuance of this law, means just what the law says it may mean, and was simply a designation of a tract within which the petitioners might establish a colony. It of itself passed title to no portion of the land to them.

In Spencer vs. Lapsley, 20 How, 270, the supreme court used this language in respect to the law under which this grant was made.

"The contract of an empresario obliged him to introduce colonists into a specific district. The colonist having a family, was entitled to one league of land, of a particular quality, for which he paid a small sum to the government. The empresario was paid five leagues and five labors for every 100 families introduced. Of course, the excess of land within the limits of the colony, after supplying the colonists and the empresario, remained to the government. The commissioner of distribution was an officer of the government, who superintended the fulfillment of the contract by the empresario. He ascertained the character of the colonists allotted to them and the empresario their shares of land, and for that purpose appointed surveyors, received returns of the survey, and executed the final titles."

Further strengthening this view of the meaning of the grant is article four of the instructions, quoted supra, which provides that the commissioners shall issue the title for land; and this simply carries out the idea running through the law, that no title passed to any of the land until the establishment of the colony.

But further, the law which we have been considering was the law of the state of Coahuila and Texas, which was passed in pursuance of a decree of the Mexican government of August, 1824, which will be found in Rockwell's Spanish and Mexican law, page 451. In that general decree of the nation, by the 12th article, it is provided that no one person shall be allowed to retain the ownership of more than eleven leagues square. Obviously one of the states, acting in pursuance of that decree, would not have provided for a larger grant.

From these various considerations it seems to me clear that the grant in controversy was not intended to be, and was not, a conveyance subject to defeasance, but that it amounted only to a designation and setting apart of the tract as a tract within which the petitioners could establish a colony in conformity to the colonization law, and upon such establishment obtain title to a fixed quantum of land within the tract. As there is no pretence that one was ever established, no title to anything ever passed.

It follows that the complaint holds nothing by virtue of this so called grant, and the demurrers must be sustained, and it is so ordered.

A true copy.

Teste: WILLIAM A. WILLARD, *Clerk.*
By F. W. Topper, *Deputy Clerk.*

The consternation brought about by the demands of the Colorado Interstate Company can only be imagined. It was similar to the havoc wrought by Reavis when he introduced his Baron of Arizona Grant not too long afterwards. If the Beales Grant had been conceeded to the Interstate Company it would have changed the lives and possibly the homes of all the people in Springer, Raton, Cimarron, Rayado, Baldy and all the settlers on the Maxwell Land Grant. Just what arrangements would have been made is a matter of conjecture. Some would have made plans to remain at all costs and it would have cost all they owned to remain; others would have resorted to Winchesters. Most would have lost ranches, homes and savings. Said the Galveston, Texas, News (March 7, 1887):

"It was heralded forth from Kansas City a few days ago that an interstate land company organization, with headquarters in that city, and of which Rufus Hatch of New York is a member, had completed the purchase of the Arkansas Land Grant, comprising 79,000,000 acres, and situated in the Panhandle of Texas, New Mexico, Colorado and embracing a portion of No Man's land, and all of the famous Maxwell Land Grant. It is said here that instead of there being a grant by the Mexican government there was never anything as a foundation for the claim except the contract between the Mexican government and Beales and his partner, by which the latter were to receive four and one half leagues of land for every hundred families introduced into the country. The contract lapsed years and years before Beales and his partner died, because of their failure to comply with the provisions."

Said a Washington, D. C. paper:

"General-Commissioner Sparks of the Land Office said today in a letter addressed to John E. Owens of Brooklyn, New York, in answer to an inquiry about a syndicate getting possession of an enormous tract of public lands: I am in receipt of your letter of the 3rd inst. inquiring how a New York Syndicate can get possession of 60,000,000 acres of public lands. I infer that your inquiry relates to a newspaper paragraph recently stating that a syndicate had purchased a private land claim embracing an enormous quantity of land, including portions of Texas, Arkansas, the Indian Territory, New Mexico and Colorado. I have to advise you that no possession has been acquired by any person or persons or 60,000,000 or any other number of acres of land under the alleged claim, and that the records of this office disclose no foundation for a legitimate claim of this character. No person has any legal right to attempt to control or dispose of public lands of the United States upon the pretext of such claims. Persons who purchase quit claim deeds from claimants of alleged private land grants do so at their own risks.

"Mr. J. F. Hadley, Treasurer of the Interstate Land Company, speaking of Commissioner Sparks' letter yesterday said: 'The opinion of Mr. Sparks is worth no more than yours. He has no jurisdiction in this matter, and it is not to be supposed that the protocol and the Mexican records would be filed in his office. He need not be alarmed about anybody getting bit. We are not trying to sell any stock.'

"'How about the statement in the dispatches that the Grant was never earned?'

"'When Grants were made in Mexico the grantee was given a deed of the property. If the condition of the Grant were not complied with and inquest of office was held and the Grant forfeited. If superior force prevented compliance with the conditions, then the title became absolute. That is the law in every country and applies to all sorts of contracts. Dr. Beales spent large sums of money in colonizing Texas and did establish a colony there. It was no fault of his if Texans destroyed it. Opinions amount to nothing. This is a matter for the Supreme Court to pass upon, and we will fight our case there." (See the interesting article in the Kansas City Times for March 8, 1887.)

Santa Fe, N.M., March 4, 1887: The press reports from Kansas City and St. Louis recently announced the claim of a vast tract of land in the Southwest by a corporation known as the Interstate Land Company, the land purporting to be a Grant from the Governor of Coahuila and Texas made in 1832 to Dr. Beales under the colonization law of that state enacted in 1825. The publication here today of the facts of the case, and the claims on which purchases from Beales' heirs base their rights to this property, place the matter in a rather different light than that already laid before the public.

"Investigation proves that this land scheme bubble was years ago exploded by the cold hand of the law and of fact, the Texas and Pacific Railroad Company alone expending nearly $100,000 to secure the opinions of the best legal minds in the land as to the validity of the claim. Among others, Hon. Wm. M. Evarts was employed to investigate the subject, and his report was adverse as to its validity.

"In 1881, the Beales' heirs donated one half of their claim to Howard Institute (Still operating as one of the finest institutions of higher learning in the United States for the progress of the Negro race. It has placed many of them in the fields of medicine, law and other professions.) at Washington, hoping thereby to secure the aid of the United States government in their endeavor to establish their title, but the effort proved futile. In commenting on the showing presented by the attorneys of the Interstate Land Company, the New Mexican (newspaper) today says:

"There is no denying the fact that the foremost legal talent in the Union was engaged in investigating this wonderful claim for the past ten years, doing their work very quietly—with singularly suspicious quiet in fact— The Company seems to rely chiefly upon the statement of the case by A. B. Bright, a lawyer of New York, whose very voluminous opinion is alleged to be endorsed by General Benjamin Butler of Massachusetts. The lawyer significantly confines himself to the position which Texas occupies in the matter. Never a word has he concerning New Mexico's standing in the premises, and how, when or where the governor of Coahuila and Texas got authority to grant away land situated within the province of New Mexico, the boundaries of which were established by decree of the Cortes of Spain in 1813 and were never changed by the Mexican government, the opinion of Mr. Bright fails to show. The governor of Coahuila and Texas had no jurisdiction over any part of the lands within the province of New Mexico. Texas attempted to extend her jurisdiction as far west as the Rio Grande river; but it failed and neither Old Mexico, New Mexico or the United States recognized any right to any such jurisdiction. The claim that Texas ever had any jurisdiction as far west as the Rio Grande, as above set forth, is fully disposed in the negative by the Act of Congress of September 9, 1850, defining the boundaries of New Mexico as originally established by the Spanish government in 1813.

"Thus, so far as relates to land situated within the boundaries of New Mexico, this claim under the Beales' heirs is void, a delusion and a snare to catch investors in a wild-cat land speculation. As regards Texas, Colorado and No Man's Land, there is not even a lurking suspicion that this claim can be made to hold water in the courts. Beales secured the Grant upon precisely the same conditions under which Wilson held it. The government archives admit the forfeiture of Wilson's claim for non-compliance with his colonization contract, and the record further shows that in the original Grant to Wilson it was specified this Grant should become void in case of Wilson's failure to carry out its provisions. Beales, in turn, altogether failed to colonize the Grant, hence the title to the lands never became vested in him. The people of New Mexico, who are versed in the history and the laws governing these matters, have no apprehensions whatsoever as to any effect this astonishing claim can have upon titles to land in the Territory of New Mexico." (Santa Fe Globe Democrat.)

Up in Raton the Maxwell Land Grant Company was particularly concerned especially since at face value the Beales Grant seemed to be valid and the Raton Range gave the people to understand as much. . . . "The Mexican Grant is perfectly regular, and was made March 14, 1832, to Juan Carlos Beales and Jose Manuel Royuella, and hence antedates both the Maxwell and the Mora Grants and embraces those. October 11, 1832, Royuella conveyed all his interests to Beales, who died in New York in 1879. His heirs in 1886 conveyed the concession to their present possessors. This Grant is archived in the city of Mexico, Saltillo, Austin and Santa Fe. Its genuineness is beyond dispute, and there is no doubt as to its confirmation by the Treaty of Guadalupe Hidalgo, made between the United States and Mexico in 1848.

"Unlike the Maxwell and Mora Grants, the boundaries of the Beales and Royuella Grant are fixed by determinate points of astronomical observation and natural monuments. These boundaries being natural and immovable cannot be changed by the ingenuity of modern devise, such as has been employed to enlarge the limits of certain Grants of more modern date.

"While this Grant embraces large scopes of territory upon which settlers have made improvements, it is understood that the present owners of the Grant will deal most liberally with the settlers; and it is believed that no hardships will be experienced by private individuals who have occupied portions of the embraced territories. The record shows that the present owners have, in its entirety, all the titles that Royuella and Beales got from Coahuila and Texas, under the Mexican Government, and that their title is prior to any other Grant or title. This Grant is clearly protected by the second article of the protocol to the treaty of Guadalupe-Hidalgo, which literally provides: The American Government by suppressing the 10th article of the Treaty of Guadalupe did not in any way intend to annul the grant of lands made by Mexico in the ceded territories. These grants, notwithstanding the suppression of the articles of the treaty, preserve the legal value which they may possess, and the grantees may cause their legitimate titles to be acknowledged before the American tribunals. Conformably to the law of the United States legitimate titles of every description of property, personal and real, existing in the ceded territories are those which were legitimate titles under the Mexican law in California and New Mexico up to May 13, 1846, and in Texas up to March 2, 1836.

"These considerations induce the belief that this is superior to any title extant, whatever the claimants of the Maxwell and Mora Grants, which are subordinate to the Royuella-Beales Grant, because inferior in point of time, may think certain, it is the great mass of settlers in New Mexico and Colorado, and they have reason to rejoice over the establishment of their titles through the successors to Royuella and Beales, who are understood to be disposed to clear up the vexed question of land titles in these parts, without perpetrating outrages upon the settlers.

"This claim takes in the eastern half of New Mexico (all that lies east of the Rio Grande), a small portion of southeastern Colorado, the western portion, one-third of it at least, of No Man's Land, and a strip of land in Texas lying east of the boundary of this territory.

"The title and history of this claim read well and may prove of some consequence to the settlers of this vast tract. No matter if the Supreme Court should confirm the title of the Maxwell Land Grant it would not affect the validity of this older Grant, it being prior to all others, except grants to about the amount of four million acres all told. While it may never amount to anything more than a claim, it might mean a great deal. They claim an unbroken chain of title from 1826 down, and promise bona-fide settlers that they shall have free title to their homes and land. This would in event of the substantiation of their title, relieve the uncertain feelings so prevalent upon this grant-ridden country and settle bitter feelings which have been engendered on the Maxwell Land Grant. Many eminent lawyers will no doubt differ as to whether this gigantic claim will ever secure recognized title or any part thereof but in the meantime grass will grow as well as ever. Let the fittest survive—Livestock Journal of New Mexico and Raton Range—March 4, 1887.)

Meantime the Kansas City Times reviewed the whole history of the Grant which appeared in print on the same day that the Raton paper offered so much hope to the settler and the Interstate Land Company. Said the Kansas paper:

"Nearly a year ago a Kansas City man learned (just how the editor failed to note) of the existence of the protocol and in October last he went East to investigate the matter. A search through the archives of the Land Department in Washington revealed the protocol. He then proceeded to hunt up the heirs, whom he found in New York City.

"With the heirs, Anita Exeter, James A. G. Beales and Adelaide K. Jaffray, he made a contract for the purchase of the property for $1,250,000. In November a syndicate formed in this city and organized a company to which it sold the property for $10,000,000, the members of the syndicate retaining an interest. The company was organized under the name of the Interstate Land Company of Colorado, the principal officers of which are in this city. Charles Godnight of Palo Duro, Texas, is President; N. B. Childs of Kansas City, Vice-President and General Manager; O. H. Nelson of Burlingame, Kansas, General Manager; ex-governor Thomas Carney of Leathenworth, Kansas, Assistant General Manager; S. T. Hadley of Kansas City, Secretary and Treasurer. (These also composed the Board of Directors.) The Attorneys are Hon. Alexander Graves of Lexington, Mo.; Walton, Hill & Walton of Austin, Texas and John L. Jerome of Denver, Colorado.

"The deeds from the heirs, which have been recorded in New Mexico, Colorado and Texas, show that the Grant covers 13,000,000 acres in Texas, taking in two tiers of counties on the western border of the state from the northern boundary to the 32nd parallel of north latitude; 1,221,000 acres in what is known as the public land strip in No Man's Land; 7,000,000 acres in south Colorado between the Kansas line and the Rio Grande river, and 47,000,000 acres in New Mexico, including all of the territory east of the Rio Grande, with the exception of 4,000,000 acres lying along the Rio Grande included in smaller grants made by the Mexican government prior to 1832, which were accepted by the terms of the Grant.

"The history of the Grant shows a singular oversight on the part of the United States government. The Grant was originally made to Stephen Julian Wilson on May 27, 1826, by the Mexican government. The Mexican government was independent of Spain. The next year Wilson sold a half interest to Richard Exeter, a Mexican subject. Exeter died in 1829, leaving his wife and daughter, Anita Exeter. Dr. John Beales, an Englishman who had migrated to Mexico and became a Mexican subject, was appointed administrator to the estate. A year or two later he married Exeter's widow, and on March 14, 1832, Beales and a

Mexican named Jose Manuel Royuella, for the purpose of perpetuating Exeter's estate in his heirs, petitioned the Mexican government for a re-grant of the land on the same conditions as those governing the Grant to Wilson. The Grant was made and Beales obtained Exeter's interest while Royuella received Wilson's. October 1, 1832, Royuella, for a valuable consideration, sold his entire interest to Beales, who became the sole owner of the Grant. In 1835, Beales, at the expense of $100,000, established a colony on the land at a town which he called Dolores. The Texas war of independence breaking out, the Texans forbade Beales from taking possession of the property and the president of Mexico on January 14, 1836, issued an order to General Santa Anna, commander of the Mexican armies, to use his forces to protect Beales in the possession of his property. The Texan forces, however, proved too strong and destroyed the town established by Beales at so much expense. Beales then proceeded with his family to New York and the unsettled state of the country for the next fifteen years succeeding prevented him from establishing his claim to the Grant. When the commissioners from the two governments proposed the treaty of Guadalupe Hidalgo, which was to end the Mexican War, it provided that all the grants of land made by the Mexican authorities in what was known as Coahuila, Texas, that were legal under Mexican law on March 2, 1836, should be confirmed by the United States. The tenth article, which included this provision, was struck out by the United States Senate when it ratified the treaty. The result was that the protocol, since the Mexican government refused to accept the treaty, by which the Beales Grant is protected, was drawn up and ratified by the United States.

"Singularly enough the protocol remained virtually unknown. It was not until several years after that the protocol was published in the public domain book issued in the Land Department. Even then its significance was not recognized, and probably would not have been now had it not been for the discovery of the gentleman who bought the heirs' interests. Dr. Beales recorded the Grant in Santa Fe, New Mexico, and Austin Texas, in 1870. He died in 1879 leaving a widow who afterward died, and three children, among whom were Anita Exeter, a daughter of Mrs. Beales by her first husband. The grants under which the Maxwell and Mora lands are held were made in 1841 and 1845 by New Mexico an interior state (? It was not even a province—it had the rating of a Department) of the republic. Even though they had been made prior to the Beales Grant (since the latter was recorded in 1870) they should be void for the reason that the grants are in territory east of the Rio Grande, whereas the jurisdiction of Mexico extended only to the west of the river. The grants, however, were not prior to the Beales Grant, but were made several years later and on that account are illegal. The grants owned principally by German Capitalists.

"In December Childs went to Mexico and secured copies of all the documents relating to the Grant from 1826 down to the time of the treaty of Guadalupe Hidalgo, which show an unbroken chain and line of title to the present owners."

March 18, 1887—The Interstate Land Company held a meeting of the stockholders in the office of N. B. Childs. Said the Board of Directors: "Foreigners owning tracts of land and corporations will be the owners that will have to settle with the company. The most notable among these will be the Germans claiming to own the Maxwell Land Grant, as they have no title, but that which is subject to title of the Interstate Land Company. The huge land grant purchased by the Interstate Land Company includes the immense ranches of Stephen W. Dorsey and Robert G. Ingersoll and also includes in its boundaries several cities of considerable size and of no little commercial importance. Among them are Las Vegas, Santa Fe, Albuquerque and Socorro—all in New Mexico. The company will send surveyors to these cities and also to other cities to make out surveys and every property owner will have to look to the company for a quit claim deed in order to get a clear title to his property. It can readily be seen therefore that the company has an almost endless amount of work before it and that the mere task of clearing titles will in itself require several years of time. It will be necessary to keep a large number of surveyors at work constantly in all parts of the huge territory covered by the Grant."

Maxwell Land Grant lawyers, railroad lawyers, lawyers for settlers, cattlemen and the government saved grants, cities, towns, ranches and rivers for New Mexico, Texas, Oklahoma, Colorado and Kansas. Had the Interstate Land Company won, our story would have been different or not at all.

Chapter Nine

THE MAXWELL LAND GRANT COMPANY

Northern New Mexico owes its progress, wealth and very existence, to some extent at least, to the Maxwell Land Grant Company. The Santa Fe Railroad came over the Raton Pass in 1879 and thus obtained its right of way through New Mexico because of the generosity of the Maxwell Land Grant Company. The towns of Raton, Springer, Cimarron, Maxwell, Rayado and Eagle Nest are due to the Townsite plats made by the company. Frank R. Sherwin has the undying gratitude of the company for a good many enterprises he started. He lost out on some deals but that was the aftermath of the tragedy of the death of his beautiful daughter at the Maxwell house where they lived. Mabelle Sherwin was a gracious hostess and loved by the people of Cimarron. The purge of the Maxwell Land Grant and Railway Company left Sherwin rather stranded and when the company was amalgamated into the Maxwell Land Grant Company he married Colorado's Governor Gilpin's step-daughter, left his son Frank in Denver, moved to Boston, engaged in speculating in mines and died there. Schomburg and Stephen B. Elkins became directors for a time. About 1877, W. R. Morley, a young railroad engineer with the Kansas-Pacific Railroad, was elected by the Board of Directors as Manager of the Maxwell Land Grant Company at the suggestion of Henry M. Porter, a stockholder who ran the bank at Elizabethtown. Later he entered partnership with Clouthier and started the famous mercantile store of Porter and Clouthier at Springer. Morley called to his assistance a former classmate of his at Iowa City College, Frank Springer by name, a young lawyer who became attorney for the company and the Santa Fe Railroad. He went directly to Holland to try to straighten out the affairs of the company which needed straightening out to say the least.

Many of the stockholders were not aware that they were being duped. They never suspected that there was no such thing as a steamboat on the Vermejo and that the Cimarron did not have ports for cargoes from the Seven Seas. Others wondered why they were not receiving the millions in return for their investment as Maxwell was supposed to have done and as the people who sold them their shares said they would. Springer straightened out the company single handed. But with an intelligent lawyer and a sincere Board of Directors the company was flat broke. But Morley pulled the chestnuts out of the fire for the stockholders, having ever at his side, as his guiding light, Frank Springer.

Born in Iowa in the year of Manifest Destiny, Frank Springer was to be the hope and inspiration of the Maxwell Land Grant such as no one before or since. No sooner out of college than he was recognized for his legal talent. Morley could use such a man and invited him to Cimarron. No sooner in Cimarron than he took over the editorship of the *Cimarron News and Press*. In Holland and England he told the stockholders of vast fields of gold, copper, coal, silver; of flowing water; of immense grain fields and grazing lands. This, he made them understand, more than compensated for the money they threw into the venture. With a little patience the millions they dreamed of would be a reality and endless sources of wealth would stream to them. At that time McMains and Anti-Granters were unknown. Springer married Josephine M. Bishop of Cimarron, a girl Clay Allison sought to make his wife. His shyness and her mother's coldness dampened his spirits so he tried elsewhere. That Allison would marry a polished and accomplished person as Miss Bishop is not far-fetched. He was educated. He was also a successful stockman despite his six-shooter exploits. Springer was still a young unknown lawyer. His true greatness was not to front itself until the Anti-Grant War. Looking at the two suitors, everyone would have given the preference to Clay Allison. Everyone but Mrs. Bishop. Springer later made his home at Las Vegas, without, however, giving up his ranch at Cimarron. With his equally distinguished brother, Charles, he built the famous Eagle Nest Lake Dam.

As defense lawyer in the courts in the interest of the company, Springer is the most impressive figure in the whole history of the Maxwell Land Grant. Hardly more than the age to vote, he is gazed upon by hoary headed men as their savior; lawyers with the print of legal ledgers still fresh on their fingers look to this young veteran as a man to imitate. No man was as adroit in riding the storm. Once called in to straighten out the Maxwell Land Grant tangle, he rolls up his sleeves and jumps into the thick of the struggle to labor ambitiously to ride the crest, for success in the venture also meant advantage to Frank Springer. From the day he received his sheepskin at Iowa University he maintains an upward struggle that wins for him favor from Morley, Mrs. Bishop, Miss Bishop, the Maxwell Land Grant Company, the Santa Fe Railroad and the people of Cimarron.

He wrote out two rudimentary articles of belief: The Maxwell Land Grant Company needed him more than he needed it; the company could be the making of New Mexico and bring about its Statehood. He argued with such a tigerish ferocity that had his body been combustible, a supply of water would have had to be on hand in the courtroom lest he be devoured by his own flame. His cannon-ball sentences, crashed and thundered to dispel the ranks of opposition. Anti-Granters fought a lost cause because Springer represented the Maxwell Land Grant Company.

Yet Springer had limitations as striking as his talents. Deeply versed in Paleontology, he was ill-informed in various other fields of knowledge. He read little but law books, debates and government manuals and had he broadened his views and widened his time for that deeper knowledge and type of reflection he would have branched out into the political field up the ladder of national fame as one of America's great statesmen. A prodigiously effective floor debater, he had no real strength of abstract thought and no real capacity to present such general ideas as are associated with philosophical and political thinking. He had never produced a genuine legal paper that set the pattern for later day law students. His oratory had limitations but was considered brilliant in the Southwest, so much so that it became an obsession. He gave awards for oratory to young Highlands University students at Las Vegas after that institution was established. Springer Hall there is named for him as is Springer, New Mexico. While he secured friends to him with grapples of iron, he induced them to act on practical resourcefulness rather than far reaching symmetry.

Springer was an expert of the extemporaneous. His whole proficiency, backed by invincible personal force, was for meeting all practical situations which confronted him and the Maxwell Land Grant Company with some rapidly devised measure, without looking to the ultimate consequence, since such outcomes could be met when the time came, and trusting to the company's resources for remedying all defects. He had faced such situations as a raw recruit lawyer in Iowa; he had improvised as publisher of the Cimarron newspaper, when he knew little or nothing of journalism; he had come to the front when he knew little law and less jurisprudence; he had done some quick thinking when he ceased being an Iowan and put on the garb of a New Mexican; he had pulled rabbits out of the hat in manipulating the policies of the company. But his legal combat was all he lived and died for. His one weak point was that he oversimplified the problem because he was confronted with it and overlooked the remote possibility that O. P. McMains could, and did, make the results of his victory over the Anti-Granters take on important aspects that more than once seemingly placed a life in his hands. The price of victory is often bloodshed as much as the result of defeat. Squatters on the Grant were not aware that all was settled by legal procedure any more than prospectors asked Maxwell's permission to stake out claims at Baldy, Elizabethtown and Willow Creek. After all, land is a sort of gold and no man likes to be told that legally it doesn't belong to him, especially if he absolutely and firmly believes he is in the right. The great penalty paid by the born fighter whether he be a Springer or a McMains is that he gradually accumulates a legion of enemies so that even if he has the ability to take and give blows, he still has to reckon on the final bill not of material profit and loss, but the ultimate hate or love future generations, who with impersonal perusal place in categories not a man's contributions to society but the wounds of the under-dog he so gloriously licked. That is why there will always be partisans in the Maxwell Land Grant question; simply because Springer won and McMains lost. More so since the former died so wealthy and the latter in the Russell home in Stonewall which was loaned to him so poor was he. Had the reverse been the case, the thinking would also be reversed.

The Maxwell Land Grant Company intended to profit from the mistakes of the Maxwell Land Grant and Railway Company. The Board of Directors did not intend to fall into the same pit a second time like the blind leading the blind. Stockholders in Holland did not aim to be duped by lying posters and folders. They sent representatives from their own country into the field for there was only one universal language they understood—loss and gain—A loss was a loss in Dutch as well as in English and even if it proved to be Greek it would still be a loss; never a gain. The company would scratch that word from its list. Sherwin was a failure to the company because he had the interests of Sherwin at heart. Men must be located who would eat, sleep, live solely for the interests of the Maxwell Land Grant Company. Therefore only such men would be employed whether to take care of cattle on the Maxwell Farm or to direct the vast corporation from behind a desk at Cimarron. How he did it was of no concern to them so long as he did it. The books must be drenched in black ink rather than red and they had invested enough money in the project to see the black rather than the red. One thing must be said in their favor, they were not out to eject settlers. Everyone was given ample time and opportunity to pay something for a deed in his favor according to his circumstances in life. The company was firm but not unfair, no matter what the opinion of McMains and his followers.

As the affairs of the company progressed they sold off 250,000 acres of land of the north end of the Grant to the Colorado Fuel and Iron Company for the sum of one million dollars. It was worth the money paid and repaid itself many times over in coal and timber. Land was also sold and leased for farming and to Townsite companies. The Maxwell Land Grant Company also leased and sold about 500,000 acres of coal land from all of which they raised enough cash to pay off most of their junior bonds lately issued, and still had quite a bit of property left. Not having paid much, if any, of the interest on the original $5,000,000 debenture bonds.

Frank and Charles Springer organized the St. Louis Railroad and Coal Mining Company, now known as the St. Louis and Rocky Mountain Coal Company. They leased and bought from the Maxwell Land Grant Company about 500,000 acres of land, interested some men in St. Louis in the deal, built a railroad from the Colorado & Southern Railroad west of Raton, to give them an outlet south for their coal and on down past their coal property to Cimarron and up the canyon to the gold mines. They sold their interest to the Santa Fe railroad retaining their interest in the coal mines. They built a reservoir (Eagle Nest Lake) on the Cimarron River, given Frank Springer as a bonus above his salary by the company, for conducting its suits to secure patents to their lands, and bought from Porter 52,000 acres more, all under the reservoir.

Morley was succeeded by Mr. P. Pels (Pels in Colorado was named after him as Morley, Colorado was named after Morley and Springer, New Mexico after Frank Springer). Morley afterwards built a railroad from Lordsburg, New Mexico, to the Clifton Copper Mines in the same state, as well as the railroad to Guyas in old Mexico and was later employed to build a railroad from Chihuahua to Mexico City. While with this project he was accidently killed by a gunshot. His body was brought to Las Vegas, New Mexico, for burial and interred there in December, 1883. He left a wife, one son, W. R. Morley, Jr., who was quite a football hero in his day, two daughters who settled at Datil, New Mexico, above Magdalena where Manville Rhodes used to write his cowboy stories as he rode on horseback. Pels was a tall man with a flowing beard and looked like a patriarch.

To go back to the validity of the Grant one has to remember the Treaty of Guadalupe Hidalgo. The Mexican Government had refused to ratify the treaty until they had gained a promise from the United States Government that the Spanish and Mexican land grants would receive protection from the American Government. In the protocol attached to the treaty, protection was fully guaranteed, so that a Mexican citizen holding a grant from the Mexican government would receive the same rights of enjoyment of his property under the United States that he formerly received from the Mexican government. To carry out the agreement, Congress passed the Act of July 22, 1854, providing for the appointment of a surveyor-general for New Mexico. Under this act the surveyor-general was to notify grant claimants to file their papers in the surveyor-general's office at Santa Fe, New Mexico, leading to the confirmation of their grants by Congress. The surveyor was vested with judicial authority in that he was to summon witnesses, take testimony, and pass on the grant by giving his decision as to whether it was a valid grant or not. All the documents were then forwarded to the General Land Office of the Department of the Interior in Washington, with the surveyor's comments. There Congress either approved or rejected the claim. The confirmation by Congress became a quit claim or relinquishment by that body to the grantees of any claim that Congress had to the grants, and confirmed the claimants in their rights to the land. The first survey made under the jurisdiction of the surveyor-general was, as a rule, followed by another survey leading to the patent of the land by Congress.

Governor Armijo made large grants because he received a private stipend in proportion and also to strengthen the claims to the whole region which lay between the Rio Grande and the present boundary of Texas. That the Lone Star State claimed this latter is evidenced by the Texas-Santa Fe Expedition sent out to take it by force of arms. The land given Miranda and Beaubien comprised almost the combined areas of the states of Rhode Island and Delaware. Padre Martinez protested that this land belonged to Charles Bent and the Indians. Maxwell acquired the land legally. After the American occupation and because of the Hildago Treaty, Congress required claimants to bear the expense of its survey. Maxwell deposited the required amount in the General Land Office but withdrew it because the Secretary of the Interior, J. D. Cox, on December 13, 1869, refused to permit the grantees more than eleven square leagues to each claimant on the grounds that the Mexican land laws stipulated that much as the maximum. He was overruled and Maxwell had the survey continued.

A suit in equity filed in the United States Circuit Court of Colorado by the United States Government against the Maxwell Land Grant Company to cancel the patent to the land ended up five years later by the United States Supreme Court accepting the validity of the grant because the original petition was not individual but for colonizaiton purposes, consequently making it a De Nevo Grant whereby the claimants were entitled to all the lands surveyed within the exterior boundaries. After the decision was handed down in May 1887, settlers living on the grant, many of whom had acquired the right under the government survey of 1874, opening the land for settlement, which accounted for their agitation under McMains, bitterly attacked the decision as depriving them of their property. An attempt on the part of the Maxwell Land Grant to settle with those who had just claims did not prevent bloodshed. It was some time before the company affected a settlement and entered upon a period of economic development of its coal, timber, agricultural lands, mines and the prosperity of Northern New Mexico and Southern Colorado.

On February 8, 1888, Harry Whigham, acting for the Maxwell Land Grant Company leased the famous Aztec flour mill in Cimarron, together with the ditch rights for the same, and other appurtenances for a year upon the express condition that George Grubble, leasee keep sober and attend his business and should he become intoxicated or under the influence of liquor, "then this lease shall be void from such time and the same if the rent has not been paid." Whigham was hemmed in between trying to be reasonable and trying to appease his superiors. Added to his burdens McMains moved to Stonewall, in Colorado, which was part of the grant property and continued his agitation there:

"Harry Whigham, agent and receiver of the Maxwell Land Grant Company, recognizing the Comet as the leading anti-Grant paper having the largest circulation among settlers on the alleged claim, has seen fit to request that we publish a letter from him in answer to an article which appeared in our last issue. In order to answer his unfounded charge that we are misleading the settlers. He left on the morning train. He does not anticipate any difficulty in enforcing the mandate of the court on the settlers, as they already see the folly of kicking against the judicial tricks. The editor has not seen the form of lease which receiver Whigham proposes to give those settlers on the grant who are willing to lease from him for one year, if there are any such; but he has seen the form of lease which Harry Whigham uses when he leases lots in Maxwell's North Addition (Boggstown) to Raton, and supposes the terms of both are similar. In the latter form the settler binds himself to pay rent annually in advance, and if default be made in the payment of any rent when it becomes due, Mr. Whigham may take immediate possession of the premises leased. And yet Mr. Whigham says he stands ready to make a 'fairer arrangement with any settler on the grant than the owner of private lands in the Territory' what settler can pay rent annually in advance? Whigham speaks the truth when he says that those persons who keep up an excitement and prevent an 'amicable arrangement', are the worst enemies of the people most interested. Who are the people most interested if not the parties who claim to own the Grant? For 'amicable arrangements' in his letter read 'settlers ruin'." (*Livestock Journal of New Mexico, March 26, 1888.*)

"Harry Whigham says he does not mean to eject the settlers by wholesale. Most certainly not. A locoed schoolboy wouldn't pursue that court. You can't move 10,000 people that easy. But he can serve writs of ejectment on a few ignorant people in various sections of the grant, and by giving it proper notice, so that everybody knows every move he makes so as to easily intimidate the rest. Threaten an illiterate citizen with the extreme penalty of the law for the violation of the orders of a court, and it will act more quickly than wholesale ejectment. Notice the first break Whitman made last week. The deputy-sheriff, armed with legal documents, goes over by Cimarron and serves on a poor, ignorant Mexican, who doesn't know the difference between a writ of ejectment and a Chinese laundry bill, he resists intrusion by the officer. The court then issues an order to have the Mexican appear in court to answer for contempt of court. Why doesn't Mr. Whigham take the same course with some person on the Grant who understands the English language and the law, and who would have the money necessary to employ a competent attorney to attend his interests? No. That wouldn't do. It wouldn't give the necessary notoriety to the point the agent and receiver intended to make. . . ." (*Ibid.*)

"A letter just received in St. Louis from Amsterdam, Holland, says that the Maxwell Land Grant Company is annoyed over the news of the disturbed condition of the settlers on their property. One of the share-owners has been sent over to visit the property, with instructions to act with the utmost fairness. He will be on the property next week. It is hoped there will be no further ruptures between the settlers and Mr. Whigham before the arrival of the emissary, who will undertake the role of peacemaker. All peaceful citizens will receive fair treatment at his hands. We always supposed that Harry Whigham had sufficient brains to make any settlement that might be consistent. If Whigham and his able attorney, Springer, can't do business, no philanthropic emissary need apply. Any Dutchman who takes that pair to be innocuous desuetudes, is surely 'off his base'." (*Ibid.*) (Note: This sounds like McMains.—Whigham wrote:

"The United States Government has spent more money in preparing this case than has ever been used in any case in New Mexico or Colorado. It has been decided by a U. S. Judge in favor of the Grant Company on the law and facts. Notwithstanding all the charges of fraud, the court finds on evidence that there has been no fraud. Who is to decide such matters? The courts after hearing evidence, or interested parties without evidence? Would you like to have the title to your house or cow decided in the latter way? . . . Nine-tenths of the men who yell the loudest about their homes and their rights have come and settled upon the grant since the U. S. patent recognized the title of the company peaceably and quietly. Has it occurred to you that the men who came here and found a U. S. patent for the land a title which the greatest lawyers in the land called perfect, are the ones who ought to await until the court of the last resort decides that this title is not good?————. You and some of your readers seem to blame the grant owners for the trouble the settlers find themselves in by the decisions of the courts, but you lay the blame at the wrong door. If these people have been misled by the unwarranted acts of the land department in trying to override an Act of Congress, they should blame the government, not the company. The company bought the land in good faith and paid a very good price for it. Upon what principle do you ask them to make a present of it to somebody else? The Maxwell Land Grant Company stands ready today to make a fairer arrangement with any settler on the grant than any owner of private lands in the territory. . . . " (*Ibid.*)

The answer to the controversy was a mass meeting of the settlers at a place known as Adobe House, Horseshoe Pasture on the Vermejo River. The meeting was comprised with but one object in view, the securing for themselves and each other whatever rights they had to their homes and property. From early morning till noon they could be seen approaching Adobe House from every direction. By noon a larger body of Americans and Spanish-Americans, residents on the grant, were assembled than ever before met for a similar purpose. They elected officers, made laws and drew up a constitution. Actually, it served no purpose but to stir up hatreds and controversy since, as Whigham remarked, U. S. Congress made a decision and what higher appeal had they? Behind all this agitation was the General, McMains, stirring, moving, pushing, edging, hedging, spurring on opposition against the foreigners. It was a term he constantly employed and put in the mouths of the editors who were partisan. After awhile even Americans resented the reference to Hollanders.

"If the Trinidad Citizen would study the history of the Maxwell Grant closely, it would find that Congress confirmed the grant in 1860, which was during the reign of one Buchanan, and at a time when Elkins and Chaffee had no influence in National affairs. Furthermore, if the Citizen will look into the records, it will discover that the many who filed on the land, proved up and obtained final receipts were no more than five. And further, if the Citizen will stop its cry about Dutch owners long enough to learn the truth, the fact will stand out in bold relief that the Maxwell Company is an American Corporation and that a large portion of the bonds are owned in this Country. H. M. Porter, of Denver, has $300,000 of the company's bonds. Lee, Higginson & Company of Boston are investors of considerable extent, and R. V. Martinson and others of New York have hundreds of thousands in it. And to go further, the Maxwell Company is assessed on the property both in Colorado and New Mexico and the tax collectors of both Colfax and Las Animas Counties collect taxes from the Company. Under all these circumstances, it would appear that the Grant Company has some rights that the citizen should respect. Everyone interested will, in the end secure their rights. You may require a little time to demonstrate that the majesty of the law must be respected and obeyed, but it will be done, and those illegally engaged in obstructing the execution of the law will suffer. The misguided and ill-advised men so engaged out to see the inevitable result of their wrongdoing and desist from any further participation in such conduct. We believe that a properly directed effort would secure indemnity from Congress for every settler on the grant who, in good faith located on the grant as government land. Any effort petitioning Congress or any other department to meddle with the decision of the U. S. Supreme Court is time wasted, and any unlawful interference with the Company or its property will tend to prejudice their case against securing equitable relief. Settlers think this over before going any further in the wrong direction." (Springer Stockman, September 6, 1888.)

M. P. Pels fared no better than Whigham with the settlers. To make sure that Congress was not mistaken he wrote the President. On September 27, 1887, President Cleveland answered:

"In the matter of the Maxwell Land Grant referring to your communication, as in every other, the law of the land must be supreme. The judgment of the Supreme Court of the United States on the subjects involved therein is authoritative and conclusive. Its judgment must be respected and obeyed. Those who counsel resistance to the law or by false and inflammatory statements such as are made in the handbills submitted to me, attempt to impose upon the ignorant by advising an appeal from the judgment of the highest court in the land to lawless force, are the worst enemies of those whom they have mislead. Any lawful overt act committed in pursuance of such counsel will of course, be visited with the penalty appropriate to the crime. If any wrongs are done, then redress can be obtained through peaceful method of the law which is fully adequate to protect every right of the citizen. Its faithful enforcement is due alike to the poor and the weak, the healthy and the strong. I sincerely trust the incendiary counsel (no doubt McMains) in the handbill will not produce the baleful effect for which it was intended, and that those in whose favor the court has determined these vexed questions of title will not attempt to extend their rights to cases not determined and that in insisting upon their rights they will deal kindly and generously with those who have mistakenly acted upon an invalid title."

McMains was not the one to take this sitting down. Gathering up evidence to contradict this, a year later he wrote the President on September 19, 1888:

"Because the decision of the Secretary of the Interior of December 31, 1869, the entire tract of land in New Mexico and Colorado claimed as the Maxwell Land Grant was thrown open to settlement and entry as public land in 1874, and homesteaded and preemption settlers permitted to acquire private and vested rights. The settlers claim that the Secretary's decision of 1869 upon which their rights depend is binding in law until legally reversed. If this proposition is not true, the settlers agree to give the Maxwell Land Grant Company peaceable possession of their so-called Grant. The Interior Department, since the decision of the Supreme Court, in the Maxwell grant case, admits no direct proceeding was ever instituted for the purpose of reversing the Secretary's decision. Has the Secretary's decision then, been indirectly or collaterally reversed? This, Your Excellency, is all the question the settlers wish to have authoritatively answered. If the said decision has not been collaterally reversed and the settlers claim it has not been and cannot be, we besech your Excellency to have the Secretary's valid decision of 1869 enforced and the rights of settlers dependent upon it protected. And for this your petitioners will ever pray."

McMains brought on the agitation at Stonewall that resulted in his indictment as well as hailing before the court, as participators: Morton Kephart, F. B. Chapman, Alfonso Chapman, Joseph Hagen, George Russel, Sam Bell, William Haden, Al Kelly, O. B. Abbott, James Cox, Adrian Girardet, A. Duling, and McGathy. *(Trinidad Advertiser Oct. 4, 1888.)*

RATON RANGE—SEPT. 2, 1887

It is currently reported that masked men, with blanketed horses, have been lying in wait for Mr. Pels in the Stonewall country. What good would it do them to get away with the Grant Company's agent does not appear. There can be no benefit accruing to the settlers commensurate with the risk they take in such serious violations of the law. If the agent had a posse and writ of ejectment with him we could understand how they might be tempted to assume the defensive, but that they should lead out in the aggressive is a matter of surprise. There can be no peaceable ending resulting from these hostile movements if the ball ever opens. The end will come, and it will come quickly, if such unlawful demonstrations are to be pursued in the future.

Instead of taking up some practical line of action and retaining the sympathy of the government, they are wrongly following the advice of Mr. O. P. McMains. We are informed however, that even Mr. McMains, while on his recent trip to the mountain district, acquiesced to the growing desire to obtain legal counsel for the settlers. This is a rich stage of the game for him to arrive at such a conclusion; it would seem to a common observer that he had an ample opportunity for a legal fight, which will probably never be found again, whence at his instance the government started suit in Colorado to set aside the patent. Then would have been the opportunity to exhaust legal aid. For him at this time to submit to the procurance of legal counsel can only be likened to locking the stable after the horse is gone. We cannot believe that there will ever be a re-opening, legally, of the Maxwell Grant case as far as the boundaries are concerned, and, as to whether they were really entitled to such land has become an unimportant, useless question. There is, however, a movement coming rapidly to the front to prevail upon Congress to buy this land and throw it open to settlement, which we believe will yet be carried up to a successful issue. The national treasury is accumulating $10,000,000.00 of surplus each month of the year. Congress is bound to give due consideration to the unfortunate situation of such a large body of settlers who have been defrauded by the outrageous legislative act confirming this enormous grant as a valid grant, when it was in violation of the spirit of the Constitution, uncalled for by any treaty with Mexico, and a shameful release of an immense tract of the people's domain. Congress should, and no doubt will, relieve the settlers upon this large scope of country if they will only comport themselves with discretion and secure recognition through the proper channels, and set to work in a systematic manner upon the only solution of their difficulties. i.e., the purchase by the national government of this much disputed tract. What would the temporary investment of a couple or three million dollars affect an overflowing treasury where ten millions of surplus accumulate every month? It would be an extraordinary and unnatural Congress that would refuse the just requests of a mistreated people to have their homes, which they have improved, and occupied, for so many years, placed so that they could secure proper title thereto. The money necessary to carry this out would return to the national coffers inside of two or three years, after having performed the honorable service of carrying out a great moral obligation, rendering happy and peaceful the homes of thousands of harrassed settlers and removing from an otherwise prosperous commonwealth the retarding influences of complications arising in the settlement of an immense land grant. For these reasons involving matters of such great magnitude and grave importance, we are glad to learn that letters are going to many parts of the U.S. soliciting attention of members of Congress to the condition of affairs in this section and asking legislative relief for the settlers upon this grant. Let the good work go on."

TRINIDAD ADVERTISER—FEB. 6, 1889

"O. P. McMains, S. D. Bell, and Anderson Duling were arrested in the city yesterday morning by Sheriff Burns under an indictment of the last grand jury charging them with manslaughter. The indictment grew out of the death of Squire Russell, who was killed during the Stonewall troubles last August, when a mob of the Maxwell Land Grant settlers attacked a number of deputy sheriffs that had been sent out there to disperse them and keep the peace and in which McMains, Bell and Duling were involved. The bonds of the three men were placed at $500.00 each which they easily furnished, and were released Our sympathies are and always have been with those settlers who established homes on this land when it was given for settlement and our opinion is the same now as that expressed at the time of the riots; that mob violence was wrong and would only injure the cause of those settlers who suffered.

"McMains has forced himself to the front as a leader of the settlers and at his door can be laid the trouble of last August. The deputies were sent to Stonewall by Sheriff Burns to preserve the peace and but for the determination of Mm. McMains to bring about a conflict there would have been no trouble. His ambition has seemed to be to cover himself with glory by leading an armed resistance to the law and we trust now his ambition has been fully satisfied."

After the affair at Stonewall quieted down, the Grant Company continued on in comparative peace. There were no more riots to a great extent. Law suits there were and continue to this day but these are settled in courts not with Winchesters. The Grant Company sought to colonize as Beaubien hoped to, and with more success. The Grant has done for New Mexico what Beaubien promised to do for Mexico and for this reason alone merits a monument for all time.

FARMING LANDS UNDER IRRIGATION.
COLFAX COUNTY, NEW MEXICO

UNDER THE SPRINGER DITCH SYSTEM. IMMEDIATELY ADJACENT TO THE ATCHISON, TOPEKA AND SANTA FE RAILWAY.

DELIGHTFUL CLIMATE. HOME MARKETS. PLENTY OF WATER. PRICES AND TERMS REASONABLE.

ADDRESS: THE MAXWELL LAND GRANT COMPANY,
RATON, NEW MEXICO

LANDS UNDER THE SPRINGER DITCH SYSTEM.

Located near the town of Springer, on the main line of the Atchison, Topeka and Santa Fe Railway, they are easy of access to schools, churches, and postoffices. The large coal, gold and copper mines which are being operated here make a market for all produce raised. To raise sufficient for the home market would mean the cultivation of every acre. Prices to be obtained for farm products are the very best, and the competition would be from Nebraska and Kansas, and the difference in freight and express would, of itself, represent a large profit. The price of every product raised is far higher than eastern prices, and cost of production under irrigation no more; every year's crop being assured.

These lands are all under the Springer Ditch System, and the supply of water is drawn from the Cimarron River. A large canal takes the water from the streams to a chain of large reservoirs and lakes situated on the high prairie, and from these reservoirs lateral ditches are run on uniform gades in all directions. The fall of the rivers is about sixty feet per mile, while the canal and ditches are only five feet per mile: by which it will be seen the river waters are available for irrigation at very short distances from their source of supply. The largest reservoir in the Springer System contains 7,000 acre feet; its average depth is nine feet, which can be increased to twelve feet, therby doubling its capacity. There are six smaller reservoirs containing an aggregate of about as much as the larger one; the whole calculated to irrigate a much larger tract of land than is available under the canal, which insures absolutely an abundance of water at all times, the reservoir system guaranteeing water during the dryest season.

Irrigation and Its Advantages

The advantage in favor of irrigation cannot be stated in figures, but this much can be said, that there cannot be any possibility of failure of crops, either through drouth or drowning, as is too often the case in the great agricultural states; and that the ground is kept in continuous high fertility from the constant additions of alluvial wash carried on to it by irrigation. It is estimated that lands irrigated year by year have double the productiveness of lands in the east. The natural fertility of the soil is enhanced by the fertilizing influences of the irrigating waters which keep the lands perpetually fresh, so that not only a better quality of crops but a larger yield per acre year by year can be raised on irrigated lands from the constant combination of sun and moisture, (Moisture at the roots and sunlight at the top), thus the two essential conditions of vigorous plant life are always present.

The farmer who wishes to come to this section need not hesitate because he does not understand the science of irrigation. He will have plenty of neighbors who will teach him and by close observation will learn it quickly. He will soon realize that a man who owns a farm equipped with irrigation canals and a reasonable supply of water properly stored away in the days when not needed is master of the elements.

Crops

Wheat is an excellent crop and the quality of the same is not excelled on the American continent. Thirty bushels to the acre is a moderate estimate. Oats do exceptionally well, and 35 to 50 measured bushels with a weight of from 40 to 50 pounds to the bushel, per acre, is considered a fair crop. As everything is sold here by the pound, heavy weight grain counts in favor of the farmer.

Alfalfa

Is the great standby. It is a feed for every class of animals. Hogs fatten on it, so do cattle and sheep. Horses and mules will do ordinary work on it without grain. It is a great forage for another reason, which is that the young farmer can plant a field of it when he first comes west to grow up with the country, and when he is a grandfather that same field will, with ordinary care, still be producing its three to four crops of five to seven tons annually. One irrigation in the spring and one after each crop is cut is all that is necessary for alfalfa after it is well set. It takes two years to get a good start and then it will outlive a generation.

Potatoes yielded remarkably well. Everything in the way of garden truck does well. Sugar beets and all other roots give good results. Pumpkins and squashes are enormous growers. Melons are first-class and in celery we defy the world to excel us.

Soil

The soil of this section is by nature exceedingly fertile, and capable of producing abundantly all kinds of crops, grains, vegetables and fruits possible to this altitude and latitude. The soil is a mixture of fine sand, light clay and loam, and is generally covered with nutritious grasses. Properly and judiciously watered and worked it never fails of good returns and never wears out. A year's cultivation changes the entire aspect and character of the soil in a marvelous degree, and the longer it is cultivated by irrigation the better it produces. While the soil may seem, on a superficial view, to be destitute of organic matter, it is yet of exceeding fertility under the influence of water; though it is a clay it is at the same time friable, and the nutritious substances which are yielded are generous in the extreme, possessing a wonderful power for the absorption of both heat and moisture. Without irrigation, it is true the value of the land would be nominal, being only fit for grazing with water—a universal solvent—its capacity for production is almost beyond computation.

Climate

The Climatic conditions, with reference to agriculture, are especially inviting. The average winter is short and a large portion of that is open and mild, permissive of outdoor work comfortable. The spring season opens early and the autumn holds late so that throughout practically the entire year there are comparatively few days when outdoor labor is in any sense uncomfortable.

This section has the healthiest and most beautiful climatic conditions that can be found in any portion of the United States or of the world.

The average elevation is about 5,000 feet. The hottest summers, as the vigors of winter, are tempered by altitude and a southern declivity. This diversity of temperature and consequent climatic conditions is the source of a corresponding diversity in the industries and products— staple and otherwise. The fruits, grains, vegetables and cattle is ample guarantee of the permanence and prosperity of all. This country thus holds out the two most inviting conditions essential to pleasant and successful colonization:

First. A more than ordinary certainty of financial reward of judicious investment and hard work; and,

Second. A climate unsurpassed anywhere and not equalled in the eastern and middle states for health and comfort.

The prime factor that makes this section an especially inviting one for immigration is that though it exports many articles, such as beef, wool, coal and minerals, it does not produce one-quarter of the agricultural product consumed, and has for the present to depend upon the farming portions of Kansas 500 miles away to make up this deficiency.

Right here at home the best markets will be found. The cattle and sheep men are not producers of hay, grain and fruits, nor do they even raise garden truck; but they buy oats by the ton; they buy bacon, garden truck and fruit in large quantities.

The miners who delve for coal, copper and gold are many in numbers, and they buy our produce at good prices, so that the home market will consume everything that can be raised. The market is within easy wagon haul from these lands and in the surrounding settlements, good prices for everything raised can be obtained.

Building material is reasonable, or, if you desire, you can build your building or so-called adobe, or sun-burnt brick. Dwellings built of this material resist both heat and cold, and they are cheap and comfortable.

Fuel, both coal and wood, can be obtained within easy distance at nominal prices.

The lands under the Springer Irrigation System will be sold, including permanent water rights, in tracts of from twenty acres up. Reasonable terms can be had; perfect title guaranteed. The main object of the Maxwell Company being to have the lands settled by capable, industrious and intelligent farmers, no land will be sold for speculation. The price asked for this land is about one-half what is asked for similar land 200 miles north and south under not nearly as good conditions. What this country needs are farmers—professional men we have plenty of—but we are in dire need of good intelligent farmers.

The Maxwell Land Grant, contains 1,714,765 acres; title perfect; United States patent confirmed by decision of the United States Supreme Court. Within its boundaries are the prosperous towns of Raton, Springer, Elizabethtown, Maxwell City and Catskill, and the city of Trinidad is six miles north of the Grant. In addition to the lands under the Springer Ditch hereinbefore fully described, the Maxwell Company has for sale lands under the Vermejo Ditch System, large bodies of graizng lands and timber lands. Mining claims within its mineral territory can be acquired under regulations as favorable as the United States laws. Copy of such regulation will be mailed on application.

Said the Raton Range for Sept. 2, 1887: "Mr. Pels, agent for the Maxwell Land Grant Company, was in Las Vegas last week. He was interviewing several of the business men in reference to a projection of the line of the Denver, Texas & Gulf Railroad over the Raton range via Long's Canyon to Las Vegas. Mr. Pels stated that the Maxwell Grant Company would do all it could in the way of inducing that company to build the line and thought if the people here and those along the proposed route took hold of the matter that the construction of it could be secured."

Pels was for the betterment of New Mexico through the Grant in every way possible. But he had his own troubles. Everything he tried to do was mis-represented and mis-interpreted by the Anti-Granters who felt that McMains had sufficient knowledge of the law, as well as influence in Washington, to oust the Maxwell Land Grant Company. Pels divided his time between Raton and Denver. When McMains felt that Hunt had deflated his importance with the settlers in New Mexico he went to live at Stonewall in Colorado and Pels was always sending officers after him to make him realize that useless blood was being shed. But McMains had the taste of the mob in his mouth ever since the Cimarron days following Parson Tolby's death. The Anti-Granters rode in Colorado with masks, pistols and guns, in broad daylight as well as at night. On August 24, 1888, Randolph was burnt out because he claimed that the Grant people were right and he started paying for his property. Pels was furious. He wrote his deputy at Trinidad to punish the culprits. The deputy replied that he would if the agent would send him a letter of authorization to arm twenty or thirty members more to his band.

The mob then went to Janny's place near Stonewall and told him that they would stop his mill and run him off his place if he continued to have dealings with the Maxwell Land Grant Company. People like him, they complained, made it look bad for the Anti-Granters. After all they had pioneered the valley with good intentions and homesteaded there in full compliance with the laws of the United States covering the matter. The deputy went to Randolph and Janney and obtained affidavits implicating Captain Russell, Chaplain, Henry Fisher, Ed Bonnett, James Cox, Morton Rephart, Joseph Hagen, Johan G. Hagen, Patricio Duran, Justo Sandoval, Juan Chacon, Albino Chavez, Prudencio Chacon and Julian (Frenchy) Giradet. When asked on what charges these men were to be taken he said: "Some on charges of unlawful entry, unlawful assembly with masks, pistols and guns; others for tumultuously and unlawfully preventing one Lewelling from pursuing his lawful occupation."

The deputy seemed especially interested in arresting Russell, the founder of Stonewall, and former soldier at Fort Union in New Mexico. The result was the death of Russell which seemed ironic indeed since he came through all the campaigns and skirmishes with Indians during his army days without a scratch. The charge against Russell seems to be that he threatened Janney and prevented him from showing papers. Wrote an old settler from Elizabethtown on February 26, 1886:

"Myself and quite a few of the settlers in my neighborhood have been talking for a few weeks about this Anti-Grant matter and wondering what was going to come next. Among the many things that we talked of was the county newspapers and how they stood on this question. It comes very natural for us to believe that newspapers are run for money, just as any other business would be, and that a paper would be likely to print whatever brought the biggest price. There are a couple of papers printed in this county, which come to our town, and which we read, but we have come fully to the conclusion that they are for the Grant, and, of course, if they are favorable to the Grant they are against the settler. I will say to you that we haven't noticed anything in your (The Comet) columns lately that was very positive either way. We want you to say one way or the other. There are about twenty-five of your papers taken up here and I know that if you would come straight out against the Grant, and go for it right up to the handle, your paper would be taken twice as much. I know four or five that said so. I haven't got much respect for a paper that is always standing on the fence—just ready to go whichever way the wind blows. I want you to write me just how you stand—plain out. If you do, I will tell you that we will all stick to you. I wish you would tell me, also, if there is any talk about the settlers organizing, and what they are doing in the other parts of the Grant, or what they are going to do. We don't want to be behind any other locality, for the Anti-Granters are just as strong here as anywhere. If you do say anything in your paper about the matter, speak out plain, and then we will know that you have some backbone left; for if there is one thing that I like better than another, it is to see a man or a newspaper stick up and fight for his rights."

To which the editor replied that his paper was very much in sympathy with the settlers and he would come straight out with them even "up to the handle but only if the officers of the Maxwell Land Grant Company took any steps against the settlers that they were not justified in doing."

Whigham was tired of being accused of mistreating settlers. He knew that if he went to visit them individually he would not get beyond the first home because there were some who were not beyond killing him for the sake of keeping their homes. He tried in vain to have the settlers understand that the strong arm tactics of the law officers were not due to instructions from him. The Maxwell Land Grant Company was in a ticklish position. The grant was theirs. The highest court in the land proved that. The original patent of the United States of America for the Maxwell Land Grant ended: In testimony thereof, I, Rutherford B. Hayes, President of the United States, have caused these letters to be made Patent and the Seal of the General Land Grant Office to be herewith affixed. Given under my hand, at the City of Washington this 19th day of May in the Year of Our Lord 1879, and the Independence of the United States 103. Witnessed by William H. Cooks, Secretary; S. T. Clarke, Recorder of the General Land Office."

Whigham felt that he could not respect those who had no respect for the signature of the President of the United States.

The first Placer lease made by the Maxwell Land Grant Company was between the company and Thomas Lowthian and William Middleton who leased the mining claims on Grouse Gulch below Bloomfield's and above Gallager & Greeley's mining claims. The same that were opened by Mr. Bloomfield in the summer of 1872 and the Moreno mining district for the year 1873. It seemed inconsistent to Whigham that all these mining companies should go through legal red tape to work their claims while the squatter was enriching himself from the sale of cattle, grain and produce to which he was not entitled since he had no right to the land. It is interesting to note that no one believed that there was oil on the land. The first oil lease was not let out by the company until May 23, 1903 to A. C. Majors. Whigham, in an effort to stop abuse from the Anti-Granters, wrote an open letter from Cimarron (March 22, 1886) which only served to infuriate the Anti-Granters the more. He said:

"Some persons, through the papers and otherwise, are now busily engaged in trying to take advantage of the present situation of affairs regarding the Maxwell Land Grant, to stir up excitement and disorder in the community. As usual with that sort of people, they manufacture the most of their facts without any regard to the truth. As a rule, these are also persons who have little or no property at stake, and are always willing to push somebody else forward to do the fighting and stand the expense and other consequences. It is not true, as is now so industriously circulated, that it is the intention of the receiver to proceed to eject settlers of the Grant by the wholesale. I am directed by the court, which appointed me to collect pay for the use of the lands belonging to the Maxwell Land Grant Company, and I have given notice accordingly. If the lands embraced in the United States patent which that company holds belong to it, the occupants should pay for the use of it. If they do not, I cannot collect rents. If the right to collect rents or occupy the property is disputed, we must appeal to the courts, and let the question be settled according to the laws under which we all live, and which are made by the people themselves for the protection of all alike.

"People say that the Maxwell Land Grant Company ought not to take any further steps until the patent suit is decided by the Supreme Court of the United States. They accuse the Grant people of always winning their cases because of the superiority of their lawyers, the settlers being too poor to litigate against them. They must not overlook the fact that the patent suit is carried on by the government of the United States, which is certainly as wealthy and powerful as any Grant company. It has for lawyers in the case the Attorney General of the United States and his whole force of assistants, besides special counsel, who gives his entire attention to it. The government has spent more money in preparing the evidence in this case than has ever been used in any case in New Mexico or Colorado. It has been decided by a United States judge in favor of the Grant company on the law and facts. Notwithstanding all the charges of fraud the court finds on the evidence that there was no fraud. Who is to decide such matters; the courts after hearing the evidence, or interested parties without evidence? Would you like to have the title to your house or horse or cow decided in the latter way?

"Nine-tenths of the men who howl the loudest about their homes and their rights have come and settled upon the Grant since the United States patent recognized the title of the company peaceably and quietly. Has it occurred to these people that the men who came here and found a United States patent for the land and a title which the greatest lawyers in the country called perfect are the ones who ought to await until the court of last resort decides that this title is not good?

"No doubt it would be pleasing to a great many if the owners of the Grant could be persuaded to be still, while somebody is disputing the title and let them grow rich out of the free use of the grass and finally be able to plead the statute of limitations against the Grant owners when all other questions have been settled. Are these gentlemen, who want the owners to wait th decision of the Supreme Court, willing to give a bond that they will pay up all the back rents if it is decided in favor of the company? They probably prefer that we should go on as heretofore paying the taxes on all the property which they get the benefit of grazing.

"The settlers blame the Maxwell Land Grant Company for the trouble they find themselves in by the decisions of the courts, but they are wrong. If these people have been mislead by the unwarranted acts of the Land Department in trying to override an Act of Congress, they would blame the government and not the company. The Maxwell Land Grant Company bought the land in good faith and paid a very high price for it. Upon what principle are they asked to make a present of it to somebody else?

"The Maxwell Land Grant Company will help anyone complying with the law and make easy settlement with all those who wish to retain their property."

Judge J. H. Hunt, realizing that McMains had lost the case, consulted lawyer Thomas Catron of Santa Fe asking him to re-vamp the case, but the lawyer was not interested. Many settlers were in dire straits and could not pay their bills. One believed that the Maxwell Land Grant Company would be willing to pay McMains what he had spent in the case if he would give up his agitation, which all thought he would do when he failed in Washington. Mrs. McMains said: "I would gladly accept every dollar I can get from the Maxwell Land Grant Company. For a long time I have tried to get Oscar to give it up and quit prating on Grant matters and to take to the lecture field which would be the best thing for him, but he will have none of my advice."

That Mrs. McMains was a much neglected person and subject to the whims of an over-enthusiastic husband, everybody agreed. Everytime she begged her husband to give up the generalship of the Anti-Granters he stormed at her and told her to stick to her duties as a housewife. Hunt gave him five dollars from a miner at Blossburg which McMains said was meant for his wife and the reason why she had turned against his espousing the cause of the Anti-Granters was because men like Hunt were feeding her fancy ideas while he was away trying to help the settlers. The domestic life of the McMains couple was not a happy one.

"The Maxwell Land Grant should not pay less than $25,000 taxes. Placing the exceedingly low value of $2,000,000 on this immense and valuable property at 1¼ percent would produce that amount. We doubt whether the company would sell it today for five millions. What justice is there in taxing the private individual nearly the full value of his property and then letting a wealthy foreign corporation escape with a paltry tax? Placing the valuation at $5,000,000 at 1¼ percent the taxes would be $62,000, and last year they only paid the pitiful sum of $9,000 in round figures. We want to call attention of the public to the fact that justice and fair dealing demand that there should be a change in the public policy which has been pursued towards this corporation." (Live Stock Journal of New Mexico April 1, 1887.)

"On Tuesday evening last, Hon. O. P. McMains addressed a mass meeting of the citizens of Raton at the Rink. The old agitator is certainly to be admired for the pluck which he has shown in this cause, and the good grace with which he faces an audience which as he himself has said had begun to look almost cross-eyed at his futile efforts in behalf of the settlers.

"He stated that this was his last stand and appeal to the chief executive of the nation for the execution of the law as intended and demanded by the Constitution. He maintains that Cox's decision, as Secretary of the Interior, and Head of the Land Department, that this is public land and open for settlement under the land laws. It had never been set aside by competent authority and is final as an adjudication of the Beaubien and Miranda Grant; that he rests his whole case upon the issue of an answer from the president to the question: 'Is the decision of Secretary Cox final or not?' This is all he wants to know. If the president says that it is then he is willing to drop the matter and retire. McMains believes that the Supreme Court willfully ignored and repudiated the fact that this was shown not to be an impresario grant, but a simple grant to two individuals upon which to raise sugar beets. That it was stated to him by a reporter who attended the Maxwell case in the Supreme Court that one of the justices on the bench had said that he regarded the action of Commissioner Williamson, in ordering a survey for the Grant, as a revocation of the decision of Cox. Said McMains: 'Oh, the idea of an inferior officer in the Land Department arbitrarily reversing and revoking the decision of the head of that department!' McMains believes that the president will answer yes or no to this question when it comes up in such simple form. He does not regard it as a complicated question of law for the courts to interpret, but a matter so plain that the chief executive can answer in a minute." (Live Stock Journal of New Mexico May 27, 1887.)

The Cox decision was thrown out. After this McMains went to Colorado in an effort to agitate the settlers there. He had nothing more to do with the people of Vermejo, Cimarron, Blossburg, Raton, Eliazbethtown, Springer and other settlements on the Grant. They had deserted his cause and were not worthy of his attention. Actually they came to see his fight as a waste of time and decided to settle with the Grant people.

There was a time when even the United States sued the Maxwell Land Grant Company over the limitations of the Grant. J. A. Bentley was the special U. S. Attorney in the case, assisted by Hon. Wm. A. Maury, the Assistant Attorney General of the United States. These were the points of their argument:

1. This suit is brought to set aside the patent issued to Charles Beaubien and Guadalupe Miranda, on the 19th day of May, 1879, for the Mexican Grant confirmed by Congress as Private Land Claim No. 15—June 21, 1860, and the survey by Deputy U. S. Surveyors John T. Elkins and W. G. Marmon, executed in September and October 1887, upon which the patent was based.

2. The relief is asked upon the ground that the patent covers a large amount of land not included by the Grant and not covered by the Confirmatory Act of Congress.

3. The Mexican Grant was for twenty-two square leagues—97.424 8/10 acres, as was confirmed for that quantity and no more, as we shall contend. Whereas the patent was issued for 1,714,764 99/100 acres, an excess of 1,617,340 14/100 acres.

4. The government alleges and proves as will appear, that the patent issued for this great excess of land by mistake and inadvertance, into which the officers charged with the duty of issuing patents were led by misapprehen-

sion of the law as the extent of the confirmed Grant and their authority in the premises, and the fraudulent representations of the proprietors of the Grant relative to its extent and the locality upon the ground of its outboundaries as designated in the original Grant papers, and the false and fraudulent survey by the Deputy U. S. Surveyors, by which they falsely located said outboundaries in substantial conformity to the pretensions of the Grant proprietors, and included some hundreds of thousands of acres outside of and adjacent to the true outboundaries designated by the Mexican authorities. Whether, therefore, the quantity of land to which the Grantees are entitled is limited to 22 leagues, the maximum of two Mexican grants, or comprises all of the lands within the outboundaries as designated by the Mexican authorities, the case is a proper one for relief.

5. The original Mexican Grant was for 22 leagues and no more.

6. The Mexican league was not the same as the American.

7. The Act of the Mexican Congress of 1824, and the regulations of 1828, constitute the only authority since their passage for granting of Public Domain in the Mexican Republic.

8. Public officers are mere agents; their power limited by the law, and the government is not bound unless their acts are within their statutory powers. This rule has been recognized and applied by the courts whenever the question has arisen. And it has peculiar significance in cases involving the Mexican Grants, which the faith of the government is pledged by the Treaty of Guadalupe Hildago to recognize and uphold. Without the enforcement of this rule in these cases, the government would be exposed upon every side to the most gigantic frauds. The magnitude of the Grant claimed in this case illustrates the ruinous consequenses which would flow from the adoption of a contrary rule.

9. There is no California case where a Grant to one person of more than 11 leagues was sustained, and the general language of the Court alluded to must be regarded as having reference alone to the case under consideration. Upon reason and authority it is clear that the Grant at the date of the Treaty of Guadalupe Hildage, was for 22 leagues and no more, whatever the quantity of land embraced in the natural boundaries mentioned by the Mexican officials. And if the Grantees are entitled to the quantity of land now sustained upon the subsequent proceedings of this government in relation to the confirmation of the Grant.

10. The confirmatory proceedings under the Acts of Congress July 22, 1854 and June 21, 1860, operated simply to confirm the original Mexican Grant and not a Grant de novo—for the excess of land comprised within the out boundaries specified, either in petition for the Grant, or in the act of juridicial possession.

11. The confirmatory proceedings consist of two parts —a) The proceedings of the Surveyor-General of New Mexico—under Section 8; Act of July 22, 1854—b) The Act of June 21, 1860 confirming Private Land Claim No. 15.

12. The Surveyor-General of New Mexico proceeded under these provisions to inquire into the Beaubien and Miranda Grant, and on the 17th of September 1857, made his report thereon, transmitting the claim for the action of Congress. . . . The Grant having been confirmed by the Departmental Assembly, and having been in the constant occupation of the Grantees from the date of the Grant until the present time, as is proven by the testimony of witnesses, it is the opinion of this office that it is a good and valid Grant according to the laws and customs of the government of the Republic of Mexico, and the decisions of the Supreme Court of the United States, as well as the Treaty of Guadalupe Hildago of February 2, 1848, and is therefore confirmed to Charles Beaubien and Guadalupe Miranda and is transmitted for the action of Congress in the premises. . . .

13. There is no interpretation of the recital; no enlargement or change of the Meaning of the Mexican Grant proceedings but on the other hand there is a distinct and explicit annexation, so to speak, to the Grant papers, of the laws and customs of Mexico, the decision of the Supreme Court of the U.S. and the Treaty of Hildago, as the rule and the light by which the Mexican Grant—the confirmation of which he was recommending—was to be interpreted.

14. In the Beaubien and Miranda case the Surveyor-General's report attempts no interpretations of the papers and proceedings of the Grant—He simply declares it "valid" and no interpretation enters into the confirmation by Congress except as to the "validity" of the Grant.

15. The general features of the country where the Grant is situated should first be brought to mind. The Raton mountains are a spur of the Sierra Madre or main range of the Rocky Mountains, shooting off to the eastward upon the 37th parallel of north latitude. For a distance of about 30 miles from the Rocky Mountains to the Raton Pass, south of Trinidad, they are in general, an easy, flat top, wooded ridge, issuing to about 8,500 feet above the sea, and some 2,000 feet above the valleys of the water courses at the foot, with here and there breaks upon either slope, where the waters run the summit into the Las Animas river on the north side and into the Colorado on the south. East of the Pass they suddenly rise up to the height of more than 9,500 feet, spreading out a considerable width both north and south. Here upon the top of the mountains are extensive table lands with precipitious edges, varying in height from 500 feet to 1,500 feet. This formation extends eastward along and near the 37th parallel for 70 miles or more, gradually decreasing in height. Just south of the Raton spur another spur of the Sierra Madre puts out to the south for the distance of some thirty or forty miles, where the main range makes off in a southwesterly direction, this enclosing the Moreno Valley, while on the east is the Colorado river, and on the south in the Rayado, Cimarron and Ponil rivers, all forming a junction and emptying into the Colorado near the southeast corner of the patented Grant.

16. On August 18, 1869, Maxwell, then proprietor of the Grant, caused a false desino sketch map of the Grant

to be placed among the records of the Land Office in Washington.

17. A comparison of the map so forwarded with the true map, or desino of the Alcalde, constituting a part of the Grant papers, shows that it was false in several essential particulars, viz. The south boundary of the true desino is 10⅛ inches long, while the south boundary of the false one is only 8⅝ inches in length, while the northern boundary is of the same length in both maps, and the northern and southern boundary in both are parallel.

18. The western boundary on both intersects the north and south boundaries at right angles while the intersection of the eastern and southern boundaries in the true desino form an acute angle of —— degrees abd a false map of —— degrees.

19. The true desino shows three characters upon the western boundary, which unquestionably were intended by the alcalde to represent noted mountain peaks through which the boundary passed, and upon or near which the Colorado, the Vermejo and the Ponil rivers have their respective sources.

20. It is not necessary to speculate as to the degree of criminality which attaches to the surveyor-general for this false map. It is sufficient that L. B. Maxwell, then the proprietor of the Grant, was a party to the furnishing of it.

21. In view of what has since transpired in respect to the location of the Grant, the twisted false map was intended to pave the way for the substitution of the Una del Gato creek flowing into the Chicorica creek and thence into the Colorado from the east, for the alcalde's Una del Gato (Catspaw) river, which flows into Colorado from the north, joining the latter at the great bend where that river leaves the base of the Raton divide and flows southwestward, and while the omission of the characters signifying the mountain peaks in or near which the several rivers head, virtually tying the north boundary to the summit of the Raton mountains, was to furnish opportunity to locate the northwest corner upon a mountain peak far to the northward, in order to extend the out boundaries of the Grant in that direction.

22. Alterations in the map forwarded to the Commissioner of the Land Grant Office were not the result of accident; an inspection of the two maps will satisfy any person that both skill and design were employed in their making; at the same time preserving the general configuration of the map, so that the alterations might not be detected upon a casual examination.

23. December 31, 1869—The Secretary of the Interior decided that the confirmed claim was for 22 leagues and no more—11 to each grantee.

24. Following this decision, on January 5, 1870, Jerome B. Chaffee and his associates, contracted with Griffin, whose contract with the surveyor-general has been suspended by the Commissioner, for the survey of the Grant.

25. In order to fully appreciate the enormity of the fraud of their survey and plat, and comprehend the deception practised upon the Land Department at Washington, D. C., by the filing of it there, as the true survey and plat and compare it with the alcalde's plat which had been deposited at the request of Mr. Maxwell a few months previously, at the same time bearing in mind that the alcalde's map (the false one being a twisted copy presenting the same general features) had been prepared without an actual survey, at a time when little was known of the country in particular by civilized men, except as to prominent mountains and passes, and the existence of more important streams, with a particular knowledge of the locality at certain points, and merely speculative knowledge as to the remainder of its length. While that of Mr. Griffin had been prepared from an actual survey made by himself, after knowledge and speculation had become particular knowledge in regard to the whole face of the country.

26. He goes on to mention the mistakes Anton Karl and J. J. Major produced an actual survey of the country in 1883—etc. He points out that every mistake was actually intended to falsify the Grant.

27. The designation of the three mountain peaks upon the western boundary, which had the effect to tie that line, both as to locality and strength, is another evidence that the alcalde's intention was called to details as well as to generalities, and constructed his map with great regard to the topography of the country.

28. It is a matter of common notoriety as well as clearly indicated upon the face of the Mexican Grant papers and desino that the chain and compass were not employed in making the Mexican Grants. Land was comparatively valueless except such as had water channels. These having their sources in the mountains, the out boundaries of the Grants were always described by prominent mountains and streams nearest to the particular location of the land; the title which was intended to be transferred, while the interior geography consisted mainly, if not exclusively, of the water channels flowing upon or through the Grant from the mountain ranges named in the out boundary calls; and this, as before stated, for the obvious reason that the water channels gave the value to the land. Without them it was worthless for either agriculture or grazing.

29. The alcalde's desino of the Beaubien and Miranda Grant is not an exception. It is in evidence, and it is a well known historical fact that at the date of this Grant, and for many years afterwards, the country promised within the out boundaries, to use the words of one of the witnesses—'was inhabited only by Indians, wild horses and buffalo.' except at the Rayado and vicinity, where some settlements of civilized men were located as early as 1843.

30. An occasional hunter had indeed visited different localities in pursuit of game and brought back to the towns some account of the topography of the country, but there was little certain knowledge relative to the particular geography, except along the 'trails'. And the geography of the desino was therefore made up of a few prominent, well known physical features filling in the intervening space fore or less correctly in their general effect, according as the judgment of the draughtsmen was more or less correct in his determination of the sources and the courses at different points of the various water channels within the out boundaries. The desino in this case, having his authority, and no greater, we claim it fixed the northern boundary of the Grant without question, at the summit

of the Raton mountain; that was a feature well known and seen from afar off; and the eastern boundary so close to the eastern bank of the Colorado river as to exclude all land watered by any other streams. A bare inspection of the alcalde's map in view of what is known of the manner of the production of such maps, and their political purposes would seem of itself, to be conclusive evidence, upon these points. It omits to take notice in any way, of any of the numerous streams, large or small, flowing into the Colorado from the east below the great bend, while upon the north it shows that that boundary was intended to be located at the very sources of the waters flowing from the top of the Raton mountain southward. Besides, the original petition for the Grant describes the north line as following a summit from the northeast corner of the top of the mountain on the west.

31. In 1867, Maxwell made a private survey of his Grant, and fixed his northern boundary upon the summit of the Raton mountain, establishing stone mounds thereupon in the immediate vicinity of the 6th mound of the Las Animas Grant. In 1854, Maxwell giving orders to his sheepherders, pointed out the line of the Raton mountain as his northern boundary.

32. Elkins and Marmon assert that they located the out boundary line in conformity with instructions received from the Commissioner of the General Land Office and surveyor general, regardless of their true location upon the ground, and that they used the field notes of the Griffin survey as well as his plat, which was exhibited to them by Mr. Springer, the attorney for the proprietors of the Grant. . . . They accepted for the purpose of their survey, the out boundaries of the Grant, and for the information received from witnesses by them furnished. They commenced their survey on September 19, 1877 and concluded it on October 11, 1877—covering a distance of 226 miles in 22 days including Sundays, over a country, which according to the notes of their survey, and according to the notes of Griffin, the general atlases of the country, and the topographical maps of Messers Karl & Major, was of the most difficult character, over high mesas and mountains, in many places entirely inaccessible to the human foot, the survey over which line had occupied Griffin from May 25, 1877 to September 25, 1877—six times as long. They followed Griffin except at points where the Commissioner directed a departure.

33. The errors of this survey in the region of the third mound and Raton peak connected with the false naming of localities in the neighborhood are not to be construed as mere mistakes, but as intended falsehoods, and therefore a fraud upon the government.

34. The articles of association of the Maxwell Land Grant Company and the minutes of the first meeting of its Board of Directors held May 29, 1880 in the Netherlands show that it was organized out of the bondholders of the Maxwell Land Grant and Railway Company, who had, as such bondholders, employed Frank R. Sherwin and Lucien Birdseye to buy the Grant for them, at the Master's sale, made in pursuance of a decree of foreclosure of the mortgages of the Maxwell Land Grant and Railway Company, under which the bonds had been issued. The decrees of the foreclosure show that F. H. Ziegelaar, P. G. Gerlings, A. A. DeSalangre, V. A. Van Hall, L. VanLimburg-Striun, all of whom, except Salangre, were incorporators or directors, were also holders of 6158 out of 7000 bonds secured by the first mortgage, and that the same parties owned 2707 of the second mortgage bonds out of a total of 2,750. It appears that the patent was delivered to Lucien Birdseye by the Commissioner of the Land Grant Office as the representative of the bondholders; so that the bondholders are directly connected with the issue of the patent, and chargeable with actual knowledge of the proceedings leading to its issue.

35. They were all speculators. They knew the U.S. government upheld the Cox decision of December 31, 1869 of the Grant as less than 100,000 acres—so they are culpable.

It looked bad for the Maxwell Land Grant Company. Everyone went around with a worried look—everyone but Springer. He sat down and wrote out a brief that was to settle once and for all the Maxwell Land Grant ownership. Here is his defense taken from his own notes as he wrote them:

NOTES ARRANGED AFTER HEARING THE OPENING ARGUMENTS OF MAURY AND BENTLY FOR THE GOVERNMENT, MARCH 10, 1887.

A

1. History down to the Patent   A complete
   1. Petition and Grant 1841 ⎫ proceeding under
   2. Juridicial possession 1843 ⎭ Mexican law.
   3. Denouncement and approval by Departmental Assembly.

Note—An *empressario* Grant—should have been transmitted to the Supreme Government and may have been.

   4. Treaty of Guadalupe Hildago 1848
   5. Surveyor General Act of 1854
   6. Beaubien and Miranda's petition to Surveyor General April 1857
   7. Surveyor General's Decision September 1857
   8. Act of Congress Confirming June 1860
   9. Maxwell's efforts to get survey.
 10. Sale of Maxwell Land Grant and Railway Company 1869
 11. Secretary Cox's Decision 1869
 12. Griffin Survey 1861
 13. Secretary Delano's Decision 1871
 14. Decision in Tameling Case 1876
 15. Secretary Schurz's Order 1877
 16. Instructions Maxwell Land Grant Company 1877
 17. Elkins and Marmon's Survey 1877
 18. Protests and Contests—Our survey 1877-1878
 19. Patent May 9, 1879
 20. Sale to Maxwell Land Grant Company 1880
 21. This suit 1882

2. The Pleadings
   Original Bill 1882
   Complete Proofs 1883
   Amended Bill 1884
   Demurrer

Hearing in Circuit Court October 1885
1. Grounds of attack on Patent
   a. Want of authority
      1. Because void above 22 leagues.
      2. Mistake of Law including lands outside of the true boundaries.

Fraud—

Because survey erroneous and land officers led to adopt it by reason of false statements in field notes, and by previous claims of owners that another false survey was correct.

Patent issued on one authority, for a grant made absolute by Act of Congress.

Survey neither fraudulent in procurement nor erroneous in fact.

That the survey and patenting of confirmed grants are, administrative matters alone, that complete jurisdiction is vested by law in the Land Department to locate the boundaries on earth's surface and to determine all questions of fact presented by this record and its action has the force of judicial determination.

All these matters of fact were actually presented to, and considered by, the Land Department and its judgment is not reviewable by the courts upon any suggestion of error or fraud, unless the fraud be as such extrinsic matters as prevented a fair determination.

3. THERE ARE ONLY TWO REAL QUESTIONS
   1. Was there want of authority?
   2. Was there fraudulent procurement?

The eleven league question

The Grant was by specified boundaries through all proceedings of both governments.
   a. Effect of judicial possession
      Cases cited
   b. Mexican proceedings—Equal a patent.
      Denouncement and approval by Departmental Assembly.
      Re-granted by government.
      Rec. 386-388

Prima Facie Gov. grant at Acts of Treaty because
   a. Shows no quantity on its face,
   b. fact of excess must have been first officially determined.
   c. good under former government until disavowed.
3. Presumptions attacking them.
4. Valid in part according to bill.
5. Could have been perfected by Supreme Government of Mexico before cession.
6. U. S. Congress succeeded to this power and did it.
7. Suppose the Grant wholly void originally i.e. suppose law of 1824 to 1828 repealed before Grant.
8. Act of Congress cured all defects.
   Sovereign power breathed into it.
      breath of life—if dear—2 Pet. 6:27 see end of notes.

9. Confirmation and Quit Claim.
   May have been treated by authority of both governments as an *Empressario Grant,* and as such not limited to 11 leagues.
10. Tameling Case.
    Falacy of their whole argument lies in their misconception of the words "according to law." This does not mean "provided it does not conflict with some law." It means that *in view of* in *harmony with* or *under* and *by virtue* of those *laws* and *customs,* the Grant was only authorized and is valid.
11. Reports of the Committees.
12. Intentions
    a. of Mexican authorities shown by language use.
       1. Granting words
       2. Individual possession
       3. Approval of Departmental Assembly and re-grant.
    b. Of Surveyor General shown by his decision
       1. According to Mexican laws and customs.
       2. No limiting words.
    c. Of Congress shown by
       1. Confirmation and Quit Claims
       2. No method provided for segregating 11 square leagues except in No. 17 which shows that attention of Congress was directed to the limitation and that it did not choose to apply it in this case.

Fraudulent Survey

To show ground of relief Government must show
1. That survey was in fact false
2. That it was made in pensance of acts in themselves fraudulent and adopted solely in consequence of those acts.

We win if we show that *either* of these facts does not exist.

Survey not erroneous to the Prejudice of the U. S.
   a. Dominant boundary cals—
      Chicorica
      Una de Gato
      S. G. Instructions Rec. 309
1. U. S. Witnesses
   (seven cases listed on notes)
2. Defacts Witnesses
   (five cases noted)
3. War Department map.
4. Hayden's map.
5. Mearn's map.
6. Counterminous Grants.
   a. Vijil & St. Vrain
   b. Sangre de Cristo
7. Deseno—Miranda & Beaubien
8. Proof of N.E. Corner by
   Silva
   Wooten

BENTLEY'S THEORY

A. If supported by any facts, would only prove that there were *two possible locations* and doubt as to which is correct thus making a clear case for judgment and discretion.

B. To vitiate for mistake, it must be *clear* mistake—on facts about which there is *no dispute.*

If a mixed question of law and fact the action of land office must stand.

Fraud charged in Par. XVII of Bill.
  a. Elkins & Marmon map.
  b. Surveyor General and Com.G.G.O. not in fact deceived by anything done by Elkins & Marmon.
  c. All the errors charged may have been result of bad judgment, incompetence or negligence of U. S. Surveyor.
  d. If made without procurement or motive they are *not fraud,* however erroneous.

Bentley now claims that the whole range of mountains and mesas dividing the water flowing into the Las Animas from those flowing into the Colorado was the *Chicorica* or *Chacuaco Mesa stated by the Alcalde.* This distinctly disposes of frauds Nos. 2 & 3, 4 & 5 of Par. XVII in the Bill.

No. 1 is the charneas cruk which is not a boundary call at all.

No. 6—is that the course from N.E. corner to Fisher's Peak is 1 degree and 33' too far out as given in field notes —though Archibald found the monument on the ground as stated by E. & M.

No. 7—is that their course far from N.M. boundary to N.E. cov. is 1 degree 27' too far for in—this excluding the lands included in that angle from the survey!

These seven are *all the frauds* charged upon the surveyor.

What becomes of the case???

The U. S. Congress took up the Grant which the Surveyor General had reported to them as having been made by the Mexican authorities and confirmed it. That is to say made it perfect and complete.

If it was only inchoate before it thus became perfect.

If defective in whole or in part its *infirmaties were cured.*

If void before the life giving breath of sovereign power made it valid. (six cases quoted)

Brief for argument upon Demurrer to Amended Bill

Before Judge Brewer at Leavenworth July 21, 1884

History of proceedings as shown by the record from 1841 to filing of Bill—

After the lapse of 36 years, and after all these proceedings on the part of the owners of the Mexican title to procure its recognition by the U.S.—after all the known steps have been taken to perfect and *settle* the title that court is asked to sit in judgment upon the acts of a coordinate branch of the government and to take from the parties in interest the evidence which the U.S. has given that their Treaty obligations have been discharged. charged.

NATURE OF U. S. PATENT FOR CONFIRMED MEXICAN GRANT TWOFOLD

1. *A deed* and in such it is a relinquishment of all the right, title and claim on the part of the U. S. to lands embraced within its boundaries—a *quit claim*—a conveyance.

2. *A record* of the action of the Government in performing its obligations under the Treaty and the law of nations.

It is the evidence which the government furnishes the claimant of its action respecting his title. Before it is given, numerous proceedings are required to be taken, before the tribunals and offices of the government, and it is the last act in the series, and follows as the result of those previously taken. It is therefore record evidence of the government's action. By it the government representing the sovereign and supreme power of the nation discharges its political obligations under the treaty and the law of nations. By it this sovereign power which alone could determine the matter, declares that the previous Grant was genuine; that the claim under it was valid and entitled to recognition and confirmation by the law of nations and the stipulations of the treaty and that the Grant was located, or might have been located, by the former government so as to bebrace the premises or they are surveyed and described, as against the government, this record, so long as it remains unvacated, is conclusive, and imparts absolute verity.

(2 cases cited)

PART TWO

JURISDICTION OF THE COURT TO REVIEW THE ACTION OF THE POLITICAL DEPARTMENT OF THE GOVERNMENT.

Not derived from any *special* grant of powers by Congress. But must rest in the *General Equity* powers of the court.

Effect of acquisition of Mexican Territory upon property rights.

Law of nations—

Treaty of Guadalupe Hildago—8th and 9th sections.

The change of sovereignty did not effect the rights of the inhabitants to their property.

They retained all such rights, and were entitled by the law of nations to protection in them to the same extent as under the former government. The treaty, in express terms, guaranteed to the inhabitants of such territory *"free enjoyment of their liberty and property."* The term "property" as applied to lands embraces all titles, legal or equitable—perfect or imperfect. It comprehends every species of title inchoots or complete. It is supposed to embrace those rights which are executary as well as those which are executed. In this respect the relation of the inhabitants to their government is not changed. The new government takes the place of that which passed away. (Two cases cited.) This obligation was binding upon the new government and was to be discharged at such time and in such manner as its political department should surfit.

Various methods adopted to this—

In California—powers partially vested in certain tribunals, but reserving for a time matters of survey and patent to the political department.

In New Mexico and Colorado—Powers wholly reserved to the political department.

Acts of Congress—July 22, 1854—creating Surveyor-General to ascertain the origin, nature, character and extent of all claims to lands under the laws, usages and customs of Spain and Mexico.

To make a full report of all such claims as originated before the cession.

With his decision, as to the validity or invalidity of each, under the laws and usages and customs of the country, before its cession to the U. S.—and transmit them for the Act of Congress.

Act of June 21, 1860—confirming grants as reported by Surveyor-General.

Act Rev. State., 1878 SS 2447—Patents for confirmed grants to issue upon plats or survey approved by Surveyor General if found correct by the Commissioner of the General Land Office.

Such a patent therefore, is not a sale by the United States of land it owned, but is a final recognition by the government, through its legislative and executive departments of the title to land it never owned, or pretended to own, but which was private property it was bound to respect.

U. S. Circuit Courts in California have disclaimed authority to review the action of the Land Commission and District Courts in determining the validity and location of a Mexican Grant or its extent, when acting in the special capacity prescribed by the Act of 1851.

A fortiori the U. S. courts of General Jurisdiction cannot review the action of the political department of the government where the entire authority to investigate, determine, confirm, locate, and patent grants was reserved to it.

If the U. S. Court can do it, any State Court, with general equity power can, and would have its spectacle of State Courts practically adpidicating the validity and propriety of its acts, of the political department of the government in discharging its treaty obligations.

Powers of this court inadequate to complete justice.

Cannot make new survey or furnish parties with patent for lands it finds comet.

Cannot compel Law Office to do so.

Cannot restore parties to former situation.

Courts have no authority to interfere with surveys, unless by express status.

No power to review action of Land Department for *mere errors.*

If jurisdiction exists—does the bill present a *case for its exercise?*

Statement of Subsistance of bill—

In framing this bill, the opposition has undertaken to lay the foundation for a destruction between this and decided cases and by cunningly drawn allegations, in the guise of statements of fact, in the apparent hope that they would render the bill safe against attack by demurrer. We will of course be referred to the familiar rule of pleading that a demurrer admits the allegations of the bill. But this is not an absolute rule. It must be taken with the qualifications that:

Demurrer does not admit

1. Matters of interference and argument, however clearly stated—nor

2. The accuracy of our alleged construction of an instrument, when the instrument itself is set forth in the bill, or a copy annexed, as against a construction required by its terms—nor

3. The correctness of the ascription of a purpose to parties, when not justified by language used. (Cases cited.)

The Act of juridical possession was the only segregation known to Mexican Law. (Case cited.) Nor

Allegations construing the Grant differently from the terms expressed in the papers evidencing the Grant and attached to the bill. Nor

Allegation of area granted—which is to be deduced from the Grant itself and the Act of Congress. (Cases cited.) Nor

Allegation impeaching the truth of findings of Surveyor-General in his decision attached. These findings are conclusive until reversed by Congress. (Cases cited.)

The grounds upon which this court is asked to cancel patent are:

1. Mistake of law—*Inadvertence, misapprehension of duty* and *authority* on part of U. S. officers.

2. *Fraud and misrepresentation.* What are the functions of U. S. officers charged with the examination of Mexican grants and with surveys and patents?

Surveyor-General—Act of 1854—Comm.G.L.O. Act re. Patents Rev.St. SS 2447.

More than fifty years ago the sup.C.U.S. announced as the result of all prior adjudications the broad principle that where power or jurisdiction is delegated to any public officer or tribunal over a subject matter, and its exercise is commuted to his or their discretion, the acts so done are binding and valid as to the subject matter. The only question which can arise between an individual claiming a right under the acts done, and the public, or any person denying its validity, are power in the officer and fraud in the party. All other questions are settled by the decision made or the act done by the tribunal or officer, whether *executive, legislative, judicial or special,* unless an appeal, or other version *by* some appellative or supervisory tribunal, is prescribed by law. (Cases cited.)

And though this doctrine has been affirmed and declared again and again by that court, it has never been stated with greater precision and force.

It has been applied specifically to the U. S. Land Officers, to all public matters relative to the disposition of the public lands, and the settlement of Mexican titles, in a long line of decisions, holding that their acts, and decisions, within the scope of their authority are conclusive. (Cases cited.)

In all these cases there is a qualification that the action and decisions of these officers may be corrected by courts of equity in a direct proceeding, for mistake, fraud, or imposition.

But this is admitted to be an extraordinary power, only to be exercised in cases that are perfectly clear, and the court say so. (Cases cited.)

It is a sound principle that where there is a mixed question of law and fact, and the court cannot so separate it, as to see clearly where the mistake of law is the decision of the tribunal to which the law has confided the matter is conclusive.

But this proposition may be regarded as settled by these cases:

That the action of the U.S. Land Office in matters within their authority, has the same weight as a judicial decision and can only be attached for reasons upon which a judgment could be attached.

And it must be further remembered that these cases mostly arise upon a construction of the powers of these officers under the ordinary land laws of the U. S. and not of the acts of the political department of the government in discharging its treaty obligations—as to which the argument to be deduced from this is vastly stronger.

Ignorancia juria unamilmera excusat is a maxim both of land equity. (Cases cited.)

Mistake to be relievable in equity must not have arisen from negligence, where the means of knowledge were easily available. Must be *clear* mistake, on facts about which there is no dispute. (Cases cited.)

But there was no mistake here.

The mistake of law alleged is that the Com.G.L.O. issued patent in the belief that the Grant was good for all the land within boundaries, instead of 11 leagues to each grantee. The Act of Congress June 21, 1860 confirming the Grant shows on its face value that Congress not only confirmed the Grant by its boundaries, but *intended to do so.* This appears from the private restriction of Vijil and St. Vrain to 11 leagues each. Petition of Miranda and Beaubien to Surveyor-General describes the Grant in full and states that the *quantity is unknown.* This was before Congress as part of the Surveyor-General's decision recommending the Grant for confirmation. What did Congress confirm?

The Grant as Thus Recommended.

If the Grant had been void before, this confirmation would have made it good.

Confirmation equals Grant de novo. (Cases cited.)

Misapprehension of Duty & Authority.

Comm.Gen. of Land Office had for a guide in addition to the law itself, and decisions of the Supreme Court—

    a. Decision of Secretary of Interior in this case.

    b. Opinion of Att. Gen. of U. S.

Inadvertence—No authority for setting aside. State works through its patents though issued by mistake to one not entitled. (Cases cited.)

Misrepresentation—Will not vitiate unless relied upon by its opposite party. (Cases cited.)

Com.G.LO. *did not* rely on it because he ordered a different survey from Griffin's.

With these preliminaries we may now consider the force in effect for the purposes of the case of

The Frauds Charged in the Bill.

a. That Maxwell and all subsequent parties knew that the origin of their titles was the proceeding of the Mexican government before the Treaty and that the history, extent and limitations of the Grant were as set forth in the bill, and that it only contained 97,424 acres located and selected on the Rayado, Cimarron and Ponil rivers.

This is badly pleaded so far as contrary to what the documents themselves disclose for the parties also knew the Grant as shown by the papers attached;—decision of Surveyor-General thereon Act of Confirmation by Congress.

Patent itself.

They knew that these were the acts of the officers and authorities charged by the U. S. with determining the validity, extent and location of the Grant, and they had a right to rely on these acts as conclusive. (Cases cited.) They also knew in addition to the foregoing, but which are matterd app. knowledge or notice. (Cases cited.)

Maxwell bonded the Grant to Chaffee who proceeded to have the Griffin survey made, and represented to U. S. officers that it was a camch survey of outboundaries and that the Grant extended to them.

The law required Grant claimants to deposit money to pay cost of survey. These representations are not such as if made to annul the patent, for, they were matters equally within knowledge of the U. S. officers. They were matters in regard to which the officers had no right to rely on theirs, but were bound to act on their own knowledge.

That surveyors Elkins and Marmon ran the lines of the out boundary falsely and fraudulently and returned false and incorrect notes thereof:

No inducement or collusion charged;

No reason why they should falsify;

No connection with any parties in interest—All such matters charged in old bill abandoned in new.

The matter of survey and boundaries was one of which the U.S.L. officers had special and peculiar means of knowledge.

Fraud must be alleged with particularity as to time, place and circumstance. It is not enough to use the word —fraud—The facts, supposed to constitute it, must be set forth so that the court can determine whether they amount to fraud in law. (Cases cited.)

No notice of alleged frauds charged upon defendants.

Notice to individual stockholders or directors not enough to bind corporation. (Cases cited.)

The plat of this patent survey, accompanying the field notes, was therefore the survey of Gen.Com. L.G.O. and shows the facts of topography very fully, and shows that most of the things charged in this bill on this head, were known to the U. S. officers when patent was issued. Courts do not sit to determine whether discretion of surveyors has been accompanied with them—discrimination, or the highest of wisdom. In surveys of Mexican Grants the juridical possession controls the U.S. officials unless otherwise stated in decree. (Cases cited.)

The government has been allowed privileges and immunities in this suit, which would have been accorded to no individual and with all deference to the views of the learned judge who permitted the bill to be filed, I think the liberality of the court has been carried too far already. At all events, it is now time that we should get back to the principle which has been established by a long line of decision from . . . . . to the Beeher case in this circuit, that when the government enters the courts of the country as a litigant, it puts itself upon the same footing with private individuals and has no other or greater rights than the humblest citizen. It comes not as a dictator, but as a petitioner. I do not believe that the U.S. has the right to vex and harrass its citizens with suits liable to the same consequence for dilatory practices . . . or error. And this the more in a class of cases which are notoriously instigated and prosecuted in the name of the government for private ends. To say that the governmen can file bills in chancery, lending its name to every irresponsible agitator or blackmailer who asks it, covering with clouds of doubt and suspicion the titles it is bound by solemn obligations of a Treaty to respect and to make good, blazoning forth to the public gaze the names of the individuals charged with fraud and the most stupendous and iniquituous character, without a syllable of proof to sustain them when challenged—and can keep its suits in court, to the ruin of private interests, while it makes one dilatory motion after another, and while— its agents go on fishing expeditions throughout the country, hoping to bring to light some reason why the suit was ever brought —to say that the government can do this of right, which no citizen can do, is a doctrine for which I find no authority. The government has immunities—it is true— it may even have prerogatives but when it voluntarily enters the doors of the court of equity as a suitor it leaves them on the outside. It comes with head uncovered like the poorest citizen. It ought to come with hands as clean. The government has always sought to confirm valid titles and not defeat them. (Cases cited.)

Needless to say, Springer won the case and the Maxwell Land Grant Company operates to this day. Wrote William Falconer from Carinton, Fordown, Kincardeneshire to officials of the Maxwell Land Grant Company in England:

About 40 percent of the estate is rolling prairie, well watered by numberless streams, and all of it heavily grassed, the bottoms along the streams being natural meadows. The remainder and western portion of the estate is among the foothills of the Rocky Mt. Range, which forms the western boundary. A series of canyons form natural highways through the foothills from the rolling prairie on the east, and what is called the Park country, next to the mountains on the west. These canyons and foothills are sufficiently wooded to form abundant shelter for cattle, and the grass there is even finer in quality than on the prairie. . . .

The black gamma grass, so highly prized for its sweetness and fattening qualities, characterizes the entire estate, even the table lands on the tops of the mesas are in many places thickly covered with it, but the variety of other grasses especially in the parks is great. At some points the famous blue grass of Kentucky, which was accidently introduced here, has made great headway.

While on the estate I mingled a great deal with a small number of ranchmen who have long been residents in that section. Some of them as much as twenty-five years, and from them learned that it had never been necessary in that climate to house or feed cattle in the winter, and no losses had ever occurred from exposure in the most severe winter. The prairie portion of the estate is seldom whitened with snow. . . .

I have considered the leases granted by the Maxwell Land Grant Company to the Maxwell Cattle Company, and I estimate that, allowing for every reservation named in the lease, the total acreage controlled by the Maxwell Cattle Company at a peppercorn (a dollar a year) for the term of thirty-eight years, can never be less than 1,400,000 English acres, which will easily carry 80,000 head of cattle. I cannot estimate the value of such a lease, at less than £250,000, if it were to be bought and paid for in money.

Chapter Ten

GENERAL OSCAR PATRICK McMAINS

When Cotton Mather, Richard Mather, Increase Mather and Samuel Mather, the famous divines of New England, shuffled off the mortal coil, they must have lingered in thereal places hoping in time to come upon one at whom they could cast their cloaks so full of oratorical gifts and powers. For some unknown reason the man who fell heir to their type of fiery preaching lived in Indiana. He was intelligent as they were; always had the fires of hell ready for some unfortunate sinner as they did; bellowed away to the ends of the earth as they did; carried a fight to its bitter end like the Mathers; never believed in lost causes any more than the divines; refused at any time in his life to admit that sometimes he could be wrong. His name was Oscar Patrick McMains. Of Scotch-Irish parentage, he did nothing to influence the history of Indiana but chance brought him to New Mexico and there he brought the Territory into focus to place it into the inter-national limelight. There is no monument to him, no street named after him and very few people in New Mexico are aware that he ever existed. Over in the capitol building, gathering dust, are records of his acts when he was in the legislature; in every newspaper in the land that was printed at the time he was making history, one comes upon the headlines that he made and wonders how such a little man who merited so much print should be erased so quickly from the pages of history. That is the way of a transgressor. For in the eyes of the law, both Federal and Territorial, McMains was wrong—very, very wrong. But to O. P. McMains he was right—very, very right. This he maintained to his dying day; for this he would not die, but live. Actually the whole history of the Maxwell Land Grant centers around him. Beaubien, Miranda, Maxwell, Allison, Pels, VanHouten and all the others are but spokes in a wheel of which he is the hub.

The Methodist-Episcopal church called for volunteers to work in New Mexico. The first to answer the call was Rev. Thomas Harwood. Later on he was followed by Rev. Tolby and Rev. McMains. The influx of prospectors, cowboys, ranchers, outlaws, lawyers, dance hall girls, gamblers and merchants into the Cimarron area due to the gold strikes at Baldy, Eliazbethtown and the Moreno Valley made it imperative that ministers of the Gospel from the various denominations come to look after the spiritual wants of the members of their faiths settling in Northern New Mexico as well as the mining area around Socorro and Lincoln. Tolby was very well liked by many. The mystery surrounding his death has not been solved to this day.

"Our dearly beloved Brother F. J. Tolby is dead. He was shot and killed on the 14th day of September, 1875, while returning from one of his appointments at Elizabethtown. He had labored nearly two years at Cimarron and Elizabethtown and did the church good service. He was a rising man, bold and fearless in the pulpit and out of it. He had made many friends on his circuit and in the territory and was hopeful for the future of his work: but in the midst of his hopes and labors, in the noon-day of his life he was cut down, but, like a warrior, fell from his saddle in the midst of the strife. Earlier in the year I had visited Cimarron and had a good visit with Brother Tolby and his family. . . . After which I went East to visit my relatives and friends after an absence of twenty-three years. At Chicago I learned of the assassination of our dear brother, Tolby. I hurried home as fast as I could and found the country in great excitement. Mrs. Tolby and her three children were literally crushed. All the territorial papers were full of the probable causes which lead to his assassination and utterances against the perpetrators of such a dastardly deed.

"We had heard that a certain Mexican (Cardenas) from Taos had said, on his return to Taos from Elizabethtown country where the murder took place, that 'A Protestant heretic had been killed.' This being before it was known in his neighborhood led us to believe that he must know something about it and hence we decided on a trip over to his place. So I had one of the boys at our school go over with me. We went via Cimarron, Elizabethtown, spent a few days at Taos, but couldn't find the man who had spread the news. The man was afterwards found, tried, and shot in the dark as he was being taken from the courtroom at Cimarron to the jail. The fact is that the excitement was so great that hardly anyone was safe. Quite a number of supposed innocent parties were suspected; some left the country in excitement and several others lost their lives. Even some of the members of the courts were suspected, and their lives threatened and such was the excitement that it was thought unsafe to hold the courts next approaching and they were moved from Cimarron over to Taos. Two other suspected men, Mexicans also, have been killed. (Reference here to Griego and Vega.) The excitement and danger were greatly intensified by the unwise efforts upon the part of Rev. O. P. McMains who spent much of his time in trying to ferret out the case and bring the guilty parties to arrest.

"If there were others mixed up in the case other than the three who lost their lives as heretofore given, I have always thought the unwise methods of Mr. McMains served to cover up the tracks of evidence and they have never been found.

"With many other theories as to the assassination of Mr. Tolby I give my own which to me has always seemed the most reasonable. A cause for murder is malice, gain, or political intrigue. In the murder of Mr. Tolby none of these could hardly be the cause. He was a man loved by all so far as we could possibly learn. The murder occurred about eight miles below Elizabethtown and the horse was led up into a near canyon and tied and left. As to political tricks and intrigues that could hardly be named as he was not a politician. But there is a fourth motive which is often resorted to in this country. . . . "

Rev. Harwood who wrote the above proceeds to explain that upon one occasion when Tolby and he were talking, the Cimarron circuit rider told him that he had witnessed a pistol fight in which a native (i.e. Spanish American) had wounded an American. The Spanish-American rushed his intended victim and would have ended him had not Tolby suddenly appeared and stopped him. He felt it on his conscience as a duty to go before the grand jury at the next court session and have the fellow indicted. Tolby was the only witness. It would be well to have none at all, so the fellow, who was hermano-mayor at his penitente morada (A morada was a private chapel built away from a town for the exclusive use of the Hermanos. Here they conduct their meetings every month, usually the first Sunday of the month, and hold their rituals during the Lenten season. While not as secret as some societies many writers who know very little about them portray them as beating themselves to death, nailing themselves to crosses on Good Friday and always acting with a mystifying "hush-hush" air that baffles even the most intelligent readers. Penitentes are normal American citizens loyal to their family, Church and country.) schemed to do away with him, or have some of his fellow penitentes do it for him. He had a friend who may also have been his nephew well known between Elizabethtown and Cimarron as he was the mail carrier. This express-rider and circuit-rider often met on the highway in performance of their respective duties. He would know exactly when and where to do the deed. Harwood's theory is as good as any advanced, and a lot better than many since he knew the country and the people better than most.

The minister's personal effects were intact. Nothing was stolen. The news of the atrocity sounded as drums along the Mohawk—the echo of which transcribed itself over and over again in ranch, dugout, mine-shaft, saloon, dance hall, town, county, territory, nation. It was the pillar of fire by night; the cloud by day to stir men's imaginations, move their tongues, feed their mob instincts, lasso their vigilantes and shoot off their guns. Anti-Granters remembered how the good parson was ready to negotiate the purchase of a large tract of land along the Vermejo in Colfax county to re-habilitate the Utes and Jicarillas whom he considered badly treated and who got the wrong end of the stick in the sale of the Maxwell property to a corporation. He was often heard to say that the land rightly belonged to the Indians in the first place. The murder, unsolved as it is to this day, touched off hatreds that still persist. Contrary to public opinion the murder of Tolby did not bring McMains to New Mexico as many authors claim. McMains was already in New Mexico five months prior to the murder. Tolby and McMains were friends. Rev. Harwood is of the opinion that Tolby served as a chaplain in the Civil War. If he did it was not from Indiana nor Ohio nor Illinois. A search through the War Department records from these states fails to show up the names of McMains and Tolby as much as some authors insist that they served from Indiana. If they were in the war, and I do not doubt that they were, it was from either Wisconsin or one of the New England states. Neither McMains nor Tolby lived in Indiana during the Civil War nor prior to it. Tolby could not have been a chaplain, nor McMains for that matter. Tolby was born in 1842. He was nineteen years of age when the war broke out, hardly an age for an ordained minister, but a likely age for a private. It is possible that he may have been given leave during the last year of the war to return to the seminary for ordination, then get back into the army as a chaplain. This would explain Harwood's view. He was thirty-two when he came to Cimarron and thirty-three when he was killed.

My own theory is that he was ordained a minister of the Methodist church after the Civil War; that he studied in the seminary with McMains; that both worked for their church in Indiana prior to volunteering for New Mexico; that Tolby came to New Mexico several months ahead of McMains as a minister; that McMains did not come to New Mexico as a minister but as a printer. When Tolby was killed McMains was the printer at the Cimarron News office. Why he did this instead of preaching has not been explained. He was younger than Tolby by two years, but looked older. There seems to be evidence that he also served in the Civil War. He was of Scotch-Irish parentage, well educated and had ambitions as a writer, editor and publisher, all of which became realities when he founded The Comet — the present Raton Daily Range. When Bishop Bowman heard of the murder of Tolby he wired McMains to investigate the affair simply because Rev. Harwood was in Chicago at the time.

McMains was a medium sized, heavy-set individual with bad teeth and a thunderous voice, who immediately pointed his finger at one Cruz Vega. The body of Vega was found on October 1, 1875, hanging from a telegraph pole, a little over a mile from Cimarron, the county seat. The case should have been tried there, but when McMains was pointed out as the man principally responsible for the death of Cruz Vega, he asked for a change of venue to Mora county. He was found guilty in the fifth degree and fined three hundred dollars; but Judge Waldo held that the verdict did not say of what the defendant had been found guilty, so McMains was to go on trial again; this time at Taos, where Judge Parks dismissed the case on April 1, 1876, for lack of sufficient evidence. Wrote Rev. Harwood:

"McMains came to New Mexico and made his home in Cimarron, New Mexico, early in 1875. He was a member of the Colorado Conference. He was appointed as a supply at Cimarron and Elizabethtown. He was a fine preacher, a better preacher than pastor. He was often rash, often imprudent, not safe as a leader, and too strong to be lead; but in the main he meant well. He had the faculty of getting himself and others into trouble much easier than he could get us out. Some time after the Tolby affair he held me up before a public congregation as a 'weakling' and as having no backbone. Two things I could never stand to be called, a 'coward' or 'lazy.' I had surely shown my courage in circulating a subscription all over the country collecting money to pay a two hundred dollar debt for Mr. Tolby and to send the family, the wife and two girls to their home in Indiana. I made a hard and costly hundred mile trip to Santa Fe to plead with Judge Waldo and Attorney General William Breeden to admit Brother McMains to bail and succeeded——. . . . But last of all and best of all Brother McMains found himself a good wife (in Cimarron) and I had the honor of performing the marriage ceremony. He purchased some property in Stonewall, Colorado, and died only a few years ago."

"Some fifteen years ago, McMains, whose name has acquired such a forlorn notoriety, was a Methodist preacher in good standing. His zeal to discover the murderers of another Methodist preacher by the name of Tolby, caused him to take part in a most brutal and treacherous murder. He suspected a poor Mexican of knowing something about the murder of Tolby. He decoyed this man out of the settlement. He called a band of desperadoes to assist him, and then commenced an examination by torture. They dragged the witness by the neck; they hung him up and let him down; they beat him with revolvers; they shot him and left him dead and hanging to a telegraph pole. McMains was not only a part of the band that did all this, but he planned and instigated the whole affair. Of course his excuse was that his intentions were good, and he did not think it would go so far. McMains was finally, after much trouble, indicted, and placed on trial for murder. McMains was a martyr! McMains was persecuted! A Methodist Bishop (Bowman) went from St. Louis to Washington to invoke the aid of authorities there to save poor, persecuted, innocent, sanctified McMains. The powers in that city decided to give full support, and the attorney general of the United States at once telegraphed measures for the immediate release of the afflictd McMains. Now commences an interesting little study that will give some senators a headache in this Anerbeen business. The attorney general of the United tSates at once telegraphd to the U.S. attorney for the District of Mexico to stay all proceedings in the case of McMains until further advised from this department.

"The said U.S. attorney for the said District of New Mexico replied that he had the honor to inform the department of justice that he had no connection whatsoever with the case; that McMains had been indicted under the Territorial laws of New Mexico and that the case against him was being prosecuted by the attorney general of New Mexico. A telegram was then sent to this latter. He telegraphed back that he worked for the governor of New Mexico. A telegram was sent to the governor who replied that McMains had been indicted by a grand jury and that he was actually on trial for the said crime." *(Letter of Judge S. E. Axtell, January 31, 1891.)*

Bishop Bowman was deeply concerned over McMains. He was in constant communication with Rev. Harwood, the superior of the Methodist-Episcopal Missions of New Mexico. Young, fiery, untamed, married, McMains made it a point to go from house to house enlisting sympathy for his cause—the first major one he had ever undertaken —and the last state became worst than the first. McMains no more settled the death of Tolby any more than he settled the Maxwell Land Grant case for the settlers. He seemed destined to align himself to lost causes. Wherever he went blood was spilt; homes burnt; law-suits filed; bad feeling aroused. Some people have the happy faculty of arousing hatreds; McMains was one. When Bishop Bowman came to Santa Fe with Bishop Simons, he had a conference with McMains and was impressed enough to induce Harwood to give him the parsonage vacated by Tolby's death, although it was against Harwood's better judgment:

"I did not justify McMains in his unwise and dangerous method of trying to ferret out the assassins. My advice was for us to go right on in our missionary work as if nothing had occurred, but at the same time keep our eyes and ears open for all we could see and hear and as 'murder will out', I thought we would be more apt to get on the track of the murderers in that way than in any other. Mr. McMain's plan was to quit everything else and hunt down the assassins. And when his constant declaration was that he knew who the murderers were it was but natural that the prosecuting attorney, who was likewise just as anxious to find out who they were, would cite Mr. McMains to appear before the grand jury to state what he knew. His refusal to state what he said he knew on the ground that it might involve himself was what lead to his indictment by the grand jury of murder in the first degree and for that he was tried, but not convicted.

"It is wonderful how high the excitement ran. In order to make it appear that certain parties were guilty of murder even dreams of an old lady and seances of an aged gentleman were brought to bear in the private arguments . . . The lady's dreams were strange, but dreams should weigh nothing when human life is at stake. The seance was also equally as strange. Before Mr. Roberts and I had returned from our trip over to Taos, soon after the murder had occurred, to try to find out what a Mexican had said about the assassination, the spiritualist claimed to have been in a seance and saw that a party had come up from Taos to the Taos canyon to waylay us. This word being told in our neighborhood, while Mrs. Harwood did not believe at all in spiritism, still she could not help feeling uneasy about us. Mr. Roberts was a young student and preacher at school; he had been ordained a deacon at Cincinnati on our way home from the East in 1875. (When Harwood found out about the death of Tolby he broke off his vcaation and hurried back to New Mexico.)

"The facts of the scare were as follows: As we were going down the Taos creek out of the mountains, Mr. Roberts said, 'I saw some Mexicans hiding in the bushes.'

He seemed quite excited, catching up his rifle. I said, 'Don't shoot until I tell you.' The horses were trotting pretty fast down grade and all at once when we turned another turn in the road, a Mexican almost turned a somersault out of the bushes into the road. They were fishing for trout with hook and line and one fellow had caught one and sprang out to take the fish off the hook. We inquired for the man we were after, but they knew nothing of the man nor of Mr. Tolby.

Mr. McMains succeeded Tolby at Cimarron and Elizabethtown. Rev. McMains had been unwise in his methods of the investigation of the murder of Rev. Tolby. I was just as anxious to assist in the investigation as Mr. McMains was or any one else could have been, but we differed widely in our methods. I am quite sure that I was the first one to make any special effort to find the murderers, or to pay out a dollar, as in my dangerous trip to Taos, as spoken of heretofore. The country was thrown into a fearful condition and at times it seemed with the light of a match it might set the whole country ablaze. People on the stage coming into the country were afraid to come through Cimarron, headquarters of the excitement.

"Mr. Swope, the stage agent, came to see us and to have me, if possible, stop McMain's foolish efforts to ferret out the murderers. But after he was arrested and imprisoned, for the courts had been changed from Cimarron to Taos for judicial purposes, and succeeded in getting a change of venue from Taos to Mora, and when he was imprisoned at Santa Fe, one hundred miles away, I, at my own expense, pleaded with the judge and prosecuting attorney and secured the privilege of bail and he was released under $20,000 bond.

"Suffice it to say that he met all the charges manfully and after appearing before the courts at Taos, Santa Fe, Mora and in Colfax county, the case was discontinued under Judge Bradford L. Prince.

"Thus the grave charge against a minister of the Gospel for murder in the first degree, confined in prison first, without the privilege of bail; second, admitted to bail of $20,000; third, brought before the courts of three counties; kept under a cloud for nearly two years, in the final analysis simmered down simply to imprudence, rash and unjustifiable. Had he listened to my advice his troubles might have been avoided, some lives probably saved and the law had its proper course.

"Mr. McMains had many friends and while in prison he was well cared for, and I was censured because I refused to pay him his missionary salary while he was under indictment for murder. How could I? That was contempt of court. Both Bishops Bowman and Simons approved of my course and said that I had acted wisely in the case. Before Bishop Bowman left Santa Fe he said, 'I don't see how I can appoint Brother McMains to Cimarron and Elizabethtown but I wish you would.' I did so knowing that a strong petition went up to the Missionary Society asking that it be done. Mr. McMains' case had by this time been thrown out of court. Some time after this he rode down fifty miles to have me perform his marriage ceremony."

Rev. Harwood was at this time residing at Tiptonville near Watrous. In one volume of his work he seems to indicate that he went to Cimarron to perform the marriage ceremony while McMains was still gathering evidence in an effort to solve the murder; in the next volume he says that McMains married following the ejectment of the case. We must remember that he wrote these events forty years after they took place so we must look for some discrepancies. No doubt he married before. In those days, even though rough and lawless, a girl hesitated before marrying a man who spent any time at all in jail. But if she were married to him when he went to prison, upon his release he continued on as if nothing had happened. It was the code of the Victorians and this was the height of the Victorian Era. Dickens, Thackery, Collins, Butler, and others were the rage, fad, and even gospel of womanhood in America during this period, Cimarron not excepted. Be that as it may, he was married when he broke off from the Tolby case and began to champion the cause of the squatters and settlers on the Maxwell Land Grant. That was in 1879. From the time he was released from jail to his first out-cry against the Maxwell Land Grant Company he carried out his work as a preacher, making friends wherever he went and soon his part in the Tolby aftermath was forgotten. He did not storm against the characters who visited Lambert's bar in Cimarron any more than he did against those who frequented the bars and dens of Elizabethtown. He watched with joy the approach of the railroad and hoped for bigger and better things for Cimarron when it arrived. He seemed friendly with the officials of the Maxwell Land Grant and Railroad Company. Only when this sold out to the Maxwell Land Grant Company does he make his appearance as Agitator for the settlers. He had been favored by the officials of the former company; ignored by the latter. This hurt. He had asked for a deed to some land along the Vermejo as well as a place near the present site of Raton but was repulsed both times. He had ambitions of becoming a cattle baron and the company knew it. It was all well and good for him to become a rancher of tremendous proportions but not on their land. He was then told that the land he was using did not belong to him (He could produce no deed to it.) and he would have to vacate it. He dared the company to take it away from him. The war was launched.

Before taking leave of Rev. Tolby to study McMains as the leader of the Anti-Granters let us see what the Cimarron News and Press had to say about the death of Tolby. The paper that should have had glaring headlines —the paper of which McMains was the printer, not the editor, merely commented on September 18, 1875:

"Rev. T. J. Tolby, Methodist-minister of this place and Elizabethtown, was murdered last Tuesday at the head of the canyon about twenty miles from here on the Elizabethtown road. It was supposed that he was murdered for plunder but his horse was found about 600 yards from where the body was found, tied to a tree, and the saddle found about 100 yards in another direction. The body was brought in this morning and will be buried this afternoon, with Masonic honors, he being S.D. of the Cimarron Lodge. It is thought that his murderer is a white man and was paid for the job. Mr. Tolby leaves a wife and two small daughters (which number conflicts with some authors who say that there were three small girls). He was one of the men interested in buying a tract of land on the Vermejo for a colony of Indians." On November 4th, the same paper said:

"On the night of October 30th, Cruz Vega of Cimarron was hung to a telegraph pole by a vigilance committee for being an accomplice in the death of Rev. J. F. Tolby. He was employed to watch some corn on the Ponil, and with his employer, William Lane, was taken and examined and confessed that he was present and saw the murder of Tolby, which was committed by Manuel Cardenas, and alleged that he was hired by parties in Cimarron. Cardenas was arrested in Taos, but for want of evidence he was not held and has been discharged some weeks since."

Meantime both the Santa Fe and the Rio Grande railroads were racing towards the Raton Pass. When McMains was told that he possessed land unlawfully, he took to studying Spanish Land Grants. Convinced that the law permitted only eleven square leagues, he studied maps with an eye on the route that one of the railroads would have to take. Pacing off the land he found that just north of the Stockton ranch would put him out of jurisdiction of the Maxwell Land Grant Company's claims. It would if they only had eleven square leagues. There he built his home. He was never blessed with children. One day as he was building his corral, he was told by officials of the company that he was on private property. McMains invited the officials to his home. There he picked up his shot-gun, pointed it at the men and calmly told them that he would give them two seconds to get off his property. From that moment he ceased being Rev. O. P. McMains and became General O. P. McMains, Agitator For The Settlers. Said Henry M. Porter in his *Pencilings of An Early Western Pioneer:*

"The settlers were encouraged and led by a preacher by the name of McMains, who had some ability as an orator of the 'open air variety', and who went all over the country denouncing the company for trying to sell and lease lands they had bought and paid for, and calling the whole scheme a swindle on the part of the company. He found nearly all the squatters willing to believe his story and follow his lead and organize to resist the payment for lands or rents, or accept titles from the company.

"For many years many suits were brought by Mr. Frank Springer, to collect pay and quiet the title to the land in the local courts, and after much litigation and delay the Supreme court rendered a decision giving to the company all the land they claimed under the description given originally by metes and bounds.

"McMains then got up a petition, signed by all the squatters, asking the Supreme Court to open up the case and allow a new trial, as they had discovered fraud and had new evidence to offer, to show the illegality of the title to this vast estate upon which thousands of poor men had made their homes, and would be made to lose them by dishonest methods of the Grant Company. The petition was granted, the second one ever given a re-hearing of a Supreme Court decision. In a new trial all was gone over and the former decision sustained, which caused many months of delay and expense.

"The company then commenced to make sale of its lands to the squatters and give them a long time to make payments and at a low rate of interest. In the meantime the English owners became negligent in the management of the estate and no interest having been earned or paid, the Holland bondholders became discouraged with the enterprise."

McMains had a powerful voice like the sudden peal of thunder that broke, with clanging sound, the stillness of the night. He bellowed and roared like an angry air-wave, causing his listeners to quake in genuine fear of temporal and eternal judgments; he terrorized and frightened until he was looked upon by his followers in the Anti-Grant movement as the Appointed of God, the Avenger, the Scourge of the Granters, searching his own heart and mirroring it as the Caesar who would lead his legions to a sweeping victory; the glory of the Anti-Granters; the Colossus with one foot set firmly in extraditing them from the captivity of Amsterdam; the other set in solid rock of their faith in him, while underneath flowed his people and his people pushed on by the rapid stream of his words, power, force, learning and leadership. At first he was not troubled by the squabbles of the squatters but being in Cimarron it was not long before he permitted himself to be dragged into the net not so much because he was interested in their cause as his own. And if he won Colfax county would be forever grateful to him. Possibly even erect a monument to him or name a city after him. He might even be rewarded with an immense tract of land and live in even greater splendor than Lucien B. Maxwell ever dreamed was possible. When he came to a dead end, he was too well oiled as an agitator not to devote his attention to some lost cause and the cause he sponsored was close enough to home.

He had saved up enough money for something he knew he would do some day. To own his own newspaper. The Santa Fe Railroad came through as he so shrewdly guessed it would but he had a moment's disappointment when the Otero Optic made its appearance. When the editor decided to move to Las Vegas McMains felt that now the road was clear and the Raton Comet was the voice he would use to fight the Grant people. From the start it was a success simply because all his followers were also his subscribers. Many more subscribed just to read what he had to say. Promptly he dedicated the sheet to the public as the official organ of the Anti-Granters. With this newspaper and through a series of lectures he managed to keep in touch with Cimarron. After a time he was forced to admit to himself that he couldn't do the two things and do justice to any one of them. He decided to sell the paper but only to an Anti-Granter. He must also control the policies of the paper. The name of the sheet was changed to The Raton Guard. Squatters who had enlisted under his standard collected money for him to make trips to Washington, Chicago, Omaha, Kansas City—anywhere, everywhere that he could find material and officials who would listen to his plea. Added to this he had himself elected to the Territorial legislature in order to keep his finger on the pulse of the governing body of New Mexico as well as to introduce a bill into the House that would oust the Grant Company once and for all. But he had not counted on Tom Catron, Elkins, Springer and others who had more power than he believed existed even in Washington. In Santa Fe he failed dismally. Back to Raton he went, buying his paper from the people he sold it to and re-naming it The Raton Comet. In his very first editorial he wrote:

"Greetings to our friends; defiance to our foes. Here is The Comet again with the same old motto: Open War Against Secret Fraud. The Fraud is a towering giant, a majestic two million acres known as the Maxwell Land Grant. It has fed on fraud; fraud will kill it. Its demise, however, can be hastened by a newspaper as well as legal treatment and hence the Comet will go for the diseased and unwildy corporiety of the Maxwell Land Grant and heavy."

Meantime he devoted a little time to his ranch south of Raton. He bought the best stock and registered his brand MAX. Why? Did he feel confident of victory and expect enough of the estate in recompense as to call it His Maxwell Land Grant? Why MAX instead of OPM? This brand is interesting. If the Maxwell Land Grant Company had any objections to it they never made them public. McMains continued collecting from Anti-Granters for trips to Washington in an effort to induce the Land Office there to reverse the decision it had made in favor of the Maxwell Land Grant Company. In 1882, while McMains was attending court sessions at Cimarron, five men rode to his ranch and made off with all the stock as rent due the Maxwell Land Grant Company. If McMains persisted in living on the ranch he would have to pay rent. In April of that year he made a speech at Cimarron so vitriolic that the Maxwell Land Grant Company decided that he was a menace to the peace of the area and would have to be removed from the region. They advertised that on April 19, 1882, all of his effects would be auctioned off as payment due them. All over and above would go towards the land and he could apply for a deed to the place. With this down payment he would not be considered as a squatter. Two hundred of his adherents gathered together at the auction and the only things more conspicuous than they were the gleaming Winchesters in their arms. The sale was started by Sheriff Wallace and Deputy Bowman. Wallace began:

"Who will bid on the mare next to the fence?"
Silence.

Several men changed the position of their rifles. The sheriff seeing that he availed nothing, produced a form and read out the reasons why McMains forced the company to hold the auction. He made certain to add that he was only performing his duty. The spokesman for the two-hundred told him that his duty was now performed and he had best get on his way. Nor must he think of a repeat performance for they would not be as patient the next time. If the Grant Company dared to send him back again they would march on Cimarron and put a bullet through every Pro-Granter they found there. At this time McMains was in the height of his power. The editor of the Raton Guard wrote:

"The Maxwell Land Grant, from the day of its fraudulent existence, has been noted for taking every little, mean, and dirty advantage that it has in its power. And as the last, low fling at the settlers, just on the eve of the trial of the case in the United States court in Colorado, and just a few days before the bill in equity could be filed, they served their ejectment notice in the northern end of town. . . . The case will come up in Cimarron next week, but if at that time the bill has been filed, or an order received from Attorney General Brewster to stay proceedings, as he ordered the suit, we think the court will continue the cases. McMains, not being present when the officers of the law arrived, was not dispossessed, but they levied on his hay and his goods and they say they will put him out when he returns. The settlers need feel no alarm for the days of the Maxwell Land Grant are numbered." No doubt a number of settlers would have come to terms with the Maxwell Land Grant Company had not McMains insisted that the Grant was a fraud and the decisions of the courts would swing in their favor. In Colorado as well as New Mexico newspapers took up the cry that made them feel that their cause was not a vain one. Said the Trinidad News on March 21, 1882:

"O. P. McMains, who is familiar with the whole history of the Grant and its outrage from the beginning, has followed them (i.e. Grant officials) like a sleuth hound. He has been prosecuted, persecuted and imprisoned by the swindlers but never faltered in his work, meeting with but very little encouragement, poor in purse, armed only with the spears of justice and truth; yet, he has battled with these monied giants and has at last succeeded in turning the attention of the government to the monstrous and infernal iniquity they have perpetrated."

On the day following this editorial McMains succeeded in collecting together a number of ranchers and business men whom he convinced were imposed upon by the Grant people, and in Bayne & Franks Hall in Raton he gave a long speech reviewing their cause and stated his reasons why he believed that they would come upon the ultimate victory. If they were united into an organization, he told them, they would be a political force in the land and as civic leaders they would rally all the people from Springer to Trinidad to their standard. He was authorized by the organization that was formed because of his speech to inaugurate Anti-Grant clubs at all the voting precincts on the land in question both in Colorado and in New Mexico. On April 6, of that year, he boldly announced a meeting to take place at the county clerk's office in the Colfax county courthouse at Cimarron, stating at the same time that the place was supported by tax-payers and as public property any citizen had the right to call a meeting there if he so desired. A large crowd attended the meeting at which McMains repeated substantially what he had said in Raton. J. H. Hunt was chosen president of the organization; E. Donagher was given the berth of secretary. As a political force it accomplished nothing and died a-borning.

At another mass demonstration held in Raton McMains

was so overcome to see the vast throngs that welcomed him that he was unable to speak for a few minutes. He told the assembled audience that this was the proudest day known to his manhood because it proved that he had sincere followers who were convinced as he was that they were maintaining, at all hazards, the rights granted them by the Constitution of the United States. They were entitled to self-protection and self-preservation. He made every effort in his speech to be calm, cool and to indulge in no personalities. The time was not ripe for the settlers to handle the matter for themselves with any show of intelligence, and to devise means for the promotion of their common cause, he would call upon Sheriff Wallace to see what he had to say. The sheriff told the people that he was in office because the people had recognized him as an Anti-Grant man. He would rather die than see their rights abused or violated, insisting withal that McMains was one of his best friends. His position as sheriff forced him to serve ejectment papers. Whereupon some one from the back of the hall yelled, "Then die. You have turned against us." Others took up the cry with, "Hypocrite! Hypocrite!" Suddenly everybody was yelling: "Down with him! Away with him."

Here was a riot in the making. Hunt realizing that violence would result started to yell: "We want McMains; We want McMains."

McMains restored order by coming up to the platform and making another speech. The meeting broke up in an orderly fashion and the day was saved.

"From *Hill's Leading Cases,* we publish a report of the Commissioner of the General Land Grant Office for the use of the attorney general in the suit to vacate the patent issued on July 1, 1875, for the Canon del Agua Rancho, on account of frauds. The method of adjusting these land grants under the Act of 1854, allows entirely too large a margin for corrupt officials. We have always been of the opinion that there were other private land claims patented about the same time as the Canon del Agua, in which it will appear in time that the surveys were approved, and the patents issued on grounds other than appear on record.

"The survey of the Beaubien and Miranda, or Maxwell Land Grant, a vast tract of land lying in New Mexico and Colorado, was also patented about two years ago without adequate examination and in spite of protests, letters and papers from this country showing that the survey erroneously included, in the southwest corner, Elizabethtown, and Elizabethtown Valley, rich in minerals. This valley is V shaped, pointing north, with a chain of mountains on each side, and these papers showed that the boundary there, described in the Grant, ran on the east side of the valley instead of on the west, as surveyed. It is true that these protests were not formal, because all the lawyers of the country were either employed or intimidated by the Land Grant Company; but they were such as under the practice of the General Land Grant Office, it was customary to make the basis of an investigation. But the survey was approved and the patent issued without any time being given for the opposition of the settlers and miners in the valley to take legal steps." (*Raton Guard,* November 25, 1881.)

The above was the type of editorial actually written by McMains but signed by the editors of the paper as part of the fight to uphold the settlers. Anyone who dared print anything favorable to the Grant was attacked. When the Albuquerque Review decided that McMains would never win his fight, this is how it was answered:

"The Albuquerque Review is premature in its announcement. The application was not refused. (i.e. the Attorney General of the United States was supposed to have refused O. P. McMains' application asking the government to set aside the Maxwell patent of May 19, 1879.) The Attorney General has not as yet expressed an opinion in the matter. It is said by some that Mr. McMains is not able or competent to cope with the opposition. This may be so, but there is only one man who has fight enough to contend with such a corrupt corporation in trying to establish a bogus claim. Let it be known however, that Mr. McMains is too shrewd to undertake this matter alone. He has two of the best attorneys in the country, one from New York and one from Washington and they are still confident and have every reason to believe that they will be successful in defeating the Land Grant in the interest of the people. The Review will please make a note of this that the people may not be deceived." (*Ibid.*)

"There is nothing new from Washington regarding the Maxwell Grant matter. McMains is still at his post of duty, and though writing encouragingly to his friends, has not as yet forwarded anything that will justify us in stating anything definite. Just here let us state that we have noticed articles in several of the Territorial papers, especially the Mora County Pioneer, a vile out of the way sheet, reflecting upon Mr. McMains, a gentleman whose unblemished character is far above such vile slander as the heavens are above the earth. The Pioneer got its information from the News and Press, published at this place (Raton), and in doing so, the Pioneer should have remembered that the information gained from a paper which lies to the people of the town in which it is published, is not reliable authority upon which to formulate and express opinions. The people of Colfax county know Mr. McMains, and are not afraid to trust him with money to fight the bogus land grant and work in the interest of the people. Whenever you see stated in a newspaper, wherever published, that the gigantic swindle, the Land Grant, has been successful in establishing its erroneous claim, you can mark it down as a lie.

"It was only yesterday that one Harry Wigham, Secretary of the Land Grant Company entered the portion of the town claimed, and by all honest and well-informed people believed to be owned by W. W. Boggs, and informed the settlers that if some payment was not made by next Tuesday, that they would be ejected. He informed them that the suit had been decided and that there was no other alternative but for them to pay up or leave their possessions. Let not the people be deceived by false prophets and a bogus company. Pay not a dollar and be not afraid of ejectment. It is only a foul plot to plunder and rob you. The whole truth in a nutshell is that the

Land Grant Company anticipates defeat, and is endeavoring to bull doze the people into buying lands for which they will be able to give no title, while they yet pretend to hold some brief authority. The Raton Guard, the people's organ, will inform you when the matter in court has been settled, and until then pay not a farthing. No sensible man will pay a dollar to the Land Grant Company or any of its servants until the matter in litigation is settled, not only by the attorney general, but by the courts forever. This corporation is trying to lead the people into believing that if money is paid on land, and if they do not get the title they will refund it. This they might possibly do, but until the matter is settled, your money is safer in your pocket. Again, let no man who claims possessions in what is known as Boggstown pay a dime to the Maxwell Grant Company until they are reliably informed that this company legitimately owns the land. This report that the cause in litigation has been settled, is false to the very core, and there is no more foundation for it than the false alarm they gave the people, through its paid organ, the News and Press the week before last. Let the people mark these men and in the future know them.

"The News and Press was made up last Saturday principally of an article on the DuChaillu banquet and the editor of that sheet, with his usual native modesty, made himself the hero of the occasion, and took particular pains to give a full account of all that eminated from his college fed brains." *(Raton Guard, November 25, 1881.)*

When the editors of the Cimarron paper decided to cease publication, the presses gathered dust in the abandoned press room. Shortly after the coming of the railroad, a young man anxious to make his way in the world as a newspaper man heard of the printing press and bought it taking it to Raton where he thought it was most needed. He had no sympathy for the paper put out by McMains calling it a propaganda sheet rather than a newspaper which was exactly what it was. Cannis had brains and used them. He was backed by a college diploma as well as the ability to write editorials. He was not prejudiced. For this reason the Maxwell Land Grant Company advertised in its paper and sent him the news of the goings-on about the Grant. McMains and his supporters objected to this and soon took to calling the Raton News and Press the official organ for the Maxwell Land Grant Company as the McMains paper was the official organ for the Anti-Grant organization. Two newspapers in the little town at the time was not a novelty. Indeed, the novelty is that there were only two. Later there were to be more. In the end the Raton Daily Range, the paper founded by McMains was to survive—as a newspaper, and a good one at that. The only victory and monument McMains ever achieved.

"In the issue —of the Raton News and Press of two months ago (October 7, 1881) an editorial appeared on the Maxwell Land Grant question, and while reading said editorial it occurred to me how ridiculous and non-sensical it was, for the News and Press to endeavor to build up public opinion in favor of the Maxwell Land Grant Company which is recognized and considered to be, by nine-tenths of the people of New Mexico, the most gigantic and fraudulent land swindle ever perpetrated in this or any other country. It is true that if the title to land in this town and vicinity could be perfected or even quieted, it would be of immense benefit to this place in building and improvement. . . . To be obliged, yes, even compelled, to shut our eyes to the real facts in the case and allow ourselves to be whipped, as it were, into complete submission to the ideas of this great Land Steal Company and votaries, is a little too much, it seems to me, to ask the citizens of Raton and New Mexico generally. From the tone of the editorial referred to, it is apparent that an attempt at gang law is being resorted to and that the person or persons who dare raise their voice louder than a whisper in proclaiming their opinion in this matter of great public concern and interest does so at the peril of being considered an enemy to the advancement of Raton, and thereby bring upon themselves the censure of the people of the locality. The News and Press may succeed in establishing this as the correct doctrine for itself and others interested in having it so; but as it will never succeed among the class of people, of which the writer is one, who believe it is their duty as American citizens to hold up before the great American people in their true light these infamous and wholesale land robberies, which beyond all questions of doubt are today the greatest scourge and impediment to the real progress and development of this country that the people have ever been called upon to battle against.

"The statement in the News and Press to the effect that the great question has been settled in favor of the company for now and forever; because the attorney general of the United States refuses to take steps to set aside the Grant title is of no practical importance whatsoever for the reason that it does not follow by any means that because the attorney general refuses (if he has refused) to interfere against the company at present, that therefore the Grant is not fraudulent and this inaction on the part of the attorney general in no way exculpates them from the charge of fraud or gives them a good title. . . . The attorney general knows full well that the matter is now in court and that the same question is there involved that would be raised in proceedings against the Maxwell Land Grant Company, and that it would be useless expenditure of time and money to multiply suits in court involving the same questions when the decision in one case will be a precedent in the other.

"It is a well known fact that when the town of Otero was laid out a few years ago on what was known as the Stockton claim of one mile square, the north line of the Maxwell Grant was on the north boundary of the said claim as the deed of the Maxwell Grant to Stockton clearly proves. . . . It is well known and can be readily proven when the proper time comes that Mr. Maxwell never claimed any land north of where Otero now stands." *(Raton Guard, December 7, 1881—Clearly the work of O. P. McMains.)*

Said the editor of the Las Vegas Optic: "It seems that the Raton News and Press is a paper favoring the Grant. Mr. Canis' Raton Citizen's Improvement Association died for want of encouragement. Some men would kill heaven and all its archangels." But the editor of the other Raton paper was more severe: "George F. Canis, editor of the News and Press is a tramp of uncertain origin—a hired hand of the Land Grant." Canis took exception to these remarks and said so editorially, whereupon McMains gathered together a number of his followers and marched to the office of the News and Press. Canis realized that they were bent on destruction and promised to retract in his next editorial if they would not destroy his press. Shortly afterwards he sold out the paper working in the editorial department of the Las Vegas Gazette. There he soon made himself obnoxious to the editor of the Las Vegas Optic and moved on to Socorro and worked on one of the newspapers of that mining community. He was soon involved in a duel with the editor of the Socorro Sun, but that editor was killed after a Christmas Eve service three days prior to the date set for the duel. Canis went to Deming where he started another paper and became postmaster but before long was burned in effigy by the vigilantes. He evidently stayed on for a time then returned East.

McMains was cited for delinquent taxes by the county of Colfax—Precinct No. 6 for 1880-1881 to the tune of $13.56. He evidently paid it for his name does not show in the next list. The Chicago Tribune, the Omaha Bee and the Washington Times now took up the cry in favor of McMains. Said the Chicago paper: "The people aggrieved have shown fight—the poor against the rich. They have sent Rev. O. P. McMains to Washington to plead their cause. McMains is a minister of the Methodist Episcopal church, an earnest and straightforward man of fine literary attainments. . . . Mr. McMains now goes to the press and the country. He states that New Mexico is in danger of being covered by fraudulent grants, that the defeat of this grant monopoly means the defeat of one hundred others and the opening to settlement of grazing and mineral lands to the people to whom they of right belong."

As time went on and McMains semeed to avail nothing people began to raise doubts as to his ability. Some still clung to their leader: "No one save the low down characters who have been brought in by the Maxwell Land Grant Company can doubt that McMains has been honest and sincere in his endeavors to defeat the Grant and have their limits re-established upon their legitimate lines. . . . " Reference is made here to the Bat Masterson mob brought in to protect the settlers who had legitimate claim to their land. The vigilantes were organized, mob violence ruling for a while, resulting in the killing at Springer, then the county seat, of the brother of George Curry, who became governor of New Mexico, and several others. The governor of the Territory was ready to send out the militia from Santa Fe as well as enlisting the aid of several companies of soldiers from Fort Union, which latter were rushed to Springer and remained there until the disturbance subsided.

"Is McMains trying to organize a mob? We think not. Whatever will be done will be done in self defense. But this is a question for him to answer, not us. So far we have no cause to find in him, on the other hand we do not favor mob law either. Self protection is the right of every man and he who will not use it is a fool." Raton Guard April 12, 1882.) Feeling at Cimarron, Springer, Elizabethtown and Raton was tense and sharp as a razor's edge. Tavern brawls ended as partisan fights. There were only two types of men Granters and Anti-Granters. Up and down the length and breadth of the Grant went McMains with his message and his hopes. The Grant had to go because there was no such thing as a Maxwell Land Grant, and he would prove it. Again, McMains sold his land and bought other property known as Crow Creek Meadows, several miles west of Dorsey. Again, the Maxwell Land Grant Company told him he was trespassing, but this was like waving a red flag before an angry bull. He insisted that they had no right to tell him where to settle. The company brought a court injunction against him.

TERRITORY OF NEW MEXICO
    TO
OSCAR P. MCMAINS, AND TO HIS CONFEDERATES, AGENTS, SERVANTS, AND EMPLOYEES, AND AIDES, AND ABETTORS AND TO EACH AND EVERY ONE OF THEM GREETINGS. . . .

WHEREAS the Maxwell Land Grant Company has lately exhibited and filed in the office of the clerk of our District Court, within and for the County of Colfax, its bill of complaint against you the said Oscar P. McMains, and your confederates, agents, servants and employees, and aiders and abettors, praying to be relieved touching certain matters therein alleged, and we being willing that the relief therein prayer for all shall be granted:

NOW THEREFORE, you, the said Oscar P. McMains, and you, his confederates, and aiders and abettors, and each and every one of you, are strictly restrained and enjoined from in any manner occupying, holding or possessing any lands within the limits of the Beaubien and Miranda Grant as described in the Patent therefor issued by the Government of the United States, and not conveyed by the Maxwell Land Grant Company, or its grantors to the other parties, and especially any lands known as the COW CREEK MEADOWS situate between the Vermejo and Red Rivers, containing about six-hundred acres, more or less, being the same land or ranch formerly occupied by William Cayard, and afterwards by the Dubuque Cattle Company, and upon which there have been made other extensive and valuable improvements, consisting of a two story dwelling house, stables, water tank, out houses, fences, etc., or from in any manner interfering with the said Maxwell Land Grant Company or its employees, or those claiming under it, in the free use and enjoyment of the said lands, and the hay, grass, and water thereon, or from cutting, removing, or appropriating to your own use the grass or hay growing thereon, or from herding or pasturing upon the said lands, or any other lands within the boundaries of the said Grant as aforesaid not heretofore conveyed as aforesaid, any cattle, sheep, goats, horses or other animals, without the permission of said Maxwell Land Grant Company, or from constructing, placing or maintaining upon the said lands, or any portion of the lands within the boundaries of the said Grant, not conveyed as aforesaid, any fences, or in any manner obstructing or preventing the horses or cattle of the said Maxwell Land Grant Company, or those claiming under it, from grazing, feeding upon the said premises, or any other part thereof, or from freely passing or re-passing thereon, or having access to the waters of the said well and water tank. Hereof fail not at your own peril.

(signed)   HON. S. B. AXTELL
Chief Justice of the Supreme Court of the Territory of New Mexico

(signed) C. M. Phillips
Colfax County Clerk
        S. Burkhart
        Deputy

You have guessed it correctly; McMains ignored the order and continued on as if he had never received it. He was again hailed before the court at Las Vegas on Tuesday, August 5, 1884. This time he seems to have obeyed the injunction for we hear of him no more at Crow ranch. Naturally, this only served to embitter him the more. Rev. Sinnock, who came to Raton for his health, took over the pastoral duties of McMains who was devoting all his time to fighting the Maxwell Land Grant people anyway. His trips to Topeka, Chicago, Omaha, Denver, Trinidad, New York and Washington became more frequent. He made such a nuisance of himself in Washington that the persons he called upon there made it a point to be out when they knew he was in town and he never came without advertising the fact. The Washington Globe Democrat newspaper printed an open letter from him addressed to the president of the United States. It was a letter of calm dignity not characterized by the nervous aggressiveness which generally marked his articles. The manner in which he poured out his heart and pleaded with the president to ease the burden of his prayers awakened sympathies of even those opposed to him. He proceeded to show how his efforts to have Cox's decision (which was decided in favor of McMains and the settlers but overruled by the Brewster decision) enforced in the Maxwell Land Grant case. He recited in detail some of his numerous audiences with President Cleveland, also quoting some petitions sent in by the settlers.

"It is a great pity for McMains, and those who believe with him in the overruling power of the Cox opinion that he ever stumbled on the idea. The poor old fellow who has worked for years along this line, believes in it, lives by it, and must live on—doomed forever to disappointment and unrequitted hope. Cox gave the settlers a good right to settle on the land now embraced by the Maxwell lines. That is all the weight his decision ever carried or ever will carry. It will never again appear in the history of this case so far as title to the Grant is concerned. It does not come, it cannot come or even enter into the chief executive's province to answer questions of this kind. The executive cannot construe or decide legal questions. The vital question which enters into the validity of the Maxwell Grant is: Did Congress have the right to confer the land described in that tract? The Supreme Court has decided that Congress did have the right, even though it was public land. Where are you going to have that decision reversed? The Range has repeatedly set forth the fact that no power on earth can furnish relief except Congress. Until that relief is obtained the title will rest with the Maxwell Land Grant Company, and be respected in the courts. Quite a number of settlers have seen the soundness of this position and have addressed friends in Congress setting forth the situation. We so sincerely regret that Mr. McMains takes this untenable position which cannot result in anything tangible for assistance or alleviation to the settlers. Mr. McMains closed his own letter to the president with the following pathetic appeal:

" 'Long, but in vain, Your Excellency, have I offered prayer for the settlers in the dark, secret-keeping-mystery-haunted closets of the nation's houses at the capital city; but hoping this open public prayer in which the whole nation is expected to join, be speedily answered and settlers relieved of heart sickness, caused by long deferred hope . . .' (*Live Stock Journal of New Mexico*, August 26, 1887.)

McMains had trained himself in logic of the "one track mind" variety. His home training had been rigid and he was taught never to throw away an idea if he thought it sound but to follow it through with bulldog tenacity. He inherited his father's emotional propulsion that fitted him into an articulated philosophy as a shaft to a spear-head. To him conversion was a humbling of the heart, an enlightment of the mind since humiliation unaccompanied by a considerate degree of information was worthless. Protestantism, as he saw it, ran a hazard that through excess of zeal its doctrine might be perverted to erroneous conclusions. His was a cause since he dedicated himself to work among unsophisticated laymen who could never understand, even after his teaching them, that the natural mind was abysmally incompetent and that God had uttered the Truth in clear and simple dicta, why people should need ministers and leaders skilled in the sciences, in oratory, in causes such as his, in logic, in order for them to hear and understand the Word of God and correct living as citizens. A justification by faith was not for him a justification of illiteracy, especially of people in high places whose untutored minds failed to comprehend that the Maxwell Land Grant people were wrong and he was right, any more than the strong were justified in dominating the weak. In powers of concentration he felt that his learning and logic was just as good as Springer's, Catron's and Elkins'. To beat these and to unseat the hold of the Maxwell Land Grant Company ceased to be a cause; it developed into an obsession.

As a preacher, the Word of God and not of creatures, was the source from which his theology was gathered; the human reason could safely be applied to it, could be the extraction of arguments, discernment of axioms, formulation of the method, all according to the eternal rules of dialectics. People listened to McMains in spite of themselves. Yet, if his words were scrutinized closely, it became evident that all his oratory was employed with a double connection, and the contradiction between its two meanings was only thinly disguised by the generalizations he used. That is why the hundreds who flocked to hear him in the early days of his fight against the Maxwell Land Grant were carried away by his logic and continued to listen in later years but for the purpose of laughing at his sallies, ranter and vile terms against the foreigners. He was confident that whenever he ventured forth to the plane of reason the fortress of revelation remained as an impregnable refuge to which he could retreat should he be defeated in the field of activity in which he was engaged. That is why he sought to rationalize in every letter, edict or speech attacking the Grant. He struck out boldly because he felt that he was accommodating the squatters and doing them a particularly valorous service when he defended the truth of their stand against the Maxwell Land Grant Company, by his own wit without being forced to take shelter behind his calling or with a Winchester in hand, although sometimes he was very close to using the latter, but to him this was the exception that proved the rule. He did not demand acquiesence in the irrationality of foreign control as he saw it of property in America belonging to Americans, but believed thoroughly that the Federal government was not approaching the thing squarely since eleven square leagues was all the Mexican government had in mind when Beaubien and Miranda were alloted their tract.

It was all so clear in his own mind and he couldn't understand why it was not clear in the minds of the Maxwell Land Grant people. He was to dedicate the balance of his life, and wreck it, in an effort to wipe away the cloud that befuddled them. He saw that he would have to convince the president of the United States as well as the district attorney, the attorney general, the judges of the Supreme Court, and even the humble miner of Blossburg who didn't know a word of English. To McMains such a man was not a foreigner but the Holland stockholders were. Very much so. He was willing to take all in order to apprehend the machinery that worked for the ultimate end of what he considered a constitutional right that the squatters had as much right to the land as Daniel Boone in Kentucky. He had not looked for, nor hoped for, the violent convulsion of a riotous camp meeting, but an exercise, under divine guidance, through his oratory and leadership to point out to his followers as Moses of old the Promised Land and freedom; all that resulted was bloodshed, taunts, ridicule, imprisonment. But these he looked upon as the plagues of Egypt that had to be suffered in order to bask in the sunshine of victory.

The stockholders in Holland never saw the Grant. Settlers not only saw it, but homesteaded on it to increase the pulse of America and build its glory. To be under the domination of a foreign power, to have to ask men who only knew America for its wealth for the right to live on the land, and not to maintain sub-surface rights to land bought from them was more than he could stomach. For settlers to be controlled by voices from Holland made them lacking in integrity, thus marring the symmetry of the whole and voiding the pattern of a solid unity from Washington to Cimarron. That his own parents came from Scotland was not taken into consideration. The set-up of the Maxwell Land Grant spoiled the good complexion of the nation which the proper action on the part of constituted authority could bring back to the wonderful structure for which so many of the flower of American manhood gave their lives but a couple of decades before, the sweet order lines and usefulness of the original plan of the Revolutionary fathers. One nation indivisible, with liberty and justice for all. Here it was the Anti-Granters against the Maxwell Land Grant Company; here the settlers were not at liberty to pursue their agrarian way of life; here injustice reigned. The foreground of his consciousness was the task of explaining again and again that the cause was not indifferent or secondary; that he was not to be outflanked in any of his maneuvers justifying families squatting on the Maxwell Land Grant property, which in his opinion did not belong to the people of Holland in the first place. He was the liberator; the only man in the whole country with his eyes open; the St. Paul of his age to give himself over to the enemy to be mocked, beaten, imprisoned, martyred, but in the end he would be recognized for the hero he was. When the United States authorities pronounced that the land did indeed belong to the Maxwell Land Grant company, any other man would have bowed his head and said: "Causa finita est." Not McMains. He was to carry the battle into Colorado to make his last stand at Stonewall, so appropriately named for he was a stone wall to the bitter end. There he died and was buried.

"O. P. McMains, the erratic genius, and self-styled, self-constituted agent of the settlers on the Maxwell Land Grant, who think they still have a show to retain their claims through the courts, has finally come to grief in Washington last Monday morning. On that day he made his appearance at the east front of the capitol, shortly before the assembling of the Supreme Court and began to denounce the justices as corrupt, at the same time disturbing the order of the day by distributing circulars about the Maxwell Land Grant. The more he talked the more excited he became, until suddenly, there was a pistol shot fired. The police arrested the parson and he is now locked up. He became quiet after a time, and talked quite naturally. He explained that his gun had gone off quite accidently. Those who saw him in the state of nervous excitement think there was some danger of some mischief being done to the Supreme Court. McMains had been for years the champion of the settlers on the Maxwell Land Grant in New Mexico. He had been in Washington a great deal resisting the proceedings of the Holland Land Company to perfect the title to this grant. He has issued numerous manifestos signing himself 'Agent For The Settlers'. As the corporation gained point after point, the parson grew more and more violent in his demonstrations. He began by charging the land officials of New Mexico with all sorts of crimes; then he included the Land Office at Washington in his sweeping charges of corruption. He added the Secretary of the Interior, the President, and finally the Supreme Court, to those whom he accused of malfeasance. Recently he issued an address which he headed

OFFICIAL CORRUPTION: SECRETARY LAMAR AND PRESIDENT CLEVELAND. THEY ARE PARTIES TO A TRICK AND A FRAUD IN THE INTEREST OF A FOREIGN CORPORATION.

This was just before Lamar was confirmed as Associate Justice fo the Supreme Court. Since then McMains has been quiet until the scene Monday at the Capitol. In the cause of his career at Washington, he has had one or two fist fights, in which he showed his nerve and willingness to stand by his convictions or imaginings. McMain's friends here (in Raton) think he has become demented over his long brooding on the Grant question and unless taken care of, may do some serious damage to the Court or other officials whom he imagines, in his delirium, have wronged him. His career as a sensationalist in speaking or writing is ended, and the settlers' money he has expended has gone for naught! Alas! Poor McMains! *(Raton Range, April 6, 1888.)* Here is a sample of one such manifesto:

DEFIANCE AND CONTEMPT FOR ALL THAT WHICH IS CONTEMPTIBLE. SETTLERS, YOUR CASE IS WON.

The Interior Department admitted, March 6, 1888, that the decision of Secretary Cox, of December 31, 1869, upon which your property rights depend, had not been reversed by a direct proceeding. The law says it cannot be reversed by an indirect or collateral proceeding. Hence, the Secretary's decision is valid. It is law. And it must be and shall be enforced.

After having for several years past exhausted all peaceful remedies to induce public officers to compel the Maxwell Grant Company to respect the authority of a Secretary of the Interior, you have at last said to the law-defying thriving corporation:

'Hands off! Get out of these mountains!' And from Stonewall, Colorado, to the Moreno Valley, New Mexico, no Maxwell Grant thief dare show up.

THE WAR IS ON; the precious blood of settlers has been shed, and we must fight it out on the line. No quarter now for the foreign defiance to the Secretary's valid decision, who are attempting to evict American citizens from their homes, ranches and mines.

The result of your uprising against a law-defying corporation, and the public officers who are aiding them in their high-handed lawlessness, cannot be doubtful. The people of the United States, aroused at last to the enormity of the crime that is being committed by unlawful evictions, will demand, in their indignation, that these evictions, proceedings be stopped, the valid decision of Secretary Cox enforced, and your rights dependent upon that decision protected.

In your name then, SETTLERS, I hurl defiance at the foreign corporation. I say to those foreign evictionists: Your Supreme Court decision, purchased at so great a price, is a contemptible legal abortion; it is entirely too collateral. The Secretary's decision, in spite of it, is still law; so, then you bloody-handed Dutch, English and American corporate land thieves, you government defying court-corrupting, assassination-plotting scoundrels——

HANDS OFF, GIT OR BE GOTTEN.
    (signed)   O. P. MCMAINS
              AGENT FOR THE SETTLERS

When McMains availed nothing with his arguments concerning the rights of the Maxwell Land Grant Company over the land they claimed, McMains then went back to the claim of a former president of the Republic of Texas in the hopes that Texas would renew her claim to the territory and thus begin all over with Texan backing. He held that by the Hildago Treaty Texas had the right to the section of New Mexico in question. He wrote to the authorities in Texas for them to recognize the Rio Grande as the western boundary of Texas and he also maintained that even more land was due Texas since much of the land ceded by the Treaty was actually west of the Rio Grande. Texas had sent commissioners to New Mexico on August 12, 1850 to claim this land and as a result of this Congress, on September 9, 1850, settled the issue by purchase from Texas for the consideration of ten million dollars. Why didn't Texas put up a fight for what was rightly hers? McMains even went to Austin to plead with the governor to look into the matter. As a result Judge Reagan was sent to Santa Fe by the governor to investigate. On January 12, 1886, the judge formed a committee whose duty it was to find out why Texas was swindled. Nothing came of the matter. McMains again failed. But he did publish, in Trinidad, Colorado, an interesting manifesto on the subject.

MANIFESTO NUMBER 142

The Rio Grande is now the boundary between Mexico and the State of Texas from the Gulf to the 32nd parallel of the north side.

One might think from a glance at the map, that the Rio Grande, at the time of the treaty, was the boundary between Mexico and the State of Texas ONLY FROM THE GULF TO THE 32ND PARALLEL.

Congress, however, thought otherwise; for on September 9, 1850 (Stats. at large Vol. 9 p. 146) it purchased from the State of Texas for $10,000,000, all the land in New Mexico and Colorado east of the Rio Grande, between the 32nd parallel and the Arkansas River: an area of 57,000,000 acres.

By its Texas Purchase, then, Congress admitted the Rio Grande, from its mouth to its source, to be the boundary between New Mexico and the State of Texas at the time of the treaty of Guadalupe Hildago. Hence,

EVERY FOOT OF TERRITORY CEDED BY THE TREATY OF FEBRUARY 2ND, 1848, IS WEST OF THE RIO GRANDE.

Treaty protection should not, therefore, be extended to so-called Mexican grants which were within the State of Texas at the time the treaty was made. Such a proceeding in unlawful *(McKinney vs Saviego 18—How 235)*.

And now, at the eleventh hour, comes the GREAT BEALS GRANT, claiming that it, too, is a claim for about 80,000,000 acres on the east side of the Rio Grande. This grant leaves no room for the myriad other so-called grants on the east side of that river. THERE IS ONLY ONE

Grant East of the Rio Grande, and That One is the Great Beals Grant. It, Only, *is entitled to* treaty protection, although Within the Limits of the State of Texas at the Time of the Treaty!

It is high time that this unlawful proceeding of extending treaty protection to so called grants which are not within the territory ceded by the treaty should be stopped.

The Settlers on the so-called Maxwell and Sangre de Cristo grants will not submit to be evicted by a foreign corporation that is falsely claiming their pretended grants to be in the Territory of New Mexico ceded by the treaty.

Nothing short of United States troops can drive us from territory purchased from the State of Texas under claim that was ceded by Mexico. This is the only power that can compel us to submit to such an unlawful and outrageous procedure.

(Signed)   O. P. McMains
Agent for the Settlers

McMains re-organized the Anti-Granters at the meeting held at Adobe House, Horseshoe Pasture on the Vermejo on March 31, 1886. C. B. Ladd called the meeting to order and Marion Littrell, who became one of the more famous sheriffs of Colfax county, was elected chairman. Charles Hunt, owner of the Raton Comet, was chosen secretary; M. M. Salazar, interpreter. The following committee was named to draft rules for a permanent organization: J. Forstner, John Larr, J. A. Hunt, J. J. Gonzolez, M. M. Salazar, Garnett Lee, P. J. S. Montgomery, C. B. Ladd and Walter McLoud. The result of this meeting was that The Anti-Grant Mutual Protective Association came into existence, at least on paper, for it achieved nothing and died shortly afterwards. C. B. Ladd was president; J. Lowry, Abe Severs, M. M. Salazar and John Holmes, vice-presidents; George Geer, who operated a bond and real-estate office in Raton, treasurer; Chas. F. Hunt, secretary. All decided to abide by the Cox decision and passed this resolution: "We, in mass meeting assembled, do hereby suggest to Harry Whigham, as agent of the Maxwell Land Grant Company, that we desire no injunction or ejectment suits prosecuted against any members of our association of peaceable settlers on public domain until the rights of the Maxwell Land Grant Company to the lands they claim are settled by the Supreme Courts of the United States."

"O. P. McMains arrived on one of the snowbound trains from the East last evening and immediately called for a meeting to be held in the Rink. A large concourse of people attended. George W. Cook acted as chairman; J. C. Holmes as secretary.

"McMains rehearsed the matter of fact, and points of law, the decisions favorable and unfavorable to the settlers, by different Land Commissioners, sifting to the bottom and cutting to the core all the decisions and combinations of officials or courts adverse to the rights of the people. He related the fact that while he had undiminished faith in the final issue, he had cause for losing faith in men—the officials whose duty it was to do that which was laid down before them pat and plain in law—and yet it was a sad reflection upon human nature that men holding high positions of trust and admitting that they had a right to a certain ministerial act . . . in fact, were bound to do it, without having any option to do otherwise . . . yet declining not only to do what was their plain duty, but going aside, out of their way, to do what they knew to be wrong, merely for personal ends. This is what made the speaker tired. But what is to be done?

"Citing a few vulnerable points, upon which the entire contest depends, Mr. McMains thinks the case of the people against the Grant Company invulnerable. The Cox decision, which ordered the restoration of the plats to the public domain, had never been abrogated nor set aside by competent authority, and hence it holds good, notwithstanding the corrupt act of Commissioner Williamson (an inferior officer) in attempting to overthrow the judgment of his superior. No decree of any kind that is judicatory can be attacked much less reversed by a lower court. All that stands in the way is the fact of refusal on the part of Surveyor-General Julian to restore the plats of the Maxwell Land Grant back to the government. This, Julian refuses to do, and the speaker's mission to Washington was for the purpose of finding higher authority that would compel the Surveyor-General to execute Secretary Cox's order. That would put the grant people on the defensive, where they by right belong. The patent talked about so much was issued, not in compliance with, but in defiance of, law. Hence it carries with it no weight—No more than if it had been issued by a private individual. At best it was not a patent in the proper sense of the word, it was merely a quit-claiming of land, which was conveyed. If the Grant had been originally a bona fide one, then the title was never overted in the government, and could not therefore be transmitted to another. It was in fact void. An nonentity, and yet a bugbear used by corrupt officials to appress and annoy the people.

"The late decision of Judge Brewster, at Denver, amounts to simply nothing. The United States Circuit had no jurisdiction in the case. 'If the people will stand by me a little longer,' said McMains, 'I am so certain of final victory that I am willing to stake my reputation on the matter. Yes, more, I am willing to be called infamous, if the people do not win the day.' A committee was appointed to prepare an appeal to President Cleveland to be presented through Delegate Antonio Joseph for justice in the matter." (Raton Range Wednesday, January 27, 1886.)

Suddenly, all began to change. People were not coming any more to hear an orator, they were coming to laugh at a clown. They began to realize that for all his talk the Maxwell Land Grant Company still retained the land. Many decided to pay each month as requested until they had proper title; others moved away. The tone of editorials moved with the times:

"The Comet wishes its readers to clearly understand that there is a wide difference between Anti-Grantism and McMainism, though McMains claims that the two are identical.

"While the Comet is thoroughly Anti-Grant in its principles and has and intends to devote its columns and its influence to assist the cause of the settlers on the Maxwell

Land Grant in their struggle for their homes, it firmly believes that the time has come when it is no longer to the advantage of the settlers to be led by a 'boss' of the 'at any rate let us agitate' type. When two weeks ago McMains, in the anguish of defeated hopes, cried aloud, 'Oh, for a Clay Allison!' Why did no one step forward? Not because there was not as brave a man on the Grant now as there was ten years ago, but because the Winchester and the Six-shooter have retired in favor of law and order.

"The Comet is fully satisfied that from now on the courts and not the agitators will guide the destinies of the citizens of Colfax county, and while it has and never will advise the settler to go as far as the law allows in asserting his rights, it cannot in justice advise those who have their all at stake to be guided by a man whose life-long teachings lead to anarchy and mob law, and who has nothing to lose and everything to gain by disorder and tumult." (Raton Comet May 14, 1886.)

"About two years ago McMains was in his prime. As an orator he had no equal in Colfax county. The settlers on the Maxwell Land Grant believed him to be a second Savior come to wipe out the sins of the past and furnish them homes for the future, where neither Jew, Gentile or Dutchman could interfere with their flocks and herds grown sleek and fat on the sunny hillsides of New Mexico.

"They tended their flocks and herds, and sold the increase and delivered the money to him. He went to Washington and returned and made them happy by stating that he could induce Attorney General Brewster to bring a suit to have the land claimed by the Grant Company in Colorado declared public property. This suit, he told the settlers, would decide the whole question. but the authorities of Washington were very difficult to approach and he must have five hundred dollars to give to a friend of the attorney general before that dignitary could be induced to order the suit brought.

"The settlers of Colfax county raised the five hundred dollars and gave it to McMains, who, most likely, put it in his opinion, where it would do the most good. The settlers of Colfax county also gave him money to defray expenses while hunting up the evidence to be used in the proposed suit in Colorado, having told them that such a suit would settle the whole question.

"Attorney-General Brewster, relying on his promises, that he would assist the government in every possible way, and on his statements that he had documentary proof and hundreds of reliable witnesses, both Mexican and American, who would come forward and swear that everything and everybody connected with the Maxwell Land Grant Company was a fraud, ordered Mr. Bentley, of Denver, an honest and capable attorney, to bring the suit and asked for, and Mr. Bentley filed the suit asked for, and Mr. Bently filed a bill in the United States Circuit Court as instructed.

"The suit in due time came to a hearing. Matters became interesting. The Grant Company employed able counsel to defend their interests and Bentley called upon McMains to fulfill his promise and produce his witnesses and proofs. McMains, when called upon, left Denver and went to Washington. He had become suddenly as silent as the grave. For thirty years he had been printer, preacher, agitator and rustler and experience has taught him that sometimes silence is golden and when properly cultivated would produce a golden harvest.

"Mr. Bentley and the settlers relied upon McMains to furnish proofs and evidence, and, as none were forthcoming, the suit was lost. McMains now charges fraud against everyone. He says that the Colorado suit does not affect New Mexico in any way and loudly advertises the bringing of another suit in New Mexico. If such a suit were brought, would he not at the last moment be again suddenly convinced that it would be to his interests to again be silent?" (Ibid.)

"O. P. McMains well known to the general reader in Colfax county, expects to cut no inconsiderable figure in county politics during the approaching contests. He has already outlined his tactics in a recent speech where he has exhorted his followers to vote for whom they pleased for delegate and for county offices, but they must make certain that the name of A. Sever for sheriff was on every ticket. What do Democratic aspirants for official honors think of this program? Are they aware that they are to be slaughtered by their political bosses to secure another term in the sheriff's office? If they are not 'on to' the scheme they had better open their eyes at once." (Raton Range Sptember 28, 1888.)

"O. P. McMains and the strikers for the boodle office holders are still trying to fan life into the old time Anti-Grant cause by holding a political meeting in Vermejo Park, haranguing the settlers in the old Declaration-of-Independence style. It would seem to a thinking, candid public that the people of Colfax county had had enough of McMainism and the harpies who win office by keeping alive bitter prejudices upon a lost question. *(Ibid July 20, 1888.)*

"Mrs. Clay Allison, widow of the noted character of earlier days here, was booked to arrive here on July 21st. She will visit the family of Mr. Young on the Vermejo." (Trinidad News July 30, 1888.) When she did arrive she told the reporter that Clay Allison never intended to be associated with Anti-Granters in any matter or form. When he was with the vigilantes following the murder of Rev. Tolby, it was because he felt that he was fighting a just cause, and that the murderers had to be brought to punishment no matter how violently this was done. That McMains was there at the time was just an accident and Clay would have sought out the perpetrators of the deed no matter who was in Cimarron at the time. He had a great admiration for Tolby and his part in bringing the guilty to trial was an act of gratitude and respect for one of his best friends.

"O. P. McMains received a dispatch on Wednesday morning (July 25) not to leave Trinidad for Raton just yet. The old man started out for Raton on the very next train. He says that if any choose to arrest him it will only call attention to the justness of his controversy." (*Ibid. July 30, 1888.*)

"O. P. McMains, S. D. Bell and Anderson Duling were arrested in the city (Trinidad) yesterday morning by Sheriff Burns under an indictment of the last grand jury charging them with manslaughter. The indictment grew out of the death of Squire Russell, who was killed during the Stonewall troubles last August, when a mob of the Anti-Maxwell Grant settlers attacked a number of deputy sheriffs that had been sent there to disperse them and keep the peace and in which McMains, Bell and Duling were involved. The bonds of the three men were placed at five hundred dollars each which they easily furnished and were released. Our sympathies are and always have been with those settlers who established homes on this land when it was given for settlement and our opinion is the same now as that expressed at the time of the riots; that mob violence was wrong and would only injure the cause of the settlers who suffered.

"Mr. McMains has forced himself to the front as a leader of the settlers and at his door can be laid the troubles of last August. The deputies were sent to Stonewall by Sheriff Burns to preserve peace and but for the determination of Mr. McMains to bring about a conflict there would have been no trouble. His ambition has seemed to be to cover himself with glory by leading an armed resistance to the law and we trust now that his ambition has been fully satisfied." *(Trinidad Advertiser February 6, 1889.)*

"There is good stuff in McMains of Colfax county. His dogged persistance in his fight with the Maxwell Land Grant Company challenges admiration. It is such men who bear the brunt of agitation and become martyrs of needed reforms in Government. . . . So says another newspaper. That is quite true. But they are generally men with better heads than the shoulders of the noted agitator bear. His heart has been right, but his head has not been qualified for the grand mission so boldly undertaken, pluckily pursued, but ah, so grievously ended. Starting the suit in Colorado, and abandoning it as he did, forged a chain for the settlers which we fear can never be unriveted. Refusing, on account of jealousy, to be associated with competent legal counsel, he went on blindly to the Supreme Court, in legal ignorance until the fate of the settlers was decided by that court against the settlers. What admiration he has won by his pluck has been more than counter-balanced by his ignorance and jealousy. Whether it has been ambition to achieve a great triumph alone against a great corporation, or the selfish hope to reap a pecuniary reward unshared with others that steadied him on his course and made him spurn the suggestion of uniting counsel, no one will ever know. He is now in the national capital. What he can hope to accomplish with but some little money from friends among men he has so insanely abused, cannot be conjectured." *(Live Stock Journal of New Mexico taking exception to an editorial in the Albuquerque Citizen—December 2, 1887.)*

Judge Long to the Grand Jury in session at Springer, New Mexico: "It is currently and publicly reported that in July of this year the demonstration at Stonewall, Colorado, had armed men, many or all of them masked. They took into their own hands in this county of Colfax the administration of the law, here as well as there where by force they re-instated a person who had been ejected by the sheriff in the discharge of his sworn duty, by virtue of a legal writ but a few days before, after which they then paraded through the streets of Raton. Such persons should and must be punished." *(New Mexico Live Stock Journal September 26, 1888.)*

"McMains is at last reaping some of the fruit for himself which he has prepared for others. On Wednesday he was lying in the Trinidad jail with ten indictments over him, calling for nineteen thousand dollars in bond. Eight separate indictments were found against him for assault with intent to murder John Sells, Edward Brown, John Hannan, William C. Hunn and John Pembroke." Raton Range March 28, 1889.) McMains was then sentenced to serve some time in jail, after which he again returned to his hobby of agitating against the Grant. Again newspapers assailed him so bitterly that in 1893 the Clayton Enterprise told them all to leave the poor, beaten old man alone to enjoy his last days in ranter against a company which already won its case. After all, he was not leading armed mobs anymore, just standing on street corners denouncing the company. After a time he went into seclusion at his home in Stonewall, and there ended his days.

At Stonewall he did not even have a home of his own. Mr. Russell gave him the loan of one until the day of his death. On April 15, 1899, at 15 minutes past 12, McMains died of catarrah of the stomach. On the following day, Sam Bell went into Trinidad for a casket. McMains was buried on the 17th at the Stonewall cemetery, fourth grave right as you enter, next to Loganberry. No marker is on his grave now for time destroyed it. But he is still remembered. His wife went back to Missouri where she ended her days in peace and there was no more talk of Anti-Grant war.

Chapter Eleven

CLAY ALLISON

It sometimes happens in the course of history that the champion of a Lost Cause outlives, in song and legend, the great enterprise for which he is willing to shed his life's blood. No movement is without its dark moments which produces such phrases as, "My kingdom for a horse," These are the times that try men's souls," "Oh, for a Clay Allison." This latter expression was used by O. P. McMains when he felt that he had no lieutenant brave enough to aid him in his fight against the Maxwell Land Grant Company. Allison was reticent when questioned in later life about his dealings with McMains in Cimarron following the death of Rev. Tolby. He was not so taciturn with his gun. However vehement his denials to reporters in later life as a successful cattleman in Pecos, Texas and Las Vegas, New Mexico, McMains would not have sought a Clay Allison in his hour of trial had he not tested the man somewhere along the line before. True, the death of Rev. Tolby was not a Grant matter and the work Allison did for McMains as a vigilante was over with before the leader of the Anti-granters commenced his war on the Maxwell Land Grant Company, but Allison must have been with McMains when he switched over even though he was never identified as an Anti-granter. Allison lived at Cimarron. He was part of the life that went on there. Those were frontier days. He did no more nor no less than any frontiersman and certainly ended up a lot better off than many of them. The strangest thing about Clay Allison was not his life but his death. Of all the frontier gunmen that have shot their way into the pages of history, his end was the most out of character of any. He never reached the heights of Billy the Kid in public fancy but his exploits are more daring, more romantic and certainly more brave. He was not an outlaw with a gang which meant that he worked alone and fought alone. Sometimes his brother, John, is found at his side, but magazines periodically feature Clay Allison alone. He was a brave man but women always baffled him. One time when he was courting a young lady at Vermejo, the mother of the girl got her broomstick after him and told him never to come near the place again. He never did.

He was always a religious man at heart and usually when he was drinking heavily he would stand up on the bar and ask all the men in the room to join him in a hymn, even though he was no hand at carrying a tune which produced more discord than harmony. If he saw anyone who was not singing it angered him so that he usually forced the vocal cords at the point of a gun. The most popular story about Clay Allison is the tale of his visit to a dentist:

"Clay Allison, who has just left this city of Las Vegas for Lincoln county, (Seven Rivers where he bought a ranch after leaving Cimarron) is known as a holy terror when he is aroused and although increasing years and different conditions have made him less vindictive, he still has a decided fondness for getting even with his enemies, and is pretty likely to do so as a general rule. Clay was up in Cheyenne a few days ago with a bunch of steers about fifteen hundred head in number which he sold at a good profit, and as he was suffering with a toothache, while there he went to a dentist to get relief. The dentist, who was 'on the make' sized up the man as a cow man with plenty of cash and determined to make some money out of him. Instead of applying a little creosote to Clay's aching tooth he got him in his dental chair and proceeded to bore a hole in one of the cowman's best teeth for the purpose of filling it, which it didn't in the least need. He was a clumsy quack and inadvertently broke about half a tooth off. Clay got mad and left and went to another dentist who repaired the damage at the expense of twenty-five dollars and told the victim that he had been treated by an errant quack who evidently wanted to make money out of him. This fired the blood of Mr. Allison, who fairly thirsted for revenge, and he got it too. He proceeded to the quack's office, seized a pair of forceps, threw the man down on the floor, and in spite of the yells of the victim, inserted the instrument in his mouth and drew out one of his best molars. Not content with this he grabbed for another and caught one of the front teeth together with a large piece of upper lip and he was tugging away at it when the agonized shrieks and yells of the poor devil, upon whose chest Allison was pressing his knee, drew a crowd and ended the matter. The story is said to be absolutely true and Allison admitted it." (Las Vegas Optic July 7, 1886.)

The story of Allison has been told and re-told to such an extent that no two authors have related it alike. What actually happened was that Clay came over from his ranch at Seven Rivers in Lincoln County with a number of cattle he hoped to dispose of either at Cimarron or at Springer. Boggs and others had built up his hopes that he would have no difficulty in finding a buyer at either place. When he got to Springer he found that someone, possibly Charles Goodnight, had been there before him but that did not discourage him. He went on to Raton,

[145]

Trinidad, Denver and finally Cheyenne, at which place he was more than successful. His tooth began bothering him at Denver but he paid no attention to it because he felt that loss of time would also mean loss of profit and he had come too far to take a loss. Authors have placed the incident as happening at Las Vegas, Lincoln, Denver, Raton, Trinidad and Springer. Some authors have been called authorities on Clay Allison on the basis of the dentist incident. It seems that all anybody knew about him for a long time was that he was tough and knew how to pull teeth. One point overlooked by practically every author is that from the very beginning, when Allison moved from Tennessee to Texas, he was a highly successful cattleman and bid fair to become famous as such in line with Chisum, Goodnight and others who names are known to every rancher in the Southwest. His untimely death cut off his bid for fame, but it failed to wipe out the deeds that rank him with Billy the Kid, Radabaugh and other gunmen who feed the imagination of our Western writer of today.

Clay Allison was part of all the doings on the Maxwell Land Grant following the death of Parson Tolby until O. P. McMains changed his tactics from seeking the murderer of his fellow preacher to fighting the Maxwell Land Grant Company. McMains was well aware of the type of man he was dealing with and was friendly with Allison as a successful cattleman, overlooking the faults of the rancher who was usually a very nice companion until he had a few drinks tucked away. Furthermore, Allison was educated. The one strange note about it all was that O. P. McMains was a Northerner. Just why Allison overlooked this merely explains another side of his many natures. So many stories and legends have been built up about the man to cloud the facts of his life that one hesitates to give him his place in the history of the Grant. Some authors have placed him on the Grant because he murdered a man in Texas. They overlook the fact that he came to New Mexico with a herd of cattle. A man escaping capture will not be hindered by a slow-moving herd of steers. Allison killed in Colorado, Texas and New Mexico but he was never known to run away. He knew the Grant country before he moved to New Mexico. As a cowboy he had driven cattle for Charles Goodnight to the Maxwell ranch and on up to Denver. He would have bought property then as did Stockton, Chase, Davis, Ellis and Dawson, but his own herd was so poor in numbers that he decided to wait until the stock demand would boom. What finally decided him was the gold rush to the Moreno Valley and the rise of Elizabethtown. This gold rush placed the characters on the stage that brought the scenes of vigilantes, the Maxwell Land Grant and Railway Company, Rev. Tolby, Rev. O. P. McMains, Mills, Elkins, Catron, Allison, Maxwell Land Grant Company and bloodshed. Whenever Allison came to Cimarron he stayed with Boggs who was quite a frontiersman in his own right and a Southerner. He taught Allison many tricks of gunplay that were to be useful when he was sought out by gun-fighters who sought the distinction of being his conqueror. At no time in his life was Clay Allison ever a professional gun-fighter.

Eighty miles northeast of Memphis, on the South Fork of the Forked Deer river, is the trade center of a large and fruitful agricultural region that is Jackson, Tennessee. Even in 1840, when Clay Allison was born there, it was quite a cotton center, despite its small population of a few thousand. The Allisons had one of the better homes of the town and were looked up to by the aldermen. Clay's father was a cotton agent and buyer. He also had a small farm on the outskirts of the town and there Allison first came to know about cattle. There were three children—Clay, the oldest, John and Mary. Clay attended the Lane school and was considered a bright pupil. The Allisons made up part of the blue-blood society of the town and it was considered an honor to be invited to one of their socials. Polk, Clark, Cheatham, Cleburne, Breckenridge, Ruggles, Hardee and others to fight for the South in the war between the States often visited the Allisons. Clay served with Hardee's corps at the battle of Shiloh. One month before the battle General Grant entered Jackson and made it his headquarters. The town was in the hands of the Confederates following the famous battle and then re-captured by Federals under Col. Engelmann. Clay was told that he could remain at home if he promised not to give the 3rd Illinois soldiers any trouble. His father and brother were with General Forrest. After seveal days the Union men decided to search the homes for food. In order to ascertain whether or not something was hidden in Mrs. Allison's best pitcher, the corporal in charge broke it over her protests. Clay said nothing. That evening he made the rounds of the drinking places, saw the man he was looking for and shot him. His horse was fast and carried him out of danger before the Federals could recover from their surprise. Clay joined General Forrest as an Intelligence officer. On his very first mission he was caught behind the Union lines and in Federal uniform. Brought to trial as a spy he was sentenced to be shot the next day. Placed in a home with a guard to watch over him, he abided his time until the soldier drowsed, took his gun and shot him. He escaped to the hills and was identified with guerilla warfare until the end of the conflict.

Following the Civil War he found the old homestead a shambles and decided to try his luck in Texas. Many of his friends and relatives were there and seemed to be content with the move. Besides Carpetbaggers in Tennessee would never let him forget the war. It was only towards the end of his life that he mellowed towards Northerners. His first job was as a cow-hand on a ranch at the headwaters of the Brazos river. The war taught him to save. Thrifty in every respect during these early days he would never spend any money for clothes, entertainment or drinks. Women he fled from as beyond his comprehension. He had a pleasing personality and won many cowboys over as lifelong friends. Within eight months he was able to buy a ranch from a discouraged farmer who thought he would be better off with a job in Austin. Clay sent for his brother John and his career as a cattleman in the Southwest was launched. Charles Goodnight bought the cattle at a profit and the brothers sold the ranch for something bigger. He worked for Goodnight while John took care of the homestead.

It was while on one of these cattledrives for Goodnight that Clay began the startling acts of his life that were to make him a character. He also took to drinking with the boys and in the state of intoxication would do things he would later regret. Camped at the outskirts of Canadian, Texas, the hands began drinking. Allison had more than enough. Suddenly, he took off his clothes retaining his gunbelt, boots and broad-brimmed hat. He rode up and down the streets of Canadian in just that attire. Some amazed citizens called on the marshal to arrest him. They were even more startled to see him parade the peace-officer into a saloon at gun-point and force him into drinking so much whiskey that the town felt itself better off with the male Godiva than the wild shooting drunken marshal who almost sent five people to their graves. This was the first of the great exploits of Allison which gained in the telling until fanciful fiction clouded the truth. Back at camp Allison was treated as a hero. From then on he sought to be the only star in the cast and performance. Repeat performances were given at Dodge City, Hays City, Abilene, Denver and Trinidad.

This was the age of the cattle barons. Scotchmen, Englishmen, Germans, Dutchmen and Americans were buying up vast domains, forming syndicates, controlling the meat industry of America. Limitless, rolling ranges that helped them to build empires which they ruled from a lordly mansion in feudal splendor. Allison worked for a few, always increasing his profits until he found himself fairly well off in land and cattle. On one of his trips to Cimarron he noted the wonderful grass and the plentiful streams about the area. Here would be the place to set himself up as a cattle king. He bought the land from Lucien Maxwell and settled down with his brother John and a few of his favorite cow-hands near the site of what was shortly afterwards to be the village of Otero. The main factor in settling here was the fact that two railroads were working their way into Trinidad about thirty miles north which would make shipping cattle a lot easier on the men as well as the steers.

On the ranch next to his in Texas lived a short, squatty rancher by the name of Johnson. Allison and he had difficulties over a water hole. The story goes that Allison invited him to assist him in digging a grave. After which both would enter and indulge in a nice knife fight. The one to come out alive would bury the other. Allison won but skipped the country in fear of Johnson's friends. If such were the case why would he come all the way to Maxwell's? I have found no conclusive evidence that such a fight actually took place, nor do Allison's relatives know of one. It was part of the legend built up about the man after his death. In the glowing accounts of his life and death, not one makes reference to such an incident taking place in the life of the man. No warrant was ever issued for the arrest of Allison regarding his implication in the death of Johnson. Furthermore, the whereabouts of Allison were well enough known for any of Johnson's friends and relatives to have their revenge should they be in quest of it. Miguel Otero is of the opinion that Allison sold his interests in Texas to start anew in New Mexico. While I have a high opinion of the author, I cannot reconcile the fact that Allison did bring his hired hands with him, and did have a herd in an amazingly short time, too short not to have trailed them up with him. He left Texas with a definite place in mind which could hardly be the attitude of a fugitive. Otero, who knew Allison during these days, wrote:

"When sober, Clay Allison was well mannered and extremely likeable, but under the influence of liquor he was a terror to the whole neighborhood and a good man to avoid. Gradually, his name became dreaded in the whole section. He actually killed so many and was so keenly aware of the readiness of friends or relatives to 'get even' that he never stood or sat in a room with his back to a door or window." Allison, at the time he settled on the Maxwell Land Grant was six feet two inches tall, weighed one hundred and ninety pounds and had blue eyes set in a large boned square-set pioneer type face that always created the impression that he was ready to take his place in the driver's seat of a covered wagon and hit the trail westward. He had a prominent Roman nose and wore his hair long in the fashion of the day. His mustache was so large that it drooped below his chin. At times he permitted his beard, a reddish-blond tint, to grow, for he was fair haired rather than dark. He walked with a limp due to an accident he had when his gun went off, the bullet penetrating the right foot. His right eye was crossed so that the iris seemed to be just off the bridge of his nose. His ears were large and stuck out from his face a little but he managed to conceal this with his long curly hair, which he parted from the right almost from the center of his head. His upper lip was thin but did not curve at the corners which gave the impression of a rather large mouth. His lower lip was thick and protruded a little creating a shadow for his round chin. His neck fitted into a size sixteen collar. He wore expensive clothes.

Today, as one drives through Highway 85 on the way to Raton north of Otero, he can picture to himself the tall, fair-haired cattleman rounding up his cattle. Here Clay built a dugout. He and other ranchers used it as a shelter during the branding and round-up seasons. It was situated west of the Cimarron river and built into a hillside —just one large adobe room. Here also were stored provisions. Among Allison's supplies one always found whiskey—five gallon jugs. It was customary every evening for the men to wash up, eat their supper and while away their time in drinking and dancing. As there were no women about they danced with each other nor did they think it was effeminate. Sometimes they did an Indian dance around a fire using the Rebel yell instead of the warwhoop. It became particularly fascinating when they were three masts to the wind. The cook was rather obese and if there was anything he detested it was to dance with these rather merry men who used him for a bulwark rather than for amusement. One fine evening he managed to escape and found a splendid hide-out in the tall grass near the river. There he made a fine big bed and slept the sleep of the guiltless. For one hour he slumbered on until Clay Allison decided he wanted to dance with him. He bellowed out. No response. Allison decided to hunt up his dancing partner. He stumbled against the prone figure in the tall grass and the poor corpulent cook was doing a solo by the light of the moon at gunpoint.

After a time Allison sold his holdings at this particular spot and moved closer to the village of Cimarron. He watched the sale of the grant with interest not altogether blaming Maxwell for moving on. Allison seemed to get along with the manager of the Maxwell Land Grant and Railway company, and often visited him at his home which was the old Maxwell homestead. He took three trips to Elizabethtown but failing to strike it rich he decided to stick to ranching, selling much of the beef he raised to the sprouting mining communities about. He seems to have had no difficulties with the Utes and Apaches about; on the contrary many were quite friendly with him. He often went up the Vermejo to visit a girl by the name of Mamie Bishop but her mother chased him out with a broomstick one evening with the admonition never to darken her door again. Many frontiersmen had been treated that way. Kit Carson was once humiliated even more so by an Indian girl. Allison next tried his luck with the Holbrook girl. She liked him well enough but she knew of his reputation with drink. If he killed people when under the influence of liquor, what would he do to his wife? She decided not to take the chance.

During those Frontier days of adjustment, westerners sought fame by seeking out a noted gun-fighter or desperado and challenging him to a gun-duel. If he came out victorious it added to his fame and usually meant free drinks wherever he went. It also meant he could bully anyone in town, which is what he usually did. No cock ever crowed louder than he did, until a man with a quicker trigger-finger came along to deflate him. One such character was Francisco Griego better known as Pancho. He (and his family) was brought to Cimarron by Boggs to work for Lucien B. Maxwell. He was an expert shot and horseman and resented the jibes of the Texan cowboys about the place. He gathered together a few men and started a raiding party. He had killed several men before deciding on Clay Allison. He was man enough to tell Allison that he had come to try his luck with him. They went into a bar to have a drink over the deal as businessmen are wont to do. Allison noticed Pancho fanning himself with his sombrero. It was a ruse to get the drop on the cattleman, but it was too apparent. Stealthily, Pancho reached for his gun, but his over-cautiousness was his undoing. Without seeming to move Allison already had his gun out and shot him. He then went to the Justice of the Peace and had himself acquitted as acting in self-defense. Commented the editor of the Santa Fe New Mexican:

"On the night of November 1st, Francisco Griego was shot and killed by C. Allison. Both parties met at the door of the St. James hotel, entered, and with some friends took a drink, when the two walked into the corner of the room and had some conversation. There Allison drew his revolver and shot three times. The lights were extinguished and Griego was not found until the next morning. Francisco Griego was well known in Santa Fe where his mother lives. He has killed a great many men, and was considered a dangerous man; few regret his loss." But those few decided to take the law into their hands. And here is where Allison fits into the Maxwell Land Grant story. Years after the following events took place, C. N. Blackwell, a noted citizen of Raton, New Mexico, wrote to M. W. Mills, an attorney living at Springer who had been held a prisoner by Allison during the Reign of Terror at Cimarron and therefore an eye-witness to the stirring events that was to make the little town a rather dangerous place to live in indeed. The letter is dated from Springer on February 13, 1924:

"I have your letter of the 8th. In reply thereto I will recall some of the incidents connected with the murder of the Rev. Thomas Tolby. Sometime during the year 1873, there came to the town of Cimarron a Methodist itinerant minister, whose name I believe was the Rev. F. J. (just above he calls him Thomas) Tolby. He came with his family from some place in Indiana, locating at Cimarron, and preaching there one Sunday, then going to the mines at Elizabethtown and preaching there the following Sunday.

"He lived in one of the houses belonging to the Maxwell Land Grant and Railway Company and made his trips from place to place, usually on horseback. He was quite an able preacher. I should say a better speaker in the pulpit than most preachers then, and even now. He was quite liberal in his views, ready to discuss all kinds of topics, such as gambling, horse-racing, dancing, etc. He did not condemn those things as most preachers are inclined to do.

"He very frequently visited a sort of a public, front office that I had in those days (at Cimarron) and was quite familiar and friendly with the sporting class who frequented this office. Because of his liberality of views he succeeded in getting quite an audience. I think he had been a soldier in the Civil War and a Chaplain in the army. While he was a loyal citizen to his country, he did not belong to the Republican party. He was rather more in the line of what was then called Copper-head Democrats. Usually when our District Court Judge, Chief Justice Palen, who was exactly the reverse sort of man in politics, came to Cimarron to hold court, he would rush off and call at his room and there met Judge Palen and quite often my father who was a great friend to the judge was often there visiting with them also.

"Their conversation usually ran along pleasantly until they would come to the subject of politics and then Judge Palen and the Rev. Mr. Tolby would have a fierce battle of words. Yet, they would part quite good friends and Mr. Tolby would call again and again. He was such a common friendly sort of man. He even associated with more worldly men that often such men manifested rather more familiarity with him than they were justified in doing. I remember that I had seen them and heard these sporting men invite him to take a drink, or to go to a horse race. He never did anything of this kind but took no offense at the invitations.

"I think that it was on Saturday, September the 12th, 1875, when he made his usual trip on horseback to Elizabethtown, and on Sunday held his usual church service, that he left Cimarron. On Monday morning, September 14, 1875, he started back to his home in Cimarron. The contractor of the mail route was named Florence Donahue who had employed a fellow by the name of Cruz Vega to act as his mail carrier from Elizabethtown to Cimarron. This Cruz Vega started out a short distance behind Tolby that Monday morning, on horseback also, so that when the minister got down about six miles from Elizabethtown, Cruz Vega was about a half mile behind him as appeared from some evidence later on in court. About two miles further on at the mouth of the Cimarron Canyon, Tolby was shot and his body drawn up into some brush and his horse tied to a tree. Vega must have passed not far from Tolby's horse, without seeing the horse, or he murdered Mr. Tolby himself, according to the evidence that was offered. A little later in the day some men found the horse and found the body. Afterwards Vega was arrested and charged with murder. At the time Tolby was murdered the District Court had adjourned at Cimarron and gone to Taos for the purpose of holding Court there. I was in Taos attending Court at the time. I remember very well someone coming over from that neighborhood and reporting the murder. None of them seemed to take much interest in making inquiry about it except me.

"I think a reward was offered for the arrest of the murderers and this reward was about three thousand dollars. It was offered by the Masonic Fraternity. About two or three months later, I was in Trinidad, Colorado, applying for an injunction before Judge Wells in a mining litigation. A number of telegrams came to me from friends in Cimarron, advising me not to return because a mob was gathering there by the hundreds, from all parts of the country, and that it was charged that I had some complicity in the murder of Tolby, along with Dr. Longwill, Florence Donahue, Francisco Griego and others. These telegrams seemed too absurd and ridiculous to me so I took my team and buggy and started to go back to Cimarron. I ran my horses over thirty miles until they were too exhausted to overtake the coach that went to Cimarron (This coach left Clifton House near the site of the village of Otero).

"When I finally caught the coach, I turned my team loose on the prairie hitched to my buggy. When I got to Cimarron and the coach rolled into the plaza, a thousand men or more jerked me out of the coach and had the rope all ready to hang me to a telegraph pole. Some of my friends had a lot of Indians arrayed and staked out, who threatened to shoot the mob if anything was done with me. The mob agreed to appoint twelve men and to have my friends appoint twelve men to take charge of me, which was done. For a day or so I was guarded by these twenty-four men until the United States Government sent soldiers from Fort Union, who came suddenly upon the mob, who dropped their guns. It was demanded that I be given up to the soldiers, who notified the surging, excited mob that I would be held upon the order of a properly constituted command of the Court. A mob trial had been ordered and hundreds, if not thousands, of witnesses were summoned. Days were given to hearsay testimony. At that time Judge Henry L. Waldo, a young lawyer at Santa Fe, was sent up to look after my defense.

"Previous to my arrival at Cimarron Dr. Longwill, who had been charged as an accessory to the murder of Tolby, fled to Fort Union for protection. He started back from Fort Union with these same soldiers that had been sent to restore order at Cimarron, but he became frightened and turned back and went to Santa Fe as fast as a relay of stage coach horses could be given him. He landed safely in Santa Fe although pursued by some of the same mob. The mob trial lasted four or five days and was made up of the Justice of the Peace and two of the mob men. These men determined that I should be set at liberty since I had no connection with the murder, so they turned me loose and shot a man by the name of Cardenas whom they were taking to the jail.

"There was a printer working in the office of the Cimarron News at the time Mr. Tolby was murdered; a man by the name of McMains who took an affidavit that had been forced from Cardenas by Harberger and others at Elizabethtown. This affidavit charged Cruz Vega as the actual murderer of Tolby being paid for it by Florence Donahue and Francisco Griego, who in turn got their money from Dr. Longwell. It also stated that M. W. Mills was the lawyer employed and knew and advised them about the murder. In this way I became connected with the murder of Mr. Tolby. The Cimarron News was operated by the Maxwell Land Grant and Railway Company, with W. R. Morley, Frank Springer and others running it.

"At the election a short time previous, I had been elected to the legislature, running against Frank Springer, whom it was said had a large slush fund at his command. I was elected by about five to one. O. P. McMains also claimed to be a Methodist preacher. He took the Cardenas affidavit and rode over the whole country reading it to the people, fixing a day when they should gather together and avenge the death of Rev. Tolby. The day that I arrived in Cimarron was the day that the mob gathered. A few days previous to this time, McMains got Cruz Vega and gave him five dollars to husk some corn on the Ponil Creek for him. One night while he was there the mob took Cruz and hung him to a tree. At the trial afterwards, of McMains, for murder, the evidence was that he ordered a rope about Cruz Vega's neck, pulled him up to a tree, let him down and asked him to tell who had given him the money to murder Rev. Tolby. Vega said that no one had given him money and that he had not murdered Tolby. They pulled him up and then let down again asking him if Donahue and Griego had given the money and Vega said—No. They pulled him up again, choked him almost to death, and then let him down and this time he said, Yes.

"The Governor of the Territory of New Mexico wrote afterwards that it appeared that McMains decoyed Cruz Vega, dragged him by the neck; hung him up and let him down; beat him with revolvers; shot him and left him hanging dead to a telegraph pole. McMains was tried on the charge of murder on a change of venue to Mora county; found guilty of murder, but the jury failed to put in the word murder. The presiding Judge, Henry J. Waldo, decided that because of this omission it was a fatal error and in this way McMains escaped punishment for the crime he had committed. At the mob trial in Cimarron, Henry L. Waldo appeared for myself and McMains and Frank Springer appeared for the prosecution and the mob. After the close of the trial the crowds surged back and forth, rushing from place to place and all kinds of demonstrations went on. Not only threats of killing those of us who had been charged with complicity but even McMains, his associates and adherents. Only one man was shot, although assassination would have taken place were it not for the presence of the soldiers and the counsel of other good citizens. The mob suddenly changed, gathered up their arms and went back to their homes. Others were shot and hung shortly afterwards from the difficulties that had grown from this trial. Among these was the bravest man of all, Pancho Griego, who was shot by Allison in the back.

"I was only too glad to get on the coach before daybreak and go to Santa Fe. The legislature soon convened and moved the courts from Colfax to Taos county. Then came the District Court at Taos, guarded by two or three companies of United States soldiers from Fort Union. Officers were sent out to Colfax county to bring to Taos all of the witnesses and the Grand Jury took a week or two trying to investigate and locate the perpetrators of the crime of the murder of Tolby. They failed to find any indictment and nothing further was done. The soldiers had to be kept at Cimarron for several months to keep down the proposed and attempted violence that seemed to be in the air. I should add however that the mystery was never solved, even though men like M. M. Chase and hundreds of others that have passed over the Great Divide continued to say that all that was charged in the Cardenas affidavit was true and that M. W. Mills knew the perpetrators of the crime if he would only tell it. While hundreds of others have also said that I was as guilty as Cruz Vega, I can honestly say that to this day (February 13, 1924) I do not know any more about it now than I did then, or than I am telling you. Yet it has been an unfortunate fatality that has blocked my career in life off and on ever since and I have found it difficult to rise above it.

"Perhaps I ought to say further that the motive for the murder of Rev. Tolby must have been because he openly declared that he saw Donahue and Griego shoot at some Americans and that he intended to be sent before the Grand Jury in order to secure an indictment. Also it was said that because of his Copper-head democratic politics, some of the officials at Santa Fe wanted to dispose of him. No self-respecting, considerate and fair man ever entertained any credence of this theory. I know of no reason why any man, even with evil intentions, should have coveted the life of Mr. Tolby. It was a mystery at the time he was murdered and the same mystery has continued ever since. There was some evidence against Longwell which was that he was friendly with Griego and Donahue, but he was too much of a money lover to pay very much to have Rev. Tolby killed. I have dictated briefly the items that I recall and trust I have answered your inquiry."

That the lawyer shows a decided prejudice against McMains, Longwill and Allison the reader has already seen. Let us remember that Mills wrote this almost fifty years after the events took place and names and incidents became confused in his mind. This often happens. I recall interviewing several old timers who saw Billy the Kid stretched out for burial. One said he was loaded with buckshot; the other said he had a bullet in the head and another in the stomach. The Santa Fe New Mexican gives us these accounts:

"For the past week Cimarron has more or less been in a complete state of anarchy growing out of the excitement incident to the late murder of Rev. Tolby and the lynching on the night of October 30 of Cruz Vega charged with complicity in the same . . . aggravated by the killing of Francisco Griego, three days later, by Allison of Red River. On Sunday, the telegraph was employed most of the day in detailing further excitement and anarchy starting, as we gathered, among the friends of the lynched man. It is charged by the reaction party, or mob, that before the death of the lynched man he stated that other persons were implicated in the murder including some of the best citizens of Colfax county. Among them, as alleged, was Dr. Longwill, the Probate Judge, M. W. Mills, a member of the legislature, and Mr. Donahue, an old man and a respected citizen of the Territory of New Mexico. On this, at best a very doubtful statement, the two latter have been arrested on civil warrants and are now in the custody of the sheriff.

"Much apprehension was felt among the friends of the gentlemen both at Cimarron and here in Santa Fe, for their personal safety in the present excited state of things in Cimarron and the sheriff telegraphed the Secretary of the Territory that he thought that he would be able to maintain order. It is hardly necessary to say that in view of the intelligence and high character of the gentlemen named that no one here in Santa Fe for the moment believes that either of them are in any manner, directly or indirectly, implicated or in any degree have countenanced the murder of Mr. Tolby.

"It is to be hoped that moderation will prevail and that the law will be permitted to have its courts. In the present state of feeling it is especially due to the parties that they have a full and searching examination. Since writing the above we learn by telegram that Manuel Cardenas, the man who was a few days since arrested in Taos, on suspicion of having committed the murder, and discharged for want of evidence, has been re-arrested and confessed that he committed the murder. He likewise, in the spirit of justice, exonerates Longwill, Mills and Donahue from any complicity in the murder. From this circumstance, as well as from their good character and standing in New Mexico, there seems to be a well grounded suspicion of foul play and a working up of the mob by design for the purpose of ruining the characters of the parties named." (Nov. 9, 1875.)

There seems to be an armed band of men in and about the town bent on violence, lawlessness and the civil authorities, but from all we can learn compel them to do as they see fit. The citizens are terrified, and many of them have left town to save their lives. Mr. Mills and Donahue, who have been charged with complicity in the murder of Tolby, which we believe to be entirely unfounded, are in the hands of the mob, and it is said that they declare their intention not to surrender them even on a writ of habeas corpus. United States troops are on the ground and they will prevent violence and bloodshed if they have notice in time, but even their presence has not had the effect to disperse the mob who seem to have control of the prisoners and the administration of affairs. All that the accused want is but a fair and impartial examination according to law, but this cannot be had where terror and lawlessness reign supreme. They know that they can establish their innocence if they have an opportunity.

"In our article of yesterday we state the Cruz Vega, who was hung by the mob, implicated Dr. Longwill and Mills in the murder of Mr. Tolby; we since learn that this was a mistake and that Cardenas, who has since retracted, is the only person who did so. So far as we can learn the only evidence against Longwill and Mills and Donahue seems to lie in the statement of Cardenas, to somebody to that effect, and which he now retracts. It has been ascertained that this man Cardenas is an escaped convict, having been found guilty of murder on September 9, 1864, in the county of Taos, and sentenced to be hung, which sentence was commuted to imprisonment for life; this has been officially telegraphed to the authorities at Cimarron by the clerk of the Court.

"The murder of Tolby is only a pretext for this armed band to visit their violence upon peaceful citizens of Cimarron. . . . The sheriff seems powerless to do anything except by permission of the mob." (November 10, 1875.)

Here we note that O. P. McMains comes into the picture for the first time. He was a very good friend of Tolby's both growing up in Indiana together and attending the same seminary of studies for the Methodist ministry. Mills claims that he worked as a printer on the Cimarron paper. This I doubt very much for there was too broad a field for Circuit Riders in the Southwest for anyone of the ministers to waste time in an office especially when another was already in the field. If McMains were alone in the field he possibly would have worked as a printer for there was hardly enough income as a Circuit Rider for a comfortable living. That he was a printer I believe, since after the Tolby affair he took to printing a newspaper in Raton when that town was founded. But he had nothing to do with the Cimarron paper. If he did, Clay Allison would not have dumped it into the river. At least not at the time these events took place. If he did any work in the newspaper office it was when he was firmly established as Tolby's successor. He disappears from the news from 1876 to 1880. In four years it is possible that he salvaged much of the press from the river or ordered new parts and printed pamphlets at the Cimarron News and Press office. He was never connected with the paper in any way as publisher or editor, but he may have helped as printer since he knew the printer's trade. The paper belonged to the Maxwell Land Grant and Railway Company. O. P. McMains was at the office regularly and came to know every official connected with the company who visited Cimarron. He knew more about the company than any other individual at Cimarron outside of the company and its lawyers. That he was to become the arch-enemy of the company he never at that time suspected. His only interest was to find out who killed his fellow minister and friend.

It was the death of his friend that brought him to Cimarron and to Clay Allison. Allison was a religious man having been taught the fear of God from his mother's knee. He had a deep respect for Parson Tolby and often invited him to Lambert's bar not because he believed that the minister would accept but because it spoke of his constancy when he refused. Clay always liked a man who stuck up for what he believed. Often when he was under the influence of liquor he would start a hymn standing, head uncovered, on the bar inviting all in the room to join in. It meant death for anyone to refuse.

When McMains came to Cimarron to take upon himself the double duty of Circuit Rider and detective in the investigation of the death of Parson Tolby, he heard of Allison and hunted him up. The tall cowboy took an immediate liking to the diminutive, squatty preacher, even though he was on the opposite side of the fence in the war between the States. They were seen together quite often and Allison agreed that the murderer of Rev. Tolby should be sought out and punished. The Maxwell Land Grant and Railway Company seems to have had nothing to do or say about the goings on and they had every reason in the world for complaint for all the property traversed by Cruz Vega, Cardenas, Griego and Allison belonged to the company. The preacher was murdered on their property. The mob was taking over in their town and people were moving away from their Grant.

Allison was the leader of the mob. McMains convinced him that his was a holy cause and that killing a preacher was not just like killing an ordinary person. The man had dedicated his life to doing good but some one came along and took that life away. He had to pay the penalty. Clay rounded up his cowboys and a number of settlers. He was very cordial to the soldiers although the sight of their uniforms must have made his blood boil. Allison was aware that although the Justice of the Peace found a pretext for the shooting of Griego, the latter's friends were of another mind. This is one reason why the rancher kept so many men about him. Cimarron was having a Civil War of its own and the Maxwell Land Grant officials wisely let it die of its own volition. One can see that possibly Allison was correct later on in denying that he was McMains' right hand man during these days. While he seemed to be working hand in hand with McMains he actually was guarding himself against any surprise attack from the friends of Griego and Vega and they seemed to have had many. The law placed McMains on trial; not Allison. He often reminded newspaper reporters of the fact.

"Clay Allison, so well known in Colfax county, is in Las Vegas, and on Wednesday (May 12) said to the reporter of the Las Vegas Optic that he wishes emphatically to deny that he is in any sort of sympathy with O. P.

McMains in his incessant agitation of the Maxwell Land Grant question. And he especially desires to contradict the report, originated by either McMains or his followers, that he would go to Mr. Whigham, agent for the Maxwell Land Grant Company, and attempt to intimidate him in any way whatsoever in the discharge of his duties. Mr. Allison has concluded that the law should take its course, and from present appearances there is no doubt that the best policy for the settlers on the Maxwell Grant is to make compromises with Mr. Whigham, secure their homes, and end this eternal litigation warfare on the Grant of which old man McMains is the chief promoter and instigator. Allison wishes to distinctly disavow any sympathy whatsoever with McMains and his present policy of senseless agitation. Allison also desires to say that he held to these same views with reference to the old man and his Maxwell Land Grant agitation three years ago, and was only restrained from making them public by his brother-in-law who thought it might be wise to keep quiet on the subject for a while. Old McMains ought to take a tumble by this time, as he can no longer rely on Allison as his right bower." (Live Stock Journal of New Mexico May 14, 1888.)

One might say that Allison was for McMains when it came to the Tolby case, but mostly because the combined forces would protect him against reprisals from the friends of those whom he felt had to be done away with for their part in the murder of the parson, but not in anything that pertained to the Grant company for the simple reason that his deed to his property on the Grant was in order and was recognized as such. It was only such people who could not conclusively prove title that agitated which, of course, let him out.

His brother John was with him during those stormy days following the death of the preacher. How active a part he took in the proceedings is lost in the glamor that accrues to the older Clay. John makes sporadic appearances in the story, then ultimately retires to Jackson, Tennessee, and there passes out of the picture. He was never interested in the cattle business as a business but merely as a necessity. He always loved the city life and sought ways and means to get into a city whenever he could. He was not as tall as Clay, nor as heavy but he did like to take a drink once in a while, and like his brother, got rather rough under the influence of liquor. The year following the events related above, the two brothers went to Las Animas, Colorado, to put in a large order at Otero's mercantile store. Following their purchase they decided to make the rounds. Before long they were hanging on to each other for support. Wise saloon-keepers, knowing the nastiness of the boys under the influence of drink, closed shop despite a rushing business. The loss would be greater in life and wreckage. That afternoon Frank Riggs, a whiskey runner, arrived in town. Unfortunately he met up with the Allison boys and the trio began by toasting to Clay's health. He gave the proprietor a five dollar bill, saying he would call for the change as soon as he fetched his valise, which he had left at the drugstore. Once out of the saloon, he hopped a freight and was never seen at Las Animas again.

Realizing, despite the haze, that Riggs pulled a fast one, the pair continued drinking wherever they found a place open to receive them, killing time until the evening dance. While the dance was in progress, they started their own Allison style of strip tease, and in order to keep the dancers moving they fired off their revolvers now and then. Sheriff John Spear had about as much as he could stand. Calling his deputy, Charles Faber, he rounded up a posse of twenty men and returned to the dance hall. Faber ordered the brothers to put down their guns. The music continued playing; dancers continued whirling but out of line of fire. Perhaps this was the wrong thing to do. Bravery is one thing but dealing with drunken men another. Had the Allison boys been sober they probably would have admired Faber his courage. Faber fired on the two men, wounding John. The older Allison believing that his brother was dead, killed the deputy sheriff. Crying like a baby Clay took his brother in his arms trying to dress him and rush him to a doctor at the same time. The men surrounded him and made him prisoner, taking care of his brother for him. They felt rather foolish now that blood had been shed. After all they were having a good time and none of the dancers were hurt although all were pretty badly shaken up. Allison was taken to a Justice of the Peace but acquitted because it was proven that Faber had fired without warning and had secretly hoped to "get" the Allison boys in the hopes that it would make him a famous Frontier sheriff. The Justice ruled self defense and Clay spent the rest of his time there taking care of his brother.

Allison also frequented the haunts of El Morro, another community of sorts in Colorado. On one of his big sprees there he encountered "Buckskin Charlie" and immediately proceeded to the New State saloon owned by a former railroad worker by the name of Rufe Harrington. As the drinks piled up, their mellowness and friendship for each other changed and they became bellicose. This time no knives or guns were used. Allison downed Charlie and gave him such a drumming that the poor beaten man had to be taken to Trinidad for medical care. When Allison sobered up he was told what he did and went to Trinidad to apologize for having been so brutal. Miguel Otero who was at El Morro tells us that on the same day that Allison beat up the hunter "Jacob Gross, A. M. Blackwell, Frank B. Nichols, Pete Simpson and I were playing cards in the second-story room of Harrington's New State saloon, directly over the bar. Allison entered the saloon below, and in his excess of spirits, began shooting through the ceiling. The bullets came up close to the card table around which we were gathered. Looking about for a place of safety, we saw a large Charter Oak cooking stove which happened to be part of the equipment of the room. We made a run for the stove, and all five of us jumped on top and watched the splinters fly up from the floor each time one of Allison's bullets came through.

"Allison continued this drunk for more than a week. During that time he had a room at the New State hotel, to which he would retire at an early hour, after putting up his famous black horse at a livery stable. That horse was the pride of Allison's heart. It was a beauty and as well trained as a circus horse. Allison never tied him when he went into a saloon, but simply turned him loose to graze. When he wanted the horse to come to him, he would whistle through his fingers and the horse would come at full speed.

"Frequently, when on these periodical sprees, Allison would bring a bucket full of beer for the horse, but the wise animal would only take a swallow or two and then upset the bucket with his nose. Sometimes Allison would call for a bucket of fresh water and then pour a quart of whiskey into it and ask the horse to drink. But as soon as the horse smelled the whiskey he would shake his head and upset the bucket.

"One day during an epochal spree (in the same town) he met me in front of the saloon and asked me whether I wanted to drink with him. Of course I did so, whether I wanted to or not. Then Allison asked me to take dinner with him at the hotel. Again I accepted, and had a devilishly poor time, as he was excessively drunk and added to my disquietude by laying his pistol by his plate. I was on pins and needles all through the meal, but fortunately, there was no one else in the dining-room besides ourselves and the waiter, who was a great friend of Allison's. I was not uneasy about my own safety, for there was a strong friendship between him and myself. (He does not say just what he was uneasy about. Possibly that Clay would shoot someone and he being with him would be implicated.)

"It was after this drunk that Allison came over to the store (the famous Otero Mercantile store) and in an excess of generosity presented his horse to my father saying: 'Don Miguel, you are the only man living that I would give this horse to.' Of course my father declined to accept the present with many, many thanks."

One author has presented Maxwell's home as a bar. As far as I know it was never a saloon. He may have gone there for drinks with Harry Whigham, Sherwin, Goodnight, Birdseye and others but we should be sensible about characters like Allison. He wasn't always in one saloon and out the other. The huge dance hall, bar, gambling den built by Maxwell in 1865 must not be confused with his home. No doubt Allison frequented the place but no stories about the man have come from this place. Allison, when in Cimarron, spent most of his time at Lambert's bar. Another author has given Allison credit (if it can be called that) for shooting down five Negro soldiers on their way to Fort Union. The killing of these men was not the work of Allison but rather that of Davy Crockett, the nephew of the more famous Davy of Alamo fame. Allison was quite friendly with Davy merely because he was from Tennessee. It has been said that Allison had the same type of draw on his revolver as John Wesley Hardin, John Ringo and Wild Bill Hickok. This may be so, but his arm action seemed to be slower. He could draw without anyone realizing that he moved his arm. The only way he was like the trio named is that he pulled the hammer back in the motion of drawing, and the gun was fired as the muzzle dropped to level. It was gunplay used only by experts whose lives depended on the quickness of their draw. Another author remarks that dance hall girls fought one another for his crude favors. Allison was never crude, whatever else he was. Nor did he ever bother with dance hall girls. He always, drunk or sober, treated women with the highest regard, never quite mastering his awe of them.

There was no doubt that Clay Allison was a man to be feared. Over in Rayado people locked their doors every night in apprehension of his cowboys who would come in riding any time of the day or night shooting off their guns. Furniture was piled up against all entrances as an added precaution. During Allison's Reign of Terror in the fall of 1875, Doctor Longwill took to spending the nights at Rayado. The cattleman found out about it and rode out at the head of his men so as to bring the doctor back to Cimarron for justice. Allison found out where the doctor was. He knocked on the door. Mrs. Longwill answered. Was the doctor in? Yes, he was. But he was a very sick man. The poor doctor needed medical attention himself for he was abed with a severe case of small-pox. If his business was urgent she would lead him to the sick room. Allison declined the offer, jumped on his horse, rushed home to change his clothes for fear of contagion. Said one man, years later, as he reviewed his past in Cimarron:

"It was at Cimarron that many desperadoes attained prominence. One of these was Clay Allison, from Tennessee, who had killed Chunk Colbert, Griego, and others. He sought with a mob at one time or another to kill Mills and as it seems a few hours later said he was wrong and led another mob to rescue Mills because a gang of men were approaching his house and had the rope ready for the purpose of hanging him. Clay always boasted he had saved Mills' life. Allison had much power and personal following and he was immune from arrest for many years, but the federal authorities finally sent aid to Sheriff Rinehart in the person of a few companies of soldiers. These surrounded his house one morning and arrested him. He afterwards made his escape, but was not bothered since."

Sheriff Rinehart brought him to Taos on one occasion because he feared that Allison's cowboys would attempt to rescue him. It was rather a hectic ride and by the time they got to Taos the Taosenos were under the impression that Allison was arresting the sheriff. Many variations were given of this but most are just tall tales told because the average reader would like to have his gunman a superman and sheriffs have to be shamed.

Several miles south of Raton on Highway 85 one comes upon a State Marker giving the story of the old Clifton House. It stood off to the right of the road and was a stopping place for the Barlow and Sanderson Stage Line. Chunk Colbert came in one fine day and asked about Clay Allison. He was plenty handy with a gun and decided to take the crown from the rancher. Here was the logical place for the encounter since Clay's cowboys would not interfere. Chunk was a good cow-puncher himself and also knew how to drink and gamble. Like the man he hunted, most of his shooting was done under the influence of liquor. He also bragged a lot. The two had met often at dances held at the Clifton House and at the end of each dance both knew that eventually it had to be one or the other. Some of Allison's cowboys remarked that Allison was just an ordinary person with whom trouble had the habit of overtaking. Chunk owned a Kentucky sorrell, a gift from Tom Stockton, builder of Clifton House. Allison had a white Texas pony. Colbert spread it around the bar that his sorrell was the fastest horse in the West and he would match it against any horse in the country, even Allison's pony. As he had hoped someone told Clay who promptly rode to Clifton and asked Colbert if he really thought his sorrell could beat the Texas White. The discussion became rather heated.

Allison was aware that it was a ruse by which Colbert hoped to puff up his pride. He had a twenty dollar gold piece and a five dollar bill. If Chunk could match it, he would have a chance to prove what his sorrel could do. The race was to be run on a quarter mile straight track at the Stockton place south of Clifton. Two Englishmen from the rooming house were appointed judges; one to stand at each end of the track. The judges decided upon a tie in an effort to avoid bloodshed. On the way home from the track Allison told a friend of his by the name of Gillespie that he felt certain that Colbert would not rest until the duel was fought. Chunk went to the bar at Clifton, ordered drinks for all and boasted that his father was a famous killer having sent twenty-two men to Boot Hill. He himself had killed only seven, to which, when Allison heard it, he remarked that he had no intentions of being the eighth.

The following day, at noon, a little party was gotten together to celebrate the winning of the race although no victor was named. Both felt that each was the winner. The party was necessarily small because many invited declined to attend knowing that it was to be the last meal for either Clay or Chunk. The dinner was not served in the dining room of the Clifton House, but in the small cafe nearby where short orders were served to people in a hurry and where one could get a steaming bowl of chili. This tasty dish was not served in the main dining room. The tables were small booth-like affairs hinged to the wall. The rivals sat at one table. The guests decided to leave them to each other. At the far end sat one of the judges ready to run at the first sign of gun play. The two men, facing each other, placed their guns in their laps, keeping them cocked. The coffee pot was at Allison's left elbow. Colbert had already downed his first cup and decided on the second. He reached across his plate with his left hand passing his cup to Allison, who, as a gentleman, would pick up the pot and pour. This would mean the use of both hands which was what Chunk was depending upon. Allison smiled at the idea and thought it quite childish. Since Allison declined to pour, Chunk made a quick movement for his gun and fired but too quickly because the muzzle did not quite clear the edge of the table. The bullet passed through the table board and ranged upward over Allison's head. At the same time Allison brought his gun into play and the bullet entered Chunk's head just above the left eye. Colbert was buried in the small cemetery on the slope behind the Clifton House. Clay arranged his own time for meeting Sheriff Rhinehart. Nothing came of the killing since the judge at Taos, where the pair went, ruled it as in self defense. A grand-niece of Allison's once told me that often as a little child she would sit on Allison's lap and he would rock her to sleep. She was always amazed at the blueness of his eyes and how kind they were. No one considered him a bad man only a dangerous one when he was drunk. I guess that is true of any man having too much to drink.

Allison married Dora McCollough of Cimarron and the couple seemed quite content. Their first child, a girl, was born sickly. Her father took her to Las Vegas often for medical treatment. Whenever he took her to town he never entered a bar. He was suspicious of Arthur Jilson, town marshal of East Las Vegas, whose attitude was anything but friendly. Whenever he visited Las Vegas he stayed at the St. Nicholas hotel, playing the part of a refined gentleman. He transacted business at the San Miguel National Bank of Las Vegas where his friend, Miguel Otero, was cashier. He often asked Otero to accompany him about town for old times sake, as well as to act as his guardian angel.

It has been said that the only man Allison feared was Sheriff Mace Bowman who held that office some time after Rhinehart. Bowman proved to Clay on several occasions that he was quicker on the draw than he was. Allison always marveled at the strange way Bowman reached for his gun and had it in your ribs before you could flicker an eye-lash. He asked Bowman to teach him how he did it. Allison practised for weeks. When he thought that he had mastered the art he invited Bowman to a drawing duel. This was a type of duel fought with empty guns. Three times Bowman had the bead on him. This made Bowman the better man. Bowman is one of the few great Frontier sheriffs overlooked by Western writers and those looking for new material would do well to look into the life of the sheriff. When Mace Bowman died Allison was already settled at Seven Rivers in Lincoln County. Allison felt that Cimarron and the Red River district was getting a little too crowded for him and his cattle. He sold out. But he always managed to pay visits to Santa Fe, Las Vegas, Fort Union, Elizabethtown, Virginia City and the new railroad towns of Raton, Otero, and Springer as well as the coal mining town of Blossburg. It was on one of his visits to Springer that one of Kit Carson's sons who was cow-punching for him met a girl he fell in love with and Allison stood as the best man. The couple went to Seven Rivers to live. Wrote the editor of the Las Vegas Optic (May 12, 1886) on one of Allison's visits:

"The time was, perhaps, in the early and trying days of New Mexico, when men carried their lives in their hands, juries rendered their verdicts before the cases were heard in court, and men settled their differences at the point of a six-shooter, and our head-lines mentioned at the head of this column would have struck terror into the hearts of those who were the sworn enemies of Clay Allison, and even those who were not, would have feared that his presence was an indication that trouble was to follow; for he was, and is, a brave, determined man, who will sell his life dearly under any circumstances that may come up, fighting at the drop of the hat, and to the bitter end for a friend, and vindicating his rights at all hazards, none who then knew him, or know him now, can deny.

"Clay Allison has no doubt had as many tragic adventures as any man in the West, but he could not be the bad man at heart he is painted to be, and still number among his friends the character of men that he now does. The scenes and tragedies of other days, in many of which he was the hero, perhaps more from necessity than from choice, are fading gradually from his mind and he no longer cares to have them referred to.

"Five years ago with ten thousand dollars in his pocket, he passed through Las Vegas. The money was invested in a ranch and cattle on the dividing line between Texas and New Mexico, and he has since made this place his headquarters. He spent last summer in Sedalia, Missouri, paying occasional visits to his ranch and seeing that his cattle were properly handled by the men in charge. As an indication of the thrift that attended him, it may be stated that an Englishman recently offered him the neat sum of $73,000 for his ranch and cattle. Our reporter asked, 'What is the occasion of your visit to our city, Mr. Allison?'

"To which he replied: 'I am here for a two-fold purpose. I am driving across the country to the best market I can find with 1,500 head of cattle, as fine steers as were ever branded. My herd will reach Springer in about twelve days and I will make my headquarters there until the steers are disposed of. (Actually he had no luck at Springer so he drove them on to Cheyenne where, as we have already seen, he disposed of the cattle and had his experience with the quack dentist.) I also came to have my picture and a sketch of my career appear in the Stock Growers Magazine of your city. As the price charged by the journal is not made public, and as I have a proverbial delicacy about matters so personal to my humble self, I will ask some of my friends to obtain the information for me. Besides a portrait of myself I have eight men and a dog—a shepherd dog that does not talk much, but thinks a great deal, and it is my earnest desire that their portraits also appear in the same issue of the Stock Growers that mine does.'

"The reporter then asked: 'Is it true that you have withdrawn from the Lincoln County Stock Association and are opposed to such organizations generally?'

"Allison replied, 'Young man, I am. I gave notice to Mr. Anderson, the president of the organization, of my intention from that body two months before he would assent to drop my name from the books of the association. I am a free, American-born citizen of the United States, and while my brain after death may not weight as much as Tom Catron's will, yet I claim to be the happy possessor of sufficient brains to manage my own private business affairs without the intervention of any association of other cattle raisers, be such association local or Territorial. Of course if any of these fellows who delight so much in splurging around the country under broad-brimmed white hats, and in having their names and pictures emblazoned so boldly and so frequently in print, want to make an assessment against me for this, to them—a laudable purpose—well and good. I'll go down into my jeans, dig out my weasel skin and plank down my share of the amount desired. But I have set my foot down on its heel pretty lively and shall no longer submit to any systematic extortions of these cattle associations, in the forms of fees, dues, and the like.'

"The friendly visit of Clay Allison to this office this morning was much more welcome than have been visits of his to other newspaper offices in the Territory, within the memory of man."

The editor makes reference here to the time during the riots at Cimarron following the death of Parson Tolby when the editor of the Cimarron paper made some highly uncomplimentary remarks about Allison. Clay went down to the office found it locked, broke in and saw the half finished edition near the press. He distributed it to the boys for sale at several times the price telling them to make certain that it was Clay Allison's special edition and to make certain that no one would refuse to purchase a copy. He then dismantled the press dumping a major part of it into the Cimarron river. This was the only act of violence against the Maxwell Land Grant people I have known Allison to perpetrate. Actually, it was not against the Grant company so much as against the editors of the paper. Whether a new press was bought or the other salvaged from the river I cannot say. Most likely the latter since it was not very deep and a man could wade across it. The paper was being printed three years after Allison led his mobs against Donahue, Vega, Cardenas, Mills and Longwill in an effort to help McMains avenge the murder of Tolby. The press was then moved to Raton and the name changed to Raton News and Press. Bought out by the Raton Range parts of it are being used to this day. The Comet for June 8, 1883 carried this report of the death of Sheriff Mace Bowman:

"Early Wednesday morning, the citizens of Raton were startled by the report that Mason T. Bowman, our county sheriff, had died the night previous in Trinidad. The news was so sudden that many could not believe it until the report was confirmed by residents of this place who had been in Trinidad Tuesday night and were with the sheriff during the last hours of his life. The cause of his death was a hemorrhage of the lungs, an ailment that had troubled him for a good many years. For forty-eight hours previous to his death he had complained of being troubled in this way, but thinking it would soon pass off did not summon medical aid. During the afternoon of Tuesday, however, he grew rapidly worse, and Dr. Beshoar was called, but too late to be of any assistance, the sick man dying at nine o'clock that night. Mrs. Bowman and deputy sheriff Burlison were telegraphed of Mason's illness Tuesday afternoon, but the dispatch was received too late for them to take the passenger train for Trinidad that evening, and were compelled to wait for the emigrant which reached this place at 8 o'clock Wednesday morning. Mrs. Bowman did not learn of her husband's death until she arrived here, and when the terrible news was told the poor woman bowed her head with grief, and for a time could not shed a tear. It had been scarcely two years since they had been married, and her grief at his death seemed greater than she could bear.

"The remains were taken from Trinidad to Springer

(then the county seat) Thursday morning, where the funeral was held in the afternoon and attended by a large concourse of mourning friends. Mr. Bowman leaves a wife, but no children, in comfortable circumstances.

"Mason Theophilus Bowman was born in Bourbon county, Kentucky, in 1847; and was therefore in his 36th year. His parents being well-to-do people he was given a good education, spending most of his life in the school room until he was 15 years of age, when he left school and joined the Southern army in which he served until the close of the war. He fought bravely and received many compliments for his courage and good judgment. In one of the many battles in which he engaged he received a wound in the lungs which always troubled him to the date of his death and ultimately became the cause of his passing away.

"After the war closed he went to Texas where he met with many exciting adventures, being foremost of a party formed to exterminate a band of highway robbers. In the spring of 1867 he and his companions found a wealthy stockman by the name of Robert Lee, who had been overtaken by a band of ruffians, robbed and left bound to a tree in a lonely part of the country to starve. Mr. Lee, on being released, immediately organized a company of which Bowman was a member, their object being to capture and punish the gang of highwaymen. The two parties met frequently and a battle ensued each time with heavy losses on both sides. It took nearly four months to exterminate the outlaws, but they finally succeeded and received the thanks of the state authorities and citizens. It was during this campaign that he received the name of Mason, by which he became so well known that he finally prefixed it to his Christian name, and for the balance of his life was called Mason (Mace to his friends) T. Bowman.

"In the fall of 1867 he left Texas and went to Trinidad, Colorado, where he occupied official positions as deputy sheriff of Las Animas county for several years. Leaving there he came to this part of New Mexico, where he resided up to the time of his death. Here he became acquainted with nearly everyone, and it may be said that no one had more friends and less enemies than he. His personal popularity was demonstrated last fall when he was elected sheriff of this county by a large majority, and it was the universal opinion that he made the best sheriff that the county ever had. By his death the county loses an honorable and upright citizen, as well as a capable and efficient officer. A man who was himself his worst enemy —whose generosity was his greatest fault. He was beloved by his friends and respected by his enemies, and whether they be enemies or friends the citizens of the county and the Territory of New Mexico will always remember him as a kind and generous gentleman."

Mace Bowman was not Chunk Colbert's uncle as some authors have claimed. He did not come to Cimarron to avenge Chunk's death. He was well known to Clay Allison in Texas and the friendship endured when Bowman moved to Colorado. Bowman was sheriff only seven months, too short a time to have very much contact with Allison who was making plans at the time to sell out and move to Lincoln county. Allison was much older than Bowman. The few times they did meet it was always Allison who pestered Bowman to teach him his trick of gun drawing. Bowman was also a successful cattleman and left his widow well off. Allison had just settled at Seven Rivers when Bowman died. Here is a report on the death of Clay Allison found in the Live Stock Journal of New Mexico for July 22, 1887:

"A short account of the death of Clay Allison has been published in some of the territorial papers. That a man who had passed through so many dangerous scenes— scenes of bloodshed and times that tried men's very souls— should at last meet his death by falling from and being run over by a wagon is a curious winding up of a remarkable and almost unparalleled career.

"Clay Allison first came to Colfax county when the old Clifton House six miles below this (Raton) city was an important point on the old Santa Fe trail. He brought a herd of steers which belonged to Lacy & Coleman to this point for sale. It was while there that he and Chunk, a very nervy man from Texas, had their difficulty. It is related that Clay and Chunk had an old feud which had been in the family sometime in Texas; that Clay had met Chunk's uncle in Texas and the two men had their left hands bound together and fought it out with knives, which had resulted in the killing of the uncle. At any rate, Allison and Chunk concluded that they would have a sociable meal together and let bygones be bygones. They chatted pleasantly with each other, exchanging the courtesies due gentlemen of their blood, with their pistols in their laps, until Chunk concluded that it was time to vary the conventionalities and restraints of such tame proceedings and pulled his pistol up, accidently mistaking his aim. Clay, ever ready to exchange civilities of western society, returned the well meant advance by sending a bullet through Chunk's head, which, falling upon his plate, allowed the brains to form an extra dish for this sociable affair.

"In the early troubles which surrounded Cimarron when Maxwell Land Grant company and a select set of politicians were heaping infamous measures upon the citizens, Clay Allison was a Godsend to Colfax county. (The journal was definitely anti-grant.) Fearless and just in the execution of everything he undertook, he acted as a great check to the political party that was endeavoring to run the public and private machinery of the county. When excitement was high and when armed men were ready at the crack of a gun to start a war of no mean proportions, Clay Allison killed Pancho, a man who had many backers, but none of whom openly took it up.

"It was about this time that Clay turned newsboy. The News and Press which was issued at Cimarron, and was the organ only of those who were seeking to place their heels upon the neck of the individual liberty and prosperity of Colfax county, had awakened the contempt of Allison and his friends, and so this office was visited one day by him and a few followers who fed its type to the fish and suckers of the Cimarron river. One side of that week's issue was already printed, so that the blank side was appropriated by the new firm, which wrote on every paper in letters of red: CLAY ALLISON'S EDITION. And he turns newsboy, and, in company with old Joe Curtis, travels the streets of Cimarron selling copies of the paper at 25 cents apiece—more than they have ever brought since.

"It was during these troubles that the lamented Tolby met his death, and Cruz Vega who was suspected of the crime, was taken out and by force was made to confess and implicate others. McMains planned this scheme, but claims that Allison and his followers got beyond his control when they strung Vega up and then took the rope to the horn of a saddle and gave his corpse a free circle through the greasewood.

"When Colfax was attached to Taos for judicial purposes, officers wanted Clay for some of his acts but did not want him bad enough to kill him or be killed. Santa Fe officials did not lack authority to do anything at the time so a company of colored soldiers went after Allison and surrounded the house of I. C. Lacy, where he happened to be. They demanded unconditional surrender but they were talking to a man who had never made one. He agreed to come out however and go with them on condition that he be allowed to retain his arms, which was granted. While en route with Sheriff Rhinehart to the Taos court, Clay took the sheriff's hat, used it for a spittoon, and then returned it to the official head of that officer.

"At one time Mason T. Bowman, who was true steel to the core and noted for his gameness under fire, met Clay at a dance. Each one envied the other his reputation for nerve and during the evening 'bowled up' pretty well and before morning were having a little dance together with nothing but their underclothes and pistols on, which latter they flourished and handled in no awkward manner. Those who witnessed this little war dance momentarily expected one or the other or both killed, but it ended up without any tragedy.

"When Clay was in any of the towns and was drinking it was his favorite amusement to have fellows kneel down and drink, and dance awhile to amuse him—sometimes varying the entertainment by making some fellow drink whether he was dry or not.

"At Las Animas, a few years ago, a sheriff went into a saloon and dance hall to arrest Clay and his brother John. The officer was backed by his commission and a double barrelled shot gun. Clay say him enter and shouted to his brother to warn him. John threw his right side toward the officer just in time to receive a load of buckshot in his shoulder, disabling his right arm. But with his left he sent several bullets into the region of the officer's heart, while Clay was attending to the same line of business by sending in a few shots. It is needless to add that the officer was killed, for there was generally a mortality attending any picnic with the Allisons. John still carries a load of buckshot from which he suffers once in a while. He is now in Tennessee on a farm.

"In looking back over these violent scenes in which Clay Allison was such a prominent actor one cannot fail to be impressed with the fact that with all his reckless and desperate acts he was a man of warm heart, generous impulse, clear intellect and of unquestioned honor, and, when not in liquor, a thorough gentleman. He was a man who was universally respected for his justness and integrity.

"As the West settled up, Clay concluded to settle down and discard the reckless and dissipated path of life and married Miss Dora McCullough who resided in the Vermejo part of this county (she was born in Missouri.)

"But it seems as if death lurks by the wayside and comes in the most unexpected forms, and this brave man who faced death in so many trying places at last met the grim spectre in the most commonplace way."

Allison lived in Pecos, Texas at the time of the accident. He had sold out his holdings in the Seven Rivers country and returned to the land from whence he first came into New Mexico. His widow and two daughters continued the ranch. After a long period of mourning, Dora Allison re-married J. L. Johnson, a merchant in Pecos. The couple moved to Fort Worth, where the former Mrs. Allison lived until her death. The sickly sister recovered her health and made a happy marriage as did the other Allison girl. So, Clay Allison passes on after a brief but stormy stay on the Grant, but long enough to help make up its history.

Chapter Twelve

LIVING TOWNS OF THE GRANT

1. RATON, NEW MEXICO

Twenty miles south of Trinidad, Colorado, the traveler, after an arduous journey over the Raton Pass looks into a beautiful valley that seems to retain its freshness despite the hustle and bustle of modern day living and in the center of the valley sits the city of Raton. Today it is known for its horse racing, cattle industry and the hub of the New Mexico coal region, but the Indians that first crossed this area knew it as the mountain shaped like a rodent, which translated into Spanish meant Raton. Here the Navajo came in search of game; buffalo once roamed the valley before migrating to the plains of Kansas; no Pueblos were built in the area, at least not after the eruption of Mt. Capulin. I am of the opinion that there are buried pueblos here possibly eighty feet below the level of the plans very much preserved as was Pompeii by the lava of Vesuvius. Apaches, Kiowas, Comanches often roamed the area. The Indians called the place Chuquirque which became a landmark for those going to the Taos fair for annual trade. The name applied to the high peak east of Raton so shaped like the head and back of a field-rat. It was definitely not named by Spaniards. Only after the coming of the Americans was it explained away as a place infested by rodents. Coronado came close to the site of the future city about where Dillon is, but had nothing to say about it. Why should he, there was no gold gleaming against the sun, only silver streams and green grass.

Soon the Indians beat a regular path over the pass, for here were deer, turkey, buffalo, bear, elk. Here, too, were the swift, clear trout streams of the Vermejo, Little Cimarron, Ocate, Rayado. Governor Antonio Valverde Cosio made use of this trail in marching from Taos, east through the Cimarron country to Dillon, over the pass to Trinidad in 1719. It is from his report that we first know of the Las Animas river by name.

"On the twenty-fifth of the month (September 1719) the said senor governor (Valverde) with all his camp left the spot and river of La Soledad (the Rio Colorado—Red River—Valverde reached the stream near Dillon) and marched about nine leagues. He crossed a mountain ridge with so many forests, ravines, canyons, and narrow places that it was necessary that day to divide the cavalry into ten groups to get it over such a difficult trail. In this the soldiers worked considerably in order not to lose so many beasts—with which care and divine favor assisting, they succeeded in bringing the horses safely over the mountains, going as far as the Rio de la Animas, a name his lordship gave it, where the camp was placed thankfully, since it was a pleasant place" (near the present city of Trinidad, Colo.).

The next white men we have records of who passed through the present site of Raton are the two Mallet brothers who led a party of six from the Illinois country to Santa Fe in 1739. Whatever the French menace to New Mexico, it was removed forever when France lost all her colonial possessions to England in 1763.

Philip Nolan led a raiding party into Spanish territory in 1801. Some have said that he was hunting wild horses, but the Spaniards were not so sure. Taking the lesser of two evils they attacked him, killed him, hanged one of his party and imprisoned the rest. Lt. Zebulon M. Pike was later to meet Solomon Colly, a survivor, in Santa Fe. Whether LeLande came over the pass, or through Costilla into Taos to Santa Fe is a matter of conjecture. Purcell came over the pass as ambassador for the Comanches and Kiowas in 1805. One year later Don Fecundo Melgares took the field over the mesa with one hundred cavalry and five hundred New Mexico Militia to turn back Captain Sparks who was commissioned by the federal government to ascend the Rio Colorado and reach the continental divide. In the same year came Pike, the unsuspecting tool of Aaron Burr and General James Wilkinson. However, he did not enter New Mexico through the Raton Mesa marching to the present site of Canon City (Colo.) he struck westwards (Salida) in search of food looped back on his trail to camp at the former turn-off point (Canon City). Going along the San Luis Valley he came to the Rio Grande which he insisted was the Rio Colorado, territory claimed by the United States. Although the closest Pike got to Raton was the site of the present St. Charles & Greenhorn, below Pueblo, his report was to awaken the East and interest the United States in the Southwest. Profit, expansion, adventure—Pike's report helped to give us the Santa Fe trail and indirectly Raton.

Captain Becknell had marvelous success in trading with the Comanches in 1811. He reasoned that if it was so profitable dealing with Indians, how much more so, further south, amongst the New Mexicans. Consequently, in 1812, he brought his goods to Taos avoiding the mountain route. By 1822 the Santa Fe Trail was making history. In 1824 came the first organized trade. In 1821, members of the exploring party of Major S. H. Long reported coal in the vicinity of the Raton mesa. This introduced mining expeditions to Raton long before the establishment of the town.

For twenty-five years traders, pioneers, adventurers sprinkled blood, sweat, tears, and lives over arduous table land always encouraged by the fact that this was the last obstacle of a difficult journey. Each wagon left an imprint, each imprint stamped the inevitable. President Pierce's goal from ocean to ocean meant incorporating this very Trail into the Federal government. Then came the war with Mexico. Over the Pass, came "The Army of the West" led by S. W. Kearny. One of his men wrote in his Journal: "August 18 (1846) Had Armijo's heart been as stout as the walls of rock which nature gave him to aid in the defense of his country, we might have sought in vain to force this passage. But the bird has flown, and the trees cut in the way made the belief strong that they never from the first had any idea of fighting us. The defile was narrow, and from the cliffs above they might have hurled rocks of a ton in weight upon us. But the heart was not there, or every inch of the ground from the Raton to Santa Fe would have been disputed."

Another member of the army of the west wrote:

"August 7 (1846) Our march today has been through a valley, except in places where it was impassable, and then over mountains. One place was so very steep that our wagons had to be let down by means of ropes, and other places seemed to be equally as bad. But upon the whole, it has been a very pleasant march. Breathing the pure air untainted by the dust we have been so familiar with, drinking clear mountain water, and resting under the shade of tall pines are luxuries that we, as soldiers, have not been accustomed to—and rare indeed. There are some small oak bushes in these mountains, but their growth never seems to exceed six inches in diameter. Camped at the foot of the Raton mountain, or Mouse mountain as called by the Mexicans, but in size it resembles but little a mouse. Had plenty of wood, water, grass."

In this same year Susan Shelby Magoffin accompanied her husband Samuel on a trading expedition. The Santa Fe journey was her honeymoon. She wrote from Bent's fort in Colorado:

"Thursday July 30—(1846) This is my nineteenth birthday! The fort is crowded to overflowing. Col. Kearny has arrived and it seems the world is coming with him. Volunteers are under his command now only as he, on his arrival dispatched them under Captain Moore ahead, for the purpose of repairing fifteen miles of the road called the Raton, a bed of rocks impossible for the wagons of which there are a goodly number to pass——

"Thursday night—July 13 (1846) Camp No. 7— Left Camp early this afternoon. Came to camp again at sunset, just at the entrance of what is called "The Raton," a difficult pass of fifteen miles through the mountains. Our tent is on the top of a hill—surrounded by most magnificent scenery. On all sides are stupendous mountains—we have been rather uncomfortable today (14th) —a wagon was turned over this morning, and the bed and bows are so much broken as to cause a delay of some hours to repair it sufficiently to travel on. The "Raton" is not the best place in the world to keep such articles new; almost every fifty or hundred yards there are large stones, or steep little hillocks, just the thing to bounce a wagon's wheels up, unless there is the most careful driving.——

"Saturday 15—Camp No. 9. Still in the Raton traveling on at the rate of half mile an hour, with the road growing worse and worse—worse and worse the road! They are even taking the mules from the carriages this afternoon and half a dozen men by bodily exertions are pulling them down the hills. And it takes a dozen men to steady a wagon with all its wheels locked—and for one who is some distance off to hear the crash it makes over the stones, is truly alarming——We came to camp about half an hour after dusk, having accomplished the great travel of six or eight hundred yards during the day—

"Monday 17—Camp No. 11—A most beautiful marching this has been and fine for the animals, cool and pleasant and we have traveled well considering it is in the 'Raton'——. I have been on top of another high mountain. I shall be quite an experienced climber when we leave the 'Raton.' It has been my daily exercise since we entered the mountains.

"Wednesday 18—Camp No. 13. Out of Raton at last! We have been in it five days——We may now bid goodbye to any game; that is one redeeming quality of the Raton —the furnishing us with wild meat—we have had fine, clear, cool water too, and slightly impregnated with sulphur, not a very disagreeable quality to me."

In 1854 Hayden brought the Raton area again in the limelight by assuming that the coal beds extending from Montana to the New Mexico area by asserting that they were of the Tertiary age of rocks. While this assumption was proven false, it nevertheless focused attention on the region about Raton. In 1865, R. E. Owen found, near the top of Raton Pass fossil plants which he thought were in shale of Cretaceous age, which three years later, John L. Le Conte said were only middle-Cretaceous age. Le Conte was the man who found coal-bearing rocks in the Raton field in the vicinity of the present hamlet of Yankee. Others on scientific expeditions in this locale before the establishment of the city were Hayden (1868); Lesquereux (1872), who described 21 fossil plants from the Raton Mesa region; L. L. Stevenson (1873), Endlich (1877).

Richard Lacy Wooten, the Virginia-born frontiersman was more familiarly known as "Uncle Dick" often passed through the old trail. It was a relatively fair mountain road possibly because of the work of Captain Moore's crew. The more he saw of it the more he realized that it was a natural highway from southeastern Colorado to New Mexico. If he could hew out a road through the pass, which barring grades, should be as good as the average turnpike of the '60's, he could make money from the caravans going through. He went to the legislatures of Colorado and New Mexico for charters to cover the rights and privileges which he demanded for this project. The New Mexico Territorial laws showed no such charter. This was bad for old Uncle Dick a few years later for he was to have trouble with the Territory in 1873 about the existence of such a charter. In 1866 he built his home on top of the mountains and constructed his famous toll-road over the pass, cutting out hillsides, blasting ledges of rock, building bridges by the dozen, felling trees, working difficult grading. Opening the road brought the stage to New Mexico, and the stage brought road-agents so that at an unsuspecting moment at one of the curves on the pass, when the horses were slowed down, bandits would appear from the thickets and demand the express company's strong box. A law was passed February 1, 1873:

"Any charter which may be held or owned by Richard Wooten or any other person or persons under the general corporation act of this territory over any portion of the Trinidad and Raton mountain road running from Red River in the territory to the town of Trinidad (Colo.) and passing by the house of the said Richard Wooten, shall not be received as evidence of the existence nor as the charter of any corporation or company and the said charter or so called charter is hereby declared null and void."

One of the stage lines was the Barlow & Sanderson. When Doniphan's contingent of the Army of the West entered New Mexico they camped at the site of the present Fairmont Cemetery just east of some willow trees and a spring. The willow trees and the spring are now gone—replaced now by some houses on what is known as Maxwell Avenue on the North side. Here in the '60's the government erected a forage station. Probably with the secondary intention to rest horses and men after the difficult descent down the pass, for a string of forts were to be built in the new territory to subdue the Apaches, Utes, Comanches, Navajos. A corral and store-house were built in which to warehouse provisions for the traveling wagon-trains whose duty it was to keep the United States Army supplied in New Mexico and the far West. The Barlow and Sanderson Stages made use of this station, not as a regular stop but as a watering place and emergency station. The regular stop was at the Clifton House further south.

How many travelers must have peeped out the stage windows dreaming of a ranch! And Willow Springs was ideally situated for a farm. Water in abundance, pasturage for grazing; the soil was rich, too. Some must have made up their minds then and there. Taking down their carpet bags from the stage, determined to call this place home, they set with a will to build a two-roomed jacal log house. Perhaps they had visions of a large trade with travelers. Whatever their hopes, they must have become disheartened and sold out to a Mr. Sears. He removed the jacal and built a four roomed log house facing the spring. Soon the water from the springs began to diminish, so a seventy foot well was dug at the spot which opened up a new water supply.

John Thacker, a pioneer from Iowa, came over the pass from Colorado where he had been living, and thought of buying the Sears' property. He brought seven hundred head of cattle along with him. While the family lived at the springs house—he himself, with several cowboys stayed near the site of Fairmont Cemetery where Col. Doniphan's had encamped in 1846 for there seems to have been a spring there at the time. Mr. Sears did not move away for he was still at the Willow Springs house in 1872. The Thackers did not stay longer than a year. In 1874, the owner of the Willow Springs ranch is on record as offering water for sale to travelers for twenty-five cents a bucket. This brought about the postponement of many talks and even morning oblations until something cheaper could be had down the line at Clifton House. In 1877, William Boggs owned the Willow Springs property until the Maxwell Land Grant Company had him ejected about 1885.

Early in 1878, George J. Pace came to Willow Springs and opened a store in the west room of the ranch house which he rented from William Boggs. When Pace was ready to open his store, a negro was killed near Willow Springs. There being no other place to put the body it was laid on the counter of the store for the night. It was buried on the hill just above the ranch house. When the stage passengers got out to stretch their legs at Willow Springs, they were not fed simply because it was more of a watering place for the horses and mules rather than a regular stage stop. The appointed stop was at Clifton House. When Pace opened his store, a petition was taken up requesting a postoffice at Willow Springs. The petition was granted. George J. Pace was named postmaster and if he had not shortly afterwards removed South to Otero, it is possible that today Raton would have been Willow Springs instead. Enough homesteaders must have been about for the government to officially recognize Willow Springs.

The Clifton House was built in 1867 by Tom Stockton, on the Red River, as a convenient headquarters for ranchers and stockmen attending cattle roundups in the spring and fall. It was a three story adobe structure six miles South of Willow Springs. Here the Barlow and Sanderson stage line made an official stop. Mesick operated the Barlow and Sanderson stage office there. Instinctively he saw the tremendous possibilities of accomodating over night transients. He leased it from Stockton. Six sleeping rooms and a dining room, a bar, the Clifton House was the half way stop from El Morro, Colorado and Cimarron in New Mexico. Here the stockmen got their mail. Here were weddings, funerals, parties, dances, horse-racing, killings. Clifton House even had its own boot-hill. However, the killings were not the fabulous number writers would have us believe. Here too, was a store but prices were so high that many of the cattlemen found it more economical to take their wagons over the pass to Trinidad for supplies. Here too, they could gossip on the veranda. Nearby were the Barlow and Sanderson barns, out-buildings, and blacksmith shop. Here the stages changed to four fresh horses if going south, or six mules if going over the pass. A separate saloon and store were added later, as well as several houses of natives who always served chili if travelers craved the dish. Mathias Stockton (Tom's brother) and Miss Dove Stout were married at Clifton House. Joe Adams was running the Clifton House in 1877 and 1878. In between times, the Stocktons took over. They ran the place after Adams left. With the coming of the railroad to Raton the usefulness of Clifton House and the Barlow and Sanderson Stage line rapidly found itself fading into the past.

Meantime things were humming up north. The Santa Fe and the Rio Grande railroads were at war. The Barlow and Sanderson stage had the best route from Colorado to Santa Fe. Besides, the coal-fields around Trinidad would mean freighting into the Southwest. General Manager Strong jumped into a Barlow and Sanderson Stage taking Don Miguel Otero, Sr. with him to sound out the New Mexico legislature regarding the Santa Fe's possibilities in the state for the Southern Pacific looked upon the entire Southwest as its own private child. Strong immediately contacted his lawyers, organized the New Mexico and Southern Pacific railroad to build from Raton Pass to the Arizona line. Back in Colorado, Strong had courage. He called on Robinson the engineer who in turn was to contact Uncle Dick for his road. That was on February 26, 1878.

The Rio Grande was building over the Veta Pass, down to Alamosa and Fort Garland. It had already surveyed a route across Raton to Cimarron (New Mexico) in 1876. Abruptly it stopped. No plot was filed, nor was Uncle Dick who owned the toll road consulted. While surveyors for the Rio Grande were running new lines along the inclines of Raton mountain Ray Morley of the Santa Fe was drawing sketches and making notes under their very noses—as a sheepherder. Kingman came in from Cimarron (New Mexico) to help build the railroad over the pass. Kingman, Robinson, Morley for the Santa Fe—McMurtrie and De Remer for the Rio Grande. The Santa Fe men approached Uncle Dick. Said Robinson "The Santa Fe will make it up to you." Said Wooten "I guess I'll have to move out for the locomotive to move in."

In December 1878 "Uncle" Avery rode the first engine over the switch back, down over the pass, into New Mexico, and the toll-road was gone forever. Material, powder, manpower could now be shipped to the lower entrance of the tunnel being blasted out. The headings met on July 7, 1879 the date we give as the founding of the city of Raton.

Strong had not forgotten Miguel Otero's help with the New Mexico Legislature for the Santa Fe railroad. Consequently, when the railroad lay track beyond Willow Springs, Otero became the first railroad town and station to be built in New Mexico. So, in 1879, it was a boom town. Stores, saloons, dance halls. Dolores Martinez, who weighed a good three-hundred and fifty pounds had the most popular resort in Otero. She was known to many as "Steamboat." Russ A. Kistler, who later founded the Las Vegas *Daily Optic*—got his start at Otero on borrowed money. He issued the first copy of the *Otero Optic* on May 22, 1879. When Otero became a ghost town he removed to Las Vegas.

A. A. Robinson, chief engineer for the Santa Fe had to select a permanent site for division headquarters. To move from Otero to Willow Springs would save five miles round trip between these two points for the pusher engines on the ascent to the tunnel. Furthermore water from the rimrock on Bartlett mesa just north of the site aided Robinson in giving Willow Springs the preference over Otero. The name Raton replaced Willow Springs probably because Raton Range, Raton Peak, Raton Mesa, were close by or because the name was a daily occurence among railroad men coming over the pass. Immediately a tent-city mushroomed. Pace came back from Otero in early 1880 with his post-office and his store; this time not going to the Willow Springs place but to what is now the 100 block on South First Street. If we gauge the founding of the town by Pace's post-office, then Raton was founded in 1880. Swiftly, the Santa Fe pushed forward the work on the machine shops and round house. More and more people came in, living in tents and box cars. Fullbright built a shack to serve short orders to the construction gang. He was affectionately known as "Pigsfoot" because more often as not the construction gang would be served pickled pigsfeet. He is not to be confused with "Piggy" Jones the brother of "Hog" Jones who took over the Clifton House to start a hog farm. To further insure the town as a positive thing, a number of railroad officials formed the New Mexico Townsite Company and dickered with the Maxwell Land Grant Company for a deed to three hundred and twenty acres of land "situated upon the line of the New Mexico and Southern Pacific Railroad, near the base of the Raton mountains." A plot was filed with the deed of the Townsite Company providing for a townsite west of the railroad, three blocks wide and four long. The Townsite Company apparently was not too sure. Cimarron certainly had a larger plot. A few months later, when the town boomed, this plot was substituted for one of forty-three blocks, running from the railroad west to Sixth Street and from Clark Avenue to a half block beyond. John Jeffs, who came to Raton in July 1880, is quoted as saying: "Three inhabitants have already pitched their tents before me." With the filing of the plot, houses and stores were moved in from Otero, the railroad town five miles to the south. Saloons, stores, rooming houses, spread alng Firsto Street. The town started spreading. Cornell and Weaver set up a painters and decorating establishment; Servell and Collins started the Raton bank; P. L. Beatty opened up the Grand Central restaurant; B. Asher opened up a newsstand; S. R. Lyons lined up all the Spanish-American farmers to the Colorado border for his fruit and vegetable stand; Jack O'Rielly did well for a time with his Five Cent Beer Saloon, but he thought it tied him down, so he sold it; White came in with his photography gallery. A newspaper called the Raton Guard was rousing both settler and gunman to a war against the Maxwell Land Grant; H. Erdman found a place to open his boot and shoe shop; D. F. Bloomer started the city's first barber shop. A frontier town would collapse without lawyers so Chas. M. Bayne, Edwin N. Franks, W. J. Clarbourne, G. C. Stocking posted their shingles. The railroad brought in doctors too: C. B. Hohlhousen, J. L. Holcomb, J. J. Shuler. C. Nairn dealt in flour and grain; hungry people hung around L. Ludwig's bakery to catch the bread as he spaded it out of the oven.

Even then people were beginning to call it the Gate City. R. Ferguson sought to popularize this name when he called his restaurant, The Gate City. Miss Nellie Ward opened her dress shop, Mallet and Van Haren would make out very well with their undertaking parlor for between the cowboys riding in on payday and gamblers from Vegas, Dodge City and other frontier towns, not only was the little village shot up, so were many of the inhabitants.

Yes, Mallet and Van Haren could rub their hands in glee. Business would be fine. Bayne and Frank put up a hall and started the Raton Social Club with H. D. Peri as President, J. Dowling as treasurer, C. Bayne as secretary. E. Leonards opened up a laundry. A few Chinamen did likewise. Leonards then went into the clothing business. J. P. Burnan and the Cohn brothers opened up mercantile stores. J. H. Remsburg became Raton's first milkman. McMartin put some blue paint over the store brought up from Otero and called it The Blue Front Store. W. H. Bannister went into competition with the Raton Dry Goods Store against Mitchell and Norwards Dry Goods. R. C. Schroeder opened up a drug store. W. H. Lelton monopolized the meat market while J. M. Dillman went into the carpenter and building trade.

It wouldn't be a frontier town without liquor houses. There was T. McAuliffe's "Mountain Monarch"; the "Little Brindle." The Moulton House also had its bar as did the Central Hotel, the Union Hotel, and other places whose names are lost.

People were church abiding always. Methodists made arrangements with Bayne and Franks for the use of their hall every Sunday. Rev. A. H. Boyle came in from Trinidad each Sunday to hold Episcopal services in the public school house. Miss Darling was the school teacher. A. Craignyle, J. C. Wells, Dora Asher, Carry Thompson, H. H. Bannister got together in November 1881 to organize the Baptist Congregation. The Catholics had their Mass in their homes first by a priest from Trinidad, then by the priest from Springer until they built their own St. Patrick's Church.

People did not limit their residences to the south side of the track. In 1881, Harry Whigham notified the people on the east side of the track that the land would be surveyed by the railroad as an addition to the Raton Townsite. Mallet and Van Haren had their first recorded unnatural death when a Chinaman shot a man at Crane's who had relieved him of $100 of his hard earned savings. The Willow Springs Ranch was fast losing its nomenclature for Boggstown, named after W. W. Boggs. Already the four hundred people that made up the town were looking ahead for the county seat. November 25, 1881, the Raton Guard wrote:

"The Red River Chronicle is further informed that Raton is ahead in this (Colfax) county and will be the county seat after the legislature meets."

The history of Raton would have been quite different in those early days, if Rev. T. J. Colby, a Methodist minister, who rode the circuit between Cimarron and Eliazbethtown, had not been murdered. Rev. Oscar P. McMains was commissioned by his bishop to ascertain the cause of Tolby's death. Dropping his work as a preacher, he turned detective. Picking up clues here and there he convinced himself that a certain Cruz Vega was the murderer. On October 1, 1875, Vega was found hanging to a telephone pole, almost a mile north of the Ponil River in Colfax County. A finger of guilt pointed to McMains. He was arrested, tried before a jury in Mora District Court on a change of venue (very common in those days) from Colfax County. He was found guilty in the fifth degree and fined $300. He was to go on trial again at Taos, but Judge Samuel Parks dismissed the case. McMains was to be the cause of sudden death for three men, the cause of the Colfax County-Maxwell Land Grant trouble, a headache for the church with which he was affiliated, and a mob ruler in Raton, for while the Tolby case was never solved, McMains soon forgot his confrere in the larger and more important warfare against the Maxwell Land Grant Company. To pursue this war, he settled just to the south of Raton, and started the first newspaper in Raton as a propaganda sheet against the Grant Company. To oust the Company from Colfax County became his creed, his food, his obsession, and his downfall.

McMains went up and down the length and breadth of the Grant seeking out voters favorable to the cause of the Anti-Granters, inducing them to place their votes for only such candidates as would promise to take care of the settlers and make it miserable for the Maxwell Land Grant company. McMains was elected to the legislature but took no interest in Territorial affairs that did not better the cause of the Anti-Granters. Following his term in Santa Fe he returned to Raton to editorials such as this:

"The Maxwell Land Grant fraud is doomed on unimpeachable recorded testimony that the patent has by high judiciary authority already been decided to have been obtained by fraud in the survey, and this fraud in the survey renders uncertain the boundaries of the Maxwell Land Grant as confirmed by Congress to decree the Granters their Grant not by what is uncertain metes and bounds, but by what is certain, i.e., eleven square leagues." (Raton Comet Feb. 24, 1882.)

"The sign, 'Willow Springs Ranch' on top of the long, low log cabin near the track just north of the town looks quite pretty and the words are musical. There is something pathetic about the sign. Anything that reminds one of the good old days that are gone never to return is pathetic and the Willow Springs Ranch carries one back to the stage-coach and the ox-train, to old fashioned people, to all the romance and the incident that hangs around the Wayside Inn.

"Mr. and Mrs. Boggs have Willow Springs Ranch in their keeping. Alas! We are brought to an abrupt halt and are reminded that the Goths and the Vandals to whom no relic of the past is sacred, whose only object is present plunder, are trying to wrest the old homestead from its present owners. It was once valuable in the days of the iron-horse as a town site, and now Mr. Boggs must undoubtedly be the finest in the territory, as the proprietor surrender to the land sharks.

"'This land,' says Boggs, 'was never leased. I went to Sayors myself when I was about to purchase it of George Greer, and asked him about the ranch and he told me it was government land; that Maxwell never claimed any further than Red River. When Maxwell sold to Tom Stockton and Miller, he claimed that this northern boundary line followed Red River up into the mountains.'

"The Nolan Grant in Mora county was 600,000 acres. In county matters I wil have little or nothing to do with politics. We are for a People's Party against land holders. In our open war against secret fraud we expect the opposition will make it pretty hot for us. Villainy backed by wealth is a formidable antagonist. THE COMET WILL:

STRIKE: Till the last Grant foe expires.
STRIKE: For our ranches and our fires.
STRIKE: For the justice that our sires
STRUCK FOR ON THE 4TH DAY OF JULY 1776.
(Raton Comet July 21, 1882)

"Mr. William Burbridge has rented Cook's new building and will fit it up as a model bar and billiard hall. It intends to spare neither labor nor capital to make it complete in every detail. The counter was made here by Mallett and Lawlor, and is a superb piece of workmanship. Three side boards have already been received from Cincinnati which cost nearly a thousand dollars, and everything else will be gotten to correspond. When open, the whole room will be principally marble, cutglass and French mirror, and will be tony in every respect. If men will drink, we wish the new house success." (Raton Guard, February 10, 1882.)

Burbridge was a gentleman. The worst crime in the world for him was to have a stain on his cravat, a stray hair out of place, soup forming tear drops on his mustache. He was courteous to all his customers taking liberties with none and expecting all to keep and maintain their distance. He favored only one man—that was because he was under obligation to him. It began in Texas. Burbridge and Mentzer ran a saloon in the Lone Star State. One day a customer walked in and after ordering a few drinks began abusing Burbridge. He looked upon the tavern keeper as an enemy and insisted that a duel be fought. But the meticulous William was above such roudiness. He brushed the lint—imaginary, of course for he would rather be seen dead than be caught with a speck of dirt on him—off his black, broadcloth jacket, and told his abuser that it was beneath the dignity of any Burbridge to engage in such sordid affairs. It just wasn't done, don't you know.

But Gus Mentzer, his partner decided that the customer was in an ugly mood and would only be content with Burbridge's blood. He went over to the table and was invited to a drink. He accepted. He took another, followed by a few more. The customer continued to call Burbridge names, and began playing with his revolver in the hopes that Burbridge would reach for a gun. Gus seeing that the result would be tragic for his partner reached for his gun and called upon the customer to shoot it out with him. The customer was carried out as Mentzer cooly blew into the barrel of his smoking revolver and told Burbridge that he had saved his life, a fact that Burbridge readily recognized. After that the pair moved to Raton.

Now William was seriously worried about the "Kid's" drinking. He had always called his younger partner "The Kid." With the new tavern catering to the elite, it was not good for business to have a drunkard about. Just how he explained away the many drunks he sold liquor to he never said. But it is possible that he was trying to make a gentleman of his partner. He warned Mentzer that if he did not stop drinking heavily he would dissolve the partnership. To which Gus would always reply that the business was his by right because if he had been killed in Texas Gus would have become sole owner. One day Burbridge carried out his threat, dissolved the partnership and had Mentzer thrown out. This hurt his pride as much as the seat of his trousers. He re-entered the saloon.

A short distance away the Wallace Sisters were giving a performance at the McAuliffe & Ferguson Hall. They had previously engaged to play at Cook's Hall but at the last moment the plans were changed. It was early summer and they were performing before a large audience. Suddenly the sound of shots mingled with the lines of the artists. The show must go on. And it did, but they were playing to an empty hall. As famous as they were there was always something more dramatic about bullets. The Bank Exchange Saloon was having a drama all its own.

Burbridge would not accept Mentzer's invitation to fight it out on the street. The duel, much to the distaste of both, since the mirrors that would be shot up were so expensive, would have to be fought in the ornate establishment. R. P. Dollman, who ran the Little Brindle bar was also deputy sheriff at the time. He happened to be in the Bank Exchange when Mentzer came in to invite Burbridge to fight it out. He yelled at Burbridge perhaps because he realized that Mentzer was drunk whereupon good old William became ruffled and fired at him instead of at Gus. Patrons ducked under the tables; others made for the street. Glasses, water system at the bar and other things were hit by the three way wild exchange of gun fire. One bullet struck Mentzer without doing serious damage. Seeing that he accomplished nothing he took to his heels. The patrons came out from hiding and the crowd from the theatre joined forces and offered themselves as a posse under Dollman's direction. All the buildings were searched; the boxes and packing cases lined along the streets thoroughly examined, but no Mentzer.

Suddenly some hawkeye spotted the "Kid" among the packing cases at the Depot. A shout went up and the manhunt was on. At this juncture, the evening train pulled into the depot. Crowds jumped on it, looking behind every seat, in the wash room, even under the train. It was like the hounds looking for the fox. Dollman came to the conclusion that he was in the woods some distance beyond the tracks, and as it was already quite dark, the search was called off for the time being. Back they went to the Little Brindle Saloon to drink to Dollman's health, since his life was just as endangered as Burbridge's. This was near the Bank Exchange. So, for an hour the deputies of the brass rail relived the incident, probably expanding their part as the drinks piled up. With worked up imaginations they re-visited the Bank Exchange to inspect the damage. All quieted down for a while, and "Lord Louie" resumed in the music hall above the Bank Exchange.

Suddenly, the drinkers in the back of the saloon stiffened. There at the bar was Gus himself demanding a stiff drink. What he got was a volley of lead. J. H. Latimer closed in, but was wounded by the "Kid" who seemed to have a charmed life. None of the bullets from the group now closing in on him, hit him. Gus was on the defensive. An orderly retreat was in order. He fled across the street into the railroad yards just across the depot lawn. The switch engine had just pulled in. Engineer Mulvaney had just taxied his wife up to town in the engine from their box car quarters a mile down the tracks to get groceries from the mercantile company situated between the two saloons. They were at the store at the time the shooting started. The Wallace sisters must have been in tears. To Gus, the engine was salvation. He disappeared behind it. Hugh Eddleson, a partner of Moulton's of The Moulton House, spotted Mentzer in the locomotive. The Kid was also wide awake and a bullet hit Eddleson in the Esophagus. The others who had come around when Hugh had yelled "There he is," stopped to examine the stricken man. This gave Mentzer an opportunity. He sat to make his getawawy on the engine but Mulvaney had left the reverse lever of the engine in a neutral position. Working at the throttle availed nothing.

It would be well to remind the reader that June 26, Monday night, was the date of the Mentzer affair. The paper published the account during the week on June 30, Friday, but give it very little publicity. Turner, the gambler, who prodded Mentzer on and even gave him the guns, was arrested in Las Vegas July 6, 1882. The day following the affair 1,200 people met to organize the Vigilantes — E. Parson presided — Joe Osfield was acting secretary — J. K. Pare, J. R. Givens, C. Duncan, M. McMartin, A. H. Jones, J. Osfield Jr., George Pace,, John O'Reilly, John Jeffs and D. F. Reed were committeemen (Raton Comet —June 30, 1882).

The Kid was sober enough to realize that he was in a precarious position to say the least. S. H. Jackson, of the Little Brindle Saloon next closed in on him but was rewarded with a bullet in the stomach. Jackson fell from the engine cab — dead.

Dollman had arrived by this time. He was Jackson's brother-in-law and half owner of the Little Brindle. Mentzer's gun was empty. Taking advantage of his opportunity Dollman crowded the Kid. The crowd stormed in and Metzer was subdued. Part of the crowd assisted in carrying Hugh Eddleson to Dr. J. J. Shuler's office on Park Avenue, off First Street for medical care. The larger part, feeling that the night had not played out her tragedy, accompanied Dollman and Mentzer back to the saloon. The deputy decided to shackle Gus lest he escape and cause further disturbance. He was just about to clamp the shackles to the Kid's leg when in walked Harvey Moulton. He was a locomotive engineer, a relative of Eddleson's and with him owner of the Moulton House hostel. He was also local Justice of the Peace and the first person in Raton to dig for water. Moulton Avenue is named after him. Hearing what happened to his partner he decided to bring Gus to justice then and there. A mob seconded his action as they marched to the Little Brindle where the Kid was kept prisoner, and as justice of the peace, he demanded that Gus Mentzer be turned over to him to be hung for his crimes. Dollman, hearing the noise left the back way, probably suspecting what was taking place and hoping to obtain aid. This left Mentzer alone with deputy William Bergen. Moulton broke in and insisted that as justice he had the right to have Mentzer hung. He wanted the prisoner. Bergen seeing that he would lose the prisoner, shot Moulton who reeled; just before he fell he crossed his hands and returned the shot sending a bullet thru Bergen's stomach. Mentzer must have shook his head thinking how bad it was for men to kill each other over him. He stepped over the wounded prone men and escaped to Williams and Fick's butcher shop. The crowd had no time for him at the moment. They were busy getting Bergen to the office of the Raton Coal and Coking Company where he died on Tuesday at 10:00 A.M. All the butcher could gasp was, "Why, Gus, we've been looking for you all evening." Mentzer pleaded for help and that he be hidden somewhere until it was safe to skip town. Williams instead grabbed a rope with which a customer that day had led a pig to his shop to be butchered and threw it to the crowd that now surrounded his shop, suggesting they would need it. However, he turned Mentzer over to Dollman. The mob relieved Dollman of his prisoner.

The rope was placed around Mentzer's neck. He was pulled out to the First Street boardwalk. They sure had a time with him for he fought like a tiger till the very end. He was conducted to the front of the Raton Bank on the corner of Clark Avenue and First Street. The rope was thrown over the bank sign, but it crashed under the Kid's weight — A boy was boosted up to the post on which the sign rested. He fastened the rope over the top. Up went the Kid. He tried loosening the rope about his neck. His strength failed. The body hung there till Tuesday morning. Mallet and Van Harem had coffins for all five. Bergen was buried at Blossburg. Mentzer, Moulton, Eddleson, Jackson in Raton. The whole town was out for the funerals. All work suspended for the morning at the Santa Fe shops. Rev. O. P. McMains had funeral services for Moulton and Eddleson. Rev. J. A. Callen had the services at Blossburg for W. Bergen. These were the largest funerals ever witnessed in the area. On July 6, 1882 Dollman resigned his office as deputy sheriff to give all his time to the Little Brindle saloon and possibly because he had enough of bloodshed. Mentzer was twenty-six years old at the time of his death.

The multi-killings did not disturb McMains in the least. He was only interested in anything that pertained to the Anti-Granters cause. Said the Raton Comet: From several events reported to have happened in town during the past few months it would appear to outsiders, or rather to those not acquainted with our town that Raton is a terrible bad place and that life and property is conceded of no importance by the bloodthirsty inhabitants of this burg. This impression has gone abroad through the disjointed, garbled, maliciously false statements found in several newspapers and in no sense of the word does this sort of thing do justice to our people who are as intelligent, upright and law abiding citizens as can be found in the world . . . George F. Canis, editor of the New Mexico Press and News, is blamed mostly. He published a supplement of seven columns to his paper on October 30, 1882, wherein he charged Rev. O. P. McMains with murder, etc. McMains' friends are a little mad and so is everybody who is opposed to this beautiful country being stolen by the millions of acres by the vampires and land grant pirates of New Mexico. McMains has had to suffer martyrdom on more occasions than one, by his exposure of corruption and fraud by which the people of Colfax county were threatened to be engulfed. When Parson Tolby, several years ago, was way laid and shot in the back while performing the duties of his heavenly mission, McMains nobly came to the rescue and was instrumental in tracing the murderer of his brother minister. This was an act on his part which has placed him at the mercy of the terrible bad element that infested this country at the time. When McMains went to Canis asking for proof of his statements Canis said he did not have them whereupon McMains addressed a large gathering telling them the facts that led to the killing of Parson Tolby and the arrest of Cruz Vega as the murderer. When he finished, Canis got up and addressed the crowd and apologized for his writing and promised to write a retraction. Mace T. Bowman, the deputy, was present. Everybody here knows that Canis did not do this of his own accord but with instructions he dare not disregard. He was used as a catspaw to pull some one else's chestnuts out of the fire. Instead of injuring McMains it is on the whole the very best thing that could be thought of to elect the Rev. McMains as a representative of the people of this country to the legislature at Santa Fe.

But the agitation, instead of cooling down, mounted like a wind-blown blaze. The Pro-Granters called in James H. Masterson, the brother of "Bat" Masterson, former town marshall of Dodge City, Kansas. The gunfighter immediately formed a company of National Guards making sure to secure the permission of Gov. Lionel A. Sheldon. The company consisted of commisisoned officers and five non-commissioned men plus thirty-five privates. When, however, muster roll call was published on Monday, February 23, 1885, it was discovered that a number of privates existed only on paper; that the company was fraudulently organized and the rumor spread that it was probably a secret army to overthrow the Maxwell Land Grant Company that was supposed to have hired them. It seems that they were won over to the cause of the Anti-Granters. It was said that Masterson's gun went to the highest bidder so that it was hard to say just on whose side he was on. Masterson went about with gun and threatening words.

Drums along the Red river. A beat to quarters for the Anti-Granters as well as for the Granters. The McMains bubble was ready to burst. Jim Masterson was now deputy sheriff. Over and against Masterson towered the lanky cowboy from along the Vermejo well known to the Red river forces. He would come to Raton of an evening with Marion Litrell, who later became one of the more famous sheriffs of New Mexico; Robert E. Lee, the gentle Southerner who always welcomed a trip to town; John Dodds, the quiet one, who always dreamed of a great cattle industry for New Mexico; Ed King, the young cowboy loyal to his employer and sincere with his friends; Garnett Lee, the cool calculating one, tall in the saddle, his blue eyes never telling his likes or dislikes; Abe Howe, who rode as fiercely as he talked; John Curry, who came down from Colorado way with his young brother George who preferred to remain in Raton rather than ride the range. George Curry climbed to the top and became Governor of New Mexico. There were other popular cow-punchers who joined Rogers a-riding up and down First Street just shooting away before settling down to witness a quasi-opera put on by strolling players, or to view a play at the Rink. (See Raton Comet Feb. 28, 1885.) Masterson was not too happy about the way the boys would always take over the town. Besides, there were a number of other charges against him well worth looking into.

Rogers was over in Chihuahua (present East Raton which was then divided into three districts: Fairmont, Chihuahua and Buena Vista) when he came face to face with Masterson at Williams & Sargent's Dance Hall.

"Someone tells me, Masterson, that you plan to kill me on sight. I am not here to kill citizens or to fight citizens but only to kill those people who are continually saying that they aim to kill me on sight."

Rogers was wanted for killing Miller, shooting Smith, Hixenbaugh and for assault on Masterson. One Saturday night when he was in town he went with the boys to see a play. He left during the first act, went to the sheriff's office and gave himself up for trial. Brought before court on the above mentioned charges he pleaded not guilty and was permitted his liberty on a one thousand dollar bail.

The Anti-Granters felt that they had something to crow about. The Maxwell Land Grant Company, so they said, imported Masterson and his gunmen; misled the Territorial Governor to the extent that he invested military power in the venture which power was used for ejecting settlers from their homes.

Monday evening, March 9th, Masterson was walking down First Street. D. W. Stevens was walking up, having just closed the doors of his mercantile establishment. Suddenly Masterson turned, struck Stevens on the head with the butt of his six-shooter and kicked him into the gutter. Silence.

Word of this attack reached George Curry who worked for Stevens as a clerk. He jumped into action, calling a mass meeting of the vigilantes. Before the meeting was called to order, Curry, who had obtained a considerable sum of money from Stevens, bought up every Winchester, shot-gun, rifle, cartridge and shell on the shelves of Carey's hardware and every other hardware store in town.

Up to Cow Creek went Curry's riders, like modern Paul Revere's to arouse the settlers. They rode on the wind to Rayado, Vermejo, Ponil, Elkins, E'town, Cimarron and Blossburg. Everywhere and anywhere where there was a man with a horse and a will. Shadows in the night fast moving in the moonlight and blood was on the moon. For McMains this was his greatest triumph, even beyond the day Clay Allison rode at his side in Cimarron. At the vigilante meeting it was agreed to arrest Masterson and every one of his so called militiamen. Curry tracked down Masterson to the Moulton House hostel and demanded his surrender. Six hundred determined vigilantes had gathered at the Rink. O. P. McMains put a motion in order to close all saloons. The committee voted on this and dispatched a contingent to carry out the order. From the time that the first train tooted into Raton it had never been known that a man couldn't get a drink at one bar or another. Now for the first time in its young history Raton was completely dry. Fifteen guards were named to escort Masterson over the line to Colorado. Rogers was appointed captain. One hundred and fifty men patrolled the streets. Every Masterson sympathizer they found was rounded up and escorted out of the city. All the militiamen were herded in one group and three hundred vigilantes marched them over the Pass with a warning to stay out of New Mexico. Just why every Pro-Granter was not killed that night is only explained in the fact that there were a number of level-headed captains among the vigilantes.

The Ides of March as terrible now for a number of men as it was for Caesar. The scene shifts to the county seat at Springer. Two cowboys from Cow Creek who used to be friends met on the streets of Springer. The argument that broke their friendship came up. Jesse Lee was now deputy sheriff at Springer. John Dodds had come into town with Sam Littrell for some corn, Littrell's presence may have had something to do with closing the argument for both men went their respective ways. Dodds proceeded to get drunk, and shoot up the town. In one of the saloons he met Carter the Constable, and shouted to all that would listen that he had beat up the officer in the fist fight. A warrant was sworn out for his arrest for disturbing the peace. He was apprehended, brought before a justice, pleaded guilty, paid his fine and started home with his corn. The day was Sunday.

On the way out of town Dodds was overtaken by Lee and Carter, who tried to arrest him on a complaint made by the latter. This was too much for Dodds. He pulled out his six-shooter and backed up the men while he returned to town to call up Captain Dick Rogers of the Vigilantes in Raton. Rogers started for Springer through the Red River route in order to pick up some boys at the Cow Creek Ranch. He succeeded in getting Tom Whealington, John Curry and Bob Lee.

The Anti-grant war broke out again. People took sides so by the time the Vigilantes got to Springer every trail had its cowboys riding into town to take one side or another. From an issue between Lee and Dodd, it fanned out into granters and anti-granters. Lee had arrested Dodds and put him in the county jail at Springer. A mob swarmed around the prison. Jack Williams, United States Deputy Marshall in Springer consulted with Rogers. Word had gotten around that Rogers would attempt what Moulton had attempted before in the Mentzer case. Williams advised against it. Williams knew Lee and felt he could talk to him. Rogers also knew Lee for he had saved his life but two weeks before in Raton. Turning to the mob Williams said "One of you come with me." Without waiting to see who it was he turned towards the jail. It was Richard Rogers.

In the jail as a fortification were "Duce" Hixenbaugh, Ernest Anthony (the horse thief), Jesse Lee, Kimberly, McCall. Said Rogers: "Don't Shoot! We did not come for trouble, we want peace." Three guns pointed out the window. Lee at the controls. Suddenly Rogers dropped, a bullet through the heart. Whealington came up on his horse, jumped off, picking up Rogers, who had been wounded, to bring him out of rifle range. John Curry, gun in hand came up to cover for Whealington. Another shot, and Curry fell mortally wounded. Tom Whealington fell over the body of Rogers, to join him in the ride to the great beyond! This was too much for George Curry. He rushed the jail followed by Bob Lee, and John Howe, shooting as they neared it. They availed nothing. John died in his brother's arms 2:00 A.M. the next morning at the Springer Hotel. George Curry went to the telegraph office and contacted the Vigilantes from Raton. Forty came under the leadership of John McKown and Charles F. Hunt. They had but to view the bodies of Rogers, Curry and Whealington to know that those in the courthouse must suffer the same fate. They took over the Santa Fe railway station, the telegraph office.

Behind the scenes, district attorney Melvin W. Mills watched all. With telegraph and railroad closed to him, he had one choice. Prevent wholesale killing he must, and would. Hitching a team of horses he set out for Wagonmound, twenty-six miles away. The telegraph there was at his disposal. Acting governor Losch contacted General Bradley, Commander of the military department of New Mexico, soon armed troops marched up from Fort Union to Watrous where they boarded a train for Springer. The soldiers had trouble with the Vigilantes, who prevented them from entering the jail and courthouse. The Commander of the troops pleaded with the Vigilantes to name a committee to confer with his officers named Marian Littrell, Chas. H. Hunt, Thomas P. Gable, George Curry. As a result of the meeting, the courthouse defenders gave themselves up and were arrested by the soldiers, taken to Vegas guarded likewise by Littrell, Curry, Edward King, James Smith and William South. Lee, McCall, Kimberly stating through their attorney that the court would be prejudiced against them in Colfax County obtained a change of venue to Taos County. Watrous village had just received its name but one year previous, named after Samuel Watrous who had settled there in 1849 when it was known as La Junta. The junction of the Mora and Sapello rivers. The leader of the troops was Captain Joel Kirkman of the U.S. 10th Infantry.

Raton has still to see the funeral as big and impressive as that of Rogers, Whealington and Curry. The whole county seemed to be there. The Vigilantes were present en masse. Three ministers preached funeral sermons. The mines were closed down. Even the roundhouses permitted the help to lay off. Over in Taos, on May 15, 1885 the jury was in session for forty minutes. Verdict: Not Guilty. Lee, Kimberly and McPhane were free. Tom Catron was polite enough to stay out of the Springer and Raton area for the next few years.

Granters and anti-granters were still wary of each other. While anti-granters took things into their own hands they paid less attention to McMains agitation but invited him constantly to give speeches for he had the gift of keeping the flame and hatred against the grant alive by his oratory. McMains himself was destitute and lived on the charity of his followers.

"Honorable O. P. McMains returned from his protracted visit to Washington, D.C. last Monday, having accomplished his task proving to the Land Commisisoner and the Interior Department that the lands claimed by the Maxwell Grant Company, were public lands according to the decision of Sect. Cox in 1869 which decision was never reversed and consequently the insurance of the patent was without authenticity of law beyond the power of the land department." Feeling victorious the anti-granters staged a big rally inviting the Governor. The Rink was packed. There were seats for 600, but those standing were estimated at 1,200, which was practically the population of the little city. O. P. McMains brought in the land grabbing monopolies in his speech as usual. Said the Agitator: "I have carried on this great fight against land thieves and corrupt officials almost unaided and alone." Col. Hans Mattson was manager of the Maxwell Land Grant Company at the time. He was formerly U. S. Consul at Calcutta. People were beginning to tire of words. The wiser ones knew that if the government said the land belonged to the Grant Company it just did. Was McMains making a living off them? Suspicions were forming:

"Mr. McMains has indeed pursued a strange course since he commenced this fight. He has been the agent of some of us settlers, he has drawn himself up to his full height, and declared that he believed he was born and created for this special mission of unearthing and defeating the gigantic fraud of the Maxwell Land Grant Company that for every great era of national reform there sprung up some gladiator to fight its cause in the arena. But settlers, not withstanding all the enthusiasm which has bubbled up from that devoted heart, he forgot all about that great mission for which he was created when he went to Frank R. Sherwin, upon the latter's arrival at Cimarron and while struggling for mastery of his great love for the down trodden ignorant settler, in which battle he has come off victorious, then and there offered to bury the hatchet and think no more of wars; to let this immense fraud, of which he has raged so much since he started, go unfought, so far as he is concerned, if only the Land Grant Company would give him title to the ranch and vega for which the settlers were so ready to fight on — I, myself, J. A. Hunt, am among the number who will blindly continue to follow this fanatic, to the neglect of their own interests and manly independence and never tumble to the fact that he pretends to be supporting himself at Washington upon his own money!

"McMains to the Settler said; Ho
I tell you the land must go:
Just put up your wealth
I'll go east for my health
And laugh at you — Sabe, just so!"
(Raton Comet, May 26, 1886)

Feeling that he was becoming a laughing stock in Raton McMains moved up into the Stonewall County in Colorado.

What would a town like Raton do for entertainment in those days? The Santa Fe railroad was interested in bringing books, authors, plays, bands, minstrels to town. The Raton House was the Social Center in 1880 and 1881. People didn't think ten dollars was too high to pay at a banquet in order to hear some author verse his high opinions on current subjects. With the foundation of the town the Raton Literary Society held the spotlight for a while. In October 1881, the machine shops of the Santa Fe railroad were completed and to commemorate the event, a **Grand Ball** was arranged by D. H. Dotterer, master-mechanic for the employees, who invited the entire town as well as officials from as far away as Topeka. About two months later, the Raton Social Club was formed with H. D. Peri as president, J. Dowling as treasurer, C. Bayne as secretary. The dances and socials were held at Bayne and Frank's Hall. Also there was the juvenile entertainment by the pupils of Kilgor's school where home talent was encouraged and exhibited. McAuliffe and Ferguson hall was often the scene of those productions. Another social club was the Cactus Club but it had too much genius to survive long so it disbanded April 20, 1882. The Ideal Musicale Quartet Company gave its recitals at Bayne's hall. Popular in 1882 were also the Wallace sisters. Many people found entertainment in attending the Vigilante meetings or anti-granters meetings to hear O. P. McMains boom out against the Maxwell Land Grant Company. Over 1,200 people are known to have attended such meetings. Road companies were cordially invited. On April 27, 1882 the Williams Theatre Company arrived in Raton for a short stay regaling the people with such dramas as "The Hidden Hand", "Octaroon," "Uncle Joshua Whitecomb." Anything new called for a Grand Ball as the starting of the Raton Hose Company in 1883. Churches also had benefits and socials for raising funds towards the structures. A big event was the opening of the Raton Skating Rink. The Rink had about as many customers as present day movies. The Raton Guard on November 14, 1884 had this to say about the town's new attraction: "Carpenters are at work erecting a comfortable and commodious stage in the Skating Rink. Seats will be provided from time to time. Good companies will be procured and will first class entertainment given. This is something needed in Raton for some time and will add considerably to the popularity of our town place for first class companies to stop over." There was a band composed of Santa Fe employees. Baseball was popular in the spring and summer. Footraces between Raton and Blossburg teams drew crowds as well an occasional boxing match. By 1886, the Gate City Jockey Club was an established institution. Jacques Kruger, the great comedian of his day, with his New York Comedy Company entertained in Raton in January of that year. The Santa Fe railroad was also putting up a social center of its own in the reading room which was also good competition for the Rink. The Rink was also the scene of early basketball contests. The growth of the town soon proved that something more than the Rink was needed. While the billboard continued to display featured stock company attractions the newspapers began a drive for Raton's own opera house. "Raton has needed and demanded a cosy and comfortable opera house for a number of years. No more remunerative investment is offered in the Southwest." Nevertheless the people would be entertained. Felix and Eva Vincent came in for a six nights engagement, playing such emotional dramas as Lady Andley's Secret, Uncle Tom's Cabin. As an added attraction each night a dress pattern or a gold watch was given away. The company closed with the play, Inshanague. Matinees were twenty-five cents for adults, fifteen cents for children. By 1892, the Rink became known as The Rink Opera House. The Mendelsohn Quintette Club Concert Company started off the year with a bang. That is the same year that saw the Raton Reading Room and Public Library open for business. The library was turned over to the city of Raton by the Santa Fe railroad. Bicycle riding became the fashion that year. "Miss Geneva Day, is the first lady to grace a safety bicycle on the streets of Raton. This popular accomplishment is in vogue with the ladies of the East and will soon become the fad of our progressive city." On September 8, 1892, Professor Harry Miller took a long lease on the Rink and had it remodeled into a handsome, comfortable and attractive opera house. At this time a phonograph found its way to Raton so that the owner was able to advertise: "Parties desiring to use the phonograph for an evening entertainment will leave orders at the postoffice." Miller brought in more and more road companies. Grace Beebe and the Crawford Comedy Company were booked for four nights. The complete list is too long to enumerate but we will list a few for old-timers to sigh over.

King and Ellison Comedy Company playing *"Little Lord Fauntleroy"* (September 13, 1890).

Boston Ideal Opera House Company playing, *"A Pretty Persian"* (January 8, 1902).

The Sanford Dodge Company playing *"The Three Musketeers"* (March 11, 1902).

The Pay Train (March 10, 1899).

Burton and Bakers Bellringers played for three nights in September, 1901.

The Roy Crawford Comedy Company played in *Zig Zag* for a week (November 2-8, 1901).

Spectators were severe critics: *"Uncle Tom's Cabin"* as played at the Opera House this week in this city was enough to cause Harriet Beecher Stowe to come to life and enter a protest. "It was bum."

Joseph Newman Company was booked for week beginning August 27, 1904.

The Marie Fountain Theatre Company (September 26, 1904).

Lincoln L. Carter's great melodrama *"The Two Little Waifs"* (November 7, 1904).

Hoyt's *A Texas Steer* (November 16, 1904).

Miss Soda Talbott of the Jose Newman Company plays in "A Woman's Intuition" at the Raton Opera House (August 27, 1903).

Meanwhile Hugo Seaburg of the Seaburg hotel waited patiently for a dream to come true. Across the street from his hotel a structure was going up that was to be the pride of the Southwest. Special trains would be run in from as far away as Denver to see his new theatre. With a floor space of 12,000 feet, the seating capacity was advertised as five thousand. Completed, the theatre had thirty one private boxes of eight seats each. It was steam heated. The main floor seats sold for a dollar a performance; the balcony for fifty cents and the boxes for one and a half dollars. Elmer F. Oille was contracted as manager. The old Rink had competition. The population of Raton at the time was 5,500. The name of the new theatre was the Coliseum Garden Theatre. Later on it was called simply Coliseum. The best in the entertainment could be seen and heard there. The following are representatives of what was on the boards: Uncle Tom's Cabin, National Grand Opera Company presenting scenes from Faust, Parifal, Travatore, Carmen, Charles B. Hanford in *The Taming of the Shrew,* The Wolfe Stock Company in *The Millionaires;* The American Stock Company in: *The Counterfeiters, The Foxy Mr. Bower, A Bachelor's Honeymoon, Captain Rocket.* (Pie eating contests were held between the acts during scene changes.) Other plays presented there were: *New Elack Crook, The Burgomaster; The Toymaker.* The San Francisco Opera Company as well as the Comic Opera Company played at the Coliseum. Other popular plays were: *Michael Strogoff; St. Elmo; Stubborn Cinderella; Not a Man in the House; Othello; Nero, the Gladiator;* Charles B. Hanford in *The American Lord;* The Cute Little Mechanics in *The Girl at the Helm; The Lion and the Mouse;* George Thompson in *In Wyoming;* La Salle Vaudeville Company; G. M. Cohan's *Forty-five Minutes From Broadway;* Miss Marie De Blau in *Tempest and Sunshine; The Gingerbread Man;* Gus Weinburg and The Dancing Eskimos in *The Alaskan;* Bailey and Austin in *Top of the World; The Showgirl.* Movies came to the Coliseum in 1908 and operated by the Morley Brothers on open dates from stage plays. Wrestling, political meetings and boxing also took place there on open night. Countess Thamara de Swirsky, "the inspirational and Interpretative dancer, with Noble Russian blood in her veins," was the last advertised performer at the Coliseum. A Mr. Koegh and his stock company came in for a few performances. His one performance was the last. The next day the Coliseum was no more.

FLAMES PLAY HAVOC WITH THE COLISEUM THEATRE
CAUSE OF THE CONFLAGRATION UNKNOWN
GREAT DANGER FOR THE SURROUNDING HOMES

Shortly before 2:00 A.M. this morning (February 11, 1911) the city was awakened by an unwelcome alarm. When the fierce flames were finally subdued, the frame structure with its entire contents lay a mass of ruins with the adjacent residences of George Hobb on the North, and C. W. Sinnock's property across the street South, and the home of R. I. Beck across the alley immediately to the rear of the Coliseum were badly scorched and more or less ruined by the water necessarily used to quelch smouldering eves and roofs. Harry Kyle, night clerk at the Seaburg, was reading in the lounge when he was aroused by a muffled explosion. On glancing out, he noticed flames busting over in several places in the theatre. He awakened Mr. Koegh of the company who gave the performance on the night before, and together they rushed to the theatre to salvage what they could. They succeeded in saving two trunks. The rest was a total loss. The scenery, etc., was valued at $5,000. The Stock Company will cotinue at the Lyric.

One big drawing card on Sunday was the saloon, until the Sunday closing law of New Mexico was enforced. Sunday was also the day to "get away from it all." Crowds flocked to the Yankee countryside. "Special train service to Yankee, Santa Fe, Raton, and Eastern Railroad will inaugurate next Sunday, a special train service to accomodate the large number of people who like to spend the day in the cool groves and canyons surrounding the prettily situated camps of Yankee. Train leaves Raton at 9:00 A.M.

returns at 3:00 P.M. Another train leaves Yankee at 6:30 P.M." For fifty cents round trip, the people were willing to ride in box cars, packing cars, freight cars, anything the locomotive pulled to freedom from care. More amusements were forthcoming:

"Monday, September 2, 1907 will witness the opening of a pleasure and amusement park to be known as Elks Park, one mile southeast of Raton. Sixty acres of land heavily wooded; benches and seats to be constructed and a baseball diamond to be laid out; a one-fourth mile race track constructed and a merry-go-round installed and other attractions arranged to amuse the public. A dancing pavilion thirty-five by seventy-five feet is being constructed. An orchestra will be in attendance. At least one band will be in attendance on opening day. For the present a hack line will convey visitors to and from the park. The gentlemen behind the venture are James Cook, Harry Fanning, Albert Cook and William Cook."

The movie made its way south from Denver. Two brothers from Denver opened the 'Dime Theatre' as a "popular family amusement resort" showing such spectacular films as "The Wonderful Flames." Meanwhile the Santa Fe reading room continued to provide entertainment for the general public down at the reading room. "Reading Room entertainment scheduled for Friday at the Santa Fe Club House is "The Dawn of Tomorrow" by Edith Adams Stewart assisted by her daughter, Miss Jean Stewart." The Ida Kimey Concert Company also had booking at the reading room, as well as many other popular entertainers.

Another theatre vying with the "Dime" and the "Lyric" was the "Isis," which advertised itself as "The House of Features." The price into both movies was five cents and ten cents except when a very special attraction came to town like the six-reel "The Last Days of Pompei," then prices went up to fifteen cents for children and twenty-five cents for adults. The Lyric tried to keep the same prices even when such an important film as "Ivanhoe" filmed in England, played. "The Isis Theatre is featuring this week the Gans-Nelson fight. The crowds continue each evening as the Raton Concert Band gives their regular concert in front of the little theatre, and the crowds make one think they are in a large city as they jostle goodnaturedly about, and hang on from one performance to another determined to see the Gans-Nelson picture if it takes all night." The Isis opened at the Roth block which was then 129 Park Avenue on Friday, July 16, 1908. C. J. Lindale was proprietor and manager. The first showing offered "The Pretty Flower Girl"—Pathe's hand painted colored film. On the same program it offered "The Fashionable Hat," "The White Squaw," "London Regattas and Exhibitions," "What a Razor Can do,' also Illustrated Songs: If You Cared For Me and Dixie and The Girl I Love. All for the amazing price of five cents for children and ten cents for adults!

The debris was hauled away from the Coliseum and the interior rebuilt. Under new management it was reopened as the Aerodome and continued to run on the same basis as the Coliseum bringing in road shows and having boxing, wrestling, or movies on open night. Not to be outdone the Lyric closed its doors for a face lifting job. When it did reopen it advertised itself as "The Beautiful Lyric Theatre" —The House of Quality. Popular music by the Lyric Symphony Orchestra. Entire change of program every night. Continuous performance from 7 to 10:30 P.M. Admission five and ten cents." The Aerodome, possibly because its prices were one dollar for adults and fifty cents for children found it hard to compete. It passed to other hands. Manager E. L. Pitz changed the name to the Magnet and tried desperately to keep the legitimate stage in Raton. "The Girl in the Tazi" said to be the funniest comedy produced in this country for the past decade will soon be here. Mr. Pitz is confident that in bringing this merry play to this city he has secured one of the hits of the season. This hit also includes the late craez of the year, the Argentine Tango—Adults one dollar. Children fifty cents". The Lyric Symphony Orchestra consisted of C. C. Selby as pianist, Ray Parker as violinist, and Paul Cozis with a drum traps and zylophones. The Isis, The Magnet, The Magnet Junior, The Dime, The Lyric are all gone now.

When Kilgore's school presented a program from time to time it started a precedent that endures to this day. The school programs of Raton are always of the highest calibre. Replacing the theatres mentioned above were The Grand Theatre and The Princess. The Grand continued to bring in concerts, stock companies, boxing, wrestling, lectures, while the Princess catered to the film industry. At this juncture, the city fathers thought that Raton should have an auditorium.

"The finishing touches on Raton's beautiful public owned Auditorium are progressing rapidly and before we realize it, it will be ready to be dedicated to the public. A matter of three weeks or so, and the last touch will have been put on.

"The Municipal building itself is a beautiful structure but the auditorium is its crowning glory. It must be seen to be appreciated. Architecturally it is grand and artistically beautiful. And what is more to the point it belongs to the community—the people's very own. It was built on their credit but will not cost the taxpayers one cent. The rentals will take care of the up-keep and interest and also provide a sinking fund to retire the bonds. It can be truthfully said it is one of the most brilliant examples of financiering for the benefit of a community ever attempted and there is no doupt but that Raton's way of doing things will be the reason for many other cities and towns of the southwest.

"No citizen of Raton can enter this beautiful Auditorium without a deep feeling of pride and patriotism - - - The price for seats on this occasion will be ten dollars, five dollars, and two-fifty. It is the means the committee has adopted for paying for the furnishings of the auditorium and it will give an oppountunity for our patriotic citizens to show their appreciation of the city administration's energy and progressiveness in providing them the most beautiful auditorium in the Southwest". The theatre opened on Tuesday, April 27, 1915.

"Raton's rapid transition from a frontier settlement to a municipality of importance was emphasized last Tuesday evening when her beautiful new $55,000 municipal theatre finally opened to public service.

"When the curtain rang up at 8:30 very few seats on the main floor remained unfilled and the balcony was packed with a representative gathering enjoying to the utmost, the comforts of their new theatre also admiring its beauties of interior.

"For a musical comedy, "The Red Rose" is probably one of the most pleasing productions on the road. Its lyrics and comedy are fresh and splendidly produced by a strong cast. Everyone of the auditorium's 772 seats were found to be of the most comfortable kind, not crowded, as is usual in such cases, but placed in accordance with the best seating systems. Open admiration was heard for the main curtains handsomely illustrated with familar local scenes. In fact, from the orchestra pit to the utmost row in the balcony, every detail in the theatre's construction and furnishings was found to be in perfect harmony with the dominant idea entertained by its promoters—to give the people of Raton a public place of assemblage. Commersuate with the city's need for many years to come, and an institution of which her citizens might feel justly proud.

"Since the laying of the cornerstone on August 20, 1914, under Masonic auspices, by the State Guard Master, Nathan Jaffa of Roswell, the people of Raton have watched the erection of the edifice with deepening interest. The plan had its modest inception over three years ago when $25,000 was voted by the taxpayers for the building of a city hall and suitable quarters for municipal officers. After several months deliberation the plan was enlarged to include a public auditorium and a modern equipped two story fire station which now adjoins the main building on the north. These plans were carried to friction less than eight months with the result that the people of Raton now own a municipal building group providing the most beautiful and modern equipped theatre in the Southwest outside of Denver; a modern fire department building and several suites of offices which will be used largely for municipal purposes. The actual cost of the two new structures and their furnishings will approximate $55,000. The city administration compares that the building will eventually pay for itself out of the revenues derived from its use, having an annual rental value of about $4,000-$1,500 of which will be required for interest payments and the balance applied to the cost of maintenance and a sinking fund to care for the principal"—The paper further adds:

"Still greater things are ahead of us if only the same spirit of progressiveness and farsightedness prompt those who have interests of our own community at heart. It is this spirit that will bring Raton a purer and more abundant source of water supply, more manufacturing industries, more civic improvements, more wholehearted co-operaton among our people, and material benefits which should make Raton a city of 20,000 within the next ten years".

The name given the auditorium was The Shuler Auditorium to honor one of Raton's pioneer citizens and several times mayor. The son of another pioneer, Manville Chapman, completed the art work as a P. W. A. project a number of years later. These paintings are a pictorial history of Raton and the Southwest.

Sunday was always a frolic day in the early days. The Raton Concert Band paraded the streets to serenade the people. The crowd however was to be found at the railway station watching trains come and go. If you were in search of a friend you were sure to find him either at the railway station or in the wake of the band. In the summer he would be either at the race track or at Yankee. Not very exciting but friendly and the friendships lasted a lifetime. Then there was the Shakespeare Club if you liked that sort of thing.

Other places where time was spent if you belonged to the organization were: Raton Business Men's Association; Raton Encampment No. 5, I. O. O. F., Mendelson Hall for Railway Brotherhood; Hillside Lodge No. 295 for Locomotive Fireman and Engineermen; Brotherhood of Railroad Trainmen—Raton Pass Lodge No. 221; A. F. and A. M. Gate City Lodge No. 11; Raton Chapter No. 6 R.A.M.; Aztec Commandery No. 5 K.T.; Queen Esther Chapter No. 1 O.E.S.; B.P.O. Elks No. 865; Fraternal Brotherhood, Raton Lodge No. 80; I.O.O.F. Raton Lodge No. 8; Margaret Rebecca Lodge No. 8; Yeoman; Royal Neighbors; Knights and Ladies of Security Council No. 2210; Ladies Auxiliary to B. of L.E. No. 123. And later on were added Lions Club, Rotary Club, Community Concert, Knights of Columbus, Kiwanis, Boy Scouts, and Girl Scouts, Catholic Daughters of America, St. Patricks Dramatic Club.

The year 1880 was an effervescent year of turmoil, change, turbulence. Caught in the vortex of mining rushes, partisan exigency at Washington, eight great territories threw open their arms to a first line of the restless, granulated army of civilization moving westward. Added to this the railroads advertised the advantages of living in the "wide open spaces". The cattle industry reached the midway prosperity. That was the year that Garrett trapped Billy the Kid, the James brothers did well with their train robberies, and deeds performed that today make the West the glamorous and romantic past of folklore, melodrama, novels. Drift-ins from Dodge City, Salt Lake, San Francisco, Las Vegas, the Panhandle, Lincoln County, left, if not a mark, at least a blotch passing through the Gate City. Wiser citizens realized that in permitting the bad-men to shoot it out, such characters would be carried to Boot-hill and in time the town would adjust itself. Such was the experience of other towns. Pioneers, however, enjoyed a fight.

"Several fights in town last night." A jail was necessary. The city's first carcel was built behind the site of the present Elks Club house. A deputy sheriff from out of town brought in a prisoner one night, locked the lumber jail and took the key back with him. The prisoner hit upon a rouse of fire but burnt himself and the jail. Efforts made at his rescue were too late to save him.

A source of annoyance was horse stealing. The most notorious horse thief in Raton in the '80's was Ernest Anthony. The editor of the newspaper was in a constant dither about him.

"Ernest Anthony, the young man who stole a horse from the Manby Brothers and was captured in San Miguel County, and placed in the Springer jail from which he escaped a few days ago and brought here for trial is now the first occupant of the new jail." "Ernest Anthony, that infamous horse thief who is allowed to lie around the country after escaping the custody of Sever and to take the citizens property at will, was visiting down at the middle Vermejo last Sunday. If Sever don't go up and get that notorious thief before long, Billy Corbett will have to go and bring him in again." "E. Anthony, noted horse thief is still loafing around this country". Anthony was finally apprehended and sent to the State Pen in Santa Fe.

Oft times cowboy outfits came in from the Vermejo and other places to shoot up the town. One of these cowboys was Dick Rogers. Most of the drinking and celebrating was done on the East Raton. He had trouble with a man named Smith while drinking in one of the East side taverns, and as a result shot him. This set sheriff John Hixenbaugh on his trail. Several months later when Rogers was in town again he picketed his horse near the cemetery in Buena Vista as East Raton was then known and went in search of Hixenbaugh to have it out with him before he went back to the ranch. Not finding the sheriff, he whiled away his time at his favorite haunts on Garcia Street. Hixenbaugh finding out that Rogers was in search of him, went to do a little looking of his own. Taking Deputy Will Lysett with him he rode over to Buena Vista where he found Roger's horse. He waited. About midnight Rogers who had his fill of gaiety, went for his horse. Within fifty yards of Hixenbaugh he was commanded to throw up his hands. Relying on the darkness and on his Winchester, he shot at the spot from which he heard the voice and wounded the sheriff in the knee, jumping forward as he did so, thus upsetting Lysett, and setting him out of range of gunfire. As he made his getaway Lysett was left holding his horse. For Rogers to have escaped on his horse might have been fatal. Hixenbaugh was taken into town to Dr. Kohlhousen while a posse was gotten together in search of Rogers. Not long afterwards Rogers returned to hear that James Masterson, whom many considered a hired gunman, was appointed deputy sheriff. Masterson, like Hixenbaugh was gunning for Rogers. Following the familiar path to Buena Vista, the outlaw corraled the deputy in Williams and Sargent's dance hall. Said Rogers, as he drew his gun; "I did not come here to kill citizens or to fight citizens but only to kill those people who are continually saying they will kill me on sight". He put away his gun and gave Masterson a sound thrashing. Pat Garrett, on the strength of his killing Billy the Kid blew into town one day from the East, feeling out the possibility for the sheriff's job. Receiving no encouragement, he went on into the Texas Panhandle.

Masterson was not to be outdone. He pulled strings to have a company of commissioned officers and non-commissioned officers recognized by the Territorial Government. Suspicions were aroused. The company was called an Army for the overthrow of the Maxwell Land Grant Company. Masterson as captain, was called upon to post the names of his Company H. When it was found that a number of the privates existed on paper only the company became liable to indictment for forgery and perjury. Things got too hot for Masterson. Vigilantes escorted him out of town showing him the rope they would use on him if he ever dared show his face in Raton again.

Rogers added to his list when he had trouble with Miller. Raton had an attraction for him within a week of the Company H Militia affair he was in town again with Marian Littrell, Robert E. Lee, John Dodds, Tod Wallington, Ed Kink, Garnett Lee, Abe Howe, John Curry and a host of other "popular punchers" to attend an opperetta at the Rink. With such friends about him no atempt was made to arrest him. He did give himself up after the show and was charged with the killing of Miller, the shooting of Hixenbaugh, assault on Masterson amongst other charges. He pleaded not guilty and was released on a $1,000 bail. A week later Rogers was to save Jesse Lee's life, only to lose his own the following week at the hands of the same Jesse Lee in the Settlers vs. Maxwell Land Grant War. Conditions didn't improve any. One out of town editor commented: "There is a gang of fellows at Raton who seem disposed to run things in a light handed manner to suit themselves and the minions of the law up there seem disposed to turn a cold shoulder to the enforcement of law and order. Bad state of affairs this. The remedy should be searched for and applied hot. Poulticing will not do in such cases".

Over at the Howe Ranch Frank Catlin had been drinking heavily. Deputy sherriff G. W. Cook (for whom Cook Avenue has been named) was called in to quiet him. An argument ensued. Catlin went for his six shooter but the sherriff beat him to the draw. Several shots were fired. Catlin was killed. Bowed with sorrow as Cook was, this death was a crushing weight, for the body of his 29 year old son lay at his home awaiting burial. Such were the trials of a frontier lawman. Leaving his dying son he went to the Howe Ranch bar in fulfilment of duty. Startled as Raton was by Catlin's death, how could they but help admiring Cook as he accompanied the body of his boy to the grave the next day. Louis Blair was the proprietor of the Howe Ranch. One day he invited his friend Jack O'Meilly, a Santa Fe freight conductor, to his saloon for a drink. For some unexplained reason Blair asked the barkeeper for his gun and emptied it into O'Meilly. The victim was taken to Dr. Shuler's office where he died. Blair was imprisoned at Springer but was released on a $5,000 bond.

Bob Ford, tiring of life in Las Vegas, came to Raton feeling that his popularity as the slayer of Jesse James would give him a berth there. No sooner had he arrived than he got into trouble with Jack Miller, the deputy sheriff. Both felt insulted. The apology would have to be written in blood. Ford challenged Miller who readily accepted. They selected a lonely spot on the road out to Folsom with the understanding that only one would return alive. Miller was on hand but Ford failed to appear for which he was upbraided by his associates as a coward. Returning to town Miller gave Ford a permentory invitation to leave Raton for his own and the city's good. Ford had no intention of meeting Miller but confessed that he relied on his fame as James' slayer to subdue Miller. Cattle rustling, horse stealing, and sheep stealing was a common pastime in those days. It got so bad that J. B. Dawson, J. A. Salazar, J. V. Velasquez, H. W. Leight, E. D. Wright, the Troy brothers, Jose Aragon, Romaldo Martinez, Juan B. Tafoya, H. W. Kelly deposited $12,000 to be expended in awards for the arrest and conviction of any person caught stealing sheep. The Troy brothers posted an additional four hundred. Holdups were staged in a novel way: "About 1:30 A.M. Saturday morning, the Bank Exchange Saloon was robbed by three masked men who secured $362.00. One of the trio remained at the door while the other two entered together and covered the crowd, robbed the games, the saloon, the cash register; not being disturbed in the saloon all the time. All the robbers wore sweaters over their clothing and two of the men are described as quite tall while the third is thought to be but a boy. They also broke into A. H. Carey's hardware store and appropriated a fine Colt's rifle and a lot of cartridges".

Raton spread in several directions. The box-car homes of 1879-1880 were not only on the south side, but on the north, known as Boggstown, and on the east known as Buena Vista, Chihuahua, or merely East Side. Spanish-American railroad workers first settled this side, which for a time was seen as an independent town apart from Raton proper. The Maxwell Land Company controlled the land there which was not included in the right-of-way turned over to the Santa Fe Railroad. As boxcars and tents faded away, Buena Vista settled down to become Raton's Great White (and Red) Way. A dance hall was put up and the proprietors honored themselves as private deputy-sheriffs. In 1881, the Santa Fe acquired more land and Harry Whigham notified the people of Buena Vista that the land they squatted on would be surveyed by the Santa Fe and included in the Raton townsite. This didn't slow them down any. Indeed it brought a rather scathing rebuke from the Editor of the Comet; "Buena Vista in this vicinity is the Sodom and Gommorrah of this country and if it doesn't rain fire and brimstone in that locality it is not because the measure of immortality is empty. Every week discloses some new phase of misplaced confidence and uncertainty of true love".

While the cowboys were having their cattle wars, and the Maxwell Land Grant Company having its troubles with O. P. McMains, East Side now and then flared up with incidents some of which were of tragic consequence as when some local resident accused Juan Castillo of an alleged attack on an eight year old girl. The opinion was divided. Relatives of the girl sought in vengance. Friends of his, doubting the truth of the accusation hid him in a box car. He was not secreted long for about fifty Spanish-Americans worked up to mob violence took him out of the car and hung him to the alamo tree by the Arroyo on the East side. Sheriff Parker and deputy Catlin investigated the case but it wasn't until nine months later that they arrested Marcus Trujillo and Jose Sanchez as implicated in the affair. They were finally released for lack of evidence. The Maxwell Land Grant Company had the East Side plotted and mapped and straightened the streets and alleys. More business men opened up establishments and the lawlessness of the East side was confined to one street. J. E. Vigil and his wife went to a dance at Cantou's Hall on this street. A young man asked for a dance. She consented. Vigil, jealous by nature, shot and killed her. He made his escape to the panhandle of Texas. He was captured several weeks later at a dancehall as the result of an argument because a girl he was paying attention to danced with another man. Brought back for trial, he was sentenced to be hung in Raton on February 17, 1905. The hanging was postponed until April 4. The sentence was finally changed to imprisonment. That same year Sheriff Littrell and his department decided to clean up the East Side. The attempt merited a comment from the Raton Range: "If the cleaning out continues, East Raton will yet become as clean and immaculate as the beautiful snow".

Boxing was looked upon with horror in the early days but not on the East Side. The Progressive Saloon sent out secret notices of contests held in its back room. The night that Eddy Seely of Blossburg took on an ex-cop from Chicago there were one hundred and fifty spectators to witness the contest. Seely, stripped to the waist wore white body fitting tights, Latimer his opponent wore a red shirt and white long tight fitting pants. The contest was a while in getting underway because both boxers were using gloves, but the rules of the London Prize Ring which were being followed called for bare knuckles. The referee refused to enter the ring, the contestants refused to take off the gloves. Finally, Jack Murphy consented to referee. Gloves were used. In the fifth round Murphy decided that Seely won the fight on a foul. Conscientious objectors started the bottles flying and soon the melee was watched by Seely, Latimer, and Murphy. The next day many of the prominent citizens of Raton walked into their offices with black rings around their eyes. That same week a row occurred among the demimode of the East side in which Polly Wilson paralized Rosita Cantana with a beer glass, knocking her out in one round. "The fight is a result of an old feud. Both are in love with the same hombre. They both met at El Dorado Saloon where a fellow was lying, having been hacked with a hachet. Rosita, who was acting as nurse, refused to permit Polly near the patient. They decided to settle it once and for all the next time they met. Later on, Rosita hearing that Polly was in the Cowboys Exchange Saloon went after her with both fists clinched. Polly met her halfway with a beer glass. Brought to trial Polly was declared innocent". The editor adds a futher unrelated item that "it is said that there are more dead hogs, dogs, noisy boys, burros, goats in Raton than any other town in New Mexico." Jealous of the Seely-Latimer contest, Cheyenne Bill, the 'Red Handed,' a town character advertised himself as "The Terror of the Wicked West" and would take on any customer in a prize-ring contest. No one paying atention he took off for the Sioux country hoping to take enough scalps to be sold at $2.50 a piece to visitors and tourists.

Frank Cantou of the East Side, and his brother Steve were suddenly confronted by deputies John Barnum and Louis Martinez. They were told that they were under arrest. The Cantou brothers refused to accompany the officers unless they produced a warrant. About 5:00 A. M. the following morning as Frank was entering the back of his store to the rear of the building, there stood John Barnum and Martinez with guns leveled at him. He rushed for the door and as he entered four shots were fired at him. One of these shots took effect in the left lung just below the heart. He slammed the door shut behind him. A shot crashed through the panel. Whether he was shot from the outside or when he entered Cantou couldn't say. As soon as he got inside Barnum and his associates ran away. Steve and several others, who were still asleep in the house when the shooting started jumped up to see what had happened. They found Frank lying on the floor. Sheriff Hixenbaugh went in search of Barnum and Martinez, arrested them for attempting murder for they had no warrant even when they shot Cantou. As deputy for the East Side, Barnum had his hands full.

For two days, Sunday and Monday three Goodman brothers, a cousin E. L. Stuck, from Yankee enjoyed themselves on the East Side They began by drinking, then by beating up a piano salesman from Denver. Later on they entered Jim Barnetts saloon where soon a half dozen men were beating each other up when Barnum appeared on the scene. He had been standing directly across the street when "Blind Alber's" mother and the cook of the Green Light saloon called to him to quiet the rumpus in the Lone Star saloon. He ran to the back entrance of the place, pushed open the door and four men jumped on him. He pulled out his gun, backing up until he was on the platform in the rear of the Lone Star, the men fighting him all the time and trying to get his gun away from him. Finally Frank Goodman got hold of the gun, and in trying to pull it out of Barnum's hand it went off, the bullet piercing Goodman's hand and leg and hitting Watson who was taking no part in the fight but was standing on the ground level about two feet below the platform. Barnum having lost his gun, ran across the street to the 'Dobe Saloon, picked up another one and started after the Goodmans, who by this time had started up Buena Vista Hill. A shot was fired while he was gone from his own gun, in the rear of the Green Light. He caught up with two lawbreakers a few blocks away and with the help of an unidentified young man who had meantime secured Barnum's gun and joined the pursuit, he arrested them. Brought before Sheriff Gale, they as well as Barnum were detained. Robert Watson died. Immediately, the Raton paper started a crusade against the bawdy district. The proposition to move the houses outside the city limits did not meet with much encouragement from the owners of the buildings and saloons. Bad for their business they said. Barnum was released on bail. He maintained that all would have been quietly settled if someone hadn't grabbed for his gun.

The elements sometimes gave the people a rough time of it. There was that terrific storm in August 1908 that wiped out the filling in several cuts along the line on the Santa Fe, Raton and Eastern Railway so that within one hour the streets had four inches of water. The home of E. R. Lane on Second Street and the north edge of the arroyo washed away. The yard of contractor Jerls was water swept and there four wagons floated off. The havoc was still greater below the first street bridge. All the smaller wagons and foot bridges from the upper part of the Arroyo came down with the flood and were lodged against the bridge of the Santa Fe and Eastern Railways. A block above this, on Chicorica Street, the water swept ten feet above the wagon bridge, carrying away railing and leaving only the steel frame and the floor so weakening the approaches that passage over the bridge was impossible. The culmination of havoc was reached at the Santa Fe and Eastern railroad bridge. Great timbers were swung against the structure and up the bank with such force that the whole south end of the work shop of Francisco Maes, the carpet cleaner, was torn away by the flood. Here the real wreckage of houses began, and though only a few in number, the loss was quite heavy on the poor Spanish American families living in the wake of the waters. Francisco Maes, Patricio Gonzales, John Barnum, Mrs. Valdez, Samson Jacobs and others had their homes severely damaged by the water. Further over, in the lower part of the East Side Mrs. Flores, a school-teacher, awoke to find her bed soaked and practically floating. She caught up her little baby, only to lose him in the water. In the darkness she could scarcely tell its location but caught it by its clothing, and with her two older children, made her way two blocks to the house of councilman Raines where all were cared for. Sixty children spent the night in the Presbyterian church on the East Side as none could tell what might come and all were frightened. The brick plant on the East Side belonging to the Fulghum brothers sustained severe loss from standing water and washout. Down to the house of Pat Gonzalez floated the large bridge from Cook Avenue and a mass of other wreckage. The houses were a total loss. Every bridge and foot board along the whole arroyo was washed out with the exception of the First Street bridge. Latimore lost about fifty blooded chickens from his yard near the Lane house in Second Street. Lane whose five room house was a total wreck found the remains piled up against the First Street bridge. Lane, who was employed as a druggist in Cimarron, had mortgaged the property but a short time before to the Raton Loan Association.

Over in Santa Fe, J. E. Vigil had served nine years of his life imprisonment sentence. The penitentiary board in reviewing his case, realized that it had many extenuating circumstances; besides he had been a model prisoner. Acting governor De Baca gave him a parole hoping that Vigil would start life anew and a credit as a citizen.

Before the Civil War, and after, many towns tolerated houses of prostitution to protect the fairer sex, thus segregating the madames from the rest of the town. Such houses were tolerated but not desired because court records seemingly indicated that decent girls were safe from attack where those of assignation were licensed. While we don't attempt pros and cons, Raton had such a district. In 1908 the Deputy Marshall was on trial for not turning in funds collected in the fines on the East Side and for protecting the Dens which throve in the houses. Thirty-two women paid fines in February to total $272.00 All paid $8.50 each for immunity from arrest. The deputy (name withheld) turned in $187.50 from all sources. Mayor McAuliffe said that historically the people of the 4th ward requested the district to be established and lewd women to be kept in the district. Special officers were employed to prevent their getting beyond those limits. I—C—a denizen produced a receipt for the purpose of carrying on the business of a woman of the town. The payment was due on the eighth of each month. F—L—, E—M—A—G— paid the fine for the purpose of conducting business in the segregated area. The deputy was found guilty as charged. The women were indicted for keeping houses within 700 feet of a church or public building. They were fined $25.00 and costs. These women testified that at various times the City Council had promised them immunity from arrest if they paid their fines each month. This raised quite a rumpus in the city, so that the Editor of the Raton Range wrote in the April 8 issue:

"The system of licenced houses of prostitution which has been in vogue in Raton for years has fostered crimes and vice until in the past year practically every crime in the statute books of the territory has been committed in this Hell's Half Acre which is under the protection of the peace officers of the county, and without public protest from the people who claim to be interested in the morality and welfare of Raton. The action of the Grand Jury put an end to this system forever. This district has been established by City Ordinance and comprised a parting of two blocks on Garcia Street in East Raton. One dollar went to the man who collected the fine; the fine was eight dollars and fifty cents. All houses nearer than 700 foot from a church or hall were closed".

The Atchison, Topeka and The Santa Fe railroad had been interested in education from the very start. A small school was erected and known as The Raton Free School. Miss Belle Roux was to teach since she had been teaching at Otero, but she left for Chicago to marry Daniel M. Tine. Miss Anne Darling was engaged as principal and teacher. Boys and girls of all ages came in with the Santa Fe workers and early pioneers so that the question of a high school was brought up for the first time on June 7, 1882. Nor was the Raton Free School big enough to accomodate the children of the booming town. Miss F. Harless opened a select private school as well as Mr. and Mrs. T. A. Kilgore. Miss Harless closed her school after a year, leaving for Hutchinson, Kansas. Kilgore added a Miss Mc Michael to his staff, and continued as Raton's most popular school teacher. He searched for Juvenile talent, hiring McAuliffe and Ferguson's Hall to prove to the parents that their darlings could be entertaining. Any day the children got off from school apart from legal holidays was made up during the Christmas, Easter or summer holidays so that in the early years school was on well into June. What constituted a day off?

Take the time that Tom died. Tom was just a dog. Part St. Bernard, part just plain dog. He was owned by Raton's first photographer W. A. White. Wherever the photographer went, Tom went with him. In fact whenever possible Tom had to be in the picture. Soon the school children adopted Tom. He followed one or another to become as much a pupil as they. One day Tom was missing from school. Consternation! March 3, 1885, all schools were closed. The children, dressed in white carried a little white coffin to the foot of Goat Hill where Tom was laid to rest. A Tombstone marked his resting place. Vandals made away with it one night and Raton lost a symbol of how it took even quadrupeds to its heart.

Meantime a school board was chosen and correspondence started with a number of eastern gentlemen to choose the best possible candidate for the position of superintendent of the Marcy and Mc Custion Institute that was to be Raton's first high school. On July 4, 1884, the cornerstone was laid. The Raton Weekly Independent ran quite an editorial:

"Some time ago a gentleman residing in Colfax County requested a few of his friends to consider a proposal he desired to make them. A meeting was held in Burnam's Hall. An offer of $10,000 toward the building of a public school house was then made. The announcement was received with surprise, and many even greeted the news with expressions of doubt. That a man without family should make such an offer seemed barely credible. Russell Marcy, a prominent cattleman of this county, an old resident, and one who stood high in the estimation of the people was that man. So humble was Marcy about his offer that he desired no publicity save in the fact that a citizen was giving the money. But such things will come out, and soon it was published in every paper in the Territory that Mr. Marcy had given this liberal donation to the Gate City.

"A partner of Mr. Marcy, next added the sum of $5,000 to the fund, Mr. Mc Custin is also a cattleman, generous, kind, and like his associate in business, not a lover of notoriety. The A.T. and S.F. railroad has always felt a lively interest in Raton. It has located its shops here, put in a system of water works which has no superior in the Territory. When the officials learned of the generosity of these "Cowboys" a check was sent by the railroad officials for $5,000. Then came the New Mexico Town Site Company which donated a block of land for the edifice. Owing to the fact that some of the lots in the donated block had been disposed of, a little delay in the proceedings was necessary, but was finally settled to the satisfaction of all concerned. A committee was then selected and appearances seemed to indicate that a school house was really to be built. Time passed, however, and but little headway was made. The committee at this time consisted of Russell Marcy, D. W. Stevens, and G. J. Pace. Plans were invited and in due time they were examined and it was found that Mr. D. Risdon had furnished the best for the needs of the town and the amount of money to be expended, and his work was adopted. Bids were then asked for through the papers and the successful bidder was found to be the architect who drew the plans. About this time Mr. Marcy, owing to his inability to give the matter its proper attention placed G. W. Cook on the committee to represent him, and to the energy of this gentleman is due in a great measure the present condition of the building. When the work had fairly commenced, this paper called attention to the fact that some celebration should take place on the occasion of the laying of the cornerstone. A meeting was called at McAuliffe and Wheeler's Hall to consider the matter and it was decided that the event should be observed in an appropriate manner, and to this end a committee of ten was appointed to make the necessary arrangements. After consultation it was decided to have the celebration on the 4th of July 1884. This committee was selected to represent the different interests of the town and the first resolution adopted at the meeting was for a committee of seven; but when the nominations were made, to not excuse any, and to allow a full representation the ten names adopted were: Russell Marcy, D. H. Dotterer, J. C. Holmes, W. J. P. Williams, Charles Wheeler, T. P. Gable, J. I. Holcomb, C. A. Fox, T. W. Collier, M. A. McMartin. At the first meeting Mr. Marcy sent in a letter of resignation, which was accepted and the nine remaining members organized for business by the election of D. H. Dotterer as chairman, J. C. Holmes as secretary. Among the first things accomplished was the appointment of subcommittees to take charge of the work. T. W. Collier and J. C. Holmes had charge of the invitations; D. H. Dotterer, T. P. Gable, T. W. Collier, M. A. Mc Martin; music, C. Wheeler, C. A. Fox: decorations, J. L. Holmes, W. J. P. Williams; barbeque, W. J. P. Williams, W. H. Letton; fireworks: D. H. Dotterer, T. P. Gable; reception, T. W. Collier, H. H. officer, H. L. McCorn, J. J. Shuler, C. M. Bayne, W. C. Clark.

"Their labors were now fairly under way and frequent meetings were held to perfect arrangements for the grandest celebration ever held in this section of the country. Perfect harmony prevailed in all their councils. There was no dissension and everything portended a successful termination of their arduous duties. Speakers were invited, and special care was observed to ask none to participate who might in any manner allude to subjects foreign to the event. The speakers were Robert G. Ingersoll, Jose de Sena, W. H. Rogers, V. A. Hadley, Rafael Romero. Officers of the day were Rev. J. McGautheff as chaplain, S. W. Dorsey (of the Star Route fame) as president, vice presidents, D. H. Dotterer, Delos Chappell, J. Armstrong, Dolph Peterson, A. E. Burnam, B. Chandler, W. C. Wrigley, C. A. Forster, H. Wigham, A. H. Carey, J. W. Dwyer; Grand Marshal, Col. E. G. Savage; while H. P. Taylor, A. C. Voohees, A. G. Shaw, C. B. Adams, and Herbert Savage served as aides.

"A few days prior to the 4th the townspeople had made the town gorgeous in the display of evergreens, flags, and bunting. A pole was erected on First Street from which floated the Stars and Stripes. An immense arch was erected at the corner of First and Saunders Avenue, by the Beringer brothers. The railroad company sent out special trains to bring in the necessary material and citizens did labor voluntarily.

"Early in the morning of the Fourth people from the surrounding country commenced coming in. The early train from the east brought a large delegation from Trinidad, which was swelled to larger proportions when the noon train arrived. Starkville also turned out a goodly number of its people. All the towns in the neighborhood were well represented and before the hour designated for the procession our streets were thronged with a multitude of strangers.

"The hour announced for the procession arrived, but a telegram had been received that a large number of people were on the train which was expected in a few moments, and the start was accordingly delayed. In the lead rode the speakers followed by the Gate City Band in a wagon drawn by four horses appropriately decorated. The music was excellent, and the new uniforms of the members excited the admiration of the hundreds of spectators who filled every available point of observation along the line of march. A wagon containing the cornerstone, on which Thomas McCrae, the artisan who had done the cutting, was busily putting on the finishing touches.

Mr. Marcy occupied a large carriage immediately behind the stone, and with him rode Mr. Dotterer, who represented the A.T. & S.F. Next came a wagon with a banner on which was inscribed the names of the donors, under the headline of "Our Benefactors." The center was filled with a painting of Russell Marcy, executed by M. T. Hudson. This was furnished by the railroad shops and was highly complimented. The states and Territories were represented by forty-eight little girls dressed in white, each carrying a small flag on which was painted the name of the State she represented. In the center of the wagon rode Miss Della Clark as the Goddess of Liberty, and directly in front of her on less elevated seat, sat Miss Ollie Olive as the representative of New Mexico.

"The Star Clothing House had a fine display. A comical feature of this was a sheep, covered with a white blanket to represent 'sheep clothing'. Beringer Brothers had a huge clock which attracted a great deal of attention. Jos. Schroeder had a fine soda fountain on wheels. The Union House turned out "The Band of 1776" clad in fantastic costumes. Olive's coal mine was represented by a wagon on which was a burro attached to a coal car on which a miner was busily at work. Mrs. C. M. Bayne presented to the public a fine showing of millinery and dressmaking ability, on a very large float, profusely decorated with national colors. At one end of the float wee immense glass cases, filled with a fine selection of trimmed hats and bonnets, comparing most favorably with the imported hats and bonnets seen upon our streets. At the other end was a figure dressed in a very lovely costume, also a sewing machine and operator. In the center were several large baskets of flowers most tastefully arranged, near these sat Mrs. Bayne and several other ladies, all busily at work, which made the scene one of the most real and life-like of the day.

"J. R. Jones had a ranch team. He showed his hogs and cows, and himself and wife were in the operation of making butter while the procession moved. A huge boiler on which the shop boys were fastening rivets represented the boiler shops. C. A. Fox had a hardware and tin shop in the line which was most appropriately arranged, workmen were making and giving away tin cups. The photographic apparatus of Mr. White was in the line. John Labadie's tailor shop was admirably arranged. Blossburg was represented by over 300 miners from the Raton Coal Company. Also a wagon containing the requisite number of girls to represent the States. A carload of coal was shown. The turnout reflected great credit on the busy little town and added much to the success of the day. Starkville sent about 200 miners and a wagon, drawn by six mules, on which were two coke ovens in full blast. Twenty horsemen accompanied this delegation which was under the lead of Samuel Thompson, and represented the Trinidad Coal and Coke Company.

When the procession arrived on the grounds the exercises were immediately commenced. It had been impossible to provide shade for the audience, and the day was hot. No one felt disposed to grumble, however and the audience placed themselves in a position to listen to the speakers. The meeting was called to order by the secretary of the committee of ten who introduced Rev. J. McGaughey, chaplain of the day, who offered the prayer for the occasion. Mr. S. W. Dorsey made a brief address following the reading of the list of officers. At the conclusion of Senator Dorsey's remarks, he introduced as the superintendent of the laying of the cornerstone, the Governor of the Terirtory. The mason's work was done by Thomas McCrae and his assistants. The Governor then placed within the box the documents prepared for that purpose, the stone was placed in its proper position, and the master of ceremonies reported the work accomplished.

"The corner-stone is a fine piece of work, on the east side of which is engraved 'Donors: Russell Marcy, O. W. McCustin, A.T. & S.F. R.R. Co., R.T.S. Co.". On the north side was engraved '1884' Senator Dorsey then announced his portion of the work completed and said that an address would be delivered by Governor L. A. Sheldon. Governor Hadley spoke after Sheldon which came as a surprise since he had been the victim of a severe cough and he feared an attack if he should exert himself in speaking. The audience evinced their appreciattion of his effort by frequent and hearty applause. The absence of some of the expected orators was unavoidable, and is regretted. However, the exercises were lengthy enough, considering the weather, and closed with an eloquent one given by Col. W. H. Rogers. At the close of his speech the President announced the balance of the programme to be a barbeque, fireworks and a grand ball in the evening at Wheeler and Rush's skating rink. The amount of food consumed at the barbecue was 4,500 pounds of beef; five lambs; 1,000 pounds of bread; 120 gallons of coffee; 100 gallons of iced tea; besides a generous donation of cake and pie furnished by our town ladies. The victuals were served by volunteer waiters, both ladies and gents, who performed their parts well. The coffee was made by John Sigwalt, who ranks high in the cuisine depatment. After lunch the crowd witnessed a baseball game between Trinidad and the Wheeler Club. Raton won 39 to 21. McNeill was captain of the winners. Butts acted as umpire. The fireworks were displayed from an elevation west of town, from which the spectacle was visible for miles. This continued for over an hour. The closing event at the skating rink gathered the largest crowd ever seen in Raton. The immense building was crowded to its full capacity. The music was furnished by the Gate City Orchestra under the leadership of Professor Boffa. Over 100 couples took part in each dance and the party continued until three the next morning. To Mr. Wheeler is due praise for his exertions in getting ready this fine building, than which a finer cannot be found in the Territory; and there are few times in the East of larger size than Raton that can boast a better."

"The new school building is enclosed and is now rapidly being completed. It is the finest school house in the Southwest. There was no auditorium in the Institute because the first graduation exercises were held at the Rink on Thursday, May 17, 1888, the graduates being May Shy, Belle Geer, Elsie Beringer, Joe Brockett, Robert Officer, Will Stevens. School lasted nine months, being supported by local entertainment. The school census of 1889 showed 569 children of school age in the Raton school district. A portion of the East Side district was returned to Raton for it had been running independently as the Buena District School, opposite Fairmont Cemetery, with Mary Murphy of Trinidad as teacher. She taught in Raton until 1892 leaving for the Gallup schools. A private school was opened on the East Side under the auspices of the Presbyterian church on Guadalupe Street. A. C. Burnam, long identified with the Raton schools opened a language school in his accounting house in 1885 where R. W. Couthat, principal of the Institute taught Latin, Greek, Spanish, Italian, Portuguese. In April 1885, a commercial school was started, and two months later a school of Higher Ornamental Drawing, a School of Painting and Design, a School of Music and a School of Science. Special classes in Spanish for people living on ranches were conducted on Saturdays.

Professor J. P. Owens, a graduate of Princeton College, who had been teaching in the Blossburg school took charge of the Institute in 1886. The school teachers that year were; Owens, James Walker, M. B. Mason, Ida Cavanaugh and Mrs. F. R. Givens. Over in North Raton Mrs. C. E. Moore opened a Kindergarten and Primary school in her house with rates two dollars a month, payable in advance. In 1889, a movement was started to locate an agricultural college. "Raton is in the field for an agricultural college. If the legislature desires to locate the institution where it will be the greatest benefit to the agricultural interests of New Mexico. If the college is to be rewarded for political services rendered or to be settled by a trade for services to be preferred, Raton of course, will not be considered". In 1890 the schools were to be closed for lack of funds. In 1892, the teachers were: James H. Walker, Jr., principal, Charles E. Higbee, assistant, Emily C. Kern, M. L. Darling, Isabel Talliaferro, Mary O'Brien. The teachers in 1893 were: James E. Cane, Louise L. Kilbourn, E. C. Kern, Lizzie McIntire, Marguerite Voorhees, Miss Conn, Lizzie Downing, Lizzie Walker (at the Buena Vista school). Amy Wilkinsin came later. In 1898, R. H. Carter. superintendent, S. D. Burnam, Mrs. O. Sweitzer, M. A. Mitchell, Lizzie Downing, Helen Popen, Mrs. N. Conn, C. Ellenwood, Fannie Massey, F. W. McClelland, Mary Murphy (who apparently was dissatisfied at Gallup or attached to Raton). The 1890 list was: Professor S. W. Black of Kansas, superintendent, W. F. McClelland, assistant superintendent, Fanny Massey, Florence Hartsell, Helen Popen, Alice F. Lee, Mamie Howells, Mrs. Oma Switzer, Mary Murphy, Alpha Mitchell, Sally Burnam, Jeanette Ritchie, Mrs. L. Lizie was substitute teacher. Over at the Rink, Mrs. J. Johnson opened a dancing school, teaching the fine art of dancing every Saturday afternoon. The teachers for 1898 were Supt. R. H. Carter, Ass't. Supt. Wm. McClelland, Fanny Massey, E. Weight, Helen Popen, Mrs. N. Conn, Sally Burnam, E. Ellingwood, M. A. Mitchell, Lizzy Downing, Mamie Howells, Mary Murphy (Buena Vista School). In 1909, the Institute was called Central School with Professor N. B. Studebaker as principal. The teachers were Mrs. Myers, Miss Ritchie, Mrs. Bennet, Miss Auisenburg, Anne Burnam, Miss Massey. The North Side School was opened this year with L. D. Brown as principal and Miss Linwood, Miss Howells, Sadie Burnam, Miss Van Burskirk and Miss Wilkinson as teachers. Miss Cora Laughton of Coshocton, Ohio came as teacher in the Presbyterian Mission School on the East Side. Juan Arellano taught Spanish at his store on Buena Vista hill. Another private school where nothing but Spanish was taught was opened on Martinez Street. In 1902, Wililam H. Heiney was superintendent of the Raton schools. The teachers for 1904 were: Professor D. L. Lucas, Fred Morrow, Lora Davis, Bessie Davis, Mabel Benfer, Nellie Nash, Vera Nash, Emily Schwachheim, Anna Bills, Veta Bills, Anna Gohrman, Florence Frost, Ethel Vaught, Anna Burnam, C. F. Coulter, and Kate Orin.

The teaching staff for 1905: Supt. Professor Heiney, Cora Polk, assistant principal, Sarah I. Kettle, assistant principal, Mabel Benfer, Ida Caldwell, Anna Burnam, Mrs. Neville Conn, Florence Slocum, Gussie Dyer. The North Side School: D. L. Lucas, principal, Estelle Nash, Diana Bovier, Mamie Howells, Jennie Bennet. This is the year work began on the Longfellow and Columbian schools. The school teachers at the Longfellow school in 1907 were: Miss Glass, Miss Wagoner, Miss Lauderdale, Miss Jackson, Miss Haver, Miss Stump. The Columbian School teachers were: Miss Bennet, Miss Bucher, Miss Coulter, Miss Perley, Miss Benfer. The high-school teachers were: Mrs. Dyer, Miss Williams, Miss Conn, Miss Lockard, Miss Davis, Miss Thatcher, Miss Schwachheim, Miss Austin, Mr. Grover, Miss Duncan, Mrs. Meyers. The teacher at Endeavor Hall was Mrs. Myers with Miss Wendleson as substitute. The teachers in 1908 were: Miss Bucher, Miss Glass, Miss Davis, Miss Schwachheim, Miss Benfer, Miss Austin, Mrs. Conn, Miss Coulter, Miss Wagoner, Miss Thatcher, Mr. Grover, Mr. Fisher, Bessie Davis, Miss Leech, Miss Perley, Mr. Hoenschel, Mrs. Lichard, Mrs. Dyer, and Mrs. Quincy.

Chapter 57 of the State Legislature, IS. Sub. S.B. No. 29 —approved June 10, 1912, passed a bill for the establishment of a County High School for Colfax County. The Central School then became the Colfax County High School. T. W. Conway who was superintendent of the Raton Public Schools in 1913 and 1914 wrote:

The Board of Education, in keeping with the spirit of Educational progress that permeates our citizenship, contemplates at an early date to remodel that portion of the old high school building that has been used for high school purposes for the last 25 years. When this improvement is completed the entire structure will have about 35 school rooms and workshops, besides a large auditorium with a seating capacity of 750. The buildings, grounds, furnishings and various equipments of the several departments represent an outlay of more than $125,000. The enrollment for the present year (1914) is higher than for any time in the history of the school, now having gone beyond the 1,000 mark. The Colfax County High School was open for work on September 8, 1913 in quarters that had been occupied by the Raton High School for a number of years." On February 12, 1914 the new building was completed and formally turned over to the Board of Education of District No. 11 at which time dedicatory services were held. On the morning of February 16, 1914, the new high school building was occupied for the first time by the freshman, sophomore, junior, and senior classes of Colfax County High School. At the expense of more than $4,000 the manual training, domestic science, and science departments have all been thoroughly equipped with all the modern appliances for demonstrating the various phases of natural and scientific instruction. The other departments, English, mathematics, Latin and commercial, have all been installed in new quarters, and like the new departments are thoroughly equipped, and with an efficient head to each, and will now be able to render excellent services to the community."

1912 was also the year the Raton Business College started: "On the 31st of the current month, (May 1913) the Raton Business College will round out its first year of existence. Started on the first Monday of June 1912, it had an enrollment of 44 students. The school sprang into immediate popularity and within one year has received through its doors 117 of our young men and women. Its average daily enrollment had exceeded fifty, and it had given diplomas to 38 students, most of them for the grade of excellent. Forty-eight of its students are now in employment. Many who took the course did not desire employment, or were already employed in their own business. None who have taken positions have lost them through incompetency while many have been promoted in positions they have already held because of their increased efficiency."

Another school that proved popular was the Raton Industrial School. "This school conducted under the provisions of the Smith-Hughes bill is quite popular. There are two classes at the school one composed entirely of Spanish-Americans. This school teaches building trades, carpentry, electric wiring, plumbing, pipe fitting, etc."

In August 1922, Sister M. Angela Hoestetter, of the Sisters of Mercy, came from Slaton, Texas, with eight other sisters. Dr. Kohlhousen's home on Third Street bought by the sisters and converted into a grade school. The first high school pupils were registered in 1925. The chapel and south wing of the Academy were completed in 1929. The school is known as St. Patricks Academy.

It has been said that Raton at one time had thirty-nine schools. Most of these were private schools. Schools for dancing, language schools, sewing schools, etc. The most famous private school still stands. This is the one story log house on the northwest corner of Savage Avenue and North 4th Street. This is one of the few houses that was in existence before the coming of the railroad. "Buck" Forster acquired the place and repaired it in the winter of 1881. Forster was a gunman and suspected of being a highwayman.

The slope up the Pass was a hard pull on stagecoaches, an advantage many highwaymen made use of. Forster was reputed to have been in on some of the robberies. People avoided him since he had a reputation as a gunman. One day Forster got into an argument with a fellow by the name of Blackwell (no relation to C. N. Blackwell of the National Bank in Raton), who was caretaker of the Captain George W. Cook estate on the Sugarite, where he raised fruits and vegetables to sell in the new community. On the corner of Savage and Second, Forster made a pass to draw a gun, Blackwell, who was also armed, took no chances. He shot to kill. He escaped through the brush where the present home of John Morrow is located. A crowd of citizens started after him, firing into the thicket. Not aware that the man killed was Forster, they pursued Blackwell but he made his getaway. When they discovered who it was that lay on the street, no one would carry him to his little log cabin. When Blackwell was found in Colorado two years later, the authorities, believing he did Raton a good turn, said he wasn't wanted. It was after this that

Belle McCord (her maiden name may have been McAulter according to Chas. E. Howells who was one of her first pupils) opened her pay school. She was also a clerk at George Pace's post-office. When the Institute was built Leopold Biddle, a promoter and mining man from Elizabethtown, together with his daughter and son-in-law Harvey Applegate occupied the cabin. They made additions, using it as a residence. It still stands.

Another log-cabin school in 1882, was over in Stringtown and taught by Mrs. Bobb. Still another private school was taught by a man named Dunkley on the second floor of a building at the end of First Street. This later became the John Thomas Hotel. Dunkley ended up in Denver as a District Court Judge. The T. A. Kilgore school was a small one room building on Second Street across from the old Ford Garage building. The present schools in Raton are the Colfax County School (site of the old Institute), the Columbian (old North Side School), Kearny (old South Side School), St. Patricks Academy, Our Lady of Mercy (built by Mother Angela about the same time that the Academy opened), Longfellow School (old Buena Vista but not the same site).

Over in Cimarron William Henderson was watching the progress of the railroad. When the "tent city" mushroomed he picked up his press and settled in Raton. "New and Press" was short lived. In Otero Kistler was publishing the Otero Optic. Given the choice between Raton and Vegas, he selected Las Vegas changing the name to The Las Vegas Daily Optic. His choice was a matter of precaution. Otero had folded up completely in five years. Raton's future was uncertain. Any town one year old had no guarantee for the second year. Las Vegas was an old established town. Nearer to Raton O. P. McMains, Captain General of the Anti-Granters set up his Comet in the belief that the "pen is mightier than the sword." Realizing that he might even be more powerful in the legislature, he sold the Comet that very year to Donaghe and Lanstrum who changed the name to the "Raton Guard." In July 1882, he bought the paper back, changing the name to "Raton Comet," writing in the first issue: "The Raton Guard gives place to the Raton Comet. We sent to Trinidad (Colorado) to the Trinidad News Office for the old Comet head but it could not be found. We will have a head electrotyped as soon as possible. Greetings to our friends. Defiance to our foes. Here is the Comet again with the same old motto: "Open War against secret fraud. The fraud is a towering majestic 2,000,000 acres—the Maxwell Land Grant. It has fed on fraud—fraud will kill it. Its demise however, can be hastened by a newspaper as well as by legal treatment and hence the Raton Comet will go for the diseased and unweildy coporiety of the Maxwell Land Grant and heavy! The Comet will also continue the fight of the Raton Guard against the Nolan Land Grant No. 39." What a way to start a paper! The only one who suffered from the ordeal was McMains himself. The Government recognized the Grant for all his printing and fighting. He was ejected from his ranch. Realizing how often he had to be out to agitate meetings against the Grant Company (we do not doubt that in his own mind he was sincere), he took on Adams as a partner. Meantime, George F. Canis who did not see eye to eye with McMains on the Land Grant deal set up his New Mexico Press and News which he may have bought from Henderson. He carried on the fight pro-grant. In one article, Canis went too far. So thought McMains. He had suffered martyrdom long enough. He led a mob to the New Mexico News and Press office and demanded proof of its editor. Canis eyed the throng. Every one an anti-granter. McMains, when Canis explained he had no proof for calling the editor of the Comet a murderer, began relating his part in the hanging of Cruz Vega at Cimarron for the murder of Parson Tolby. Canis addressed the crowd when McMains finished. He apologized for his writing and promised to print a retraction. Deputy Bowman was present waiting for the first gunfire. Remarked McMains: "Everybody knows that Canis did not do this of his own accord but with instructions he dare not disobey. He was used as a catspaw to pull some one else's chestnuts out of the fire." The editor further comments: "no revolvers displayed." Canis had his fill of Raton and the Maxwell Land Grant controversy. C. B. Adams was the sole publisher of the Comet in 1883. McMains sold the paper to him and Adams took in his brother as partner, but not for long. Charles B. Adams was sole proprietor and editor in 1884 when he sold the paper to someone else. 1884 was the newspaper year in Raton. There was the "Raton Weekly Independent" published by J. C. Holmes; The Raton Comet published by the Adams brothers; "The Raton Daily Independent" published by J. C. Holmes; the "Raton Daily Register" published by Edwin E. Adams; and several other sheets whose existence went out with the year. In 1886 J. Hunt and Clauson purchased the "Comet", changing the name to "The Raton Range." Two years later the paper was owned jointly by R. Rogers, June H. Hunt and Captain T. W. Colliers. Hunt took over the Range and commenced to blast McMains: "O. P. McMains has left Raton for Washington, D.C. He found the atmosphere here a little chilly. The wind is blowing the wrong way. Everything has gone wrong and everybody is dishonest but McMains. He secretly had a pamphlet printed in Trinidad, for he couldn't risk having it published at Raton. Judge Hunt finds there is nothing to McMains but wind, so he squeezes some of it out, and then leaves him entirely collapsed." Nevertheless, McMains was considered quite a poet and oftimes requested by editors to write poetry for their papers. In 1885, he had Raton singing to the tune of Yankee Doodle Dandy:

> 1
> Albuquerque's a dingy burg
> Las Vegas wind and sandy
> And Springer is a sleepy town
> But Raton is a dandy.
> 2
> Old Santa puts on agonies
> Socorro looms up grandly
> But none can come up to Raton
> For Raton is a dandy.
> 3
> New Mexico is the place to go
> Raton the place to stay in
> Gate City opens wide her portals
> In Kansas its a snowing.

The Range again changed hands and in 1900 F. D. Morse was owner and editor. In 1889, another short lived paper known as "Livestock Journal of New Mexico" published in Raton on Saunders Avenue near First Street made its appearance. In 1901, The Raton Range was bought by C. E. Stivers as half owner, while F. D. Morse retained on half interest. It was styled "Colfax County's official paper." Newspaper parties were the fad at this time. "A newspaper party—at which original stanzas of poetry are required from each guest is a Raton fad. No wonder Colfax County sends so many lunatics to the asylum."

In 1899, George W. Berringer started the Raton Reporter, a weekly newspaper. Later this was published by a corporation known as the Raton Reporter Publishing Company with B. L. Connell as president, editor and business manager. A typical editorial for this paper (Raton Reporter, May 7, 1914):

"Raton is worth one million, thirty-nine thousand eight hundred and forty-two dollars, according to figures compiled in Assessor Gillespie's office. The population of the city is near 5,000 souls, and not a house in town for rent—i.e. from unconfirmed sources. Eleven churches, four high schools and one county high school, beautiful park and Carnegie library, beautiful and commodious courthouse, a city hall, jail and fire department building, broad streets, a very efficient sewerage system, fine hotels, restaurants and cafes, beautiful Santa Fe depot, reading room and athletic building and park, a brick factory, electric light company, ice and cold storage plant, lumber and planing mills. A congressional appropriation for a new federal building, a contemplated municipal building, a proposed irrigation system to take in 5,000 acres directly East of the city and many other improvements peculiar to a progressive city like Raton.

"But here comes the rub. Raton is now mortgaged for practically half the assessed valuation—all because of a franchise of the Raton Water Works Company which would expire in 1916, was made political capital of by hopeful and aspiring office holders. A bonded indebtedness of $400,000 for a municipal water works which is now drawing 5 percent interest and will eventually develop into a hardship on property owners much excess of the increased valuation the improvement contemplates. Instead of increasing the worth of property values, individual opinions are, that the same condition will prevail the same as does all property when heavily mortgaged—depreciate in value. Such contemplation, however, is of individual origin and does not hold that the opinion is prophecy or fulfillment, neither does the writer contend that 'everything' is gone to the dogs! It is never too late to right about face until the damage done is beyond retrieve.

"Because of the unsatsfactory water service occasioned by one continuous string of mishaps to the plant and reservoirs, the expenditure of large funds which were not authorized it seems from the New York office, not by any means the fault of the now managers of the Raton Water Works, the people of the city of Raton, became impatient with the service and gladly welcomed and countenanced any issue which purported to relieve the situation to the extent that a bond issue election was regularly called and held and a majority vote cast in favor of bonding the city of Raton in the sum of $400,000.

The people of the city of Raton are now told that the bonds are sold and everything is lovely. Hearsay is to the effect that instead of being sold, the bonds are juggled. In plain words, a certain bonding company is advancing money for pipe, equipment, and construction in order that prima facie evidence be before the people of Raton in the belief of a municipal plant soon to be completed.

"The source of supply of water determined under municipal issue is now the property of the Raton Water Works Company, and while the city administration contemplates no trouble in acquiring such water property, it is the belief of many that this fact will place another long, drawn out and expensive law suit on the records. It is human nature to defend one's own property and no one blames the present water works company from defending their right and title to the land, reservoirs, mains and equipment now constituting the site and service. The mandamus proceedings, which were the result of ill advised contemplation on the part of the city fathers in the erection of a municipal opera house, cost the city of Raton about enough to erect the building. In fact, the mayor stated to the writer that it cost the city so much that they could not afford to have the financial statement printed in the Reporter so that the people might know of the expenditures occasioned—the right of the people at all times. The mandamus action of the property owners was also so expensive that the city is without funds to compile and have published in book form the ordinances of the city of Raton! Neither the Range nor the Reporter publish the proceedings of the regular meetings of the council—because (permit us to lie) the city must economize. Penny wise and pound foolish was never better illustrated.

"The Reporter does not wish it said of the institution that it is against public improvement—far from it. The Reporter encourages and foments all issues designed for the betterment of the city, but does not believe that a political organization has the right to take advantages of a condition to the extent that the property of the city can be promiscuously mortgaged or juggled at the will of the organization. And to add insult to injury—never a public statement given the people that they may determine the expenditure wise or unwise. The Reporter is published in this community that the people may read in its columns such business conduct of officials as should be published. Not one man in a hundred finds it convenient to attend council meetings, but all might know what our administration were doing if the administration were to cause to be published their deliberations. As it is we hear 'this and that,' 'it is said,' "Did you hear the city books were in bad shape?", "I see Shuler got a new phaeton the other day billed to the city," and all those unpleasant and nauseating rumors which come of failure to take the public into their confidence as they should be.

"It is the opinion of the Reporter that the administration would have served the people of Raton better had they drafted a new franchise which contemplated and embraced provisions adequate with the needs and service of the water consumers, and placed such document before the Raton

Water Works Company in lieu of a further extension of the franchise. The people of Raton do not expect the Raton Water Works Company to engage themselves into thousands of dollars of expense for improvements with their franchise expiring in 1916, and a threatening administration to deal with. This fact, at the ideal moment as it were, has brought the people of the city of Raton, face to face with a real problem—a problem that cannot be solved in a day and one which will materially affect the property values in Raton for over thirty years to come.

"Mr. Lawrence, executive head of the Water Works Company stated to a representative of the Reporter, that his company stood ready to make all necessary improvements in lieu of the proper extension of franchise, and that the administration were appraised of their good intentions through correspondence, said correspondence now on file in the office of the company. Mr. Lawrence states that the city administration absolutely ignored every reasonable overture made by them and so intent were the administration upon the bond issue that business foresight and economy in the interest of the property owners of the city of Raton were absolutely ignored and the correspondence either never answered or in a most evasive way. The Reporter asks the people of Raton if this is true—Have the administration, in saddling a $400,000 debt on us done their best for the city? If the people of the city of Raton want such proof, the Reporter is ready to publish such full and complete (not partial) correspondence as was entered into by the Water Company and the administration prior to the bond action as promulgated by the administration. The cold, hard facts of any situation are not the choicest reading, but most interesting, and a detailed publication of such facts would make more noise than the dynamite explosions upon Goat Hill.

"After the pipes are laid, the equalization reservoirs in and the money spent—where comes the water? The courts do not hold (as has been represented) that a city can file on and condemn water which is now being used for the benefit of the people. The water in the Sugarite is now being used for the benefit of the people of the city of Raton. The administration will have to face these facts as they well know and in facing them (before the courts) as they will be compelled to, is going to add further expense. The truth hurts no one—and by telling of it might save Raton thousands of dollars.

"The people of Raton are in need of the real TRUTH as surrounds the water question—unbiased and impartial facts, covering the full ground, and the Reporter (who as a minister of the Gospel is called) hears that call, and as ever, stands ready to defend the best interests of the city. The Reporter has no ax to grind, no political or pecuniary ambitions. We do not (as has been represented) 'do as we are told.' Quite the reverse. When the Reporter gets so low in the pale of its duty as to pen untruths for a few paltry dollars and publishes them to the world, it is then time for yours truly to 'give up the ship' and abandon all hope. When the Reporter employs its talents in the art of lying to deceive its subscribers it will never be while yours truly is at the wheel."

In 1910 The Raton Range became a daily newspaper which it is to this day. In 1930 its editors changed the name to the Evening Gazette but the people were too used to the other name and once again it was called The Raton Daily Range. Frank Pfieffer is owner and publisher; James Barber is the editor and doing a good job of it. The Reporter has ceased publication.

Water was always a major problem for Raton. Judge Moulton experimented with the first cistern as early as 1881. That same year the Raton Comet carried this interesting item: "About 1½ miles southward of town is a work being carried on, the importance of which is only equalled by the questions with which it is being performed. Last summer, a Mr. Spencer, assistant engineer of the water service, conceived the idea of sinking a large well in the locality named mainly for supplying the railroad demand. He selected a point to which all the natural drainage of the basin tends and now a splendid supply, in fact a surplus, proves the wisdom of his choice. The present stream pump throws a stream three inches in diameter which by no means equals the inflow. The proper foundations, etc., are now being built for a large pump house which will contain engines to throw a four inch stream so that the water supply of the shops, locomotives, etc., is well assured. It only remains to secure an equally good supply for domestic use and when this is done the question of water for Raton is settled for years to come." (The Comet Dec. 16, 1881). A Colorado paper dated February 24, 1882 stated: "The newly erected water tank near the Raton bank makes the water business much more convenient and profitable to the haulers." A few months later the Raton paper remarked: "Arrangements have been made to lay water mains on First Street and put in three fire plugs, one in each block where the principal business houses are located. The first thing to do is for citizens, especially the business man, to secure hose necessary in case of a fire. Fire plugs are of no account unless we can have a hose to conduct the water. Insurance will be much less and the companies will take risk more readily when they find out that property is properly protected by water works. Some steps ought to be taken at once in this regard so that we may raise funds for a hose company." The hose must have been procured for the following year we find: "Cheyenne Bill has been employed by the citizens of Raton to keep the hose carriage clean and in order for immediate use for he is said to be only genuine dude in Raton."

The Raton Artesian Well Company was formed to meet the needs and demands of the growing town. It debated the feasibility and advisability of buying an engine and pump, using them for pumping the water from the well to supply those needing water for irrigation and other purposes. At that time (1888) there was 1,500 ft. of water in the well and it was thought by many who had given attention to the water problem that the supply was inexhaustible and that the water would flow from the bottom as fast as the stream could be pumped during the day. The company proposed to pump water during the day and manufacture electric lights at night in sufficient quantities so as to furnish Raton with lights. By 1891 Raton could boast 25 water meters. A reservoir was built on Goat Hill but by 1898 was sadly in need of repairs. A. L. Hobbs, who was superintendent of the water works, had another one built but repaired the Goat Hill container so as to hold a supply of water for city use in case of repair work on the new main line between the city and the main reservoir for this would necessitate the cutting off of the main supply. The old reservoir that formerly supplied Raton was given new retaining walls and re-cemented throughout, and covered entirely with ventilators. This reservoir had a capacity of 75,000 gallons. The Raton Water Company began the work of laying 1,000 feet of water main on Fourth Street as early as 1883. April 28, 1904 the Raton Range carried this item:

"Monday afternoon at 1 P.M. E. C. Phillips & Son, Contractors, of Longmount, Colorado, with a large force of men and teams began work on the new reservoir for the Raton Waterworks Company to be located in the Sugarite canyon, three and a half miles above the present reservoir. Raton will have plenty of water for the new reservoir has a capacity of 60,000,000 gallons which is about double the old reservoir, a supply adequate for a city of about 12,000 people and will cost about thirty thousand dollars."

Raton was then a city of about 6,000, yet for all its prediction, as the city grew, water again became a problem. In 1914 bonds were floated. The city of Raton voted an expenditure of $400,000. Eventually the problem seemed to be solved to the satisfaction of all. It was until 1945. The Bookout Construction Company seems to have done the job and Raton will have water for many years to come.

The Baptist services were held in the Craigmyle school in 1881. The Episcopalians received the services of Rev. Boyle of Trinidad. The Methodist congregation held services in Bayne & Frank's Hall. Catholics had Mass in various homes until a little brick church was erected on Third Street. J. O. Osfield and J. Boyle gave the use of their home to Father Accosini of Springer for Sunday Masses until the little church was dedicated to St. Patrick in 1883. It had a tower and two bells. When the new church was built this was sold as a private residence. It may still be seen opposite the Raton Range building, minus the tower. Other churches were built with the growth of the city for Raton boasted religious affiliations in sixty-five denomination. At times when a congregation is too small to maintain their own church it rents the hall of the public library. It is a city proud of the religious attendance of its people to the various churches.

RAYADO, NEW MEXICO

In point of settlement Rayado is the oldest inhabited place on the Maxwell Land Grant, both for the Indians as well as for the White Man. It is saved from the ranks of the Ghost Towns because of the tremendous Boy Scout movement at Philmont Ranch. Because of Philmont Rayado has become famous both nationally and internationally. Rayado is a sweet sounding name with but little meaning for people not interested in this particular section of the country. But a visit to the grand daughters of Carlos Beaubien, J. Abreu and Valdez who were born at Rayado convinced me that here was the most fascinating area in all the Grant. Times change, but these last noblewomen of the Valdez and Rayado tracts carry on, indifferent to the changes in the world about them. For they know the truth about the past and the dangers they lived through not so much to survive as to out-wit the ever hungry Indians who always made it a point to drop in for supper especially when the men were away on a business trip.

Carlos Beaubien's grand daughter is in her 70's. She is sedate, kind, amiable; her eyes sparkle as she re-lives the old days of her childhood at Rayado. She has a gracious manner, and in short, terse sentences she photographs on your mind the activities of pioneer-day Rayado that makes you believe you have thrown back time and walk the fields with Indian Agents, merchants, Santa Fe traders, Utes, Jicarillas, outlaws, ranchers, soldiers and Indian scouts. Many was the time the little mite of a girl was closeted against the sudden raids of the perpetual Indians who were interested in carrying her off to be sold to Navajos as a slave and the reasonable price of five dollars. She remembered Maxwell's rambling twenty-room house and Carson's place and the tales that were told there about her primos because she was related to Carson and Maxwell. The Abreu tract was on the Maxwell Land Grant as well as the Valdez tract. Her mother and dad once owned quite a portion of the Grant but Maxwell bought them out. They later bought back about twenty thousand acres which became their home place. This country the Abreu family knew—here they were born, went to school, grew up and married. Phillips of Oklahoma bought their place, tore it down because he wanted no other home on his ranch in an effort to re-claim the wild life and re-capture the days of the cattle barons. Perhaps because he thought of the country as primitive he turned it over to the Boys Scouts of America.

Maxwell's home at Rayado was big. No doubt about that. He was used to bigness because he was born in a mansion at Kaskaskia; his father-in-law had a big place at Taos, and he had promised his bride, Luz Beaubien, a home she could roam around in. It stood to the left of the Abreu home in plaza style as a protection against Indians and outlaws. One day three outlaws stopped the young Abreu boy who was on his way to Cimarron, built up by Maxwell after leaving Rayado, to buy medicine for his sick mother, Beaubien's daughter. The only thing that saved him from death was his age. This much must be said to advantage for the outlaws of Rayado and Cimarron, they respected women and children. While Maxwell's home was tremendous, Carson's was poverty-stricken by way of comparison. He was never able to live sumptuously neither at Taos nor in Colorado. He was too much on the go and he had a family of seven to provide for. Not that Maxwell did not have just as much, it was just the difference in the two men. Carson's home at Rayado, built of adobe, was in back of the Abreu home which faced the garrison wall on the plaza.

The Abreu home (as well as the Maxwell house) was built with an eye on protection from Indian raids. Maxwell's home contained an inner plaza as well as an outer one. With the military garrison opposite afforded as much protection as Bent's fort. The gates could be closed and wagons placed in the center of the plaza sheltered by Abreu's home, Maxwell's mercantile store and home and the military post. The corrals formed the other section.

The Abreu house as well as the Maxwell house and the military post at Rayado was mostly the work of one man by the name of John Holland. He never married and in his old age was affectionately known as "Uncle Jack." He came to New Mexico with the army as an expert carpenter and was the only soldier at Rayado that knew anything about the cannon that surmounted the walls, hence his nickname of El Artillero (Artilleryman). When the military post of Rayado was moved to Fort Union, Holland mustered out of the army and became associated with Joseph Pley, Abreu and Maxwell in the mercantile business. He later settled in Cimarron and seems to have been very prominent in the affairs of the Maxwell Land Grant Company.

The only reason why Jose Pley has been overlooked by all students of the Grant is the fact that so little is known about him. He was a Spaniard who worked his way in with some French-Canadian trappers about the time that Maxwell found his way to Taos, and became acquainted with Carlos Beaubien who gave him a job as a clerk in his store. Later he took over in the Beaubien store at Mora and became a partner of Maxwell's at Rayado. He was Lee's administrator following the Taos Massacre of 1847. Pley seems to have had little to do with the Grant on paper but there is a suspicion that he prepared much of the groundwork in sales to Fort Union, beef to the Indians, collecting rents, working up auctions, ordering stock, and running the business in general. He was married to Lee's oldest daughter. It was he who built the beautiful home, Holland being the contractor, that was later to be known as the Abreu residence. It faced the garrison wall on the south side of the plaza. Pley, having difficulty with his wife who could never get used to the wilderness, nor live down the Massacre, sold out to the Abreu family, lived for a time at San Luis in Colorado and finally returned to Spain where he ended his days.

The Abreu family that bought the Pley home has more history in its little finger than most historical families have in their whole bodies. It just has not been written up. The Abreus were connected with the revolution of 1837 when Gonzolez, the Taos Indian, was proclaimed governor. They also brought the first printing press to New Mexico. Their home was always open to weary travelers who came through over the Santa Fe trail cut-off. Because of the strategic position, the government put up a cantonment that helped to make Rayado safe from outlaws and Indians. Kit Carson said:

"I passed the Rayado country in 1844, with Lucien B. Maxwell, and saw large fields of corn, beans, pumpkins, and other products, and a great deal of land cultivated, and several houses built on the Big Cimarron river, one of the small streams on the grant. I went there and settled myself with Richard Owens, and several others in 1845; we built houses, and I alone had 15 acres under cultivation. I left in August of the same year for California. The settlement was occupied from 1844 up to this time (1857) every year. Lucien B. Maxwell settled on the Rayado, a stream within the grant, in 1849, and still lives there at this time (1857). There are about 200 acres under cultivation, about $15,000 in buildings, and about 15,000 head of stock."

Even after the American occupation, for several years, as Jose Franco testifies, Lucien Maxwell was the only resident there. Many of the smaller adobe homes Maxwell put up for the families of the people working for him. Pley must have built his house with the coming of the garrison as Holland was either in the army or employed by the army. It was in October, 1850, that Bennet came to the garrison. Therefore, the quasi-fort must have been constructed in the spring of that year. It was built of adobe. Maj. Williams Nicholson Grier was commander. Rayado was not on the main road of the Santa Fe trail, but on a cut-off run by the stage company. This road met the old trail at a point called Puertecito (not to be confused with the little village of Puertocito near La Frague, now known as Sena). Here troops met the mail coaches. Bennet himself relates that he often left Rayado with a detachment of 20 men to meet the mail on the road from the United States (even in 1850 he could not be convinced that he was not on foreign land—it must have been quaint) to protect the mail from the Indians! These raiders must have been Comanches as we will see in the story of Wagonmound.

The government never had serious difficulty with the Indians at Cimarron, although at times it looked mighty possible. Bennet could appreciate the suffering of the pioneers, for sometimes he had to travel through two feet of snow, and once he found the mail-carriers almost frozen to death and the mules in like predicament, but more starved than frozen. They took the mail on to Barclay's fort (present day Watrous), where they no doubt remained until favorable weather. Winter seemed eternal to these young recruits from Ireland, Germany, and the Eastern United tSates, who felt they were at the edge of the world here at Rayado—recruits indeed, when Holland was the only man in the fort who knew the workings of the two cannon on the walls! Later on, these men built Fort Union probably under the direction of this same Holland. After Maxwell moved to Cimarron, and the soldiers to Fort Union, the adobes in the barracks were taken down brick by brick and moved to Cimarron to build homes for the grant people. Whigham, Crocker, and others lived in them. Several of these homes still stand opposite the stone jail in Cimarron.

Rayado was not to see much of the grant war because Abreu had a clear title. However, many of the participants often came to Rayado and while the danger from Indians seemed to wear off, the danger from outlaws and cattle rustlers increased. It was to the Abreu home that Clay Allison's cowboys came in search of Dr. Longwell, who seemed to be connected with the Santa Fe ring, a crime in their minds punishable by death — six shooter death. Mrs. Longwell came to the door. What was their business? Dr. Longwell, of course. Well, the doctor would see them but he was sick in bed with the smallpox. Perhaps if they went to his bedroom to discuss their business. They declined the invitation.

So, life went on even after the Maxwells and soldiers left. Abreu invited families to come in and sharecrop with him, building homes for them as Maxwell did. As many as 50 families lived around the Abreu house at one time. A priest was sent by Bishop Lamy, Father Antonio Forchegu, who lived at the Abreu home and said Mass there. He was a big man well over six feet, with shoulders as broad as his troubles. Outlaws and Indians learned to respect him. Carson, Maxwell, Allison, and Lambert counted him among their friends. When Cimarron outgrew Rayado, he moved to Cimarron for a time. He also said Mass for the Catholic soldiers at Fort Union. Later on he was appointed Vicar General of the Archdiocese of Santa Fe. He lies buried in a vault under the main altar of the Cathedral.

To develop further the religious atmosphere, the Abreus built a little chapel dedicated to the Sacred Heart. It was blessed by Archbishop Pitaval in 1900. Father Haggerdorn came over from Springer to say Mass, and the little chapel was deeded over to the Archdiocese of Santa Fe. Father Splinters also was very well known at Rayado, as well as Father Garcia (who celebrated his 60th ordination anniversary last year in Trinidad, Colorado and is still as spry as he was when he drove his surrey to Rayado).

When Phillips bought the Rayado place, he left the church standing but not the Abreu home. With the development of the Rayado township Abreu moved to Rito de La Maquina a short way from Rayado. There he built a two-story, 14-room house. When Phillips bought the tract, he leveled it leaving two rooms for employees. The Phillips of Philmont ranch, I am told, was not the oilman, but his brother. Since the land was turned over by Phillips to the Boy Scouts of America, boys from every part of the country have an opportunity to see Carson's and Maxwell's —two of Fremont's scouts—old stamping ground. Buffalo Bill was around this country too, and it was near Rayado that their few weeks' stay each summer is well worth what they read and hear about it in the winter.

No more fitting place can conjure up in the minds of these famous scouts, the really famous scouts who preceded them; Williams, Wallace, Maxwell, Dold, Charettee, Le Doux, Carson, and a host of others whose names are in every scout-lore book in the land. The name Rayado seems to be going, however, for the name Carson-Maxwell. That seems to be the new post-office, from what I understand. Yet, neither of these lived there as long as the Indian for whom the place is named. Rayado means streaks. There was on old Indian chief, Ute or Comanche (more likely Ute since they had settled in the district), who built a hut there and isolated himself for some unknown reason from his tribe. He was tatooed about the face and over these lines he streaked multicolored paints. Hence the name Rayado. There he died. Whether his tribe buried him there or another spot has not been recorded for history.

When Bennet saw the place for the first time in 1850, he wrote: "There are but a few people at Rayado and only about 10 houses besides the soldiers' quarters."

In 1910, the Rayado Colonization company was formed. Here is a sample of their folders put out for the sale of the land:

In preparing this little booklet, we have put forth an honest effort to give to the purchasers accurate information for their guidance in making an investment, or in changing their location.

In this booklet we have included some letters from farmers and fruit-growers in the vicinity of the Rayado Ranch. We think that The Rayado Ranch, with its combined resources, which are herein explained, will produce results similar to those attained by others in our vicinity. We are conscientious in our belief that everyone purchasing a tract will be pleased with the investment.

There are many millions of men and women today working as clerks in the congested cities of the East, who know that their weekly wages are supplying them only with the necessities of life, it taking almost every dollar they receive to provide for their families. They dread to think of the days when younger men and women will take their places, days when it will be difficult for them, in their old age, to secure employment. The time to provide for your old age is when you are young and in your prime. Our object in placing this property on the market in small tracts is to give the wage-earner an opportunity to save $10.00 per month from his wages and invest it in the land. If you do not take advantage of this opportunity to purchase a home on easy terms, it is your own fault, for the price and payments are within your reach.

When you are old, you cannot depend on your friends. You all know that YOUR DOLLAR IS YOUR ONLY FRIEND. The more dollars you save, the more friends you gain. Begin saving now, and invest your savings in land, there is nothing better.

All of you have had dreams of the free country life, where you can do as you please, and breathe God's fresh air, unspoiled by the dirt and grime of the city.

We think that the APPLE will be the star fruit of this vicinity, and are confident that even your small investment, if properly handled, will prove profitable to you.

Think this over carefully and do not condemn our proposition until you have investigated it thoroughly. Too many people make the mistake of forming an opinion on a proposition before they know anything about it whatever. Don't do this, for if you will take the time to investigate, you will say that our proposition is better than we have represented it.

The population of the world doubles every twenty-seven years. There is a baby born in the United States nearly every minute, but no more land is made for it. Your boys are getting larger; they will soon want land. Emigrants keep coming into the United States by the thousands. Every hour in every day of the year the demand for land and the products of the land increases, but there is no more land.

Do you remember when Uncle Sam was giving away farms in Kansas, Nebraska and Colorado? All that is worth while is gone now; yes, they are still pushing farther and farther into the West.

At a recent opening of a large section under the auspices of the Government, there were many thousand more applications than there was land to be sold. The demand for Western land already seems greater than the supply.

Some of you are wondering why this land was not thrown open for settlement before. The facts are these: In the early days most of the land in New Mexico was given in large tracts called "grants," to individuals for services they performed for the Mexican government, and until the last few years these grants have been owned by parties who did not want to subdivide them into small tracts. It is with pleasure that we are able to offer one of these favored grants in small tracts on easy terms.

Immense fortunes have been made in the last few years by men who purchased the land while it was cheap. If you have failed to take advantage of former opportunities, here is one more chance for you to get a small tract of land on EASY TERMS.

In introducing our proposition to the public, we wish to quote Chapter 33 of Burdette's "Life of Kit Carson":

Arriving again in Taos to carry into effect at once the resolution he had formed of establishing a permanent home, he (Carson) joined his old friend Maxwell in the purpose of occupying a BEAUTIFUL ROMANTIC VALLEY, fifty miles east of Taos, called by the Indians 'Rayado'.

"Through the center of this valley flows a broad mountain stream, and for the loveliness of the scenery, or the fertility of its broad, sloping basin, or the mountain supply of timber, there can scarcely be found a spot to equal it. Carson and Maxwell established a settlement about midway in the valley, and at the present date have an imposing little village, in which the houses of Carson and Maxwell are prominent."

The above description refers to THE RAYADO RANCH, which is now being developed by THE RAYADO COLONIZATION COMPANY, Denver, Colorado.

Kit Carson and Maxwell at the time they selected this tract of land as their permanent home, had practically the entire West from which to select. The ruins of Kit Carson's home still remain as a monument to his memory, and may be seen at the present date on this land.

Having spent considerable time in selecting a body of land that would be suitable in every respect for colonization, and one that embraces all the essential features for fruit-growing, general farming and grazing, together with plenty of timber necesasry for the successful development of the colony, we recommend this tract of land.

You have heard how independent the truck farmers and fruit growers have become in the past few years, their land having increased 100 to 500 per cent in value, and no doubt you have many times desired to own such a farm, but your limited means have not allowed you to make the purchase—first, because it required more money than you could command to swing such a deal, and second, because you were required to purchase a larger tract of land than you could handle.

In order to meet the wants of PEOPLE OF LIMITED MEANS, the land will be surveyed into not more than 2,000 tracts, or divisions.

THE PRICE for the purpose of quick sale, we have fixed at $250.00 a contract; payable $20.00 down, and $10.00 per month, or a discount of 5 per cent will be allowed to parties paying all cash upon signing of the contract; no interest or taxes until deed is issued. We consider that each and every purchaser will get VALUE RECEIVED.

WE OFFER NO GAME OF CHANCE OR LOTTERY, but are selling this land in tracts as a straightforward business proposition, that will command the consideration of every person who wants to make a profitable and safe investment to purchase a home on EASY TERMS.

This oportunity is the chance that seldom comes to THOSE WHO NEED IT MOST.

ONE GOOD INVESTMENT IS WORTH A LIFETIME OF LABOR, and all we ask is for you to read carefully this booklet. WE INVITE THE CLOSEST INVESTIGATION of our proposition.

It is our aim to make the irrigated part of this ranch a veritable city of small farms and orchards — a high class community of farmers and fruit growers.

THE RAYADO RANCH is situated in the southern part of COLFAX COUNTY, NEW MEXICO, and consists of about 30,000 acres, of which about 12,000 acres are susceptible to irrigation.

About 5,000 acres are timbered land, and the balance grazing or pasture land, part of which could be cultivated.

Endeavoring to equalize the value of the different tracts, or divisions of land into which The Rayado Ranch is to be surveyed, we are dividing the land into four different classes, as follows:

Class "A". About 3,000 acres. Irrigable river bottom, or vega land, to be surveyed into five-acre tracts, or divisions.

Class "B". About 8,000 acres. Irrigable mesa, or second bottom land, including a small amount of vega, or river bottom land, not quite as desirable as Class "A", to be surveyed into ten-acre tracts, or divisions.

Class "C". Mountainous and mesa timbered land, also a few tracts of mesa land susceptible to irrigation, and pasture land, to be surveyed into 15, 20 and 30-acre tracts, or divisions.

Class "D". Grazing, or pasture land, to be surveyed into tracts of 40 acres and larger.

The size of each tract, or division, to be determined by its character and location, and other points generally used in determining the value of land, and in our judgement, all tracts, NOTWITHSTANDING THEIR SIZE, are to be as nearly of the same value as possible.

The water to be used for the irrigation of these lands will be conveyed by deed from, or certificate of stock in, The Rayado Land and Irrigation Company, which Company owns the water rights that go with the Ranch. This means that the irrigation system will be owned and controlled by the owners of the irrigated land. The shares of water stock or deed will be delivered to the purchaser simultaneously with the warranty deed.

There will be set aside daily 10 per cent of the money received from the sale of the contracts. This money will be placed in a fund with The Continental Trust Company of Denver, Colorado, to be expended and paid out by The Rayado Colonization Company, for the construction of ditches and headgates to the land to be irrigated. This 10 per cent will be considered a contribution by the holders of contracts for the development of the water and water rights, and the construction of headgates and ditches for the use of any or all the lands to be irrigated.

Each applicant when he makes his payment and executes a contract will receive from the company a receipt showing that when he has made the last payment to be made on his contract, the Company will issue to him a CERTIFICATE, stating that he shall have credit on any tract of land purchased by himself, or his accredited representative at the auction, to the extent of $250.00.

No assignment of this certificate or the contract will be binding upon the Company, unless duly made on the blank form printed on the back thereof, and presented to the Company for registration and acceptance. No assignment of less than the entire interest in this certificate or the contract shall be made by the purchaser. Any attempt to do so will not be recognized by the Company.

The Company will not issue more than one certificate for each tract of land to be sold at the auction, and in no event more than 2,000.

When all contracts are sold and paid for, the Company will notify each Contract Holder in good standing, at the address given in his contract of the time and place for such Contract Holders to meet for the auction. When the Contract Holders by themselves, or their representatives, have assembled for the auction, they shall elect by a majority vote from among their number, three Trustees, who shall appoint an auctioneer, who shall proceed to auction and sell the different tracts of land at a bona-fide competitive auction to the highest bidder for cash; provided, in lieu of cash, the holder of a contract may have credit on the amount bid in the sum theretofore paid on his contract. Payment of all sums bid in excess of $250.00 on any one tract, shall be made either in cash to the auctioneer at the time of the bid or upon such terms as may be satisfactory to the three Trustees. The bidding will be open and competitive, and no lottery, or game, or scheme of distribution by lot or chance will enter into same. All moneys derived from this sale over the contract price of $250.00 shall be placed in a fund with The Continental Trust Company of Denver, Colorado, which overbid, if any, will be repaid by The Rayado Colonization Company to the Contract Holders, in good standing at the time of the auction, pro rata, as a dividend; thus reducing the cost of each man's tract of land. Contract Holders in good standing, or their accredited representatives only, will be allowed to bid. The Company will furnish to the Trustees selected for the benefit of the Contract Holders collectively, an abstract of title, together with an opinion of a reputable attorney, that the title to said Rayado Ranch in fee simple, is vested in said Company, and that the said Rayado Ranch is free from all indebtedness.

Each Contract Holder, or his accredited representative, must buy a tract of land for each contract he holds or represents, for not less than the contract price of $250.00 on any one tract, at the time of the auction, there being as many tracts as there are contracts.

During the auction no one but Contract Holders in good standing, or their accredited representatives, can take part.

In our judgment all tracts are practically of the same value, but if a Contract Holder, or his accredited representative, at the time of the auction shall pick out a tract that he considers more valuable or desirable he may bid as much for it at the auction over the minimum price as he desires. The Contract Holders, through the Trustees, elected by themselves, or representatives, shall conduct the auction. THIS IS POSITIVELY NOT A DRAWING NOR A LOTTERY, but simply A BONA-FIDE COMPETITIVE AUCTION, thrown open to all Contract Holders, or their accredited representatives, with no arranged order for bidding, and where each and every Contract Holder, or his accredited representative, has equal rights.

Each Contract Holder, or accredited representative, may buy one tract for each contract he holds or represents. This gives the Contract Holder, or his accredited representative, the opportunity of buying his land in a body at the auction.

A WARRANTY DEED will be executed by the Company to each purchaser, for the property purchased by himself, or his accredited representative, at the auction, as soon after the auction as a complete list of the tracts sold, together with a list of the purchasers thereof, shall be furnished the Company by the Trustees, and deeds can be properly drawn. This warranty deed will be deposited with The Continental Trust Company of Denver, Colorado, to be delivered to the purchaser upon the delivery of his certificate, together with his receipt for the overbid, if any to The Continental Trust Company. The warranty deed and water right will be issued to the party named in the certificate, or his assignee, as registered on our books, or to his heirs.

The Company will also survey all of said land to be sold and furnish to each Contract Holder at the address given in the contract, at least thirty days before the time of sale, a plat of the property, also a fair description of the various tracts, or divisions, into which it has been surveyed, so as to enable each Contract Holder to have a fair idea of the value of each tract, or division, of land.

In case of an oversale of contracts the Company reserves the right to reject all over 2,000 contracts, and those received at our office at Denver, Colorado, first, shall have the preference right.

Free round-trip transportation to the land will be furnished the representative of any club of twenty or more Contract Holders in any one town to see if our proposition is as represented in this booklet, provided, that said representative shall within three days after his arrival at Springer, New Mexico, therefrom wire The Rayado Colonization Company at Denver, Colorado, that the proposition is, or is not, as represented herein. If your representative wires that our proposition is not as represented in this booklet, we will refund your money to you.

> Little drops of water
> On little grains of sand
> Make the big red apples
> On Rayado Valley land.

> Oh, those juicy big red apples,
> And the fancy price they'll bring,
> Will make you wish you had some land,
> As land is just the thing.

> We're raising Ganos and Jonathans,
> Winter sorts and fall,
> But the "Cimarron" is the apple
> It's the best one of them all.

We offer now small tracts of land
For the man of moderate means,
We'll take him to New Mexico
Where the sunshine always beams.

Water, sun and soil
Make those big red apples fine,
And if you want some of this land
You had better get in line.

SPRINGER, NEW MEXICO

Springer was founded because of the Santa Fe railroad. While the officials of that line were grateful for the use of the right of way through the Grant, it realized that unnecessary expense would be involved in laying track eastwards to reach Cimarron then westwards and south again to reach Las Vegas and Albuquerque. It is amazing the number of officials of the Maxwell Land Grant Company who were also officials on the Santa Fe. This harmony accounted for the ease with which the railroad had its say-so in exactly where it would lay tracts. Springer, the lawyer was honored on this occasion. The depot on this section of the railroad was named for him. The town took its name from the railroad depot. Chase, in his *"Editor's Run"* passed by the place in 1882 to note: "Springer is a station started a year and a half ago, when the railroad went through this locality. It has a depot, two stores, an adobe hotel, a billiard or pool hall, and a dozen little houses. It expects to be larger, but what shall build it up a passing stranger cannot see. But it has trade from ranchmen a hundred and fifty miles east. The store of Clothier & Porter did a business of $60,000 last month. A ranchman may not come often but when he does, he loads up $300.00 to $1,200 worth of goods, and departs for headquarters. The store alluded to is about 150 feet long and is full of everything used by man or beast, from a cambric needle to a four horse wagon."

D. A. Clouthier was close to the Maxwell Land Grant and a contributing factor in uniting it since through his marriage with one of the Beaubien girls, he inherited a part of the grant through his wife. A native of Canada, this French-Canadian found his way to Taos, clerked for Carlos Beaubien, then for Maxwell, started the Clouthier ranch on the Grant, and formed a partnership with Parker for a warehouse and mercantile business in Springer. At the time Springer was founded he was county-treasurer, the county seat being at Cimarron. Later he went into the Second Hand Furniture business. He was one of Springer's first citizens and should be called the founder of Springer since it through his efforts that Springer survived and became a town. To understand the growth of Springer we will itemize the accounts as they have come to us to retain the flavor of the times without embellishing the truth of the happenings. Too many incidents concerning New Mexico have been glossed so that the truth is hardly recognizable and the people are more readily attuned to believe the "George Washington Slept Here" as gospel than the fact that he was dead and buried before the place ever saw light of day. A point in question is the belief that so many people of Cimarron have that Kit Carson slept at the St. James—Lambert Hotel. If he did he came back from his grave two years after his demise to do so.

Springer—January 23, 1882—Dr. Sherman told us that he had made arrangements to build his store house which as soon as completed, will be filled with a fine line of drugs and all articles carried by first class apothecaries.

That enterprising firm, Messrs. Harmon and Small, our butchers and Livery men, are doing a lively business, as is evinced by the corral and stables being filled to overflowing nightly.

We opine for Springer within the next twelve months: a wholesale and retail hardware store and a boot and shoe store. Let them come, plenty of room and plenty of customers can easily be found.

As yet the murder of young Broeksmit is wrapped in mystery. His father P. S. Broeksmit, from Cedar Rapids, Iowa, arrived last week, and will, we are told, remove his son's remains to his Iowa home for final interment.

The addition to the depot is fast nearing completion. The old one is too small to hold the freight put off here and Springer being quite a shipping point for ranches and towns adjacent, the Santa Fe was compelled to enlarge their quarters.

Henry Kingman, superintendent of Porter & Clouthier's mammoth warehouse tells us business is simply rushing in his department.

Out of a possible attendance of 25 scholars, our school average for the past week was 21. Now that we have a school here, it would behoove stockmen around us to send their children. Board can be obtained at a very reasonable figure. Any branch can be taught from ABC's to highest mathematics, and if desired Latin or Greek. There is now no use sending children to the States to be educated.

While down at Springer this week (February 10, 1882) we met Thomas Tindall, of the firm of Tindall & Company, contractors and builders. They have been working on Porter & Clouthier's store and warehouse for about a month. An addition of 30x75 feet has been made to the rear of the warehouse, giving the store a depth of 275 feet. 30x52 feet has been added to the retail department, making the retail room 30x102 feet. The carpenter work is all first class, and Porter & Clouthier are well pleased with the job. Tindall & Company inform us that they have contracts ahead in Springer to keep them busy till late in the spring, and that there will be a great deal of building done there the coming season.

The county commissioners held a meeting at Cimarron on May 8, 1882, to consider proposals for the erection of county buildings at Springer. From George Pace, one of the commissioners we learn the following result: That the contract for all the buildings and all the work, with the exception of the steel cells, was awarded to W. H. Wilex, of Cimarron, at $9,800. This is the whole sum and substance of the matter. The contract has been awarded and the buildings will be put up at once at Springer. The awarding of this contract is contrary to our judgment—contrary to the wish and desire of the majority of voters and taxpayers of Colfax county. The commissioners who voted for the measure will yet rue their action. We do not mean to say that the commissioners who voted for the measure were insincere, for we believe them to be honest gentlemen and think they acted as they thought right. Marcy and Valdez voted for the appropriation; Pace against it. Four steel cells and corridor were erected by P. J. Pawley & Brothers for $7,800.

Over on Colbert avenue, Jackson put up his leading hotel. On the corner of Third and Maxwell, Bob Stepp sold wine, liquors, and cigars in his opera house and saloon. M. W. Mills opened up his law office in competition with William C. Wrigley, and at times was Senator Dorsey's agent for the Starr Route about Springer. Charles Ilfeld was inviting the women in to see those elegant satin dresses or to take home a sack of the finest potatoes ever put on the Springer market.

The Grand Jury was calling attention of the court to "the necessity of building a wall around our jail. The sufferings of the unfortunate devils confined there at present deprived as they are of exercise, demands a change of some kind. Humanity is shocked by torture of beasts; much more so when applied to men. Let the county commissioners order these men taken out, even in shackles, to breathe the fresh air daily. Dr. Dudlum, our county physician, has time and again called the attention of the officials to this matter."

By 1884, it was graduated from a pioneer village to big time, so that it could sit back as a quiet big brother and wink at some of the carryings-on in the newer villages, or even in itself with the cowboy feuds or the Anti-Grant war.

The Colfax County Stockman advertised itself as "The only genuine newspaper of genuine stamina in the whole of northern New Mexico." with the added admonition: "And don't you forget it." Joseph Imbery, in his barber shop on Third Street, was wondering whether the Northern New Mexico Cattle and Stock growers' association would pay the $250.00 fine for anyone reporting a cattle rustler, or turning in anyone illegally burning the grass. The grass about Springer was gamma, although cattlemen would have the visitor believe that one ton of it cured was better than two tons of timothy, and that it was the best domesticated grass in the country. One door west of the post office, J. Wagoner was not so worried. He had plenty of patrons for his Montezuma restaurant. Just now settled and complacent Springer was in 1884 can be gathered from the Fourth of July celebration:

"It was remarkably quiet; more so than is usual in other days, a majority of our American citizens having taken the advantage of cheap railroad fare and hied themselves to other localities to have their fun. Nothing was heard to disturb the quietude of the still, warm air but the firing of the national salute of thirty-nine guns in the forenoon, and the sweet strains of music wafted on the breeze from Cipriano Lara's string band, which led the members of "La Sociedad Filantropica" in grand procession around the city, each bedecked with a handsome rosette, the badge of the order, preceded by the Stars and Stripes. In the afternoon a public meeting was held by the society at the court house at which some business was transacted and several patriotic Union speeches were indulged in, interlaced with music from the band. In the evening the members of the society repaired with their families to Bob Stepp's opera house, and engaged in a very enjoyable dance, which was largely attended, and lasted until after midnight and thus ended the celebration of the day which all true Americans loved."

If July 4, 1884, was quiet for the citizens, it was a busy day at the jail. Six men were the guests. Jailer Bunn, in order to give them a little exercise, had them sweep out the jail, wash dishes, and cut wood. About 4 P.M. just after three of the men had come in from cutting wood, and as the jailer was locking the outer door, one of the prisoners struck him over the head with a large piece of wood, cutting a terrible gash but not knocking him down. The paper continues: "Laughlin, Lopez, and Garcia then jumped upon him and tried to throw him, and for five minutes a desperate struggle took place between the three convicts and the jailer, the prisoners holding the jailer in such a position it was impossible for him to reach for his revolver. They finally secured it, and after hitting the jailer a terrible blow on the head they secured him, putting irons on his hands and feet and throwing him in a cell. They then proceeded to set out guards, rob their prisoner of $160, taking one or two revolvers, and lay down the law to Brennan (another prisoner) as to how he should act, because he refused to join their efforts to escape. He was the prisoner they nearly pounded to death a few days before because he refused to come in on the plan. They waited in the jail from 4 till 7, determined to kill any person coming near the jail. After dark the five took Brennan, and making him proceed in front, they marched out, took five horses, two of which belonged to Donacio Olone, and started east. Several miles from town they dropped Brennan, who immediately rode into town to rescue the jailer Bunn. He had been gagged. As soon as Brennan hit town, he gave the alarm. It was nearly 12:00 P.M.

A large crowd gathered at the court house where Brennan was working like a Turk cutting a hole in the brick wall in order to get at the jailer, and relieve him, as the runaways had locked up everything when they left and threw away the keys. Bunn was found more dead than alive. Men started for Cimarron the next morning, and others, in company with Bunn, took the road to Vegas. Sheriff Stockton and Deputy Hixenbaugh came down on an early freight and investigated the matter satisfactorily.

"Since April, the men (four of them) had been sentenced to the penitentiary but have languished in the Colfax county jail, when they should have been in Leavenworth. They have been penned up in their cells here during this hot weather, with no exercise or fresh air, until life has become a torture, and they determined to make an escape, even if it cost them their lives rather than remain in jail." J. H. Hunt, the Justice of Peace of Raton who sentenced Brennan for robbing the Person of one Frank McSwiggan in May, revoked the sentence when he heard the part Brennan had played in releasing Judson Bunn. Whether the three were ever caught, I have not been able to find out; the records are silent. Red McLaughlin, who was in jail for stealing Bob Barton's gold watch, left a letter at Bunn's side:

"This is to certify that I, Red, do say that in all my experience I never saw a man with more courage than was shown by Jailer Judson Bunn. I acknowledge that we proved ourselves three cowardly curs of the first water in taking advantage of one man. But the truth is, we were compelled to . . . The county commissioners, together with Judge Axtell, are responsible for the act. They sent me to jail without any evidence whatsoever, and this is how I return the compliments. I am sorry Judd Bunn is the victim. I will see Judge Axtell before I leave the territory, and see him to his sorrow . . . etc."

Meantime, realizing the growth of the town, the archbishop of Santa Fe cut off Springer district from the Bueyeros parish and turned it over to the Rev. A. J. Accorcini, who came to be known as the "Pastor of Colfax County." His district was larger than many present-day archdioceses. A church was erected; Mrs. Alfred Clouthier was engaged as organist, Mrs. Keller, Mrs. Luna, and Mrs. Cowan banded together as an Altar society. By 1886, Father Accorcini was inviting in priests from Watrous and Tiptonville for Solemn Masses. The growth of Raton and Blossburg caused him to relinquish much of the care to the extent that at times Springer had to go without its Sunday Masses. The church was dedicated to St. Joseph.

On March 29, 1886, Father Accorcini wrote: Henceforth I shall be at Blossburg and Raton on the third Sunday of the month, so that there will be no services in Springer on the third Sunday. My parish is big and extended. I have sent in my resignation of Elizabethtown as a portion of my parish. I will visit Ute Park once a month instead of Elizabethtown."

On May 30 of that year, the people were impressed with his First Communion class. April, three years later, the Catholic Church society of Springer purchased five acres of ground above the town and west of the railroad for a cemetery. By August of that year, the new church and parochial school on the hill northeast of town so attracted settlers that the trend for building moved in that direction, so that today the church seems to be near the center of town.

Before the county seat controversy, the town had over 1,000 population. A local editor boosted it by writing: "This town is located on the Cimarron river, has a fine system of Holly waterworks, two churches, fine system of public schools—with a $10,000 school building in the progress of erection—cement works, stone quarries, fire clay, coal and alum near at hand. Two bridges span the Cimarron at the town, and a magnificent farming country of undulating plains, all under the great Springer ditch system, surrounds the town."

To give the pros and cons of the fight with Raton for the county seat would open old wounds. Was Raton justified in moving the seat from Springer? Since the seat is now at Raton it would be best to save it for the Raton Story. My only comment is that the people of Springer are not unworthy of a county seat.

Padre Garcia, who recently celebrated his 60th anniversary of ordination at Trinidad, Colorado worked for a time at Springer after Father Accorcini. Father Cellier and Father Lambert also saw service there before the coming of the Oblate Fathers from Texas. The Oblates of Mary Immaculate still work at Springer.

In November, 1906, Springer saw disaster. A fire originated in the kitchen of a small restaurant spreading its flames to the main store of the Floersheim Mercantile company, the warehouse of Talle, the saloon of Candido Olona, the mercantile company of Salazar and Warder, and two of three other business houses. Despite the fact, Springer went on even when a short time later a money panic closed down improvements in every town in the United States, Springer put on new life and sought in various ways to prove that a town can try and succeed. Old Lady Elizabeth Pascoe, who had settled near what later became Elizabethtown, and ran the Springer hotel from 1883, was an inspiration. She died at Ft. Collins, Colorado, in 1908. Springer incorporated in 1910. The new opera house was known as Porter's and later as the Springer. It does not exist today.

In 1907 a paper noted: "The old county courthouse built in the time when Springer was the county seat at the cost of $20,000, and which was abandoned since the removal of the seat to Raton, is fast falling into decay and the building will soon be a total loss to the community." Someone has pointed out the courthouse as a school." It would be nice to see the edifice as a Colfax county museum, since Raton does not have such interests. It would be a monument to the heritage that is Springer's."

The Sisters of Mercy have charge of the parochial school at Springer. At Springer also is the State Industrial school. Here Byrch Telford is trying to rehabilitate the boys. One does not feel imprisoned here. There is nothing confining about the place. It struck me as a big boarding school with farm attached. Telford may have an answer for all the other schools of the country, and Springer will not forget to honor him.

The idea of moving the county seat to Raton did not set too well with Springer. Led by Salazar, the county clerk, every effort was made to guard the courthouse so that the records would not be transferred to Raton. But despite Salazar's vigilance the records were taken to the Gate City. Springer hurt at the injustice had a little ditty which told just how they felt about it. Everytime a citizen of Springer met another they asked if the permission for taking a walk or for speaking, eating or sleeping came from Raton. The ditty expressed very well what they had in mind:

I

The injunction got a big black eye,
    Carry the news to Raton
And Colfax people now eat pie,
    Carry the news to Raton.

II

Carry the news to Collier,
    Carry the news to Voohees
Carry the news and give them the blues
    Carry the news to Raton

III

They tried to wipe out the town of Springer
    Carry the news to Raton
But in all their efforts they couldn't swing her
    Carry the news to Raton.

IV

Carry the news that will give them the blues
    Carry the intelligence to the Commercial Club
Carry the news that will give them the blues
    Carry the news to Raton.

"We understand that C. F. Remsberg of Raton, the foreman of the last Grand Jury, now says that the recommendation by that body to enlarge the courthouse, was slipped in without his knowledge. This is a lame excuse at best, but proceedings of that body leaked out, and at the last session the clerk, Albert Shaw, refused to embody the recommendation in the report, but as it passed with fifteen majority, the foreman very promptly compelled Mr. Shaw to do so. And now Mr. Remsberg says, like any boy being caught in the act, 'it wasn't me, 'twas him.' (*Colfax County Stockman, July, 8, 1893.*)

"On Tuesday night just after twelve o'clock an alarm of fire aroused people from their beds, when it was discovered that the Aztec Hotel building was the victim. When discovered, the kitchen, a brick addition to the building, was burning, and if there had been water the fire could have been easily quenched as the wind was quite strong from the west, while the fire was on the east side of the structure. But there was no water and the fire had full sway, for men could do nothing and in a few moments the whole of the large building was in flames and it was totally destroyed.

"The house was unoccupied and how the fire originated is not questioned. It was an incendiary act beyond doubt; but whose hand did the devilish work is yet to be ascertained. The building belonged to M. W. Mills, district attorney, and it is probable that the incendiary fire was the act of some one of those whom he has to prosecute. G. W. Abbott saw the fire first. He was coming up the street when he saw an explosion and a high flame flare up. He started for the fire alarm bell, but immediately noticed that it seemed to be all dark again in that direction so he did not ring the alarm but went up to the building to investigate. He then found fire burning under the kitchen floor and hastened to the fire bell and rang out the alarm. There can be no doubt of the incendiary origin of the fire. The building was insured for $1,000. (*Ibid, May 27, 1893.*)

"Springer has a large number and a great variety of dogs—some pedigreed—and she also has quite a sufficiency of lazy hogs and bum cows. If Springer was incorporated these things would not be thus; hence incorporate and do not let the county capitol be among the drags. (*Ibid, April 11, 1891.*)

"Honorable O. P. McMains, a former well known citizen of this country, was last week sentenced to jail for six months by the United States Court at Pueblo, Colorado, for intereefering with a United States Marshall. He has evidently found that bucking against Uncle Sam is somewhat different from intimidating Colfax county officials. (*Ibid, April 25, 1891.*)

Rev. A. Hoffman and Rev. Hyde have been engaged in good work in Springer during the past two weeks and their efforts will soon show up in a fine church building, if nothing more. They have held revival meetings here, enlisted the sympathies of many who were supposed to be case-hardened, made their meetings and their visits attractive and popular, so that when they undertook to raise money to build a church it was found to be very easy work. They are pleasant gentlemen, strong in their faith and take no undue advantage of Satan unless he is down and physically helpless, as we have been during their stay here. (*Ibid.*)

The record appearance on the boards by our local dramatic club was even more flatteringly received than the first, and the playing was proportionately better. If the members improve with each appearance as they did between first and second, the troupe will soon be in condition to go on the road and storm the towns.

The play of The Turn of the Tide, is a heavier one than Among the Breakers, requiring more study and acting and calling for a better display of talent, and the various numbers showed no lack of zeal in proportion. There might have been more animation put into the scenes here and there, but these are not professionals drawing salaries from $2 to $200 a week. They will do better as they become more accustomed to facing audiences.

The lady actresses were Mrs. R. A. McConnell, Mrs. G. W. Young, Miss Ella Roseberry and Miss Lutie Sturges. They say that Mrs. McConnell as the real quiet body was very much at home, and Mrs. Young as Frisky was true to nature. The heavy emotional parts sustained by the younger ladies were more closely criticised than the others, with the popular verdict in their favor.

Of the gentlemen on the stage there were none that could be called sticks, though they might have been improved. Abbott was too impulsive in combat, while his adversary Chilson, lacked in impulsiveness making a mismatched team. Joe Kremis had evidently taken real life lessons in his'n; Morton Roseberry as Pepper was immense; someone remarked that Morton was a 'born-nigger' but that is hardly possible; Walter Sever did the burglar act well enough for one not in practice and Wright in his sort of second hand lover parts didn't seem to care much about it anyway.

The company is good enough for any town in New Mexico, and will fill their little theatre at every performance. They give us something to gossip about, too, which is something in a small community where topics get thread bare if not renewed. (*Ibid, February 28, 1891.*)

Springer the county seat was laid out in 1879, and was made the seat of government in the year following. Springer is on the Cimarron river, ten miles north of the southern boundary of the county. The altitude is about 6,000 feet above sea level. For about six years the town was only an out-fitting and shipping point, and no attempt was made to utilize its advantage for permanent residences and business, but upon the settlement of the title of the Maxwell Land Grant in the United States Supreme Court, by which one third of the county was confirmed to the Grant claimants, affairs took a different aspect, and people came to look upon Springer in the light of a home. One of the first moves was the incorporation of a water works company by the resident citizens and in one year from the time the first steps were taken a first class Holly system of water works was in operation, and has been paying investment from the start.

Following the water works came other improvements of public and private nature, all contributing to the public welfare; lots were fenced, gardens made, trees planted and streets graded. A volunteer fire departmnt was organized with hose cart and 1,000 feet of the best hose, fire hydrants planted in positions to give ample protection from fire to the entire town.

The Cimarron river is bridged here with one structure of 400 feet in length, and another iron bridge is under contract. There is a good school with a fair and average attendance. The population of the town is 1,000.

Springer is the trade center for a radius of about 500 miles except on the north. It has a large cement mill, the capacity of which is 400 barrels and employs, when running full about 30 men. There are extensive quarries and mines of cement, limestone, fire clay and alum in the immediate vicinity, and coal mines 20 miles away.

The only artesian water in New Mexico (i.e. in 1891) was struck on the Taylor ranch, a short distance (3 miles) from Springer, in June last (1890). The bore is but 251 feet deep and has discharged continuously a seven inch stream of water since it was first opened. Other wells are under contract in and around town.

Two of the grandest irrigation systems in America have been put up in successful operation here and by their works we prove them. The Vermejo system was first built and put into successful operation here. It has a large ditch or canal tapping the Vermejo stream at the foothills and running out on the high prairie where it feeds a system of 14 reservoirs, saving all the surplusage of water not used during the season for irrigation purposes. On this system the Maxwell Land Grant Company, two years ago, enclosed a farm of thousands of acres which was planted to all kinds of grain, forage, vegetables and fruits. Heretofore farming and fruit growing had been confined to the valleys along the natural water courses—this was the first experiment on the dry prairie and it was that the high table lands are better adapted to agriculture and fruit culture than the bottom lands, on account of the greater warmth of the soil, more easily worked, quicker response to irrigation and better absorbent qualities. The crops yielded immensely. Nothing failed, and the second year was a repetition of the first on a greater scale. There is not another such farm in the arid regions.

The Springer Land Association's big ditch takes its waters from the Cimarron fourteen miles above Springer. Connected with this great coral is a system of large reservoirs which receive and hold the surplus waters of the season. Like those of the Vermejo system they are of such vast proportions that an entire season's failure of water would not run them dry after filling. On the town of Springer the ditch has gained an elevation of over 100 feet above the river. The ditches run on a grade of about five feet to the mile. The main ditch and laterals are 46 miles long. The largest ditch is 24 feet wide at the bottom.

Last year the Springer Land Association followed the example set by the Maxwell Land Grant Company on a smaller scale as regards farming, but much larger in the line of gardening. Col. Dwyer (after whom Dwyer Avenue was named in Raton), the general manager, started his plows on the 30th of last March. His determination was to plant everything in the line of vegetables and grain that is grown in the temperate zone, and he carried out his intentions. Here is the result; the grand total from everything:

Oats——75 acres on sod
36 bushels to the acre
39½ lbs. to the bushel
Corn——50 acres
40 to 45 bushels to the acre

Wheat and barley, large yields. Three cuttings of alfalfa.

Vegetables—The finest grown anywhere and yields very large.

In this work the colonel had the assistance of Mr. Prendergast, a theorectic and practical gardener. About 1,000 fruit trees were planted in the spring. They all thrived during the season. These two farms (Maxwell and Grant's and Dwyer's) have attracted much attention and through their agency thousands of acres of land have been sold.

The fruit region does not appear to be bound by altitudes. We have some of our best orchards over 7,000 feet. In the higher altitude apples, pears, peaches, crabs, cherries and all the varieties of berries yield plenteously; while in the lower valleys the various plums, nectarines, apricots, etc., as well as the fruits above mentioned are successfully grown. There is no finer flavored fruit in the world than that raised near, and shipped from Springer.

The town of Springer is handsomely laid out; the streets 120 feet wide and running at right angles. It is 25 miles to the base of the snowy mountains, and the view as superb. The sun shines 365 days in the year. A whole day without sunshine is almost unkown. Society is good, and conduct is well ordered. It has been a bad frontier town, but its days have passed on, never more to return.

A new school building, adequate to accomodate all the school children of the town, will be constructed within the next three months. Here, too, is the sportsman's paradise. Within a radius of 20 miles of Springer are 50 lakes, the home of geese, ducks, swans, and all other feathered game in countless thousands. The mountain streams are filled with trout; the prairies are dotted with antelope, while the mountain forests are the homes of deer, bear, and other noble game. (Henry Sturges in the Colfax County Stockman, August 1, 1891.)

The prettiest sight that Springer people have seen for many a year was on exhibition Thursday, when they saw the grand old flag of the country—Old Glory—floating from the mast of their new school house. *(Ibid, September 18, 1893.)*

Springer has enjoyed a continual round of festivities this week. Two nights were treated to a Mexican sleight of hand performance which was good; Tuesday night the Tennessee (Negro) Jubilee Singers played to a very large house, which was very good; Wednesday and Monday nights Prof. Buckley gave us lectures on spiritualism, also lectured Tuesday afternoon opposite the Springer House in the open air, on Thursday a good crowd gathered at the new school house and lovers of dancing enjoyed themselves until along into the next day. The ball was given by the school house force, most of them also taking part in the festivities. Everything was free, and the boys conducted things in grand style and showed that it is needless to go farther than the hardy workingmen for entertainment. The entertainment was a success socially, and we think in every other way. *(Ibid.)*

A scene in the court house in Springer (March 24, 1892). The judge—(J. Long)—"Gentlemen, if any of you have any reasonable excuses to offer why you should not serve as jurors, you can now state them."

Mr. Marks—"Your honor, I am the only baker in town and ask to be excused on that account."

Judge Long—"Can't excuse you. These appear to be well bred (Pun on bread) people anyway. Besides a change of diet may be of benefit to them. Next."

Mr. Morton—"I ask to be excused because I am the only banker in town."

Judge Long—"Can't do it! Sit down! In these times bankers cannot be better employed than serving as jurors, where lessons can be learned and the people can know where they are. Keep your seat. Next."

Mr. Talle—"I ask to be excused for the reason that my store needs me and I haven't any clerk."

Judge Long—"All right, you may step down. The court is not disposed to deprive a store of its only occupant. Advertise and then you will not be so lonesome."

Springer has one industry which, if properly developed, will prove of immense benefit to the town and will net big returns for the investors. Some time ago a few plaster settlers were added to the cement plant and it was found that our gypsum deposits of which large beds are found in the immediate vicinity, when properly treated yielded a superior quality of plaster.

This plaster is used with two parts sand and makes a wall harder than rock itself. Our new school house has been plastered with it, and after the first coat was dried the plasterer took a piece of common flooring, which he broke to pieces upon the wall without frazling the wall in the least. This and other severe tests proves beyond question that Springer plaster is of the most superior quality.

A plaster is made at Gipsum City, Kansas, that is about equal in quality to the Springer article, but while they charge about $18 a barrel, our plaster can be delivered F.O.B. at Springer at $7 and still realize a fair profit. The small quantity made was quickly disposed of, with orders still pouring in, so it is intended to start the kettles again at an early day. There is still much of prosperity in store for Springer, and with a little energy, push, and pluck we can build up industries to the benefit of the town and community, and particularly to the benefit of those who put their shoulder to the wheel." *(Ibid, October 7, 1893).*

Last Sunday our representative, in making his rounds, called on the force of workmen at the new school house. Mr. Lake, the foreman, allowed us the privilege of inspecting every department, from the large commodious basement to the culinary quarters. On dropping in this very interesting place we were turned over to the hospitality of Mr. Smith, who is in full charge; this gentleman took us in as the long lost prodigal and killed and cooked for us until he began to wonder what was going to be left for the rest. He explained the different schemes he had in view and the different ways he had of making this and that. We will not attempt to give the bill of fare at this time but Mr. Smith has promised us a meal off and on if we would not mention his name, so he was told that he would not be mentioned; also the same with Mr. Lake. We did not meet any of the other gentlemen employed there, but we are told that they were all nice fellows and a jolly crowd. It will pay everyone to call around there at mealtime, and we will assure you good treatment at their hands. *(Ibid, January 29, 1893)*

On Monday afternoon an alarm of fire startled the town, when it was discovered that Robert Stepp's barn was burning. The fire burned rapidly and soon created a breeze which carried the flames to the ice house and Rev. Hyde's stable near by.

In Stepp's stable were his two horses and in a pen adjoining were several pigs which fell victims to the fire. Mr. Hyde succeeded in saving his horse. Stepp also lost a set of double-harness and other things that were in the barn.

The nearness of the dwelling houses placed those buildings in danger and all efforts were turned to saving them. Mrs. Stepp was carried from a sick bed to a neighbor's and all furniture carried out of the residence of Messrs. Hyde and Stepp. The store tenement house west of the burning barns also took fire, but was extinguished before much damage was done. The house is occupied by Mrs. Bay and Mr. Norman, the latter suffered considerable loss by having his furniture damaged.

The origin of the fire is understood to be from the children of Stepp smoking cigarettes in the barn and the loss is about $1,000. Let this loss be a lesson to the parents. *(Ibid, July 29, 1893)*

Wednesday night about midnight an alarm of fire again startled our citizens and called them from their beds. It turned out to be a fire in the new building erected over the ruins of Stepp's ice house, which consumed the new and what was left of the old building and a lot of lumber. It was supposed that what was the cause of it was fire that had lain dormant in sawdust since Monday. *(Ibid. Or did the parents refuse to take the lesson?)*

The Comedy Company that played here Thursday night in the guise of the St. Louis Comedy Company was undoubtedly a first class fake. It would be an easy matter for anyone to place the trio who composed the outfit, as a very 'bummy' set. They claimed to be billed for Las Vegas last night, and if the citizens there appreciate a bum show they should have seen this one. Several of us went, though we were ashamed of it. *(Ibid, August 5, 1893)*

It rained hard last Sunday night and the jail leaked again, letting out two prisoners through a hole in the south wall. It must have been the rain that caused the leak, for how else, in view of previous breaks could the prisoners leak out? Their names were Felix Cosby, alias Maxwell, cow-thief, and Les Dilman, a bad man from Raton.

Sheriff McCuisten was absent when the prisoners escaped

and was not at all able to blame for their getting out. He came here promptly and offered a reward of $50 for their capture. The description is as follows: Felix Cosby, half-breed Indian, is about 5 ft. 7 in. high, dark complexion, dark eyes, black hair, dark moustache, thin and straight, weight about 160 lbs., wearing white cowboy hat, high-heeled boots, and blue overalls. Les Dilman is dark complexioned, dark hair, dark eyes, twenty-one years old almost smooth faced about 5 ft. 5 in. high, weight about 135 lbs., wears grey-stripped pants, dark hat, well worn, old shoes almost worn out. *(Ibid)*

Yesterday was a proud day for Springer, and indeed for the county and territory as well, for each magnificent institute of learning that rears itself in overland of sunshine should be a course of congratulation to the entire commonwealth, as well as for the locality in which it stands. Its benefits not only accrue to its immediate neighborhood as a means of educating the young, but it stands as a testimony for the whole territory, telling home seekers from the efete East that we of New Mexico realize the advantages of education and although in a comparatively new country of untried resources we are fully alive to the importance of providing good school facilities for our young. But to Springer and District No. 24 belong the congratulations that their pluck and energy has provided the fire building and its dedication to the long and useful service in the purpose for which it is designed.

Yesterday morning at sunrise, the emblem of education, the beautiful Stars and Stripes were raised over the cupals of the school house, and, as in graceful folds it fluttered out on the breeze it brought pride to the heart of man. All the bells in town rang forth in merry tones welcoming the peeping sun that was to witness Springer's proudest day. At noon the bells were chimed again, and still again as sunset when the flag was furled from over the building, where God willing, it may float hence a hundred years. During the day many visitors had arrived and were assigned by the committee on entertainment to our hospitable citizens.

Long before seven people had begun to gather and 7:30 every inch of sitting and standing room of the upper floor was occupied. The teacher's rostrum was placed in the hall, so that two rooms were available for the audience. Order being established, Father Hoelterman invoked the divine blessing upon the assembly and upon the long and continued use of the building as an education of the people. After the opening remarks by the chairman, contractor F. W. Pierce, in a neat address, made formal delivery of the building by passing the keys to the chairman of the school board, A. J. Clouthier, who in his acceptance made an appropriate reply. Miss Edith Kremis rendered the solo 'Red, White and Blue,' with a full chorus. W. C. Wrigley of Raton, made the first address of the evening, choosing for his subject, 'Education and Its Influence Upon Inherited Character.' After the song 'Come Where the Lilies Bloom,' by the choir, John Morrow, M. P. Pels, and M. W. Mills, delivered short extempore addresses, interluded with songs by the Spanish Quartette and a solo by Mrs. A. J. Clothier, Governor O. A. Hadley followed with the second address, confining himself more particularly to the importance of education as a basis for republican government. The song 'America' by the audience, and Rev. A. A. Hyde closed with a prayer and benediction.

After the close of the formal exercises, the young, some in feeling only, gathered in the rooms below and a most enjoyable dance was indulged in until a late hour; thus most happily closing a day that long will be remembered, both on account of its importance in the history of Springer and its place in education.

In our gratification over the final competition and appropriate dedication of our new school building, it would be an injustice were we to overlook one who had done so much to enable us to get such a satisfactory school house at such a comparatively small cost. We refer to the architect and builder Floyd W. Pierce of Trinidad, Colorado. Much has been said descriptive of the structure, so all we can say here is, that those who have any building to do, will be but consulting their interests to secure the services of Mr. Pierce. We are satisfied that he can refer to any citizen of school district No. 24, Springer, Colfax county, New Mexico, and particularly to the school board and others with whom he has come in contact in a business way. A word should also be said for Robert Lake the able foreman who had immediate charge of the work.

The building is of home burned red brick, 14 inch walls, stone trimmed and the main structure is 50 feet by 65 feet. It contains 5 rooms 26 by 30 and can accomodate 400 pupils. In addition to the regular school rooms there is a class room 15 by 20; 4 cloak rooms, 4 commodious closets for teachers and two halls 20 by 29; there is also a large furnace and fuel room in the basement 26 by 30. The building consists of two stories, each twelve feet in the clear, and from the ground to the top of the tower it is a little over 60 feet. Standing as it does on the hill back of the town it presents an imposing appearance and can be seen for miles in every direction. Captain Sturges made a creditable presiding officer.

M. P. Pels and his daughters, Mrs. Clutton and Miss Pels, were among Springer's distinguished guests. County Superintendent John Morrow made many friends in his well chosen remarks upon education and educational methods.

Gov. O. A. Hadley, in that happy way which is all his own, held the attention of his auditors despite the lateness of the hour when he took the rostrum. The address of Hon. Wm. C. Wrigley opened up a broad field for thought as to the inflembleness of the character of the few, and the susceptibility of education of the many.

Col. M. W. Mills confined himself principally to a comparison of the old and the new. Telling of the early towns of Colfax County that without schools proved to be a mushroom growth.

Hon. M. P. Pels spoke chiefly of the self-congratulation that the people, not only of the town or country but of the whole territory could indulge in at being able to show the Eastern tourists such magnificent school buildings as those in Raton and Springer.

Little Ruth Kremis did well with her patriotic solo. The solo by Mrs. A. J. Clouthier was the musical event of the evening. Her full, rich voice filled the building and was the only part of the exercises heard in the back rooms. A. B. Beringer of the Raton Reporter was among the invited guests. Putting the rostrum in the hall and seating the audience in the two rooms proved to be a great mistake. Although at least 300 people attended the exercises, but only a few so fortunate as to get seats in the hall heard the exercises, and as far as hearing the speeches was concerned, at least 200 of them might as well have been at home, but still good nature prevailed and after the splendid dance all agreed that they had enjoyed themselves. *(Ibid, November 25, 1893).*

As arranged last Tuesday evening the ladies of the Methodist church gave a supper at Cowan's Hall. An unusually large crowd patronized the ladies in their commendable effort, and the net proceeds amounted to a little over $51. It is thought that this with the church improvement fund on hand will be sufficient to purchase the needed chairs. *(Ibid, October 14, 1893)*

The Catholics of Springer are making an effort to add some much needed improvements to their church building here. It is intended to line the walls on the outside with brick and make some other changes which will greatly improve its appearance and convenience. Funds are of course in demand and all good people interested in church work are solicited to lend their aid, even though their subscription may be small. *(Ibid)*

The men of Springer can congratulate themselves that at least we have a first class barber, J. A. Jenkins is located in one of the back rooms at Nemecio Olona's and but one call upon him will convince you that he is the man to patronize. *(Ibid, November 11, 1893)*

Dr. L. Himes, M.D.
Dr. H. P. Mickey, M.D.
Kermis Bros., drugs, medicines
A. V. Rivas, watch maker, jeweler
J. Phillips, Flour and Seed, Undertaking and embalming, coffins and caskets.

Springer Mercantile Company is fitting up an ice house in the rear of the Montezuma Hotel.

Mrs. Sarah D. Solano, wife of Cipriano Solano, killed J. Cornelio Gonzalez, a brother-in-law, in Springer last night, with an axe in protection of her home. Jury verdict was justifiable self defense. *(Raton Range, September 3, 1903)*

E. B. Garcia of Southern California University will be principal of the Springer public schools. *(Ibid, September 7, 1903)*

Well the real time is going to happen next. Friday evening, July 31, at Porter's Opera House in Springer when the second annual cowboy dance will transpire. Louis Brown, the most noted promoter of all the Southwest, will have charge of the floor. *(Springer Stockman, July 30, 1903)*

The old county courthouse, built in the time when Springer was the county seat, at a cost of $20,000 and which was abandoned since the removal of the seat to Raton, is fast falling into decay and the building will soon be a total loss to the community. *(Ibid, August 8, 1907)*

Fire started at 7 A.M. in the kitchen of a small restaurant. The flames spread to the main store of Floersheim Mercantile Company, the warehouse of Talle, the saloon of Candido Olona, the mercantile company of Salazar and Warder, and two or three other business houses. *(Raton Range, November 26, 1903)*

The village of Springer has been incorporated. Springer must be prepared to have salaried officials. This will fix editor Hutchinson with some "home" graft to grow caustic over and he will be busy at home. Good luck to the town and may it show its pluck until it becomes a city. *(Ibid, January 4, 1910)*

There will be a meeting at the Springer Opera House on January 6, 1908, for the purpose of organizing a commercial club.

Tomas Salazar, son of M. N. Salazar of Springer was fatally shot and Gabriel Gonzalez was dangerously wounded and Albert Harman seriously wounded at Springer Saturday night about 10 P.M. in a pitched battle which was the outcome of the feud which had existed since the murder of Dolf Harman by Gonzalez on August 11, 1907. It is said that Albert Harman began the shooting. Gonzalez had killed Adolf Harman in the barroom of the Springer Hotel while Harman was trying to eject him from the saloon. Gonzalez obtained a change of venue to San Miguel county and was tried and acquitted. At the trial it had developed that A. Harman had killed Esteban Trujillo, a deputy sheriff at Springer on January 22, 1897, and on that account and because of other trouble at various times a feud sprang up which involved Gonzalez. *(Ibid, January 22, 1908)*

MAXWELL, NEW MEXICO

This is the story of a little city, so small and seemingly unknown, that when the St. Louis, Rocky Mountain, and Pacific Railway had maps made of its route, the company entrusted with the job, failed to mark the site of the city on the map. Large cities relegate little places into the background, but history in such places is often made by people settling there from such places as Maxwell. People are very much surprised to hear that a community the size of Maxwell can put out a history that sometimes proves more fascinating, more exciting than a city of international reknown. Our little city is on Highway 85, thirty-two miles south of Raton, and boasts a population of less than five-hundred people. It is comparatively new as towns go in the Sunshine State, but it has a history that combines the frontier, industry, enterprise and the American way of life with a spice all its own to make it just a little different from the rest of the towns that mushroomed near it. Just recently it held a celebration in honor of the re-opening of its famous irrigation ditch that attracted national attention.

As can be surmised the name stems from Lucien B. Maxwell, once the owner of the fabulous Maxwell Land Grant. In 1888, the Maxwell Land and Irrigation Company, an organization controlled for the most part by stockholders from Holland, began making surveys of the present site of the city for irrigation purposes. Gradually, the people came to call the place Maxwell Station because of the Santa Fe railroad depot. The irrigation company suddenly realized that the spot was centrally located for business purposes as well as an ideal spot for the central offices of the Maxwell Land Grant Company. From an irrigation project it found itself with a general store, still in operation, together with a saloon, hotel, and livery stable. Even before the townsite company went all out to sell the town, Maxwell Station was making history.

On Sunday, December 24, 1882, P. M. Hackett, a section foreman at Maxwell Station went to Raton to have a tooth extracted. He took six of the nine men working under him along with him on the hand-car. While in town, his men got to drinking, and when they were ready to return they made sure that they took additional fortitude with them. It being Christmas Eve, Hackett bought a gallon of whiskey and some cigars to make the next day a merry one at the section house. The party reached Maxwell Station about eight o'clock that evening, and as they were waiting for supper, Mrs. Hackett suggested that as Pete, one of the hands, was duty bound to walk the track on Sundays and as he had walked all that day, he should be given a drink and a cigar. This was done. But Pete liked the liquor so much that he demanded another drink, but was refused. At this point his comrades became angry and set up a howl for firewater, and swore that nothing would prevent them from having that article of red joy, or at least the money with which to procure some.

Mrs. Hackett, aware of what she started, sought in vain to pacify them telling them that there was no liquor in the house. They insisted that they would have budge or blood. Pete and his brother-in-law, Andrew, were foremost in the demands, and when they were told there was no whiskey, they said they would have it or the money, or kill Hackett. Andrew picked up a hammer and commenced pounding the table and door, Pete picked up the fire shovel and a six-shooter, and together they declared war. Hackett, who was in the kitchen at the time, hearing the row in the dining room went to investigate. At this point the pair started for him and to get out of their way, Hackett jumped through the window and then told his ten year old son to reach out his Winchester to him. This the lad did, and with rifle in hand, the foreman went around the house and again entered the kitchen, hiding himself in the closet to hide from the infuriated natives.

Pete heard Hackett enter the kitchen, and laying down the fire shovel he picked up the candle on the table and holding the light in his left hand, with the revolver in the other, he entered the room to look for his quarry. Pete saw the closet door close, and with an oath said: "I've got you now. Your money or your life." He no sooner said the words when Hackett fired his rifle, the ball entering Pete's heart. Hackett then jumped over the body and rounded up the other men and herded them upstairs. He then took a chair and sat at the edge of the dining room table with an eye on the stair way. Mrs. Hackett dragged the body outside, and the family had a meeting as to what was best to be done. It was decided that Hackett should return to Raton and give himself up. He was taken to the county jail at Springer, to celebrate a Christmas far different from what he had planned. Hackett remained in jail until April when it was decided that he could await the next term of court if he could produce a $5,000 bond. As nothing came up later he was evidently let go in favor of self-defense.

The townsite company elected James L. de Fremery as president, and a plat was made of the future city. Other towns took exception to the new idea, looking upon it as another get-rich-quick real estate deal. Anti-granters were particularly noisy. In vain did the company seek to convince the press that it was out to help New Mexico and to develop the land. Wrote the president from New York:

"The rumors that have reached my ears are none other than that the Maxwell City Land and Improvement Company was organized for the purpose of booming Maxwell City, selling lots at high prices, making a handsome speculation, and then letting the town take care of itself. I wish to deny those charges.

"It will be sufficient to disprove these assertions by calling the attention to the work which this company has already accomplished, and the amount of money that has been embarked in this enterprise. We have purchased no less than one thousand acres of the Maxwell Land Grant Company. All of this land has been fenced in, and is now being broken. We have built a commodious and attractive hotel; a very large livery stable is nearly completed, and in the immediate future we propose erecting a large two-story brick store building. Ground has been left for public squares, and it is our intention to plant these as well as the streets with shade trees. Everything is being done to make Maxwell City a lovely place to live in.

"The water supply will be ample and of excellent quality. A large reservoir, which will hold over ten million gallons, is in the course of construction. It will give a pressure of nearly one hundred feet in the town. The water to be used for town purposes will pass through large filters of the latest and most approved patterns, which will render the water the best for drinking purposes in Colfax county, and has been sufficiently proven by analysis, and there will be an abundance of it.

"The lots are being offered at exceedingly reasonable rates, in order to attract new comers, and it is our intention to lease our farming lands on exceedingly low terms. We are doing everything we can to assist in the devolpment of that section of the country, and we trust that false rumors will not persist. If those who settle in Maxwell City have as much energy as the people of Raton to the north, there will be no doubt as to its future."

The news flashes that were of vital interest to the inhabitants of the new town may not be worthy of our notice today, but they were part of the village gossip, and put together they paint for us a picture of the goings-on that are now but history:

"The quiet of the city was somewhat disturbed Saturday by a run-away. One of Mr. Dawson's teams thought matters were moving too slowly for the general good. Bruce Dawson carries the only mark of the accident, but he is still in the ring . . . Sunday brought the usual crowd to the Maxwell House, where Sunday dinners seem to have a fascination . . . The large iron columns for the store front have arrived. The building is one story high now, and will have attained its full heighth by the Fourth of July . . . Maxwell City is thawing out, and the long looked for mother earth is becoming visible in spots. Ice is frozen eighteen inches and the Maxwell City Ice Company is laying in a good supply. L. S. Preston and family have moved into J. van Houten's commodious cottage on Third St. (Preston, N. M. and Van Houten, N.M. are named after these men) . . . The day school has been very well attended during the bad weather. Miss S. E. Gladden directs the course of the young ideas. Rev. Hyde, of Springer, has arranged to preach in Maxwell City once a month. The young ladies of Maxwell City are almost out of sight since the leap year ball proved to be such a success. The boys smile as they did not have to foot the bills."

Trivial things, yes, but not to those who had to sell their homes somewhere, and pack all their belongings in wagons and carts to come to a frontier town not knowing who their next door neighbor would be, and to harmonize living conditions to suit the taste of a man from Germany, or Texas, or Kansas, Poland, New York. Anywhere and everywhere, Maxwell City was certainly cosmopolitan.

"The offices of the Maxwell Irrigated Land Co. were well filled Saturday afternoon with farmers from nearby ranches, who came to discuss sugar beet culture, and to listen to the remarks of J. E. Gauger, chief agriculturist of the Holly Sugar company. The meeting was called to order by J. I. Cowen. After stating the purpose of calling the farmers together, which was to interest them in growing beets, he called upon Mr. Gauger to take charge. Mr. Gauger presented the new beet contract of the Holly Sugar Co., and read it explaining each section as he went along.

"The contract is much better than the one offered last year. In the matter of freight rates, the company will pay half, and the grower the rest. The Santa Fe made a rate of a dollar a ton on beets to the factory. "Mr. Gauger said he believed Maxwell was favorably situated for growing beets. From experiments made last year it was proven that beets of a high sugar test could be grown. The freight rate is low, and this would undoubtedly produce a satisfactory tonnage. He urged the farmers to consider the matter.

"H. S. Johnson, who is employed by the Santa Fe to encourage and instruct beet growers, told what he thought about beet culture. Mr. Johnson is a beet grower of years experience and has a farm at Rocky Ford (Colo.) where he has made a lot of money in the beet business. He enlarged to some extent upon what Mr. Gauger had said, and promised to all those who would plant beets that he would give them all the assistance and advice they would need so that they would have a good crop. He said he was ready to sign contracts with any who wanted to plant beets. He secured a number of contracts" (April 2, 1909).

"The bank building at Maxwell is nearing completion and in a short time it will be ready for business. The safe and fixtures have not yet arrived. The stockholders elected A. S. Hall, J. I. Cowan, Charles Wolf, William Van Bruggen and Fred Haines as directors. The bank will start with a captial of thirty thousand dollars."

"The Maxwell baseball fans were disappointed last Sunday on account of the proposed game with Springer not coming off, and some of them even went so far as as to go to the ball park, and while disappointed in not seeing the game as promised, were allowed to pass the werisome hours by watching the local boys do practise stunts on the diamond. The season is practically ended at Maxwell now, so far as baseball is concerned, and football will probably be in the limelight until the holidays.

"Harry Brennen, who is having his property painted on Maxwell Ave., will renovate it, and fix it up by painting the inside and papering. This is a great, big roomy house, and would make a fine rooming house for rental. Part of it is occupied. The Whitely property having been lately occupied by Mr. Stevens and family from Oklahoma. The Van Bruggen cottage on Coyote Ave. is occupied by Mills and Davis.

"The services at the church last Sunday morning and evening were quite good although the attendance was a little slim. The Junior Endeavor of last Sunday was well attended and speaks well for the Juniors. These meetings should all be well attended, as they are very interesting and helpful. Miss Bessie Jackson who led the meeting of the Christian Endeavor last Sunday evening, read a paper on "How We Can Help Our Pastor," which was very good.

"A meeting was held at Abreus last Wednesday night to discuss general plans for the Maxwell Free Library. The people of Maxwell are showing a good spirit in this movement, and it looks as if the idea will be pushed to a finish as some of our Maxwell people are becoming personally interested and are going from door to door for books, magazines and papers to start the library."

"Mrs. Lizzie Pyper is teaching twenty-six pupils in the public school. She is an excellent teacher (1893). Eleven families have contracted for and will buy lands in a body north of Maxwell, three miles. They will put up their own ditch and reservoir system; the water being taken from the Red River. . . . Rev. Mr. Sanders, pastor of the Christian Church at Trinidad, Colo., preached several nights last week. . . . The Maxwell City Sunday School had an election of officers last Sunday. Nearly all of the old officers were re-elected. Mrs. McCloud is superintendent and Mrs. Powers secretary. . . . A musicale and basket social will be given in the hall Saturday night, Sept. 30. Baskets with lunch for two will be sold for twenty-five cents. The proceeds will be used to buy a dictionary for the public school."

"Happening to be in Maxwell City on business last week, and having a few leisure moments on our hands, we strolled over to the Maxwell City flour mills. The miller, D. B. Powers met us at the door and showed us over the entire plant. As yet no work has been done, but a large quantity of wheat and fuel has been accumulated and the machinery put in motion several times will be made in a few days. While we must confess our inexperience in mills and milling, we still could not be but struck by the undoubtedly perfect appointments of the mill. It is of course of the roller system, and Mr. Power will turn out a high patent flour that will stand the test with products of any eastern miller. While there we were shown samples of New Mexico and Kansas wheat. The latter was of a grade we were accustomed to see in the States, but on seeing the New Mexico article we were indeed astounded; it was so large of grain, plump, and of a beautiful golden color, and with such wheat there is no reason why New Mexico flour cannot compete with any first class flour of the world. This is not an extravant conjecture, when we remember that our territory carried off the first prize for wheat at the Chicago Exposition, where all the world was in competition. We bespeak for Maxwell City mill a large patronage. Nor are our good wishes tainted with anything of jealousy, for Springer will soon have a milling plant of its own, and there is ample room in our broad irrigated valleys to raise more than sufficient to heap the hoppers of each to overflowing. (Oct. 7, 1893)."

"As will be seen by our advertising column, the new flour mill is all completed and before this issue of the Stockman is fairly circulated one of the most important industries of Colfax County will have turned on the steam and Maxwell City will be in the market to buy all kinds of flour, meal and feed; or to exchange the one for the other on a basis advantageous to the producer. In a conversation last Tuesday with Mr. D. B. Powers, the prinicipal owner and manager of the mill, he stated to a Stockman representative that the mill would certainly start on Monday, October 30, at which time he was assured the miller would be on hand, his tardiness being the only cause of the recent delay. Mr. Powers is a practical miller himself but his time will be occupied in the outside work and business management of the concern. The Maxwell City Milling Co. which is the name of the new company will at all times pay the highest cash price for wheat, corn, oats, barley and in short, any kind of grain the farmer may raise. The company will also have for sale the best high patent flour, as well as half-patent and intermediate grades, corn meal, bran, feed, and all other mill products. While the mill is not prepared to do custom work, Mr. Power will make a specialty of exchanging flour, meal, feed, and other grains for any grain offered, at live and let live prices. He does not expect Colfax County people to patronize him at a loss, but if his flour is as good and as cheap as flour shipped into the territory then he hopes the home industry will be given the preference. All he asks is a trial. (October 28, 1893)."

About this time a group of businessmen interested themselves in a railroad to run between Maxwell and Taos. The leader in this enterprise was William Cameron, and he undetook the tremendous task of surveys, right of way, recording deeds, and other such important preliminary work that goes with the construction of a railroad. So the little city went on its merry way convincing the rest of the country that it was a nice place to live in. Now and then the peace of the community was broken by a pistol duel or knifing, but that didn't seem as important as when a dam burst and the town was out of water for three weeks. The future of the place hung in the balance then. But willing hands went to work and the community was saved. The years passed on seemlying uneventful but the people were doing things here that towns of larger size hesitated to start. There was the orchestra started by L. T. Sheves, who played the trombone. P. D. Peterson played the drums; C. P. Smith and his wife played the violin and piano, and H. L. Phelps played the mandolin. "The new curtain drop at the Davis Opera House has been finished and is now ready for service. The central picture shows a deer, surrounded by a lot of wolves, and the deer is making a fight for his life. A hunter appears on the scene, but whether he is going to kill the wolves and set the deer free, or intends driving off the wolves and killing the deer himself is not clear. Anyway, it is an interesting picture. Around the picture are the usual business ads, all from Maxwell business houses. The curtain for the back of the stage is being painted." (April 1, 1915).

The city of Maxwell was incorporated in 1914. The following year E. A. Hudkins was elected mayor. N. E. Harrison saw the possibilites in the new newspaper called the Maxwell Mail and bought it, naming his brother, Max G. Harrison as editor. J. Gordon Smith was elected village clerk. That was the year that construction started on the Menapace Hotel. Twelve guest rooms it had on the second floor while the lower floor was filled with lunch rooms, offices and kitchens. Of interest were the city ordinances. Here is a sample of one:

"Be it ordained by the Board of Trustees of the Village of Maxwell that license be obtained for each merry-go-round—ten dollars per day, for each day or fraction thereof Each day shall end at midnight. Proprietors of billiard, pool, bagatelle and pigeonhole tables, and any and all similiar tables, used or played upon for consideration, shall pay five dollars per annum or fraction thereof for each such table and each such year shall end with the municipal year. Every variety theatre shall pay fifty dollars per annum or fraction thereof. Each auctioneer holding auction sales on the streets, alleys, or public grounds shall pay two dollars for each day or fraction thereof. For any shows, lectures, concerts whatsoever or any performance of any kind or nature or selling anything of any kind or nature whatsoever whether admission fee is charged or not, and whether voluntary contributions are solicited or not five dollars per day. For each show of any wild or tame animal, fowl, beast, bird, human monstrosity, or freak of nature, performance of horsemanship, feats of activity or strength, athletic feats, and all similiar shows, or exhibitions, three dollars a day."

William Van Bruggen was elected second mayor of Maxwell. Shreve, the muscian decided to go into the drug business. After four years of struggle he emerged with a bigger and better drug store in the Paulson Building. J. Gordon Smith bought the Maxwell Mail from Harrison and installed himself as editor. A village jail was constructed, but it seemed unnecessary. Just when the populace thought that a fellow by the name of Archuleta would be the first occupant, he paid his five dollars fine leaving the jail without an occupant. Commencement exercises were held at the Davis Opera House. Also at the opera house were conducted dancing classes under the direction of Edith White and D. A. McMillen. Of interest too, for the moment was the tension between Miss Shirley Miller, principal of the school, and the school board. She was replaced, after her voluntary resignation, by R. L. Krigbaum, former principal of the schools at Desmoines. Mrs. H. S. Bartless was postmistress but resigned in favor of moving to Albuquerque. In the first drawing of the war in 1917, the following Maxwell boys were called: Albert Louis Martin, William E. Rutherford, Fred L. Rosier, E. E. Malsom, Marcos Romero, F. E. Mumford, C. A. Marshall, Victor Trujillo, Clodoves Casadoes, Jose T. Gallegos, Max

Cardenas, Elutario Lopez. One of the first buildings to be put up in Maxwell was the brick livery barn on the hill. For years it housed the finest steppers in the country. Cowpunchers coming into town to make a night of it put their ponies in the big barn before filling up on fire water and unlimbering their guns; the stage line to Chico used the barn for headquarters. But with the event of the horseless carriage the old landmark was changed into a garage. Dr. M. T. McDowell bought the big Vrockett house on upper Tenaja Ave. for the purpose of opening a hospital in Maxwell. Services for Catholics were held at the Davis Opera House every Sunday morning at nine o'clock. If Communion was to be brought to the sick, a member of the family rode into Springer on the day before and notified Father Cellier. The Menapore Hotel opened on Monday, February 8, 1915. The proprietor put up a sign that the place was exclusively for men and he would tolerate no women, young or old about the premises. On the following week; the Catholic men of Maxwell held a mass meeting at the Maxwell hotel for the purpose of interesting the town in a Catholic church. The meeting proved a success for the little city has a church taken care of by the Oblate fathers from Springer that would do justice to a larger community. When school opened in the fall of 1915, there was an enrollment of seventy-six pupils. Mrs Turner taught music once a week, and Drawing twice a week. Miss Jessie Chaffee was principal, and taught the eighth and ninth grades, assisted with the tenth, and between times managed to get in the sixth and seventh. Mrs. Jennie Turner took care of the first and second, while Miss Mildred McCready handled the fourth and fifth.

"Dr. M. T. McDowell lay in a pool of blood for several hours Monday morning while Charlie Smith administered first aid and kept the doctor from bleeding to death while waiting for help to arrive from Springer and Raton. Before the bank opened for business on Monday morning, Dr. E. T. Bruce entered by the side door to transact some urgent business before starting out on his morning calls. While still at the teller's window, Dr. McDowell came in. There had been some unpleasant feelings between the two doctors for some time. An argument followed. Dr. Bruce had an open penknife in his hand sharpening a pencil. It is alleged that he struck Dr. McDowell in the face with the knife. Dr. Panton responded to the hurry call making fifteen miles here in his car in twenty-three minutes. He is from Springer. Dr. Hobbs of Raton also responded to the call. A dozen or more stitches were needed, and Dr. McDowell was not removed from the bank till nearly noon. The bank was closed all that time. Dr. Bruce went home regretting the affair. There was no arrest made." (Maxwell Mail—March 23, 1916).

"Charley Davis, marshall of the village of Maxwell, had a lively set-to with a character, name unknown, in front of the Davis Opera House, Saturday night, during which time the stranger took a jab at Charley with a wicked looking knife. Fortunately, the officer was quick enough to avoid the thrust, although his coat was cut so close to the skin that he shivers yet every time he puts his hand on his fifth rib. Having backed away from danger, Charley reached for his gun, but meantime his prisoner had turned and started to run. At the rate he was going, the bullet had small chance of reaching him. The shot served to attract several willing helpers and a search was started for the fugitive. He was discovered hiding in a ditch in front of the mayor's house. At the command to get to his feet he responded so slowly that Charley gave him a sharp tap on the head with his 'billy' which put that useful weapon out of use and convinced the lawbreaker of the seriousness of monkeying with the law. After mentioning the shortcomings of the prisoner in general and detail accompanied with well directed prods with his gun, used in place of the broken billy, the marshall forced the captive to jail where he was locked up for the night. Sunday he was fed and watered regularly, and should have passed a peaceful night. Perhaps he did, perhaps he didn't. Whether he did or didn't is still a guess, for he was not there Monday morning to tell about it. He was gone. Vanished. Vamoosed. Skipped. Marshall Davis says he went off duty about four o'clock Monday morning and went past the jail to see if everything was in order. Through five inches of solid cement he could hear the regular breathing of the prisoner. He then went home to breakfast, after which he put some choice bits on a tray and carried the food through the morning sunshine to the jail. He thought he was carrying it to the prisoner, but when he got there the prison was bare and the nice little prisoner was gone. Sometime between the time of four and eight the jail lock was broken, not only the outside lock, but the cell lock also, and nothing stood between the prisoner and liberty. The jail doors were secured by a big hasp and staple, and an ordinary padlock which was locked. It is believed that some friend or friends of the prisoner had come along after the marshal went off duty and pried the locks off with a pick. It would have been an easy thing to do if one could work without interruption. A reward was offered for the return of the prisoner and officers in the neighboring towns are asked to be on the lookout for him." (Sept. 4, 1917).

A reward of twenty-five dollars was offered for the arrest of the person or persons who broke the locks, and an additional twenty-five for the return of the prisoner. No one put in a claim.

"One of the busiest, happiest and most prosperous towns in the state was Maxwell in the fall of 1913 and the spring of 1914. There was plenty of water, all the farmers had big crops and the prospects for continued successful farming were very bright. Land values were firm and business and building lots in town were changing hands with gratifying frequency. New business houses were built, new people coming in and new homes were going up both in town and country. Then came the loss of the Hebron dam. Water shortage followed year after year. Farmers began to leave the tract after trying in vain to grow crops with insufficient water. Many who had invested their few hundred or thousand gave up the fight and sacrificed all they had put in. Some lost all they had paid and are still in debt to the company. Farm houses on the Maxwell tract by the dozen now stand empty, with the yards overgrown with weeds and the broken windows telling the story of desertion and blasted hopes. In town several small business houses struggled along for a while and then died. The cobbler was the first to go; two restaurants followed soon afterwards. The two lumber companies consolidated; the hardware store was absorbed by other established businesses; the plumber closed his shop and moved to Dawson; the Baptist church disbanded and its building is now used as a blacksmith shop; the postoffice which had been third class for some time now dropped back to fourth class; the butcher shop closed its doors and finally the newspaper gave up its fight for its existence and ceased publication. During the three years the town was going downhill several lodges gave up their charters until now only one lodge, the Knights of Pythias, continues and even this lodge has not enough members left in town to fill a quorum. But all the time there were stouthearted farmers and business men who believed that Maxwell was not dead, but only sleeping. Water is what we need. And when the dam will be re-built the good old days will return. Now the Hebron dam is to rebuilt and Maxwell will thrive once more. (Oct. 17, 1916).

So, the town that refused to be licked, continues. A large concern known as Maxwell Farms helps keep the community alive. Several years ago it was found that turkeys do so well at Maxwell that a large turkey industry gives promise of some day making the community one of the larger shipping centers in that line in the country. Maxwell once had the title of The Sugar City. In writing the story of Maxwell, the Raton Daily Range, December 2, 1910, had this to say:

"The old Maxwell ranch, near the exact geographical center of Colfax county was the scene of the first irrigation project of any magnitude in Colfax county. Like many other first attempts it was not the success that its designers hoped for.

"The fact that certain of the original plans have been abandoned, that new work has replaced the old, and that now the water distribution and conservation are entirely successful, describes completely the difference in methods employed, or the evolution in irrigation plans during the last two decades.

"The Maxwell Irrigated Land Company has been in possession of this splendid tract of land embracing 22,000 acres, only two and one half years, and in this brief period a fortune in cash has been expended by the owners. The completion of their unique irrigation system will call for an outlay of over $750,000. The corporation is formed of wealthy men who are financially able to carry out the entire project without reference to land sales—a most fortunate circumstance for all purchasers.

"When the original owners selected this tract for their initial operation they had approximately 500,000 acres to chose from. The water supply and its availability, splendid character of the soil, its beautifully level surface, and the fact that the main line of the Santa Fe railway formed the eastern boundry of the great property, were elements that lead to its preference.

"About 40 purchasers of tracts, 40 to 320 acres each in extent, have in 1910 harvested very profitable crops, in spite of the fact that it was one of the dryest years ever known, and are happy, prosperous and enthusiastic believers in the future development of the entire tract. The policy of the company in not selling land, or agreeing to deliver water to the full amount of even present capacity, enabled them to supply all the water required in this extreme season.

"Meanwhile the progress has been rapid in extending the storage system and, whereas they had 8.000 acre-feet and will be 15,000 in the spring of 1911. With this capacity of 8,000 feet only 4,500 acres were cultivated, though that area will be largely exceeded in 1911. Several new settlers are now putting in crops on virgin soil, and many will begin to plow early in the spring. The complete system of storage provides for the impounding of 30,000 acre-feet, and so large are their main in-take ditches that six-days of flood water in the Vermejo and Red rivers will fill every lake of the dozen full to the brim. A large reserve remained in the reservoirs after this season's irrigation, and every minute the ever flowing current of the Vermejo is contributing to the storage supply. On November 4, 1910, the writer witnessed the irrigation of newly sown winter wheat. That same day the mountain sources were covered with snow, more was falling steadily, and a two-inch coverlet was spread over the fields that night. The users could see the supply replaced, even as they drew upon the storage.

"The special money crops recommended are: winter and spring wheat, sugar beets, alfalfa and Mexican beans, and, of course, apple culture, all tested thoroughly in this locality and found highly profitable. The fact that many of the Maxwell farmers are experienced growers of alfalfa and sugar beets, and orchardists from the famed irrigation centers of Colorado, tells a plain story. They sold their high-priced farms at fancy figures and here secured what they have found to be superior advantages at one fourth to one third the price per acre. One instance exemplifies the spirit of 'hustle and get there,' prevalent among the settlers on the Maxwell tract. A newcomer from Kansas, J. M., achieved the following results in thirty days from his arrival on the ground: A neat and commodious farm house, costing 1,100 dollars, enclosed and ready for the finish; barn buildings better than average completed; 105 acres ploughed, and sixty-five of it sown to winter wheat and irrigated. Sam Gerritson eighteen months ago purchased a tract of 320 acres. He rented a portion of it in 1909. This season he handled it himself. He cut about 200 tons of alfalfa and hay, had a fine crop of oats from a large tract of newly broken ground, which was planted after the middle of June, made $50 an acre from a few acres of beans, and has several stacks of exceptionally fine wheat; 160 acres is sown to winter wheat which will undoubtedly produce heavily next year; he has experimented with garden truck of various kinds in an exceptionally well kept garden.

"Few properties anywhere are so well located as far as transportation facilities are concerned. The Santa Fe railroad main line forms the eastern boundary of the property. The St. Louis, Rocky Mountain & Pacific tracks are only a mile or two from the northwest corner of the tract. The El Paso and Southwestern parallels the Vermejo river on the west, only a short distance from the company's lands—three lines of railway, connections for everywhere, fencing in this unique tract. The last named road has in contemplation a line through the property, and a spur of one and a half miles from the Santa Fe will place all the choicest beet lands within easy reach of the ideal site chosen for the beet sugar refinery that will be built within a short period.

"The Maxwell Company is the first to cultivate sugar beets on a commercial scale, 275 acres being planted in 1910, and the crop is now going to Colorado refineries at the rate of two or more cars a day. The yield is fully equal to that in the Arkansas valley, and the percentage of the sugar content much higher, the quality superior in all respects. After paying freight of fifty cents per ton the the Maxwell growers received an average of twenty-five cents net per ton more than the local growers near the refineries obtained in 1909, and it will do better in 1910. An average sugar content of 17.5 percent as against 12 to 15 percent tells the reason why.

"The smoke of the coke ovens at the celebrated coal mines of Colfax county is in plain sight of the Maxwell townsite, on the eastern line—farthest from the mine pits. An abundant supply of never-failing spring water of great purity is delivered with sufficient gravity pressure to reach the third floor of buildings. Lime is accessible within a few miles from Maxwell. These conditions, combined with the fact that the Maxwell tract alone could furnish beets enough to run a large factory —although there are thousands of acres of good beet soil on adjacent properties—makes it evident that Maxwell will soon be known as the Sugar City—for short, as that will be an easier name to remember. Just tell a Maxwell farmer that he cannot grow this or that in this climate and he will proceed to prove the contrary forthwith.

"Maxwell is a 'born city'—a city from its inception, although the population is small in numbers. The business buildings, constructed of high grade local made brick, are modern and handsome. The Farmer's Bank & Trust Company's fine structure cost $15,000 and is both substantial and ornate, equipped with all modern conveniences, including steam heat, gas lighting, etc. It is wired for electricity and it is expected that in a year or two the gas plant will be superseded. The Maxwell Irrigated Land Company occupies elegant and spacious apartments in this bulding. The streets are broad and lined with cement sidewalks in the business section. All of the business buildings have sewer connections, sanitary considerations being an important element in the company's plans. The city water supply comes from crystal springs a short distance east of the city, owned by the Maxwell Water Company. The water is perfectly pure and palatable, the supply adequate for a city of 3,000 people, and gravity pressure will deliver the fluid to the third story of buildings, affording ample fire protection as well.

"School facilities are admirable and the present (1910) attendance averages sixty-five pupils. A high school will probably be opened by January 1st, all arrangements having been concluded. There are no vacant buildings in Maxwell, and the demand is always greater than the supply. Half a dozen would-be tenants made application for houses in October who could not be accommodated. The company's policy is broad and comprehensive, liberal and progressive, and with the peopling of 20,000 acres of the Maxwell Lands, mainly in 40 acre tracts, by such a class as that already attracted to the farms by the great many advantages enjoyed, the Sugar City will soon be populous as it is now a thriving and bustling community."

STONEWALL, COLORADO

From the diary of Mrs. Russell of Stonewall, Colorado:

"One morning when things were really beginning to look a bit more hopeful, 10,000 pounds of shelled corn in the storage room at Tecolote, New Mexico, where we had our store, caught fire, from spontaneous combustion. We tried to save part of it, but great piles of blackened corn smouldered behind the store for weeks. Richard (Russell) then bought 80 head of hogs and fattened them on the damaged corn. When they were sleek and fat he hauled them to Fort Sumner and sold them to Lucien Maxwell, receiving $1,000 for them. . . . The store at Tecolote was sold in 1871.

". . . This valley a woman told us was called San Juan Valley, after Don Juan Gutierrez, one of the earliest settlers of Trinidad. Richard was a bit reluctant to drive so far out of our way. The wagon was heavily loaded and the road to the valley would wind uphill all the way. However, the woman drew such a glowing word picture of the place that we felt that it must be a second Garden of Eden. . . . The mid-afternoon of the next day we caught sight of the famous stone wall. It stretched before us, a majestic line of towers and turrets, behind which, lay an ocean of blue mist. Behind the mist, the white-capped Sangre de Cristo peaks lifted hoary hands. . . . We were not the first settlers in Stonewall Valley. We found a kindly white trapper living in a tiny cabin just below the wall, and I remember how pleased we were to locate in this new Garden of Eden near the lonely, kind white man. His name was J. A. Weston and he was a hunter-trapper. It was in his honor that the present town of Weston, Colo., was named. J. A. Weston's son runs the local blacksmith shop in Weston to this day. On the exact spot of trapper Weston's cabin stands the Murdo McKenzie summer home. Mr. McKenzie having searched the world over for the lovliest place on earth to build a summer home, chose that place in Stonewall Valley. John Sanger came from Tecolote and helped build the cabin.

"The morning was startingly cold and the children and I huddled over a great fire Richard built. How prodigal he was of wood. Log after log was laid upon that fire. That day we looked for a place to build a cabin, and at last found a level place by a clear, cold spring. There we decided to build our home. Richard re-named the valley that morning calling it The Valley of the Great Stone Wall, and Stonewall Valley it has remained ever since.

"George A. Storages came with his family from Tecolote. Before spring Richard filed in on a relinquishment claim below the wall and built his home there. His wife lived 60 years at Stonewall—Elinor Augusta Russell was born there in 1872—the first white child born in Stonewall. Then Harold, Damewood, Oliver Earl and Marion Ethel. Richard became storekeeper and postmaster. He established a sawmill and a planing mill. George Storzes established the flour mill. With $1,000 she received at Tecolote, Mrs. Russell went into the cattle business. She bought two hundred head. She also entered the dairy business with George and sold milk and butter at Trinidad. We sent freight wagons with wheat, flour and butter at Trinidad. We sent freight wagons with wheat, flour and butter to old Fort Lyon in exchange for buffalo meat and provisions—freight loads of butter to Taos or Santa Fe in exchange for red chili peppers, Spanish onions and Mexican beans."

More and more settlers came. The first Stonewall school organized in 1876. The term was three short months. The first death in Stonewall was in 1876. A log fell on a young lad who was helping to cut wood. By 1883, Stonewall had a Sunday school, schoolhouse, church, hall, stores. Social life was found in neighborhood sings and a literary society. The first marriage was that of Katie Russel to Danny Harvey in 1883.

In 1888 came notice from the Maxwell Land Grant Company to abandon Stonewall. A 24 hour notice that appeared in a Denver paper, two hundred miles away. On August 24, 1888, six armed men, described as Maxwell Land Grant deputies—led by sheriff William Hunn of Las Animas, arrived at the Coe Hotel in Stonewall. The settlers gathered at night and Capt. Russell urged the deputies to return to Trinidad. While he was talking two shots were fired. Russell died five days later. Over five hundred men were at his funeral. McMains preached his funeral oration. Stonewall exists to this day as a summer resort.

Chapter Thirteen

GHOST TOWNS OF THE GRANT

This chapter would constitute a book in itself. Just where to start is a problem. We wish to include towns that once existed but now not even a marker shows the spot where they once stood. Such are not strictly speaking Ghost Towns. A Ghost Town is an abandoned town with streets, stores and other signs of civilization except inhabitants. In other words one merely has to occupy the place to bring it to life. The Grant has very few places as such. Many of the places we list here haven't even a board left and are completely destroyed. Elizabethtown has a few homes left and may be called a Ghost Town. The same may be said for Rayado which as a town comes under our listing but not as the very much alive Philmont Boy Scout Ranch. There is no particular reason for the order of listing except that we list them as we have gathered information about them. We will first cover the towns in New Mexico, then Colorado.

CLIFTON HOUSE, NEW MEXICO

When the W.P.A. New Mexico Writers Project decided to do a book on New Mexico, Kenneth Fordyce was named to cover the area which included Clifton House. He interviewed Claude Stockton, Frank Stock- W. A. Chapman, Manville Chapman, E. Shuler, Mabel Shearer and several others. The work is now in the hands of the American Historical Society and kept at the library of the New Mexico Museum in Santa Fe. It is too good to chop up for my needs so we will give it to the reader in full.

Thomas Stockton built the Clifton House; he located it about three miles east of Red River on the west bank of the Red River (Canadian). The spot is about fifteen miles south of the Colorado line. The altitude is 6,292 feet above sea level.

A secretary of a Chamber of Commerce would have envied the Clifton House in the 1870's because of the important part the Clifton House played in the community life of northern New Mexico. When anything took place, it usually happened at the famous old stage station during the years between 1866 and 1880. Just inquire of old-timers or residents who had relatives in New Mexico in those years and you will hear such answers as these: "Yes, we stayed a night or two there when we came into New Mexico and ate our meals at the boarding house," or "I took the stage from Clifton when I went to the J. B. Dawson home on the Vermejo in 1872" or "We got our mail at Clifton for several years." And on and on. Weddings and funerals were held there, cattlemen gathered on the verandas to discuss cattle prices, and to relax after the hard labors connected with the semi-annual round-ups. Families came to Clifton to trade at the store when they could afford the high prices, although many drove to Trinidad where they could fill their wagon with provisions at a saving. The blacksmith shop was a necessity to the ranchers at times and drew them to Clifton. It was a place where news was exchanged, where the lonely ranchers and their wives; the women would sit and exchange recipes and remedies, the men would talk over plans for profitable disposal of their cattle. Clifton was the place where social events usually took place, including the horse racing. Little girls in starched dresses talked dolls and little boys in overalls bragged of their knowledge of horses and cattle and their ability on their father's ranch. The grown people got together at Clifton and talked over plans for the next dance or maybe the next wedding that was to take place at Clifton. Even the notorious element of the territory spent some time at Clifton House lending tales of the place an air of danger and roughness. (Most of the tales were greatly exaggerated.) Some traveling minister occasionally held services at the Clifton House. It was the center of the ranch-life and had a large part in all community affairs, such as they were at the time.

There was no settlement between El Morro, Colorado (near Trinidad) and Maxwell's place at Cimarron; it was thirty miles to either of these places and so the northern New Mexico people welcomed a place in their midst to be the center of "things."

W. H. Stockton lived in Tennessee. He sold his plantation and his slaves and moved to Texas just before the Civil War. He took his entire family with him; this included Thomas and Mathias Stockton. In Texas, the Stocktons settled on a ranch near Ft. Worth and they lived there during the Civil War. Another Tennessee family, the Stouts, came to Texas just after the Civil War and settled near the Stocktons. They all later came to New Mexico.

In 1866, Tom Stockton, who was born February 20, 1832 and was then thirty-four years of age, had come up from Texas to the green pastures of northern New Mexico with his herd of cattle, liked the place, saw its possibilities and stayed. Already other cattlemen had settled there,

[203]

scatteredly, for the same reason. There were no fences and that necessitated a fall and spring roundup; the drives starting east of the Dry Cimarron river and ending near the Raton mountains. This led to the need of a place for the cattlemen to get together and do their branding and finally relax when the labors were over. The result was the building of the Clifton House. Tom started the house in 1866 and finally completed it in 1870 (according to his nephew, Claude Stockton). That was a long time, but consider, the work was done at times when the cattle needed no attention (or could do without attention) and many of the materials including the sawed lumber, thick wide shingles for the roof, the glass for the windows, and the furniture had to be hauled to Clifton in road wagons from Fort Leavenworth, Kansas. It was a long hard haul with poor trails and the Raton mountains climaxed the trip with added difficulties. It was a tremendous task but those early pioneers and cattlemen knew how to do hard work and seemed to like it. Anyway, they got the job done.

Tom had help after the first two or three years. His father, W. H. Stockton, and his brother, Mathias, followed him to this new land of opportunity. They came and settled on places of their own in the immediate neighborhood and lent what help they could to Tom at the Clifton House.

The Clifton House was an ideal place for the stockmen to gather when it was completed. Broad stone steps on the eastern or front side of the house led up to the wide veranda which extended across from and along the north and south sides. There was also a veranda around the second floor. Thick adobe walls made deep windows and assured a pleasant cool atmosphere inside in the summer and warmth and protection from storms in the winter.

The basement which was used for a store-house was only partly below the ground and that gave elevation to the main floor. As the ceilings on both the main floor and the second floor were unusually high the Clifton House was a very tall building as well as being much larger than anything that had been built within 100 miles, except Lucien B. Maxwell's mansion at Cimarron.

The hallway or entry, in the center of the first floor, was where the wash basins and the roller towel were kept for the use of the guests who wished to refresh themselves. From this hall, the stairway led to two large bedrooms upstairs, each with four or five beds. The one room was for men and the other was for women. Guests in that day were thankful for a comfortable bed in which to get a good night's sleep; if they had to share their room with other paying guests, although strangers, that did not seem to matter in the least.

On one side of the hall downstairs was the parlor, later used for an office and saloon. On the other side were two bedrooms, again with several beds to better accommodate the large groups that sometimes came there at one time. At the rear of the hall was the large dining room, in which many boarders could be served at one time. One either side of the dining room was a bed room, making a total of six bed rooms. The frame structure back of the dining room was the kitchen which had been built on last. There was a fireplace in nearly every room.

When Tom Stockton built the Clifton House he had not overlooked the possibility of Indian raids in northern New Mexico. Not so long before there had been horrible massacres not too far away, and a place such as Clifton House with its thick adobe walls, its provisions in the large basement, and its water supply in the kitchen was a welcome addition to the unsettled community. A man felt safer if there was some place to take his family and stay in at least partial safety while the Utes and Commanches did their prowling and killing.

The cattlemen and the people of the vicinity made the Clifton House a busy place at times. Then too, there were the government men who traveled back and forth over the Santa Fe Trail, the traveling men (or drummers as they were once known), and the invaders who were looking for a place to start a new home, or a climate to help them physically, or those who were coming in or going through, traveling and looking for adventure and experience in this western land that was being settled.

The Barlow and Sanderson Stages, running up and down the Santa Fe Trail, increased the numbers traveling in and out of New Mexico. Clifton House being midway between El Morro and Cimarron offered the logical place for a stage stop. Barlow and Sanderson had a station at Uncle Dick Wooten's place on the Colorado slope of the Raton mountains, that was the first one out of El Morro (Trinidad). A station was planned for Cimarron and one at Crow Creek. This left Clifton House as the remaining spot where a stage station was needed. They tried to space their stations about twelve to fifteen miles apart. So it was arranged that Clifton House be the regular stage station. A man by the name of Messick leased the front room of the house for the office, and the bed rooms, dining room and kitchen for the purpose of feeding the pasesngers and lodging them.

Barlow & Sanderson built their barns, outbuildings and blacksmith shop nearby. Activity at the Clifton House really sped up and more than ever the place was the center of business and social activity of northern New Mexico.

The trips of the stage coaches were timed so that the coaches arrived at the Clifton House at meal time, or at nightfall, so that the passengers could get a good night's rest at this fine hotel. The stages, which were to go on immediately, found little delay for four fresh, well-fed horses, if for the southern run, and six mules if for the mountain run to Dick Wooten's, were harnessed ready to take the place of the tired, hard-driven animals which had just come off the trail.

The service travelers enjoyed at the Clifton House was the most remembered part of the journey across northern New Mexico in the 1870's. Rest could be enjoyed there in good beds. Fine foods, some of which were grown locally and others—delicacies—which had to be hauled in from the end of the railroad were to be had at the Clifton House tables. Many old-timers tell of the high prices for supplies at the store at Clifton and the high cost of lodging at the Clifton House including the meals, but it must have been worth a little extra to get good food, comfort, and service away out in this unsettled country for many paid it and very few complaints were remembered.

By 1872, Clifton had developed into quite a community; there was the Clifton House, the barns and blacksmith shop, store and saloon, and the houses of a native or two, one of which served meals to any who craved Mexican dishes.

It was in this same year—1872 (on August 22nd)—that Mathias Stockton, brother of the builder of the house, and Miss Dove Stout were married at the Clifton House. This was quite a social event in itself and called for the attendance of almost everyone within fifty miles. Thyke, as Mathias was called, took his bride to his ranch over on the lower Sugarite (Chicorica) about eight miles east from the Clifton House.

Things moved along rapidly at the Clifton House for the next few years. Business was good, there was lots of traveling and many people came and went at the famous stage station—Clifton House.

Our next report of the station is that a man by the name of Joe Adams was running the Clifton House in 1877 and 1878. It is also true according to the Stocktons that members of the Stockton family ran the place in between times, and also after Adams left.

Then came 1879 and the rails were laid and trains began to play back and forth between Otero (north of Clifton) and the east and it was no longer necessary to rely on horses and stages for transportation and hauling. The end of the stage line was at hand, another day had dawned and with it, more modern ways; the usefulness of the Clifton House was rapidly becoming a thing of the past.

It did not take long for the place to become deserted. After the activity of the 1870's ceased there seemed no reason to continue the place and there really was not. So soon it was deserted entirely.

The Clifton House remained empty for a year or two and then two men moved there and started in business. They were hog raisers. They were the Jones brothers. The people of Raton (which had sprung up by that time), soon got to calling them Hog Jones and Piggy Jones. Piggy was called thus because he was the cut-up of the pair; Hog got the more serious name because he was the business man of the partnership. So the famous stage station became a hog farm.

No one seems to remember just how long the Jones boys stayed at Clifton. The place was empty in the late 90's and fire of unknown origin destroyed most of the buildings. Time and the elements did their part and through those first years of the 20th century the Clifton House gradually settled back to the ground from which its adobe bricks were made. Today very little remains to help indicate the exact spot where but a few years ago such an active community existed, where such a fine hotel stood to give comfort and rest to weary travelers in a land so new to Americans.

"Grandmother" Stockton who lived in Northern New Mexico from 1870 until she died in 1933, has left with her grandson many interesting tales about those first years in the territory. She came to New Mexico with one of the cattle drives from Texas; she entered the territory at a point about where Roswell is located today. They came up the Pecos and Canadian rivers and arrived at Clifton in the winter of 1870.

Those early days at Clifton were difficult ones. There were no conveniences, not even like they had in the East. Food-stuffs which could be grown and secured nearby and staples could be bought at the Clifton store but delicacies were rare. Those who could afford it sent wagons, once a year, to the end of the railroad, especially after it reached Las Animas, Colorado, to bring back gingham, denim, shoes, hats, hardware, glass, sawed board, furniture, manufactured articles, and other food necessities.

The principal industry in Northern New Mexico at the time was cattle-raising. Many cattle had been driven in and from Texas after the Civil War. The country was all open range. Everyone's cattle ran together. No one thought of building more than enough fence for a horse pasture. Newcomers, who attempted to build fences in that day, were sure to find them cut between each post before they were completed. It was an unwritten law that there be no fencing of the range. Large round-ups were held each year where the calves were branded and where steers were selected for market. All who owned cattle participated. After the round-up, each cattleman would drive his cattle back to the home range. Often the cattle would have strayed a distance of a hundred miles or more.

Ranch houses were far apart and life was lonely for the women and children. The Indians gave very little trouble in Colfax County. The Utes and the Navajos lived there at times but they were peaceable. They were a nuisance, however, to the housewives near whose homes they camped, for they invariably entered any home without knocking. No trinkets or small valuables could be left lying in sight, for they would disappear when the Indians left.

The Comanches made one raid in Colfax County in the 70's. They stole and killed wherever they went. Near Folsom they cut a man's hand off, tied him to a wagon, and set fire to it. The Indians committed another murder near the present site of Koehler (coal-mining camp). Government soldiers arrived in a few days and put a stop to these atrocities and punished the Indians.

No regular services had been arranged for the various religious denominations in the community in the 70's but large crowds attended, partly from curiosity and many from a longing for spiritual uplift, when an occasional Episcopal rector or Methodist minister, traveling through the country, would hold a service. Catholic priests frequently held Mass also on their way through the section.

No schools were started in the 70's, but those with sufficient means could send their children to Trinidad, Colorado, or elsewhere for schooling.

Life of the early settlers was dull and monotonous. Travel and communication were slow and difficult. Exciting happenings of which we hear today were few and far between. The pioneer little realized that in fifty years people would look back to his day as a romantic and exciting time in which to have lived.

Contrary to the belief that the Clifton House was the headquarters for badmen, and the scene of many robberies and killings in those early days, those who lived there during that time report a very quiet but busy existence with fewer violent crimes than are common in our cities today.

Some would have it believed that the place was literally

strewn with the bones of many victims who were robbed, beaten, and killed as they passed through this northern part of the territory. It was once told that the dining room table was placed in front of a curtain and that wealthy guests would be purposely seated so that they could be attacked and killed by husky individuals concealed behind the curtains. But the worst that can be authentically reported is two violent deaths at, or near the Clifton House, and the burial of many bad men who were killed in Northern New Mexico and brought to the cemetery at Clifton for burial.

Both of these killings which were referred to hinge around the well known Clay Allison and Chunk Colbert. These two were bitter enemies, each waiting an opportunity to get the drop on the other.

The first killing was done by a sheriff from Trinidad; neither Clay nor Chunk were present. Chunk was in trouble in Trinidad; the sheriff wanted him; he had heard that Chunk was at the Clifton House, and he came over after him. The sheriff arrived after bed time, inquired of the proprietor if his man was there, disregarded the negative answer, took a candle in one hand and his cocked gun in the other, and started through the house to see for himself. He was nervous; it was a nervous job to go looking for Chunk Colbert at night or anytime. He opened a bed room door, saw a man in bed, and in his nervousness, fired. He killed one of the waiters, a young man who had come to New Mexico for his health. This was Clifton's first shooting. (The Allison-Colbert shooting has been covered in the chapter on Clay Allison.) Clifton House was often used as a picnic grounds as we gather from the Raton Comet for June 29, 1883:

"The employees of the Santa Fe road held a meeting at Loeb & Myer's store Tuesday evening to complete arrangemens for holding a celebration the coming Fourth of July. They decided to give a free excursion, have a basket picnic, grand ball and a general good time. The committee on transportation, Messrs. T. Saunders, M. T. Hudson, and W. R. Andrews, reported that a special train consisting of an engine, and two coaches could be secured, and the committee on arrangements, Mr. Dotterer, chairman, reported the Clifton House the best place for having fun. The committee on girls said that their female friends would furnish all the grub necessary, so that everything is settled and a good time is now assured. The train will leave here between 8 and 9 o'clock in the morning and go to the Clifton House. After reaching that place and the crowd gets settled, J. Osfield, Esq., will deliver an oration appropriate to the occasion and will be followed by other speakers. After the speeches everybody will drink a bottle of pop and then sit down to dinner. Good music has been secured and dancing will commence in the afternoon and continue until sometime the next morning. No intoxicating liquors will be allowed on the grounds, and a special force of officers will be sworn in to preserve order. The celebration, while it is being given by the railroad employees, will be attended by citizens of Raton and vicinity. Put on your picnic clothes, fill your biggest basket full of lunch and go to the Clifton House and enjoy yourselves."

The Stocktons never had any difficulty about their property at Clifton since they were fortunate enough to have bought from Maxwell prior to his selling the Grant. In all the transactions with the Maxwell Land Grant & Railway Company, the Maxwell Land Grant Company and the Maxwell Cattle Company one must keep in mind the number of ranchers and stockmen such as Curtis, Whitman, Dawson and Stockton who lived on the Grant as rightful owners of the land they bought from Maxwell.

WILLOW SPRINGS, NEW MEXICO

The site of Willow Springs is covered today by the very much alive city of Raton. Several old-timers point out different spots as to exactly where the hamlet stood. Kenneth Fordyce gave the W.P.A. Writer's Project as good an explanation as any.

Just how early Willow Springs enticed occasional travelers in northern New Mexico to the two big willow trees whose shade offered a spot for relaxation and whose spring offered a refreshing drink, is not known, for it may have been producing its cool mountain water for years. It is known that it was a favorite stopping place for thirsty travelers even before there was any kind of building there.

Willow Springs was located at the mouth of a canyon which today is called Railroad Canyon as the Santa Fe railroad's right-of-way is up through this canyon to the Raton Pass Tunnel at the New Mexico-Colorado state line, nine miles from Raton. In fact, the spot where the ranch house stood is a few hundred feet east of the main line tracks today. A yellow frame house stands on the spot today directly opposite Soldier Hill where at one time the ranch house stood, nearer to the arroyo than now, for the arroyo has been straightened out. In taking the curve out of it, they have moved the arroyo away from the exact location of the spring or well, which at one time was near enough to feed the arroyo with its then abundant flow of water. The spring was where Maxwell Avenue and North Third Street intersect today.

It is known that the spot was first used as a government forage station (no doubt paying Maxwell rent for the use of it) and that a corral and a store-house, which might be called a barn, were built there in which to store provisions for the traveling wagon-trains which were keeping in touch with the United States Army in New Mexico and the Far West.

Brig. General S. W. Kearny and Col. A. W. Doniphan entered New Mexico with an army in 1846 and after the trying experience of bringing the army and supply-train over the Raton mountains, a day of rest was ordered and that day of rest was taken at a camp just east of the Willow Springs where water was obtained. Of course, after the army went on and was stationed at Santa Fe where the general took possession of New Mexico for the United States, and later at Fort Union (north of Las Vegas) constant communication with the East was maintained and messengers and supply-trains came over Raton Pass and therefore by way of Willow Springs.

Willow Springs was an ideal place for a home . . . good water, wonderful pasturage for cattle, then too, anything would grow in the rich soil of New Mexico with water on it and water was plentiful. Just how many lived there in those first days of occupation cannot be said but in 1871 we learn that a Mr. Sears, known as "Sears at the Springs," had been living at the spot in a jacal log house which it is said had only two rooms. He was not the first occupant; someone had lived there before him as early as the 1860 s. (This would not be hard to believe especially since the soldiers from Fort Union built the highway over the Pass, and Uncle Dick Wooten was building his toll gate to facilitate travel.) Sears gets credit for removing the jacal and building a four roomed log house which faced the spring. Also along the way sometime, someone decided that something must be done about the diminishing supply of water from Willow Springs and a seventy foot well was dug at the spot which opened up a new water supply. There were other springs above and below Willow Springs along the arroyo and they and Willow Springs supplied the arroyo with an abundance of water. Willow Arroyo, later called Willow Creek, always had water running between its banks in those early days.

In 1871, John Thacker, an Iowan with the true spirit of a pioneer, came over the Raton Pass from Colorado where the Thackers had been living and settled on the Willow Springs Ranch which they later acquired from Mr. Sears. The Thackers brought 700 head of cattle with them and stayed in New Mexico. They did not live at Willow Springs long, perhaps a year. Charles Thacker, the son of John Thacker, gives the date as 1871, and says that he and other cowboys lived back near the hills, in the neighborhood of the present Fairmont Cemetery, where there was a good water-hole. Perhaps Mr. Sears was still at the ranch house in 1872. The John Thackers may have been living with him or they may have moved into the Willow Springs Ranch house later than that from some other house on the ranch, for Mr. Fayette Gillespie, who came to New Mexico with his father in October 1872, states that Mr. Sears lived at Willow Springs at the time, and that the Thackers bought it after that. This creates a slight discrepancy in the dates when the transfer took place, and it is impossible to correctly state the undisputed date.

It is recorded that in 1874 the owner of Willow Springs Ranch was offering the water for sale to travelers for twenty-five cents per bucket. It is also said that many postponed their baths and even their morning splashes in washpans until cheaper water was obtainable.

The Willow Springs Ranch is often referred to as a stage station of the Barlow & Sanderson Stage Line. According to Mr. Judd Lyons who came into New Mexico in 1877, Willow Springs was only an emergency station. The first station on the stage line (in New Mexico) was at Clifton House. The drivers often stopped at the Willow Springs Ranch House, if they were on time, to give their mules or horses a drink of water and allow their passengers to get out and stretch. Willow Springs was not a regular station; no meals were served to passengers of the stages, nor was it a scheduled alighting place.

Mr. Judd Lyons, who was born in Vermont in 1857, and came to the area in 1877, says that the Willow Springs Ranch House was then owned by Mr. William Boggs, who was originally from Maryland. Mr. Boggs must have stayed on the Willow Springs property until about 1885, when the Maxwell Land Grant Company claimed ownership of the land and put him off. A group of Anti-Granters led by the Rev. O. P. McMains, put Mr. Boggs back in the house and from the roof of a Willow Springs building, the group armed with Winchesters defied the deputies to come and try it again. The deputies took a look at the group, held a conference and decided that they did not relish the job too well or at least well enough to attempt it, and abandoned the idea for a time. But finally Mr. Boggs had to vacate. This was just one incident in that Maxwell Land Grant War which was such a serious thing and which caused so many deaths in northern New Mexico through those first settlement years.

Back to Willow Springs Ranch . . . according to Mr. Lyons, Mr. George J. Pace came to Willow Springs early in 1878, and started a store in the west room of the ranch house which he rented from Boggs. Pace had operated a store for a Mr. Graft in both Las Animas and Trinidad, Colorado, and Mr. Graft had staked Pace to a bill of goods to open a store in northern New Mexico. George J. Pace got his store ready to open, and he related to Walter L. Johnson of Raton a few years ago how on the first day that he was open for business a negro was killed near the ranch house and there being no other place to put the body, it was laid on the counter of the store for the night. Of course, it was removed and buried early the next morning on the hill just above the house. The hill is now called Soldier Hill.

Mr. Lyons relates how earlier than 1878, everyone for a hundred miles had to go to Clifton House for his mail. At that time Clifton House was being run by Joe Adams. The stages brought mail in and left it at Clifton. As soon as Pace opened his store a petition was circulated requesting a post office at Willow Springs. Mr. Lyons, a young man out West for his health and working for one hundred and fifty dollars a year, was one of the signers of the petition. The post office was granted and Willow Springs was the post office that year. Pace was named as postmaster. It was a great conveience to people living in the vicinity.

Mr. Lyons says that the first passenger train came over the switch-back and down into New Mexico in February 1878. He was here and all his information has proved very reliable, yet the general impression has been that the first trains came over in 1879. (Which they actually did, despite Mr. Lyons. One just has to search the records maintained by the Santa Fe railroad. Too much of the W.P.A. information has been taken from old-timers who remembered events rather than dates. Talking to old-timers is wonderful but misleading. I once questioned six old-timers about a hanging they witnessed: Two said it was on a Sunday morning, one on a Tuesday, one on a Wednesday, one on a Friday, the other wasn't too sure whether it was Tuesday or Wednesday. All were off on the date from one month to three years.) However, to back up his statement is the fact that Otero, fifteen miles down in New Mexico, was a town for about twelve months before it was moved back to the present site of Raton and it is a fact that this migration of the town of Otero took place in the spring of 1880. So the first tracks must have been built down the Raton mountains in 1878 on to Otero late in that year; the town of Otero survived during 1879, and moved back to the foot of the Raton Pass in 1880.

As soon as Otero started, which was when the railroad built to that location and established a division point, Pace left Willow Springs and moved his store and post office to Otero, and early in 1880 he moved them back to the new city of Raton, and opened his store on South First Street (now the 100 block) and did not go back to Willow Springs.

William Howells tells of coming to Raton on January 16, 1882, and getting his first job at the Willow Springs cafe. The Santa Fe round-house was being built at the time and a Mr. Lewis and a group of stone masons from Colorado and Kansas were in Raton doing work on the stone building. This group of men boarded at the old William Boggs place. The meals were served in the long front room of the four-roomed log house. Later when this room could no longer accommodate the group which came to dine there, a larger boarding house was quickly and rudely constructed and this served as the dining room. It was located between the log house and Willow Creek.

It is told how Mrs. Boggs disciplined her help with the long pieces of kindling which they burned in the wood stove. This was true when the drinks had been passed to her or just when they were obtainable. After one experience with the owner and her stick of kindling Howells sought employment elsewhere. The Willow Springs cafe or boarding house must have been one of the first places in which to eat in what is now the city of Raton.

Willow Springs changed hands many times in those early years. We find the Gillum family moving into the place in 1890. They have come over from their first New Mexico home on the Vermejo and moved into Willow Springs. There were Mr. and Mrs. Gillum, two daughters and a son. The son, Shell, living in Raton, has pointed out the exact spot where the house stood, where the spring or well was, and the original course of the arroyo. He also related many tales of the place and how the arroyo was dry during most of the 1890 years; how the spring or well produced water only during the rainy season, and how by 1895 it had dried up entirely.

Mr. Gillum tells of an orchard that his father planted on the two acres immediately south of the ranch house in 1891. Apple trees were imported and set out but when the drying-up process of the spring-well and the arroyo took place there was insufficient moisture for the development of the trees and they died. Other orchards were doing well in the country but they were located where conditions were more favorable, particularly along the lower Sugarite creek, four or five miles to the east, and the Vermejo river, thirty miles to the south.

Mr. Judd Lyons who lived four miles east of the present site of Raton on the Forster place (now the Ellis Jones ranch) from 1877 says that the amount of water that ever came from Willow Springs was grossly exaggerated. He sometimes doubts now that there ever was a spring at that exact spot but that there was one up the canyon and one some distance south. If he is correct then all those who called the place Willow Springs were badly misled. Perhaps it was only a well after all. But it must have supplied water to many to get the reputation that it enjoyed.

When the Gillums moved into Willow Springs ranch-house it was a four roomed log house with barns and outbuildings. A photograph taken of the Gillum family a short time after they came to the place and supposedly taken at the house shows the walls of adobe. It had either been done over with adobe or the picture shows the view of one of the out-houses which were built of adobe. The house is gone now and new residences have been built along the railroad on a public thoroughfare which is called Railroad Avenue. They face the railroad tracks. They are now part of the busy little city of Raton.

The Willow Springs Ranch House was the first spot on which man lived in Raton. It was truly the birthplace of Raton. Those who lived there went about their everyday business of living, little realizing that they were making the first history of a city and so they did not record their comings or goings, and often not even their names. Memories, which are sometimes confused by the passing of too many days and months and years have furnished the few facts that are known about Raton's birthplace. It is unfortunate that more facts cannot be recorded and preserved about Willow Springs and time will even erase the memory of the name.

OTERO, NEW MEXICO

Otero had the distinction of being the first town of the Santa Fe railroad on the Maxwell Land Grant and in New Mexico. Even after the railroad decided to change for Raton the town survived for a few years. It was named to honor the first Miguel Antonio Otero who did much to bring the Santa Fe to New Mexico. Let his son tell the story for us:

In recognition of the part my father had played in this railroad development, the first railroad town and station to be built in New Mexico was named Otero. It was about five miles south of Raton, and the commission houses thought it a good policy to establish branches at Otero. I was among the clerks transferred from El Moro to Otero for, as I seemed a hopeless case so far as going to school was concerned, my father had decided to put more responsibility upon me in the business. So I was designated bookkeeper and cashier for the branch house at Otero, although I was then only eighteen years old.

Otero was a booming town for the next few months, or, to be exact, until the railroad reached Las Vegas. It was here in the spring of 1879 that Russ A. Kistler made his first appearance in New Mexico. He called at the office one day and asked for Mr. Otero. As my father was not in town, I asked if I could serve him. That led Mr. Kistler to tell me of his trouble. His press had arrived and was on one of the freight cars in the railroad yards, but he was unable to obtain it until he could pay the freight charges.

He very frankly said he was hard up just then and had not enough money for his next meal. He had hoped to negotiate a small loan with my father. I inquired how much he needed and he replied, "Twenty dollars," adding at the same time that if I would let him have the amount he would either return it in a few days or allow my father to take it out in advertising in the paper he was going to start. I thought the case was a meritorious one and agreed to let him have the amount he needed, accepting his proposal to take it out in advertising.

The first issue of the Otero Optic came out on May 22, 1879, and it ran successfully until, with the general exodus from Otero, Kistler transferred his establishment to Las Vegas and renamed the paper The Daily Optic.

I remember a humorous incident that happened at Otero during the summer of 1879. One of the large stockholders of the Santa Fe railroad living in Boston sent his son to Otero to learn the railroad business, under the special care of the railroad agent, requesting him to give the young man some kind of light work in the office and at the same time see that he took daily horseback rides so that he might regain somewhat of his failing health. He was a student at Harvard and was somewhat run down physically. We wanted to make his visit pleasant for him, but failed utterly, for he was one of those knowing youths, perfectly well satisfied with himself in every way, who knew a little more than the average westerner. He held himself aloof from the common herd and particularly shunned the "vulgar commisison-house boys."

The railroad agent who had the responsibility of caring for the young man was, as is usually the case, looking out for his own advancement with the company. So he agreed with all the bombastic utterances, and humored the visitor in every way, to our great disgust.

One evening we held a meeting in our office for the purpose of laying plans to take the young Bostonian out on a real "snipe hunt." Certain members of our clan were appointed to feel him out gradually, and at last he became greatly interested. We told him that many of the boys objected to his joining the party owing to his attitude in the past in avoiding our company. This seemed to soften him, and he intimated that in the future he would try to tolerate us. So we finally consented to allow him to accompany us merely as a looker-on, but if he liked it, we might get up another party while he was there.

The night was settled on, and we all agreed upon the meeting place. At once we started east, crossing Red River and then going southeast for about four miles to the sand hills and brush. Every detail had been carefully prepared, and every man knew his part perfectly. The Harvard student was being entertained regarding the peculiarities of this particular kind of snipe, the methods we would have to use to capture them, and the hard work involved in driving them. This last fact became the ground for a lively controversy as to who should hold the bag, which seemed the easiest part of the whole performance.

Many of the party scattered and soon the whistling commenced. The word was passed about that a large flock had been seen running south. Soon we all started to whistle and the Eastern lad was asked to join us, as this was done to hold the birds together.

At this point a general dispute arose as to who should hold the bag, several insisting that it was their turn. No one would give in. Finally, one of them threw the bag on the ground saying: "Well, take it. I am through." Then the young man from good old Boston came to the rescue and volunteered to hold the bag himself, saying that he felt that he could do much better at that part than he could at chasing the birds. Some further discussion ensued, and, after considerable wrangling, it was agreed that inasmuch as he was a stranger and an invited guest, it would be only proper to allow him the privilege of holding the bag. So each one became alert in showing him the easiest way to hold the bag and impressing upon him the necessity of whistling all the time.

After getting him into the proper position, we left him holding the bag. We circled all around him once, then started briskly for home, leaving the young man all alone. When we had reached the outskirts of the town, we heard a bunch of coyotes and grey wolves howling loudly near the place where we had left the young Bostonian, and many of the party became alarmed and suggested that we go back. But just then something passed like a flash of greased lightning; it was the young man speeding for dear life, pale and nearly dead with fright. It was a good lesson and from that night on until he returned to his eastern home, he was a changed individual, and really enjoyed our company.

Before concluding my recollections of Otero, I must relate a good story connected with our old Brobdingnagian denizen of the dance halls referred to in a preceding chapter as Steamboat. She had been a familiar figure on the old frontier for many years, and as the years passed her shadow grew not less but greater. Everyone knew her beaming, good-natured face, and her tenderness was proverbial.

She deserves a page in the history of the old frontier, for casually speaking the greatest old specimen dangling on memory's string was the fair, fat and forty, Steamboat, who was at Hays, Kansas, in 1868. She was really an adjunct to the commission houses, starting with them from the first and continuing at every move until reaching Las Vegas in 1879.

She really was a fragile old girl and would not have weighed more than three hundred and fifty younds on the platform scales. Her name was Dolores Martinez and she was an exceptionally bright native woman or she would not have remained so long in the dance hall business and its subsidiary attachments.

It was in the fall of 1878 that she managed to get her three hundred and fifty pounds avoirdupois over Raton Pass from Trinidad and into the new town of Otero, and there she established a dance hall. It was not long before her place of amusement was the most popular resort in the lively little place. All the tough characters on the border camped there that winter and enjoyed the rough and tumble amusements at Steamboat's sale de baile on Main Street. The usual run of promiscuous shootings and gun play occurred among the trigger-conscious citizens who frequented the joint, although I do not recall that anybody was ever killed there, which seems passing strange, considering the greater part of the owl-eyed strangers and frequenters who danced attendance at Steamboat's art gallery.

One bright afternoon in spring a gayly attired dude strayed in, fresh from the East, and took a seat just as any well-behaved wall-flower should have done. He amused himself by rubbering around with his legs crossed and minding his own business in the orthodox fashion as became a refined young man of good breeding. The hammer-clawers saw at a glance that he was an inoffensive tenderfoot, and the dance went on with joy unconfined.

A big lug of a cow-puncher came in just as an overgrown horsefly alighted on the tip of the patent-leather shoe, which was sticking out in everybody's road. The cow-boy saw a streak of sunlight fall softly on the insect. Immediately the degenerate son of the range pulled his trusty six-shooter and took a heavy crack at the harmless fly, remarking that he bet that he could get it. Mr. Cowpuncher got more than he bargained for, because in that instant, he had stampeded the whole congregation of brave men and fair women. The single door at the rear was the only way out. They made a dash for it like a flock of scared sheep in a mad race for their lives. The second old buck stumbled and fell in the narrow doorway, and the others rushing behind tumbled over his prostrate form until he was buried six or eight deep upon the squirming, excited humanity—men and women all piled up in a heap like the dead in the sunken road at Waterloo. As for poor Steamboat—where, oh, where was she in all her sadness?

She was near the front door when the rumpus started, and having neither time nor desire to linger longer in such tight quarters, she let out an awful squeal, much like a hungry coyote when scenting a dead horse, gave way to the terror of the instant, and made a dash for the rear exit as the other frantic inmates had done. She was off to such a late start, however, that the gangway was choked. She saw a slight opening at the top, and made a flying leap for it. Steamboat was pretty nimble on her feet for such a big chunk of woman, and it was remarkable how gracefully she sailed through the air. It seemed as though the flight of time had passed for one brief moment, and then the "sylph-like" form of Steamboat landed on her ample frontage squarely on top of the wriggling heap of men and women. For an awful moment she poised there, balanced in mid-air, half in and half out. The louts yelled like so many hyenas, but it was to no avail. Just then the villian, who was still following her, took deliberate aim and creased her anatomy with a speedy bullet. With a display of feminine agility that was really astonishing under such trying circumstances, the old girl lost her toe-hold and fell backward with a crashing thump on the hard floor.

The cavaliers who were not injured in the wild charge, picked up her tenderly, lifting her elephantine body with much care they carried her into Doctor Robin's field hospital next door, which was always on tap for such emergencies. Cock-eyed Charlie Hall, the head nurse, when no one else was around, patched up the shattered old Steamboat, so as to get her safely out of drydock and back to port in an hour or so, a little the worse for wear and tear of a hard trip, but, if I may say the figure, like an ambitious prize fighter "slightly disfigured but still in the ring." The town gave the "old landmark" a great reception that night. As for the tenderfoot, the cowboy and the horse-fly, they all got away and were seen no more.

But wild life continued to go on and killings did take place as we gather from the Cimarron News and Press of November 27, 1879: "On Thursday last a shooting affray took place in the town of Otero in which Harry Bassett, the livery stable keeper, was killed and Zeneas Curtis severely wounded. As near as we can get at the facts they are as follows: Marion Littrell had been appointed deputy sheriff and in company with Will South and Zeneas Curtis were in Otero with the intention of arresting some men for whom they had warrants. This sheriff's party had consulted Bassett, who was also a deputy sheriff, some hours previous in regard to making the arrests, and afterwards accused him of acting in bad faith to them; some unfriendly words were exchanged when Bassett pulled his pistol and shot Curtis in the side, and before Bassett could shoot again one of the other party fired at him with a rifle, shooting him through the lungs. Bassett fell senseless, he afterwards regained consciousness, but died the following morning. Curtis's wound is a painful one, but no fears are entertained as to his ultimate recovery.'

DILLON CANYON, NEW MEXICO

Dillon was a coal mining village southeast of Blossburg at the end of the spur line that brought the coal cars to the main line of the Santa Fe railroad. Very little has been written about it and it survived but a short time due to the fact that most of the mining was changed to the Blossburg area. It was a little village at the edge of Dillon Canyon where the miners worked the coal fields. We must draw on meagre bits of information to fill the gap. Dillon was named after one of the officials of the coal company and not after anyone connected with the Maxwell Land Grant Company.

"At the saw-mill, Mr. Fry is in full charge, and having a large experience in the business, conducts the affairs of the company in a most satisfactory manner, and is much esteemed by all who know or have dealings with him . . . A dance will be given Friday night before Christmas (1881), and arrangements have been made for a coach to take those invited from Raton up and return them. It is expected that a large crowd will be present and a nice evening may be expected . . . At Dillon Canyon tomorrow is pay day, and the boys will draw their mite and many of them spend Sunday in Raton. With them pay day means a great deal. They all make good wages and have but little temptation or inclination to spend it. Hence at the end of the month there is scarcely a man who has not saved a snug little sum, and there are but few of them who have not the sense to know how to use it. We entertain great respect for all the lads at the Canyon, for as a whole they are an intelligent, jovial set and possess many sterling qualities lacking in those who laugh at honest work, and who judge a man by the clothes he wears. Through life we wish them all a prosperous journey, and hope they may be successful in returning home with good health and much good. After that silence. We hear no more of the place but it is still on the map. Ranchers speak of having their place over at Dillon, but today it is only a name. It flickered for a brief moment then died out. The center of its activity was transferred to Blossburg. At the rate that Raton is growing it will soon encompass the Dillon area.

CATSKILL, NEW MEXICO

This was one of the very few towns on the Maxwell Land Grant that had any direct connection with the company. The town got its start in the summer of 1890, when it was platted by the Maxwell Land Grant Company and tracts were leased in the nearby forests for the development of lumber companies to Wilder, McAlpine, Abeyta and Vasquez who set up lumber mills and attracted many workers to the area. Said the Trinidad paper (September 19, 1890):

"The little town of Catskill has sprung up in the past few weeks as the entrepot of the timberlands of Southern Colorado via the new Maxwell extension. The new city now comprises all the accessories of a modern frontier town. Business houses of every description, save those dispensing beverages of an intoxicating nature, and numberless private residences are making it quite a town. The chief business of the section to which the town is the entrepot lies up the Red River, west of Catskill, and it is the development of the lumber resources of a densely wooded section of the country.

"At Catskill Mr. Wilder is putting in the machinery for an immense sawmill. Two miles up the river Mr. McAlpine is busily engaged with a crew of men setting up two sawmills. Still two miles further Abeyta and Vasquez are placing the machinery for another sawmill, and a short distance up the same river the same firm have almost completed a mill whose capacity will be 15,000 feet of lumber per day. Abeyta and Vasquez have also another mill on the same stream which will be ready for operation this week. The latter mill, about twelve miles from Catskill, is supposed to be the terminus of the road. J. G. Allard of Raton, will be interested in two of the above mentioned sawmills, having made a lease of wood for extensive lath mills."

"The new town of Catskill is moving right along. A school house is being erected and a water system, mains, etc., are being put in. Several restaurants, a blacksmith shop, feed stores and two large mercantile stores have already been established. Three Raton gentlemen will soon put up a large store against the railroad track. Trains are now coming in on the new road, and a telegraph car is among the improvements of the town. As Catskill will always be a mountain division point of the U.P. and the center of a large farming trade, its future importance is well assured." *(Raton Range, October 3, 1890)*

"At last the much talked about Maxwell branch of the U.P. railroad is completed to the end of the original survey —the new town of Catskill. It is an excellent piece of engineering and its construction compares with any stretch of road on the entire system.

"Bright and early yesterday morning Agent J. F. Linthurst, Trainmaster Frederick and an Advertiser (Trinidad, Colorado newspaper) representative boarded Conductor John Burk's train and in a few moments were speeding towards the 'front'. This was the first regular train that had been run the entire length of the branch.

"The train first stopped at Sopris (Colorado) then Martinsen (Colorado) and then at Pels (New Mexico). Up to this point there is a gradual grade. Here, however, commences the steepest grade on the system, possibly with the exception of the Georgetown loop. To the left of the Pels station and high up in the neighboring mountain one sees what appears to be a wagon road leading to some forest that surmounts it, but upon closer inspection finds that it is a part of the railroad. Indeed, Agent Linthurst himself could not realize for sometime that it was a railroad. He remarked to Conductor Burk that it was a 'pretty high wagon road.' The good-natured John smiled an Hibernian smile and striking the agent on the back said, 'Why, Linty, can't you tell a wagon road from a railroad?' Mr. Linthurst was surprised and after gazing steadfast for a time said, 'You are right, John, I see the rails now.'

"The ascent of the steep grade began and as the train nears the high bridge, which is about halfway to the top of the mountain, a view is obtained of the valley below that is beautiful in the extreme. The engine, in charge of engineer Hamburger, labors on with its heavy load and finally the summit is reached which is 8,161 feet high, almost two thousand feet higher than the city of Trinidad. The decline then commences and in a few minutes Catskill is reached.

"The little town is beautifully situated, lying in the midst of the Red River valley. Surrounding it are large forests of pine trees which in a short time will be cut down to supply the saw mills. Business in the little village is already quite brisk. Several sawmills are in the course of construction and when completed Catskill will present the appearance of a true Western town, full of thrift and energy.

"The Maxwell branch, as stated, is one of the best stretches of road on the Union Pacific system. Trainmaster Frederick declared that, considering that it was but a new road, it was in excellent condition, in fact better than some old roads. This speaks volumes for contractor DuRemer, who built the road, and for his able assistant, Pete Hennessy, under whose direction the track was laid. The trains are manned by careful and competent trainsmen so that for a pleasant trip there is none more enjoyable than the ride over the Maxwell branch.' *(Ibid, October 10, 1890)*

"It is gratifying to learn that a seven foot vein of fine bituminous coal has been developed immediately within the townsite of Catskill. The discovery was made by the Acme Fence Company while sinking a well. This will give the new town a wonderful impetus and bring the inexhaustible resources of Colfax county into prominence." *(Ibid)*

The Acme Fence Company sent William McCullum and Harry Whigham to Catskill to establish a factory there that would furnish enough work for one hundred men. There were also some dark days in the village as the time when James T. Gibbons shot and killed David Barker in a quarrel over a worthless dog. It was Thursday, November 20, 1890, when Mrs. Gibbons, with her little daughter, went to Barker's butcher shop to buy some meat. Their dog tagged along and for some unknown reason bit one of the butcher's children. Gibbons upon learning of the incident grabbed his gun and shot at the dog three times without effect. Barker took his Winchester and also took after the dog. Gibbons saw him and asked: "Did you kill the dog."

"Yes, and I will kill you too," answered the butcher.

He started to re-load his rifle. Gibbons, seeing that he meant to carry out his threat, ran around the back of the house, but the door was locked. He had no choice but to plant himself squarely against it and wait for Barker. As the butcher turned the corner Gibbons shot, the ball entering in the ear and lodging at the base of the brain. In default of a $5,000 bail, Gibbons was taken to the Springer jail. It was later seen as a plain case of self defense. William Morris, who killed Ed Jones at Baldy was captured by Sheriff McCuistion at Catskill and taken to Springer, then the county seat.

E. G. Segerstrom opened a drugstore at Catskill. J. M. Waldcorn was named the first postmaster. William Buttler of Catskill has just finished digging his potatoes and from six acres has 60,000 pounds of the finest potatoes ever grown in this or any other country. Mr. Wall of Muscatine, Iowa, arrived yesterday and in a few days will go to Catskill to superintend the construction of the Acme Fence Company. The main building will be 350 ft. by 40. Albert Lawrence succeeded Waldcorn as postmaster on June 1, 1893. On July 4, 1891, a fire broke out that destroyed the saloons of Ira Gave and John Hixenbaugh. Dunn's store was threatened but the building was saved. Catskill is assuming metropolitan airs. A race course, dancing pavillion and baseball grounds are the latest acquisitions. After June 5, 1891, Catskill will have a daily mail from Trinidad, Colorado. The Catskill Ladies Band is a sensation. So is the Catskill Cornet Band. The public schools of Catskill are showing excellent progress under the management of Professor Chapman and Miss Florence York. The ladies of the W.C.T.U. invite all to the ceremony of the placing of the cornerstone for the Union Church (March 27, 1894). H. G. Franenburger replaces Lawrence as postmaster of Catskill. Mrs. Oliver Silvernail is principal of the Catskill schools (1897). The residence of Ernest Chapman was consumed by fire (Nov. 2, 1891). The Southern Hotel of Catskill is making out fine with its Saturday night dances. Catskill will be abandoned after October 1, 1901. The lumber companies and railroad will continue on at Sopris, Colorado. The Colorado and Southern Railroad tried to save the town by putting in new improvements, building a splendid park and a large modern hotel, but somehow it settled down to being a ghost town and remained such after 1905. Catskill was named by one of the men who platted the town because it reminded him of the area surrounding the Catskill Mountains along the Hudson river in New York.

PELS, NEW MEXICO

This little hamlet was named for the manager of the Maxwell Land Grant Company. It was a station on the railroad, a center for lumber and a little coal mining. The winters were too severe and the place gradually settled down to a ranching area. Modern maps fail to list it. The Maxwell Land Grant had hopes of a great lumber industry there but with too many irons in the fire it had to abandon the attempt.

ELKINS, NEW MEXICO

This was named for the famous lawyer who made an effort to establish a large ranch in the area, prior to moving to West Virginia. Never really a town nor even a village, the United States government thought enough of it to establish a post office there. One or two stores, a blacksmith shop and a carpentershop made up the village. Of course there was a saloon and place for the Saturday night dances.

BRILLIANT, NEW MEXICO

So many people confuse Blossburg with Brilliant. Both have disappeared, but they were two different towns. There were no paved streets in Brilliant but the houses were pretty much in line like those of a city street. There were quite a few families and one could live comfortably in a five room apartment for seventeen dollars a month. The Rocky Mountain Coal Company had its rules about using coal which was not out of keeping at all both for cooking and for heating. There was a tremendous store where one could buy all sorts of things but when that closed down the people went to Raton to make their purchases. The store was then used for church services. There was a wonderful school at Brilliant with four teachers for the eight grades. It was a more substantial building than one would hope to look for in a mining town.

The people of Brilliant were the most generous next to Dawson in aiding causes. They always gave to help anyone down and out and were especially devoted to the Red Cross, the Community Chest, the March of Dimes and other such civic drives. They kept their homes spic and span and always managed to invite guests for dinner. For a time it looked as if Brilliant would be the largest coal mining town in Northern New Mexico but by 1948 it joined the ranks of Ghost Towns. No one knows why these things happen. There is still enough coal at Brilliant to supply all the railroads in the United States for the next six years. Some day the Rocky Mountain Coal Company may open up the town again and laughter will ring through the canyons that surround the quaint village.

CUNNINGHAM, NEW MEXICO

Northeast of Clifton House was the Cunningham ranch and railroad station. It was never known for much except for a daring train robbery which netted the robbers just $45. "A most brutal holdup and robbery occurred on a C. & S. freight at Cunningham, on the Rocky Mountain Route, at midnight, Monday night (August 10, 1908). S. S. Dorsey, and brother, J. F. Dorsey, of Vernon, Texas, were the victims, and they charge two C. & S. brakemen, who were in charge of caboose No. 211, on the C. & S., foothills of the Rocky Mountain range through its entire length.

Even in the camps of competing projects and in general throughout the county one hears no criticism, no adverse comment, but general tribute is paid to the combined natural beauties of the property and the enterprise of its owners in so rapidly developing its magnificent possibilities.

It did not take but a cursory glance to assure those who originally came to inspect the ground that they had found ideal conditions, and the bargain for the purchase of the 18,000 acres involved was concluded in record time. The project was started less than four years ago (1907) and has been the admiration of many ever since.

The crops harvested from the thirty or more farms on and a hobo, who they could identify, as their assailants.

"The Dorseys who are intelligent ranch boys of good appearance, shipped out of Texline, Texas, Monday afternoon, with a train of cattle, expecting to be carried with the train to Trinidad, Colorado, on their way to Rocky Ford where they expected to work. After helping load the cattle and getting settled down on their trip, they were told by the train crew that they must put up cash for their trip, and after considerable argument gave the brakeman two dollars. At DesMoines the train was switched from the C & S to the Rocky Mountain, because of a washout between Des Moines and Trinidad, and here a cargo of hoboes, numbering about forty, were allowed to board the train by the brakemen.

"After the train had passed Cunningham, the junction of the Rocky Mountain and the Santa Fe, Raton & Des Moines, the Dorsey brothers were approached by the brakemen and asked to give up more money for their ride to Trinidad. The boys refused, and were jocularly told that they had a gun, and finally submitted to a search by the brakemen, who were then aided by a man who seemed to have charge of the cattle on the train. Finding that the boys were unarmed, the brakemen left them for a few minutes returning later with their pick-handle clubs. This time they demanded money from the Dorseys, and when refused, one of them struck the older Dorsey a terrific blow on the head, which put him out of commission for the time being. The Dorseys were then stood up and searched, and forty-five dollars and fifteen cents taken from them. The brakemen then led their victims back to the caboose, but within a few car lengths from the end they were told to jump off. The train was going at the rate of about twenty miles an hour, and the men were forced off the steps. Neither was seriously injured by the fall, and they struck out across the hills for the Santa Fe railroad, arriving at Otero at daylight. From Otero the men walked to Raton, arriving there with a good appetite for breakfast . . . Up to Tuesday afternoon the men who did the deed had not been captured . . ." (Raton Range, Aug. 12, 1908.)

MIAMI, NEW MEXICO

The Raton Range tells us the story of this community which once attracted so much attention and is now but a few scattered houses. A sign on Highway 85 points in the general direction and an old dirt road leads you to it. Great things were expected of it but so were they of E Town and a hundred others.

Among the dozen or more corporation and private irrigation projects in Colfax county (on the Maxwell Land Grant), none has attracted more attention on account of its instantaneous popularity than that of the Farmers Development Company, controlling the famous Miami Ranch, located ten miles west of Springer, in one of the most beautiful of the many beautiful valleys that open from the the ranch in 1910, speak louder and more practically than any other voice can of the proof of that both in theory and reality the company's plan is practically flawless. Of the 10,000 acres that will eventually be under irrigation, about 2,500 were under the plow this season. In less than three years therefore, one fourth of the original project has come under the plow, and the diverted waters of the Rayado have reclaimed land that has produced thousands of dollars worth of produce where only a few head of cattle ranged before. Monster stacks of alfalfa greet the eye at every turn. Other great stacks of oat and wheat straw speak mutely but eloquently of the thousands of bushels of grain either marketed—cashed in—or now in the barns and granaries of the prosperous farmers.

There is always to be found in a new community like Miami, one or two farmers whose crops are a little better than those of their neighbors, and in the Miami colony this year the one man who carried off the chief prizes at the county fair is B. F. McEndarfer whose eighty acre farm is a model in all respects.

FRENCH, NEW MEXICO

Colfax county contains a great many refutations of the theory that large stock raisers care for nothing else than cattle, and cherish only contempt for the plodding knight of the plow, said the Raton Range for December 2, 1910. Captain William French, one of the most prominent stockmen of New Mexico, who had been largely interested in cattle raising for twenty years in the Socorro area, and still owns several square miles of fine range in that county secured a "bit-o-ground" in the Cimarron valley a few years ago, in all about 130,000 acres, which he fenced into farms and pastures, and forsook the traditional long-horn breeds for the docile and beefy "white-faces" . . . After selling 50,000 acres of the Antelope Valley end of his ranch to the French Land & Irrigation Company, he still has 80,000 acres of fertile valley . . . French is a jolly Englishman, a brother of General French of South African fame and a royal entertainer in every way. The French Land & Irrigation Company whose tract of 50,000 acres between Maxwell and Springer on the Santa Fe railroad was formerly owned by Captain French for whom the corporation as well as the townsite was named is doing a brisk business.

French is known as The Junction City and is located at the intersection of the El Paso & Southwestern with the Santa Fe as the main line. The company's land lies on the west side of the Santa Fe tracks in a triangle formed by the two railroads. The town of French is exceptionally well built, most of the structures being of cement blocks and are very substantial and attractive in appearance. A 40 room hotel, several fine stores, an auto garage, a planing mill, a lumber yard, a grain elevator and fine residences make up the town.

Do not forget the Catholic Ladies Aid Society supper—Chicken supper and apron sale at Armon Brooks store. W. A. Cole, of the contracting firm of Cole and Work is engaged in building a reservoir and dam for the Canfield Development Company. The Dawson payrol of $34,000 was taken from the station at French in a daring holdup by three men. They held up several pasesngers and guards and dynamited the station and took the Wells Fargo strongbox. Three masked men sought to induce Smith, who was in the telegraph office, to open the door. When he refused to do so they put a stick of dynamite under the floor and blew down the door. Smith, uninjured, ran to the restaurant nearby for help, but no one there had a gun. The bandits took the trail to Eagle Tail Mountain. Two years later Bub Farmer was indicted by a Grand Jury for complicity in this holdup. Wells Fargo offered one thousand dollars for each bandit captured.

With the ice in excellent condition for skating on French's lake east of Cimarron, coupled with the fact that the moon has turned night into day has drawn a large crowd every night last week to enjoy its fine skating . . . Many thousands of acres of the French Tract are being sold for a settlement eight miles from Cimarron for the townsite of French. The French Land Irrigation Company is employing hundreds of hands on the irrigation reservoir and water system. French organized a baseball team and started its high school in 1910. Dr. Polard set up his clinic there.

Another postoffice has been established in Colfax county. The growing importance of the newly developed section of the country owned by the French Land & Irrigation Company has made it necessary to establish a postoffice at French and this rapidly growing town has at last been placed on the map. John Friege has been apopinted postmaster . . . Ray L. Gibbons has contracted for a residence on 1st Street, East, and will commence building a home twenty-four foot square in the near future. He is one of the first pioneers of French having been the first gentleman known to bring his wife to this town . . . R. J. Dobell succeeds Friege as postmaster. Miss Allen and Miss Fiddler taught music at French. Miss Allen also taught the Eighth, Ninth and Tenth grades in the highschool. Charles Cardonetti put up the blacksmith shop and became the village smithy. Louisa Allen, the school teacher, married Ed Radcliff and Alice Fiddler married Frank McElroy. John and Harry Brennan bought out Coffen & Co. General Merchandise.

As the result of an important meeting held this week (May 13, 1915) in Raton between farmers of the French Tract and the creditors of the old French Land & Irrigation Company. An agreement was entered into with most of the old creditors for a cash settlement of the former indebtedness at thirty five cents on the dollar. The money involved, which approximates $70,000, must be deposited with the receivers within the next nine months. The discharge of this obligation will remove the most serious handicap under which the new company, organized under the name of the Antelope Valley Irrigation District has been laboring for the success of the little community of French . . . The Winona Hotel was run by the Woods family . . . He changed the name from Winona to the American Hotel. Pearl Miller was a school teacher at French. The big mercantile store at French was known as Coffin & Co. Rev. Lochridge was in charge of the Methodist church at French . . . The houses at French which have been empty for the past year or so are beginning to fill up and French is coming to life after a period of business depression which has made it hard for the faithful few to hang on. J. T. Donaldson has bought a two-story building of the French Land & Irrigation Company and will use the lower floor for a store and the upper floor as a public hall. The Morrow building on Main Street now occupied as a pool hall has been purchased by the French Amusement Company. Fred Vogedling is the business manager. This is a newly organized company whose purpose it is to advance the social side of French. The Ladies Aid Society of French gave a play called Diamonds and Hearts in Donaldson Hall. Rev. Saville acted the part of the villian in a perfectly natural and life-like manner.

Most of the plowing has been finished and the farmers of French are now seeding oats, spring wheat and barley. The reservoirs are about full to their capacity and with the early spring and ample amount of water for irrigation another bumper crop is assued for the Antelope Valley this season. Arrangements have been made to stock the reservoirs with black bass this spring. The reservoirs will also be equipped with some good boats so as to make a place of recreation for the farmers of this district. J. H. Jenkins, who is an experienced fisherman and trapper, has been placed in charge as care-taker and over-seer. Word has been received from John Morrow, receiver of the French Land & Irrigation Company, that he will let the contract to complete reservoir No. 3 just as soon as all the land owners on this tract have paid last year's water maintenance fee. It is to be hoped that every land owner who is delinquent will forward his remittance to Mr. Morrow at once as it will be a great advantage to every land owner to have this reservoir completed this spring.

The newspaper at French was known as The French Farmer. It was published at Maxwell in the office of the Maxwell Mail newspaper there. It was published for eight months by J. Lee and when he moved to Las Vegas it was taken over by Mrs. E. J. Owens who also ran the French Hotel. Rev. J. L. Meredith took over the Protestant services after Rev. W. E. Saville went to Silver City. The boys from French in the first draft in 1917 were Roland Roscoe Hutson, Herman Causey Hughes, Richard Charles Garford and Lyman Alonso Davis . . . The safe in the depot at French was blown to pieces Wednesday (June 3, 1918) by someone who evidently expected to get a good haul. He must have been very disappointed for all his labor for all he got was one dollar and fifty cents. Sticks of dynamite and a bull's eye lantern were left behind as the robber made his getaway.

Try as it might the idea simply could not catch on so

that French was doomed from the start to take its place among the Ghost Towns of New Mexico. One reason for this was the constant struggle over water rights. Another was that too many boom towns were offering the best farming in the world all at the same time and practically in the same area: Pittsburg, Abbott, Gladstone, Miami, Folsom, Clayton, Mosquero, Roy, Gallegos, Des Moines, Capulin, Maxwell, Colfax, Colfax City, Dorsey, Farley and a host of other "built up on paper" places that are names for the most part today. Another reason was the rise of the coal mining towns. Why struggle on a farm when one could work for good wages six days a week and know exactly how much was coming in each week? Mining was not the risk of farming. Dawson, Brilliant, Gardiner, Van Houten, Blossburg, Yankee, Sugarite and many other mines that always had an opening for another hand. Then, too, the location was tragic. Sandwiched between Springer and Maxwell it had small hope for expansion for if it spread one way or the other it would eventually be swallowed up by one or the other cities.

YANKEE, NEW MEXICO

The Yankee coal mines began operations in 1907, when the Yankee Fuel Company was formed with J. E. Southwell as sales agent. Said the Raton Range of October 7, 1908: "The Yankee company maintains offices in Raton, but the mines are located at Yankee, nine miles distant from the Gate City. The mines have been in operation but two years, and the coal mined is of such a good quality that it is already in much demand, and large shipments are made daily to Arizona, Colorado, New Mexico, Texas, California and Old Mexico.' . . . "Probably the most interesting and exciting ball game played here this summer was that of Sunday, when the Remsberg Mercantile Company team of Raton defeated the Yankee Fuel boys by a score of 14 to 10. The attendance was exceedingly large, for in addition to the crowd that came from Raton by train, many drove into the camp from the surrounding country, to say nothing of the automobile parties and a party of cowboys from the neighboring range of the Linwood Cattle Company. The latter attracted nearly as much attention as the ball players and several bucking bronchos tried in vain to unseat their riders. Brown, the umpire, was evidently new in the business and many of his decisions were unsatisfactory to both sides, in fact several wrangles were started over them. Early in the game Captain Leason of Raton, who was playing with the Remsberg team, was hit in the left eye by a ball which put him out of business for practically the rest of the game. He was taken to the office of Doctor Drake, who bandaged the injured member, after which he returned to the field and was an interested spectator. Errington, who for Yankee, was not in his usual good form, much to the disappointment of his admirers; Weimer, who played second base for the coal miners, did some excellent work and was greatly appreciated. Merrow also showed himself to be a good all around player . . . " (Ibid, Aug. 21, 1907.) Other news items regarding Yankee:

The new pictures have arrived that will adorn the walls of a Yankee Amusement Hall. There are many rare and beautiful paintings in the lot. Construction work is being rushed on many new houses in the camp. The warehouse is practically completed and work on the new company store has begun. Work is being hurried on the extension of the railroad track to the new mine that has been opened in Reynold's Canyon. The track is partly laid to the new mine, while the grading work is nearly finished. A spur will be laid to the new warehouse which will make the camp of easier access to visitors. F. L. Lawther is in charge of the amusement hall . . . There have been so many people coming to Yankee in the past few weeks that part of them have to live in box cars on account of the shortage of houses. Thanksgiving day was really celebrated at Yankee. Yankee was the guest of the Yankee Fuel Company and the whole town was royally entertained. Invitations were sent the employees and their families only. Tables were spread in Yankee Amusment Hall for three hundred and twenty-five. The menu was printed and put up in dainty form. Music was by Miler's orchestra and the Glee Club and was continuous during the dinner from four to six. Over four hundred pounds of turkey was served. Pigeon and turkey shooting were part of the afternoon amusement; twenty-six turkeys becoming the property of those who shot them. The dinner was served by officials of the company, aided by W. S. Getchell, superintendent of the Yankee mines. Also assisting as waiters on this occasion were Boyle, Jeffies, Weimer, Edmonds, Frank Gumm, Harry Gumm, Rupert Roberts and Harold Hague.

Yankee is recognized as a model example of a modern mining town. The Yankee Fuel Company has built this town as the basis of its operations, hailed royally by its miners as THE TOWN of the West. Here everything is done to care for the welfare of the working men. The fuel company has furnished the town with an amusement hall, a club house of which any eastern city might well be envious. This building is built of sturdy materials and equipped with attractions that prove of interest and enjoyment to the miners. A library, restaurant, cafe, billiard room, bowling alley and dance hall may all be found in this building. The walls of the rooms are covered with pictures, copies of the works of the great masters. Here in the winter time the miners assemble for recreation, which cannot help but be of benefit to them from an educational as wel as moral viewpoint.

In the summer many interesting baseball games take place on the diamond before the club house, where enthusiasm and support of the Yankee team reigns supreme. Yankee loyalty to its baseball team is well warranted, for the miners have a proud record in defeating all comers this past season. The company owns and controls many thousands of acres of land surrounding the town and on the line of the Santa Fe, Raton & Eastern Railroad. Ernest M. Merrow is the general manager of the company and will liked.

One may still see the coal tipple in Yankee today. Also the foundations of the houses. There is an amusement hall where dances are held every Saturday peopled by gaiety seekers from Raton. A family or two still holds out but the big mining town that was the pride of the area is gone.

The scenery is there for those who love to take picnic baskets for a Sunday's outing. No matter how still the place seems it is always alive with natural beauty. The land seems to have reverted to the Santa Fe railroad which has a long term lease on it, although it does no mining. Several enterprising individuals like Genta of Raton continue to do some private mining with permission of the railroad but they do not have the equipment of large companies consequently many accidents take place that seem to place a curse on their efforts. The Stocktons graze their cattle here; boy scouts camp here and clubs use the area for their outings. The Maxwell Land Grant Company retains some rights over the area but I believe they pertain to sub-surface rights for minerals other than coal.

BALDY, NEW MEXICO

Baldy is one of the oldest Ghost Towns on the Maxwell Land Grant; it is also one of Grant's most exciting places from the viewpoint of legend and history. Mining and prospecting for gold began in the area shortly after Fort Union was established. W. E. Claussen gives us an account of Baldy in the May, 1947 issue of the New Mexico Magazine.

The system of working and openings around Baldy today encompass a huge area and contain many mines, all of which have operated under separate management and names. Yet the very old residents of the section who worked for the Baldy and Aztec mines in their youth recall today that all of the mines at some time or other had run into evidence of much earlier diggings antecedent to their own period by many years. The area is redolent with the lore of gold—the tales handed down from father and grandfather. Old sluice boxes and other constructive work relative to placer mining have been discovered that suggests a very early time and primitive nature to the work undertaken. South and east of Baldy Mountin, in a dense forest, there are some diggings of a very crude nature resembling early Chinese placer mines. Trees growing in these digigngs are more than four hundred years old.

Old Baldy Mountain itself has seen the ebb and flow of life, the comings and goings of mankind in quest of fortune for no man knows how many untabulated generations. Towns came into being along the lengths of Ute Creek. Two early ones are barely remembered by the oldest living natives. Yet their ancient graveyards still lie beside the stream, proving the location of the sites. The number of graves would indicate the towns either flourished for a number of years as fair-sized communities, or their death-rate was extremely high even taking into acocunt the early mining man's love for six-gun and hard liquor.

About three miles down Ute Creek from the Baldy mines there once stood a village of possibly 600 people. There was a saloon and a store, and the main activity was placer mining and logging. Another three miles down the stream was another village of from 600 to 800 miners. Like the first, this had its saloon, its store, and a post office as well. But the main center of population was Baldy town itself, high on the firred shoulder of Baldy Peak — just under timber line. Baldy witnessed and boomed with every strike. It probably was at its peak in 1880 when its population reached 2,000. The flow of life pulsed through its log-walled streets until the early days of World War II. In 1941 when the government needed other minerals, the old town was sacrificed for the good cause. Its lumber and scrap iron were sold to the government.

Hotel Baldy was for the Elite, with its barroom and its two dining rooms. Inside the barroom was a line painted on one wall across which were printed the words Altitude 10,000 feet. High, windy, lusty! From the height of its present ruined doorway one may look south and west across vast distances where fir-clad mountains rise in ridges to touch the azure of the sky. One imagines the mirror-like reflection of water below must be Eagle Nest Lake. But no, that sparkling blue jewel is some lesser body surrounded by its virgin wilderness of mountains.

Besides the main hotel there were two boarding houses with bunksto house one hundred men. Two saloons had opened as well as a general store and they did a flourishing business. Crude cabins built of logs and chinked with mud to hold out winter's biting winds sprang up in a mushroom growth about the main part of town. The place was never empty from 1880 on. Supplies were freighted in over tortuous roads to keep its store and barrooms supplied throughout the long winter months. In addition game was shot and trapped to feed its teeming hundreds.

"Uncle' Fine Hammell was up at Baldy town in 1918 and helped bury more than four hundred people who died from influenza. At some periods during severe winters the winding road must have been impassable because of heavy drifted snowand we of this generation of the motor car can but surmise the feeling of isolation that must have possessed many when the leaden skies brought the prospect of being cut off from the rest of the world.

Today there is but little left of Baldy town. The slender, bare chimney of the Baldy Hotel stands by itself, totally misplaced amidst its growth of young trees pressing in. A few bent pipes, a pile of rusty, discarded drills, a litlte rotting timber. Quiet as a graveyard—this is all one takes along to remember of this place where thousands struggled and lived in high hopes with the ever magic word Gold before their eyes . . .

In 1903 hopes were built up again with new discoveries around the Baldy area. Newspapers played up immense discoveries that started a gold rush to New Mexico once again. Baldy again became an important mining town, but prospectors realiezd before long that it was their hopes and not their pockets that bulged. After 1903 the town settled back to join the ranks of the has-beens.

VIRGINIA CTIY, NEW MEXICO

This mining village was named for Maxwell's daughter, Virginia, in whom he had placed his hopes for a prominent marriage, but like the town she melted away into the arms of the soldier from New England stationed at Fort Union.

Chase in his *Editor's Run* writes: "Five miles below Elizabethtown, Virginia City was started, where a dozen or fifteen houses went up in haste, and hastily came down the next year (1872). We passed through Main Street, but there was nothing here to mark the former existence of a village, except one slight depression in the prairie turf, where some aspiring candidate, for worldly wealth has improvised a cellar. Not a post, not a stick, or a stone could we see in the once hopeful Virginia City; nothing but prairie grass and stillness."

Virginia City—January 1, 1868—This has been a glad day for the miners notwithstanding the storm. Recent importation of "Tangle-leg" coupled with new arrivals of miners and the greetings from old friends met, have had the effect to render the town quite lively. However, everything passed off quietly so far as fights were concerned. The recent discovery of new and rich digigngs on the Moreno, beow Spanish Bar, has created great excitement, and hundreds are staking off claims where two months ago no one dreamed of looking for gold. Scores of hardy men are coming in daily and already the mines present the appearance of Colorado in 1860.

Most of those from Colorado bring small stocks of groceries so that now coffee can be had at forty-five cents a pound; sugar at forty; hams at thirty-five and other goods inproportion. There is no chance for starvation. The snow interferes materially with prospecting, yet many are out determined to make their "strike" before the spring. Lucien B. Maxwell is now engaged, through his agent, Col. J. D. Henderson, in issuing leases to the miners, and thereby settling all disputes in regards to jumping.

The low rate at which these leases are given, two dollars per month per claim of two hundred feet, and the guarantee given to protect the miners in their titles gives universal satisfaction. New quartz lodes are found almost daily and great anticipations are held by the lucky finders. The richest yet found yielded thirty-seven cents to a quarter of a pound of rock. Gentlemen from Colorado here, who profess to be "knowing ones" predict great quarts discoveries this year.

The interest in the sale of lots at Virginia City to come off on the sixth of January increases daily if we judge from the number of those present and enquiries made in regard to prices. Many are now getting out timber to build, as soon as the sale takes place, and it is no idle prediction to say that one hundred houses will be erected before spring. If the influx of people continues this spring as it is doing now there will be not less than two thousand people in Virginia City before long. All with whom I have spoken are delighted with the news of General Clever's success in securing his seat in Congress, and they feel certain of getting postal facilities and an appropriation to make a good road to Cimarron. Miners do not like toll roads and as this Territory is a ward of the government think it ought to get a moiety of its favors.

The well known energy and eminent ability of General Clever will be thrown in favor of the miners and ere spring sets in we hope to have a daily mail line from Cimarron instead of the "Pony Express" at ten bits a letter that we now have. I hope this also means a new country with two precincts. A movement is already afoot to start a paper in Virginia City to advocate the interests of miners and to start our new Moreno county we so much desire (but which they never got). The paper will be run by two boys from Colorado who know the business. (They never got there so Virginia City was not able to toot its own horn.)

Virginia City—April 18, 1868—If half of the fifteen houses in this place we try so hard to call a city have roofs it would be speaking well for the town. This place is laid out on the east side of Moreno Creek, and gently sloping to and about one half mile from it. The streets (at present under two feet of snow) running east and west are named for the letters of the alphabet and those running north and south by the cardinal numbers. There is only one store here, but no hotel, stable, restaurant or barber shop to greet the weary traveler, but after diligent research you can find some corner to sleep in, while your poor animals stand in two foot of snow, with no hay and only a quart or two of bad corn. Prices are extremely high as you can gather from this list:

> Flour, $10 per hundred lbs.
> Coffee, .65 per pound
> Sugar, .45 per pound
> Bacon, .45 per pound
> Vinegar, $1.00 per pint
> Lumber, $35.00 per 1,000 ft.
> Beef, .15 per lb.
> Corn, .07 per lb.
> Oats, .07 per lb.
> Hay, .08 per lb.
> Shingles, $10.00 per 1,000
> Molasses, $5.00 per gallon
> Picks, $4.00 each
> Shovels, $4.00 each

Virginia City was one of the few undertaking by Maxwell that failed. Not so much because there was no gold as the fact that he was already thinking at the time of the sale of the Grant. Constant law suits, claim jumping and the influx of undesirables helped to make up his mind. It was at Virginia City that the men who bought the Grant saw for themselves its tremendous mineral value. Only later on did the Maxwell Land Grant Company come to recognize its agricultural value. Had Maxwell not sold the Grant Virginia City would have progressed into one of the major mining towns of the Southwest. Instead it had the shortest life of all the Ghost Towns on the Maxwell Land Grant tract. So brief was its existence that two out of three writers of the area were totally unawares that it ever existed.

COLFAX, NEW MEXICO

The story of this village is best told by a reporter of the day: The town of Colfax is advantageously located at the junction of the St. Louis, Rocky Mountain and Pacific, and El Paso & Southwestern railways, near the center of Colfax county, only six miles from Dawson in the Vermejo valley. Fifteen miles to the westward is Cimarron, and an equal distance to the south is the town of French, on the Santa Fe main line.

Although the town itself boasts but one general merchandise store, it is a good one, carrying a large and varied stock and doing a thriving business. An auto garage and livery stable are run in connection. There is a good school and church, and the surroundings should cause the building of a solid and prosperous town.

There are numerous ranches in the valley and dry farming is being practiced successfully on a large scale by Charles Glasgow, who is the principal factor in all that pertains to Colfax.

Formerly engaged in farming and stock raising in eastern Kansas, he was attracted to New Mexico by the healthful climate and chose the vicinity of Colfax for his venture, after thoroughly satisfying himself that the locality was perfectly adapted to growing such crops as he had formerly raised in Kansas, without irrigation, as reliably as he could there. After studying the possibilities for three seasons, he purchased two years ago a half interest in the Ruston ranch, a tract of 9,000 acres, situated within the triangle bounded by the railways above named and closely adjacent to the Maxwell Irrigated Land Company's great property.

Although the season of 1910 was one of the dryest ever known to this county, his crops proved that his judgment had been quite correct. In many crops he netted an average of $20 per acre—as well as he could do on $100 land in Kansas. He will market 500 tons of alfalfa and vega hay, bringing him $15 and $16 per ton respectively. He now owns the entire property, having purchased his partner's interest.

The New Mexico Land Sales Company at Cimarron made a plat of the town of Colfax as they hoped to see it. These were the streets running north and south: Maxwell, Letts, Koehler, Johnson, Irwin, Harlan, Gillespie, French, Elkins, Douglas, Chase, Beaubien and Abbott. These were the avenues running east and west: Atlanta, Beaumont, Cimarron, Dawson, El Paso, Frankfort and Green. This was the sales talk written up for prospective buyers:

Colfax is located in the Vermejo valley about 500 feet from the Vermejo river, a permanent mountain stream which heads in the snow-capped mountain range known as the Sangre de Cristo. It is on the St. Louis, Rocky Mountain & Pacific Railroad, near the junction of that road with the Dawson railroad, a part of the El Paso & Southwestern system. These two railroads connect with the A.T.&S.F., Colorado & Southern and the Rock Island systems. The town is in the heart of the richest coal mining and agricultural district of Northern New Mexico. It is only five miles fom the extensive coal mining and coking camps of the Dawson Fuel Company where there are already 4,000 people. The rich agricultural lands in the valley belong to Charles Springer & Company, the Ruston Ranch, Maxwell Farm Land Company and the 50,000 acres of the French Land & Irrigation Company, some adjoining and all near and tributary to this town, are being subdivided into tracts suitable for farms and are being sold to settlers. This town would have been taken up before and really settled but for the fact that the former owners of the land and of the large tracts surrounding this place have always, until now, refused to subdivide and sell the same. The town is laid out on a level plateau near the foothills covered with evergreen timber.

It is true that this is very choice land, in fact it is the cream of the whole Southwest, and it is because the cattle kings have held on to the best until the last. It will go all the faster on that account. Now is a good time to buy because the cattle barons don't know how good it is or how many times it is going to double in value in the next few years. They bought it cheap when they were young men and while they knew it was the finest gazing land in all the world, and the best watered, they did not realize that it was good for anything else and they thought they were getting the best of the bargain when they sold it to the Eastern real estate dealers for ten dollars an acre, but it will raise sugar beets, alfalfa, wheat and oats, barley, rye, fruits and vegetables, and the farmers will raise more cattle on the side than all the great ranches put together numbered in their herds. The cattle barons wondered where the world would get its supply of beef when they went out of business, but every 40 acre farm where the baron ran a cow and a calf, is raising from a dozen head up on its stubble fields and around its straw stacks, besides horses and hogs and poultry, and next year the stock will be fattened on the pulp from the sugar factories and the output of cattle from this section will be greater by tenfold than it was in the reign of the cattle kings. In the fall the farmers go hunting in nearby mountains where speckled trout, deer and wild turkey abound and every now and then one finds a gold mine or a copper mine and don't have to run a farm anymore.

ELIZABETHTOWN, NEW MEXICO

This is perhaps the most famous of the Ghost Towns on the Maxwell Land Grant. Elizabethtown had all the glamor, killings, dance hall girls, stage coach robberies that the most avid Frontier fan could want. The town merits a book in itself and perhaps someday New Mexico University will give this chore to one of its students as a thesis for a doctorate. The discovery of gold in the area changed the whole course of the history of the Maxwell Land Grant. Indians were indirectly responsible for Elizabethtown. Coming as they did each week or so over the western slope of Baldy in search of game and to pick up rations at the government agency at Cimarron, the Utes and Apaches now and then picked up some rich copper float to watch the eyes of the White Man glitter. They never told where they found the stuff but enjoyed the bribe offered.

Once they took some to Fort Union, showing the copper to William Kroenig, W. H. Moore, John Buck and others stationed about the fort to watch their reaction and to exchange it for some fire-water. Besides this they received some money, promising to show the soldiers where they found the mineral. It was agreed that one man and one Indian would go to the place so that a claim could be staked out. As the Indians did not consider Maxwell as the owner of the land but rather that it belonged to them and they were the ones tolerating Maxwell there were no qualms of conscience about private property. Besides it would have made no difference to the men for they considered that gold was where you found it and they expected no opposition from anybody.

A mine was located and known for years afterwards as "Copper Mine." More recently it took on the name of "Mystic Lode Mine." Kroenig lost no time in developing the property and toward the end of 1866 he sent Bronson, Kelly and Kinsinger to work on the annual assessment on the mine. Evidently Maxwell was unaware that all this was going on for in none of the docket books of the county do we find that he brought these trespassers to court. The county courthouse at the time was at Taos.

About forty miles due west from the present town of Maxwell one comes upon a little stream of water known as Willow Creek. It rises in the Baldy watershed and flows into the Moreno river. The three adventurers arrived at this creek one afternoon and looked up to Mt. Baldy. The sun was just disappearing behind the peak, so it was decided not to scale the heights that evening but to pitch camp right there by the flow of the inland creek. One of the three, while cooking supper, picked up a pan and decided to wash some of the gravel along the edge of the creek. Coronado must have turned in his grave for what the man washed was gold!

Copper was forgotten; the men became prospectors. They had not counted on placer mining so they decided to return to Fort Union promising to keep the discovery a secret.

Alas for promises! At Fort Union they showed the gold to all who cared to look. Which meant that it was on display all day long. The news soon spread all over New Mexico and Colorado and it was not by way of telegraph or newspapers but somehow seemed more rapid. And so, the spring of 1867 saw all eyes focused on Willow Creek. Scenes of the 49ers were repeated. Gold! The magic word that brought more people to New Mexico than the Hildago Treaty. North, East, South, West — the center of the United States in 1867 was Mt. Baldy. Bronson, Arthur, Brown, Robinson and Hamilton from Fort Union made the first location on the creek, measuring their claims in a westward direction from the big pine tree which ever since was known as "Discovery Tree."

Below their claim Thomas Reese, Bill Huron and Herman Heller marked theirs. These were followed by Harrison and Dougherty, and the south side of the gulch was taken over by Matthew Lynch and Tim Foley, who had been mining previously to this on the east side of the Baldy range prospecting for the famous Aztec lode. The rush continued. Above the Discovery Tree, the territory along the creek bed was taken up by various parties all along to the very head of the stream. Others from Fort Union went a little further on to the west and north of the creek to make the first discovery on the site of Elizabethtown.

And what of Maxwell all this time? He simply succumbed to the gold fever. He staked out claims and mounted the band wagon. If there was gold to be had he was going to get it especially since it was on his property. He set up a land office and leased out parcels of land since he could do nothing about the influx of miners without bloodshed. He wrote to St. Louis for some nephews to come and assist him but they were as much in the way as his son Peter who knew ranching, merchandise and herding but was lost when it came to gold mines. So Maxwell went along with the crowd and the fever so infiltrated his blood that he went to the Black Range and at San Vincente helped establish the mining town of Silver City.

J. E. Codin, Pat Lyons, Fred Pheffer, and "Big Mitch" of Fort Union, the discoverers, termed themselves "The Michigan Company" and called the locality "Michigan Gulch." Prospectors were a dime a dozen. Most of the fortune hunters were located around Grouse Gulch and Humbug Gulch because each of these places had a stream of water. So many prospectors thought that there was not enough gold at this latter gulch to pay working it that they termed it "Humbug." Yet the "Humbug" was to prove the richest of all the diggings.

The camp grew. Lowthian, Turpin, Schumann, Porter, Gynch, Greeley, Regan, Garry, Sullivan, Cosgrove and others swelling the ranks and becoming restive about law and order. John Moore, George Buck, Herburger and Duber got together to discuss the possibilities of a new town. T. G. Rowe made the plat and survey. Then came the problem of a name. After much discussion it was decided to call the town Elizabethtown after Elizabeth Moore, the oldest daughter of John Moore, who later married Joseph Lowrey. A complete staff of city officials was elected, and Elizabethtown had the distinction of being the first city in the territory to incorporate. The population was about 5,000. Shortly afterwards a slice was cut off from both Mora and Taos counties to form Colfax county to honor vice-president Colfax.

War does not change a man as much as gold. The gold fever—it does things to a man. Take "Wall" Henderson as an example. He was a peaceable man, minding his own business, and working a claim a short distance down the creek. Some characters from Colorado, knowing that Henderson and a few companions were working a rich vein, "jumped" the claims. One morning Henderson visited the "jumpers" and warned them about trespassing. This was not to the liking of one of the newcomers. He hit Henderson with a shovel. Not satisfied with this he decided to finish him off. This time Henderson did not make peace parley. A six-shooter said all. A jury in Mora acquitted him.

He returned to Elizabethtown and abuse. The friends of the slain man made life miserable for him. One day, while pouring down drinks in a saloon, Ned O'Hara got into an argument with him over the affair and punctuated his words with a rock. Out came the six-shooter again and O'Hara was bleeding over the left eye, but not killed. From this moment on Henderson developed a persecution complex. He went from tavern to tavern, gave way to moroseness, and went about with a chip on his shoulder. He even joined a gang of outlaws up Ute Creek. When Joseph Stinson, the proprietor of a saloon in which he was drinking passed a remark, Henderson took immediate offense and emptied his revolver into him. Exit Henderson. All because of the goldbug.

Then there was Joseph Antonio Herberger. He was a member of the vigilantes. "Pony" O'Neil was wanted for murder. Herberger was instrumental in his capture. He hid between two buildings and as O'Neil went by he hit him with a brick, and while still "out," the vigilantes picked him up and strung him to a tree and riddled his body with bullets. In August 1869, Herberger beat a Captain Keefer to death in his saloon, knocking him down with a chair and finishing him off with a stick of stove wood. And all over a whiskey bill. Yet Herberger's bar was popular and no one intentionally ever tried to get a drink from him without paying for it. Herberger failed to strike it rich and perhaps was brooding over the idea when the captain told him he would pay him some other time.

Charles Kennedy probably intended well when he opened his travelers rest home at the foot of the divide, on the east side of the road from Elizabethtown to Taos. We have it on hearsay that Vice-President Colfax slept there. What goldbug bit Kennedy when he pondered the idea that robbing tourists would be better than digging a claim? Just how many strangers he put away is a secret he took to the grave with him. Some family quarrel brought his native wife to Elizabethtown to report his crimes to the authorities. They found two skeletons under the house, and in a fireplace still warm when the vigilantes arrived, were found many human bones. Kennedy was taken to Elizabethtown and placed in jail. When the vigilantes heard that his lawyer was spending freely for his release, they marched to the jail and dragged him through the streets of Elizabethtown until he was choked to death. The town was just two years old at the time. Later Kennedy's skull was dug up and sent to the Smithsonian Institute in Washington.

After a time the city settled down, coming a long way from the first house built by John C. Codlin and the first store set up by John Moore. Lambert put up a hotel there and prospected between times, but having no luck went to Cimarron where he opened the famous St. James Hotel which endures to this day. E'town carried on.

There was the famous "Montezuma" owned by Frank Dericks, and the brick mercantile store of Gottlief & Uhfelder known as the Great Western Supply Store; the E'town Hotel, the mercantile store of Herman Frolick, the Miner's Inn, Pearson & Gillen's Mercantile Company; the Popular Resort of J. W. Williams, with its brass rail and brass spitoons better known as The Senate. The Senate and the Montezuma both boasted gambling tables.

Dr. L. L. Cahill came in from Michigan as the physician and surgeon of Elizabethtown. When not busy cutting up somebody he ran a drugstore and was official postmaster besides. No railroad penetrated the town which makes us marvel when we consider the size and extent of the mining machinery taken into the area. At the turn of the century, the Moreno Valley Stage Line brought in the mail from Springer, the nearest railroad center of any importance. The distance was fifty-four miles.

Rev. J. A. Accorsini was called the Apostle of Colfax County. Actually Father Fourchegu and others were there before him but they did not organize and plan the way he did. How much territory he covered can only be imagined if we add the present Union county of today to the Texas border line, and over to Puerta de Luna. He later asked the priest at Taos to take over Elizabethtown for him which was done with the archbishop's approval. Father Accorsini wrote that after March 22, 1888, he would cease coming to E'town.

Vigilantes, outlaws, and county officials were soon smoked into the past and the residents settled down to placer mining in earnest. One of the Lynch brothers (who was afterwards killed by a falling tree) purchased the famous E'town & Red River Ditch at a receiver's sale, because the original owner went bankrupt for $10,000. This gave him control of the water in the district. The ditch had a discharge capacity of 4,000,000 gallons every twenty-four hours. It coursed its way through the district for forty miles and made a fortune for the Lynch family. Herman Mutz built an imposing structure of native white sand-stone taken from his ranch.

Over in Raton the Remsberg Mercantile Company sent Peter J. Perry to open up a branch store at Elizabethtown. A party of capitalists from St. Louis, headed by Henry Koehler, made a permanent survey for the Elizabethtown & Raton railroad. All went well—too well perhaps for Elizabethtown never dreamed of being practically wiped out by fire. But then what town does? It is said that a defective flue in the hall used for entertainments on the second floor of the Remsberg store started the holocaust. Said the Raton Range (Sept. 3, 1903)

"A Colfax county gold mining town was almost wiped out by fire Tuesday. Only one business institution is left standing. Remsberg & Co. are the heavy losers. The fire originated from an unknown source possibly from a defective flue. The fire started on Tuesday afternoon at about 2:15 P.M. in the hall used for entertainments on the second floor of the Remsberg store building and thirty minutes after the discovery of the fire the building and all it contained except about $700 or $800 worth of dry goods were totally destroyed. H. B. Phelps, the manager of the store, and William Walker, a clerk, with great difficulty and considerable risk to their lives, got the company's books and money from the safe, and with the assistance of willing hands, were able to salvage dry goods to the amount of several hundreds of dollars. The building was a two story structure on the corner of the main business street of the town. The flames spread to the Mutz Hotel, a two-story building adjoining. From there the fire spread to Harry Brianard's place, then to Bemsberg's, Gottleib, and Uhfelder's general store. Across the street in the next block the Moreno Hotel caught fire from flying embers and in one hour and fifteen minutes from the time of the discovery of the fire all the buildings mentioned were reduced to ashes. The only mercantile establishment left in town is the store of Herman Froelick."

Other prominent citizens who owned valuable property in E'town were H. H. Argue of Buffalo, New York, who owned extensive placer grounds. M. Forrester of Denver, owner of the Ajax mine; Charles J. Dodd who had a number of interests but sold out and moved to Socorro; W. C. Whitecarver and John A. Gysin of Trinidad, Colorado. M. Bass was the schoolteacher and continued so even after the fire when the town made an attempt at a comeback. John E. Codlin who built the first house in E'town was a veteran of the Civil War. He served four years under

General Sherman, coming to New Mexico in 1865, after the close of the conflict. Chase, in his *Editor's Run* has these remarks about E'town:

"In 1871 houses began to disappear from E'town, and in a year or two the village of 2,000 people or more, dwindled to as many hundred. An Irishman named Lynch managed to secure the possesison of the water ditch for twelve thousand dollars and has continued mining ever since. His wealth is variously estimated from $50,000 to $1,500,000. We visited his works, saw the operation of gulch mining, and the Irishman who owns the mine, who talks, looks and acts like any other Irishman. Our hotel accomodations at E'town were first rate. The ground floor of the building contained two rooms, a kitchen in the rear, a combination dining room, bar-room and a post-office in front. But the beds were good, and the landlord, Stone, an American, had a German wife who knew how to cook. It makes one lonesome to walk the streets of Elizabethtown. Although not an old place, it is deserted and, instead of the crowded streets, or crowded houses, rum shops, gambling saloons, and hourly knock-downs of a few years ago, a sort of graveyard stillness, deserted buildings, and general tumble-down appearance is everywhere observed. There is one store, part of another hotel, the tail end of a barber shop, the outside of a Catholic church, a barn, a good deal of glass, and other fragments of former prosperity left, but the pith, the vitality of village life has departed, no more to return, unless more water is brought from the Red River, or some large companies are formed to begin pounding up the quartz rocks by stream."

VERMEJO PARK, NEW MEXICO

The Vermejo area was cattle country from the beginning. "The Vermejo correspondent of the Springer Stockman (June 1, 1883) writes the following concerning things up that way: The lakes in this vicinity have been dry since last October, but thanks to the recent rains, they are now full of water, enabling the cattle to forsake the boggy, bottomless springs and streams which have lured so many of their bovine mates to their deaths by the appetizing verdancy of their surroundings, and graze far out upon the prairies abounding—the higher lands—with last year's grass, the glades and arroyos, with fresh, green grazing, and no necessity of traveling eight or ten miles for a drink of water. This will also dispense with the need of keeping men to guard these boggy places, to a great extent, for the purpose of pulling out cattle, and be no small saving to owners. Nearly all the cattlemen in this section consider the crisis as now passed, and hope to begin spring operations at an early date."

"D. B. Griffin was in (to Raton) from his store on the Vermejo last week making preparations for a big time up his way. Here will be singing, the reading of the Declaration of Independence, speaking, and all together just a celebration as our forefathers would have celebrated on the Fourth of July." (Ibid, June 29, 1883) "At Vermejo Park the settlers up there had quite a celebration in the good old fashioned way. The exercises consisted of singing, reading of the Declaration of Independence, speech-making, a basket dinner and a big dance in the evening. Several parties from Raton went up there, but as they have not yet returned, it is impossible to give a full report of the good time had." (Ibid, July 6, 1883) But the report that came in wasn't as delightful as The Comet expected. For the sake of history, and because Vermejo Park made up part of the Maxwell Land Grant as well as to retain the type of reporting of the day we will give in full the report published in the Raton Comet for July 13, 1883:

The Fourth of July wasn't a very good day for a picnic up in Vermejo Park this year, though everyone there had done their best in making preparations for a great time. The place selected for the exercises, dinner and dance was a beautiful one, and Mr. and Mrs. Gentry had spared no pains in preparing their home for the comfort of the many patriotic souls that were sure to come early and stay late. But about the time everybody had arrived a moist sort of rain set in, which continued during the first part of the day, and this had a tendency to dampen the spirit of good nature that was so visible early in the morning. The rain drove most of the ladies indoors, but as the men folk have a weakness for water out there, and regard a good rain a God send at any time, they turned in to celebrate both the shower and the Fourth.

The first really exciting event of the day was a foot race. Eugene Twitty being matched against Gus Brackett, and a good deal of betting was done on the result. Twitty was the favorite and odds were given on him, but Brackett fooled the boys and demonstrated that he was no slow coach himself by getting to the home stretch easy winner. Brackett afterwards downed Vic Lee and the younger Twitty when his trainers led him from the track. But we didn't see any big running until June Hunt and Den Griffin scored up for the fat man's race. They got a good start, and the way in which they tore up the damp earth paralyzed the spectators. Griffin proved to be the best muscled behind—in fact June is altogether too coupled for a short distance race and the heat was a clear walk away for Griffin.

This was the last foot race for the forenoon, and horses came next. Vic Lee had learned that a horse with a well-curved hind leg ought to run, and he picked one from his herd whose legs curved all ways. This nag is properly called Eli—for he gets there. The first race was with a handsome pony belonging to Gus Dawson, and Eli did himself and his proud rider good by putting a couple of lengths of daylight between himself and Dawson's horse at the outset, as well as the outcome. Eli also beat Uncle Jack Young's racer before he was turned out to grass.

A good deal of anxiety and interest was manifested in the foot race for a beautiful gold-lined silver cup, run by the girls. About twenty, ages varying from eight to forty years, scored up and took a standing start. The first was declared a dead heat, Juda Young and Nellie Armstrong leading the crowd, but making a tie race of it, and another start was taken. This time Juda came out a little ahead, amid loud cheers and a great rustle of petticoats. The two girls however were each given a beautiful cup and they each deserved it.

Frank Terhune won the magnificent cake prepared by Miss Gentry for the swiftest runner. At times when the clouds cleared away, the organ was brought out under the trees, and the old-time patriotic songs were sung by the entire assembly. The grand dinner that had been prepared by the ladies was made up of the best of everything the land affords, and the only criticism possible is that it was too good—it took a fellow too long to get over it.

The Declaration of Independence was well recited by June Hunt, which was followed by an eloquent address by D. B. Griffin. He is an accomplished orator and at times during the address one could fancy that he almost heard the great American bird cackle. After a few more out of doors sports had been indulged in the crowd adjourned, some to bed but the majority to the ballroom where they kept time with the fiddle until morning. A more hospitable or patriotic people cannot be found than those in that mountain region.

On the 5th, after passing a few pleasant hours at Mr. Shy's place, we started up the river bound for Poniel Park, accompanied by Mr. Shy. The ride up was pleasant enough, but coming back, we surely had an experience. New Mexico weather. Coming this way from Castle Rock ranch one passes down a canyon about half a mile to the Vermejo. The canyon is a very wide smooth one and the slope on the hillside is gradual and the hills low. When we reached the head of this canyon it began to rain, and we hope to be paralyzed if in less than three minutes the water on the side hills was not fully four inches deep, and on the level ground there was so much of it we couldn't find the road. Before we got over the half mile to the Vermejo we came to a gate, and at this spot the ground was still dry, but before Mr. Shy could open the gate the water was knee-deep to the horses. The Vermejo was out of its banks at that point in less than ten minutes, but as it is an extremely crooked brook we succeeded in driving down the five miles to the open park ahead of the flood, which came a few moments later with force enough to have drowned the whole outfit. In a number of places hail had drifted in banks four to six feet deep, and it was almost impossible for the team to flounder through. This may sound like a pretty wet story for one to tell who drinks nothing but water, but it's a true bill.

And now we will give you a fish story. After the creek got back into its banks Mr. Shy's boys went over into the potato patch and picked up great baskets full of trout that had been left on land by the creek's going down as rapidly as it had risen. They were all alive and it must be that a countless number were left to decay along the flooded parts of the Vermejo. The lower fords could not be crossed with a wagon until Saturday.

Since the big rain, which to our knowledge continued until Saturday morning, the grass and the crops are looking up wonderfully. But dry as the season has been, stock in that section does not appear to have suffered much from the drouth. We left our team and family at the comfortable home of Captain Armstrong and climbed over the burro trail to Pat Lyon's ranch in Van Brimer canyon. Pat calls this place the "Devil's Punch Bowl" but in fact it is one of the finest stock ranches on earth. Mr. Lyons raises the finest horses in the country and his beeves always sell at the highest prices. By sticking faithfully to the stock business in Van Brimer canyon Pat Lyons has become independently rich, and he has earned all he owns.

Mrs. Armstrong hasn't had as good luck with her chickens as the men folk had with their stock. Two weeks ago she had between five and six hundred beauties. One night last week 190 were stolen from their roosts, and a few days later some varmint, thought to be a weasel, got into her coops and killed about two hundred more. At this rate Mrs. Armstrong will be left without a chick on earth.

The time of the bonds on the "Cokers" cattle and ranches expired on the Eleventh of this month but whether the money from the Maxwell Land Grant Company was forthcoming or not we have not as yet learned. Bonds were given on the herds of the Hunt boys, Jack Armstrong, Vic Lee, J. B. Dawson, Z. Curtis, and others, all of whom own as good stock as there is on the range, and if the sale is not soon completed it is doubtful if the boys sell at all.

D. B. Griffin is doing a big business at his store on the Vermejo, and when the patent to the Maxwell Land Grant is set aside, he will own the finest kind of farm and stock range in the county, provided his present negotiations prove successful.

Says the New Mexico Guide Book of 1940: Vermejo Park is a magnificent private club and game preserve extending eastward forty miles from the eastern slopes of the Sangre de Cristo Mountains. W. H. Bartlett, millionaire grain operator of Chicago, bought the ranch in 1900 after his physician had warned him concerning his health, and lived there for eighteen years. Bartlett built a home for himself, and for each of his sons, with guest houses, an electric plant, an ice plant, a fish hatchery and made other improvements. The streams were stocked with bass and trout, and, operating under a park license, Bartlett drew up his own game and fish laws. After Bartlett and his sons had died in 1918 the property was in the care of trustees until 1927, when a group of Los Angeles capitalists, headed by Harry Chandler, president of the Los Angeles Times-Mirror, purchased the ranch and incorporated it into a private club, using Bartlett's home as a clubhouse. The original seventy-five members included Will Rogers, Cecil B. DeMille, Douglas Fairbanks, Max C. Fleischman, Will Hays and Andrew Mellon. The property totals nearly a half million acres. Today the ranch includes a large game preserve, where 5,000 elk, 15,000 mule-deer, 20,000 wild turkeys, pheasants, bears, wildcats, and other animals roam freely.

Mrs. Brackett tells of life at Vermejo in 1874. The first house in which the Brackett's lived on the Vermejo was made of logs, and it had a dirt floor and a dirt roof. When it rained the water soaked the sod above and the dirt fell over the house. The home-made beds sat right on the dirt floor and the children sometimes slept on the dirt floor—i.e. until one day when Mrs. Brackett was cleaning out the house and found young rattle snakes under the provision box. The snakes would crawl in frequently through the log joints and enjoy a nap in the warm cabin. The Indians ordered the Bracketts off the place but in time friendly relations were established. After a while they dropped in at all hours of the day or night for coffee of which they were extremely fond. Indians usually brought dogs along and these killed the chickens. But nothing could be done about it for if the dogs were killed it would probably mean the death of the Bracketts. After the death of Mr. Brackett his wife often scared away the Indians by telling them that her sons had small-pox. They dreaded the disease and often fled when told about it. But in time the government moved the Utes and Jicarillas and Mrs. Brackett was able to live in peace. A school was built in 1875 for the Vermejo children although before that time the mothers of the children had to do what they could by way of educating the young ones . . . When a cow or hog was butchered and dressed, it was the custom to give the neighbors a quarter which was hung up in a tree until it was all used. This was a good way to keep the meat especially in the winter time. Strangers and travelers would often come along and buy meat, venison, beef or pork. Butter was sold at seventy-five cents a pound. After the Bracketts lived there for fourteen years they were told that they were on Maxwell Land Grant property and they had to move. They bought land from the Grant company twelve miles below Dawson.

SUGARITE, NEW MEXICO

The Sugarite area was made up at first of cowboys and ranchers before it became a mining center, as we gather from the Live Stock Journal of New Mexico for April 17, 1885: The Sugarite outfit met at the old McMain's ranch at 10:30 Wednesday morning, and a meeting was called to order by W. J. Parker, who nominated Col. J. W. Dwyer for chairman of the meeting. Col. Dwyer was elected, and Joel W. Shakelford made secretary. The following gentlemen, cowboys and owners of cattle controlled by the Sugarite outfit were present: W. J. Parker, H. D. Thacher, O. A. Hadley, H. Himpstedt, A. W. Knox, T. B. Gable, G. E. Lyon, T. Shaw, A. H. Hartley, H. Alexander, S. F. Knox, E. Winter, M. B. Stockton, J. A. Judd, T. McAuliffe, C. M. Bayne, H. B. Downing, E. J. Segerstrom, H. K. T. Lyons, John Smith, J. McFedris, J. W. Dwyer, A. G. Shaw, E. C. Griffith, J. Sandusky, H. T. Woods, C. deForesta, V. W. Mizer, W. W. Sames, W. Finley, C. Remsberg, E. Strong, Hugh Smith, A. Cox and Charles Spencer.

Parker stated that he believed that the outfit should organize themselves into a social organization, with a president, vice-president and secretary, a treasurer and executive committee. By this means there would be more system to the manner of working the range, and controlling the number of cattle, bulls, etc., needed to properly stocking the country run by the outfit. He made a motion to that effect and it was adopted. The meeting then proceeded to the election of officers with this result: Pres. E. Winter; Vice-Pres. J. E. McKown; Secy. F. S. Knox; Captain, W. Parker; Executive Committee, J. W. Shakleford, A. Shaw, C. Thacker. The following resolutions were presented and adopted: a) to eliminate all misunderstandings that took place at previous meetings; b) to entitle all members to benefits in the organization.

It being reported that cattle were bogging to a great extent on the Sugarite, Una de Gato and Red River, those districts were apportioned to members of the association, each one taking as his district that portion assigned to him for keeping water holes open last winter. The question as to who would furnish the horses and wagons to be used by the outfit this winter was brought up, but as a number of representatives of larger outfits were not present, the matter was referred to the Executive Committee.

Reports came from people living up the Sugarite Canyon that they had four inches of snow last night (April 29, 1909). The snow flurries which continued throughout yesterday and part of today made travel on horseback or in buggies disagreeable and changed the atmosphere a great deal. Old residents said this morning that the freeze and cold wave was the coldest for April that they could ever remember. The fruit will not be hurt but if the cold wave continues damage might be done.

VAN HOUTEN, NEW MEXICO

Last Saturday a special train hauling the private car of Superintendent E. J. Dedman of the St. Louis, Rocky Mountain & Pacific railroad drew into Cimarron about noon. The special carried officials of the road who were out on an inspection trip over the Rocky Mountain and the Cimarron & Northwestern roads. The party consisted of General Manager J. Van Houten, Superintendent E. J. Dedman, President Henry Koehler and St. Louis men of affairs. The train was run over the Cimarron & Northwestern to its end and returned to Cimarron about five o'clock, leaving for Raton that same evening. When asked what the special object of the trip was Mr. van Houten smiled and said "We are just looking around." (Raton Weekly Range—Jan. 29, 1909)

Van Houten became quite an active coal camp, employing as many as seven hundred men. Even to 1950 it was still mining coal and seventeen families lived there at the time. It still retains a large recreation hall, a school, a saloon and a store. Of all the Ghost Towns on the Maxwell Land Grant it is the only one that shows any signs of activity, which makes it hard to classify as a "has-been" but the activity is nil compared to what the camp used to be, so we retain its name on this list.

THOMPSON, NEW MEXICO

This was never a very large place. It was a railroad station on the Rocky Mountain railroad that came in from Des Moines, New Mexico. Used as a shipping center for cattle, it never boasted a store and seemed doomed from the start.

HEBRON, NEW MEXICO

Hebron was a farming area and well known for its great ditch from the Red River. "Dr. R. A. Morley, of Las Vegas, has purchased about twenty thousand acres of land from the Maxwell Land Grant Company, seven miles south of Raton, and will place it upon the market in farming tracts as soon as he returns from the east. The land surrounds Hebron, located on the Santa Fe, and is under ditch from the Red River. In addition to being an excellent irrigating proposition, the land in question is in an area which has been for years successfully farmed by the Campbell process. The promoters of this tract of farming land recognize that it will also be of benefit to Raton. It is the beginning of the marketing of thousands of acres which lie to the south of this city, all under fair water prospects, and all exceptionally good soil either for irrigation or scientific farming." *(Raton Range, Feb. 12, 1908)* . . . Mr. Morley will colonize this tract for its owners. Small farms will be laid out and improvements made and the land will be thickly settled in a short space of time. Mr. Morley is assisted in his business by his brother, L. H. Morley, of Fulton, Illinois. Mr. Morley said: 'I have not handled a more convenient tract of land from the point of railway facilities than this one. The tract is bounded on the east by the Santa Fe railway, on the west by the Rocky Mountain railway and through its center runs a line of the Santa Fe to Van Houten. We shall have at least four stations on these different roads on this tract. The land is ideal for farming purposes and every acre is tillable. We shall expect to bring out settlers beginning next week and a great deal of land will be under plow by the first of June." *(Ibid, March 21, 1908)*

UTE PARK, NEW MEXICO

Ute Park was never properly a town but more of a resort. "The excursion to Ute Park on next Tuesday will be a rare opportunity to see one of the primitively beautiful places in New Mexico. So long has the wonderful country south of Raton been inaccessible except by wagon, that the privilege of traversing it by train and at a very low fare will induce many to attend this picnic and see the historic and grand sights of Cimarron Canyon." *(Ibid)* . . . Ute Park was reached about 10:30. Along the road, especially in the vicinity where the picnic was held, the scenery cannot be surpassed. Ute Park is the one ideal spot for a day's outing—the time and place where cares are all forgotten . . . About five hundred pleasure seekers left Sunday morning on the Brotherhood of Railway Trainmen excursion to Ute Park. Besides rambling around under the shade trees the party amused themselves at dancing, witnessing the baseball game between Yankee and Van Houten, and wading in the water or taking part in the various contests." *(Ibid, June 24, 1908)* The New Mexico State Guide has this to say:

"Ute Park was named for the Ute Indians, who lived on the east slope of near-by Mt. Baldy. The rebellious Ute resisted their white oppressors, and an Indian Agency and military force were maintained at Cimarron to keep them subdued, until they were finally moved to a reservation in southern Colorado and Utah. The village of Ute Park, opposite the mouth of Ute Creek, is the terminus of an A.T.&S.F. railway branch and is a distributing point for freight for Moreno Valley, Red River and Taos."

Now and then there was a shooting because of cattle rustling, but Ute Park was always considered the picnic grounds of northern Colfax county. There were times when the Maxwell Land Grant people wished that they hadn't sold the land and kept it for some wealthy oil man as an estate, or even maintained it for the state, but ranchers know the value of their property and no inducement will tempt them to sell. Ute Park is still the paradise it was and will remain so if Fourth of July picnickers will be careful with their fires and vandalistic instincts.

LYNN, NEW MEXICO

This was the northernmost of the settlements on the Maxwell Land Grant in the New Mexico area. A farming district, north of Raton, it was on the border and became quite the rival of the village of Wooten, the first village on Grant land in the Colorado area. The little newspaper, The Lynn Rattler, gives us bits of homey information about the little community, but the sheet suddenly took off to Wooten and became known as The Wooten Rattler.

Edward McNamara did not go to Kansas to get married. Henry Jacobs sold his trotting cow yesterday. She was a very fast cow. Ask Jacobs how fast. The young ladies of the Smith family have completed their lawn tennis court and croquet grounds and as soon as the rainy season is over some pleasant goes are expected. McNamara and Clark have re-opened the Murray Hill Hotel and big feeds are the order of the day. The asphalt boulevard will be completed in time for our street fair this fall. The Lynn Silver Cornet Band serenaded a few of the residents on Quality Hill Saturday night. The music rendered was exquisite and brought many comments and donations from music loving people. The bass drum was busted and the trombone player had his left eye blackened by the shower of bouquets. Other such comments may be found in the Lynn Rattler for 1903 and 1904.

VAN BREMMER PARK, NEW MEXICO

This is also a picnic and ranch area. Here and there ranches are seen that would make wonderful dude ranches for vacationists. If New Mexico keeps growing in population as it has been since World War II this may be the future of the locality.

PONIL, NEW MEXICO

This little village was often the meeting place of the Anti-Granters. Many of the squatters finally settled with the Maxwell Land Grant Company and went in for large scale ranching. Ponil also had a school that also served for sort of a community center for meetings, dances and socials. Many families of long standing are found in the area having settled there several generations back. The Ponil country always held fascination for cowboys and much of the rustling on the Grant took place here. Now and then a killing or hanging took place as the result.

BLOSSBURG, NEW MEXICO

Indians used this area as a camping ground long before Onate found his way to San Juan. About the time that General Armijo gave the Grant to Charles Beaubien and Guadalupe Miranda the Utes and Jicarillas considered it part of their domain and often hunted here. The ill-fated Villasur expedition crossed the spot in 1750. Kit Carson, Maxwell, LeDoux and Owens considered the spot as a settlement in the hopes of obtaining the Santa Fe Trail trade, but it was too far away from water so they settled at Rayado instead. Soldiers from Fort Union camped here when they built the Fort Union-Raton Pass highway. The Long Expedition found coal there in 1827. After Uncle Dick Wooten built his toll road many caravans cut across the site of Blossburg to avoid paying toll.

The first serious attempt at colonizing the place came through the efforts of the St. Louis, Rocky Mountain & Pacific Railroad Company, through its branch company known as The Raton Coal & Coke Company. The Santa Fe railroad and the coal company had a rough time of it. Every time that the railroad succeeded in collecting a section gang, the foreman of the mine at Blossburg came along and offered the men higher wages so that the railroad had to hunt up another crew. By 1881, Blossburg was a thriving little community and cute newsy notices began to make their appearances in the Raton papers that help to give us an insight to those early days:

"Blossburg would be happier with less whiskey, less gambling, and fewer bulldogs . . . Blossburg has increased the female population by fifteen. Several of these young women are of marirageable age. The bachelors are in high glee . . . The Blossburg Dancing club had a sociable last night at the boarding house owned by Owen and Hutchinson . . . Sol Reese is about to open a boarding house and grocery store at Blossburg. Sol is one of the solid men of Dillon, and we wish him luck . . . C. J. Fry, general clerk and superintendent of the Raton Coal & Coke Company's new mill, is about to move into one of the new houses opposite Mr. Griffin's store . . . Until now marriage in Blossburg was impossible for lack of material; the women were all married; benedicts wouldn't die and divorces unknown but on Sunday last Ike Price, the mining boss returned from Pennsylvania with a fresh supply of women belonging to the families of miners, carpenters and mechanics he brought along. Now is the time for the single men to single out their future wives.

During the last week of January 1882, Henry Wise founded the newspaper known as The Blossburg Pioneer. His office was at the sawmill. Now and then O. P. McMains came to agitate against the Grant but the miners paid no attention since they were not squatters but merely workers for a company. If McMains had a case let him take it to the officials; they just worked at Blossburg. The Blossburg Band was well known in the area. It played in Davis Hall on Saturday nights and people came in from Springer, Cimarron and Raton to hear the music. Now and then there was a killing as the time Jake Wyruch was murdered. Officials did not like the idea one bit because it meant that the men knocked off from work to attend the trial in Raton. Usually they made a holiday of it and many found their way to the liquor stores which meant that they would not report for work for days at a time. One time the little river flooded and caused much damage and suffering:

"The river commenced to rise yesterday, and at sundown it was higher than it was ever known to be. By 10 P.M. it was a raging torrent, sweeping away bridges, fences, outhouses, chickens, turkeys, hogs and all that came in the way. The saddest feature of the flood is the loss of the infant child of Mrs. John Elmgren. She was carrying the child, and, with the assistance of two men, was attempting to cross the river. The current of the stream was so swift that all three were thrown from their feet, and the child was thrown from the arms of its mother. In the darkness it could not be seen, and the mother, frantic with grief at the loss of the child, was only constrained from again rushing into the current of the stream by the united efforts of the two men who were with her. The damage to property in this place will be great, and the loss will amount to hundreds of dollars." (Raton Range)

Thomas McClain opened up a meat market; H. O. Schultz started a successful truck garden; G. R. Troast had the barber shop; Amos Jones was elected president of the Blossburg Building and Loan Association. The first school put up in Blossburg proved too small and a larger, two-story frame structure built. The first superintendent was D. L. Strine. All the meetings for the baseball association, the Masonic brotherhood, and other fraternities were held in the school. A. Cox opened a butcher shop first door south of the postoffice. October 31, 1889 saw such a blizzard that the mines were shut down, lights became a problem and water scarce. For three weeks all was at a standstill. It was worse than the epidemic of small-pox that hit the town a few years before.

Two or three times the company felt that Blossburg was a burden and sought to close it for good. But it always managed to hold on. Finally it moved its stores to Brilliant where it made a last stand. But in 1948 Brilliant too closed down for good and was added on the list of Ghost Towns much to the sorrow of many miners who gave the best years of their lives to the company. The Sacred Heart Church was demolished as well as the school and churches of other denominations. Weeds have become the grave markers for a place that was lively, joyous and prosperous. Only a few ranchers stalk the area now in quest of stray cattle. Now and then an old miner takes a ride there to remember the place where he married, raised a family and earned a liivng.

GARDINER, NEW MEXICO

Shortly before coming to Brilliant one noticed what looked like immense bee hives which were the coke ovens for Gardiner. As he turned in past these he crossed the railroad tracks to the large mercantile store, then the school and up to the hospital. The hospital was an immense building and would grace the public square of any town, for it was solidly built and really up to date. Some citizens of Raton wanted the Rocky Mountain Coal Company to donate it after it was abandoned for a Boy's Town but the company did not quite see it that way and sold it to someone who took it apart, stone by stone, and built quite a night club at the south edge of Raton. Of course the night club will be for the benefit of the good people of Raton and the juvenile delinquency problem in Colfax county will have to be solved in other ways. To have given the little ghost town of Gardiner with all its houses, store, shops and school to the City of Raton for a Boys Town would have been a feather in the cap of the company and certainly have put the buildings to use. The company had to tear them down eventually.

A number of homes were in use right up to 1949, and the company doctor came in several mornings a week from Raton at eleven o'clock sharp to look over the sick. He used but one room of the hospital. Mass was said on Saturdays for the Catholics at the home occupied by Santiago Martinez. As the town was but four miles from Raton many of the people from other denominations went there for services. The town was named for an official of the Rocky Mountain Coal Company.

KOEHLER JUNCTION, NEW MEXICO

This was mostly famous for its packing house. The Raton Range for December 2, 1910 carried an item concerning it: "A modern packing plant is operated at Koehler Junction, on the St. Louis, Rocky Mountain & Pacific railway, practically in the center of the county by the Rocky Mountain Supply Company, of which H. M. Letts is manager. The daily capacity is 50 cattle, 250 hogs and 200 sheep.

"Located within a few miles of Dawson, Koehler, Van Houten and the other great coal camps, a large home demand is only partially met by its products. The plant is built with a view to expansion with the growing trade offering, and is as complete for its size as any in the country. The main buildings are of stone, and the construction thoroughly substantial. A complete ice-making and refrigerating plant places the company on an independent basis so far as ice supply is concerned. A model poultry yard contains nearly a thousand fowl of various kinds, and is a very profitable adjunct of the plant. Situated in the heart of a cattle, sheep and hog-raising country, it has no important competition nearer than Denver, Colorado. For this reason the prices paid for livestocks are higher in proportion than those received in distant markets, the freight saving on shipment of the stock, and return of products leaving a good margin which is divided with the rancher and the farmer.

"From eight to ten cents a pound is paid for hogs on the hoof, and thousands more would be slaughtered every year, if they were obtainable locally. No branch of the stock business pays better than hog raising, nor so well for that matter, on the capital invested. Two litters of six to ten pigs a year that will bring $15 to $25 each, at eleven months old, is certainly a profitable crop, and they can be raised and fattened as cheaply in Colfax county as anywhere on earth. With the greater peopling of Colfax county by farmers who understand pig raising, this business is destined to attain large proportions, and a considerable enlargement of the plant will be necessary in the near future."

DORSEY, NEW MEXICO

This little village was named for the famous senator who founded the Star Mail Route. Dorsey was a railroad man who settled near Raton to become a stock man. But he was too much for industry and decided to go back to it. He sold out his interests in New Mexico but the name remained. Soon a post office was granted, a school built, settlers moved in and it looked as if it would become quite a town. Today it is but a shipping center for cattle.

DAWSON, NEW MEXICO

"GONE, DAWSON died today (April 28, 1950, as quoted from the Raton Range). The miners rolled out of No. 6 on the final man trip this afternoon. This is the end—and the thing many people simply refused to believe could happen even when it was going on right before their eyes. No more coal will come out of Dawson. Phelps Dodge crews will salvage the mobile machinery, chiefly mechanical loaders. They will probably not even bother to pull out the rails—too expensive.

"The next thing will be to get the people moved. They have been given the chance to stay in the company owned houses until June 30. Then they will have to leave. Presumably the houses and other buildings will be sold or torn down. Phelps Dodge isn't going to pay property taxes on a town that is dead. The big power plant will stay for a while at least. The Springer REA Co-op and the Frontier Power Co. are still dickering over it. The REA wants to buy it. There is enough coal on the ground to run the plant for ten or twelve months longer. After that, if the power plant is still needed, the fuel will have to be shipped in. A group of Dawson men propositioned Phelps Dodge to lease the mine for a small scale operation. The company said no. There isn't much more you can say about this; the bleakest day in Dawson's history. It is a sad day for Colfax county.

"The mining business is that way. Plenty of other towns have died in Colfax county. The deaths have brought hundreds of minor, individual tragedies. But Raton and Colfax county are still there. The first mining town to boom and die was a gold-mining town—Elizabethtown, a rip-roaring frontier city that teemed with more than 3000 persons at one time. It was Colfax county's first capital and was toppering toward the grave when Raton began to take on civilized airs. E-town's bones lie bleaching even today in windswept Moreno Valley.

"There are others. There is Baldy, another gold town that died. You have to look hard today to find a trace of the once flourishing place which even boasted a mill to process the gold ore. The list of coal mining towns in the Raton area that are no longer alive is impressive. Look at them: Yankee, gone; Sugarite, only a few stark foundations and a crumbling tipple to mark the spot; old Brilliant, practically no trace left; Gardiner, a tiny cluster of buildings left; Van Houten, a ghost of its once bustling self. With the closing of the schools at Dawson on May 12, the exodus leading to the complete evacuation of the once prosperous coal mining town will be under way. The press and magazines have recorded the decision to abandon coal mining in what was reputedly in its day the largest coal mining camp west of the Mississippi river and one of the most modernly equipped. Karl F. Guthmann, editor of the Roy Record, who watched Dawson grow into a properous town of 8000 people, visited the town last week at a time when a crew from Life magazine was taking pictures for a feature story. He says:

" 'Sad is the plight of many of the miners and others who have been residents of the camp for as long as 40 years. One of the old timers told, with tearful eye, of the large number who are without funds even to move their household effects to another town. Most of the number are inexperienced at means of livelihood other than jobs found about the mines and many are too old to make application for other employment. Many have applied for work at the nearby Koehler mines, but for various reasons have been rejected—principally because the present crew at the mine is now employed by three days a week. Already houses, both frame and cinder block, are being torn down and moved away; mining machines have been moved outside the pits and the lamp house and machine shops have been boarded and only a few grocery items remain in the once well-stocked store. With the closing of the schools on May 12 the exodus leading to the complete evacuation will be under way. The telephone exchange is being abandoned and life will be extinct in the once active Masons, Eastern Star, Forester, Knights of Columbus and Alianza-Espano lodges. The only activity which will remain in the once flourishing camp will be the modern power plant which supplies current to many towns and REA lines throughout Colfax and Harding counties . . . Deploring our national policy, one of the idle miners cited our benevolent acts abroad in the effort to buy friendship while others at home are ignored and neglected. He told of Marshall Plan dollars being poured into a coal project in France where the modern coke ovens and other scientific apparatus is being installed to extra the scores of biproducts of coal, these to be sent over here to flood American markets in order to provide livelihood for Frenchmen!' " (See the Albuquerque Journal for May 10, 1950)

Following the Civil War the trend was westward because too much damage had been done in the East and many thought that by coming to New Mexico, Utah, Colorado, Texas and California, they might make something of their lives so shattered by the conflict. One young man, J. B. Dawson by name, dreamed of apples, chickens, cattle. With a fresh start in life in a place remote from terrible memories, there would be so much to live for. He was connected for a time with Charles Goodnight but the drive for the cattleman from Texas was too much for him. He got too much of it in the army. He would rather do it the easy way and on his own land. He heard stories from soldiers at Fort Union and Santa Fe Trail traders of the wonderful cattle land along the Vermejo. He saw Lucien B. Maxwell, bought a home site and felt at peace with the world. On January 17, 1869, a tract of land, indefinite in description passed from the Maxwell Tract to J. B. Dawson. The deed was recorded on Lincoln's birthday of that year. The price was $3,700. Dawson had the impression that he was buying one thousand acres, but when the Maxwell Land Grant Company's lawsuits were over he found that he had bought 20,000 acres.

Dawson was aware at the time that he bought the property that Maxwell had the same property under consideration for three prospective buyers by the names of Miller, Maulding and Curtis. He got in touch with them, and bought their rights from them under contract. He added more stock, ploughed up more ground, planted more fruit trees. Eventually his place became known as the Cimilarie Ranch. Mrs. Dawson wrote years later:

"Two-year-old apple trees planted out here will bear some apples the third year, and by the time they are six years old will bear a barrel a piece. Pears will do the same when they are seven years old. I sell the apples for five cents a pound in the adjoining towns of Raton and Trinidad, or four cents a pound at the farm. I do not consider that it cost anything for cultivating my orchard, for the beans, corn, etc., which I raise on the ground between the trees more than pay for the care of it. Plums, peaches, cherries, strawberries, gooseberries, currents, and grapes have all done well with me and command a ready sale at good prices. I think the advantage is in favor of farming here, as we have some rain, and irrigation to fall back on. I consider this country ahead of any other for the fruits named above."

Maxwell knew there was coal on the property and often used some of it to heat his home. Dawson, Curtis and several others also mined some coal on the property for their private use. Word of this got around to the Maxwell Land Grant Company which is what started the law suit since Dawson did not let out that he had paid for the property. The company was under the impression that it was leased or rented and ordered him off his own ranch. Charles Springer and Andrieus Jones acted for Dawson which helps to explain his victory. These lawyers were also to work for the Maxwell Land Grant Company and become rich in doing so. Others were later attracted to the place because of the rich coal vein and the fight was on to induce Dawson to sell.

"President C. B. Eddy of the El Paso and Northeastern railroad, accompanied by a party of other railroad men, visited Colfax county last week to inspect the Dawson coal lands, recently purchased by the railroad. Mr. Eddy, in an interview, (with a reporter from the Las Vegas Optic—June 20, 1901) stated that the money is on hand for the construction of a line of railroad to these coal fields, and the likelihood is that the road will miss Las Vegas (which the citizens of that fair city did not favor) a distance of fully twenty miles. A town site has been purchased and laid out on the Dawson ranch by the new owners of the Dawson fields. As Mr. Eddy is a town builder and boomer who always 'gets there' in his projects, it may be predicted that the new town in Colfax county, through his efforts, and backed by the railroad he represents, will be one of the important towns of New Mexico."

"The Dawson Fuel Company filed incorporation papers in the office of the Territorial Secretary, J. W. Raynolds (June 18, 1901). The capital is $1,900,000 divided into 10,000 shares. Headquarters are at Alamogordo (future home of the A bomb), in Otero county. The incorporators are: Clarence D. Simpson, Charles B. Eddy, Benjamin S. Harmon. (These may be called the fathers of the City of Dawson.) The Directors are: Simpson Eddy, Thomas B. Watkins, B. H. Williams and Peter Thompson. The company will engage in mining coal in Colfax county where it has acquired the Dawson coal fields." Shortly afterwards the Dawson Railroad Company was formed.

"The Dawson Railroad Company filed incorporation papers at the office of the Territorial Secretary, Saturday (July 13, 1901). The incorporators and directors are: C. Simpson of Scranton, Pa., who subscribed to $126,000 worth of stock; T. Watkins, also of Scranton; C. Eddy, of Alamogordo; B. Harmon, of York, Pa.; Alexander S. Grieg and Ernest J. Dedman, both of Alamogordo. The other subscribers are: Francis H. Ross and John Frederick, of New York. The capital stock is $3,000,000 divided into 30,000 shares of which $130,000 has been subscribed and ten percent of the amount paid to the treasurer. The company intends to build a road 130 miles long from Liberty in Guadalupe county where it will connect with the Rock Island railroad, and the El Paso & Northeastern extension to the Dawson coalfields in Colfax county. The headquarters of the company will be at Alamogordo. Work on the proposed railroad is to be commenced as soon as the El Paso & Northeastern and the Rock Island extensions are completed. Those interested in the railroad are people who recently bought the extensive coal fields at Dawson."

Springer has acquired from the Dawsons, on October 29, 1896, a deed to one-half interest in all the sub-surface rights to minerals on the ranch. He may have been instrumental in interesting buyers for the coal fields. It has been said that Charles Springer, Mary Chase Springer, (his wife) and J. B. Dawson sold the Dawson property to the newly organized Dawson Fuel Company for the sum of $400,000. Dawson conveyed land for a townsite for an additional $5000, keeping for himself his home, some farming land, his orchard, and some grazing land, amounting in all to some 1,200 acres. Mrs. Dawson, regardless of the fact that she was now in the chips, threw in another clause before signing away the property. Ever the farmer's wife, she asked for, and obtained, the exclusive right for a period of ten years, to sell milk in the town to be, which town was to be called Dawson.

"The work of laying the ties and rails and building the bridges on the Dawson branch of the Rock Island is being pushed. The depot at Dawson will be a handsome structure. There are about five hundred people already living at the new mining town (August 21, 1902). About one hundred cottages have been erected by the fuel company and more are in the process of erection. The coal tipple has been completed and about fifty men are employed opening up the coal vein preparatory to taking out coal. It is reported that a town will be laid out somewhere between the Bell ranch and the Santa Fe crossing. The company expects to have the line open for traffic by the First of November."

"The first consignment of coal consisting of twenty-nine cars arrived at Santa Rosa from Dawson last week. The coal is of excellent quality. The opening of the Dawson coal fields and the prospective production of coal along the Santa Fe Central Railway will relieve the chronic coal stringency along the Rock Island line in New Mexico" (Jan. 15, 1903)

"Fire broke out in the mine at Dawson from some cause not definitely known. Supposition is that the fire was started by a curtain in the mine being accidently set afire. The flames rapidly spread, and the five hundred miners employed there made a hasty exit, with the exception of three: Serapio Ragel, Miguel Salazar, and a Negro, who never came out. Saturday afternoon the superintendent and a number of miners started in to rescue the imprisoned men and to put out the fire, but after going quite a distance inside the entry, a terrible explosion occurred throwing the party to the floor with violence, several being severly injured, and all, when they came out, being more or less scorched. While mine No. 1 had been closed, there is no curtailment in operations at the camp, the entire force of miners being put to work in the other mines. (Sept. 4, 1903).

"The Stag Canon Fuel Company of Dawson purchased a brick plant to be located at Dawson for the manufacture of brick for the company's use. All coke ovens in the future will be built of this brick, the shale for which is most abundant there. The plant was sold by G. W. Nushaw of Dayton, Ohio, for the C. W. Raymond Company of Dayton. Its cost is $10,000 and it will be installed at once. Mr. Nushaw has sold a large plant to our local cement company which will be ready for use in May." (Jan. 18, 1909). But to go back a few years to the establishment of the town:

"The Dawson Railroad Company filed incorporation papers at the office of the Terirtorial Secretary, Saturday. The incorporators and directors are Clarence Simpson of Scranton, Pa., who subscribed to $126,000 worth of stock; etc." as we found out above. But these men were not idle. They sent out contractors and working crews so that before long Dawson was quite a mining community even though it changed hands several times. By 1910, it was recognized as one of the largest towns of its type in the Southwest, and it did all the things that are generally done in a town its size.

"Walter Byers was killed at Dawson (April 18, 1910) by a single shot from the gun of Thomas O'Neill, who was fortified by a few drinks. It seems that the two became involved in a heated discussion that brought on the fatal results. Deputy Sheriff Frank Vance took O'Neill into custody and brought him to Raton. Byers was forty years of age and tipple boss at the mine. He leaves a wife and eight children. O'Neill served for a time as bartender at the mining town, but later gave it up for the life of a cowboy."

"The Phelps Dodge Smelter syndicate has gained control of the roads formerly held by the New Mexico Railway & Coal Company, whose lines extend from Dawson, New Mexico, a short distance south, to Raton; then to El Paso. The smelter people will now build from Dawson to a point south of Durango (Colo.) to tap the immense coal fields there. When the announcement was made a few days ago that the Phelps Dodge syndicate had relinquished a right-of-way through New Mexico from Farmington to a station near El Paso to the Denver & Rio Grande, railroad men wondered, but with the announcement that the smelter people have acquired lines which will permit them to get the coal from near Durango, the situation is clearly understood. The New Mexico Railway Company is owned by the El Paso & Northeastern; the El Paso & Rock Island; the Dawson Railway and the Alamogordo & Sacramento Mountain Railway. By the acquisition of those lines the smelters and mines of New Mexico, Arizona and Mexico will be further supplied with Colorado coal. C. D. Simpson, president of the New Mexico Railway & Coal Company has given out the following statement from New York:

"'For upwards of two months I have been getting options on the stocks and securities of the various companies which are owned and controlled by the New Mexico Railway & Coal Company with the view of re-organizing the company on a four percent bond basis. For several months the New Mexico Railway and Coal Company has been negotiating with the Phelps Dodge & Company for a long term contract to supply their large demand for coal and coke for their Arizona copper mines, smelters and railroads, and during these negotiations, after I had obtained options on a large majority of all the securities, we came to an agreement by which Messrs. Phelps, Dodge and Company purchased the entire capital stock of the New Mexico Railway and Coal Company, carrying with it the ownership and control of the above mentioned companies.'" (May 25, 1905)

"J. Parker Wells of Dawson has just secured the contract for furnishing the miners of Dawson with meat and he estimates that he will be able to dispose of thirty-five beeves weekly. He said: 'There is plenty of native beef, rolling fat in the country, and especially in the county of Colfax, that I can purchase, but I do not expect to leave Colfax county for any of my supplies. This will leave the money at home and in this way I believe that my securing the meat contract will be of benefit to the town of Dawson and the county and the cattlemen. Dawson is growing fast and there is not an idle man in town. There are from three to five trains of coal going out daily and every man in the camp is in a prosperous condition. The script which was used so long in camp is done away with and every man is paid in cash. But if a man wants credit coupon books these are issued to him and held out of his wages. Several new business blocks are in the course of construction and there are many new cottages being erected which will be occupied by the miners. The water supply is also being developed and will be made adequate to supply a city of twice the population of Dawson.'" (July 11, 1906)

"Dawson, the big coal camp and town of Colfax county, is evidently planning to remain the biggest coal camp in New Mexico. More than two hundred new houses are being built to accomodate the miners, and there are as yet many who have to live in tents until houses can be built. It is believed, however, that the houses will be built to comfortably take care of all before winter sets in. The Southwestern Fuel Company is building a commodious office in a central location, and here all company business will be tranacted, instead of being scattered all over the town. A large number of clerks and stenographers are now employed in the various departments. The new hospital will soon be ready for use. It is a new hospital and will comfortably house a large number of patients. Four new mines are now being opened by the company about one mile up the Vermejo, and a track is being graded to the new location. Two hundred new cottages will be built near the new mines at once, and it is believed the output from these mines will greatly increase the total output of the camp. The Southwestern Mercantile Company is building a new warehouse near the present store building of the company. This warehouse will cost in the neighborhood of five thousand dollars and will fill a long felt want. The storage capacity has been too small for the needs of the business transactions by the company and the new building will facilitate the handling of merchandise of all kinds.

"Dawson will soon be the best lighted small town in the Southwest. The immense electric plant of the company will furnish light to every house in the camp, and all the streets and alleys, public places, stores, about the vicinity of the mines will be lighted from a central system. Work of wiring the town is about completed, and the current will be turned on the new lines. The fuel company will soon build a new washer, much larger in capacity and more modern than the present one. It will cost thousands of dollars but will be one of the finest in the Southwest. Skilled mechanics and tradesmen are scarce in Dawson and more are welcome. A seventy-five foot addition has been built to the Dawson Hotel to help accomodate the guests." *(Raton Range, July 18, 1906)*

The people of Dawson were always sports-minded. From infancy boys wore baseball gloves or threw basketballs around. Many miners were able to retain their jobs because of their baseball ability. Large posters announced games; newspapers gave every game more publicity than national events. The town also boasted one of the best bands in New Mexico. Many of the Italian miners were competent musicians and known far and wide. The band went on all baseball trips so that the attention of the spectators was divided between listening to the music and watching the wind-up of the pitcher.

There was the day that the blacksmith shop caught fire; the tragic day of the murder of Mrs. Frank di Julio, Antonio di Julio and Bartolo di Julio. Dawson people will long remember P. Grover, M. Sullivan, A. Martin and A. J. Smith who taught in the Dawson schools. The teachers in 1917 were: G. L. Fenlon, S. Hanna, S. Cooper, A. Devlin, E. Pitts, G. McDermott, A. Nair, N. Nutter, F. Sitko, H. Henry, H. McGarvey, and N. D. Edwards. The day that the big, beautiful new theatre was opened the Wolfe Stock Company gave the first performance. That was in 1907. The name of the play was "Our Boys." One of the greatest disasters of Dawson and New Mexico was the terrific explosion at the mine on October 23, 1913, which entombed over three hundred men. Relief crews from all the Swastica Coal Company camps the surrounding area were called upon for help. The total loss of life was definitely set at 286. But Dawson soon lived the disaster down and work was resumed. All went well until railroads started to convert to diesel and other companies would under bid for contracts. A sixteen million dollar industry of the bi-products of coal was going to be built up until it was found that there was not enough water to take care of the plant. Doom was inevitable. The end came although quicker than people suspected. Dawson is no more.

MARTINSEN, COLORADO

This village was named after an official of the Maxwell Land Grant. In the heart of the Colorado coal and ranching region it might have been quite a settlement had not Raton and Trinidad been so close as shopping and shipping centers. Towns cannot grow too close together in the Southwest because the industry is essentially cattle and each steer needs so many acres for grazing. Lack of water will back down many places.

PELS, COLORADO

Pels was also named for an official of the Maxwell Land Grant Company. The village was started as a shipping center for the trains running into Catskill, New Mexico. From Pels the trains could hook up to the main line at Trinidad. With the railroad gone the town had served its purpose. A few ranchers still inhabit the region and someday large lumber and coal camps may open up there.

SAN FRANCISCO, COLORADO

This is a little ranching community that devotes a little time to mining coal. The area is quite undeveloped not because it isn't rich but because too many other places are being worked. Some day the Grant company will commercialize it.

WOOTON, COLORADO

At the foot of Raton Pass this place was named after old, lovable, "Uncle Dick." He signed his name Wooten, but for some reason the place was spelled with an o at the end. Here the famous scout maintained his toll gate, hotel, dining room very much in the order of the Clifton House in New Mexico. The wagons along the Santa Fe Trail that didn't take the Rabibt Ear route, or go around him to avoid the toll tax, rested. Railroad men came to love the place. Ranchers often came here for Saturday night dances and socials. The lonely grave one sees near the old manor house is that of a soldier killed by his own men out of hatred. The feud began in New Mexico and had its tragic end here in Wooton when the soldiers were escorting a stage to Denver. Colonel Owensy rebuilt the famous Wooten ranch and spent many happy days there. The place will eventually become a resort area for it is one of the most beautiful spots in the Southwest.

RINCON, COLORADO

This place is also in the coal region and extensive ranching is carried on there. At one time there was hopes that it would blossom out into one of the major camps of Colorado but it never came up to expectations possibly because too many other camps close to railroads or spur lines were operating at less expense. Should coal once again become the industry that it was at the turn of the century this may become quite a city.

AMERICAN, COLORADO

This settlement was near the present site of Morley. From the piles of slack one sees and from the remains of the coke ovens along the highway this must have been a tremendous coal camp. Whether because the vein ran out or because Morley seemed better situated, the camp closed down and Morley was founded. Today a cafe, gas station, garage and motel are on the site. Perhaps the proximity to Trinidad may make quite a suburban area of the place. If Trinidad expands towards Raton then someday this place may become part of that city. Several years ago a big sign read: Site of the Great American Mine. But that too, is gone.

THE CREEKS ON THE GRANT

While the problem in New Mexico seems to be water, the Maxwell Land Grant tract has many streams which while not enough for the ranges, fields and coal camps are certainly more than found in other sections of the state. We list the creeks here in Colorado and New Mexico. Middle Fork, San Francisco, Acequia de los Apaches, West, Castle Rock, Hart, Lowrey, Mills, Muddy, Pine, Nigger, Humbug, Grouse, Mexican, Willow, Comanche, Tolby, Sawmill, Cieneguilla, Nine Mile, Palo Flecha, Lorencito, Gonzolez, Mestas, Ancho, Gorillo, Bonito, Ute, California, Clear, American, Beaver, Coyote, Patten, Martinsen, Colorow, Saruche, Chicken, Clear (Colorado to distinguish it from the one in New Mexico), Tin Pan, Williams, Canfield, McCune, T.B.L., No. 9, Sheep Spring, Potato, Jones, Ramba, Gardiner, Cottonwood, Chicorica, Raton, Little Crow, Sugarite, Coal, Tenaja, Urraca, Stout Canyon, Blind,

Dead Horse, Five Dollar, Sheep, Twitty, Chimney, Prairie Dog, Spellman, Juan Baca, Juan de la Cruz, York, Curtis, Gooseberry, Hoyle, Mercer, Stag, Sprig, West York, York, Ercenoso, Caliente, No. 16, Bend, Moreno, Sawmill (near E'town as apart from a creek of the same name up near Catskill), Dyke and Big Ditch. A few are unnamed. Why not name one for yourself?

THE RITOS OR RIVERS ON THE GRANT

Ponil, Uno de Gato, Vermejo, Leandro, Ricardo, Oro, Bernal, Middle Fork, South Fork, Costilla, N. Cerrososo, S. Cerrososo, N. Ponil, Middle Ponil, S. Fork Ponil, Agua Fria, Rayado, Cimarron, Red, Long's Canyon, Cimarroncito, North and West Fork Cimarron, and Abreu.

THE CANYONS OF THE GRANT

Box, Saltpeter, Stout, Railroad, Prairie Crow, Potato, Tin Pan, Dutchman, Coleman, Long's, Valdez, Van Bremmer, Burnt, Dillon, Coal Creek, Caliente, Dean, Cimarron and Cerrososo.

THE PARKS OF THE GRANT

Vermejo, Van Bremmer, Baldy, Garcia, Agua Fria, Ponil, Ute, Castle Rock, Red River.

THE MESAS OF THE GRANT

Bartlett, Cedar Hills, Rayado, Gonzolez, Uraca, Clear Creek, Black Mountain, Chicorica.

THE LAKES OF THE GRANT

Eagle Nest, Dorsey, Charette.

SOME OF THE LARGER RANCHES ON THE GRANT

Curtis, Stockton, Wrigley, McMurdo, Dorsey, White, Dover, Abreu, Clutton, Shoup, Brackell, Springer, Chase, Porter, Clouthier, Service, Littrel, Lucy, Dawson, Coleman, Franklin, Lee, Bea, Torres, Smith, and Carey.

THE ST. LOUIS, ROCKY MOUNTAIN & PACIFIC COMPANY

The St. Louis, Rocky Mountain & Pacific Company owns a larger coal area than any other corporation in the country, more than 500,000 acres, and this vast possession lies wholly within Colfax county. On practically the whole area are three different seams of high-grade bituminous coal ... The coke produced is sold to smelters and refiners in Arizona, Mexico, Texas, Montana, Colorado and Utah. Coal is shipped over a territory equal to one-sixth of the entire area of the United States serving a population of six million people. The following named railroads draw on these mines for fuel supply: A.T.&S.F.; Colorado and Southern; El Paso & Southwestern; Rock Island; Kansas City; Mexico & Orient and others.

The Santa Fe railroad is rushing to completion its Texas cut-off, which will form the shortest rail line between the Colfax county coal fields of the St. L. R.M. & P.R.R., and the port of Galveston. When the K.C., Mexico & Orient railroad is completed, an outlet to the Pacific coast trade at Topolobampo will be available.

The St. Louis, Rocky Mountain & Pacific railroad, an allied corporation, operates 102 miles of track, all but twenty of which are in Colfax county, connecting with the Santa Fe, El Paso & Southwestern, Rock Island, and Colorado & Southern railways, within a few miles of the lines and traversing the finest agricultural section of the country from Ute Park on the west to Des Moines, in Union county, on the east, where it connects with the Colorado & Southern. It is also the "lumber road" of northern New Mexico, connecting at Cimarron with the Cimarron & Northwestern railroad, operated by the Continental Tie & Lumber Company. Seven locomotives and 600 cars are employed in the traffic, and all rolling stock and other equipment is first class in all particulars.

A marked recovery from the depressed conditions of 1907, which so seriously affected both coal and lumber interests, has been made, and the operations of the St. L., R.M. & P. for the fiscal year ending June 30, 1910, shows a handsome surplus after all fixed charges were met. The principal mines of the company are the Van Houten, Koehler, Brilliant, Blossburg, Gardiner, Dutchman, Sugarite and Railroad Canyon, all of the number being operated in 1910. The Raton, or Blossburg seam, lowest of the coal measures is the most fully developed, and the scene of the principal operations. The vein is from four to fifteen feet thick. The Tin Pan seam, 455 ft. above the Raton, is opened at Brilliant, where extensive operations are now being conducted. The coal seam varies from four to six feet in thickness. Both above named seams are persistent throughout the company's property. The Potato Canyon seam is 355 feet above the Tin Pan and ranges from four to six feet in thickness. This seam has been well prospected, sufficiently to demonstrate its regular persistence, but no mine workings have yet been opened.

The heaviest producer of the group is the Van Houten mine, only two miles from Preston, a station of the St. L., R.M. & P. R.R., fourteen miles southwest of Raton. A spur of the Santa Fe line runs direct to the mine. Here the vein is four to fifteen feet in thickness, and five openings are operated. In rush seasons as high as 4000 tons a day have been mined in this property. At Gardiner, fourteen miles from Van Houten are 200 coke ovens that are supplied from this mine. In 1910 the gross coal mined at all the company mines, will amount to 1,500,000 tons. The coal put on the rails, will total 1,200,000 tons, and

150,000 tons of coke will be sent to market, a marked increase over the production of 1909, which showed nearly 12 percent advance over the figures for the year previous.

In Prairie Crow Canyon, about twenty-two miles southwest of Raton is the Koehler mine, second only to Van Houten in importance and output. The Raton seam is operated through three openings, being from four to eleven feet in thickness. A large coking plant south of the town is an important factor in the Koehler output. Perched on a high bluff at the Canyon's mouth, the town of Koehler would be selected by many as a home site, merely for the scenic attractions. The population is prosperous and contented, the word "home" meaning much to the residents, who find comforts far exceeding those usually found outside of mining camps in towns of similar size. The water supply is excellent, electric lights are furnished in all the houses, the homes are neat, cozy and well furnished, showing that a superior class of mine workers is attracted by the liberal policy of the management.

The Brilliant mine is well developed and thoroughly equipped and preparations for active mining in 1911 have been completed. A force of fifty men is now employed. The Dutchman mine is in good condition and can be put into operation within a few days at any time. The Sugarite mine of the company's group is three and a half miles northeast of Raton, leased to the Raton Coal Company, which hauls the coal in teams to Raton, supplying the retail demand. The position of the St. Louis, Rocky Mountain & Pacific Company is a commanding one. With its operated mines developed and equipped far ahead of present demand, three or four in reserve, that may any day be added to the producing list; with a practically inexhaustible supply in its immense domain, and an ever increasing market, it is at once a dominant factor in the coal market of the west.

A few short lines of railway in the country can boast of equal scenic attractions to those offered along the 106 miles of track that constitutes the St. Louis, Rocky Mountain & Pacific, having its present eastern terminus at Des Moines, Union county, where it connects with the Colorado & Southern, and at the western end of the terminus is at Ute Park. Raton is the general headquarters. Westward from Raton, which you leave behind at 2:30 P. M., the rails skirt the base of the foothills, winding along the brows of high mesas from which views across forty to sixty miles of vales and hilltops are obtained. To the northward a series of canyons are opened to the eye, one after the other for many miles, each presenting some new feature to appeal to the artistic appreciation of all nature lovers.

The Rockies are in turn inspiring, awesome, grand, stupendous or beautiful—but never wearisome to the trained traveler . . . . Leaving Cimarron the twelve mile journey to Ute Park follows the windings of the river of that name at every fresh turning or crossing of the swiftly running stream . . . It was in Mid-October that the writer first saw Ute Park, the core of the New Mexico section of the Rocky Mountains. It presented a painter's dream of color riot beyond the power of men to adequately describe. (Raton Range December 2, 1910)

THE MORE FAMOUS RANCHES ON THE GRANT

(a) THE MAXWELL RANCH

(From the Cimarron News-Press Dec. 6, 1907)

One of the most interesting and picturesque regions of all New Mexico is the large tract of one million, seven hundred thousand acres known as the Maxwell Ranch through which the old Santa Fe Trail ran. Dead many years, Lucien B. Maxwell, belonged to a generation and a class almost extinct, and the like of which in all probability will never be seen again for the reason that there is no more frontier to develop them. Several years prior to the acquisition of the territory by the United States, the immense tract comprised in the geographical limits of the ranch was granted to Carlos Beaubien and Guadalupe Miranda, both citizens of the province of New Mexico and agents of the American fur company. Attached to the company as an employee, trapper and hunter was Lucien B. Maxwell, an Illinoisan by birth, who married a daughter of Beaubien. After the death of the latter, Maxwell purchased all the interests of the joint proprietor, Miranda, as well as those of the heirs of Beaubien, thus becoming at once one of the largest land owners in the United States. At the heighth of his influence and wealth during the War of the Rebellion, when New Mexico was so isolated and almost independent of care or thought by the government at Washington, he lived in great magnificence, like to that of the nobles of England. The thousands of arable acres comprised in many of the fertile valleys of his immense ranch were farmed in a primitive sort of way; principally by native Mexicans. He employed about five hundred men, and men now living that used to work for him say that he was not a hard master, but on the other hand was kind and considerate of their wants and that his many workmen really loved him as he was ever their friend and advisor. The sources of his wealth were his cattle, sheep and the products of his area of cultivated acres, principally barley, corn, oats and wheat. These grains he sold mainly to the quartermaster and commissary departments of the army in the large military district of New Mexico. According to the estimates of his Mexican relatives during the Civil War he sold one thousand horses, ten thousand cattle and forty thousand sheep. His wool clip must have been enormous. He possessed a large and perfectly appointed grist mill, which must have been a great source of revenue, for wheat was one of the staple crops of his many farms. This three story stone grist mill is still standing and in good condition at Cimarron. The lower story is occupied by the Cimarron Mercantile company as a store room and the two upper stories are leased by the C.M.A. association for social purposes. This mill was run by water coming through a flume from the Cimarron river nearby. In the summer of 1867 there was great excitement over the discovery of gold on the Maxwell ranch and adventurers were beginning to congregate in the hills and gulches everywhere. The discovery of the precious metal on his estate was said to have been the first cause of his financial embarrassment. It was the ruin also of many other prominent men in New Mexico, who expended their entire fortune in the construction of an immense ditch forty miles in length from the Red River to supply the placer diggings to the Moreno Valley with water, when the melted snow of Old Baldy range had exhausted itself in the late summer. The scheme was a stupendous failure; its ruins may be seen today going from Elizabethtown to Red River City and in the deserted valleys, a monument to man's engineering skill, but the wreck of his hopes. For some years previous to the discovery of gold in the mountains and gulches of the Maxwell ranch, it was known that copper and large quantities of coal existed on this ranch. While there has never been much copper mined here, there has been (and will continue to be for many years to come) immense quantities of the finest coal in the country mined from the hills and mountains which composed the old Maxwell ranch. Mr. Maxwell built his manor house in the old village of Cimarron on the bank of the river of the same name. It was large and roomy, purely American in its construction, but the manner of conducting it was strictly Mexican. Some of its apartmetns are said to have been elaborately furnished, others devoid of everything except a table for card playing, and a few chairs. The kitchen and dining room of his establishment were detached from the main residence. There was one dining room for the male portion of his attendants and guests of that sex, and another for the female in accordance with the strange Mexican custom. Not far from this manor house were a group of buildings, houses for his hired men, stables, mill, store and blacksmith shop and it is said that the grounds surrounding these buildings were a constant resort and loafing place of Indians. The Maxwell house at Cimarron is still standing although it is very much out of repair. Until a few weeks ago when a fire occurred in this house it was occupied by three families. Mr. Maxwell selling his ranch to an English company and his removal to another part of the Territory, together with an account of the intervening years between his removal and his death, as well as a delineator of his character is reserved for a future number of the News and Press.

(b) THE HECK RANCH

Four miles southwest of Cimarron is the Heck ranch. This ranch consists of thirteen hundred acres, much of it rich soil capable of producing excellent crops of all kinds of grains and vegetables. It has two large orchards, the trees being right in their prime. Last year (1906) the trees bore a phenomenal crop of several varieties of the most merchantable apples, but this year the trees failed to bear any fruit on acount of the late frost in May last. This year the farm has produced two hundred and fifty tons of hay, four hundred bushels of corn, much wheat and barley and all kinds of vegetables. During the summer and fall months, several gallons of milk and a load of vegetables were sent to town daily. (i. e. to Cimarron) Last month there was shipped to Denver one hundred and thirty head of cattle which were very fat and in number one condition.

This ranch has an abundance of runinng water besides a large reservoir, well filled with water near the barns and corals. At present it has two hundred head of cattle, six work horses, a large number of milk cows, many hogs, geese, ducks, sixty turkeys and hundreds of hens and chickens. The land here is capable of raising very fine sugar beets. Connected with this ranch is a leased pasture near Elizabethtown of four thousand acres where the cattle graze during the summer months. Some of the finest horses and mules raised in this region come from this ranch. Only a few days ago a fine span of horses raised here were sold for four hundred dollars.

The mansion house is a two-story adobe with many large and spacious rooms, well adapted for work as well as for cosy and comfortable life. The barns, the wagon and tool houses, creamery, and other out buildings are many and in good state of preservation. This ranch is owned by Mathias Heck, who was born in Cologne, Prussia, June 19, 1829, and came to this country in 1844. After living in sereval states he came to New Mexico in 1862. He served in the Civil War as a member of Company K, First California Cavalry. (He was with the volunteers that came with General Carleton in an effort to drive the Texans out of New Mexico and save Fort Union. Colorado did the fighting for them at Glorieta, Peralta and along the Rio Grande. Although the Californians arrived too late they stayed around for a long time just in case. This was the second instance, the first being after the Mexican War, when soldiers mustered out to take up farming and family life in New Mexico.) He was honorably discharged from the army at Santa Fe in July 1866. In 1867 he went to work in the mines at Elizabethtown. From there he went to Ocate where he spent nine years in keeping a mercantile store and ran a hotel. In 1878 he located on his present ranch near Cimarron. Mr. Heck although 79 years of age, enjoys excellent health for one of his age. Although unable to do much work, he has his eye on business and walks about his many acres with a firm and elastic tread and bids fair to enjoy many more years of life, which is the hope of his many friends.

Mrs. Heck is a remarkable woman; although several years past seventy, she runs her house and does a good share of her house work as though she were only forty. They have one daughter who lives at home and one son who lives in the neighborhod and takes general care of the ranch.

(c) THE X A RANCH

The X A ranch is on the Ponil river and consists of twenty-seven thousand acres divided into two tracts, one called the Twitty place, ten miles from Cimarron, the other called the Lane place, nineteen miles from Cimarron. The land is owned by the Maxwell Land Grant Company but is leased for a term of years by O. B. Bishop of Cimarron, James K. Hunt, assistant cashier of the First National Bank of Raton and Eugene G. Twitty, probate clerk of Colfax county. The new railroad (R.Mt., ST.L.&P.), for a space of about twelve miles, runs through the center of this ranch. The pastures of this ranch are well adapted for the grazing of large bunches of cattle. The grass is fine the year around with plenty of water. The ranch will support from twelve to fifteen hundred head of cattle. A portion of the ranch contains excellent land for cultivation. Last year (1906) a large crop of rye and oats were raised yielding forty bushels to the acre. Some of this land would produce a fine crop of sugar beets. All kinds of vegetables can be grown here in their season. There are twenty-five saddle and stock horses on the place, together with milk cows, geese, ducks and a large number of hens and chickens. The buildings consist of two log houses, several barns and sheds and many outbuildings. Recently there was shipped from this ranch to Omaha three carloads of cattle which were in very good condition. O. B. Bishop is the manager and part owner of the stock. He spends most of his time at the ranch while his wife and children live in Cimarron during the greater part of the year so that the latter can enjoy the advantages of the public schools.

(d) THE LORD RUSTAN RANCH

Rustan was a nobleman from England who put some money in stock in the Maxwell Land Grant Company, then decided to come over and see the land for himself. He liked what he saw and bought land sending for his family to come over from England to live on the Vermejo. He sold the ranch on December 18, 1907. "An extensive land deal has taken place at Vermejo, New Mexico, in the sale of the Lord Rustan ranch of 9,000 acres, and a fine herd of graded cattle, to Rev. R. A. Morley, D. D., of East Las Vegas. The land lies surrounding this junction point of the St. Louis Rocky Mountain & Pacific Railroad with the Dawson Railroad. The property will be sold to colonists. It is reported that the Rustans will return to their former home in England. Charles Springer of Cimarron, with a number of stockmen, as stockholders in the company, is building a packing house near Koehler, a few miles north of Vermejo. The plant will have sufficient capacity to furnish meats for the mining camps and railroads towns and, in fact, the whole of Colfax county." (*Raton Range, December 25, 1907—Apparently Christmas didn't mean anything to newspaper men in thise days. A Christmas greeting meets the eye as if the editor were forced into it not as something of good cheer. The editorial for the day is entitled: A Modern Fleet.*)

(e) THE URRACA RANCH

George H. Webster, Jr., is an enthusiast on the subject of the Urraca ranch which he owns. His enthusiasm is abundantly justified for it is without doubt one of the finest country estates of its size in the United States. In fact, there are but few estates of any size, anywhere, that embrace so many advantages and its possession should satisfy the ambition of any man. In its present (1910) state it is an ideal ranch, farm and home, and its future development is already provided for, as accurately planned as human foresight can devise.

Although Mr. Webster has been in possession only five years, he has completed one of the most comprehensive and extensive private systems of water conservation and irrigation thus far put into operation in New Mexico, according to Vernon L. Sullivan, territorial engineer. A resident of the teritory for eighteen years he had gained most valuable experience from a study of all its irrigation projects. For location and accessibility the Urraca ranch has few equals. The fields adjoin the south boundary of the Cimarron townsite, the residence being only three miles from the railway station. The ranch corrals were formerly a stage station of the old Santa Fe Trail, which runs from north to south through the tract of 80,000 acres. The great Scenic Highway of the Rocky Mountains will follow the trail at this point, and at no distant date automobiles will pass the home farm in daily procession by dozens, and tourists will pursue a leisurely pace in order to drink in the beauties of the mountain scenes unfolded to the westward, equalled by few stretches along the entire route.

Mr. Webster owns a vast water shed, the sources of the Cimarroncito Creek, covering many miles in area along the mountain range to foothills . . . The handsome ranch house is located in a thirty acre apple orchard of 20 to 30 years' growth . . . Within ten years time these 23,000 trees will produce annually from about 100,000 to 150,000 boxes of apples.

Other famous ranches on the Grant were the Dawson ranch, the Chase ranch and the Hartly ranch. C. M. Chase, in his Editor's Run mentions that he visited the Chase ranch on October 18, 1881. Mr. Chase is a man 45 years old and a border life experience of 30 years has given him the best qualifications for stock raising in a new country. Mr. Chase was born in Wisconsin, and his father, W. C. Chase, a native of Bradford, Vermont, being an extensive stock broker, put him into business of handling stock very early in life. Before Colorado had made much pretension as a teritory even, Chase emigrated to the far West, took a hand in corraling Indians, hunting game, mining, etc. His business took him over a large part of the country from the Black Hills to Santa Fe, New Mexico. For a number of years he was engaged in the freighting business across the plains from the Missouri river to Denver. Some fifteen years ago, being well acquainted with the greater portion of the range along the foothills of the Rocky Mountains, he selected Cimarron, New Mexico, as the finest climate he knew, and as a locality affording the richest range and the best shelter for cattle. He moved here, commenced his farm and started his wonderful herd. From a small beginning he has worked his way up to be the leading stock man in these parts. He has a residence three miles from the village of

Cimarron, in a rich canyon, from a half mile to a mile wide. His home place contains one thousand acres of land. Here he keeps forty horses and about three hundred head of cattle. The horses are designed mainly for his family and individual driving, and the cattle are the property of his children. Fifteen miles to the north he and two partners named Dawson and Maulding have a ranch of fifty thousand acres, all enclosed, about twenty miles of it having the wire fence and fifteen miles the walls of the mountains. This range takes the natural drainage of the Vermejo river; is sufficient for 3,000 cattle, and is already stocked with a herd of 2,500. This range is about half open prairie, the other half extending back into the foothills which contain numerous canyons and mesas, largely covered with pinon trees, forming the finest imaginable shelter for cattle. The ranch is considered a sort of "home pasture" and is about eight by ten miles in extent. The canyons extend way back into the foothills forming beautiful parks, little and big, from 100 to 2000 acres in extent, dotted here and there with the pinons, and are as beautiful and romantic as it is possible to form on the bosom of Mother Earth. They are simply charming, and one almost envies the life of an animal in possession of such homes. The hills rise up suddenly out of the flatlands and terminate in flat tops, miles in extent and rich in grazing capacity. Though very steep and covered with pinons, most of their sides also form good grazing.

Mr. Chase and his partner, Dawson, own a sheep ranch one hundred and eighty miles southeast of Cimarron, some twelve by fifteen miles in extent, which contains a greater number of acres than the home pasture. This ranch is now stocked with 15,000 sheep of improved breed.

With the two partners mentioned above, Mr. Chase purchased last year a tract of country one hundred and fifty miles southeast of Cimarron, and just north of the sheep ranch, embracing about sixty by thirteen miles in extent, containing in round numbers 500,000 acres, allowing ten acres to each animal. In ordinary seasons this is sufficient. The company, however, intend to allow the herd to grow, by purchase and increase of 25,000 head and then make their calculations for the future.

In addition to the above, Mr. Chase and his partner, Dawson, a man by the name of Folsom, and four others, have purchased a tract of land of about 150,000 acres, thirty-five miles southeast of Cimarron, which has not been stocked as yet, but will be this winter by purchase of stock from Texas. It will range easily 10,000 to 15,000 head. Mr. Chase has the management of these different ranges; i.e. he does the buying and selling, and has general supervision, with a boss on each ranch, to attend to all the details, such as hiring the help, who ride the fences and go around the range daily to keep an eye out for breaks in the fence, to round up cattle at stated seasons, to cut out beef to be sold, calves to be branded, etc. For his supervision he gets a salary from each company, as well as his share of the profits . . . On leaving the sheep camp, a mile ride over the prairie brought us to the wire fence of the "home pasture"—a fence sixteen miles long. An opening was made and we passed in, rode two miles, and came to the old Santa Fe station, now used as a home for Marion Littrel (the rancher who later became sheriff of Colfax county and then warden of the state prison at Santa Fe), the boss of the ranch. *(Chase does not speak here of the railroad but of the old stage station that was a resting place along the Santa Fe Trail.)*

From here we passed on through the pasture, over lonely country, entered a canyon and passed up two miles, to where the mountains draw together and form a canyon one-half mile wide. Here we found the residence of Mr. Dawson, a one story adobe house with adobe barn and adobe corral. Half of the house had been torn away and an addition was about to be built, but two or three small rooms were left. Mr. Dawson and wife, seven children, the school marm, and a visiting gentleman and lady from Trinidad, were the occupants. An addition of four full grown men to the the accomodations at hand might look to the proprietor of an eastern mansion like crowding the mourners. But Dawson said that he had lived in the country for fourteen years and had never yet turned away the first person from his doors on account of no accomodation.

After supper we all packed into a room about 12 by 14, with a fire place at one end, a crib in one corner, bed in another, secretary in a third, while a wash stand and a half dozen chairs completed the outfit. It was soon discovered that there was music in the company, and a space was cleared away in the center of the room, a Wood's organ brought from the entry, and the school marm, the Trinidad lady and the subscriber formed a trio for the execution of Gospel hymns, which drew forth rounds of applause from a "crowded house." Mr. Dawson related his experience as a hunter *(he had spent thirty years of his life with the cattle, game, Indians of northwestern Texas).*

Mr. Dawson's home place contains about one thousand acres of excellent land, and, contrary to the general rule, he does a little at farming, has a variety of fruit trees, a garden and plants some corn. Farming was common here prior to the coming of the railroad two years ago as everyone had to raise his own supplies or pay for hauling seven hundred miles from Kansas City. The wheat and corn fields have gone to weed. The untold profits on stock raising, and the ease with which the work is done make farming a small compensation. Mr. Dawson keeps on at the home place and has a few hundred head of cattle there which he has turned over to his children. He has about seventy-five horses, a lot of chickens, a pack of nine hounds, which guard the premises. Mr. Dawson is an excellent specimen of the pioneer, open-hearted, cordial in his welcome, fond of company and of storytelling. He has roughed it, pinched his way along up to the present time, but now counts his land by the townships and his cattle and sheep by the thousand.

THE RAILROADS

The first railroad to enter into the Grant proper was the A.T.&S.F. As G. D. Bradley says in his Story of the Santa

Fe: William B. Strong saw this situation, and he had the resolution to over-ride the timidity of his official superior and act at once. Had it not been for the invincible determination of Strong and the intelligent cooperation of Robinson it is quite possible that the Denver & Rio Grande and not the Atchison, Topeka and Santa Fe would have first crossed New Mexico, and become a great system. As it was, the Santa Fe crossed the divide, gained the coast and became a transcontinental railroad while the Rio Grande still is confined to three states. Small wonder then, than on February 2, 1878, Strong ordered Robinson in haste to Raton Pass, and seize and hold the Pass against all opposition. Palmer was on the alert not to be outdone if he could prevent it. He appears to have shadowed the Santa Fe plans, and late in February, he also made ready a force of men and teams and placed them in Raton Pass. It also happened the Mr. Robinson of the Santa Fe and Chief Engineer McMurtrie, of the Rio Grande, field leaders of the rival forces, traveled together on the same Denver and Rio Grande train from Pueblo to El Moro, the nearest railroad point to the scene of operations. Arriving at El Moro that evening Mr. McMurtrie went to bed while Engineer Robinson hurried overland to the home of Dick Wooten near the north slope of the mountain, a famous old scout who operated a toll road over the Pass. This was to be near the scene and ready for any emergency. About 11 o'clock that night Robinson was informed by a special messenger from Trinidad that the Denver and Rio Grande people had organized a force of graders and were moving across the country back of Trinidad to the Pass. There was no time to lose. Hurrying with all speed to Trinidad, Robinson, accompanied by a staff engineer, Wm. Morley, got together a crowd of men with shovels and returning had detailed this party at several strategic points through the Pass and were busily grading for the Santa Fe railroad by 5:00 A.M. One of the workers was Wooten, who began shoveling by lantern light near what is now the north approach to Raton tunnel. Not long after daybreak the Denver and Rio Grande forces arrived only to find their rivals in complete possession of Raton Pass—a defile that held the destinies of a great railroad. Some loud and bitter words were exchanged, but the Santa Fe men, though threatened, declared that they had first possession and would fight to retain their ground if necessary. After much blustering, their opponents withdrew and setting up camp nearby began locating a rival line over the mountain, following a stream known as Chicken Creek. But this route proved wholly impracticable and within a few weeks, on April 18th, the Rio Grande people withdrew and went north to Canon City, leaving the Santa Fe graders in undisturbed possession . . .

The big question which now comes to mind, which no historian of the Santa Fe railroad has covered, is: What if the Maxwell Land Grant Company decided it didn't want the Santa Fe railroad to cross its property? THIS WOULD HAVE CHANGED THE WHOLE COURSE OF NEW MEXICO'S HISTORY FROM 1879 TO THE PRESENT DATE.

Palmer had been a stockholder in the company. He was well known to all the Grant officials. Enough pressure from him might have influenced the Grant Company. But Miguel Otero was also known to the Grant people and just as influencial. No doubt in weighing the pleas of the two men the Company decided that what Otero had to offer was more beneficial to them financially. The Santa Fe was a larger larger system and the dream of Cyrus K. Holliday of a road from Chicago to California was beginning to materialize. This coupled with the idea that a railroad could bring in colonists and miners determined the Maxwell Land Grant Company to do business with the Santa Fe railroad people. This decision of the Maxwell Land Grant Company to give the Santa Fe the right of way through its large domain is sufficient to give it the niche it deserves in the history of the state. It also serves to blot out many of the errors its officials may have committed against certain squatters. For the company was a corporation and dealt with trespassers as such. Individually the officials of the Company were on the helpful side but were constantly hindered by agitators like O. P. McMains. We have seen the St. Louis, Rocky Mountain & Pacific. Other roads were the Ponil & Cimarron; Raton & Clifton; Cimarron & Northwestern; Mountain, Valley and Plains; Santa Fe, Raton & Eastern; Raton, El Paso & Southeastern; Des Moines & Dawson. A number of other spur lines from Trinidad to Catskill; from Raton to the coal camps at Brilliant, Koehler, Blossburg as well as to saw mill and lumber areas. But all are gone now like the Ghost Towns we mentioned, not even the rails remain to show where once tracks made marks of civilization. There were a number of other railroads on paper which is as far as they ever got.

Of all the railroads the only one that remains is the Santa Fe. Cars do run on a spur line to Koehler but just how long this will function is a matter of conjecture. There are rumors of Koehler shutting down in May 1952. Already miners are casting about for new jobs and stability. They have seen Brilliant, Van Houten, Blossburg, Dawson and Yankee fold up. If the rumors prove to be true they do not wish to be caught napping. Should this one remaining mine on the Grant close down it will be the end of the spur line also so that two industries rails and coal will join the ranks of has beens. It is always happening; Cars replace wagons; talkies replace vaudeville; television replaces the radio. Perhaps it is progress which means that something has to die for something else to live. The Maxwell Land Grant Company takes it all in stride. Even when the state of New Mexico bought much of the Cimarron canyon for picnic grounds for tourists, the Grant did not fold up. It will go on until such names like Carson, Beaubien, Dold, Miranda, Maxwell, Pels, Whigham, Waddingham, Van Houten and others become dim to the memory of our children's children until the end of time.

—*The End.*

Chapter Fourteen

THE PICTURE STORY

CHARLES H. TROTIER BEAUBIEN
He had visions of an empire when he petitioned for the Grant. He died at Taos almost as land poor as the day he arrived.

GUADALUPE MIRANDA
He was too sure of the grants he had near Mesilla and Dona Ana to care about his share of the Grant. He lost those too when he couldn't prove title. He did not get much from selling the Grant but he enjoyed peace of mind.

PABLO BEAUBIEN *and* REBECCA BEAUBIEN
Pablo might have been sole owner of the Grant had he been a little older. Maxwell did not wait for Pablo to mature before buying up his share of the Grant.

GOVERNOR MANUEL ARMIJO
To the day he died at Lemitar, New Mexico, he insisted that one-sixth of the Grant was his. Maxwell scoffed at the idea. Armijo's heirs never pressed the claim.

TEODORA BEAUBIEN MILLER
She sold her share of the Grant to Maxwell. Later Grant troubles convinced her that she did the right thing.

JACK HOLLAND
Builder of the Maxwell house at Rayado and the one
at Cimarron. He never married. He was postmaster for
a long time at Rayado on the Grant.

PETE MAXWELL
(Seated)
Big business did not interest him. In January 1883,
despite the fact that he was a wealthy sheepman, he
sold the Fort Sumner estate to Dan L. Taylor, Lon Horn
and Samuel Dess, cattle dealers from Trinidad.

PABLITA MAXWELL
She had great admiration for her father. She
regretted the sale of the Grant but made
herself at home on the new family
estate at Fort Sumner.

CAPTAIN KEYES   VIRGINIA MAXWELL KEYES

They married in the old grist mill at Cimarron despite Maxwell's wishes. Their son is General G. Keyes of World War II fame. Her marriage was more important to her than any part of the Grant.

SOFIA MAXWELL
She wanted no share of the Grant only to be left in peace.

MRS. FRANCES CLUTTON
Original owner of what is now Philmont Ranch, she loved every inch of the Rayado country.

J. G. ABREU *and* PETRA BEAUBIEN ABREU
As a Beaubien she owned part of the Grant but sold to Maxwell for a pittance. Later on they regretted they did not hold on to their share. This couple made its home at Rayado and was very happy there.

LUCIEN B. MAXWELL
Eventually he acquired the whole Grant but instead of
settling back to enjoy it sold out to the Maxwell
Land Grant and Railway Company.

CLAY ALLISON
O. P. McMains looked upon him as his right hand man. When he moved elsewhere McMains felt very much like R. E. Lee hearing the news of Stonewall Jackson's death.

PONCHO GRIEGO
Killed at Lambert's Bar at Cimarron. Some have maintained he was trying to up-hold the Grant Company. Clay Allison thought otherwise.

THE GRIST MILL AT CIMARRON
Here the Indians received their rations. Upper center the Maxwell mansion. White building far right was the old county courthouse. Cimarron was the county seat at the time

THE MAXWELL MANSION AT CIMARRON
(After a fire)
This was the showplace of the Grant during the early days.

D. A. CLOUTHIER
By mercantile enterprise at Elizabethtown, Rayado, Springer and other villages on the Grant the Clouthiers did much to spread the fame of this section of New Mexico.

CLIFTON HOUSE
The Stocktons bought their land from Maxwell long before the Anti-Grant troubles. This place became a favorite stop for stage coaches. There is a boot hill close by.

RAYADO STAGESTOP
One of the Santa Fe Trail stagestops was this station at Rayado. Here mules were changed and people fed. To the right the Abreu residence.

The D. A. Clouthier home near Springer was one of the most beautiful in New Mexico. Maxwell often dreamed of a home like this.

Raton
Raton was the Big Town in those days. It still is the largest city on the Grant. Today it houses the archives and offices of the Maxwell Land Grant Company.

There is nothing left at Dawson today. Once the proud queen city of the mining towns on the Grant, it bowed to the diesel and progress.

The Santa Fe at Harvey House, Raton
The railroad did more to build up the Grant than any other individual factor—even the discovery of Gold on the Grant.

Catskill was one of those delightful spots on the Grant that went along its merry way leaving the Anti Granters and the Granters to settle their disputes elsewhere. The Ladies' Band was quite popular at Catskill.

Even at the turn of the century travel along the Rayado was as refreshing as it was interesting. The Abreus go for a visit.

Beautiful Stonewall. Here the Anti Granters made their last desperate stand. Here Captain Russell met his violent end. Here is the final resting place of that Arch-Agitator O. P. McMains.

Every town on the Grant found a way to amuse itself. Springer was no exception.

CHARLES ABREU *and* M. M. SALAZAR

Salazar (standing) fought a losing fight to keep Springer as the County Seat. Opposition got so strong that for a time it looked as if U. S. troops would have to be called in.

Cimarron once had hopes of becoming the biggest city on the Grant. Today it is one of the most beautiful tourist centers in New Mexico.

Industry like this makes us realize why the Maxwell Land Grant Company fought for what it had.

Dawson is no more but many on old miner will remember this scene.

BIBLIOGRAPHY

A. Decisions in the Supreme Court of the Territory of New Mexico
William Bent
    vs
Guadalupe Thompson, et Al.
John Jenkins
    vs
The Maxwell Land Grant, et Al. (Jan. term 1906)
Alexander McNab, and Others
    vs
Frank Springer, and others (Sept. term 1905)
B. Decisions of the Supreme Court of the State of Colorado
The United States
    vs
The Maxwell Land Grant Company (Opinion of Hon. D. J. Brewer)
The Maxwell Land Grant Company
    vs
The Colorado Fuel Company (November 7, 1889)
The Interstate Land Company
    vs
The Maxwell Land Grant Company
    and
The Maxwell Land Grant Company
    vs
Vicente Preteca, et Al. (Printed at Santa Fe, N.M. 1890)

C. THE SUPREME COURT OF THE UNITED STATES
The Interstate Land Company
    vs
The Maxwell Land Grant Company (April 6, 1891)
The Interstate Land Company
    vs
The Maxwell Land Grant Company (October term, 1890)
The United States
    vs
The Maxwell Land Grant Company (October term, 1886)

MAXWELL LAND GRANT MATERIAL

Transcript of Title: McNally, Rand Co., Chicago, Illinois, 1880
The Maxwell Land Grant: Rand, McNally & Co., Chicago, Illinois, 1903
Maxwell Land Grant Mining Districts: Raton, N.M., 1901
The Gold Mines of the Moreno Valley: Poole Brothers, Chicago, 1894
Colfax County, New Mexico: Santa Fe, N.M. 1901
Maxwell Land Grant Mining Regulations: Raton, N.M., 1901
Raton, N. M.: El Paso, Texas, 1903

A History of the Maxwell Land Grant
(Thesis for the State College of Education) Wilfred I. McPherson, Colorado, Greeley, Aug. 1936
Maxwell Land Grant: William A. Keleher, Santa Fe, N. M., The Rydal Press, 1942
The Frank Springer Collection: Museum of Santa Fe, Santa Fe, N.M.
The M. W. Mills Collection: Highlands University, Las Vegas, N.M.
Raton Historical Collection: Raton Public Library, Raton, N.M.
The Davis Collection: Springer, New Mexico
The Vita Abreu Collection: Springer, New Mexico
The Lail Collection: Cimarron, New Mexico
The Alpers Collection: Cimarron, New Mexico

UNITED STATES DOCUMENTS:

    House Reports, 36 Congress 1 Sess., Vol. 2, Doc. 321, (Serial 1068)
    House Reports, 35 Congress 1 Sess., Vol. 4, Doc. 457 (Serial 967)
    House Reports, 36 Congress 1 Sess., Vol. 2, Doc. 228, (Serial 1040)
    Report of the Governor of New Mexico to the Secretary of the Interior, 1883
    Report of the Governor of New Mexico to the Secretary of the Interior 1885
    Report of the Governor of New Mexico to the Secretary of the Interior 1886
    Report of the Governor of New Mexico to the Secretary of the Interior 1887
    Report of the Governor of New Mexico to the Secretary of the Interior 1888
    Report of the Governor of the Territory of New Mexico to the Secretary of the Interior 1889
    Report of the Governor of the Territory of New Mexico to the Secretary of the Interior 1891
    Report of the Governor of the Territory of New Mexico to the Secretary of the Interior 1894
    Claims in the Territory of New Mexico: Washington, D.C. 1858
    Congressional Records—California and New Mexico: Washington, D.C. 1850
    Acts of the Legislative Assembly of the Territory of N.M., Santa Fe 1875
    Official Letters—Land Office—Santa Fe, July 8, 1869 to April 11, 1873
    Official Letters—Land Office—Santa Fe, Nov. 12, 1863 to July 2, 1869

Official Letters—Land Office—Santa Fe, July 10, 1859 to November 12, 1863

Circuit Court of U.S. for the District of Colorado, Oct. Term 1885

J. A. Bentley vs. Chas. Springer

United States Supreme Court—U.S. Appellant No. 974
vs
Maxwell Land Grant

Supreme Court of the Territory of New Mexico, January Term 1889, No. 376

Frank Springer's Oral Argument in the Supreme Court U.S.A.

Patent United States of America to Charles Beaubien, Dec. 20, 1880, Rec. Costilla, N.M., June 2, 1884

Will of Charles Beaubien Dated January 16, 1864, Taos, N.M., Feb. 13, 1864

Discharge of Administrators of Charles Beaubien, Jan. 12, 1869, Taos, April 5, 1889

Maria Paula Lovato et Al. to William Gilpin, Taos, Oct. 16, 1894

Frederick Muller as Guardian for Pablo Beaubien, Taos Co., March 15, 1864

Pablo Beaubien to Wm. Gilpin, Costilla Co., Colo., April 5, 1889

COLFAX COUNTY RECORDS

Mora County Mining Claims—in the Raton Courthouse.

Colfax County Mining Claims Vol. 1, 1869, Raton, N.M.

Colfax County Deed Book — Vol. 1, 1869 — 1874, Raton, N.M.

Docket and Criminal Records, Vol. 1, 1869 — 1871, Raton, N.M.

Docket and Criminal Records, Vol. II, 1871 — 1874, Raton, N.M.

Docket and Criminal Records, Vol. III, 1874 — 1880, Raton, N.M.

Docket and Criminal Records, Vol. IV, 1880 — 1885, Raton, N.M.

Docket and Criminal Records, Vol. V, 1885 — 1890, Raton, N.M.

Court Proceedings Cases 556 — 557 — 558, County Courthouse, Raton, N.M.

Deed Book A Mora County at the Raton Courthouse

Deed Book B Colfax County, 1871, Raton, N.M.

Inventory of the County Archives of Mora County, Mora, N.M.
Albuquerque, N.M., 1941

Historical Records of Colfax County, Raton Public Library, Raton, N.M.

Maps and Abstracts of the Maxwell Land Grant, Colfax County Courthouse, Raton, N.M.

PERIODICALS AND NEWSPAPERS

New Mexico Historical Review, Santa Fe, N.M., July 1946
Old Santa Fe, Santa Fe, N.M., July 1913
Old Santa Fe, Santa Fe, N.M., July 1914
Old Santa Fe, Santa Fe, N.M., October 1913
Raton Comet, Raton, N.M., July 14, 1882
Raton Guard, Raton, N.M., April 21, 1882
Raton Guard, Raton, N.M., April 12, 1882
Live Stock Journal of New Mexico, Raton, N.M., August 26, 1887
Raton Range, Raton, N.M., April 6, 1888
Raton Range, Raton, N.M., September 28, 1888
Colfax County Stockman, Springer, N.M., Nov. 4, 1893
Colfax County Stockman, Springer, N.M., March 3, 1894
Live Stock Journal of New Mexico, Raton, N.M., March 26, 1886
Springer Stockman, Springer, N.M., September 6, 1888
Trinidad Advertiser, Trinidad, Colorado, Feb. 6, 1889
Raton Range, Raton, N.M., September 2, 1887
Trinidad Advertiser, Trinidad, Colorado, October 4, 1888
H. C. Upshaw—Ranch Romance Magazine, N.Y., June 7, 1940—Lucien Maxwell, Duke of Cimarron
Frank D. Reeve—Federal Indian Policy—In New Mexico Historical Review, Santa Fe, April, 1938
New Mexico Magazine, November 1935
New Mexico Magazine, June 1931
Cimarron News and Press, Feb. 7, 1907, Cimarron, N.M.
Cimarron Citizen, March 4, 1908, Cimarron, N.M.
Clayton Enterprise, Clayton, New Mexico, April 25, 1891
Pamphlets and Tracts Collection—Listed as the Texas Purchase Collection, University of Colorado, Boulder, Colorado
The Fordyce Papers—American School of Research, Santa Fe, New Mexico
Field and Farm Magazine, September 1888

SECONDARY SOURCES

Abel, Anne H.: Official Correspondence of James S. Calhoun, Washington, D.C., 1915

Anderson, George B.: History of New Mexico, Its Resources and Its People, Vol. 1. Pacific States Pub. Co., Los Angeles, Calif., 1907

Bancroft, Hubert H.: North Mexican States and Texas, Vol. 1, San Francisco, California, 1889

Bancroft, Hubert H.: History of Mexico, Vol. V, 1824-1861, San Francisco, California, 1885

Bancroft, Hubert H.: History of Mexico, Vol. VI, 1861-1887, San Francisco, California, 1888

Bancroft, Hubert H.: Arizona and New Mexico, 1530-1888, San Francisco, California, 1889

Bancroft, Hubert H.: History of Nevada, Colorado, Wyoming, 1540-1888, San Francisco, California, 1890

Bandelier, Adolph S.F. and Bandelier, Fanny B.: Historical Documents Relating to New Mexico, Carnegie Institute of Washington, D.C., 1923

Coan, Charles F.: A History of New Mexico, Vol. I, The American Historical Society, Inc., Chicago, Ill., 1925

Duffus, Robert L.: The Santa Fe Trail, Longmans, Green & Co., New York, 1931

Garrard, Lewis H.: Wah-Ta-Yah and the Taos Trail, Harlow Publishing Company, Oklahoma Pub Co., Oklahoma City, Oklahoma, 1927

Grant, Blanche (Editor): Kit Carson's Own Story of His Life, Taos, New Mexico 1926

Harwood, Rev. Thomas: History of the New Mexico Spanish and English Missions of the Methodist Episcopal Church from 1850 to 1910, 2 Vols., El Abogado Press, Albuquerque, New Mexico, 1908

Fish, Carl Russell: The Rise of the Common Man, 1830—1850, Macmillan Co., New York, N. Y., 1927

Haley, J. Evetts: Charles Goodnight—Cowman and Plainsman, Houghton, Mifflin Co., New York, 1936

Lavender, David: The Big Divide, Garden City, New York, 1948

Inman, Col. Henry: The Old Santa Fe Trail, Crane and Company, Topeka, Kansas, 1916; also
Macmillan Co., London, Eng., 1897

Kendall, George W.: Narrative of the Texan Santa Fe Expedition, Harper and Brothers, New York, 1844, 2 Vols.

Nevins, Allan: Fremont: The West's Greatest Adventurer, Harper Brothers, New York, 1928, 2 Vols.

Nevins, Allan: The Emergence of Modern America, 1865—1878, Macmillan Co., New York, 1927

Dunham, Harold H.: Lucien B. Maxwell; Frontiersman and Businessman, The Brand Book, Denver, Colo. March 1949

Otero, Miguel A.: My Life on the Frontier, 1864-1882
Press of the Pioneers, New York 1935

Otero, Miguel A.: My Nine Years as Governor of the Territory of New Mexico, 1897—1906
Albuquerque, New Mexico, 1940

Porter, Henry M.: Pencilings of An Early Western Pioneer
World Press, Denver, Colo., 1929

Priestly, Herbert I.: Coming of the White Man, 1492-1848, Macmillan Company, N.Y., 1929

Riddle, Kenyon: Records and Maps of the Old Santa Fe Trail, Raton, New Mexico, 1948

Ryus, W. H.: The Second William Penn, Kansas City, Mo., 1915

Rhodes, E. M.: Penalosa, Santa Fe, New Mexico, 1934

Schachner, Nathan: Aaron Burr, Frederick Stokes & Co., N.Y., 1937

Stanley, F.: Raton Chronicle, World Press, Denver, Colo., 1948

Stanley, F.: One Half Mile From Heaven: The Cimarron Story, World Press, Denver, Colo., 1949

Schlesinger, Arthur M. and Fox, Dixon Ryan: A History of American Life, 12 Vols., Macmillan Co., N.Y., 1946-1947

Twitchell, Ralph M.: Leading Facts of New Mexico History, 3 Vols., The Torch Press, Cedar Rapids, Iowa, 1912

Twitchell, Ralph M.: Spanish Archives of New Mexico, 2 Vols., The Torch Press, Cedar Rapids, Iowa, 1914

Vestal, Stanley: Kit Carson: The Happy Warrior of the Old West, The Riverside Press, Cambridge, Mass., 1928

Beadle Dime Publishing Co., Life and Times of Christopher Carson—American News Press, N.Y., 1867

Troncoso, Francisco Del Paso (Compiler): Epistolario de Nueva Espana, 1515—1818, 16 Vols.
Antigua Libreria de Jose Purrua e Higos, Mexico City, Mexico, 1939

Bradley, Glenn D.: The Story of the Santa Fe, The Gorham Press, Boston, Mass., 1920.

www.ingramcontent.com/pod-product-compliance
Lightning Source LLC
Chambersburg PA
CBHW081151290426

44108CB00018B/2509